Ego Functions in Schizophrenics, Neurotics, and Normals: A Systematic Study of Conceptual, Diagnostic, and Therapeutic Aspects
by Leopold Bellak, Marvin Hurvich, and Helen A. Gediman

Innovative Treatment Methods in Psychopathology.
edited by Karen S. Calhoun, Henry E. Adams, and Kevin M. Mitchell

The Changing School Scene: Challenge to Psychology
by Leah Gold Fein

Troubled Children: Their Families, Schools, and Treatments
by Leonore R. Love and Jaques W. Kaswan

Research Strategies in Psychotherapy
by Edward S. Bordin

The Volunteer Subject
by Robert Rosenthal and Ralph L. Rosnow

Innovations in Client-Centered Therapy
by David A. Wexler and Laura North Rice

The Rorschach: A Comprehensive System
by John E. Exner

Theory and Practice in Behavior Therapy
by Aubrey J. Yates

Principles of Psychotherapy
by Irving B. Weiner

Psychoactive Drugs and Social Judgment: Theory and Research
edited by Kenneth Hammond and C. R. B. Joyce

Clinical Methods in Psychology
edited by Irving B. Weiner

CLINICAL METHODS
IN PSYCHOLOGY

CLINICAL METHODS IN PSYCHOLOGY

Edited by

IRVING B. WEINER

Case Western Reserve University

A WILEY-INTERSCIENCE PUBLICATION

JOHN WILEY & SONS New York · London · Sydney · Toronto

Library of Congress Cataloging in Publication Data:

Main entry under title:
Clinical methods in psychology.

  (Wiley series on personality processes)
  "A Wiley-Interscience publication."
  Includes bibliographies and indexes.
  1. Clinical psychology. I. Weiner, Irving B.
[DNLM: 1. Psychology, Clinical. 2. Psychotherapy.
WM100 C639]

RC467.C577   157'.9   75-28366
ISBN 0-471-92576-4

Printed in the United States of America

10 9 8 7 6 5 4 3 2 1

To David Shakow

With appreciation for his contributions to clinical psychology as a science and as a profession.

Contributors

JAMES N. BUTCHER, PH.D., Professor and Director of Graduate Education in Clinical Psychology, Department of Psychology, University of Minnesota

JOHN E. EXNER, JR., PH.D., Professor and Director of Clinical Training, Department of Psychology, Long Island University; Diplomate, American Board of Professional Psychology

RONALD E. FOX, PH.D., Professor and Coordinator of Education and Training, Department of Psychiatry, Ohio State University; Diplomate, American Board of Professional Psychology

GEORGE FRANK, PH.D., Associate Professor of Psychology, New York University; Diplomate, American Board of Professional Psychology

MARVIN R. GOLDFRIED, PH.D., Professor of Psychology, State University of New York at Stony Brook; Diplomate, American Board of Professional Psychology

MALCOLM D. GYNTHER, PH.D., Professor of Psychology, Auburn University; Diplomate, American Board of Professional Psychology

RUTH A. GYNTHER, M. A., Formerly Instructor in Psychology, University of Missouri of St. Louis

AGNES D. JACKSON, M. S., Research Associate, Department of Psychology, Rutgers University

BERNARD LUBIN, PH.D., Professor and Director of Clinical Training, Department of Psychology, University of Houston; Diplomate, American Board of Professional Psychology

GAIL R. MAUDAL, PH.D., Crisis Intervention Center, Hennepin County General Hospital, Minneapolis, Minnesota

PETER E. NATHAN PH.D., Professor and Director of Clinical Training, Department of Psychology, Rutgers University

IRVING B. WEINER, PH.D., Professor and Chairman, Department of Psychology, Case Western Reserve University; Diplomate, American Board of Professional Psychology

ARTHUR N. WIENS, PH.D., Professor and Director of Training, Department of Medical Psychology, University of Oregon Medical School; Diplomate, American Board of Professional Psychology

Series Preface

This series of books is addressed to behavioral scientists interested in the nature of human personality. Its scope should prove pertinent to personality theorists and researchers as well as to clinicians concerned with applying an understanding of personality processes to the amelioration of emotional difficulties in living. To this end, the series provides a scholarly integration of theoretical formulations, empirical data, and practical recommendations.

Six major aspects of studying and learning about human personality can be designated: personality theory, personality structure and dynamics, personality development, personality assessment, personality change, and personality adjustment. In exploring these aspects of personality, the books in the series discuss a number of distinct but related subject areas: the nature and implications of various theories of personality; personality characteristics that account for consistencies and variations in human behavior; the emergence of personality processes in children and adolescents; the use of interviewing and testing procedures to evaluate individual differences in personality; efforts to modify personality styles through psychotherapy, counseling, behavior therapy, and other methods of influence; and patterns of abnormal personality functioning that impair individual competence.

IRVING B. WEINER

Case Western Reserve University
Cleveland, Ohio

Preface

This book surveys the major methods of assessment and intervention currently being employed in the practice of clinical psychology. To achieve broad coverage of the field, the chapters delineate theoretical, research, and applied aspects of the methods with which clinicians work, and they address the needs and interests of both beginning and experienced practitioners.

To these ends, each chapter discusses the historical development of a particular method of assessment or intervention, theoretical similarities and differences among leading proponents of the method, research findings bearing on the utility of the method, and specific recommendations for putting the method into practice in clinical settings. Although the authors organize their material differently, they all write both as practitioners concerned with helping people in psychological distress and scientists concerned with systematic empirical investigation of clinical methods.

For the beginning clinician each chapter offers an introduction to the central concepts, techniques, and lines of research on which the major psychological methods of assessment and intervention are based. Of additional value for the clinically experienced reader, the chapters also summarize the present state of the literature, offer guidelines for future directions in training, research, and practice, and include extensive bibliographies useful for reference purposes.

The chapter topics are selected to represent those methods of assessment and intervention that, as judged from prevailing clinical practice and volume of publication, are being most widely used and studied. The first part of the book, which deals with methods of assessment, consists of chapters on the assessment interview, projective techniques, measures of intelligence and conceptual thinking, personality inventories, and behavioral assessment. The second part of the book deals with methods of intervention and comprises chapters on individual psychotherapy, group therapy, family therapy, behavior modification, and crisis intervention.

Sincere appreciation is expressed by the authors to the many colleagues who read portions of the manuscript in draft form and to the many secretaries who contributed invaluable clerical assistance. We also gratefully acknowledge permission to reprint their copyrighted materials extended by Academic Press, Inc.; the American Psychological Association; Holt, Rinehart & Winston, Inc.; McGraw-Hill Book Company; Pergamon Publishing Company; and *Psychology Today*.

IRVING B. WEINER

Cleveland, Ohio

July 1975

Contents

CLINICAL METHODS
IN PSYCHOLOGY

PART ONE

Methods of Assessment

CHAPTER 1

The Assessment Interview

ARTHUR N. WIENS

There are many fields in which interviewing is an important professional skill, and many areas of research contribute knowledge regarding interviewing. The student of the interview, and this includes all clinical psychologists, is well advised to keep himself informed of the new knowledge being presented in a great variety of professional journals and books. This chapter accordingly reviews some aspects of interviewing practice and research with the keen awareness that even as it is being written new findings are being reported.

For many years there seems to have been an implicit assumption that interviewing is an art rather than a science, hence that it cannot be taught but can only be gradually acquired through personal professional experience. This assumption must certainly be questioned as one reviews the current interviewing research literature in which behavioral scientists report on their efforts to study specific aspects of the interview interaction. With a specification of interview behaviors it becomes possible to assess the interview effects of a variety of interviewer and interviewee characteristics and tactics. It is also reasonable to assume that the beginning interviewer can study and should know various aspects of the psychological forces at work in the interview. Such knowledge can then be a basis for acquiring and using insightfully the specific techniques of interviewing.

An important underlying assumption in this chapter and in the research on the interview during recent years is the view that the interview is an interaction process between the interviewer and interviewee, clinician and patient, psychologist and client, and so on. That is, both participants share actively in the process of interviewing, and both participants are influenced by each other; the end product of the interview is a result of this interaction. This assumption of mutual interaction is also referred to as the relationship aspect of the interview and, in this chapter, is viewed as a most critical consideration for the interviewer. The relationship established between the interviewer and the interviewee determines whether or not the purposes of the interview can be achieved. Relationship considerations hold from the first interview encounter, and thus make artificial an attempt to distinguish between assessment and therapy interviews. An interview that is only "diagnostic" will probably make the patient feel like some kind of specimen of psychopathology and actually make it difficult for him to share his concerns with the interviewer. From the first meeting between clinician and patient (or any other interview pair) the focus must be on the development of a shared feeling of understanding of the patient.

This chapter is organized under the following general topics: general considerations; anatomy of the interview; nonverbal communication; interaction, tactics, and training; and the initial clinical interview—some specific considerations. An attempt is made in each instance to refer to specific research programs to allow the reader to identify additional sources of review and study. An attempt is also made to evaluate the research findings for possible clinical implications that can provide a basis for developing specific clinical interview guidelines.

GENERAL CHARACTERISTICS OF THE INTERVIEW SITUATION

Almost a half-century ago data were published by Rankin (1928) showing the relative proportion of time spent by adults in various types of communication, including listening, reading, speaking, and writing. The average percentage of waking time devoted to each form of communication was computed for a total of 60 days as recorded by 21 different people with miscellaneous occupations, including teaching. In these records the time listed as conversation was divided in two, with half recorded as talking and half as listening, on the assumption that one generally listens about half the time and talks about half the time during a conversation. For this group of records nearly 70% of the total waking time was spent in some form of communication. Listening was the most frequently used of the four language arts (approximately 42%). Talking ranked second, reading third, and writing fourth. Oral language stands out very conspicuously as being the most used form of language.

The probable number of two-person conversations going on in close proximity to the reader is enormous. Furthermore, the number of interviews taking place at any point in time is very large. Matarazzo (1965) has pointed out that since antiquity the interview has been used professionally by philosophers, physicians, priests, and attorneys. Within the twentieth century many new professionals have been added to this interviewer list. These include psychologists, psychiatrists, social workers, sociologists, anthropologists, nurses, economists, newspaper reporters, salesmen, welfare caseworkers, finance company interviewers, and so on. A listing of interview situations would be almost endless.

Because of the virtual omnipresence of the two-person interview, one would assume that much is known about interviewing and that, by now, it must be a relatively exact science with specified rules of procedure to follow. Alas, not so. It still remains very much an individual art, and there are relatively few universal dictums to guide the novice interviewer. However, a great variety of professionals (and laymen) do have excellent talent and skill in interviewing. The novice interviewer can learn by example and study from many different sources and should by no means limit himself to psychology textbooks or psychology instructors. For a current nonpsychology and very public example, one might pay close attention to the interview skills of Dick Cavett on his national television program as he elicits verbal responses from a variety of interviewees, some of whom are presumably motivated to be frank, open, and expressive and others of whom are quite reticent.

Interview versus Conversation

The term "interview" has a history of usage going back for centuries. It was used originally to designate a face-to-face meeting of individuals for a formal conference on some point. Later the term became familiar in its journalistic usage as reporters interviewed people to obtain statements for publication. Virtually all current definitions of the interview include reference to a face-to-face verbal interchange in which one person, the interviewer, attempts to elicit information or expressions of opinion or belief from another person, the interviewee.

An interview resembles a conversation in several ways. They both typically involve a face-to-face verbal exchange of information, ideas, attitudes, or feelings and contain messages exchanged through nonverbal as well as verbal modes of expression. However, a crucial characteristic that distinguishes an interview from a conversation is that the interview interaction is designed to achieve a consciously selected purpose. There may be no central theme in a conversation, but in an interview the content is directed toward a specific purpose and is likely to have unity, progression, and thematic continuity. If the purpose of the interview is to be achieved, one participant must assume and maintain responsibility for directing the interaction (asking questions) toward the goal, and the other participant must facilitate achievement of the purpose by following the direction of the interaction (answering questions); that is, one participant is the interviewer and the other the interviewee. There are no comparable status terms or selected role behaviors in a conversation.

The nonreciprocal roles of the two participants in an interview relationship result from the fact that, in one form or another, the purpose of the interview is to benefit the interviewee. The profession of the interviewer entails an obligation to perform clearly defined services for the client. Whereas the interviewee may reveal a great deal about himself from a wide segment of his life, the interviewer typically limits his revelations to his professional life.

Furthermore, whereas in conversation a person may respond in a spontaneous and unplanned manner, an interviewer deliberately and consciously plans his actions to further the purpose of the interview. The interview itself is planned to occur at a definite time and place and, unlike a conversation which can be started and terminated at will, an interview once initiated must be continued until its purpose has been achieved or until it is clear that the purpose cannot be achieved. An interview requires exclusive attention to the interaction, and for the interviewer to become bored or to terminate the contract for personal reasons leaves him open to a charge of dereliction of professional responsibility. Finally, because an interview has a purpose other than amusement, unpleasant facts and feelings are not avoided. There may actually be a necessity to introduce unpleasant facts and feelings if doing so will be of help. For a fuller exposition of these points and the fact that conversations sometimes turn into interviews or that interviews can be conducted in many different settings (office, bus, supermarket, on the way to the hospital, etc.) the interested reader should consult Kadushin (1972).

Interview Validity

Research workers and clinicians need to have some idea of the extent to which the interview constitutes a valid measuring instrument. More specifically, one might ask about the validity of a particular interview technique, interview topic, or interview situation or context. A question that must be considered is whether answers in an interview have any relationship to the interviewee's actual behavior, the underlying attitudes that govern his behavior, or the factual events concerning which he is asked to report (Maccoby & Maccoby, 1954). For example, it has often been recorded that eyewitness reports are notoriously unreliable and that omissions and distortions in such reports become more pronounced with the passage of time. It is also well known that interviewees typically want to put themselves in a favorable light before the interviewer and may therefore distort or conceal attitudes and behavior. Likewise, research on psychological assessment indicates that answers to personality test items may be affected by a person's tendency to give what he believes to be the proper or socially desirable answer. Rosenthal (1966) has shown that, even in very carefully controlled experimental research studies, experimenters tend in subtle ways to influence their subjects' behavior toward support of the experimental hypotheses. The results of verbal conditioning studies clearly show the necessity of paying careful attention to the interviewer's behavior and the clinical setting as determinants of the obtained interview material. Matarazzo and Wiens (1972) have reviewed a series of studies in which it was demonstrated that slight changes in interviewer verbal behavior clearly modified interviewee speech output characteristics. Hence it cannot simply be assumed that an interviewee's behavior is determined solely by his thought content.

Kahn and Cannell (1961) point out that the concept "true value" becomes quite obscure when one wishes to assess and measure attitudes. An interviewee's response to solicitation of feelings about his supervisor might be influenced by his public and private sentiments on this topic. It is also more than likely that he does not have a single, enduring, or true opinion about his supervisor, but that his attitude depends on the immediate situation. For example, different attitudes would probably be expressed on such different occasions as being recommended for a promotion, being reprimanded for a mistake, having just heard an eloquent sermon on brotherly love, and sitting together in a union meeting to promote demands for a wage increase. The attitude expressed on each of these occasions would, however, have a validity of its own and, in a sense, each would be true because each existed. The problem for the interviewer is to decide which of these attitudes he wants to measure and which attitude has target value. Once the objective has been defined, there is then a true value that constitutes the target.

Some research attempts to assess accuracy of interview data by comparing results obtained through personal interviews with information from independent objective sources (see Kahn & Cannell, 1961; Maccoby & Maccoby, 1954). For example, victims of auto accidents tend to exaggerate the amount of work time and pay they lost, and as many as 40% of respondents may inaccurately report contributions to a community chest, 17% inaccurately report age, and even 2% inaccurately report possession of a telephone. Problems of validity of self-report seem to be especially prevalent in studies of human sexual behavior.

Finally, one must consider how aware the interviewee is of his own behavior and motives. It has been suggested that, in the spheres of behavior where repression and other defense mechanisms are at work, it becomes most important to check interview findings against overt behavior. There is the celebrated instance of a mother being interviewed concerning her child-rearing practices. During the interview she held her small son on her lap. The child began to play with his genitals. The mother, without looking directly at the child, moved his hand away and held it securely for awhile, meanwhile talking to the interviewer. Later in the interview, the mother was asked what she ordinarily did when her child played with himself. She replied that he never did—he was a very ''good'' boy. She was evidently entirely unconscious of what had transpired in the very presence of the interviewer. Similarly, people may be unconscious of the ways in which they express aggression, or the ways in which they attempt to obtain approval from others.

Kanfer and Phillips (1970) have written an excellent discussion of the methodological problems involved in using a person's self-report as an indicator of his actual experience. They too conclude that, when a person describes his experiences or his internal states in an interview, care must be taken to recognize this behavior as a response that is under the control of both the person's history and the interview situation and not to accept it as a true record of past or internal events. The interview must be considered a measurement device that is fallible and subject to substantial sources of error and bias. This does not mean, however, that the interview should be discarded as a means of collecting information. The interview, like other measurement techniques, has great value and unique advantages. What is needed is to learn more about the sources of interview bias and influence and to develop methods of eliminating or accounting for them.

Standardized and Nonstandardized Interviews

An essential feature of the standardized, or structured, interview is that the interviewer asks questions that have been decided on in advance and are repeated with the same wording and in the same order from one interview to the next. This form of interview can be used when the same, or nearly the same, information is to be elicited from each interviewee. It can also be used on successive occasions with the same interviewee. The interview data collected are usually fairly easy to quantify. Standardized, or structured, interviews typically allow information to be compared from case to case; they are more reliable than unstandardized interviews, and they minimize errors of question wording. Usually they are not used in exploratory research or initial interviews or before the data to be collected have been carefully defined and articulated.

Unstandardized, or unstructured, interviews allow the interviewer freedom to reword questions, to introduce new questions or to modify question order, and generally to follow the interviewee's spontaneous sequence of ideas. It is often assumed that such spontaneous discussion allows the interviewee to follow more nearly his natural train of thought and may allow him to bring out interview material that is more predictive of what he would say or do in real-life situations. The flexibility of the unstructured interview may also allow the interviewer to adjust his techniques to the interviewee's particular situation. In some cases, he may omit topics that do not seem applicable, and in other cases he may introduce related topics not originally planned for.

Actually, it seems that most experienced clinical psychologists probably have adopted a semistandardized interviewing style or format. Listening to a clinician interviewing a series of patients, one can probably soon discern topic areas that he routinely introduces and questions that he asks in almost the same way of every interviewee. Without a semistandardized format or interview guide, the interviewer is very likely to overlook topics he should cover. However, the experienced clinician is also aware that he can best maintain rapport with an interviewee by formulating questions in words that are familiar to the interviewee and habitually used by him, and by taking up topics when the interviewee indicates a readiness and willingness to discuss them. The semistandardized interview gives more discretion to the interviewer in formulating the wording and sequence of questions in this way, and it accordingly requires a higher level of experience, skill, and training than is required in following a more standardized interview format. Required in particular are an overall conceptual grasp or theoretical context and considerable prior knowledge of the subject matter of the interview.

Peterson (1968) suggests that most clinical interviewing should involve an intermediate degree of structure. With total client spontaneity it is essentially impossible to define, teach, use, test, or improve interview strategy, and with a rigid interview structure the interviewer may cover the questions in a predefined schedule but remain totally ignorant of what matters to the client. Peterson suggests that the assessment needs to determine specifically what the person is doing (both thought and behavior) and then to examine in fine detail the antecedent, concurrent, and consequent conditions under which the behavior to be changed occurs. The actions and reactions of other people in the client's environment are important, including both what the patient does to and with others and what they do to and with him. Finding out what people are doing to each other can be a difficult and time-consuming task, but such systematic inquiry in relation to possible treatment modalities is an essential task for the clinician to pursue. With this purpose in mind, Peterson describes an interview strategy involving an initial *scanning* operation which consists of inquiring of the patient and referral sources about the nature of the problem behavior and the circumstances that precede and follow it. The scanning operation is followed by an extended inquiry which includes a more detailed and individualized study of the client and others most centrally involved. The third phase of the interview sequence consists of *periodic reappraisal* following introduction of treatment measures. The fourth phase is a *follow-up* study. It is clear that he does not propose or utilize a single initial interview as his assessment procedure.

Peterson (1968, pp. 121–122) presents the basic content of one possible guided interview outline, which the interested reader should consult for details. The outline includes two major headings: "Definition of Problem Behavior" and "Determinants of Problem Behavior." The definition of problem behavior includes assessment of the nature of the problem as defined by the client, of the severity of the problem, and of the generality of the problem. The determinants of problem behavior include identifying conditions that intensify problem behavior, conditions that alleviate problem behavior, and the perceived origins, specific antecedents, and specific consequences of problem behavior. Suggested changes and suggested leads for further inquiry are also noted. The novice interviewer will be glad to know that possible wording of questions for assessment of these different interview areas is included in Peterson's presentation.

Recording Interview Data

A question that arises in the minds of most novice interviewers has to do with how to record or report interview findings. Many interviews are summarized from memory, the interviewer attempting to remember as much as possible of what the interviewee has said and to make notes on the content after the interview. Arguments advanced in favor of recording from memory are that taking notes in the interview might upset the interviewee, destroy his confidence in the anonymity of the interview, or produce an unnatural atmosphere (Maccoby & Maccoby, 1954). However, recording from memory has the disadvantage of permitting more distortion due to the interviewer's biases than does immediate recording. Furthermore, points that were significant or dramatic to the interviewer are likely to be sharpened, and other points dropped out. Aside from memory distortions, a considerable amount of interview content is inevitably lost, and it is also essentially inevitable that the temporal sequences of the interview will be rearranged. In particular, points are likely to be brought into conjunction and made to seem related which were separated and unrelated in the actual interview.

Experienced interviewers who take notes during the interview report few instances of the note taking impairing rapport. Not infrequently interviewees may comment on the note taking, sometimes to ask that a given point not be recorded, but more often to ask if they are going too fast for the interviewer to keep up. Some interviewees find it flattering that someone finds their comments important enough to write down, and perhaps most give a bit more consideration to their responses. Probably the majority of interviewees regard it as perfectly natural that the interviewer take notes.

At times it is useful to tape-record interviews. Professional ethics requires that such recordings be made only with the knowledge and consent of both participants. Fortunately, experience shows that the presence of a microphone is seldom a deterrent to the interview. Where there is some reaction to the recording, the interviewer is much more likely to remain aware of and nervous about the microphone than the interviewee. The interviewee is usually willing to accept the recording apparatus on the interviewer's explanation of its importance. If the subject matter of the interview is likely to be very personal, it is advisable to tell the interviewee that, if he wishes to "speak off the record," the microphone will be turned off. Experience indicates that interviewees seldom avail themselves of this opportunity, but that it helps them to feel somewhat freer. Rating from recordings also permits researchers to take advantage of emphasis, intonation, pitch, and pauses as cues which are valuable for some data analysis purposes.

Richardson, Dohrenwend, and Klein (1965) emphasize the importance of visual information as well in understanding interview data. They use as an example an analysis of interview transcripts in terms of the number of lines of type used respectively by the interviewer and interviewee. One interviewer/interviewee ratio revealed that the interviewer said almost nothing compared to other interviewers. On observing this interviewer, however, Richardson et al. noticed that she offered the interviewee an almost continuous nonverbal commentary by nodding her head, gesturing with hands and arms, and changing her facial expression and posture. This commentary indicated her knowledge of the subject matter and her interest, support, and understanding.

In 1946 a course for Veterans Administration personal counselors was planned by the staff of the University of Chicago Counseling Center. The course lasted for 6 weeks, and Blocksma and Porter (1947) measured some differences in counselor interview behavior before and after instruction. This was the first objective research on attitudes and behaviors of counselors before and after training. The specifics of the training course are not reviewed here, but it is of interest to note that the trainees took a paper and pencil test which required them to select a response to given client statements. In every case the student selected from among five different response classes assumed to communicate different intentions of the counselor: moralization or evaluation; diagnosis or formulation; interpretation or explanation; support or encouragement; and reflection or understanding.

Blocksma and Porter's data indicated very little relationship between what, on the paper and pencil test, the students *said* they would do and what they *actually* did in interviews with clients. For example, during the pretraining evaluation they selected 89% reflection responses in the written test, but only 11% reflection responses in the interview. Marked changes took place in the students' interview behavior over the 6 weeks of training. In their pretraining interviews the students' comments were 84% directive and 11% nondirective, whereas in the posttraining interview their responses were 30% directive and 59% nondirective. These investigators also found that on the pretest 60% of the responses suggested that the student was thinking *about* the client and evaluating him, whereas on the posttest 61% of the responses indicated that the student was thinking *with* the client and allowing him to evaluate himself. Of particular interest here is the finding that the students could not reliably predict their actual interview behavior. There seems to be no substitute for actual observation and recording if interview data are to be faithfully retained.

Rapport and Relationship

All interviewers make some estimate of the degree to which the interviewee has cooperated and actively participated in the interview. It is almost universally assumed that the establishment of good rapport between the interviewer and the interviewee is important in interviewee participation and has the highest priority in an initial interview as well as in subsequent interviews as, for example, in interview therapy. Research interviewers, as well as clinical interviewers, assume that the emotional interaction between themselves and their interviewees affects the pattern of communication between them. In research assessment interviewing, the research interviewer endeavors to obtain community acceptance and support for his project, and he is careful not to become identified with any one particular community group. For example, in an industrial interview study, he seeks support from union as well as company officials. Typically an appointment time is set so that the interviewee is relatively free and uninterrupted. The nature and purpose of the study for which he is being interviewed is explained, with care taken not to give too long or complex an introduction; brief introductions usually work best. If the personal needs of the interviewee can be met in some way (including altruism), such an explanation can help to induce rapport. Finally, interviewers who are confident and expect to obtain interviewee cooperation usually do elicit active interviewee participation.

Clinical interviewers have long assumed that the relationship is the communication bridge between people. If the relationship is positive, each person is likely to be more receptive to the message being sent. A positive relationship might be characterized by feelings such as being relaxed, comfortable, trustful, respectful, harmonious, warm, or psychologically safe. If the relationship is negative, there is less desire and readiness to hear what is being said. A negative relationship may be characterized by such feelings as being hostile, defensive, uneasy, mistrustful, disrespectful, discordant, or psychologically threatened. A positive relationship frees the interviewee to reveal himself without defensiveness or distortion, because of the implied promise of acceptance and understanding and freedom from punishing criticism, rejection, or reprisal. Motivation to participate in the interview may also be derived from the interviewee's opportunity to talk about topics in which he is interested but seldom has the opportunity to discuss fully.

From the standpoint of the interviewer, a positive relationship has the effect of intensifying the interviewer's influence, making his suggestions more appealing and his techniques more effective. A good relationship also makes the interviewer a more potent elicitor of imitative behavior in accordance with which the interviewee can learn to model himself. Another effect of a good relationship and an atmosphere that reduces threat and anxiety is that the atmosphere acts as a counterconditioning context. Discussion of problems and situations that normally evoke anxiety, in a relationship context that counters anxiety, may lead to these problems and situations now evoking less anxiety. This phenomenon is quite similar to the counterconditioning seen in behaviorally oriented relaxation and desensitization procedures.

An excellent discussion of the essential qualities of an interviewer-counselor is offered by Tyler (1969), who notes that it is often difficult to analyze what good interviewers do because the essential qualities involved in a good relationship are attitudes rather than skills. Essential attitudes include acceptance, understanding, and sincerity. The interviewer quality of acceptance involves a thorough-going basic regard for the worth of human individuals and particularly for the individual interviewee sitting in the office with him. The accepting interviewer does not view his interviewee with cynicism or contempt. In fact it has been suggested that, if the interviewer has not discovered something about the interviewee that he can like by the end of an initial interview, the session has not been successful for the establishment of a relationship.

The quality of understanding (or empathy) involves the effort to grasp clearly and completely the meaning the interviewee is trying to convey. Understanding is a sharing process in which the interviewer puts himself in the client's place and tries to see the circumstances as he sees them, not as they look to an outsider.

The quality of sincerity, which has also been called congruence, refers to interviewer consistency, or the harmony that must exist between what an interviewer says and does and what he really is. Gilmore (1973) makes an interesting distinction between acceptance and understanding on the one hand (e.g., you can accept or understand somebody), and sincerity on the other (e.g., you cannot sincere somebody or something). The interviewer can only ''be sincere'' and, although this quality is hard to define, it might be considered an interviewer characteristic to the extent to which the interviewer communicates a valid and reliable picture of what he is really like inside. The reader is urged to study the extended discussion on this topic by Gilmore (1973, pp. 178–225), in which she also makes some suggestions on the development of greater personal sincerity.

A practical implication of this discussion is the implicit conclusion that no one interviewer can be all these things to all people. There is no evidence to support a belief that interviewers can function equally well with all types of interviewees. A somewhat related question might be whether there are some assessment and therapeutic intervention procedures that are less dependent on the nature of the relationship between the participants. Behavior therapists, for example, might appear to minimize the importance of the relationship, treating it as a general rather than a specific condition for therapy. Patterson (1968) discusses this issue in considerable detail and marshals both evidence and arguments to suggest that the behavior therapist is highly interested in, concerned about, and devoted to helping his client. He has the same interviewer characteristics we have referred to above. In short, behavior therapists are involved in relationships with their clients and behavior therapists are human; they are nice people, not machines.

Communication

In any clinical interview situation, as well as probably in any interpersonal situation, communication takes place between the participants. If one examines the many forms communication can take (both verbal and nonverbal), it becomes impossible to conceive of a two-person interaction that does not involve communication. Obviously, some forms of communication are more effective than others, and perhaps some are not consciously intended at all. The main skill an interviewer must develop is to convey effectively that he understands and accepts what the client is trying to say. This clearly extends beyond the factual content of the client's statements; it extends to, and perhaps most importantly includes, feelings that are often hard to put into words.

There are great individual interviewer differences in communication styles and also changes within each interviewer from one client to the next. It is probably not possible yet, if it ever will be, to suggest very specific rules of good communication. Yet, as Tyler (1969) has outlined, there are some general communication practices among experienced interviewers which are worth noting. For example, an interviewee often makes a series of comments that may involve both fact and feelings of some variety. When he pauses, the interviewer decides how to respond. The most often preferred response is a brief interviewer comment which can put together several of the feelings or attitudes that have been expressed. Short of a brief summarizing comment he should at least indicate his understanding of some one feeling by responding to it. If the interviewee's comments involve several people, it behooves the interviewer to respond to the interviewee's side of the relationship.

Tyler (1969, p. 19) offers in this regard the example of a client talking about his difficulties with an unreasonable police officer. The interviewer could comment, "He must have been a very unpleasant person," and expect to obtain more information about the officer's attitudes and motives. Or he could comment, "You seem to dislike people of that sort intensely," and expect to gain a better understanding of how the interviewee reacts.

The specific words the interviewer uses to achieve his purpose are important. A basic communication consideration is the use of words for which both participants in the interview have a common definition. It is difficult to know whether this is the case without frequently exploring the meaning both parties assign to words. In addition to the obvious consideration of a common definition, it is important for the interviewer to consider whether his use of words is likely to put the interviewee on the defensive. Words such as *coward, stupid,* or *effeminate* are best not used unless the interviewee has introduced them. Tact is desirable in all interpersonal situations, including the interview.

The interviewer also often finds that some of his own anxieties, struggles, and aspirations are being stimulated, and his impulse is to talk about himself. This impulse is best resisted in favor of keeping the focus of the discussion on the interviewee, this being one of the differences between and interview and a conversation. It is furthermore not good interviewing practice for the interviewer to recount his experiences with other interviewees, even though the problem situations appear to be similar. A basic assumption about any interpersonal partner is that what he has done to someone else he is likely to do to me.

Another task of the interviewer is to decide how to respond to silence.

If the interviewee is reflecting on what has been said, he should be allowed the silent opportunity to do so. If the silence is based on some aspect of duress or confrontation, the interviewer is best advised to maintain communication by not allowing the silence to continue. It is highly unlikely that communication will be enhanced or a positive relationship furthered by an interviewer's insisting on waiting out his interviewee. Again it can be repeated that many different words can be used to convey understanding and acceptance, and phraseology does not have to be elegant. Good interviewing does require careful listening, however, both to the individual words and statements of the interviewee and for themes that may recur. In Tyler's words (1969, p. 42), "Listen, think, respond. It is the hardest kind of work, but worth the effort."

RESEARCH ON THE ANATOMY OF THE INTERVIEW

Researchers of the interview have examined many different aspects of dyadic interaction. Traditionally, investigators have focused on *what* the interview participants say, that is, on the content aspects of speech. Research on content analysis has included the study of variables such as frequency of usage of grammatical units (verbs, pronouns, adjectives, and other grammatical units) and themes (references to parents or other significant humans), distress-relief words, past- or future-tense usage, affectionate or hostile words, so-called manifest or latent meanings, degree of inferred empathy or lack of empathy toward the conversational partner, and anxiety-laden versus neutral themes and topics, and so on.

Other investigators have studied human speech and interview interaction with a focus on *how* something is said. Physicists, electronic engineers, experts in acoustics, students of high-fidelity sound recording, and others have recorded speech and played it into oscilloscopes and other electronic equipment in order to analyze its formal components such as its frequencies, intensities, timbre, and related acoustical qualities. Matarazzo and Wiens (1972) have reviewed some aspects of the research just referred to and have presented references for more detailed review for the interested reader.

Temporal Characteristics of Interview Speech

Another area of noncontent interview research (research on the formal properties of speech) is the study of the different rates (timing) of verbal interaction. It is easily recognized that some interviewees talk and act rapidly, whereas others are slow and deliberate. One can also observe that, in many cases, people whom one does not like or cannot get along with say exactly the same things as the people whom one likes. Actors may take a short play, play it first as a tragedy and then, using the same words, play it as a comedy. Here the language is seen as unimportant, and the timing is the factor that makes the difference in its effect on the audience (Chapple & Arensberg, 1940, p. 33).

My colleagues and I have for many years conducted research concerned with the reliability and validity of inferences based on structural-temporal dimensions of the interview, namely, frequency and duration of single units of speech and silence. Three major speech variables have been studied in many different interviewee and interview situations: duration of utterance (DOU), reaction time latency (RTL), and percentage of interruptions. The mean speech duration (DOU) is defined as the total time the interviewee (or interviewer) speaks divided by his total number of speech units. The mean speech latency (RTL) is defined as the total latency time (the period of silence separating two different speech units) divided by the number of units of interviewee (or interviewer) latency. The percentage of interruptions is defined as the total number of times the interviewee (or interviewer) speaks divided into the number of these same speech units that were interruptions of his partner. The interested reader should consult Matarazzo and Wiens (1972) for a detailed definition of a speech unit, which is the basic datum in this interview research.

Clinical observers who have watched these experimental (also real-life interviews which form the basis for clinical decisions) interviews have been unable to discern the particular interviewer behaviors that have been standardized. In fact, minimal but significant interviewer standardization was introduced so that it would be possible to compare interview findings from one interview to the next. Specifically, the interviewer is asked to use open-ended questions and a nondirective interviewing style, that is, to follow the discussion topics as the interviewee introduces them. In clinical research interviews, however, the general topic areas are constant across interviews (e.g., topic areas such as "family," "occupation," "education").

In addition to using the prescribed speaking style, the interviewer is asked to speak in utterances of 5-seconds' duration, to respond to the interviewees with less than 1-second response latencies, and not to interrupt the interviewee. The interviews are observed through a one-way-vision mirror, and the observer activates the keys of an interaction recorder (Wiens, Matarazzo, & Saslow, 1965) which records on paper tape the time when either person is speaking or silent. A sequential unit-by-unit speech analysis is provided by computer printout. For individual investigators not wishing to utilize an electronic recording system, it has also been shown that a word count from a typescript of an interview gives a good approximation of the average DOU (Matarazzo, Holman & Wiens, 1967). Wiens, Molde, Holman, and Matarazzo (1966) have also demonstrated that all three speech measures can be taken directly from tape recordings of interviews to yield scores equally reliable and equivalent to those obtained by an observer of the live interview through a one-way-vision mirror.

A major purpose of these studies was to develop an interview format and recording technique that would allow the speech behavior of an interviewee to be recorded in a sufficiently reliable and stable manner so that such speech behavior could form the basis for further study. A series of reliability studies of the procedure is summarized by Saslow and Matarazzo (1959). In the first of these studies two different interviewers examined the same new patient in an outpatient psychiatry clinic using the standardized interview format described above. The two interviewers had no knowledge of the content of each other's interviews, and each talked about what he would typically discuss in such an initial assessment interview. The two interviews (of approximately 35-minutes' duration) were conducted 5 minutes apart. The product-moment coefficient of correlation between the interviewee's DOUs in the two different interviews was .91. The correlations for the other speech variables were equally high. This study was replicated using intervals between interviews of 1 week, 5 weeks, and 8 months. These studies suggested that the verbal interaction measures employed reflected stable and invariant behavior characteristics under the real-life, minimally standardized interview conditions in which these patients were studied. It was also apparent that there were wide individual differences in speech, silence, and interruption behavior.

Modifiability of Temporal Speech Characteristics

Subsequent studies revealed that, despite this high test-retest reliability, planned changes in the interviewer's own speech behavior during any given single interview could produce striking corresponding changes in the speech behavior of the interviewee. These planned changes in the interviewer's own speech behavior have included increases and decreases in his average DOUs, increases and decreases in his RTLs, and increases and decreases in his speech interruptions.

In one series of studies it was found that, by doubling or halving the duration of each of his own single speech units (from a mean of 5.3 seconds to 9.9 seconds to 6.1 seconds, respectively, in each of the three 15-minute periods of a 45-minute interview), the interviewer was able to influence the mean DOU of interviewees in the three comparable periods of the interview (24.3, 46.9, and 26.6 seconds, respectively). The positive results of this study were cross-validated in two additional studies in which the interviewer unobtrusively controlled his single speech unit durations to approximately 10-5-10 seconds and 5-15-5 second durations in the three parts of his planned interview.

That such interviewer-control effects are not limited to face-to-face employment interviews was revealed in another study (Matarazzo, Wiens, Saslow, Dunham & Voas, 1964) in which it was demonstrated that the DOUs of an orbiting astronaut were correlated with changes in the DOUs of ground communicators. In an ingenious extension of this last study, Ray and Webb (1966) showed that how much or how little President Kennedy talked in response to a reporter's questions in his 1961–1963 series of press conferences was clearly related to the length of the questions posed by the reporter. Such effects are clearly out of the realm of conscious awareness.

Planned changes in the interviewer's own RTL (reaction time before he responds to the interviewee), utilizing preplanned interviewer RTLs of 1-1-1, 1-5-1, 5-1-5, 1-10-1, and 1-15-1 seconds in separate studies, also produced the predicted increases and decreases in the corresponding interview RTLs of the interviewee. The frequency of an interviewer's interruption of the interviewee likewise revealed that, with surprising regularity, the interviewee's interruption rate covaried with that of the interviewer.

One possible implication of these findings for clinical interviews is that the interviewer could conceivably induce depressed patients to talk in longer utterances or manic patients to talk in shorter utterances by modifying his own DOUs. Another possible implication of these findings for an ongoing interview series would be the deliberate pairing of interviewers having specific known characteristics with patients whose own speech characteristics presumably could best utilize such an interviewer-interviewee combination.

Other speech modifiability studies have employed head nodding and saying "Mm-hmm" during the experimental periods of a standardized interview and have demonstrated that these are powerful tactics which can increase interviewee DOUs. In other work an experimentally induced set, in which an interviewee was led to believe that he would talk to either a "cold" or "warm" interviewer, was found to influence markedly the interviewee's RTL.

Concurrent with the studies just noted, the clinical interview research program was extended to the study of ongoing psychotherapy in which the two participants met not just for one encounter, as in a single assessment interview, but for an extended series of interviews. These interviews were entirely unstructured, and the interviewer had preplanned neither the content of his comments nor their temporal characteristics. Three psychotherapists were studied, two with two patients each and one with three patients, for a total of seven patient-therapist pairs. The results of this research (Matarazzo, Wiens, Matarazzo, & Saslow, 1968) revealed a synchrony or tracking over the sessions in the speech behavior of the two speakers. That is, each person's RTLs showed sizable differences from one day to the next but also a remarkable correlation with increases and decreases in the RTLs of his interview partner. Frequency of interrupting behavior likewise showed such synchrony across the numerous psychotherapy sessions of the therapist-patient pairs.

Individual Differences among Groups

An early question in this research program was whether the highly reliable average DOUs for each interviewee could be useful for differential diagnosis. This question was examined in a study of the interview speech behavior of five different groups of interviewees: 19 state hospital, backward, chronic psychotics (schizophrenics); 40 neurotic and acutely psychotic patients from the inpatient and outpatient psychiatric services of a general hospital; 60 outpatient clinic neurotics; 40 normals (applicants for sales positions at a Boston department store); and 17 normals (applicants for sales positions at a Chicago department store). The results revealed clear differences among these five groups. Whereas the two normal groups did not differ from each other, each of them differed significantly from each of the three patient groups. Specifically, although the range of individual differences in each diagnostic group was very large, the median value for DOUs increased steadily from the presumably sickest group (the back-ward schizophrenic patients), in which it was the shortest, to the neurotic and acutely psychotic group, the outpatient neurotics, and finally the presumably healthiest (the two normal) groups, in which it was the longest. As noted, the variability within each group was too large to allow accurate individual diagnosis by DOU alone. Nevertheless, the results are encouraging to those investigators who wish to develop objective indices to aid in differential diagnosis.

Nathan, Schneller, and Lindsley (1964) have reported comparable data from assessment interviews they conducted with mental hospital patients. Their patients talked less when discussing personally related, stressful content than when discussing presumably neutral content, and less severely ill patients had a higher rate of talking than more severely ill patients. Kanfer (1960) reported that female mental patients talked at a 25%

slower rate when talking with an interviewer about relationships with men than when talking about their present illness. Craig (1966) reported differences in the DOUs and RTLs of mental patients related to whether an interviewer gave them personality interpretations that were congruent or incongruent with their own perceptions. Kanfer (1960) and Pope, Blass, Siegman, and Raher (1970), studying psychosomatic patients and recording periodic free-speech monologues, found differences in speech and silence behavior associated with whether the patient was clinically rated as being in a state of anxiety or depression. In another study, based on interview data from normal subjects, Pope, Siegman, and Blass (1970) demonstrated similar differences in speech behavior under anxiety-stimulated and under neutral conditions.

Two studies in this area have examined individual differences among groups of nurses. In the first study Wiens, Matarazzo, Saslow, Thompson, and Matarazzo (1965) interviewed groups of staff nurses, head nurses, and supervising nurses. Standardized interview procedures were used, and the interviewer was asked to start each interview with a request that the interviewee describe her nursing activities on a typical working day. Beyond this, the interviewer was asked to make his comments nonchallenging, open-ended, and limited to the interviewee's past comments or to some new, general topic which followed naturally from her past comments. In general, the supervising and head nurses did not differ significantly from each other, but the staff nurses differed significantly from both of these groups in their speech and interruption characteristics. Specifically, the staff nurses interrupted the interviewer fewer times, spoke in shorter speech units (and consequently talked more often than members of the other two groups), and utilized less of the total interview time for their own speech. This research did not answer the question whether the differentiating interaction characteristics were inherent in the individual nurses and had led to some of them being appointed to administrative positions and others not, or whether the appointment to an administrative position stimulated the development of the verbal interaction patterns that characterized the supervising and head nurses.

In a second study with nurses, Molde and Wiens (1968) investigated the temporal verbal behavior of two groups of nurses, psychiatric and surgical, engaged in widely different work settings. As was predicted, the psychiatric nurses had a greater verbal output in the standardized interview than did the surgical nurses. The latter group was found to interrupt the interviewer more frequently and to exhibit a shorter RTL in responding to the interviewer's comments than did their psychiatric counterparts. It seemed likely that some of these observed differences could be accounted for on the basis of occupational demands on the nurse's verbal behavior, although it is not clear what interrelationships exist between innate or idiosyncratic factors and environmental influences on speech behavior, or how they interact.

Of interest in this regard are studies such as that by R. G. Matarazzo, Wiens, and Saslow (1966), which explore the effects of training in psychotherapy skills on the actual performance of a student interviewer in an interview or therapy setting. Matarazzo et al. observed a 100% increase in the RTLs of student interviewers between a "naive" first series of interviews and a second series of interviews after they had received 8 weeks of intensive instruction in psychotherapy skills. Inasmuch as this change was accompanied by a gross drop in the mean percentage interruption units by the student interviewers, it seems reasonable to conclude that the training they received in psychotherapy interviewing skills dramatically affected the temporal interaction characteristics of their speech. It is possible to speculate that both these differences and the differences observed between psychiatric and surgical nurses in their interruption and RTL behavior are attributable to degree of familiarity with psychotherapeutic interviewing procedures.

Some Relationships between Noncontent Speech Variables and Interview Content

An early attempt to study the relationship of the content of an interview to the concurrent noncontent speech behavior of the interviewee was reported by Kanfer, Phillips, Matarazzo, and Saslow (1960). In this study an interviewer was asked to vary his style of speaking from neutral to interpretive while discussing relatively standardized content with two groups of student nurse interviewees. In one part of the interview the interviewer used neutral statements and in another part, continuing with similar content, he made interpretations about the student nurse interviewee's motivations and life-style. The results indicated a significant drop in the interviewee's mean DOU under the interpretation condition as compared to the neutral condition.

In related work Manaugh, Wiens, and Matarazzo (1970) attempted experimentally to induce a momentary motivational state in two of four college groups studied. The experimental but not the control groups were instructed by a research assistant, through a brief set of written instructions, to attempt to deceive an interviewer about their education by stating initially that they had completed 1 year more of college than in fact they had, and subsequently to answer all other questions in this content area so as to be consistent with this initial deception. The data analysis revealed a significant effect on the speech behavior of these college student interviewees in the education content area for *both* the control and experimental groups. Namely, all groups talked with a longer mean DOU and a shorter RTL when discussing education content. Thus, even if the education-deception set influenced behavior in the two deception groups, the empirically recorded effect of education content itself, as found in the two control groups, was so powerful as to have masked what otherwise might have been a successful experimentally introduced motivational set in the two deception groups.

In a follow-up study Matarazzo, Wiens, Jackson, and Manaugh (1970a) selected two topic areas ("college major" and "living setting") which were assumed to be equally salient among a sample of undergraduate college students. However, again transcending the effort to induce motivational states, it was found in both control and experimental groups that "college major" was a content topic of apparent higher intrinsic saliency for the 80 subjects than was the topic "living setting." The differential saliency was clearly revealed in differences in their temporal speech behavior, specifically, longer DOU and shorter RTL when discussing "college major." Concurrent with this study, a large number of job applicants were being interviewed for the civil service position of police patrolman. These interviews, of 45-minutes' duration, were unobtrusively divided into three 15-minute segments during each of which a different content area ("education," "occupation," "family") was discussed. The results confirmed further that the temporal dimensions of speech can be differentially affected by the content topics under discussion (Matarazzo, Wiens, Jackson, & Manaugh, 1970b). Specifically, these job applicants spoke with a shorter RTL and a longer mean DOU while discussing their occupational histories than at other times. These results were cross-validated and were interpreted to mean that the topic "occupation" was more salient for these interviewees, in this particular situation, than the topics "education" and "family."

The outcome of these studies suggested that an aspect of these subjects' motivational or personality-emotional state was being revealed in their noncontent interview speech behavior. Subsequently, a procedure was developed (a Topic Importance Scale) whereby persons were asked several weeks or months in advance to rate the importance or personal saliency of a wide variety of topic areas. Interview topics were then chosen to tap high- and low-saliency ratings, and corresponding predictions were made about interview temporal speech characteristics these people would display. The predictions correctly anticipated that interviewees would have a longer mean DOU when talking about high- as opposed to low-saliency topics as they had previously rated them (Jackson, Wiens, Manaugh, & Matarazzo, 1972).

It has been suggested that, as the complexity of a verbal task increases, whether the greater complexity is based on cognitive or emotional factors, speech may become more internalized, and that external speech (DOU) consequently decreases and internal thought processes increase (reflected in longer RTL). Goldman-Eisler (1968) in this regard studied silence and hesitation phenomena in speech and has concluded that silence is used for higher cognitive activity. In an interesting cross-cultural study with Dutch subjects, Ramsay (1968) showed that there are significant differences between extroverts and introverts in the length of silences between their utterances. His view of the introvert is that such a person is thoughtful, thinks before speaking, and weighs his words more carefully than the extrovert; in this way, he concludes, the introvert's speech patterns are consistent with other aspects of his behavior. Siegman and Pope (1965) similarly found a significant negative correlation between extroversion and duration of silence in an interview situation.

Aronson and Weintraub (1972) have for years studied verbal styles associated with different pathological behavioral patterns such as impulsive outbursts, delusional symptom formation, and depression. Whereas they score speech behavior along many dimensions, of particular interest here is that depressed patients can be differentiated by their low rate and quantity of speech (the exception being the agitated depressive patient). By contrast, the impulsive patient is likely to have a high speech rate.

Siegman and Pope (1972) studied the effects of anxiety on speech. They acknowledge that anxiety is generally assumed to have a disruptive effect on speech, inasmuch as speech is a finely coordinated behavior and anxiety is expected to disrupt such behavior. They also argue that, if anxiety is regarded as a drive state, it might be expected that an increase in anxiety level increases verbal output at the same time it produces an increase in speech disturbances (e.g., corrections, repetitions). Anxiety, in other words, may have both a facilitating and disruptive effect on speech. The Siegman and Pope research data supported their reasoning, and they concluded that in normal subjects both low- and high-anxiety arousal are associated with speech productivity, speech disruptions, and an accelerated speech tempo.

There is of course great interest in assessing whether the speech variables discussed above relate to such interpersonal interview characteristics as empathy, transference, warmth, unconditional positive regard, experiencing, and other interview process variables. Matarazzo and Wiens (1972) conclude that there is preliminary evidence that this may be the case. For example, it has been demonstrated that a modest increase in an interviewer's DOU produces a significant increase in the interviewee's speech output, or DOU. One possible dynamic underlying this phenomenon may be a greater satisfaction that the interviewee feels with the longer

DOUs of the interviewer. Truax (1970) has reported finding a similar relationship between duration of therapist talk and the therapist's independently rated level of accurate empathy. Therapists who talked more per session were rated as showing higher levels of accurate empathy, and their patients showed greater degrees of overall improvement than patients of therapists who talked less. Although research in this area has only recently begun, the studies cited above to illustrate a somewhat larger body of literature serve as an initial body of evidence relating *noncontent* speech behaviors to a variety of interview variables traditionally assessed from the *content* of the same interview.

STUDIES IN NONVERBAL COMMUNICATION

The challenge of assessing reliably the presence of identifiable human attitudes, motivational states, and other personality characteristics has attracted investigators in many branches of social and psychological sciences since the turn of the century. Personality tests (objective and projective), a variety of self-report questionnaires, attitude surveys, and the like have all been used with a modest degree of utility and common acceptance (see Chapters 2 and 4). There has been general recognition that the efficacy of all of these procedures is highly dependent on the cooperation, personal awareness, and active participation of the individuals to be assessed. Faced with these limitations, behavioral and social scientists have looked for clues to individual personality and motivational states in overt behaviors that are not typically under the conscious control of the individual. Of particular interest in this respect has been the question of how validly to infer an individual's attitudinal or motivational state from more-or-less subtle nonverbal behaviors emitted during social interactions and, especially, psychological interviews. Specifically, psychologists and others have attempted to identify channels of information other than the consciously controlled channel of verbal content. During the past decade, research in nonverbal communication has generated convincing evidence that facial expressions, body posture and movements, and styles of speaking can serve as valuable sources of information. The development of sophisticated audio and video recording equipment has been necessary to record interviews adequately for later and more detailed analyses.

Psycholinguistics and Paralanguage

Perhaps many persons would say that it is of obvious importance to study language in order to understand human behavior. It appears that psychologists have come to this realization somewhat belatedly, although the growing prominence of the field of psycholinguistics suggests that there may now be a major interest in language. One psychologist who has greatly increased our awareness of the importance of language is George A. Miller (1973) who writes:

> . . . There presently exists a behavioral procedure that can exert powerful control over people's thoughts and actions. This technique of control can cause you to do things you would never think of doing otherwise. It can change opinions and beliefs. It can be used to deceive you. It can make you happy or sad. It can put new ideas into your head. It can make you want things you don't have. You can even use it to control yourself. It is an enormously powerful tool with a universal range of application. . . . Far from thinking of it as an evil or threatening thing, most people regard this particular kind of control as one of the greatest triumphs of the human mind, indeed, as the very thing that raises man above all the other animals. [p. 4–5]

Miller was, of course, talking about human language which is a basic essential for much human communication.

Language among humans is characterized by many individual differences. A major source of difference is that people talk different languages and come from diverse cultural backgrounds. This is obvious when we think of individuals from foreign countries and how difficult communication can be when two people do not speak the same language. Even within a given country there are many regional and ethnic language differences which must be understood for effective communication. The study of intercultural communication is obviously imperative, for example, for the businessman or the politician who wants to conduct business overseas. The study of ethnic language characteristics may be equally imperative for the psychologist who wants to communicate with members of ethnic minority groups. One statistical aspect of language that has been widely explored is the size of the vocabulary. Most of us are sensitive about the number of words we recognize and use, and psychologists who measure intelligence typically find that estimates of vocabulary size are among the most dependable indicators they possess. Many assessment interviewers actually utilize a selection of test vocabulary words for a quick, general estimate of intelligence. For example, the vocabulary list from the Stanford-Binet Test of Intelligence is easily used for this purpose because the number of words correctly defined can be readily translated into an equivalent IQ score.

However, it is not easy to obtain a reliable estimate of the number of words a person knows. As Miller (1969) has pointed out, people have multiple vocabularies, one for talking, one for reading, one for writing, and so on. The differences in the size of the several vocabularies within one person are sometimes larger than the differences in the same vocabulary among different people. It is a general rule of verbal learning that recognition is easier than recall; a word may be recognized by a person even though he cannot use it himself. A large recognition vocabulary despite relatively small talking and writing (recall) vocabularies allows a person to understand a wide range of speakers even though he could or would not have used their words. Intelligence, age, and education are major factors correlated with differences in the size of vocabulary.

The person with a large vocabulary is likely to have a more diversified speaking style than the one who is restricted to a small vocabulary. A person with a limited vocabulary reuses a word sooner, on the average, than a person who has a large vocabulary. It is possible simply to count the number of words that intervene between the successive use of a common word such as "the." On the average, more words intervene between successive uses of the word "the" if the speaker has a diverse vocabulary. A closely related index is called the *type/token ratio* (TTR), which provides a more direct measure of diversification. The TTR is the ratio of the number of different words (types) to the total number of words (tokens) in the passage. Typically, a total sample can be divided into subsamples of equal word length, and the TTR for each segment can then be determined and these several values averaged together for a mean segmental TTR.

Other statistical measures of verbal style include sentence length, styles in punctuation, and verb/adjective ratios. Regarding the latter, the verb/adjective ratio is usually higher for spoken than for written language. The more time one has to produce the symbols, the more qualification he puts on them. The comparison of different kinds of writing shows the largest variations. As noted by Miller (1969), for example, the dialogue in plays shows a ratio of 9 verbs per adjective, whereas scientific writings show only 1.3 verbs per adjective. Legal statutes, which deal with the acts of human beings, have 5 verbs per adjective, and fiction about 3 verbs per adjective. Theses written for the master's degree have 1.5 verbs for each adjective, but by the time candidates reach the Ph.D. level, the ratio is reduced to 1.1 verbs per adjective. In one Ph.D. thesis a cautious writer was found to use two qualifications for every construction, a verb/adjective ratio of 0.5. It is important here to note that this indicator of statistical style changes with the type of writing, and this ratio cannot be used to indicate changes in emotional stability, for example, unless the verbal tasks are carefully equated.

Kasl and Mahl (1965) have urged attention to what might seem to be irrelevant or nonlexical aspects of speech, particularly speech disturbances. Under the heading of flustered or confused speech they include a number of distinct speech disturbance categories. These include the familiar "ah" or some of its variants such as "eh," "uh," or "uhm." Also included are sentence changes that consist of a correction or change in the content of expression and which must be sensed by the listener as interruptions in the flow of the sentence. Repetitions, stutters, word omissions, sentence incompletions, slips of the tongue, and intruding incoherent sounds rounded out a total of eight speech dysfluency categories that Kasl and Mahl scored in their research. In terms of absolute frequency, they found that one or another of the disturbances occurred, on the average, for every 16 "words" spoken, which is equivalent to one disturbance for every 4.6 seconds an individual spends talking.

Kasl and Mahl also reported that, under conditions of manipulated anxiety, the frequency of all speech disturbances except for "ah" showed a sizable increase. An additional interesting finding was that the "non-ah" ratio of speech disturbance was not affected by whether the experimenter was present in the room or was in a monitor room, whereas the "ah" ratio of speech disturbance was distinctly affected. This led them to speculate that various facial expressions, movements of the head, and so on, are cues that may give feedback to a speaker. When the experimenter was in the monitor room, then, providing no listener feedback to the speaker, perhaps more uncertainty was introduced about the effects of his speaking on the listener, and the use of "ah" enabled the subjects to pause briefly to determine what to say next. This hypothesis is consistent with the earlier reference to the work of Goldman-Eisler, who has suggested that silent pauses in speech become lengthened with greater cognitive activity.

Voice is generally thought of as a purely individual matter, yet one can ask whether the voice has a social quality as well as an individual one. Intuitively people probably attach a great deal of importance to voices and to the speech behavior they carry. For example, if a speaker's voice can be characterized as raucous, it is difficult not to infer automatically some negative personal attributes of that person. Two research approaches to attempting to differentiate verbal content from voice quality have been to ask speakers to convey emotion while speaking meaningless content (e.g., reciting the alphabet or saying only numbers), or to use electronic filtering techniques to mask meaningful speech frequencies while preserving affective tone. Employing the first approach, Davitz and Davitz (1974) showed that reading the alphabet can carry affective meaning when subjects are instructed to instill such meaning into their reading. In their study all feelings were identified more consistently than chance alone would predict. Additionally, some errors in identification were consistent, namely, fear was most commonly misidentified as nervousness, love as sadness, and pride as satisfaction.

Fascinating clinical extensions of those observations are found in two studies, one by Milmoe, Rosenthal, Blane, Chafetz, and Wolf (1974) on the "doctor's voice," and the other by Milmoe, Novey, Kagan, and Rosenthal (1974) on the "mother's voice." In the first study, doctors whose voices were rated as less angry and more anxious were more successful in referring alcoholic patients for further treatment than were doctors with angry, nonanxious voices. Alcoholic patients were used as subjects on the assumption that, being sensitized to rejection, they would be especially aware of the subtle, unintended cues conveyed by the doctor, whether cues of sympathy and acceptance or cues of anger and disgust. The positive relationship between inferred anxiety in the voice and effectiveness with alcoholic patients may relate to the notion that an effectively functioning healer whose manner of speech is perceived by others to have an anxious, nervous quality may be seen by the patient as showing marked concern. The second study indicated that mothers whose voices were rated high on dimensions of anxiety and anger had children who showed various "signs of irritability," such as crying and becoming upset at separation. Other examples of voice quality communication are the familiar modifications in voice level, tone of voice, speed of communication, and the like that are appropriate for funerals, weddings, receptions, formal interviews and so on.

The interview situation is almost invariably one in which the participants listen to each other talk and can also hear their own voices. Mahl (1972) reported research in which he studied interviewees who were talking but unable to hear the sound of their own voices. Reviewing a variety of studies on delayed auditory feedback, partial deafness, temporary hearing loss, and the like, he called attention to the deterioration of speech quality in the deafened person and the corresponding importance of continual auditory feedback in the preservation of developed speech patterns. Mahl's study involved interviewing college students in four conditions: (a) sitting in the usual face-to-face arrangement; (b) facing the interviewer but being unable to hear themselves because sound was masked through earphones they were wearing; (c) being unable to see the interviewer who sat behind them; and (d) being able neither to see the interviewer nor hear themselves talk. Students were interviewed three times, so that novelty of the situation was not a factor. In the noise conditions, the masking noise was administered at all times except when the interviewer spoke.

A variety of linguistic changes was observed in this study, including the fact that the masking noise produced louder speech, flattening of intonation, a shift toward lower social status dialect, prolongation of sounds, changes in pitch, various vocal noises, slurring, change in rate, and fragmentation of phrasing. Significant behavioral-psychological changes were also observed, including greater affective expression without auditory feedback (this also involved more direct emotional response to the interviewer); freer associative responses, indicated by increased verbal productivity and increased spontaneity in the communication of highly personal information; increased cognitive confusion; and "thinking aloud." The latter phenomenon was infrequent but quite striking when it occurred, because it involved unintended and unconscious utterance of content and, in one instance, a subject disclaimed even the thoughts involved. Mahl concluded that the disinhibition shown was related to the feedback deficit and that normal auditory feedback plays an important role in the regulation of many *vocal* dimensions of language behavior, in the control of the vocal expression of affects and thought, and in the maintenance of a sense of self and reality. Possible implications of this study for the interviewing situation include the observation that a person is less aware of cues emanating from his speech partner when he is talking than when he is silent, and also that when a person is talking he is less aware of stimulation arising from within himself than when he is silent.

There are many other situations in which the study of paralinguistic characteristics is important, and an excellent overview of these situations is provided by Duncan (1969) in a discussion of various nonlanguage or nonverbal communicative functions. Weitz (1972) has suggested that, in interracial situations, the paralinguistic channel may carry more accurate information than the more socially controlled verbal channel. Her informal discussions with blacks have confirmed the observation that tone is often closely attended to as reliably indicating whether the interviewer's attitude is hostile, patronizing, or genuinely friendly. Weitz also concludes that there is individual variation in sensitivity to such paralinguistic and nonverbal channels, with the more dependent member of the dyad having the most to gain by being attuned to the other's emotional state and to the affective tone of the interaction.

The importance of noncontent (tonal or vocal) characteristics of speech is also suggested in the findings of a study by Mehrabian and Wiener (1967). In that study single-word contents with three degrees of attitude (positive, neutral, and negative) each were combined with three degrees of attitude (positive, neutral, and negative) communicated in tones of voice. Stimulus words used were "honey," "thanks," and "dear" (positive content); "maybe," "really," and "okay" (neutral content); and "don't," "brute," and "terrible" (negative content). Different subjects were instructed so they would attend to (a) both the content and tone of the stimulus words, (b) the content only, or (c) the tone only. The findings indicated that the independent effects of tone generally were stronger than the independent effects of content. Interestingly, the responses of subjects who were instructed to attend to all the information (tone plus content) showed no differences related to content. The variability of response to tone and content combined was determined primarily by variations in tone. These results demonstrate the relative importance of non-content variables, in this case tone, when assessing the emotional meaning of verbal behavior. A familiar example to the reader will be the use of the phrase, "That's just great," which can only be interpreted if one knows the vocal characteristics of its utterance.

Mehrabian (1972) also introduced and explicated the concept of immediacy as broadly describing the extent to which communication reflects closeness of interaction. Generally speaking, a face-to-face discussion is more immediate than one via videotape, which in turn is more immediate than a telephone conversation, which is more immediate than a letter, and so on. Verbal examples of variations in immediacy are personal pronouns "I" and "we," which are verbally closer than "he," "she," or "it," and phrases such as "my country," "our country," or "their country" or "I feel," "I think," or "It is my opinion." As Mehrabian has defined immediacy, it refers to the degree of intensity and directness of interaction between a speaker and the object about which he speaks. Generally, there is more immediacy in statements about persons one likes than about those one dislikes. More immediate statements are also generally judged to be more positive in tone or to reflect a more positive speaker feeling.

An interesting related topic is the form of address people use when speaking to each other. This varies with the language being spoken; consider for example, the use of such second-person pronouns as *du* and *sie* in German or, in English, the choice between second- and third-person use in directives, for example, "one should not" or "you should not." Also, of course, the form of address varies in terms of the use of honorifics, title and last name, or the use of the first name. Slobin, Miller, and Porter (1972) have pointed out that it is apparently a sociolinguistic universal that the address term exchanged between intimates (familiar pronoun, first name, etc.) is the same term used in addressing social inferiors, and that the term exchanged between nonintimates (polite pronoun, title and last name, etc.) is also used to address social superiors (p. 263). Slobin et al. showed that in a business setting where nonreciprocal address patterns occur, status is unequal. Age is also a factor in this regard, but apparently not as important as achievement; in most dyads in which the superior person is the younger, naming is symmetric, that is, there is mutual use of either title and last name or first names. An interesting additional finding was that, although the person of higher status is the pacesetter in linguistic address, the person of lower status might take the lead in self-disclosure in an effort to increase intimacy.

Selzer (1973) reminds interviewers that all interview behavior should be for the benefit of the patient, and that any interviewer behavior that does not meet this criterion has no place in a clinical situation. He then goes on to suggest possible emotional meanings for the interviewer of addressing a patient by his first name, beginning with the need to feel superior. This need may arise particularly in the insecure therapist who fears his patient may be more intelligent, more successful, or better endowed in some way than he is. In addition to possibly minimizing the patient, the use of first names may also minimize the patient's difficulties. That is, a need to assume that the patient is suffering a temporary childlike disturbance may be implemented by addressing the patient as if he were a child. The use of first names may also avoid therapeutic commitment by conveying to the patient that he and the interviewer are merely chatting.

The use of first names may also imply an offer of friendship which can carry with it the implied demand that the patient reciprocate. However, friendship relationships may pose a problem for the patient, both in general and with specific reference to his feeling that he must not do or say anything to jeopardize his friendship with the interviewer. He might then hesitate to discuss topics that might offend or alienate the interviewer. Finally, the status differential implied by the use of first names may push the patient into a greater state of dependence or regression at the expense of his working toward greater maturity and reliance on his own judgment. Selzer acknowledges that these are speculative concerns and that the use of first names may be warranted in some instances. He also makes the good point that the interviewer should have a good reason for addressing his patient by whatever form of address he uses.

Facial Expression and Visual Interaction

It has been suggested (Weitz, 1972) that nonverbal behavior can be seen in some sense as predating verbal behavior and perhaps as being a more primitive response system. For example, under stress people often resort to nonverbal signs, such as screaming or crying, with accompanying facial expressions, rather than undertaking a complex verbal analysis of the situation. Comparative psychologists and ethologists have been interested in facial communication among animals, and social scientists within the fields of anthropology, sociology, and psychology have been interested in possible cross-cultural universals in facial expression. For example, the "eyebrow flash" of recognition on greeting seems to be characteristic of all studied cultures and primate groups. The work of Ekman and Friesen (see, e.g., their 1969 publication) is frequently referred to in reviews of facially displayed affect. In their human cross-cultural research Ekman and Friesen demonstrated that there is consistent recognition of facial expressions of such primary affects as happiness, surprise, fear, sadness, anger, disgust, and interest. They have also developed a Facial Affect Scoring Technique (FAST) to study more systematically the identification of affect and the various aspects of the face that contribute to an observer's judgment of expressed affect.

There are various facial phenomena to which an interviewer (and interviewee) pay attention. This chapter has already called attention to some effects of interviewer head nods. Another very common behavior is the smile, which to many interviewees can communicate such acceptance messages as, "I like you," or, "This is enjoyable." Or a smile can indicate the opposite, as noted by Birdwhistell (1970):

. . . My mother took great pride in her role of gracious hostess. She would say firmly, "No matter how much I disagree with a guest I never allow an unchristian word to cross my lips. I just smile." Well, my mother's thin-lipped smile, which could be confined to her mouth, when accompanied by an audible input of air through her tightened nostrils required no words—Christian or otherwise—to reveal her attitude. [p. 52]

Very likely, most interviewers would think first of visual interaction, or looking into an interviewee's eyes, if asked to say what they attend to in facial expression. It is interesting to note, for example, the emotional reaction produced when one person in a dyad is wearing dark glasses. Almost automatically, the person wearing the dark glasses becomes the observer and the other person becomes the observed person, even though the person without the dark glasses might ostensibly be the interviewer. The reader can note for himself his personal discomfort if an interviewee does not offer to remove dark glasses; it is as if he is on the other side of a one-way screen. Argyle and Kendon (1967) and Exline (1974) have presented excellent overviews of gaze behavior, as well as reports on their own research on this topic. The act of looking (what a person is looking at) can be quite easily identified by most people and is often the start of some focused interaction. Eye contact has an important role in signaling verbal interaction. Typically, the listener signals that he is paying attention by looking at the talker's mouth or eyes. When the time comes for the talker to be a listener, there will usually be an eye signal. The talker will look toward the listener, and the latter will signal that he is ready to talk by glancing away. Once a discussion is underway, each person looks at the other's eye region in glances of varying length, usually between 1 and 7 seconds. The person listening gives longer glances then the one talking and tends to look considerably more.

Typically, the person in a small group who receives the most looking time by an experimenter, for example, is judged as the person toward whom the experimenter feels most positive. In group discussions, power coalitions are likely to be signaled by the pattern of looking behavior among the members of the discussion group. The mutual look is a well-recognized signal of involvement with each other and, other things being equal, the longer the periods of eye contact, the greater the level of mutual involvement. Conversely, people who avert their gaze may be signaling a "walling off" of themselves, a fear of rejection, or generally a wish not to be seen. Autistic children typically avert their gaze. Exline (1974) calls attention to a study in which members of a dyad were looking at each other when they received the signal to speak. Dominant subjects were the first to break the gaze, perhaps because they realized that to continue looking was a cue for the other to speak and it was assumed that the dominant subjects would not give the floor to their partners. It may also be suggested that with increased cognitive difficulty with the topic under discussion there is a decrease in the amount of time the speaker looks at his listener.

As Miller (1973) points out, even the pupils of the eyes communicate. When a person becomes excited or interested in something, the pupils of his eyes increase in size. In one study, subjects were asked to state their preference for two pictures of a pretty girl; the only difference in the pictures was the dilation of the eyes. The preference judgments clearly favored the picture of the girl in which her eyes were dilated, although the judges did not consciously realize what the difference in the pictures was or what stimulus cue determined their preference.

Gestures, Body Movement, and Spatial Relations

Writings on gestures and body movements in oratory, mime, and dance date back to early Greece and Rome. One modern-day example of communication in body and hand movement is in Hawaiian dancing; "watch the hands." Many researchers working in this area of nonverbal communication have tried to introduce some kind of grammar to record, note, and study these phenomena experimentally. Prominent among these researchers are Birdwhistell (1970), Ekman (1969), Scheflen (1972), and Mehrabian (1972). An excellent overview of gestures and body movements in interviews has been presented by Mahl (1968).

The use of the hands may be a relatively independent channel of communication, as it is in the signs and finger spelling used by the deaf. Typically, however, such movements occur outside the awareness of conscious intention of the interview participants. A wide range of individual differences in body movement can be observed among interviewees (and interviewers). For example, Mahl (1968) describes such interviewee behaviors as patting and stroking hair, fingering the mouth, finger-ring play, keeping a coat on or off, crossing legs, rotating foot and ankle, finger tapping, shaking the head, shrugging the shoulders, palms up and out, folding the arms, and many more. The language of body movement has a large vocabulary. Some gestures, of course, are ritualized and, in a sense, serve as a direct substitute for the verbal meaning associated with them: the bow, shrug, smile, wink, military salute, pointed finger, thumbed nose, stuck out tongue, and so on. Other gestures are more culturally specific, such as the hand shake or the slap on the back, which are gestures of intimacy and friendship to an American but might be highly offensive to an individual of another culture who does not wish to be touched. There are probably more than 200 such mannerisms and gestures that can be studied.

Some clinicians have suggested that postural rigidity or tension may be an important measure of how difficult it will be to induce changes in a client. The reader might also try to imitate the changing positions of a client to try intuitively to infer his unverbalized feelings. Some typical body positions that have been interpreted in this way include the forward lean, which is generally viewed as being an attentive, approach posture; drawing back or turning away, which is viewed as a negative or withdrawal posture; the expanded chest, erect head, and raised shoulders, which may suggest pride or arrogance; and the dejected posture, typically characterized by forward leaning trunk, bowed head, drooping shoulders, and sunken chest. Relaxation is often conveyed by asymmetry in posture. Generally, a person assumes more of an approach position with another person he likes than with one he does not like. Higher-status members in a dyad usually show more relaxation than lower-status members, and moderate relaxation often accompanies the emotion of liking or approach. Extreme relaxation in posture is likely to be assumed in talking with persons who are disliked or not respected. Very tense posture is typically seen with persons in situations that are threatening.

Hall (1966), an anthropologist, has studied the spatial relations he found in various kinds of interaction among people in different cultures. Each culture appears to have its own implicit norms regarding permissible proximity between two speakers. For Americans, Hall has distinguished four zones: 0–½ feet for intimate; 1½–4 feet for personal; 4–10 feet for social-consultive; and 10 feet and over for public interaction. For example, two strangers will converse impersonally at a distance of about 4 feet. If one of them moves closer, the other will back away. Hall suggests that communicators who violate these implicit distance limits will elicit negative feelings from the persons to whom they are talking.

Regarding cultural and group differences in these norms, several studies have shown that persons greeting each other maintain different distances; for example, in one study Mexicans stood closest to each other, whites next closest, and blacks farthest apart. Typically Latin Americans have a closer impersonal discussion distance than North Americans, and it is virtually impossible for a North and South American both to be comfortable when they talk to each other unless one can adopt the zones normal for the other. Among two North Americans a personal conversation can be shifted to an impersonal one by the simple procedure of moving back to a distance of 4 or 5 feet. If the discussion partner cannot follow, he will probably find it quite impossible to maintain a personal discussion at that distance. There also appear to be some sex and age differences in regard to spatial proximity, with male-female pairs assuming the closest positions, then female-female, and finally male-male pairs. Children seem to assume the closest positions to each other, then adolescents, and finally adults. It has also been found that interviewees who come into the office expecting a negative evaluation are more likely to select chairs further removed from the interviewer than those expecting a positive evaluation.

Kinzel (1970) has extended the concept of spatial proximity to the idea of a body buffer zone in violent prisoners. In comparing the measurement of the body buffer zones of eight violent and six nonviolent prisoners, he found the zones of the violent group to be almost four times larger. In the violent group the rear zones were larger than the front zones; in the nonviolent group the front zones were larger. He suggested, on the basis of daily clinical observations of prisoners, that physical proximity to another inmate was at least as powerful a trigger of violence as were threats, thefts, or other more overt provocations. Violent inmates spoke of their victims as "messing with me" or "getting up to my face" when they were actually at conversational distances. Kinzel poses such possible clinical implications as distinguishing violent from nonviolent individuals by body buffer zone measurements and using periodic zone measurements to document the effect of psychotropic medication, need for incarceration, evidence for change or improvement, and so on.

Obviously, to become conversant in the language of nonverbal communication, one would have to become aware of how the various channels of communication relate to each other. Some interesting research in this regard has been reported by Mehrabian (1972). He demonstrated that tone of voice (positive, neutral, or negative) was less potent than facial expression depicted on photographs (positive, neutral, or negative). Each of the subjects in his study heard neutral content words expressed with one of the three degrees of attitude while seeing a photograph with one of the three degrees of attitude. Analysis indicated that the facial component had a stronger effect than the vocal component. Estimating relative weighting in message communication, he concluded that the message received was weighted 55% by the facial expression, 38% by the tone, and only 7% by the content. If these results have any generality for real-life communication situations, they suggest the importance of careful observation of nonverbal components, especially if these components are inconsistent with the verbal content component.

Another study which demonstrates how the various channels of nonverbal communication can be used is reported by Hetherington (1973). In this study observations of nonverbal behavior were used in combination with other information to discover the effects of the loss of a father on adolescent girls. Hetherington found that the absence of a father, especially if it occurred before the girl was 5 years old, resulted in social awkwardness with men. If the absence was due to the death of the father, the girls tended to be frightened of men; absence due to a divorce was related to being clumsily erotic with men. With respect to nonverbal behaviors, girls whose fathers had died, when interviewed by a man, tended to choose a seat far away from the interviewer, keep silent, sit stiffly upright, turn their shoulders away from the interviewer, establish little eye contact, and smile rarely. Girls who were fatherless as a result of divorce, when compared to the preceding group or control subjects from intact families, tended more often to choose a seat close to the interviewer, be talkative, assume an open, sometimes sprawling posture, lean forward, look into the interviewer's eyes, and smile. Fatherless girls in general, when compared to girls from intact families, tended to show mannerisms such as plucking at their clothes, pulling and twirling their hair, and pulling at their fingers.

Friedman (1969) presents an interesting extension of concern with nonverbal behavior into the area of physical diagnosis. According to him, one of the most lethal causes of coronary artery disease is a behavior pattern he calls "Type A." He claims that almost all men under 60 who have heart attacks are Type A's and, unless the behavior patterns associated with this personality type can be altered, none of the other precautions against it can forestall the disease.

What behavior does the Type A man show? He is ambitious, competitive, impatient, and aggressive, and he is involved in an incessant struggle against time and/or other people. His sense of time urgency is perhaps his most dominant trait. Almost always punctual, he is greatly annoyed if kept waiting. He usually feels dreadfully behind in doing all the things he thinks he should; he worries inordinately about meeting deadlines. Delays in restaurants, at airports, or in traffic irritate him. Similarly, he is impatient with people who do not come to the point quickly in conversation. He tends to talk rapidly and eat rapidly, rarely remaining long at the table. The Type A man does not usually spare the time to indulge in hobbies and, when he does, he prefers competitive games or gambling. He dislikes helping with routine jobs at home because he feels his time can be spent more profitably. In fact, he often tries to do several things simultaneously (reading while eating or shaving, for example), and frequently engages in two lines of thought at once with the result that he listens inattentively— particularly when he deems the conversation insignificant. He generally strives frantically for things worth having (a beautiful home, a better job, a bigger bank balance) at the expense of things worth being (well-read, knowledgeable about art, appreciative of nature). Often he pays little more than lip service to the human values of love, affection, and friendship. And he is chronically dissatisfied with his socioeconomic status, no matter how relatively high it is. Finally, and most devastating to his depersonalization, he is obsessed by numbers—billings per month, clients served, merchandise sold, money earned—and tends to judge his life by these number values.

Over the years Friedman and his colleagues have devised a structured oral interview, administered by trained personnel, as the best approach to behavioral typing. Whereas in broad terms they distinguish the Type A man from "Type B" (who tends to be calm, relaxed, and patient even though he may also work hard and long), their scale actually has five categories. Their interview queries a man about his work and leisure habits and about his attitudes toward time and pressures, but it is analyzed more for the intensity and emotional overtone of the responses than for the actual verbal answers. Emphatic, often explosive, replies are typical of the Type A man; his voice, for example, is often loud or even hostile. Also, because his impatience makes him anticipate what others will say, he frequently interrupts the interviewer to answer questions before they are fully asked. The Type A man's motor behavior (gestures, grimaces, and other body language) is also analyzed (table pounding and fist-clenching are typical Type A gestures). Additional description of the Type A personality is probably beyond our purpose here. Similarly, how to change from Type A to Type B, with much less risk of coronary artery disease, is also beyond our purpose here. This research does again, however, indicate the importance and possible diagnostic utility of careful observation of nonverbal behavior.

As noted repeatedly in this section, verbal communication uses only one of the many kinds of signals that people can exchange; other signals can reinforce or contradict the verbal message. These subtle signals are especially important in psychotherapy, where a patient tries to communicate his emotional troubles but may find it difficult to express in words the real source of his distress. A good therapist (and interviewer) learns to listen for more than the content of words alone, and he learns how to use nonverbal signals to help him interpret the verbal signals. Unfortunately, no one has yet put together all the research findings reviewed above so that the novice interviewer could systematically use them in behavioral assessment. Each interviewer probably uses some aspects of nonverbal evaluation and interpretation with semiawareness. Perhaps by more conscious concern we can make our intuition even more reliable. Nonverbal communication is not to be denied; actions speak louder than words.

ROLES AND TACTICS IN THE INTERVIEW INTERACTION

Thus far the discussion in this chapter has been addressed largely to the effects of interviewer behaviors on the interviewee. It is well to keep in mind, however, that this is not a static or one-way effect; rather, the interview interaction can be viewed as a dynamic process which is constantly changing throughout the course of an interview. It should furthermore be kept in mind that this dynamic state of affairs holds true for the interviewer, and that influence between the interviewer and interviewee is a reciprocal relationship constantly being modified in response to cues each receives from the other. Most novice interviewers readily admit that the interviewer has an influence on the interviewee, but it is less frequently recognized that the interviewer's behavior depends in significant measure on the interviewee's behavior. For example, when it is assumed that patients in psychotherapy engage in inner-determined free association to arrive ultimately at the causal bases for behavior, it may also be assumed that what the interviewer does has little effect in determining the nature of these associations. In this framework the recognition of reciprocal interaction and influence may be disquieting, because it eliminates the simple expediency of assigning blame to the client if the interview does not achieve its purpose. It is difficult to assert that the client's defensiveness, his wish not to get well, his transference problems, and the like, are the entire basis of an interview's being stalled if the interviewer and interviewee are assumed to be partners in what is or is not accomplished.

Ideally, in a mutual interview relationship both participants feel some responsibility for a successful interview outcome and both feel some personal autonomy and responsibility for their own behavior. The kind of mutual interaction that develops in this situation has been popularized in

Berne's (1964) ideas and writing on the "games people play," in which it is always assumed that there have to be two players. These games are often quite ritualized, and they may be either complementary, mutually satisfying transactions or transactions with explicit and implicit meanings which involve incompatible behavioral demands. In contrast to Berne's games, however, in most assessment and therapy interviews every effort is made to achieve game-free authenticity. Viewed from the standpoint of the interviewer, this means that he is active in motivating a full interviewee response and that he makes clear to the interviewee that any points of view he wishes to express on relevant topics, and any degrees of enthusiasm or hostility, are equally acceptable. As has been previously asserted in this chapter, the interview interaction has a purpose, and the interviewer has the major responsibility in keeping the interview on target. Discussing counseling interviews, Gilmore (1973, p. 230) has aptly stated in this regard that "failure to discern the difference between communicating as a means to an end and communication as an end in itself, can block the forward movement of counseling and lock the client and counselor into a race track course of endless circular laps. . . ."

Interviewer Role

Despite the assertion that the interview involves reciprocal interaction, it is helpful to look at interviewer and interviewee roles separately. Kahn and Cannell (1961) call attention to two major functions of the interviewer role, communication and measurement. The measurement or assessment role requires the interviewer to direct and control the communication process toward specific objectives. He must be clear about his assessment objectives and, through his careful formulation of major questions, ensure that the flow of communication is directed to these specific objectives. In most instances the interviewer probably teaches the interviewee what the latter's role involves. He does this in part by communicating to the interviewee, either directly or in some subtle fashion, when he has responded to an inquiry completely. Additionally, the interviewer remains nonresponsive to irrelevant interviewee responses or digressions, until the interviewee recognizes and adapts to this pattern in the interaction. This description of interviewer behavior assumes a situation in which the two participants have established a purpose for the interview that is mutually understood and accepted.

Invariably (see Maccoby & Maccoby, 1954) the interviewee places the interviewer in a role with status implications; in a medical school setting, for example, the interviewer typically finds himself placed in the role of an expert, the doctor. In this regard it is of interest to recall that, in general, people are more anxious to communicate to those above them in the social status hierarchy than to those below them. Again, however interviewer and interviewee characteristics must be considered jointly. For example, a young interviewer may exert less status influence in an interview with someone older than he than with an interviewee of his same age or younger. Sex and social status effects are equally relative. However, it is obvious that the interviewer occupies some role in the interview, whether he consciously defines it or not.

It also follows that the interviewee has certain legitimate expectations of the interviewer, including the expectation that he is able to convey warmth and acceptance and that he is sincere in his interpersonal relationships. An additional legitimate expectation is that the interviewer is competent in interview skills and familiar with a variety of methods for starting an interview and keeping it moving. Beyond this, the interviewer is expected to have expert knowledge related to the purpose of the interview. If the interviewer appears naive, the interviewee will have cause to doubt whether his statements will be understood. However, if he is overbearingly expert, he may come across as knowing everything, which can also block communication. Ideally, the interviewer should be seen as an expert seaking additional information from an informed person who has detailed knowledge or opinions to contribute. And who is more expert about the interviewee than he is about himself?

Assessment interviews require in particular a thorough knowledge of normative expectations (see Kadushin, 1972). If a child is toilet-trained at 20 months, is this late or early? If he starts to talk at 15 months, is this indicative of developmental lag or normal development? To know what is unusual, unexpected, or atypical, one needs to know the usual and typical. A background of knowledge is very important to the clinician's task, and it is to be lamented that the emphasis on feeling and doing in psychology has introduced in some quarters an antiintellectual downgrading of interviewer knowledgeability. Good interviewing is impossible without a considerable amount of knowing and thinking.

It must also be asserted that the professional interviewer needs to maintain a degree of emotional neutrality toward those whom he serves. It has long been recognized that the physician refrains from treating other than minor illnesses in his own family because of the possibility that his emotional involvement would affect his judgment and the quality of his treatment. So it should be in psychological practice, although emotional neutrality is not easy to achieve and it is not to be equated with coldness. It means, rather, that the interviewer's subjective feelings are under sufficient control so that he is free to focus on the patient's needs. One of the consequences of an overly close relationship with clients is that it becomes increasingly improbable that difficult questions will be asked. Furthermore, accepting the potential for social or personal relationships with patients is likely to accentuate the interviewer's tendency to like or dislike some kinds of interviewees. Sometimes these likes and dislikes can be based on generalized prejudice and thus lead to denial of a given client's individuality.

There are also several potential personal satisfactions that the interviewer must guard against. One of these is simple narcissism, or using the power and control one has in an interview to impress the client with how much knowledge or experience he has in the area of discussion. A related danger is seeking testimonials from interviewees as to how helpful and gratifying the interview has been. Novice or unsure interviewers are particularly prone to act in this way, and they may also be tempted to induce such flattery by allying themselves with the client against the institution the interviewer represents, whether a particular agency or "the establishment" more generally. Interviewers may also curry favor by engaging in a conspiracy to withhold information or by failing to follow up worrisome or debatable questions. In general, certain areas may remain unexplored because of fear that the attempt to introduce the material will evoke hostility toward the interviewer. Because of the possibility of these and similar negative consequences, social contacts between interviewers and interviewees are not to be encouraged. It is likewise desirable for the interviewer to be outside the power hierarchy of the interviewee, lest the interviewee avoid topics for fear he might discredit himself.

It should also be noted that the typical interview situation is one in which the interviewee becomes to some extent dependent on the expert knowledge of the interviewer. This dependency usually consists of a partial suspension of personal judgment in deference to the interviewer, heightened susceptibility to the interviewer's influence, and willingness to disclose personal information that would otherwise be kept private. It is accordingly incumbent on the interviewer to be loyal to his clients, and in particular to respect the professional ethic of confidentiality. The professional interviewer expects and receives a higher level of trust from those he serves than do most other professionals. Because of the high expectations the public holds for the professional psychological interviewer, laymen are particularly outraged when they believe a given professional places monetary or other personal rewards and satisfactions (including sexual relationships) above humanitarian concerns. Furthermore, as Adler (1972) has pointed out, the professional interviewer's work is rarely subject to evaluation and regulation by others. The implied self-responsibility for his work with patients and his professional responsibility to his profession and to his colleagues must not be taken lightly.

To turn briefly to some research reports regarding the effect of role expectations, Kanfer and Phillips (1970) note that the flow of communication in an interview is heavily determined by role assignment. Kanfer asked female nurses to discuss personal experiences in dyads and, when they acted as peers in these discussions, the nurses spent about the same amount of time talking and listening. When he asked them to adopt complementary patient and therapist roles, however, he found a significant shift in relative speaking time. Specifically, the subjects talking as patients talked about 60% of the time as contrasted with 30% talking time in the therapist role.

Heller (1972) studied extensively the effects of various interviewer and interviewee behaviors. His method has been to have previously instructed clients interviewed by experimentally naive interviewers who were asked to adopt various interview tactics. One interesting finding was that, with subjects who had a prior set toward admitting personal inadequacies and weaknesses, interviewers instructed to be passive, friendly, or silent were particularly successful in eliciting open problem discussion. The more ambiguous situations, providing least feedback, seemed most to facilitate these clients' self-disclosure. In a follow-up study Heller found that more reserved interviewers, as contrasted with more open, friendly interviewers, elicited more subject self-disclosure. He interpreted the reserved interview situation as mildly stressful and suggested that this mild stress facilitated expression in those subjects ready to talk about themselves.

With interviewees in general, however, active-friendly interviewers are probably clearly preferred over passive-hostile interviewers. The latter's passivity, lack of communication, and lack of orientation cues tend to be felt by most interviewees as presenting a somewhat punishing situation. However, whereas interviewer control, structure, and activity have generally favorable effects on the interview, this is so only up to the point where an interviewer becomes overly dominating, inflexible, and unresponsive to the interviewee's needs. By and large, more structure may be needed in early portions of the interview, as naive interviewees learn what is expected of them, and less structure after they have become familiar with their role.

Certainly there are great interviewee individual differences, including age, intelligence, and experience in the interviewee role. Assessment interviews, which require certain content areas to be covered, may require more interview directness than therapy interviews. Firm interview direction may also be needed in times of crisis when emergency action is necessary. Heller has pointed out in this regard that greater verbal productivity has been observed under friendly and "warm" interview conditions than under reserved and "cold" interview conditions, provided that the warm and friendly conditions were first in the sequence. Productivity was not recovered if the sequence of the conditions was reversed. Kadushin (1972) has also reported that a high degree of extroversion and sociability is not related to high interviewer competence. Greater interviewer competence tends to be associated with an interest in people that is scientific and objective rather than highly emotional or personal. Higher intelligence, variety of interests, and a wide range of experiences seem also to be associated with the capacity to empathize with a greater range of people.

Interviewee Role

The person in the interviewee role, if he is to be successful in this role, has to have some capacity to communicate, to translate feelings and thoughts into words, and to organize his communication. Given these abilities and a competent interviewer, the interviewee will gain satisfaction from his role through an increase in his sense of personal adequacy. It can also be noted that there are some interviewees who are so dogmatic or socially insensitive that it is difficult for them to recognize and perceive interviewer expressions of desirable attitudes. Given interviewee preferences, however, it is likely for them to choose interviewers who do not show disrespect by being insincere or in a hurry or by interrupting, yawning, or being late for interviews. Further individual interviewee preferences tend to vary with the problems involved. For example, in the area of personal problems the interviewee might be concerned most with the interviewer's affective characteristics, whereas in areas of educational-occupational problems focus might be on the interviewer's cognitive skills and knowledge. Clients from deprived social backgrounds may show initial preference for interviewers with strong political power who command access to jobs, housing, or an increase in income (Kadushin, 1972).

Interviewee variables such as social class, verbal facility, and intelligence have been related to the probability of an interviewee's being referred for or continued in psychotherapy. With reference to a continued series of interviews such as in psychotherapy, Strupp (1963) has suggested a greater probability for success if the interviewer and patient have mutually congruent expectations of what is expected and if the patient is intelligent, well educated, psychologically minded, able to communicate his feelings, recognizes his problems as psychological, and wants psychological help. Heller (1972) suggests further that specific kinds of interviewee behavior evoke predictable interviewer behaviors. For example, in a study in which clients enacted specific roles, he found that interviewers who were faced with dominant or dependent client behavior responded, respectively, with either passive or hyperresponsible behavior; when faced with hostile or friendly client behavior, they responded, respectively, with hostile or likeable, agreeable behavior. Matarazzo, Wiens, Matarazzo, and Saslow (1968) have noted variations in the verbal output of patients, which appeared related to the level of interviewer verbal output. Namely, when patients talked little the interviewer talked more, hoping to stimulate them; when patients were more verbally active, the interviewer's tendency was to talk less, so as not to impede the patients' productivity.

Interviewees vary widely in the ease with which they can establish a new relationship. The person who has grown up in a small family, or in an urban setting, or who has moved frequently, or whose work involves dealing with many people may have had a great deal of experience in forming new interpersonal relationships. Conversely, the person who has lived only in a small community, or has essentially only long-time associates, or does not work in a setting where he meets new people may experience relatively more difficulty in forming a new relationship. Similarly, the assessment interviewer will soon learn that there are assessment cues which can be gleaned from the nature of the relationship (or verbal interaction) with different interviewees. Some verbal and vocal characteristics are seen rather commonly with certain diagnostic groups; for example, the depressed patient typically demonstrates short DOUs, long RTLs, and so on.

Interviewees also approach the interview with a great variety of motivations. Some interviewees may have sought the appointment, whereas others may have been instructed to appear. The adolescent delinquent may be an involuntary interviewee, as may also the parents of a child when there is concern over possible child abuse. In all cases the interview has been affected by the events that have preceded it. Additional interviewee attitudes are shaped by immediate determinants associated with the interview situation itself, such as waiting for long periods in noisy, unattractive waiting rooms on uncomfortable, hard benches. The highly anxious patient may find even a short wait quite intolerable. These and many other interviewee variables may occur to the reader as he considers the stimulus qualities that different interviewees present.

Interview Tactics

There are extensive published sources and supervisor opinions which the interested reader can consult regarding questions about interview tactics. Assessment interviews are done for a great variety of purposes, and different tactics may be appropriate for each of them. The theoretical or conceptual framework the interviewer holds is also a major determinant of how he structures his interview. Additionally, the broad literature on psychotherapy can be profitably reviewed for a host of suggestions on interview tactics.

An excellent early text on client-centered counseling and interviewing was written by Porter (1950), and the novice interviewer is encouraged to go back to this early text for a clear exposition of assumptions about personality and of interviewer tactics derived from these assumptions. A central hypothesis in Porter's presentation is that each person has within himself the capacities to order and reorder his behavior without external manipulation by another. The interview aim that follows from this assumption is to keep the client expressing and exploring his attitudes as freely as possible. If an interviewer utilizes some sort of reassurance, persuasion, moralization, instruction, or coercion, he is making an assumption as to limiting factors in the capacity of the client to continue on his own. When the interviewer attempts to *understand* the client as the latter perceives the situation, however, he operates on an assumption that the client does not need energizing from an external source but has the capacity to continue on his own. In this frame of reference the interviewer is forced to deal with the reality the client holds no matter how much insight the interviewer may have into the errors of perception the client makes, and it is the meanings that the client has come to assign to his life experiences that constitute the reality to which he responds.

By contrast, a behavioral orientation or social-learning approach places emphasis on external variables shown to exercise control over behavior. The assumption then is that psychological functioning involves a reciprocal interaction between behavior and its controlling environment. According to Kanfer and Phillips (1970), behavior assessment serves four main purposes:

(1) identification of therapeutic target responses and their maintaining stimuli; (2) assessment of functional relationships among response classes and among discriminative and reinforcing stimuli; (3) determination of available social resources, personal assets, and skills for use in a therapeutic program, as well as of limitations and obstacles in the person and in the environment; and (4) availability of specific therapeutic strategies or behavioral techniques most consonant with the personal and environmental factors in the patient's life situation [p. 504]

Kanfer and Phillips indicate that in their approach to behavioral assessment they nevertheless make use of a wide range of historical, social, cognitive, and biological factors in addition to directly observable behavior. The approach by social-learning theorists has been to construct a model of assessment which includes attention to etiology, assessment, and therapy, and provides an effective link between these three facets of the total situation.

Porter (1950) suggested that virtually every verbal response used in any interaction falls into one of five basic categories: evaluative, hostile, reassuring, probing, and understanding. Clearly he favored the last response, whenever possible, in a clinical interview situation. An even more general categorization of interviewer comments consists of classifying them as open-ended or closed-ended questions. Open-ended questions ask the interviewee to recall something or to produce it spontaneously. Closed-ended questions ask the interviewee to recognize something. As noted in the earlier discussion of vocabulary skills, a recall task is more difficult than a recognition task, but at the same time is usually more productive in eliciting interviewee attitudes. The open-ended question encourages the interviewee to say more and does not overly limit the area or topic to be discussed. A typical open-ended question might be, "What brings you to see me?" In contrast, a closed-ended question could be, "Did your doctor send you to see me?"

An open-ended question is designed to encourage the spontaneous flow of information from the patient with as little direct interviewer questioning as possible. It is assumed that, if the interviewee is allowed to describe his problems in his own words and in his own way, more of his total situation will be revealed. As the interviewer listens carefully, he gradually pieces together a total picture. Closed-ended or yes-no type questions are not necessarily to be avoided altogether; in fact they are often the most efficient means of determining whether something is or is not the case. However, they typically do not contribute to a spontaneous flow of communication from the interviewee.

In addition to open and closed questions, many other interviewer verbal tactics have been described in the literature. An excellent review of several of these appears in Gilmore's book (1973), including misused questions, paraphrasing, describing behaviors and feelings, perception checking, verbatim playback, summarizing, formulating a choice point, facilitating transitions, gaining a figure-ground perspective, requesting a contrast, and introducing concrete examples. The interested reader is encouraged to review Gilmore's description of each of these tactics. She also includes many excellent discussions of alternative ways of obtaining information. For example, information about friendships or meaningful interpersonal relationships might well be obtained by asking such questions as, "Who takes care of you? . . . Whom do you take care of? . . . Who could get in touch with you any time of the day or night? . . . Who knows if your head aches? . . ." (p. 11).

There are also some ways of asking questions that are almost guaranteed to elicit some negative feeling in response. For example, a question like, "According to your record you have not lost any weight—why do you keep eating so much?" will almost surely antagonize a patient and put him on the defensive. The problem with putting a patient on the defensive is that he will probably say very little and may also not tell you what he really thinks. Asking "why" questions typically antagonizes a patient because they call on him to account for his behavior. It is difficult to begin a question with "why" and still avoid overtones of accusation. It is usually better for the interviewer to indicate that he does not yet understand and wishes more information. The novice interviewer is encouraged to experiment with beginning questions with the word "how" rather than "why." "How did this happen or come about?" is a question more likely to elicit an informative response than the same question begun with the word "why."

It is, of course, necessary for the interviewer to use words that the interviewee understands. Thus his questions should be brief, simple, and limited to one, clear, concise question at a time. It may be necessary to rephrase a question several times before the desired flow of communication is established. Along with this verbal interaction, the interviewer should maintain good eye contact with the interviewee while they are talking to each other. Good eye contact consists of spontaneous glances which express an interest and desire to communicate. Poor eye contact can comprise never looking at the interviewee, staring at him fixedly, or looking away from him as soon as he looks at you. Likewise, a desirable postural position involves sitting with one's body facing another person, hands gesturing occasionally, being facially responsive (e.g., smiling and frowning as appropriate), and occasionally leaning toward the interviewee to emphasize a verbal point or to indicate a nonverbal positive approach.

Training

As noted earlier, there are many discussions regarding the specifics of interviewing as these are implied by a particular theoretical or therapeutic orientation. Ivey (1971) and his associates developed a training program for teaching general interview skills. In his book on innovations in interview training, Ivey emphasizes particularly the notion of "attention" as central to the interaction between interviewer and interviewee. The basic skill of microcounseling he describes is termed "attending behavior," and it is defined behaviorally as eye contact, physical attention, and verbal following behavior. This concept makes use of the observation that interviewees talk about what the interviewer attends or listens to, both verbally and nonverbally. Once attending behavior has been learned, novice interviewers are taught to pay selective attention to emotional aspects of the interviewee comments, that is, to reinforce emotional components of the interviewee's behavior. Tyler (1969), among others, emphasizes this same kind of interviewer behavior.

Ivey points out that accurate reflection of feelings may be too difficult for some novice interviewers. When this is the case, he recommends teaching "sharing behavior" and "expression of feeling."The emphasis here is on teaching interviewers how to express themselves more clearly and how to recognize an emotion. Many other tactics are defined in Ivey's efforts to develop the skills of "direct, authentic, mutual communication." It should be added that Ivey's approach defines skills that can be taught to many different populations. He believes that the interviewer who learns the above basic skills will find that these skills allow him to deal with many more diverse situations and interviewee populations than he might have thought possible.

R. G. Matarazzo (1971) has published a general overview of research on the teaching and learning of psychotherapeutic skills. Her review overlaps the study of teaching interviewing skills generally and is recommended to the serious reader and student of interviewing. She notes that "some of the important variables in effective teaching programs appear to be *selection* of psychologically healthy individuals and combined *didactic* and *experiential* training for a specific, *well-defined* role." (p. 920).

SPECIFIC CONSIDERATIONS IN THE INITIAL CLINICAL INTERVIEW

In a very real sense, the initial clinical interview begins with the telephone call that sets up the office appointment. This call may be from the office of another professional, but often the patient is asked to take the initiative and arrange for his own appointment. It is then important to convey to the patient-caller that his call was expected and that you are pleased to hear from him. In most instances such a telephone call is a personal acknowledgement of psychopathology made with considerable trepidation, and the initial interview should not be arranged for some time in the distant future. The interviewer must convey his interest in the patient by his availability. In fact, if the interviewer has a long waiting list, he should offer the patient the option of referral to another professional.

Before the initial meeting with the patient, the interviewer must do such preparatory work as carefully studying the referral letter or other available patient data. Some patients directly express their annoyance at being asked questions that have already been answered for the record, and probably most patients feel lack of interest on the part of the interviewer that he did not bother to review their chart. Interviewer preparation should also involve the study necessary to become informed about the probable symptom or problem areas the patient may present, for example, bed wetting, alcoholism, and ulcers. If possible, the interviewer should try to imagine what the patient may be thinking or wishing to accomplish in the interview, and how he can respond. Similarly, the interviewer should have clearly in mind what he hopes to accomplish, so that he can convey clear expectations to the patient. If psychological testing is to be recommended, there should be initial arrangements for time commitments, consulting, and so on. The general idea here is to have a plan of procedure. Such a plan facilitates the interview and provides a frame of reference for the patient's comments and for observations of his behavior in the office.

There are many theoretical frameworks from which to observe and categorize interview behavior with respect to its emphasis or focus, and a host of initial interview situations call for different interview behaviors. The focus here is on the clinical-psychological interview that has as one of its functions the assessment of psychopathology. Although a review of the various definitions of psychopathology is beyond the scope of the present discussion, Spitzer and Endicott (1973) have proposed a useful conceptualization in which they suggest that the essential quality of all psychopathological behavior is that it is judged to be undesirable in some fashion. Thus psychopathology can be undesirable either to the person experiencing it (e.g., a painful emotion) or to other persons with whom the patient interacts. They emphasize that the focus of observation in identifying psychopathology is on behavior, but that this includes private experience (thoughts and feelings) as well as directly observable behavior. The interested reader is encouraged to study Spitzer and Endicott's extended discussion of psychopathology and the manner in which they differentiate it from behavior that is deviant merely in the sense of being statistically infrequent.

The interview framework proposed by Spitzer and Endicott includes observation of subjective distress, impaired thought processes, impaired relations with other people, abnormal motor behavior, inappropriate behavior or affect, impaired ability to carry out goal-directed activities, and impaired ability to test reality adequately (Spitzer & Endicott, 1973, pp. 398–399). The assessment of these psychopathological characteristics involves attention to all the interview interactions discussed in this chapter. For example, in the assessment of subjective distress the interviewer should pay attention to verbal content and also to facial expression and bodily posture. He could also do content analysis of a segment of the interviewee's speech and note any dysfluencies that occur.

In this last regard, impairment of an interviewee's thought processes may be clearly demonstrated in speech that is unintelligible because it is disorganized. Even in instances of mild impairment, there may be juxtaposition of statements, excessive or unnecessary details, inability to proceed directly to a goal idea, and so on. At times the interviewee, although not showing these obvious speech problems, reports feeling that he cannot concentrate or that his thoughts are racing. Objective and subjective correlates of these kinds are reviewed by Spitzer and Endicott (1973) for each of the psychopathological characteristics they identify. Also noteworthy is the structured interview schedule they have developed, which consists of a series of statements and questions for use in clinical assessments.

Coming back to several general considerations, we note the interviewer must recognize that his effect can be psychotherapeutic or psychonoxious. He must give thought to the personal and professional code of ethics that guides his behavior with patients. He should be clear in his own mind about the ethical limitations of social, physical, or business contact with his patients and about such issues as confidentiality and other patient and institutional rights. He should also be aware of his personal limitations, inasmuch as no interviewer or therapist has the techniques or the know-how to be successful with all patients, and some should best be referred to other clinicians. The interviewer should have learned to listen carefully with his full attention, so that his comments will follow directly from what the interviewee has been saying. The interviewee must be allowed an opportunity to have his say, which usually means an uninterrupted opportunity to review his presenting complaint. It is also imperative to know how the interviewee is using specific words and to obtain precise descriptions of disturbances and complaints so that it is possible to have behavioral referents for the patient's expressed feelings.

In summarizing the purposes of the initial clinical interview, it should be noted that they are to gather information about the patient and his problems that is not available from other sources, to establish a relationship with the patient that will facilitate assessment and treatment, to give the patient an understanding of his psychopathological behavior, and to support and direct the patient in his search for relief.

The Patient Approaches the Interview

Most patients probably have some stereotyped concept of the interviewer as a "shrink," "mind reader," or something else more or less flattering. It is important to assess sensitively the patient's attitudes from his initial behaviors, such as whether he is eager, distrustful, vigorous, feeling coerced, or whatever. Often it is useful to ascertain what the patient was told when he was referred and with what expectations or preparatory set he has come. Many patients coming to see a psychologist implicitly or explicitly have concerns that they may be judged to be "crazy." In addition, the individual patient probably has his own enduring readiness for certain interview behavior; for example, the self-pitying neurotic may talk endlessly about his bad luck, his illnesses, and the overwhelming nature of his problems.

By and large the interviewer should assume that there is no such person as an unmotivated patient; he should view his task as that of attempting a match of interviewer and patient motivations. There is always a reason ("motivation") for the patient having appeared to be interviewed. Admittedly, there are times when the only definable motivation appears to be curiosity about what the psychologist will say or do, but it is up to the interviewer to nurture whatever motivation is present. Not infrequently the patient tries to shift responsibility for further treatment or change to the interviewer, in which case it is useful to stress the concept of mutual participation. Some interviewers and therapists even model, sometimes by film, the appropriate role behaviors of a patient in the interview. Such a procedure certainly calls attention to the fact that roles are learned; in fact, there seem to be few inherent or instinctive "patient" behaviors.

The Interviewer Approaches the Interview

There are perhaps a few people who still think that what the patient does is independent of the stimulus value of the interviewer, but probably not very many. It behooves each interviewer to know the usual patient responses he elicits. Knowing his own stimulus value, the interviewer can better focus his full attention on the patient and take every opportunity to observe the patient rather than himself. There can be role problems for the interviewer, particularly with regard to personal curiosity, decision making, judging, being the saintly helper, and so forth. Above all, however, objectivity must be maintained. The interviewer must constantly keep one foot in reality and not become completely caught up in the terrors or delights of the patient's world. If the patient has an emotional outburst, it is up to the interviewer to remember or try to understand what precipitated the emotional outburst, including whatever stimulus he presented.

It is not uncommon in an interview situation for the patient to cry while giving his history. This may embarrass the interviewer and make him sufficiently uncomfortable to want to move to another area of discussion. Crying, however, signals in most patients an important area for discussion, and the patient should be helped to pursue further exploration in this area. As Enelow and Adler (1972) point out, one time when it is mandatory for the interviewer to remain silent is when the patient has stopped speaking because he is overwhelmed or about to be overwhelmed by emotion. Appropriate interviewer silence may allow the patient to express the emotion and then go ahead to discuss things he could not bring himself to discuss before. If, however, the patient wishes to withhold his feelings, he has the opportunity to do so.

There are instances in which it may be helpful to give the patient permission to cry, in a sense, by a comment recognizing how bad he feels or by the nonverbal communication of offering a tissue. The extent to which a patient is helped or the interview facilitated by such a show of emotion depends on the interviewer's ability to facilitate it and on what he does after the emotion has subsided. A supportive response is almost always helpful. For the interviewer not to acknowledge crying and make some accepting comment about it is quite devastating; the patient almost always, in the absence of interviewer acknowledgment and acceptance, feels that he has made a fool of himself. However, a supportive attitude at such a time with a supportive comment such as, "I understand," or "I know that was upsetting," is very helpful in furthering the development of rapport and a working relationship.

Like crying, anger furnishes a valuable clue in the total picture of the patient and his response to life stress. This is a situation in which it is highly important for the interviewer not to become angry in return. It is important for the interviewer to recognize the emotion and to consider whether he in some way stimulated the anger, or whether it reflects some difficulty or personality trait of the patient. It may be useful for the interviewer, in the latter case, to recognize that he is not the personal target of the patient's anger. It is then easier for the interviewer to avoid retaliating or responding angrily. This restraint in turn facilitates the patient's looking at what he is saying and considering the meaning of his feelings in the particular situation. Giving information and accepting the patient's anger are two methods for containing it. It is important for the interviewer not to take it as a personal affront and respond in kind.

The Interview

The initial clinical interview is in many respects perhaps the most important encounter between patient and interviewer. In the first place, if it does not fulfill the patient's expectations to some degree, it is likely to be the only interview. It can generally be assumed that this interview should allow the patient maximum spontaneity in presenting himself. An opening question such as, "What is the situation that brings you here today?" tells the patient that the interviewer is interested in him and his problems and encourages him to discuss anything he feels may be important. As a rule of thumb, the fewer the interviewer's utterances to keep the patient talking, the better, especially early in the interview. An open-ended-question approach allows the interviewer to learn quickly which problems the patient considers most important and gives him information about the way the patient approaches his problems. If the patient can express himself well, very few questions may be necessary.

An important behavioral attitude for the interviewer is to encourage patient specificity by frequently asking for examples of the problem situations the patient is describing. If the patient talks about arguing frequently with his wife, the interviewer does not begin to understand the real nature of the problem until he obtains specific examples of two or three actual arguments. If a patient says that he is "nervous," the interviewer should not accept the statement as sufficient but should inquire how he experiences his nervousness. An especially useful source of data on functional impairment is to ask the patient for a detailed account of a present typical day and compare this with a detailed typical day before the onset of symptoms. It may be necessary to ask the patient to start this description from the time he arises and continue in a step-by-step fashion throughout the day until he retires. Tenacity and firmness are frequently necessary in order to obtain the exact sequence of activities, the time consumed by each, whether this was a solitary time or with whom was it shared, and so forth. It is best to ask about a specific day, usually the one before the day of the interview, as this is often the day most easy to recall.

As R. G. Matarazzo (1972) has pointed out, after completing an elaboration of the chief complaint, the interviewer may profitably ask for an outline of landmarks in life development. This can include such matters as early family circumstances and relationships and the patient's role in the family; illnesses and accidents, especially as they may have affected the patient's relationship to his family or peers or his self-concept; friendships, separations, and loss of significant others through death or geographical moves; educational successes and failures; marriages, divorces, and children; and work successes and failures. All these events, in outline up to and including the present, can help the interviewer to grasp the kinds of major stresses to which the patient has been subjected, the behaviors for which he has most consistently been rewarded or punished, and his characteristic methods of fulfilling needs for security, self-esteem, affection, and approval. It should help him to understand what factors maintain the present maladaptive behaviors, and also help him to determine whether there is sufficient variety and challenge in the patient's life situation. Throughout the interview there should be careful attention to possible recurrent themes, because there are usually predictably recurrent, unique problem situations which arise from the patient's pathological life-style. In many instances the interviewee probably cannot define such themes clearly on his own and has to depend on the interviewer to recognize them and call them to his attention.

Given a conceptual framework, it is generally easier for the interviewer to follow, as they come up, the leads the patient presents for discussion. Given a framework for data collection the interviewer can conceptually fit information where it belongs, even though it may emerge in random sequence. Maintaining the flow of discussion can involve many of the interviewer tactics discussed in this chapter, including various verbal comments (see, for example, Gilmore, 1973) as well as vocal or nonverbal behaviors. An essential aspect of all of these interviewer tactics is the conveying of empathy, understanding, and sincere interest.

Finally, the patient must be able to anticipate termination of the interview; practically, this is easy to accomplish by the interviewer's pointing out when time is running short (approximately 10 minutes before the end of the interview). This gives opportunity for the patient to bring up any additional topics he wants to discuss in that session. Although the interviewer has been summing up periodically during the course of the interview, there needs to be a final summation. Each person who consults an expert expects and is entitled to an expert opinion about his situation. The interviewer must summarize with the patient his perception of the main aspects of the problems that have been presented, including both expressions of emotion and descriptive content, and his recommendations for a therapeutic program or some other potentially helpful course of action. The interviewer and patient should make every effort to achieve a common understanding of the diagnostic formulation and treatment recommendations. If this congruence is not achieved, there is less likelihood of the patient's following through on the recommendations. Part of the summing-up process is to elicit the patient's reactions and to stress the importance of his perceptions and feelings and the need for mutuality in planning a therapeutic program.

REFERENCES

Adler, L. M. The social context of the clinical interview. In A. J. Enelow & S. N. Swisher (Eds.), *Interviewing and patient care.* New York: Oxford University Press, 1972. Pp. 177–207.

Argyle, M., & Kendon, A. The experimental analysis of social performance. In L. Berkowitz (Ed.), *Advances in experimental social psychology,* Vol. 3. New York: Academic Press, 1967. Pp. 55–98.

Aronson, H., & Weintraub, W. Personal adaptation as reflected in verbal behavior.

In A. W. Siegman & B. Pope (Eds.), *Studies in dyadic communication*. New York: Pergamon Press, 1972. Pp. 265–279.

Berne, E. *Games people play*. New York: Grove Press, 1964.

Birdwhistell, R. L. *Kinesics and context: Essays on body motion communication*. Philadelphia: University of Pennsylvania Press, 1970.

Blocksma, D. D., & Porter, E. H., Jr. A short-term training program in client-centered counseling. *Journal of Consulting Psychology*, 1947, **11**, 55–60.

Chapple, E. D., & Arensberg, C. M. Measuring human relations: An introduction to the study of the interaction of individuals. *Genetic Psychology Monographs*, 1940, **22**, 3–147.

Craig, K. D. Incongruencies between content and temporal measures of patients' responses to confrontation with personality descriptions. *Journal of Consulting Psychology*, 1966, **30**, 550–554.

Davitz, J. R., & Davitz, L. J. The communication of feelings by content-free speech. In S. Weitz (Ed.), *Nonverbal communication*. New York: Oxford University Press, 1974. Pp. 99–104.

Duncan, S. Nonverbal communication. *Psychological Bulletin*, 1969, **72**, 118–137.

Ekman, P., & Friesen, W. V. The repertoire of nonverbal behavior: Categories, origins, usage, and coding. *Semiotica*, 1969, **1**, 49–98.

Enelow, A. J., & Adler, L. M. Basic interviewing. In A. J. Enelow & S. N. Swisher (Eds.), *Interviewing and patient care*. New York: Oxford University Press, 1972. Pp. 29–50.

Exline, R. Visual interaction: The glances of power and preference. In S. Weitz (Ed.), *Nonverbal communication*. New York: Oxford University Press, 1974. Pp. 65–92.

Friedman, M. *Pathogenesis of coronary artery disease*. New York: McGraw-Hill, 1969.

Gilmore, S. K. *The counselor-in-training*. New York: Appleton-Century-Crofts, 1973.

Goldman-Eisler, F. *Psycholinguistics: Experiments in spontaneous speech*. New York: Academic Press, 1968.

Hall, E. T. *The hidden dimension*. New York: Doubleday, 1966.

Heller, K. Interview structure and interview style in initial interviews. In A. W. Siegman & B. Pope (Eds.), *Studies in dyadic communication*. New York: Pergamon Press, 1972. Pp. 9–28.

Hetherington, E. M. Girls without fathers. *Psychology Today*, 1973, **3**, 46–52.

Ivey, A. E. *Microcounseling: Innovations in interview training*. Springfield, Ill.: Charles C Thomas, 1971.

Jackson, R. H., Wiens, A. N., Manaugh, T. S., & Matarazzo, J. D. Speech behavior under conditions of differential saliency in interview content. *Journal of Clinical Psychology*, 1972, **28**, 318–327.

Kadushin, A. *The social work interview*. New York: Columbia University Press, 1972.

Kahn, R. L., & Cannell, C. F. *The dynamics of interviewing: Theory, technique, and cases*. New York: Wiley, 1961.

Kanfer, F. H. Verbal rate, eyeblink and content in structured psychiatric interviews. *Journal of Abnormal and Social Psychology*, 1960, **61**, 341–347.

Kanfer, F. H., & Phillips, J. S. *Learning foundations of behavior therapy*. New York: Wiley, 1970.

Kanfer, F. H., Phillips, J. S., Matarazzo, J. D., & Saslow, G. Experimental modification of interviewer content in standardized interviews. *Journal of Consulting Psychology*, 1960, **24**, 528–536.

Kasl, S. V., & Mahl, G. F. The relationship of disturbances and hesitations in spontaneous speech to anxiety. *Journal of Personality and Social Psychology*, 1965, **1**, 425–433.

Kinzel, A. F. Body-buffer zone in violent prisoners. *American Journal of Psychiatry*, 1970, **127**, 59–64.

Maccoby, E. E., & Maccoby, N. The interview: A tool of social science. In G. Lindzey (Ed.), *Handbook of social psychology*. Reading, Mass.: Addison-Wesley, 1954. Pp. 449–487.

Mahl, G. F. Gestures and body movements in interviews. In J. Shlien, H. Hunt, J. D. Matarazzo, & C. Savage (Eds.), *Research in psychotherapy*. Vol. 3. Washington, D.C.: American Psychological Association, 1968. Pp. 295–346.

Mahl, G. F. People talking when they can't hear their voices. In A. W. Siegman & B. Pope (Eds.), *Studies in dyadic communication*. New York: Pergamon Press, 1972. Pp. 211–264.

Manaugh, T. S., Wiens, A. N., & Matarazzo, J. D. Content saliency and interviewee speech behavior. *Journal of Clinical Psychology*, 1970, **26**, 17–24.

Matarazzo, J. D. The interview. In B. B. Wolman (Ed.), *Handbook of clinical psychology*. New York: McGraw-Hill, 1965. Pp. 403–450.

Matarazzo, J. D., Holman, D. C., & Wiens, A. N. A simple measure of interviewer and interviewee speech durations. *Journal of Psychology*, 1967, **66**, 7–14.

Matarazzo, J. D., & Wiens, A. N. *The interview: Research on its anatomy and structure*. Chicago: Aldine-Atherton, 1972.

Matarazzo, J. D., Wiens, A. N., Jackson, R. H., & Manaugh, T. S. Interviewee speech behavior under conditions of endogenously-present and exogenously-induced motivational states. *Journal of Clinical Psychology*, 1970, **26**, 141–148.(a)

Matarazzo, J. D., Wiens, A. N., Jackson, R. H., & Manaugh, T. S. Interviewee speech behavior under different content conditions. *Journal of Applied Psychology*, 1970, **54**, 15–26.(b)

Matarazzo, J. D., Wiens, A. N., Matarazzo, R. G. & Saslow, G. Speech and silence behavior in clinical psychotherapy and its laboratory correlates. In J. Shlien,

H. Hunt, J. D. Matarazzo, & C. Savage (Eds.), *Research in psychotherapy.* Vol. 3. Washington, D.C.: American Psychological Association, 1968. Pp. 347–394.

Matarazzo, J. D., Wiens, A. N., Saslow, G., Dunham, R. M., & Voas, R. B. Speech durations of astronaut and ground communicator. *Science,* 1964, **143,** 148–150.

Matarazzo, R. G. Research on the teaching and learning of psychotherapeutic skills. In A. E. Bergin & S. L. Garfield (Eds.), *Handbook of psychotherapy and behavior change.* New York: Wiley, 1971. Pp. 895–924.

Matarazzo, R. G. The initial clinical interview: A general guide. In Interaction models: A student guide to interviewing. Symposium presented at the meeting of the American Psychological Association, Honolulu, Sept., 1972.

Matarazzo, R. G., Wiens, A. N., & Saslow, G. Experimentation in the training and learning of psychotherapy skills. In L. K. Gottschalk and A. A. Auerbach (Eds.), *Methods of research in psychotherapy.* New York: Appleton-Century-Crofts, 1966. Pp. 597–635.

Mehrabian, A. *Nonverbal communication.* Chicago: Aldine-Atherton, 1972.

Mehrabian, A., & Wiener, M. Decoding of inconsistent communication. *Journal of Personality and Social Psychology,* 1967, **6,** 109–114.

Miller, G. A. Statistical indicators of style. In N. N. Markel (Ed.), *Psycholinguistics: An introduction to the study of speech and personality.* Homewood, Ill.: Dorsey Press, 1969. Pp. 167–193.

Miller, G. A. *Communication, language, and meaning.* New York: Basic Books, 1973.

Milmoe, S., Novey, M. S., Kagan, J., & Rosenthal, R. The mother's voice: Postdictor of her baby's behavior. In S. Weitz (Ed.), *Nonverbal communication.* New York: Oxford University Press, 1974. Pp. 122–126.

Milmoe, S., Rosenthal R., Blane, H. T., Chafetz, M. E., & Wolf, I. The doctor's voice: Postdictor of successful referral of alcoholic patients. In S. Weitz (Ed.), *Nonverbal communication.* New York: Oxford University Press, 1974. Pp. 112–121.

Molde, D. A., & Wiens, A. N. Interview interaction behavior of nurses with task versus person orientation. *Nursing Research,* 1968, **17,** 45–51.

Nathan, P. E., Schneller, P., and Lindsley, O. R. Direct measurement of communication during psychiatric admission interviews. *Behavior Research and Therapy,* 1964, **2,** 49–57.

Patterson, C. H. Relationship therapy and/or behavior therapy. *Psychotherapy: Theory, Research, and Practice,* 1968, **5,** 226–233.

Peterson, D. R. *The clinical study of social behavior.* New York: Appleton-Century-Crofts, 1968.

Pope, B., Blass, T., Siegman, A. W., & Raher, J. Anxiety and depression in speech. *Journal of Consulting and Clinical Psychology,* 1970, **35,** 128–133.

Pope, B., Siegman, A. W., & Blass, T. Anxiety and speech in the initial interview. *Journal of Consulting and Clinical Psychology,* 1970, **35,** 233–238.

Porter, E. H. *An introduction to therapeutic counseling.* Boston: Houghton-Mifflin, 1950.

Ramsay, R. W. Speech patterns and personality. *Language and Speech,* 1968, **11,** 54–63.

Rankin, P. T. The importance of listening ability. *The English Journal,* 1928, **27,** 623–630.

Ray, M. L., & Webb, E. J. Speech duration effects in the Kennedy news conferences. *Science,* 1966, **153,** 899–901.

Richardson, S. A., Dohrenwend, B. S., & Klein, D. *Interviewing: Its forms and functions.* New York: Basic Books, 1965.

Rosenthal, R. *Experimenter effects in behavioral research.* New York: Appleton-Century-Crofts, 1966.

Saslow, G., & Matarazzo, J. D. A technique for studying changes in interview behavior. In E. A. Rubenstein and M. B. Parloff (Eds.), *Research in psychotherapy.* Vol. 1. Washington, D.C.: American Psychological Association, 1959. Pp. 125–159.

Scheflen, A. E. *Body language and social order: Communication as behavioral control.* Englewood Cliffs, New Jersey: Prentice-Hall, 1972.

Selzer, M. L. The use of first names in psychotherapy. In H. M. Ruitenbeek (Ed.), *The analytic situation: How patient and therapist communicate.* Chicago: Aldine, 1973. Pp. 64–69.

Siegman, A. W., & Pope, B. Personality variables associated with productivity and verbal fluency in the initial interview. *Proceedings of the 73rd Annual Convention of the American Psychological Association,* 1965, 273.

Siegman, A. W., & Pope, B. The effects of ambiguity and anxiety on interviewee verbal behavior. In A. W. Siegman & B. Pope (Eds.), *Studies in dyadic communication.* New York: Pergamon, 1972. Pp. 29–68.

Slobin, D. I., Miller, S. H., & Porter, L. W. Forms of address and social relations in a business organization. In S. Moscovici (Ed.), *The psychosociology of language.* Chicago: Markham, 1972. Pp. 263–272.

Spitzer, R. L., & Endicott, J. The value of the interview for the evaluation of psychopathology. In M. Hammer, K. Salzinger, & S. Sutton (Eds.), *Psychopathology: Contributions from the social, behavioral, and biological sciences.* New York: Wiley, 1973, Pp. 397–408.

Strupp, H. Psychotherapy revisited: The problem of outcome. *Psychotherapy: Theory, Research and Practice,* 1963, **1,** 1–13.

Truax, C. B. Length of therapist response, accurate empathy and patient improvement. *Journal of Clinical Psychology,* 1970, **26,** 539–541.

Tyler, L. E. *The work of the counselor.* (3rd ed.) New York: Appleton-Century-Crofts, 1969.

Waxer, P. Nonverbal cues for depression. *Journal of Abnormal Psychology,* 1974, **83,** 319–322.

Weitz, S. Attitude, voice, and behavior: A repressed affect model of interracial interaction. *Journal of Personality and Social Psychology,* 1972, **24,** 14–21.

Wiens, A. N., Matarazzo, J. D., & Saslow, G. The interaction recorder: An electronic punched paper tape unit for recording speech behavior during interviews. *Journal of Clinical Psychology,* 1965, **21,** 142–145.

Wiens, A. N., Matarazzo, J. D., Saslow, G., Thompson, S. M., & Matarazzo, R. G. Interview interaction behavior of supervisors, head nurses, and staff nurses. *Nursing Research,* 1965, **14,** 322–329.

Wiens, A. N., Molde, D. A., Holman, D. C., & Matarazzo, J. D. Can interview interaction measures be taken from tape recordings? *Journal of Psychology,* 1966, **63,** 249–260.

CHAPTER 2

Projective Techniques

JOHN E. EXNER, JR.

The development and use of projective techniques has played a significant role in psychology, particularly in the growth of clinical psychology. Although often marked by controversy, projective methods have generally constituted the major tools used by the clinician in his search for an accurate description of personality. This was especially true during the period from the 1930s through the early 1960s, when the major professional role of the clinician focused on the skills of assessment. Even in the present era, when the role of the clinician has broadened substantially to include much emphasis on intervention, consultation, and the like, assessment continues as a major professional function, and projective methods continue to be used as one of the nuclear approaches to this task.

The concept of projection that underlies these techniques derives essentially from a basic postulate offered by Freud (1894, 1896, 1911). Freud noted that a commonly used "ego defense" is the translation of internally experienced dangers into external dangers, thereby making them easier to deal with. Whereas Freud concentrated on the "defensive" characteristic of this process, others have described it as a more "natural" process wherein defense may or may not be relevant. In this context projection is conceptualized as the tendency of people to be influenced in the cognitive mediation of perceptual inputs by their needs, interests, and overall psychological organization. This concept of projection was crystallized by Frank (1939) in a classical paper elaborating the "projective hypothesis" and offering the label "projective methods" for a variety of techniques useful to the clinician in evoking this kind of psychological action.

Although Frank was the catalyst in offering the label and a clarification of the process of projection, implicit use of the concept predated his paper by at least 400 years. Piotrowski (1957) points out that several ancient Greek artists and authors ruminated about the impact of stimulus ambiguity on the interpretation of "objective reality," and both Botticelli and Leonardo da Vinci alluded specifically to the usefulness of ambiguous stimuli in studying the process of creativity during the fifteenth century. It is known that da Vinci used ambiguous stimuli as one of his techniques for selecting pupils, by presenting them with a stimulus and observing the imagination and talent with which they struggled to create artistic forms from it. During a major portion of the nineteenth century, a parlor game called "Blotto" flourished in Europe. It consisted of making inkblots and requiring each participant to offer associations to the blots or to create a poem that would match some feature of the blots. This popular game probably had some influence on the decision of Binet to explore the use of inkblots for testing the imagination of young subjects, and it may also have influenced others who preceded Rorschach in studying the usefulness of inkblots in attempting to understand personality.

The first formal projective technique apparently was suggested by Galton (1879), who discussed the possibility of using words as stimuli to associations. There is no indication that Galton actually implemented his own suggestion beyond mere pilot work. However, it is known that Jung used the word association technique during the period from 1910 to 1912 to develop a better understanding of the ideation of his patients. It is also clear that during that same period several clinicians, including Rorschach, became interested in Binet's work with inkblots and began working independently on the development of similar procedures. Rybakow (1910) used eight flat-black ambiguous figures as one of his many tests to study the unique characteristics of imagination. Also in 1910 Rorschach began his study of the use of inkblots to differentiate types of psychopathology. His initial work was apparently precipitated by reports from a former classmate, working at that time as an intermediate school teacher, that inkblots displayed to his students evoked a wide variety of responses from them (Exner, 1969).

A review of Rorschach's relatively short life reveals that his interest in inkblots did not resume for several years following 1911. In fact, the bulk of his important work in developing the Rorschach test probably occurred after 1917 and was completed by 1920. There were several others in addition to Binet, Rybakow, and Rorschach who attempted to discern some use of inkblots during the late nineteenth century and early twentieth century. Tulchin (1940) reports that Dearborn used inkblots at Harvard University to study the contents of consciousness, and Kirkpatrick (1900) concurrently studied the relationship of inkblot responses to the developmental process. Whipple (1910) included inkblots to test "active imagination" in his extensive battery of mental and physical tests.

Although Rorschach's monograph *Psychodiagnostik* (1921) is generally considered a major milestone in promoting interest in the use of ambiguous stimuli to explore personality functioning, it did not suddenly offer a "new face" to assessment. Considerable time elapsed before the Rorschach Test began to make a significant impact on clinical psychology. During the first 3 decades of the twentieth century applied psychology centered mainly on the use of tests to study intelligence and operations related to intelligence, such as aptitudes, motor coordination, achievement, and the like (see Chapter 3). Methods devised to study features of personality usually concentrated on single traits, such as introversion and dominance. In instances in which a personality description or diagnosis was called for, a thorough interview and social history provided the bulk of the data (Louttit, 1936). Tests that were used were generally constructed on traditional psychometric principles wherein specific scores could be judged against group means with little or no regard for the contents of the responses.

The first projective method to gain widespread use among clinicians was the Rorschach. It had been brought to the United States during the mid 1920s by David Levy. Levy suggested to Samuel Beck, then a graduate student, that the test might provide a good dissertation subject. Beck subsequently produced the first doctoral dissertation on the Rorschach, completed in 1932 at Columbia University under the direction of Robert Woodworth. A second dissertation on the Rorschach was completed shortly thereafter by Marguerite Hertz at Western Reserve University in Cleveland. A third major figure responsible for stimulating interest in the Rorschach was Bruno Klopfer who, after emigrating to the United States in 1934, began offering seminars on the test in New York City. At about that same time Morgan and Murray (1935) introduced the Thematic Apperception Test (TAT) which was based in part on the premise that people reveal something of their own personality when confronted with an ambiguous social situation. A short time later Murray (1938) offered a crystallized description of how the process of projection operates in an ambiguous stimulus stituation. Although Frank is usually credited with providing a greater impetus to the study and understanding of projective methods than Murray, Murray's description a year earlier offered to many a clarification of the process underlying the new projective instruments.

The availability of the Rorschach and the TAT began to change the orientation of clinicians away from one based almost exclusively on nomothetic comparisons and toward more intensive study of the idiography of the person. This change in direction emphasized the unique needs, interests, conflicts, and styles of organization that characterize each individual. The development of skills in using these projective methods gave the clinician new status among professionals, as he was now able to provide a more concise and unique description of the subject than was available from other sources. By the early 1940s case studies, research papers, opinions, and arguments concerning projective methods were appearing in professional literature in a virtual torrent, and during that decade and the next many new projective techniques were developed. Louttit and Browne (1947) reported that between 1935 and 1946 a 60% turnover occurred among the 20 most frequently used tests in clinical settings. Sundberg (1961), repeating the Louttit and Browne survey with data through 1959, found that between 1935 and 1959 the turnover rate among the 20 most frequently used tests had reached 76%.

In the Louttit and Browne survey two projective tests, the Rorschach and the TAT, appeared among the 10 most frequently used instruments, ranking fourth and fifth, respectively. The remaining 8 tests listed by Louttit and Browne among the top 10 included 5 intelligence tests, 1 interest test, and 2 achievement tests. The results of the Sundberg survey showed that, by 1959, 4 of the 10 most frequently used tests were projective techniques, with the Rorschach and TAT ranking first and fourth, respectively. Five of the remaining 6 tests on the list were intelligence tests, and the sixth was the Minnesota Multiphasic Personality Inventory (MMPI).

A more extensive and more recent survey of patterns of psychological tests use is reported by Lubin, Wallis, and Paine (1971). Their data, collected in 1969, revealed that 5 of the 10 most frequently used tests in clinical prctice are projective methods, with the Rorschach and the TAT ranking third and seventh, respectively. Three of the 5 nonprojective tests appearing among the top 10 are intelligence tests, a fourth is the MMPI, and the fifth test, which Lubin et al. found to be the *most* frequently used of all, is the Bender Visual Motor Gestalt, which is also used at times as a projective method.

Although the data from these three surveys provide an indication of the impact projective methods have had on practice in clinical settings, they fail to reflect the extensive controversy that has swirled around projective methodology. This controversy has been lengthy and at times bitter and, because it has never been fully resolved, has contributed to a frequently perceived schism between clinicians and psychologists whose interests point in nonclinical directions. There are many facets of this controversy that merit review, beginning with the difficulties in arriving at a satisfactory definition of the term "projective technique." Following the consideration of definitional issues and some comments on measurement principles and on the current status of projective techniques, the remainder of this chapter elaborates on the nature and utility of several commonly used projective instruments, including the Rorschach, the Holtzman Inkblot Test, the TAT, the Children's Apperception Test, the Make-a-Picture-Story Test, sentence completion, and projective drawings.

DEFINING PROJECTIVE TECHNIQUES

Theoretically, any stimulus situation that facilitates the process of projection, as described by Murray and by Frank, can be considered a projective technique. Although this form of definition has appeared very frequently in the literature, many clinicians have found it too vague or general. For others the term "projection" itself has carried a negative or unacceptable connotation because of its presumed link to psychoanalytic theory. This presumption is erroneous, however, even though some authors have defined projective methods in ways that imply a direct relationship between them and analytic theory (Lindzey, 1961; Sargent, 1945; Symonds, 1946; Wiggins, Renner, Clore, & Rose, 1971). Belief in this relationship, whether implicit or explicit, appears derived largely from the notion that the process of projection is a manifestation of the "unconscious" as defined in Freudian theory. Although it is true that people tend to interpret ambiguous stimulus situations in terms of their own needs, interests, and orientations, this process is not necessarily unconscious in the Freudian sense, nor must one conclude that an id, ego, or superego is involved in it.

The process of projection has been demonstrated clearly in studies by Bellak (1944), Atkinson and McClelland (1949), McClelland et al. (1949), Lindzey and Kalnins (1958), and many other investigators. But the validation of the process involved does not equal validation of any particular theory of personality. Just as the data from almost any observable behavior can be interpreted in terms of a variety of personality theories, so too can the data from any projective method be translated into any of a variety of theoretical positions, ranging from the behavioral to the analytic. In other words, none of the well-known projective methods, including the Rorschach, the TAT, projective drawing techniques, and sentence completion blanks, is tied to or dependent on a given theory of personality. Criticisms of the methods based on this assumption are naive and unjustified.

Some authors have avoided the problem of definition by simply elaborating the different types of projective methods that have been developed (Lanyon & Goodstein, 1971). This approach has merit in that it sidesteps the problems of defining stimulus ambiguity and open-endedness of response. Those who have attempted to define projective methods in terms of stimulus ambiguity and the response process have been confronted with the problem of discussing degrees of ambiguity. Murphy (1947), for example, implies in his definition that, the greater the ambiguity in a stimulus, the more projection occurs in response to it. Murstein (1963) and Zubin, Eron, and Schumer (1965) have challenged that assumption, and Murstein (1963,

1965) has pointed to the fact that, unless the stimulus "impact" is determined, it is difficult to separate those components of the response that are attributable to the stimulus from those that are projected. Both Murstein (1963) and Wiggins (1973) have argued in this regard that the stimulus features play some important role, at least for most subjects, in determining the class of response that occurs. Wiggins insists that some types of structured stimuli, such as an MMPI question, may have a greater probability of yielding extreme differences in responses (true versus false) than some of the stimuli in projective methods so structured as to provoke a high frequency of similar answers. This may be more an issue of "psychometry versus projection," rather than of the nature of projective techniques, but it has contributed to some of the definition problems in working with these methods.

One of the most interesting and potentially useful approaches to the definition of projective methods is found in the English and English *Comprehensive Dictionary of Psychological and Psychoanalytic Terms* (1958). The dictionary specifically differentiates a "projective technique" from a "projective test." A projective technique is defined as "a procedure for discovering a person's characteristic modes of behavior by observing his behavior in response to a situation that does not elicit or compel a particular response. . . ." Conversely, a projective test is defined as "a relatively unstructured, yet standard, situation to which a testee is asked to respond, but with as few restrictions as possible upon the mode of response." In this scheme the projective technique can include almost any ambiguous stimulus situation, whereas the projective test is an unstructured but standardized event. For many advocates of projective methods, this kind of differentiation may seem to be splitting hairs, yet it does reflect a unique attempt to circumvent the problems of definition.

Hopefully, it is obvious by this time that any precise definition of a projective method is fraught with complications. By using a backdoor approach, it might be postulated that any stimulus situation that is *not structured* to elicit a specific class of response, as are arithmetic tests, true-false inventories, and the like, may be a projective technique but not necessarily a projective test. For example, intelligence tests are generally regarded as structured methods and not included among lists of projective methods. This is rightfully so, since most items in an intelligence test call for specific right or wrong answers. However, some intelligence test items permit a relatively open-ended form of response, as does the Comprehension subtest in the Wechsler scales. In this instance the subject is permitted a wide latitude of response and, although not encouraged to do so, can easily project some of his needs and interests in his answer.

For example, the best answer to the question, "Why does the state require people to get a license in order to be married?" is that it is for purposes of record keeping. However, if a subject says, "To prevent the scourge of VD from being inflicted on unsuspecting women," then the answer is not only less than satisfactory, but also conveys something about the peculiar interests of the respondent. Although neither the item nor the subtest constitute a projective test, some aspect of projection has occurred, and it would be remiss for the examiner to overlook this source of information in his evaluation of the intellectual functioning of the subject.

Even if the issue of definition could be solved easily, doing so would not resolve some more basic controversial issues concerning the worth of projective methods. These issues have to do primarily with some fundamental principles of measurement in psychology.

MEASUREMENT PRINCIPLES AND PROJECTIVE TECHNIQUES

Whereas the history of projective techniques has been marked by considerable success in the clinical setting, a fundamental controversy has raged about their adequacy as measuring instruments, particularly in the context of comparing projective tests with the more structured "objective" methods. The topics of standardization, reliability, and validity in particular have often generated testiness between the protagonists and the antagonists of projective methods. In many instances claims from both sides have approximated the ridiculous, but have nevertheless been persistently repeated. The supporters of the approach have often unrealistically considered their methods an x-ray of the psyche that can reveal all; on the opposite side, psychometric loins have been girded tightly in the name of science, often spewing forth demands for levels of statistical excellence no technique useful with human subjects could conceivably attain.

Whereas the major focus in this debate has been on matters of validation, other concerns have also frequently been raised. The question of stimulus ambiguity, for example, has not been neglected. Different projective methods use different stimuli and correspondingly differ from each other in their respective ambiguity, and it is furthermore the case that some or possibly all these stimuli limit classes of response. A case in point is a projective method that has held up well to research scrutiny, the sentence completion blank. In this method the stimulus is reasonably well structured and provides the subject with highly specific cues, as in, "When I am alone _____," or "My mother _____," or "If only I _____." In each of these items the subject's attention is deliberately focused on a particular topic. On the TAT, in which the subject is asked to create a story about a picture, the degree of ambiguity is sharply increased over that in sentence completion, and the range of potential ideation or fantasy is much broader. A similar difference appears when the ambiguity of the TAT is contrasted with that of the Rorschach inkblots. Whereas in the TAT the subject is asked to tell a story about the stimulus, in the Rorschach he is merely asked, "What might this be?" The sort of mediation required in the Rorschach is hence substantially different from that required in the TAT.

Cattell (1951) accurately points out that, in the projective situation, the subject is asked to provide something that is not really there. In other words, he is required to "misperceive" the stimulus, and through this misperception he is encouraged to project something of himself into his response. Shneidman (1965) has alluded to this process as one that permits an "assay" of the ingredients of the subject. No matter what name is employed, however, it remains true that the subject is asked to do something with the stimulus that he might not do under other circumstances. The important question then becomes, "How are the subject's responses to be interpreted?"

In a traditional psychometric approach interpretation is based on the extent to which a summation of responses agrees with or deviates from an established norm. Single responses are not ordinarily studied or interpreted. The normative data are usually established by administering the test to a large number of subjects, representing a cross section of relevant populations, and then statistically manipulating the distribution of scores so as to establish the expectancy level for the occurrence of any given score. The more an obtained score deviates from expectation, the more interpretively significant it is thought to be. This approach has been demonstrated to be useful in interpreting both single scores and patterns or configurations of scores. The considerable success of the MMPI, for example, is generally the consequence of extensive work in studying the deviations reflected in certain profiles of scores, rather than the deviation of single scale scores (see Chapter 4).

The same approach has been used with most of the projective methods. However, the problems of establishing adequate normative standards for them have been substantial, partly because of the complexity of projective test responses and partly because of the considerable time necessary to collect adequate representative samples. Thus it has been possible for critics of projective methods to point to the limited standardization data available for many of the methods and to argue that deviations in response cannot easily be identified without such a normative base from which to make comparisons. Proponents of the methods have insisted in reply that normative data provide only a limited input to the total interpretive process, since the richness of the techniques derives from the more subtle idiographic nuances that occur in responses and that are ordinarily not included in any distribution of scores.

Both of these arguments have merit. It is true that larger and more extensive standardization samples would provide a better understanding of the stimulus impact of projective techniques and would make it easier to highlight patterns of deviant responses to them. At the same time, it is true that much of the interpretive substance obtained from responses to projective techniques is gleaned from the unique ways in which they are verbalized. Interestingly, some of the early attempts to obtain standardization data on the Rorschach, especially those of Hertz (1940), were met with considerable criticism beause of the intercorrelation of Rorschach scores and the fact that the total number of responses given varies from subject to subject (Cronbach, 1949). The implication of these kinds of criticism is that some projective methods, such as the Rorschach, are not amenable to study by many of the traditional techniques of measurement and statistical inference. The same issue has often underscored the controversy concerning the reliability and validity of projective methods.

The matter of the reliability of projective methods, or lack thereof, has often been pointed to by critics as another of the weaknesses of the approach. In the formal world of psychometrics an instrument should manifest a test-retest reliability coefficient of .85 or better. Attempts to apply this criterion to projective tests have frequently yielded less than satisfactory results. This seems partly due to the fact that the subject is no longer naive to the task in the retest situation, but it is probably related even more to changes occurring in the psychological activity of the subject. In other words, as needs and stresses alter, even on a day-to-day basis, some of the responses of the subject also change, thereby lowering the retest reliability coefficient. This is not to suggest, however, that projective methods are unreliable, for such is not the case. Numerous studies demonstrate for both the Rorschach and the TAT a substantial reliability coefficient for *specific variables,* even when lengthy periods exist between the first and second testing (see Exner, 1974; Murstein, 1963). Studies designed to test the split-half reliability of projective methods have generally been less successful, except in the case of some sentence completion blanks. The problem with this approach is that it presumes a relatively equal stimulus impact throughout a test. Whereas critics of projective methods often cite low split-half reliabilities as one of the shortcomings of projective methods, the fact is that none of these methods was designed with equivalence of the stimuli as a goal; rather, each part is expected to contribute to the whole, but not necessarily with the same weight or with the same impact for each subject.

Even more than reliability, issues of validity have been a focal point of criticisms of projective methods. Naturally, the same problem of applying measurement principles to the standardization of a given instrument also exists when the matter of validity is approached. Harris (1960), in writing about the problems of Rorschach validation, notes that many enthusiasts of the test have placed themselves in the "precarious position" of permitting the test to be evaluated by orthodox measurement standards, even though it is not designed or interpreted along these lines. This statement can probably be generalized to encompass nearly all projective methods, but it does not mean that the methods are impossible to study regarding their validity. It does mean that some of the traditional criteria of validity are less applicable to them than to other methods, and that some of the orthodox designs for evaluating validity should not be used.

Unfortunately, many of the critics of projective methods have refused to accept this premise and have instead persisted in citing apparent "failures" in testing the validity of the different methods. Frequently these criticisms have appeared to be more the product of bias and overgeneralization than the result of a careful review of the problems and the findings. Consider, for example, the following statement by Jensen (1958) in the *Annual Review of Psychology:* "In the writer's judgment the standard projective techniques . . . have been a failure methodologically and substantively in personality research. . . . In view of this poor showing, the hopes and claims that continue to be professed by the adherents of these methods are indeed cause for wonder." Jensen's remarks probably reflect the attitudes of many psychologists who are categorically opposed to the use of projective methods and who, by drawing data selectively from a relatively large number of investigations, appear to justify their conclusions.

Of a vast number of validity studies that have been published concerning the various projective methods, most can be categorized according to the three major kinds of validity: (a) concurrent validity, which in this case is concerned with agreement between findings from a projective instrument and findings derived from other sources at the same point in time; (b) construct validity, concerned with examining the meaningfulness of specific theoretical concepts and/or psychopathology; and (c) predictive validity, which is concerned with the prediction of future behavioral events from test data. Although all three kinds of validity represent legitimate forms of investigating projective techniques, a remarkably large number of the studies that have been published, especially those cited most frequently by critics of projective methods, have been designed so as to be only peripherally relevant to how the methods are actually used, or to concentrate only on part of a given technique rather than on the utility of the entire test in its full richness.

For instance, a large number of the concurrent validation studies have used diagnostic labels, generally derived from some form of consensus, as the external criterion against which findings from a given method are to be judged. As Zigler and Phillips (1960) have pointed out, however, these labels are based on manifest symptomotology and are not ordinarily indicative of features of personality, especially since individuals with very homogeneous personalities can develop significantly different patterns of symptoms. In that most projective methods are oriented to the description of the person, rather than to a description of symptoms, studies using this general design have usually not yielded results that favor the techniques, especially in the case of the TAT and projective drawings. But even against this stringent and somewhat unrealistic criterion, some of the projective methods have fared reasonably well, at least to the extent of yielding equivocal findings.

The bulk of studies attempting to evaluate the construct validity of the different instruments has been equally disappointing, not so much because of limitations of the methods, but more because the designs of the majority of these studies have converged on single traits of personality or psychopathology. Very few investigations are reported in which several dimensions of the person have been judged using data from projective methods and, in those in which such a design has been employed, the results are much more encouraging, especially for the Rorschach and the TAT. It is also important to note that the very issue of construct validity is, at best, a knotty one. Bechtold (1959) has noted that implementation of criteria for construct validity frequently narrows the interpretation of operational criteria, sometimes so much so that the results create an impractical situation. For instance, several Rorschach studies have been reported concerning characteristics of the "acting-out" person. Unfortunately, many of these studies have used the narrow criterion for acting-out of "assaultiveness to others," which neglects the broad spectrum of other behaviors (including suicide) that can reflect acting-out.

If issues of validity have been a major controversy surrounding projective methods, the element of predictive validity has formed the nucleus. Much of the framework of measurement is firmly committed to the prediction of behavior, and many clinicians have been trapped, or have trapped themselves, by the *erroneous assumption* that projective methods should have special predictive capabilities. This assumption has been encouraged, directly or indirectly, by numerous influential authors. For example, Sarbin (1941) suggested that a diagnostic statement is meaningful only when it has reference to the future, that is, when it is predictive. In so doing, Sarbin overlooked the value of making diagnostic statements merely to understand the person *as he is,* not necessarily as he will be.

One of the key figures in exaggerating the importance of prediction has been Paul Meehl, who in 1954 published his classic *Clinical versus Statistical Prediction*. Meehl reviewed 20 studies in his book, all but one of which showed the actuarial method to be equal to or better than the clinical technique (ordinarily based largely on the use of projective methods) in personality assessment. Meehl concluded by arguing that, because less complex and time-consuming techniques such as the MMPI can provide at least as accurate information as can the clinical approach to assessment, the latter should be abandoned so so as to allow clinicians more time for other important work, especially therapy. Gough (1963) and Sawyer (1966) subsequently published surveys of predictive studies which appear to support Meehl's argument, although Gough observed that no adequate test of the clinician's forecasting skills had yet been carried out.

Holt (1958, 1970[a]), in two excellent rejoinders to the Meehl argument, points out that in many of the studies Meehl cites the criterion used was extremely inadequate and in some instances even contaminated. In his 1970 paper Holt also calls attention to the fact that another survey of predictive studies, by Korman (1968), reports very positive findings favoring the clinical method. He notes with some sense of alarm that the Sawyer and Korman bibliographies show *absolutely no overlap,* even though they were published within 2 years of each other, a state of affairs that emphasizes how the literature is often used very selectively to support a particular bias. Possibly the most important point stressed in the Holt articles is the matter of *understanding* versus *prediction* as a viable scientific goal. He contends in this regard that, although the use of projective methods for predictive purposes is an interesting and worthwhile exercise, the *primary* purpose of the methods is to facilitate description and understanding of the person (see also Weiner, 1972).

THE CURRENT STATUS OF PROJECTIVE METHODS

Although projective methods have been in the focus of much controversy, they have continued to flourish in the clinical setting, as noted earlier in reference to the Louttit and Browne, Sundberg, and Lubin, Wallis, and Paine surveys. The controversies have not been resolved but, for several probable reasons, they occupy less space in the literature than previously. First, there has been a gradual accumulation of data, especially from some of the more sophisticated research designs, that have lent considerable support to the usefulness of some of the methods. Second, the area of assessment has broadened substantially, and the continued development of such objective measures as the MMPI together with the more recent development of methods of behavioral assessment (see Chapter 5) have given clinicians a greater array of techniques to use and to evaluate than they had earlier.

Third, there has been a considerable deemphasis on diagnostic labeling, so that the questions of labels occur far less frequently than previously and have given way to greater emphasis on the understanding of the person. Fourth, psychodiagnostic assessment is currently being done much more selectively than was formerly the case. There was a period during the 1940s and 1950s when almost every patient entering a clinic or hospital was routinely referred for psychological testing. Often the kinds of questions asked in these referrals were either unrealistically demanding or so elementary that they could be answered easily using data from other sources, such as a good history or a reasonable period of observation. Finally, clinical psychology itself has changed considerably since that time. Assessment is no longer the only primary function of the clinician, as it was 20 years ago. To the contrary, assessment is currently considered by many as secondary in importance to intervention, and a wide variety of intervention techniques have replaced assessment as the major topic of clinical interest and investigation.

The end result of these historical developments has been a more sophisticated approach to assessment. Projective methods are not always used in test batteries, nor should they be, and when they are included, they tend to be selected for specific purposes that correspond to the strengths of the particular instrument. Weiner (1972) reports data in this regard to the effect that probably more people are undergoing psychodiagnostic assessment now than in the past, but that these numbers represent a smaller proportion than previously of the total patient population, which has increased. It also appears that individuals requesting psychological testing are asking more realistic and more necessary questions than had been the case. In a large number of these instances the requests center not only on understanding the subject, but also on providing information useful to treatment planning and subsequent evaluations of treatment effectiveness.

In this new era the basic assessment approach, whether behavioral or phenomenological, is to view the subject at work, so to speak; to study his modes of response in a variety of situations; and from the accumulated data to draw intelligent clinical inferences concerning his idiography. Several projective techniques frequently play a very important role in this process, including the Rorschach, the Holtzman Inkblot Test, the TAT, the Children's Apperception Test, the Make-a-Picture-Story test, sentence completion methods, and projective drawings. The remainder of this chapter reviews how and why each of these techniques is used.

THE RORSCHACH

Although the Rorschach is not the oldest of the projective methods, it might legitimately be called the "grandfather" in the projective movement. It has probably been used more frequently than any of the other projective methods, from the 1930s to the present. It has also had the stormiest history of any of the projective techniques, as has already been noted, but has probably survived controversies as well as or better than any of them.

History and Systems of the Rorschach

The 10 Swiss inkblots that constitute the Rorschach were first unveiled to the professional world in Hermann Rorschach's classic monograph, *Psychodiagnostik,* published in 1921. Rorschach conceived of his work as an experiment in perception that would lend itself to a sophisticated diagnostic approach. He used about 40 blots in his work, most of which was conducted between 1917 and 1920, and settled on the final series of 10 blots because his publisher was unwilling to invest money in the reproduction of any more than this number of plates. Interestingly, the blots with which Rorschach did most of his work differed from those in use today, in that they contained no shading features. A printing error in the original reproduction of the plates created the shading features, and Rorschach, intrigued with the shaded plates, decided to use them in his subsequent research.

Unfortunately, Rorschach's untimely death in 1922, at the age of 38, left a significant void in his yet to be completed work. Had it not been for the enthusiasm and dedication of three of Rorschach's friends, his work might have gone unnoticed or at least unpopularized. Emil Oberholzer, Walter Morganthaler, and George Roemer continued to use and teach the Rorschach technique and to encourage its further investigation. Morganthaler had been directly responsible for the publication of *Psychodiagnostik,* and it was Oberholzer who undertook to publish Rorschach's last paper (1923). It was also Oberholzer who introduced David Levy to the test, and Levy, as mentioned earlier, brought it to the United States and subsequently encouraged Samuel Beck to consider it as a possible dissertation topic.

Most of the extensive development of the Rorschach occurred after 1930 and was based generally on several basic premises Rorschach offered concerning the technique. Some writers, including Zubin, Eron, and Schumer (1965), have suggested that Rorschach might be appalled if he were to perceive how the technique has been used in contemporary psychodiagnostics. The implication is that Rorschach would not have wanted the test committed to projective theory and would be particularly disturbed by analytic interpretations of its content. Such a conclusion is probably unwarranted, even though Rorschach did make it clear that he did not feel the test to be as useful for the study of unconscious thought as other methods, such as dream interpretation. However, he did suggest that the interpretation of content could be very helpful in serving the broad purposes of psychodiagnosis. Rorschach himself did not develop any particular theory of the test; rather, he concluded that further investigation, under well-controlled conditions, would be essential before any understanding of the process involved could be derived.

The major impetus for the development of the test beyond Rorschach's work occurred in the United States. As Shneidman (1965) points out, the *Zeitgeist* of the 1930s and 1940s was ripe for the development of projective methods, largely because of the "felt inadequacies" of the objective questionnaire approach in the clinical situation. More specifically, the development of the test can be attributed primarily to the efforts of five people, each of whom approached the Rorschach in the context of his or her own training, interests, and experience. These five are Samuel Beck (1937, 1944, 1945, 1952, 1961, 1967), Bruno Klopfer (1942, 1954, 1956, 1970), Marguerite Hertz (1938, 1942, 1951, 1970), Zygmunt Piotrowski (1947, 1957, 1964), and David Rapaport (1946). Although all five have contributed significantly to the Rorschach, they have not always agreed in their views. Consequently, as each person committed part of his professional life to the test, different approaches to it evolved, approaches marked by the unique theoretical and/or methodological signature of each.

Exner (1969) has noted that, although each of the systems of the Rorschach created by these five people has formed an overlay for Rorschach's original work, the result has been the development of virtually *five different Rorschachs*. This diversity has been both an asset and a liability for the test: an asset because the divergence among the five systems precipitated controversy, interest, and investigation; a liability because the differences among these systematizers have never been resolved fully. It seems quite certain that, in the beginning, none of the systematizers closely allied himself with an approach to the test that was deliberately different from the others. But differences in training and clinical orientation caused each to conceptualize the Rorschach in his or her own special manner.

The seeds of this divergence were sown in the period from 1933 to 1939. By 1933 both Beck and Hertz has completed their dissertations concerning the Rorschach, at Columbia and Western Reserve, respectively. Beck had gone on to Harvard Medical School and, after a year there, had received a Rockefeller fellowship to go to Switzerland to study further with Oberholzer. Hertz remained in Cleveland to begin a distinguished career teaching at Western Reserve and researching the Rorschach at the Brush Foundation, a multipurpose unit for the study of children. Each had already experienced many of the complications of the test posed by questions left unanswered by Rorschach. At about this same time, Bruno Klopfer, who had received his Ph. D. about 11 years earlier at the University of Munich, decided to leave Germany because of the pressure of Nazism. He went first to Zurich, where throught the assistance of Carl Jung he obtained a position at the Psychotechnic Institute in which he was required to learn to use the Rorschach. A year later Klopfer emigrated to the United States to accept a position at Columbia University.

Klopfer's orientation was strongly affected by contemporary German psychology and the growing psychoanalytic movement. Hence it was marked largely by phenomenology, whereas both Beck and Hertz had been trained in the more conservative American empirical tradition. It was inevitable that the Klopfer approach, which emphasized the more qualitative and subjective aspects of behavior, would clash with the more rigorously positivistic orientations of Beck and Hertz. When Klopfer began his first seminar on the Rorschach in 1934, one of the seven participants was Zygmunt Piotrowski, an experimental psychologist who had obtained his Ph. D. in 1927 from the University of Poznan in Poland and who at that time was working at the College of Physicians and Surgeons at Columbia. Although he worked closely with Klopfer for about 2 years, Piotrowski found that, like Beck, he could not accept Klopfer's seeming tendency to reach Rorschach decisions hastily, and he ultimately drifted to his own approach, which is more similar to Beck's than to Klopfer's.

Beck (1935) was the first of the major systematizers to be openly critical of the approach in which Klopfer had been trained. After returning from Zurich, he accepted a position at the University of Chicago and published a paper expressing his feelings of distress that the Zurich procedures were marked too largely by the approach of "the artist" rather than that of the scientist. In that article and one the following year (Beck, 1936), he made strong appeals for consistent and well-controlled experimentation before establishing additional scoring, and he emphasized the importance of employing standardized procedures and obtaining adequate standardization data for a variety of clinical groups.

Concurrently, Klopfer, who was both a master teacher and a master organizer, recognized the need for some avenue of communication among those working with the Rorschach. Consequently, he began the *Rorschach Research Exchange*, which was to become the *Journal of Projective Techniques* and, ultimately, the *Journal of Personality Assessment*. In the first issue, which appeared shortly before the publication of Beck's initial book about the Rorschach, Klopfer offered a refined scoring system based in part on his own experience with the technique and in part on the seminar discussions he had conducted during the previous 2 years (Klopfer & Sender, 1936). This scoring system was very well organized, but it lacked the firm data base that Beck offered for his scoring system in *Introduction to the Rorschach Method* (1937). Klopfer's scoring called for far greater diversification than either Rorschach or Beck recommended.

In a later issue of the first volume of the *Rorschach Research Exchange*, Klopfer (1937) presented a paper in which he gave considerable space to a review of Beck's new book. The review was highly critical and alluded to Beck's failure to include what Klopfer considered to be some important scoring categories. Additionally, the review implied considerable disagreement with the method used by Beck to evaluate the "quality" of the use of form features in responses. This article naturally provoked a reply from Beck, in which he was equally critical of the Klopfer proliferation of scores and especially of Klopfer's willingness to have examiner's use their own experience as a guideline in some of the scoring. A series of comments on the dispute appeared in subsequent issues of the *Rorschach Research Exchange*, some of which supported Beck, but most of which were critical of him.

One of these commenting articles was written by Hertz (1937), and probably offered a clue concerning the position she was to take in her work with the test. She was somewhat critical of Beck, not so much because of his plea for objectivity but because he had not given more definitive information concerning his procedures and populations. She was also somewhat critical of Klopfer, implying that she too was concerned that some of his decisions about scoring categories and criteria might have been made without adequate data. Hertz called for compromise and resolution of the problems, a plea she was to make several times during subsequent years. Ultimately she was to develop her own approach, based at first on her psychometric orientation but subsequently shifted to a position more closely aligned with Klopfer, especially after her efforts at standardization were strongly criticized by Cronbach (1949).

By 1939 there were at least three distinct Rorschach systems in the United States, those of Beck, Klopfer, and Hertz. It was at about that time that David Rapaport emigrated to New York after completing his doctorate at the Royal Hungarian Petrus at Pazmany in 1938. Rapaport was very strongly psychoanalytically oriented, and he perceived the disputes about standardization and objectivity to be far less important than did his colleagues. Throughout his professional life he conceptualized the Rorschach as a technique useful to the diagnostic process rather than as a test to be studied and argued over. He used the Rorschach as it seemed to fit best into the "test battery," and he argued against cumbersome extensions and refinements of it. Together with Gill and Schafer he produced a historical two-volume work on diagnostic testing which remains a classic (1945, 1946). Subsequently, his most well-known disciple, Roy Schafer, contributed another milestone work, *Psychoanalytic Interpretation in Rorschach Testing* (1954). Collectively, the works of Rapaport and Schafer formed a fifth Rorschach system, although neither intended such nor devoted a major portion of his professional work to the test. The last system to be formalized was that of Piotrowski, who published his major volume on the test in 1957.

And so, over a period of slightly more than 20 years (1936–1957), five American Rorschach systems developed, three (Beck, Klopfer, and Hertz) by 1945, and the remaining two (Rapaport and Piotrowski) shortly thereafter. Whereas each system includes most of the underpinnings of the test provided by Rorschach's original work, each is clearly discrete in its own right. The Rapaport-Schafer system is probably the most dissimilar from the others, but even when the remaining four systems are compared, the differences among them are truly astonishing (Exner, 1969). These differences are by no means esoteric. To the contrary, they involve such basic features of the test as seating arrangements for administering it, instructions to the subject, techniques of encouragement from the examiner, scoring symbols and criteria, and principles of interpretation.

Unfortunately, Rorschach practitioners and researchers have frequently either not been cognizant of these different approaches or have unrealistically minimized the differences, so as to maintain the delusion that a single Rorschach exists. Thus controversy concerning *the* Rorschach has persistently focused on validation problems and research failures with little or no attention to the fact that possibly *five tests* rather than just one were being discussed. In the clinical setting practitioners have often slipped into the bad habit of naively mixing the systems, thereby creating a new, personalized Rorschach, and then interpreting that *new* test according to guidelines provided by one of the major systematizers. The manner in which the differences among the Rorschach systems have affected the teaching of the test has been well documented by Jackson and Wohl (1966), who used a questionnaire to study differences in practice and attitude among university faculty responsible for teaching courses in the Rorschach. The Jackson and Wohl data reflect a considerable dilemma in Rorschach instruction. Not only did they find striking variability in the methods of administration, scoring, and interpretation taught by the instructors they surveyed, but they also found that approximately 60% of these instructors had had little or no postdoctoral experience with the Rorschach, and furthermore that 46% would prefer to teach something else. Twelve percent of the instructors ignored scoring of responses altogether. The Jackson and Wohl data thus suggest that instead of five different kinds of Rorschach, each based on a fully developed system, there may be as many Rorschachs as there are Rorschachers.

In a related study concerning the actual Rorschach methods employed by clinicians, Exner and Exner (1972) obtained further evidence of striking irregularity in the use of the test. Twenty-two percent of those surveyed reported that they do not score the Rorschach and, of those who do score, 75% admitted to personalizing their scoring. These idiosyncratic proliferations were by no means minor, since they frequently consisted of adding features from one system to another preferred system which was kept essentially intact. More often than not, Rorschach clinicians appear to have pieced together an assortment of features from several systems and from their own experience, *even though* maintaining some allegiance to a preferred system.

For example, 166 of the clinicians surveyed by Exner and Exner defined themselves as ''Klopferites,'' that is, as essentially following the Klopfer system; yet of this group more than half were found to ''bastardize'' their Rorschach approach in some significant way. Seventy-one administer the test face-to-face, a seating arrangement strongly denounced by Klopfer but recommended by Rapaport; 63 instruct the subject to report *everything* he sees, another procedure strongly denounced by Klopfer but recommended by Beck, Hertz, and Rapaport; 31 give equal weight to all determinant scoring features, which is opposite Klopfer's distinction between main and additional determinants but compatible with Beck, Hertz, and Piotrowski; 81 use the Beck method for evaluating Form Quality and disregard the Klopfer Form Level rating; and 32 do not score at all, an omission strongly denounced in all systems. Obviously, none of these 166 Rorschachers is really a Klopferite, although all profess to be.

The divergence of Rorschach methodology into five major systems, and subseqently into a potentially astronomical number of proliferations, has not been beneficial for the Rorschach. The failure of the Rorschach community to develop a single system of the test has penalized both the practitioner and the researcher, especially since the differences among the systems have so often been ignored or underplayed on the erroneous assumption that they are relatively minor. The naive assumption seems to be that, when the ''total'' Rorschach is used, the results will be the same regardless of such variations. It is remarkable that the test has survived despite this potentially chaotic situation, and even more remarkable that the test *has not simply survived, but actually flourished.* This durability is probably due to at least two factors. First, each of the systems included much of Rorschach's basic work, thus providing some common elements for interpretation. Second, no matter what method is employed, the words of the subject are a fundamental yield. Analysis of the verbalizations is always included in any Rorschach interpretation, and in all systems special weight is frequently given to the more unique and dramatic responses, with respect both to their actual content and their appropriateness to the blot.

Recently, an effort has been completed to integrate the most useful and empirically defensible features of the various approaches to the Rorschach into a single system (Exner, 1974). This work has utilized a large pool of protocols, collected via the different systems, to study and compare the products of each approach. These data were coded for computer sorting and analysis, and decisions were subsequently derived concerning each aspect of the test, including seating arrangements, instructions, scoring, and interpretation. In many instances the accumulated literature offered sufficient empirical basis for a decision. In other instances, in which the empirical data were limited or equivocal, new investigations were undertaken.

The result of this work, referred to as the *Comprehensive System*, is an approach that draws from each of the systems, incorporating those features that, under careful scrutiny, appear to offer the greatest yield and adding to them other components based on more recent work with the test. The Comprehensive System appears to be an approach that is easily taught, that manifests high interclinician reliability, and that should stand up well to various tests concerning validity. It is not based on any particular theoretical position, but rather represents an integration of the hard-won wisdoms of those who have developed and researched the test. The structure of the Comprehensive System closely parallels that of the other systems and of the basic design for the test originally described by Rorschach.

Process and Results in Rorschach Testing

Hopefully, this lengthy history of some of the problems of the Rorschach has generated more intrigue than discouragement, for it is truly a worthy instrument when used intelligently and appropriately. What then is the process of the Rorschach, and what results can be obtained from its use? First, the procedure of administration and scoring is relatively simple and can be learned by almost any intelligent person. According to the findings reported in the Comprehensive System, seating should definitely be side by side, not face to face. The latter holds too great a possibility of the examiner's unintentionally providing nonverbal cues to the subject, which can inadvertently influence his responses. Side-by-side administration avoids this problem for the most part, and it also permits the examiner a full view of features of the blot as they are described by the subject. The instructions to the subject are brief. After some introductory remarks concerning the purpose of the examination, the examiner hands the subject the first card and asks, "What might this be?" These are the instructions used by Rorschach and Klopfer, and they avoid some of the complications of more elaborate instructions that have been recommended by other systematizers.

The test itself usually takes 45–55 minutes, unless a subject is unusually verbose or extremely resistive. Each of the 10 cards is presented to the subject twice: first during a *Free Association Period* in which the examiner simply hands each card to the subject, one at a time, and the subject reports what the blot, or parts of it, look like; and second during an *Inquiry* in which the examiner, through *nondirective* questioning, determines what part of the blot has been used for each response and what characteristics of the blot have been important to the subject in provoking the response, such as the form features, the coloring, and the shading. The examiner records *verbatim* the verbalizations of the subject during both the Free Association and the Inquiry.

After the administration of the test is completed, the responses are scored or coded. The use of the word "score" has probably been unfortunate as applied to the Rorschach. The scoring procedure consists of translating Rorschach words into Rorschach symbols; it is thus a process more similar to coding data for entry into a computer than to scoring in the traditional psychometric sense of the word. As previously noted, many of the typical psychometric tenets have only limited usefulness when applied to the Rorschach, partly because the number of responses given varies from subject to subject and partly because the probability that each kind of score will occur is not the same for all scoring categories. The majority of subjects, whether patients or nonpatients, give 17–27 responses to the entire test when the procedures of the Comprehensive System are used. Each response is *always* scored for three basic categories, and all responses are evaluated to determine if either or both of two other categories are applicable.

The first of the three scores attributable to all responses is the *Location Scoring*. This score represents the area of the blot used by the subject in his response. There are three classes of Location Scores: one indicates that the whole blot has been used (*W*), one indicates that the response involves only a *commonly used* detail area of the blot (*D*), and one represents the use of *an unusual* or not commonly used area of the blot (*Dd*). The symbol *S* is added to any of the three scores if the subject also uses the white areas around the blot in his response. In addition to the basic scoring for location, a respectable quantity of research has demonstrated that the location selections should also be evaluated for their *Developmental Quality*

(Friedman, 1952, 1953; Goldfried, Stricker, & Weiner, 1971 Chapter 2; Hemmendinger, 1953, 1960; Meili-Dworetzki, 1939, 1956). This scoring provides an index of whether the selection of location has been simple or complex and offers some information regarding the subject's level of cognitive maturity and sophistication. A method of evaluating the Developmental Quality of location selections is included in the Comprehensive System, but was not part of the previously developed major approaches.

The second of the three scores attributable to all responses is called the *Determinant Score*. It is the most complex of the three basic scores in that there are several possible features of the blot that cause someone to identify a response, and it is the purpose of the Determinant Score to indicate which of these features caused the subject to perceive the content that he reports. It has been convincingly demonstrated that the *Form* features, or contours, of the blot or blot areas usually play some role in "determining" an answer (Baughman, 1954, 1958, 1959; Exner, 1959, 1961). Accordingly, the symbol for scoring Form (F) is used in most determinant scoring.

In addition to responding to form, a subject may report an object in movement, or he may specify that the coloring or shading in the blot was relevant to his percept. Three kinds of movement are scored: human movement (M), animal movement (FM), and inanimate movement (m). Two kinds of color responses may occur, those involving the use of chromatic colors (C) and those using achromatic color (C'). The shading of the blots may be used in three different ways: to create the impression of texture (T), to give the appearance of depth or vista (V), or to make some diffuse use of the "dark" features (Y). As Form is usually involved when either color or shading is used, the scoring format provides for including the symbol for Form depending on the extent to which it has contributed to the answer. Thus a scoring of FC indicates that Form was the primary determinant, but that the chromatic coloring also contributed. A score of TF indicates that the shading features, used to create the impression of texture, were primary in the formulation of the answer, but that Form features were also involved.

In the research leading to the development of the Comprehensive System, three discrete kinds of responses were identified that had not been afforded special scoring in the other systems. One is an answer in which the Form features are used to create the impression of depth or distance. This kind of answer, called Form Dimension, is scored FD. A second newly identified response involves the use of the symmetric features of the blot to precipitate the percept of a reflection and is scored either rF or Fr, depending on how much form is involved (Exner, 1969, 1970). Third, it has been noted that the symmetry of the blots often provokes subjects to identify *two* of an object, such as two men, two dogs, and the like. These kinds of responses, called Pair responses, are given the scoring of (2).

The third category of score assigned to all responses is the *Content Score*. This score is simply an abbreviation to code the class of object reported, such as *H* for human, *Bt* for botany, *Fi* for fire, *Sx* for sex, and so forth. The decision about which content categories are scored by standard abbreviations has been based on the frequency with which they occur. Highly unique contents, such as mud, guitar, fingernails, and the like are written out in their complete form.

As the three basic scores are assigned to each response, the response also evaluated to determine if it is *Popular*, that is, if it is a response that occurs once or more in every three protocols. If so, it is given a fourth score, *P*. Popular answers are strictly defined by the frequency of their occurrence, and 13 such responses are identified in the research concerning the Comprehensive System.

Finally, each response is also evaluated to determine if some form of *Organizational Activity* has occurred in formulating it. In other words, has the subject "created" the response rather than simply picked it out of the blot? Beck (1933) was the first to develop a scoring for Organizational Activity, which he based on a suggestion in Rorschach's original work. Beck established different numerical weights for different kinds of Organizational Activity on each of the cards. Hertz (1940) later incorporated a similar scoring in her system, and Klopfer (1946) included consideration of this activity in his method for evaluating Form Quality. The Exner and Exner survey (1972) revealed that relatively few practitioners had found the scoring for Organizational Activity useful. However, some of the recent research leading to the Comprehensive System suggested that Organizational Activity scores offer significant clues to forms of inefficient response styles, and they have therefore been included as a fifth possible scoring for responses.

The complexity of the scoring for a Rorschach response generally gives some indication about the complexity of the response itself. For instance, an answer "yellow rosebud," elaborated on in the inquiry to specify the stem and the flower part, is scored *Do FCo Bt*. This scoring indicates that the subject used a commonly perceived detail area of the blot, that the response is based primarily on Form but that chromatic color also is included, and that the content is from the general class of Botany. The *o* entered after the location score of *D* indicates that the Developmental Quality of the location selection is ordinary. The *o* entered after the determinant score of *FC* indicates that the quality of Form used is also ordinary, that is, it matches the blot area selected. If the object reported were quite incompatible with the contours of the blot area, the scoring would be $FC-$, to indicate that the Form Quality is poor.

A more complex scoring is required for the response, "Two men carrying a basket toward a bright fire in the background," elaborated in the inquiry to indicate that the fire is perceived mainly because of the redness and that it is in the background because it is smaller in proportion to the size of the men. The scoring here is $D+ M^a.CF.FD+$ (2)H,Fi P 4.0. This score reveals that a common detail area was used in synthesizing manner (D+), that human movement is involved and is *active* (M^a), that part of the response is mainly contingent on the chromatic color (CF), that the contours of the blot created a dimensional effect (FD), that the Form Quality is *superior* (+), that a pair is involved (2), that two contents are included, human and fire (H,Fi), that the response includes a Popular answer (P), and that organizational activity has occurred (4.0). This kind of answer is called a *blend* response, because more than one determinant is used. Blend answers give some index of the complexity involved in the perceptual-cognitive mediation leading to the response.

Once responses are scored, frequency tallies are developed for each kind of score, and numerous ratios and percentages are calculated. These ratios and percentages represent the *Structural Summary* of the Rorschach and provide a very important input to the interpretation of the test. The Comprehensive System includes 22 ratios and percentages from which many interpretive postulates can be derived. These include such elements as the ratio of human movement to a weighted sum of all chromatic color answers (M:Sum C), the percentage of good Form Quality used (X+%), and the proportion of responses using the whole blot compared with those using common detail areas (W:D).

There is a variety of special scorings which can also be used with the Rorschach. For example, Fisher and Cleveland (1955, 1958) have developed two special scores which assess the implications of various contents for body image boundary. A sizable literature has developed concerning the usefulness of these scores (See Goldfried et al., 1971, Chapter 6). Another example of special scoring is that for "unusual verbalizations," suggested originally by Rapaport (1946) and elaborated considerably by Schafer (1954) and Weiner (1966). In a similar vein Holt (1966, 1970, 1970(b)) has developed a sophisticated procedure of scoring Rorschach verbalizations designed to provide information concerning such basic cognitive operations as flexibility, adaptive regression, and defense effectiveness.

The material presented here may convey the impression that the scoring of the Rorschach is a complex and time-consuming process. This is *not* the case. The experienced user of the test can ordinarily score all responses in less than 15 minutes and calculate the various ratios and percentages in about half that time. Thus the average length of time required to administer the test, score the responses, and complete the Structural Summary is usually no more than 70–90 minutes—a seemingly reasonable period in view of how much information is gleaned about the subject.

Interpretation of Rorschach Data

The interpretation of the data of the Rorschach requires considerably more skill than is necessary for administration and scoring. Like any test, the Rorschach does not interpret itself, and it takes the talents of a well-trained clinician, combining his knowledge about personality and psychopathology with the test data, to derive an accurate description of the subject. The process is one of both induction and deduction, in which the interpreter uses all the data available to him. It begins with the gradual formulation of postulates using bits and pieces of data and ends as the postulates or propositions are integrated in a logically meaningful way to provide information concerning a unique person. The flow of this process is made possible by the interpreter's understanding of the kinds of psychological activity that give rise to the different response features, regardless of whether these features are represented by scores or words.

Sophisticated clinical interpretation, whether of the Rorschach or any other projective method, is not a "cookbook" process, as has been recommended by Meehl (1956). There is no simple checklist of signs which can automatically be translated into an *understanding* of the individual. There are instruments such as the MMPI that can be interpreted in a "cookbook" manner to yield a series of propositional statements about the subject, sometimes even through the use of a computer. But a listing of statements is not a full description of a person and, even though they may be "printed" with an impressive reliability, such statements fall far short of the goal of understanding the subject as a highly unique individual, different from any other.

An attempt at computer interpretation of the Rorschach has been made by Piotrowski (1964) using an extremely elaborate program comprised of 434 parameters and 620 rules. The results were somewhat disappointing, primarily because many of the variables of the test were not weighted appropriately. Piotrowski then undertook a lengthy revision of his program. By 1968 the number of rules had expanded to 937, but the problem of evaluating the more subtle nuances of the responses had still not been resolved. When the program is complete, the printed statements are generalized to some extent, and the expertise of the clinician is still required to integrate them in a meaningful way. For example, a proposition that a subject is "quick to display emotion" may be quite valid, but it provides only a very narrow contribution to any understanding of the person. Among the major questions it leaves unanswered are, "Under what kinds of circumstances does this emotional display occur, and is this proclivity an asset or a liability for the person?" Other information is obviously required before useful conclusions can be drawn in this regard. For instance, if other test data reveal that the subject tests reality well, that he has a reasonable interest in others and is capable of forming healthy relationships, that he is aware of conventionality, and that he is not ordinarily overwhelmed by feelings of tension or anxiety, it would seem realistic to conclude that he probably handles his emotions effectively.

Ordinarily, data relevant to these kinds of interpretation are available in the *full* Rorschach, that is, the composite of the structural data and the verbalizations offered in the responses. The interpretation is both nomothetic and idiographic. It involves analysis of both the quantified data and of the subject's words. Use of either without the other is a negligent abuse of the test and, more importantly, a disservice to the subject.

Rorschach interpretation usually begins with a review of the Structural Summary, that is, of the scores and the ratios, percentages, and derivations calculated from them. At this point the interpreter focuses on the configuration of the data, with particular attention to characteristics that appear with frequencies significantly greater or less than expected. For instance, Popular answers are ordinarily considered as reflecting one's ability to perceive things in a conventional manner. A protocol containing no Popular responses raises the question of the subject's capability to recognize conventional modes of response, whereas a protocol in which a large number of *P* responses occurs raises the question whether the subject is overly committed to conventionality. Similarly, normative samples demonstrate that most subjects give about three times as many *FC* responses (Form-dominated chromatic color answers) as *CF* responses (those in which color is the primary feature). If a protocol contains a large number of *CF* answers and few or no *FC* responses, a question is raised regarding the emotional controls of the subject, since the use of color is related to the expression of emotion and the use of form to the process of cognitive delay and psychologically deliberate responsiveness.

It is not possible in the scope of this chapter to detail the multitude of interpretive propositions that can be developed from the Structure of the Rorschach; it must suffice to affirm that each of the different scores has relevance to certain kinds of psychological activity. However, an example of the kinds of hypotheses generated from these data may help the reader in understanding how the Rorschach can be used. The following are propositions derived from the Structural Summary of the protocol of a 32-year-old single male charged with attempted homicide. He was referred by the court with questions concerning his "legal" sanity, since he claimed no recall for the event with which he was charged (Exner, 1974, pp. 375–385).

1. He is very labile and frequently commanded by affect rather than by more organized and controlled cognitive activity.

2. He often experiences a "need to respond" based on his less well-organized inner forces, which when combined with his lability makes for a high probability of acting out.

3. He bends reality frequently, usually to meet his own needs.

4. He is very egocentric, which sometimes causes him to disregard conventionality and which also feeds into his impulsive life-style.

5. He has very limited controls, and even when he does make attempts at organization and delay, his emotions usually break through and dictate his response.

6. He has some features of immaturity and may even be described as "infantile" at times. He has very strong needs for affection which often orient his patterns of behavior.

7. He is noticeably preoccupied with sexuality.

8. His impulsive life-style serves a defensive purpose by creating a situation in which he avoids awareness of his very strong feelings of affective deprivation.

These eight postulates do not approach the referral question directly, nor do they approach the more subtle idiographic features of the subject. They do represent, however, a beginning of the interpretation of the record, which will subsequently be enriched by the analysis of the verbal material in the responses.

The verbal material in a Rorschach protocol is a major source of interpretive data. Rorschach himself was very conservative in his estimate of the usefulness of analyzing the content. Lindner (1943, 1944, 1946, 1947), however, was among the first of many workers to argue strongly for this form of interpretation. He presented a series of "classes" of answers which he proposed regarding as representative of different kinds of psychopathological ideation. Following Lindner's lead, many contributions recommended content analysis to identify diagnostic types, personality traits, and the meaning of specific classes of verbalization. Of particular note are special content scorings for anxiety (Elizur, 1949), hostility (Elizur, 1949), aggression (Walker, 1951; Stone, 1953), homosexuality (Wheeler, 1949), tension (Smith & Coleman, 1956), body image boundary (Fisher & Cleveland, 1958), and defense effectiveness (Holt, 1960, 1966). Unfortunately, with the possible exception of the Holt scoring for defense effectiveness, these special scoring approaches have yielded equivocal findings. This has not, however, negated the usefulness of content analysis, since there are other approaches to the analysis of content that have produced more positive results. These more successful approaches have sought to demonstrate a common psychological meaning for a specific class of content and, as is well summarized by Draguns, Haley, and Phillips (1967), the studies in this area examine logical group- ings of responses that appear to have a common theme or characteristic.

Schafer (1954) presents one of the most comprehensive thematic guidelines for using this interpretive approach to Rorschach content. He cites 14 broad-ranging thematic categories and illustrates how a variety of different contents may relate to such personality characteristics as de- pendency, aggressiveness, and various conflicts and fears. For example, he suggests that responses involving reference to God, police, the Ku Klux Klan, family crests, castles, and riches may all relate to an authoritarian orientation. Similarly, a clustering of answers involving jellyfish, a straw man, weak or dead branches or roots, and badly skinned animals can all relate to feelings of inadequacy or impotency. Hypotheses developed from these sorts of analysis supplement those formulated from the Structural data of the Rorschach. For instance, an interpreter can hardly neglect the rich symbolism in the following response given to a phalliclike projection in one of the Rorschach cards: "A deadly weapon; it has a spear type tip, like one that could hurt or even kill someone." On a very basic level, such a response could be interpreted as reflecting fear of masculine sexuality. On a more conservative interpretive level, the response could represent something of the subject's conceptualization of masculinity. Either or both might be correct but, like hypotheses based on the Structure of the test, both would require confirmation from other features in the record.

Some of the responses of the 32-year-old subject mentioned previously with regard to the Structural Summary can also be used to clarify the thematic approach to interpreting content. In one card this man saw a "woman modeling something"; in another he identified a woman's geni- tals, saying, "Well, doc, this is a good one, this bottom part reminds me of a . . . a . . . well, I was gonna say pussy, but I'll say vagina to make it a little better, hows that?"; and in another he saw "a couple of ovaries or something, if there were a penis there they could be testicles, but there isn't any so they must be ovaries." Responses such as these are dramatic and telling to the interpreter. The subject is obviously concerned with sexuality and, if the projective hypothesis holds true, it is his own sexuality that is at the core of his concern. But it is not only the more striking or dramatic answers that lend themselves to a content interpretation. Any Rorschach verbalization can be interpreted, just as verbalizations occurring in ap- perceptive techniques such as the TAT or in psychotherapy interviews.

The kinds of proposition that may be developed from Rorschach content are illustrated by those derived from the verbalizations of this homicide suspect:

1. He often attempts delay, but usually fails to contain his impulsiveness.
2. He is highly manipulative of others.
3. Beneath his thin facade of cooperativeness is a strong aggressive orientation toward others.
4. He is able to test reality quite well, but often disregards it in order to serve his own ends.
5. He does not appear to have developed an adequate sex role identity concerning masculinity, a factor that is probably responsible, at least in part, for his aggressiveness and his sexual preoccupation.
6. His overemphasis on sexuality is a form of concealment of his own sex role problems.
7. His feelings of affective deprivation are often overwhelming and void his attempts at presenting an acceptable facade of smooth interpersonal relations.
8. He is often aware of his orientation to nonconformity but obtains a significant reinforcement from it, which serves to perpetuate it.

None of the above hypotheses generated from analysis of the verbal material is necessarily a firm conclusion. However, it is important to point out that, like the hypotheses derived from the structure of the test, *each is derived from a different data source.* The composite of 16 propositions developed from the structural data and the subject's words complement each other considerably in this instance, and collectively they provide much information the clinician can use to understand the subject. Taken together the data convey the impression of an impulsive, self-centered, angry individual who is prone to aggressiveness to defend against his own feelings of sexual confusion and inadequacy. He is very immature, but not psychotic. He is a product of his own "irresistible impulses" who has intense needs for affection and feelings of deprivation which supercede his awareness of conventionality and reality.

This kind of descriptive information is not predictive, for the most part, although elements of it could be used for predictive purposes if necessary. In the broad sense, furthermore, this sort of information falls far short of providing a complete description of the subject. It does not reveal the historical antecedents of his impulsive life-style, nor does it identify precisely those stimuli that pose the greatest threats to him and thus trigger his acting-out behavior. If information of this kind is required, other data sources are necessary, such as a thorough history, additional psychological tests, and probably some forms of behavioral observation. Much *specu-lation* about these antecedent and precipitating elements can be drawn from the Rorschach data, but firm conclusions about them goes beyond the data and must be derived from the professional expertise of the clinician using his knowledge of people and their behaviors. The Rorschach, in this case as in most instances, goes only so far as to offer enlightenment conerning the subject's needs, wants, fears, conflicts, and general style of response under both stress and nonstress conditions. This is the typical yield of the Rorschach.

One final word concerning the use of the Rorschach seems in order. Historically, the test made its initial impact through its usefulness in dif-ferential diagnosis. As less emphasis has been afforded the issue of diag-nosis per se, the focal point of its use has shifted to learning more about the psychology of the subject as an input to the formulation of effective treatment planning. The data remain the same, but the interpretive em-phasis has shifted. More recently, a newer emphasis has been forming in assessment, namely, to obtain information about the *results* of interven-tion, and again the Rorschach has been demonstrated to be of significant worth, especially where pre- and posttreatment protocols are available for comparison (Exner, 1974). The many potential uses of Rorschach data contribute greatly to the success of the test in the clinical setting and to its place of high regard in assessment methodology.

Several variations in the use of the Rorschach have developed during its long history. The most significant of these variations have been the Harrower-Erikson method of group administration (1945) and the Consen-sus Rorschach (Blanchard, 1959; Cutter, Farberow, & Sapin, 1967). The Harrower-Erickson group technique has not proven particularly useful in either the clinical or research setting. The Consensus Rorschach is still in a phase of development and investigation. However, early reports of its potential seem positive, and it may prove useful in clinical assessment.

THE CONSENSUS RORSCHACH

The Consensus Rorschach is somewhat loosely defined as the adminis-tration of the Rorschach to two or more people simultaneously, wherein the subjects are asked to reach agreement in their responses to the blots (Farberow, 1968). Ordinarily, all participants in the Consensus have been administered the Rorschach individually at an earlier time, although some investigators reserve administration of the individual test until after the Consensus administration, and some report including no individual testing. The Consensus procedure has been used with couples, such as patient and spouse, parent and child, two friends, two roommates, and the like; and with larger groups such as entire families, patient and staff, and so on.

Blanchard (1959), who was the first to report the process, used the technique with delinquent gang members. Loveland, Singer, and Wynne (1963) and Levy and Epstein (1964) have reported on its use with families, and Bauman and Roman (1964) have reported on the patient-spouse dyad. Whereas most of these investigations have focused on the interaction process rather than on the protocol itself, Cutter, Farberow, and Sapin (1967) have noted that a wealth of data is available when the individual protocols are compared with the consensus protocol. Cutter and Farberow (1970) have reviewed the work in the development of the Consensus Rorschach and concluded that it remains fertile ground for investigation. They have created an index of "content polarities" which appears to offer some data concerning the effectiveness of the group in dealing with the Consensus Rorschach task. They also suggest that the amount of time required to achieve a consensus response may yield useful information concerning the interaction process among the subjects. Hence this technique appears to have considerable clinical potential, and it offers a substantial challenge to the researcher because of the vast array of variables it includes.

In addition to variations in the actual use of the Rorschach, several other different inkblot techniques have been developed which attempt in the main to follow the Rorschach format. These different techniques include the Beta Inkblot Test (Wheeler, 1938), the Harrower Blots (1945), the Levy Blots (Zubin, 1948), the Behn-Rorschach (Zulliger, 1952), the Howard Blots (1953), the Holtzman Inkblot Test (1961), and the Ka-Ro Inkblot Test (Kataguchi, 1970). None of these, with the exception of the Holtzman and possibly the Ka-Ro, has fared well either in the clinical setting or under the scrutiny of research efforts. The Ka-Ro was developed in Japan and is designed as a parallel series to the Rorschach. Early research indicates that, when the two tests are compared, considerable agreement is found in the structural, or scoring, features. However, the Ka-Ro appears to evoke substantially different contents from the Rorschach. Whereas the usefulness of the Ka-Ro is still to be fully demonstrated, it seems clear that the Holtzman Inkblot Test can be very useful in the clinical setting and also holds up well under research investigation.

THE HOLTZMAN INKBLOT TEST

The Holtzman Inkblot Test (HIT) appeared in 1961 as the product of Wayne Holtzman's extensive efforts to develop psychometrically sound scoring procedures for responses to inkblots. Holtzman (1959), following the lead of some critics of the Rorschach such as Zubin (1954), noted that much of the confusion concerning the Rorschach and projective instruments in general could be attributed to failures to identify the method as a projective technique rather than as a psychometric instrument. He pointed to the many obstacles involved in quantitative studies of a test that uses only 10 blots and permits the subject to offer as many or as few responses as he wishes. Holtzman emphasized that this process results in a set of scores that are unreliable, have sharply skewed distributions, and may not possess the properties of rank-order measurements. His solution to this problem has been to create a larger number of blots and to permit the subject only one response per blot.

The HIT consists of 45 blots, some of which are symmetric and others asymmetric. Like the Rorschach, the HIT cards are handed to the subject one at a time but, unlike the Rorschach (except for the Rapaport method), the inquiry is done *after each response*. Two trial blots are used to familiarize the subject with the process before the first of the 45 blots of the test is administered. Responses are scored for 22 possible variables, generally classifiable into categories similar to those used with the Rorschach: location scores, determinant scores, content scores, and special scorings for anxiety, hostility, pathognomic verbalizations, and the barrier and penetration scores devised by Fisher and Cleveland to study body image boundaries. One of the very appealing features of the HIT is that there is a parallel set of 45 blots (Form B) that has been demonstrated to have considerable equivalence to the basic Form-A set.

The research concerning the HIT has followed designs very similar to those used in Rorschach research. For instance, Thorpe and Swartz (1966) have established a relationship between perceptual development and certain variables of the test, comparable to the Developmental Quality scoring in the Rorschach. Also in common with the Rorschach, it has been reasonably well established that the HIT human content response varies almost directly with social and interpersonal interests (Fernald & Linden, 1966). An excellent longitudinal study of developmental trends in the HIT has been reported by Sanders, Holtzman, and Swartz (1968). Mosley (1963), using a discriminant function analysis, has developed a HIT formula for the classification of schizophrenics, depressives, and normals. He reports an 88% correct rate when comparing normals to schizophrenics and a 71% correct rate when comparing normals to depressives.

Gamble (1972) provides an excellent review of a variety of research concerning the HIT. He points out that, although the accumulated literature regarding the HIT is reasonably extensive, there is no clear conclusion to be drawn about the worth of the test when compared with the Rorschach.

Gamble indicates that many more "direct comparative" studies are required before such a judgment can be reached. Zubin (1972), in a discussion of some of the newer approaches to personality assessment, expresses a sense of disappointment with the validity studies reported concerning the HIT. Zubin correctly points out that most of the studies in which positive results have been obtained have been based on data derived largely from a content analysis of the protocols rather than ". . . on the formal scores of the properties of the inkblot. . . ." The Zubin conclusions may be somewhat overdrawn, but they do appear accurate with respect to understanding the person as an idiographic entity.

In contrast to the Rorschach, the HIT is a relatively young instrument, yet to be tested fully in the clinical setting. It may not be more widely used by clinicians as a replacement for the Rorschach, in part because it is somewhat more time-consuming to administer and score. More probably, however, it has not received a wider acceptance among practitioners because of the long-standing tradition of using the Rorschach as *the* prime projective test. The more stringent psychometric approach underlying the HIT may have caused many of the followers of projective methods to reject it out of hand, assuming somewhat automatically that it reflects a non-projective orientation. In truth, however, the HIT remains an appealing inkblot approach, particularly because of its parallel forms. Gamble (1972) suggests that future research with the HIT should be addressed more directly to issues of clinical personality description and diagnostic classification, the implication being that such studies will increase the test's attraction to the practitioner.

THE THEMATIC APPERCEPTION TEST

If the Rorschach can be considered the "grandfather" of the projective techniques movement, the Thematic Apperception Test (TAT) must be considered a coequal in that movement, for it also has a long and distinguished history. Although there were antecedent attempts to use pictures as stimuli to ideation (Binet & Henri, 1896; Schwartz, 1932), none made a major impact prior to the TAT. The TAT was created by Henry Murray and Christiana Morgan in the course of their studies of personality carried out at the Harvard University Clinic during the early 1930s. It was first published in 1935, but did not have a significant influence on clinical practice until the end of that decade, by which time several studies demonstrating its utility had been reported, particularly those of Harrison (1940) and Rotter (1940).

The TAT consists of 30 pictures, most of which show people in implied action. The 30 cards are divided so that the examiner can create specific groupings for male and female subjects and for children, adolescents, and adults. Originally, Murray suggested that 20 cards, including one blank card, be administered to the subject in two sessions, separated by at least 1 day, and that the subject be encouraged to devote about 5 minutes to each card. Most users of the test have found Murray's technique to be overly time-consuming, and the general practice is to administer 8 to 12 cards in a single session without a time recommendation to the subject.

The instructions for the test have remained essentially unchanged since its inception. The subject is told that he will be shown a series of cards, and that the test is one of imagination. His task, then, is to create a story about the picture which includes what is happening at the moment, what has led to this event, what the characters are feeling or thinking, and what the outcome will be. When the blank card (Number 16) is used, the subject is requested to imagine a scene and then create a story about it which contains each of the four features required for the other stories. Murray also suggested encouraging the subject to create a "dramatic" story; however, many examiners have perceived this request as overly threatening to the subject, and it is usually omitted from the basic instructions. Murray postulated that the subject will become so engrossed with the task as to lose much of his defensiveness and project qualities into the characters in the story that apply to himself, in other words, to interpret the ambiguity of the stimulus in terms of his own experiences, needs, fears, and the like.

The TAT has not been subject to nearly as much criticism as the Rorschach, probably for two reasons. First, the TAT did not develop with as much interest in or emphasis on scoring as the Rorschach. Thus the basic subject matter that has so often been a source of criticism for the Rorschach—its scoring—has essentially been nonexistent for the TAT. Second, many of the more outrageous claims concerning the breadth of information obtainable from the Rorschach have not been advanced concerning the TAT. Murray, in particular, was conservative in his claims and approached his subject in a dignified, scholarly manner which was respected by those around him. There was no "in-fighting" concerning the most appropriate method of using the TAT as there was with respect to the Rorschach. Consequently, over the years it has been possible for researchers to study the test under little more pressure than was generated by critics of projective methods in general.

Scoring Systems and Approaches to Interpretation

Several scoring systems have been developed for use with the TAT stories. Morgan and Murray offered the first system, which was comprised of weights for each of a series of possible *needs* and *presses* apparent in a story. A need is defined, for purposes of the TAT, as a "force emanating from the hero of the story," and a press is defined as "a force or forces emanating from the environment." Murray indicated that needs may be expressed in the stories as an impulse, wish, intention, or description of overt behavior. He listed 19 needs, including, for example, needs for abasement, achievement, aggression, dominance, avoidance of harm or blame, passivity, sex, and succorance. According to the Murray scoring, each such need is rated on a scale from 1 to 5 when it occurs in a story, with the actual rating being determined by the intensity, duration, frequency, and importance that the particular need manifests in the story. Thus only a suggestion of the need in the story is scored 1 point, whereas its frequent mention or dramatic expression is scored 5 points. Presses, which include such items as association, dominance, rejection, and physical injury, are also scored on a 5-point scale according to criteria of intensity and frequency.

In addition to comprising frequency tallies and weighted scores for needs and presses, the Morgan and Murray scoring approach to the TAT also includes such elements as identifying the sex of the hero, the prevailing kinds of outcomes, the consistency of simple or complex themes, and the repetitive expression of interests and sentiments. The assumption underlying this approach to scoring is that those elements of greatest importance to the subject occur most frequently in the composite of stories given. Murray maintained that although some needs and presses manifest in the stories are "literal" translations from the subject's past or present experiences, most are symbolically representative of these things. He was not oriented toward the use of the test as a diagnostic tool, in the narrow sense of the word, which is probably another reason why the TAT has not been criticized as frequently as the Rorschach. To the contrary, Murray was among the first clinicians to stress the use of assessment procedures to explore the personality and understand the complex ramifications of its operations, rather than to make diagnoses, and above all to gain some experience of another human being. He did not claim great reliability or validity for the TAT method but, in a more conservative almost humble manner, offered it as an approach to experiencing a person in greater detail than was possible by most available methods of that era.

Whereas the Rorschach is notable for having been proliferated into at least five basic systems and countless individually personalized approaches, the history of the TAT reveals even greater diversification. Shneidman (1951) indicated that the TAT of the late 1940s could be approached and interpreted in at least 20 different ways, each reflecting a published approach encouraged by its author. Later Shneidman (1965) suggested that this extensive proliferation was due to the fact that, after its publication, the TAT quickly became "everybody's favorite adopted baby to change and raise as he wished."

Some approaches to the TAT have been strictly qualitative, in that they have emphasized content analysis, whereas others have also included some form of scoring. Among the more well-known systems for the TAT, other than Murray's, are those proposed by Bellak (1947), Henry (1947), Tomkins (1947), Wyatt (1947), Stein (1948), Aron (1949), Eron (1950), Piotrowski (1950), McCelland, Atkinson, Clark, and Lowell, (1953), Fine (1955), Dana (1959), and Pine (1960). The formats of these approaches are highly varied. For example, the Piotrowski, Bellak, and Henry approaches all focus exclusively on some manner of content analysis; Piotrowski, however, offers just a set of rules and leaves the specifics to the interpreter, whereas Henry provides formal and detailed interpretive guidelines. Henry recommends evaluation of the amount and quality of production and attention to the organization of the stories and their emotional tone, to the "action core" of the story, to the hero and his or her interpersonal contacts, and to the dynamic structure of the content, both direct and symbolic.

In contrast, the Eron, McClelland et al., and Dana approaches reflect very formal quantitative approaches to the TAT. Eron, for example, uses a normative approach in which rating scales for evaluating each story for emotional tone and outcome have been developed. The McClelland approach, which has been especially popular among researchers and was originally developed to study the need for achievement (n-Ach), uses a method whereby each story can be placed into one of three basic categories. The Dana approach focuses on the subject's organization of the task, the perceptual "range" manifest in the stories, and the extent to which personalization occurs in the stories.

Harrison (1965), pointing to the fact that the TAT is "in no sense standardized," suggests that, because of the considerable variation in methods of administration and interpretation, it would be preferable to refer to it as the Thematic Apperception *Technique* rather than as the Thematic Apperception *Test*. Whatever name used, the literature on the TAT is enormous, encompassing more than 1500 books and articles. An interesting segment of this literature converges on the stimulus characteristics of the pictures and the relationship between their stimulus value and the analysis of responses to them. Murstein (1963), among others, has argued that the pictures should be scaled for each of the various dimensions of personality they are particularly likely to tap. Such an approach has been used when selected TAT pictures have been employed to study specific needs, including achievement (McClelland et al., 1953), affiliation (Veroff, 1958), and power (Atkinson, Heyns, & Veroff, 1954). However, the task of scaling each card is very cumbersome, and most researchers have not chosen to undertake it. Rather, as Dana (1968) reports, most TAT studies concerning specific needs have used cards selected somewhat subjectively to serve the intended purpose of the research. Unfortunately, the majority of these selections seem to ignore data concerning normative responses to each of the cards as has been reported by Eron (1950) and Murstein (1972).

There is little doubt that the TAT reflects a wide variety of need states. In addition to assessing achievement, affiliation, and power, the TAT has also received confirmation as a measure of needs for sex (Clark, 1952; Strizver, 1961), sleep (Murray, 1959; Nelson, 1961), hunger (Atkinson & McClelland, 1948; Epstein, 1961; Epstein & Smith, 1956; Sanford, 1936) and fear (Fenz & Epstein, 1962). Typically, these studies have included some arousal condition designed to insure the existence of the need state being measured. For example, Rosenfield and Franklin (1966) used a form of sociometric ratings that emphasized the possibilities of both acceptance and rejection to study the need for affiliation.

Other TAT studies concerning personality characteristics have been designed to examine the concurrent relationship between elements manifest in the TAT stories and other criteria. For instance, Miner (1956) and Witkin et al. (1962) have demonstrated that the emotional state of the subject influences his stories substantially. In this regard, Murstein (1968) has reported that hostile college subjects with hostile self-concepts offer more hostile stories on the TAT than do hostile subjects with friendly self-concepts.

Clinical Applications

As also noted by Murstein (1963, 1965), the TAT has not demonstrated much utility with respect to specific issues of psychiatric diagnosis. However, this fact should not be surprising or disturbing to advocates of apperception methods, since the sorts of needs and presses manifest in TAT stories, whether approached quantitatively or qualitatively, do not necessarily have a direct correlation with psychopathological states. There is a considerable body of literature that confirms the usefulness of the TAT in differentiating the stories of neurotics, schizophrenics, and some types of characterological problems (Harrison, 1965), but most of this work does not deal directly with specific issues of the diagnostic label. Rather, these studies are intended to demonstrate that the overall composite of the TAT stories offered by people with problems is generally much different from that of stories provided by nonpatients.

One of the major limitations of TAT research is that it has been *trait-specific* and consequently of minimal use to the practitioner in the clinical setting. It is probably for this reason that most clinicians have avoided the cumbersome task of scoring each story and instead have followed the leads of Piotrowski, Bellak, and Henry by taking a qualitative approach in their interpretations. It has been in this context that the TAT has flourished as a clinical assessment technique. In this more *global* method of analysis, the interpreter usually proceeds on several basic assumptions, outlined by Lindzey (1952), which include the general postulates inherent in the projective hypothesis plus several postulates specific to the TAT.

For instance, it is presumed that the subject identifies with the hero of the story and that the characteristics attributed to the hero contribute reliably to an understanding of the subject. It is also assumed that all stories are not necessarily of equal importance in revealing the desires, conflicts, and emotions of the subject; that, as on the Rorschach, responses that do not coincide well with the actual characteristics of the test stimuli are particularly revealing, since they are determined more by the subject's personality than by the stimulus material; that stories may represent both long-standing characteristics of the subject and characteristics precipitated by more immediate events; and finally, that many of the features identified from the stories may not be reflected directly in conscious thought or in overt behaviors. Lindzey has offered support for all these postulates, and subsequent work has tended to confirm each of them.

Nevertheless, clinicians using the TAT must be careful not to lose sight of several important nonpersonality variables that can influence the stories of subject. For instance, sex differences have been reported to influence many TAT variables (Lindzey & Goldberg, 1953; Lindzey & Silverman, 1959; Moss & Kagan, 1961; Weisskopf-Joelson & Wexner, 1970), and social class differences also appear to affect the length and general content of stories (Fisher & Fisher, 1960; Korchin, Mitchell, & Meltzoff, 1950; Mason & Ammons, 1956; Reissman, 1958). Possibly even more important than these influences is the impact on the subject of events immediately preceding the test administration. Murstein (1963), reviewing a substantial literature on this topic, concludes that numerous situational factors, including features of the examiner, can have a distinct effect on the quantity and the characteristics of a subject's TAT productivity. A more recent example of the effect of examiner behavior is noted by Fiester and Siipola (1972), who administered the TAT under different conditions of time pressure, ranging from complete freedom of time to the pressure of specific time limits. Relative to the free situation, the stories obtained under time pressure showed less control of aggression and more "immature" resolutions of conflict states.

It is very important for the TAT interpreter to have some information concerning the immediate circumstances of the subject before drawing any firm conclusions from his data. Two stories for the same card given by the same subject, a 24-year-old secretary, serve to illustrate this point. The first administration of the test occurred approximately 10 weeks after she had learned that her husband, an Air Force pilot, had been killed in the Viet Nam war. She was examined at the request of her physician because she had been complaining of a variety of physical symptoms including headaches, upset stomach, leg cramps, and insomnia, for which no organic basis could be detected. Her story for Card 8GF, which depicts a young woman sitting in a chair with her chin in her hand and looking off into space, was:

It seems to be a girl sitting in a chair, not doing much except thinking. She's been doing her housework and she's tired and wondering what life will be for her. She doesn't seem to be getting anywhere and she wonders if anybody really cares for how hard she works, because if they do they never seem to tell her. She wishes she could get away but she doesn't know where she'd go and she can't forget her responsibilities to her family. I suppose that she'll get up after a while and go and finish her housework, but she won't be happy doing it and if she doesn't watch out she'll go through life without anything except feeling sorry for herself.

In this story the subject's feelings of isolation and her needs for recognition are quite evident. The hero is dominated by her own needs to assume a socially approved role, that of a housewife, and she conveys this need in a gloomy, pessimistic tone. She manifests a conflict between this need and needs for freedom or autonomy. It is a depressing and almost sterile story that indicates the experience of helplessness and the potential for a hopeless existence. Knowledge of her immediate situation encourages the translation of these data into the proposition that her physical complaints may be symptomatic of her confusion concerning her life role, and that resolution of this confusion is impaired by a continuing experience of sorrow and anger, probably related to the loss of her husband. This proposition would of course require considerable support from other data before being considered a valid interpretation. Assuming that it is true, however, a major unanswered question is whether these characteristics are *reactive*—that is, a direct consequence of the husband's death—or whether they are a more fundamental kind of response style common to her basic personality.

Data regarding this question were gleaned from retesting 11 months after the original examination, conducted as part of a research project on short-term intervention methods. After the first examination the subject had been seen individually by a therapist for seven visits, once per week, and participated in transactional group therapy for 3 months (14 sessions). Her second story for Card 8GF was:

I don't remember this one from before, hmm, it seems to be a woman daydreaming a little. She's probably thinking about painting the room and she's trying to settle on a color or pattern, she wants it to look nice. Apparently she's in the process of redecorating her house, maybe she and her husband have just bought an older place and they are fixing it up. This looks like it might be a study or playroom and she wants it to be bright. I think that she has just thought of a pattern because she seems to be smiling, like she's pleased with her idea. When her husband comes home she'll explain to him what she wants to do with the room and he'll kid her about how thorough she's being about everything. I think it will be a nice room.

This story has a much more optimistic tone than the first one did. Although it is still clearly marked by a need for recognition, the sense of depression and helplessness evident in the first story does not occur, and a theme is conveyed about a more confident hero. The need for some form of freedom or autonomy expressed in the first story appears to have been realized, at least partially, although the more fundamental need to please others is still apparent. It is also interesting that in her first story she identifies the heroine as a "girl," whereas the character of the second story is a "woman." It is also interpretively important that she does not remember the card form the first testing, as if to repress or push away the reexperiencing of her more painful feelings. On a more symbolic level of interpretation, the fact that she is "redecorating her house" and "wants it to be bright" appears to be a very positive sign. Again, it is important to understand her circumstances for, if she is socially or emotionally isolated, the seemingly positive conclusions might be tempered by questions about excessive withdrawal to fantasy. The anamnestic data, however, revealed that she was still working as a secretary, was sharing an apartment with two other women who worked in the same office, was dating frequently and with one man in particular, and was no longer manifesting any of the symptoms that precipitated her referral.

These are the kinds of data and interpretations that may be derived through the use of the TAT. It is frequently postulated (see Harrison, 1965) that the TAT provides a view of the person different from what is evident in the Rorschach or other inkblot methods, mainly because it involves more extensive verbalization related to a *common theme*. This greater frequency of words tends to make specific needs and conflicts more readily apparent to the interpreter. Nevertheless, since some of the needs and presses evident in TAT stories are very likely to be products of immediate circumstances, adequate interpretation requires that the circumstantial products be carefully sorted out from the more basic or fundamental characteristics of personality reflected in the stories.

One of the special features of most projective methods, and especially of the Rorschach and the TAT, is their relative immunity to attempts at willfull falsification or an orientation to give only socially desirable kinds of answers. Several well-done studies (Davids & Pilner, Dunlevy, 1953; 1958; Ni, 1959; Reznikoff, 1961; Weisskopf & Kieppa, 1951) have demonstrated that, although some faking is possible under laboratory conditions, the TAT generally is very difficult to falsify. It seems realistic to conclude that, when the Rorschach and the TAT are used as companion devices in an assessment battery, the possibilities of falsification occurring consistently are extremely remote.

There have been numerous variations of the TAT, and Harrison (1965) reports that over 60 different sets of pictures have been published. Some of these variations have been structured for specific purposes, such as by Ammons (1950) for use in vocational guidance, by Lesser (1958) to study aggression, by McClelland et al. (1953) to study n-Ach, by Newman (1954) to study attitudes toward authority, by Alexander (1952) to study adult-child relationships, by Johnson (1950) to study prejudice, and by Henry and Guetzkow (1951) to study small-group interaction. Others have followed a technique of redesigning some of the pictures for use with special groups, such as by Symonds (1949) for use with adolescents, by Thompson (1949) for use with black subjects, by Briggs (1954) for use with Navy enlisted men, by Lessa and Spiegelman (1954) for use with South Sea Islanders, and by Mauri (1960) for use with Japanese subjects.

Some of these variations have evolved into very distinct tests, but few of them have received widespread study or use. However, two TAT variations require special mention because of the considerable amount of work that has been done with them: the Children's Apperception Test and the Make-a-Picture Story test.

THE CHILDREN'S APPERCEPTION TEST

The Children's Apperception Test (CAT), developed by Bellak and Bellak (1952), consists of pictures in which all the characters are animals shown in humanlike action situations. The conceptualization of the test is related to psychoanalytic theory and is based on the assumption that children provide stories for animal scenes more readily than for those depicting people. This assumption has been seriously challenged by several studies that show no differences in the productions of children for animal or human pictures (Biersdorf & Marcuse, 1953; Boyd & Mandler, 1955; Ouchi, 1957). Nevertheless, the CAT has been found useful in studying differences in twins (Magnusson, 1960) and for evaluating children labeled schizophrenic (Gurevitz & Klapper, 1951), emotionally disturbed (Kanehira, 1958), and speech-handicapped (Fitzsimmons, 1958).

The approach to CAT interpretation recommended by Bellak (1954) is essentially the same as his system for interpreting the TAT. Attention is focused mainly on content analysis, with emphasis on the status of the hero and the conflicts manifest in the themes, and special consideration is given to the outcome as it relates to the status of the hero.

THE MAKE-A-PICTURE-STORY TEST

Harrison (1965) describes the Make-A-Picture-Story (MAPS) test as a "do-it-yourself version of the TAT." The subject creates his own pictures by using one or more of 67 cutouts of humans and animals and placing them on background pictures selected by the examiner. The MAPS was created by Shneidman (1952), who recommends using at least 10 background pictures. One of the basic assumptions underlying use of the MAPS is that it has more appeal to subjects than the TAT, especially since the variety of combinations of cutouts and backgrounds offers much more extensive stimulus variability. This same variability, however, makes for enormous problems in any attempt to standardize the test or assess its validity.

Shneidman has proposed a format for scoring and interpretation, although he acknowledges the possibility for nearly as many approaches to the MAPS as exist to the TAT. Clinical studies have been reported on the use of the MAPS with neurotic, normal, and schizophrenic subjects (Conant, 1950); female homosexuals (Ferracuti & Rizzo, 1958); suicidal patients (Farberow, 1950); and children in guidance clinics (Spiegelman, 1956). Generally, the MAPS appears to have gained the greatest clinical use with young clients who are hyperactive or resistive to giving stories for the TAT. Whereas it is more time-consuming to give the MAPS than either the TAT or CAT, the productions for it are also generally longer and provide a greater bulk of data for interpretation. The technique allows for many variations, such as the use of plastic or wooden figures rather than cutouts and, in the context of examining children, it resembles some of the techniques used in play therapy situations.

SENTENCE COMPLETION METHODS

The sentence completion method has a long history in psychology which extends back to some of the work of Ebbinghaus (1897) who attempted to use the method to evaluate intellectual variables. Its first uses as an approach to the study of personality appear to have been by Payne in 1928 and by Tendler in 1930. The frequency with which this method is employed in clinical settings has increased steadily since the late 1940s and early 1950s, during which time many different sentence completion tests (SCTs) have been developed. The Sundberg (1961) survey indicated that SCTs as a group ranked thirteenth in frequency among tests used in clinical settings, and the later Lubin, Wallis, and Paine (1971) survey revealed that this composite of SCTs had moved up to eighth in frequency of use.

The relative popularity of the sentence completion method is due to at least four factors. First, and most importantly, practitioners have found it to have considerable clinical utility. Second, it is very easy to administer and has the added advantage of allowing either individual or group administration. Third, it appears to be considered a worthwhile approach both by those who advocate projective techniques *and* by those who hold with a psychometric orientation. In this latter regard, Goldberg (1965) has gone so far as to suggest that the relationship between the projective hypothesis and the sentence completion method "seems questionable." The fourth element that has contributed significantly to the wide use of the technique is the relative ease with which it can be studied empirically, and an abundant research literature has accumlated concerning several specific SCTs.

The ease and economy with which SCTs can be constructed have led to a substantial proliferation of sentence completion methods. A great many SCTs have been created to tap broad issues in personality assessment and psychodiagnosis, while many others have been formulated to study more highly specific features of the individual. Within the standard format of the SCT, different forms utilize a considerable variety of stem contents, some of which are tailored to particular subject populations. For example, the college form of the Rotter Incomplete Sentences Blank (ISB) (Rotter & Rafferty, 1950) contains stems such as, "I like . . .," "The future . . .," "This school . . .," "Dancing . . .," "Marriage . . .," "I secretly . . .," and so on. The Rotter ISB is also among the shorter SCTs, containing only 40 stems, whereas many others are considerably longer. For instance, the Lorge-Thorndike SCT (1941) uses 240 stems and is much more varied in content than the ISB, and the Rohde-Hildreth Completions Blank (1946), which is a revision of Payne's original 1928 work, contains 64 stems.

As further illustrations, the Stein SCT (1947), developed originally for use in the OSS during World War II and later used in the Veterans Administration, contains two sets of 50 stems each. The Sacks Sentence Completion Test (SSCT), which was also developed for use in Veterans Administration facilities (1949, 1950), contains 60 stems. Other well-known and extensively used SCTs include those of Forer (1950) and Holsopple and Miale (1954). In contrast to these broadly oriented tests, other more specialized SCTs contain stems that have considerable homogeneity in relation to a specific topic. For instance, the Self-Focus Sentence Completion (Exner, 1973) was designed specifically to investigate the characteristic of egocentricity and uses 30 stems, all of which contain a self-reference (*I, me,* or *my*). Other specialized SCTs have been developed to focus on attitudes toward school life (Costin & Eiserer, 1949), attitudes toward mental hospitals (Souelem, 1955), and attitudes toward career choice (Getzels & Jackson, 1960).

In a thorough review of sentence completion methods, Goldberg (1965) has noted that most SCTs are neither objective nor standardized according to orthodox psychometric principles. Among notable exceptions is the Rotter and Rafferty ISB, which includes an elaborate objective format for scoring responses and for which extensive normative data have been presented. Most of the highly specialized SCTs have also included an objective and formalized scoring approach, as they have usually been developed primarily for research purposes. The majority of the more standard and general SCTs do not have specific scoring formats, however, and depend instead on interpretation of content. Yet within this group of SCTs there is considerable variation in the suggested approaches to content interpretation. Holsopple and Miale are particularly liberal in depending on the clinical judgments of the interpreter. Other SCT authors, including Stein, Sacks, and Forer, have attempted to group their stems into specific content categories, such as interpersonal relations, fears, sex-role identity, and self-concept, to guide the interpretive task. These authors generally recommend evaluation of the subject's responses as they cluster to yield trends of information relating to each of these categories.

A major unanswered question concerns the extent to which a subject can control his response to an SCT stem. Rotter and Rafferty (1950), who unequivocally regard the sentence completion method as falling into the category of projective techniques, nevertheless warn that answers to it may reflect more of what the subject is willing to provide than "that which he cannot help giving." Carr (1954, 1956, 1958) has approached this question in terms of the "levels hypothesis," which suggests that personality is arranged at different levels of psychic functioning and that these different levels become manifest under different stimulus conditions. Stone and Dellis (1960) tested this levels hypothesis with various projective techniques, including the Rorschach, the TAT, and the Forer SCT. Asking blind judges to estimate degree of psychopathology from the test data of 20 hospitalized psychiatric patients, they demonstrated a remarkable agreement among the judges, and their findings also supported the hypothesis that a positive relationship exists between the degree of stimulus structure in a test and the extent of "impulse control" manifest in responses to it. In other words, the greater the structure, the more deliberate or conscious the response and the greater the subject's control over it.

These findings, as related to the sentence completion method, are similar to observations reported earlier by Meltzoff (1951). Meltzoff administered a 90-item SCT to four groups of subjects, each of which received different instructional sets. He concluded that subjects who so wish can "censor" their SCT answers to a considerable degree, and are particularly likely to do so under alerting stress conditions. This finding, considered in light of the Stone and Dellis work, offers support to the Rotter and Rafferty view that the SCT protocol consists largely of what the subject is willing to reveal.

Goldberg (1968) has noted that a neglected SCT research area concerns the relationship between SCT responses and the reality of the subject's experience. Nevertheless, Goldberg's earlier work (1965) includes an impressive list of studies which taken together lead to the conclusion that, the SCT approach is not only a valuable tool for personality assessment, but also one "that compares favorably to other standard instruments." It also seems clear from Goldberg's review that different SCTs are not equally useful or valid for all situations. The researcher may select a particular SCT to study various issues of personality or adjustment, whereas the practitioner may find another SCT superior for the kind of assessment required in his work. On balance, however, the future of the sentence completion method appears to hold continued promise, regardless of whether it is considered a projective method, and it seems unlikely, in view of the extent of its past acceptance, that it will be marked by as much controversy as has surrounded many other projective techniques.

PROJECTIVE DRAWINGS

In contrast to the relatively calm acceptance of the Sentence Completion method, considerable controversy has surrounded the projective drawings approach. Probably no other method, with the possible exception of the Rorschach, has been so controversial and, as with the Rorschach, this controversy has generated a large body of research. Among the classic drawing techniques is the Draw-a-Man test devised by Goodenough (1926) for estimating the intellectual levels of children. Goodenough used the amount of detail and complexity included in children's drawings of people to formulate a method of scoring that yields an IQ estimate. Proceeding somewhat indirectly from Goodenough's work, Machover (1949) subsequently suggested that a clinical evaluation of human figure drawings could be used to provide detailed information about personality and adjustment. Her technique, the Draw-a-Person (DAP) test, has gradually become one of the most frequently used projective methods in clinical settings. Sundberg (1961) reported that it ranked second in frequency of use among all psychological tests, and Lubin, Wallis, and Paine (1971) found it to rank fourth in their survey of test usage.

One of the appealing features of the DAP is the relative ease with which it may be administered to either adults or children. The subject is instructed to draw a person and, after this first drawing is completed, he is instructed to draw a person of the opposite sex. Several variations of this routine may also be employed. For instance, subjects may be asked to draw two people on the same paper, or children may be asked to draw an entire family. Some examiners prefer to ask the subject to begin by drawing "yourself." Another variation of the procedure involves asking the subject questions about the figure(s), such as, "What kind of person is this?" or asking the subject to create a story about the figure. Machover (1951) has developed two lists of questions, one for adults and a second for children, which may be used if the optional inquiry is employed.

Much of the controversy concerning the DAP had focused on the various interpretive hypotheses offered by Machover in her 1949 monograph. She provides postulates concerning each of the features of the drawing, such as the facial parts, the head, the neck, arms, legs, fingers, trunk, shoulders, breasts, hips, buttocks, clothing, and the like, and also concerning the symmetry of the drawing, stance, perspective, size, placement on the page, line quality, use of shading, erasures, and so on. The basic assumption underlying these hypotheses is that the subject's drawing of a person represents an expression of his self or his body in the environment, and hence that any special or unusual emphasis in the drawing conveys information about the subjects preoccupations, conflicts, and self-attitudes.

Swensen (1957, 1968), who has been the conscientious monitor of the extensive DAP literature, has contributed two excellent reviews of the test. In his first review (1957) Swensen concluded that the bulk of evidence did not support most of Machover's specific hypotheses and that, even where support had been noted, the findings were equivocal. He suggested in this review that the method could best be used in conjunction with other instruments as part of a test battery, or as a "rough screening device" to gain quick information regarding the overall functioning of the subject. In a critique of Swensen's review Hammer (1959) contended that many of the works he cited had not been appropriately designed to study the DAP, and that many of his conclusions were overdrawn or excessively concrete with regard to the validity of Machover's postulates. Hammer had previously published a very thorough statement concerning the clinical usefulness of projective drawings (1959), and he has continued to be a champion of the method.

Swensen's second review (1968), which covered the literature after 1957, is slightly more positive than the first about the potential utility of the DAP technique, but it continues to note that most empirical data contradict the interpretive usefulness of specific "signs" on the test. He indicates that global ratings of DAP performance appear to be more reliable than signs, hence more valuable in the formulation of clinical judgments. Interestingly in this regard, he notes a consistent finding that relatively well-adjusted subjects tend to produce drawings of relatively good artistic quality; yet the better the quality of a drawing, the more conflict indicators it is likely to include, because superior drawings usually contain more details. In a review published concurrently with that of Swensen, Roback (1968) similarly concludes that most available research fails to support the Machover hypotheses. Roback also concurs with Hammer, however, that well-designed validity studies of the DAP represent an extremely small proportion of reported evaluation research concerning the technique.

There have been many variations of the projective drawings technique. For example, Buck (1948) introduced the *House-Tree-Person* (HTP) test in which the examiner conducts an extensive interview after the drawings have been completed. Wagner and Shubert (1955) have developed a special scale for evaluating drawings from the DAP on a 0 to 8-point scale. Caligor (1952) devised the *Eight Card Redrawing Test* (8 CRT), which calls for the subject to produce eight drawings of each sex. This technique appeared to hold considerable research promise, but the amount of time required to administer it and the complexity of its scoring system seem to have minimized its appeal for the practitioner. Kinget (1952) created a *Drawing Completion Test*, based on the Wartegg gestalt stimuli, but this measure too has seen little use in the clinical setting because of the complex scoring it entails. Finally of note are several finger-painting approaches (Napoli, 1946, 1947, 1948; Kadis, 1952) which have been suggested mainly for use with children or severely disturbed hospitalized adults.

CONCLUSION

It seems important to include in any summary of the preceding material mention of a fact that should have been conspicuously implicit throughout. To wit, any attempt to discuss the merits or deficiencies of projective methods *in general* is probably doomed from the onset. The history of some of these methods has been marked by considerable success in both clinical and research endeavors, whereas other methods have been subject to dispute and limited use. In many instances the controversies that have erupted concerning a given instrument have been founded largely on bias rather than on science and, altogether too often, criticisms of a single technique have been naively generalized to encompass all projective methodology. Consequently, it seems important to stress that each method should be evaluated *in and by itself* rather than under some broader umbrella that includes all inkblot methods, all apperception techniques, all sentence completion blanks, or all projective techniques. The proliferation of projective methods has been excessive and has probably served to confuse rather than resolve issues. Fortunately, during the same period that the projective movement has matured, clinical psychology has also come of age, thus hopefully creating a professionally "healthier" atmosphere in which the different instruments will be used and researched with fewer biases and more creative intellect than has previously been the case.

REFERENCES

Alexander, T. The adult-child interaction test. *Monograph of Social Research in Child Development,* 1952, **17** (17).

Ammons, R. B. A projective test for vocational research and guidance at the college level. *Journal of Applied Psychology,* 1950, **34,** 198–205.

Aron, B. *A manual for analysis of the thematic apperception test: A method and technique for personality research.* Berkeley: Willis E. Berg, 1949.

Atkinson, J. W., & McClelland, D. C. The projective expression of needs. II. The effect of the different intensities of the hunger drive on thematic apperception. *Journal of Experimental Psychology,* 1948, **38,** 643–658.

Atkinson, J. W., Heyns, R. W., & Veroff, J. The effect of experimental arousal of the affiliation motive on thematic apperception. *Journal of Abnormal and Social Psychology,* 1954, **49,** 405–410.

Baughman, E. E. A comparative analysis of Rorschach forms with altered stimulus characteristics. *Journal of Projective Techniques,* 1954, **18,** 151–164.

Baughman, E. E. The role of the stimulus in Rorschach responses. *Psychological Bulletin,* 1958, **55,** 121–147.

Baughman, E. E. An experimental analysis of the relationship between stimulus structure and behavior on the Rorschach. *Journal of Projective Techniques,* 1959, **23,** 134–183.

Bauman, G., & Roman, M. Interaction product analysis in group and family diagnosis. *Journal of Projective Techniques and Personality Assessment,* 1968, **32,** 331–337.

Bechtold, H. P. Construct validity: A critique. *American Psychologist,* 1959, **14,** 619–629.

Beck, S. J. Configurational tendencies in Rorschach responses. *American Journal of Psychology*, 1933, **45**, 433–443.

Beck S. J. Problems of further research in the Rorschach test. *American Journal of Orthopsychiatry*, 1935, **5**, 100–115.

Beck, S. J. Autism in Rorschach scoring: A feeling comment. *Character and Personality*, 1936, **5**, 83–85.

Beck, S. J. Introduction to the Rorschach method: A manual of personality study. *American Orthopsychiatric Association Monograph*, 1937, No. 1.

Beck, S. J. *Rorschach's test. I. Basic processes.* New York: Grune & Stratton, 1944.

Beck, S. J. *Rorschach's test. II. A variety of personality pictures.* New York: Grune & Stratton, 1945.

Beck, S. J. *Rorschach's test. III. Advances in interpretation.* New York: Grune & Stratton, 1952.

Beck, S. J., Beck, A. G., Levitt, E., & Molish, H. B. *Rorschach's test. I. Basic processes.* (3rd ed.) New York: Grune & Stratton, 1961.

Beck, S. J., & Molish, H. B. *Rorschach's test. II. A variety of personality pictures.* New York: Grune & Stratton, 1967.

Bellak, L. The concept of projection, an experimental investigation and study of the concept. *Psychiatry*, 1944, **7**, 353–370.

Bellak, L. *A guide to the interpretation of the Thematic Apperception Test.* New York: Psychological Corporation, 1947.

Bellak, L. *The Thematic Apperception Test and Children's Apperception Test in clinical use.* New York: Grune & Stratton, 1954.

Bellak, L., & Bellak, S. *Children's Apperception Test.* New York: CPS Company, 1952.

Biersdorf, K. R., & Marcuse, F. L. Responses of children to human and animal pictures. *Journal of Projective Techniques*, 1953, **17**, 455–459.

Binet, A., & Henri, V. Psychologie individuelle. *Annee Psychologie*, 1896, **3**, 296–332.

Blanchard, W. The group process in gang rape. *Journal of Social Psychology*, 1959, **49**, 259–266.

Boyd, N. A., & Mandler, G. Children's responses to human and animal stories and pictures. *Journal of Consulting Psychology*, 1955, **19**, 367–371.

Briggs, D. L. A modification of the Thematic Apperception Test for naval enlisted personnel. *Journal of Psychology*, 1954, **37**, 233–241.

Brown, S. W. The use of an incomplete sentences test for the study of attitudes toward negroes. Unpublished doctoral dissertation, Ohio State University, 1950.

Buck, J. N. The H-T-P Technique: A qualitative and quantitative scoring manual. *Journal of Clinical Psychology*, 1948, **4**, 319–396.

Caligor, L. The detection of paranoid trends by the eight card redrawing test (8 CRT). *Journal of Clinical Psychology*, 1952, **8**, 397–401.

Carr, A. C. Intra-individual consistency in response to tests of varying degrees of ambiguity. *Journal of Consulting Psychology,* 1954, **18,** 251–258.

Carr, A. C. The relation of certain Rorschach variables to the expression of affect in the TAT and SCT. *Journal of Projective Techniques,* 1956, **20,** 137–142.

Carr, A. C. The psychodiagnostic test battery: Rationale and methodology. In D. Brower & L. E. Abt (Eds.), *Progress in Clinical Psychology,* Vol. II. New York: Grune & Stratton, 1958.

Cattell, R. B. Principles of design in "projective" or misperceptive tests of personality. In H. Anderson & G. Anderson (Eds.), *Projective techniques.* New York: Prentice-Hall, 1951.

Clark, R. A. The projective measure of experimentally induced levels of sexual motivation. *Journal of Experimental Psychology,* 1952, **44,** 391–399.

Costin, F., & Eiserer, P. Students attitudes toward school life as revealed by a sentence completion test. *American Psychologist,* 1949, **4,** 289.

Cronbach, L. J. Statistical methods applied to Rorschach scores: A review. *Psychological Bulletin,* 1949, **46,** 393–429.

Cutter, F., & Farberow, N. L. The consensus Rorschach. In B. Klopfer, M. M. Meyer, & F. B. Brawer (Eds.), *Developments in the Rorschach technique. III. Aspects of personality structure.* New York: Harcourt, Brace, Jovanovich, 1970. Pp. 209–262.

Cutter, F., Farberow, N. L., & Sapin, D. Explaining suicide by Rorschach comparison with survivors. Paper presented at the meeting of the California State Psychological Association, San Diego, January 1967.

Dana, R. H. The perceptual organization TAT score, number, order, and frequency. *Journal of Projective Techniques,* 1959, **23,** 307–310.

Dana, R. H. Thematic techniques and clinical practice. *Journal of Projective Techniques and Personality Assessment,* 1968, **32,** 204–214.

Davids, A., & Pilner, H. Comparison of direct and projective methods of personality assessment under different conditions of motivation. *Psychological Monographs,* 1958, **72** (11).

Draguns, J. G., Haley, E. M., & Phillips, L. Studies of Rorschach content. Part 1: Traditional content categories. *Journal of Projective Techniques and Personality Assessment,* 1967, **31,** 3–32.

Dunlevy, G. Intentional modification of Thematic Apperception Test stories as a function of adjustment. Unpublished doctoral dissertation, Purdue University, 1953.

Ebbinghaus, H. Ueber eine neue Methode zur prufung geister fahigkeiten und ihre Awendung bei Schulkindern. *Zeitschrift fur Psychologie und Physiologie,* 1897, **13,** 401–459.

Elizur, A. Content analysis of the Rorschach with regard to anxiety and hostility. *Journal of Projective Techniques,* 1949, **13,** 247–284.

English, H. B., & English, A. C. *A comprehensive Dictionary of psychological and psychoanalytic terms.* New York: Longmans, Green, 1958.

Epstein, S. Food-related responses to ambiguous stimuli as a function of hunger and ego strength. *Journal of Consulting Psychology*, 1961, **25**, 463–469.

Epstein, S., & Smith, R. Thematic apperception as a measure of the hunger drive. *Journal of Projective Techniques*, 1956, **20**, 372–384.

Eron, L. D. A normative study of the Thematic Apperception Test. *Psychological Monographs*, 1950, **64** (9).

Exner, J. E. The influence of chromatic and achromatic color in the Rorschach. *Journal of Projective Techniques*, 1959, **23**, 418–425.

Exner, J. E. The influence of achromatic color on Cards IV and VI of the Rorschach. *Journal of Projective Techniques*, 1961, **25**, 38–41.

Exner, J. E. Rorschach responses as an index of narcissism. *Journal of Projective Techniques and Personality Assessment*, 1969, **33**, 324–330.

Exner, J. E. *The Rorschach systems*. New York: Grune & Stratton, 1969.

Exner, J. E. Rorschach manifestations of narcissism. *Rorschachiana*, 1970, **IX**, 449–457.

Exner, J. E. The self-focus sentence completion: A study of egocentricity. *Journal of Personality Assessment*, 1973, **37**, 437–455.

Exner, J. E. *The Rorschach: A comprehensive system*. New York: Wiley, 1974.

Exner, J. E., & Exner, D. E. How clinicians use the Rorschach. *Journal of Personality Assessment*, 1972, **36**, 402–408.

Farberow, N. L. Personality patterns of suicidal mental hospital patients. *Genetic Psychology Monographs*, 1950, **42**, 3–79.

Farberow, N. L. Consensus Rorschach in the study of problem behavior. *Journal of Projective Techniques and Personality Assessment*, 1968, **32**, 326–357.

Fenz, W. D., & Epstein, S. Measurement of approach-avoidance conflict by a stimulus dimension in a test of thematic apperception. *Journal of Personality*, 1962, **30**, 613–632.

Fernald, P. S., & Linden, J. D. The human content response in the Holtzman Inkblot Technique. *Journal of Projective Techniques and Personality Assessment*, 1966, **30**, 441–446.

Fiester, S., & Siipola, E. M. Effects of time pressure of the management of aggression in TAT stories. *Journal of Personality Assessment*, 1972, **36**, 230–240.

Fine, R. A scoring scheme for the TAT and other verbal projective techniques. *Journal of Projective Techniques*, 1955, **19**, 306–309.

Fisher, S., & Cleveland, S. E. The role of body image in psychosomatic symptom choice. *Psychological Monographs*, 1955, **69** (402).

Fisher, S., & Cleveland, S. E. *Body image and personality*. New York: Van Nostrand Reinhold, 1958.

Fisher, S., & Fisher, R. L. A projective test analysis of ethnic subculture themes in families. *Journal of Projective Techniques*, 1960, **24**, 366–369.

Fitzsimmons, R. Developmental, psychosocial, and educational factors in children with nonorganic articulation problems. *Child Development,* 1958, **24,** 481–489.

Forer, B. R. A structured sentence completion test. *Journal of Projective Techniques,* 1950, **14,** 15–29.

Frank, L. K. Projective methods for the study of personality. *Journal of Psychology,* 1939, **8,** 343–389.

Freud, S. (1894) The anxiety neurosis. *Collected papers.* Vol. 1. London: Hogarth Press, 1953. Pp. 76–106.

Freud, S. (1896) Further remarks on the defence of neuropsychoses. *Collected papers,* Vol. 1. London: Hogarth Press, 1953. Pp. 155–182.

Freud, S. (1911) Psychoanalytic notes on an autobiographical account of a case of paranoia. In *Collected papers,* Vol. 3. London: Hogarth Press, 1940. Pp. 387–396.

Friedman, H. Perceptual regression in schizophrenia: An hypothesis suggested by use of the Rorschach test. *Journal of Genetic Psychology,* 1952, **81,** 63–98.

Friedman, H. Perceptual regression in schizophrenia: An hypothesis suggested by use of the Rorschach test. *Journal of Projective Techniques,* 1953, **17,** 171–185.

Galton, F. Psychometric experiments. *Brain,* 1879, **2,** 149–162.

Gamble, K. R. The Holtzman Inkblot Technique: A review. *Psychological Bulletin,* 1972, **77,** 172–194.

Getzels, J., & Jackson, P. Occupational choice and cognitive functioning. *Journal of Abnormal and Social Psychology,* 1960, **61,** 119–123.

Goldberg, P. A. A review of Sentence Completion methods in personality assessment. *Journal of Projective Techniques and Personality Assessment,* 1965, **29,** 12–45.

Goldberg, P. A. The current status of Sentence Completion methods. *Journal of Projective Techniques and Personality Assessment,* 1968, **32,** 215–221.

Goldfried, M., Stricker, G., & Weiner, I. B. *Rorschach handbook of clinical and research applications.* Englewood Cliffs, N.J.: Prentice-Hall, 1971.

Goodenough, F. *The measurement of intelligence by drawings.* Yonkers-on-Hudson, N.Y.: World Book, 1926.

Gough, H. G. Clinical versus statistical prediction in psychology. In L. Postman (Ed.), *Psychology in the making.* New York: Knopf, 1963.

Gurevitz, S., & Klapper, Z. S. Techniques for and evaluation of the responses of schizophrenic and cerebral palsied children to the Children's Apperception Test. *Quarterly Journal of Child Behavior,* 1951, **3,** 38–65.

Hammer, E. F. *The clinical application of projective drawings.* Springfield, Ill.: Charles C Thomas, 1958.

Hammer, E. F. Critique of Swensen's "Empirical evaluations of human figure drawings." *Journal of Projective Techniques,* 1959, **23,** 30–32.

Harris, J. G. Validity: The search for a constant in a universe of variables. In M. A. Rickers-Ovsiankina (Ed.), *Rorschach psychology*. New York: Wiley, 1960. Pp. 380–439.

Harrison, R. Studies in the use and validity of the Thematic Apperception Test with mentally disordered patients. III. Validation by the method of "blind analysis." *Character and Personality*, 1940, **9**, 134–138.

Harrison, R. Thematic apperceptive methods. In B. Wolman (Ed.), *Handbook of clinical psychology*. New York: McGraw-Hill, 1965. Pp. 562–620.

Harrower, M. R. *Psychodiagnostic inkblots*. New York: Grune & Stratton, 1945.

Harrower, M. R., & Steiner, M. *Large scale Rorschach techniques*. Springfield, Ill.: Charles C Thomas, 1945.

Hemmendinger, L. Perceptual organization and development as reflected in the structure of the Rorschach test response. *Journal of Projective Techniques*, 1953, **17**, 162–170.

Hemmendinger, L. Developmental scores. In M. A. Rickers-Ovsiankina (Ed.), *Rorschach psychology*. New York: Wiley, 1960. Pp. 58–79.

Henry, W. E. The Thematic Apperception Technique in the study of culture-personality relations. *Genetic Psychology Monographs*, 1947, **35**, 3–135.

Henry, W. E., & Guetzkow, H. Group projection sketches for the study of small groups. *Journal of Social Psychology*, 1951, **33**, 77–102.

Hertz, M. R. Discussion on "Some recent Rorschach problems." *Rorschach Research Exchange*, 1937, **2**, 53–65.

Hertz, M. R. Scoring the Rorschach inkblot test. *Journal of Genetic Psychology*, 1938, **52**, 16–64.

Hertz, M. R. *Percentage charts for use in computing Rorschach scores*. Cleveland: Brush Foundation and the Department of Psychology, Western Reserve University, 1940.

Hertz, M. R. The scoring of the Rorschach inkblot method as developed by the Brush Foundation. *Rorschach Research Exchange*, 1942, **6**, 16–27.

Hertz, M. R. *Frequency tables for scoring responses to the Rorschach inkblot test*. (3rd ed.) Cleveland: Western Reserve University Press, 1951.

Hertz, M. R. *Frequency tables for scoring Rorschach responses*. (5th ed.) Cleveland: Case Western Reserve University Press, 1970.

Holsopple, J. Q., & Miale, F. R. *Sentence Completion: A projective method for the study of personality*. Springfield, Ill.: Charles C Thomas, 1954.

Holt, R. R. Clinical and statistical prediction: A reformulation and some new data. *Journal of Abnormal and Social Psychology*, 1958, **56**, 1–12.

Holt, R. R. A method for assessing primary and secondary process in the Rorschach. In M. A. Rickers-Ovsiankina (Ed.), *Rorschach psychology*. New York: Wiley, 1960. Pp. 263–315.

Holt, R. R. Measuring libidinal and aggressive motives and their controls by means of the Rorschach test. In D. Levine (Ed.), *Nebraska symposium on motivation*. Lincoln, Nebr.: University of Nebraska Press, 1966. Pp. 1–47.

Holt, R. R. Yet another look at clinical and statistical prediction: Or, is clinical psychology worthwhile? *American Psychologist*, 1970, **25**, 337–349. (a)

Holt, R. R. Artistic creativity and Rorschach measures of adaptive regression. In B. Klopfer, M. M. Meyer, & F. B. Brawer (Eds.), *Developments in the Rorschach technique*. Vol. III. New York: Harcourt, Brace, Jovanovich, 1970. Pp. 263–320. (b)

Holtzman, W. H. Objective scoring of projective tests. In B. M. Bass & I. A. Berg (Eds.), *Objective approaches to personality assessment*. Princeton, N.J.: Van Nostrand, 1959. Pp. 134–171.

Holtzman, W. H., Thorpe, J. S., Swartz, J. D., & Herron, E. W. *Inkblot perception and personality*. Austin: University of Texas Press, 1961.

Howard, J. W. The Howard Inkblot Test. *Journal of Clinical Psychology*, 1953, **9**, 209–255.

Jackson, C. W., & Wohl, J. A survey of Rorschach teaching in the university. *Journal of Projective Techniques and Personality Assessment*, 1966, **30**, 115–134.

Jensen, A. R. Personality. *Annual Review of Psychology*, 1958, **9**, 395–422.

Johnson, G. B. An experimental projective technique for the analysis of racial attitudes. *Journal of Educational Psychology*, 1950, **41**, 257–278.

Kadis, A. L. Finger painting as a projective technique. In L. E. Abt & L. Bellak (Eds.), *Projective psychology*. New York: Knopf, 1950. Pp. 403–431.

Kanehira, T. Diagnosis of parent-child relationships by CAT. *Japanese Journal of Case Studies*, 1958, **3**, 49–63.

Kataguchi, Y. *Psychopsy: Manual for Ka-Ro Inkblot Test*. Tokyo: Kaneko Shobo, 1970.

Kinget, G. M. The Drawing Completion Test. New York: Grune & Stratton, 1952.

Kirkpatrick, E. A. Individual tests of school children. *Psychological Review*, 1900, **7**, 274–280.

Klopfer, B., Ainsworth, M. D., Klopfer, W. G., & Holt, R. R. *Developments in the Rorschach technique. Vol. I. Technique and theory*. Yonkers-on-Hudson, N.Y.: World Book, 1954.

Klopfer, B., & Davidson, H. H. Form level rating: A preliminary proposal for appraising mode and level of thinking as expressed in Rorschach records. *Rorschach Research Exchange*, 1944, **8**, 164–177.

Klopfer, B. et al. *Developments in the Rorschach technique. Vol. II. Fields of application*. Yonkers-on-Hudson, N.Y.: World Book, 1956.

Klopfer, B., & Kelley, D. *The Rorschach technique*. Yonkers-on-Hudson, N.Y.: World Book, 1942.

Klopfer, B., Meyer, M. M., & Brawer, F. *Developments in the Rorschach technique. Vol. III. Aspects of personality structure*. New York: Harcourt, Brace, Jovanovich, 1970.

Klopfer, B., & Sender, S. A system of refined scoring symbols. *Rorschach Research Exchange*, 1937, **1**, 142–148.

Korchin, S. J., Mitchell, H. E., & Meltzoff, J. A critical evaluation of the Thematic Apperception Test. *Journal of Projective Techniques*, 1950, **14**, 445–452.

Korman, A. K. The prediction of managerial performance: A review. *Personnel Psychology*, 1968, **21**, 295–322.

Lanyon, R. I., & Goodstein, L. D. *Personality assessment.* New York: Wiley, 1971.

Lessa, W. A., & Spiegelman, M. Ulithian personality as seen through ethnological materials and Thematic Apperception Test analysis. *University of California Publications in Cultural Sociology*, 1954, **2**, 243–301.

Lesser, G. S. Application of Guttman's scaling method to aggressive fantasy in children. *Educational and Psychological Measurement*, 1958, **18**, 543–552.

Levy, J., & Epstein, N. B. An application of the Rorschach Test in family investigation. *Family Process*, 1964, **3**, 344–376.

Lindner, R. M. The Rorschach Test and the diagnosis of psychopathic personality. *Journal of Criminal Psychopathology*, 1943, **1**, 69.

Lindner, R. M. Some significant Rorschach responses. *Journal of Criminal Psychopathology*, 1944, **4**, 75.

Lindner, R. M. Content analysis in Rorschach work. *Rorschach Research Exchange*, 1946, **10**, 121–129.

Lindner, R. M. Analysis of Rorschach's test by content. *Journal of Clinical Psychopathology*, 1947, **8**, 707–719.

Lindzey, G. The Thematic Apperception Test: Interpretive assumptions and related empirical evidence. *Psychological Bulletin*, 1952, **49**, 1–25.

Lindzey, G. *Projective techniques and cross cultural research.* New York: Appleton-Century-Crofts, 1961.

Lindzey, G., & Goldberg, M. Motivational differences between male and female as measured by the Thematic Apperception Test. *Journal of Personality*, 1953, **22**, 101–117.

Lindzey, G., & Kalnins, D. Thematic Apperception Test: Some evidence bearing on the "hero assumption." *Journal of Abnormal and Social Psychology*, 1958, **57**, 76–83.

Lindzey, G., & Silverman, M. Thematic Apperception Test: Techniques of group administration, sex differences, and the role of verbal productivity. *Journal of Personality*, 1959, **27**, 311–323.

Lindgren, H. C. The use of a sentence completion test in measuring attitudinal changes among college freshmen. *Journal of Social Psychology*, 1954, **40**, 79–92.

Little, K. B., & Shneidman, E. S. Congruencies among interpretations of psychological test and anamnestic data. *Psychological Monographs*, 1959, **73** (6).

Lorge, I., & Thorndike, E. L. The value of responses in a completion test as indications of personal traits. *Journal of Applied Psychology,* 1941, **25,** 191–199.

Louttit, C. M. *Clinical psychology.* New York: Harper, 1936.

Louttit, C. M., & Browne, C. G. Psychometric instruments in psychological clinics. *Journal of Consulting Psychology,* 1947, **11,** 49–54.

Loveland, N., Wynne, L. C., & Singer, M. T. The family Rorschach: A new method for studying family interactions. *Family Processes,* 1963, **2,** 187–215.

Lubin, B., Wallis, R. R., & Paine, C. Patterns of psychological test usage in the United States: 1935–1969. *Professional Psychology,* 1971, **2,** 70–74.

Magnusson, D. Some personality tests applied on identical twins. *Scandanavian Journal of Psychology,* 1960, **1,** 55–61.

Machover, K. *Personality projection in the drawing of the human figure.* Springfield, Ill.: Charles C Thomas, 1949.

Machover, K. Drawing of the human figure. A method of personality investigation. In H. H. Anderson & G. L. Anderson (Eds.), *An introduction to projective techniques.* Englewood Cliffs, N.J.: Prentice-Hall, 1951. Pp. 341–369.

Mason, B., & Ammons, R. B. Note on social class and the Thematic Apperception Test. *Perceptual Motor Skills,* 1956, **6,** 88.

Mauri, F. A method of diagnosing the interrelations in the members of a family. *Bulletin of Education of Nagoya,* 1960, **31,** 83–92.

McClelland, D. C., Atkinson, J. W., Clark, R. A., & Lowell, E. L. *The achievement motive.* New York: Appleton-Century-Crofts, 1953.

McClelland, D. C., Clark, R. A., Roby, T., & Atkinson, J. W. The projective expression of needs. IV. The effect of the need for achievement on thematic apperception. *Journal of Experimental Psychology,* 1949, **39,** 242–255.

Meehl, P. E. *Clinical versus statistical prediction.* Minneapolis: University of Minnesota Press, 1954.

Meehl, P. E. Wanted—A good cookbook. *American Psychologist,* 1956, **11,** 263–272.

Meli-Dworetzki, G. Le test Rorschach et l'evolution de la perception. *Archives of Psychologie,* 1939, **27,** 111–127.

Meli-Dworetzki, G. The development of perception in the Rorschach. In B. Klopfer et al. (Eds.), *Developments in the Rorschach technique:* II. *Fields of application.* Yonkers-on-Hudson, N.Y.: World Book, 1956. Pp. 104–176.

Meltzoff, J. The effect of mental set and item structure upon response to a projective test. *Journal of Abnormal and Social Psychology,* 1951, **46,** 177–189.

Miner, J. B. Motion perception, time perspective, and creativity. *Journal of Projective Techniques,* 1956, **20,** 405–413.

Morgan, C., & Murray, H. A. A method for investigating phantasies: The Thematic Apperception Test. *Archieves of Neurology and Psychiatry,* 1935, **34,** 289–306.

Mosley, E. C. Psychodiagnosis on the basis of the Holtzman Inkblot Technique. *Journal of Projective Techniques and Personality Assessment,* 1963, **27,** 86–91.

Moss, H. A., & Kagan, J. Stability of achievement and recognition seeking behavior from early childhood through adulthood. *Journal of Abnormal and Social Psychology,* 1961, **62,** 504–513.

Murray, E. J. Conflict and repression during sleep deprivation. *Journal of Abnormal and Social Psychology,* 1959, **59,** 95–101.

Murray, H. J. *Explorations in personality.* New York: Oxford University Press, 1938.

Murstein, B. I. *Theory and research in projective techniques (emphasizing the TAT).* New York: Wiley, 1963.

Murstein, B. (Ed.) *Handbook of projective techniques.* New York: Basic Books, 1965.

Murstein, B. I. Discussion of current status of some projective techniques. *Journal of Projective Techniques and Personality Assessment,* 1968, **32,** 229–232.

Murstein, B. Normative written TAT responses for a college sample. *Journal of Personality Assessment,* 1972, **36,** 109–147.

Napoli, P. J. Finger painting and personality diagnosis. *Genetic Psychology Monographs,* 1946, **34,** 129–231.

Napoli, P. J. Interpretive aspects of finger painting. *Journal of Psychology,* 1947, **23,** 93–132.

Napoli, P. J. A finger painting record form. *Journal of Psychology,* 1948, **26,** 31–43.

Nelson, C. Thematic sleep responses as a function of time without sleep. In S. Epstein (Ed.), *The influence of drive and conflict on apperception.* Washington, D.C.: National Institute of Mental Health, 1961. Pp. 8–9.

Newman, C. A study of the relationship between attitudes toward certain authority figures and adjustment to the military service. Unpublished doctoral dissertation, New York University, 1954.

Ni, L. *Study on concealment of the subjects in telling stories on the TAT pictures.* Taiwan: National Taiwan University, 1959.

Ouchi, G. A study on CAT. II. A comparison with TAT. *Bunka,* 1957, **21,** 194–207.

Payne, A. F. *Sentence completions.* New York: New York Guidance Clinic, 1928.

Pine, F. A manual rating drive content in the Thematic Apperception Test. *Journal of Projective Techniques,* 1960, **24,** 32–45.

Piotrowski, Z. A Rorschach compendium. *Psychiatric Quarterly,* 1947, **21,** 79–101.

Piotrowski, Z. A new evaluation of the Thematic Apperception Test. *Psychoanalytic Review,* 1950, **37,** 101–127.

Piotrowski, Z. *Perceptanalysis.* New York: Macmillan, 1957.

Piotrowski, Z. Digital computer interpretation of ink-blot test data. *Psychiatric Quarterly,* 1964, **38,** 1–26.

Rapaport, D., Gill, M., & Schafer, R. *Diagnostic psychological testing.* 2 Vols. Chicago: Yearbook Publishers, 1945, 1946.

Reznikoff, M. Social desirability in TAT themes. *Journal of Projective Techniques,* 1961, **25**, 87–89.

Riessman, F., & Miller, S. M. Social class and projective tests. *Journal of Projective Techniques,* 1958, **22**, 432–439.

Roback, H. B. Human figure drawings: Their utility in the clinical psychologist's armamentarium for personality assessment. *Psychological Bulletin,* 1968, **70**, 1–19.

Rohde, A. R. Explorations in personality by the Sentence Completion method. *Journal of Applied Psychology,* 1946, **30**, 169–181.

Rorschach, H. *Psychodiagnostik.* Bern: Bircher, 1921. (Trans. Hans Huber Verlag, 1942.)

Rorschach, H., & Oberholzer, E. The application of the form interpretation test. *Zeitschrift fur die Gesamte Neurologie und Psychiatrie,* **82**, 1923.

Rosenfield, H. M., & Franklin, S. S. Arousal of need for affiliation in women. *Journal of Personality and Social Psychology,* 1966, **3**, 245–248.

Rotter, J. B. Studies in the use and validity of the Thematic Apperception Test with mentally disordered patients. I. Methods of analysis and clinical problems. *Character and Personality,* 1940, **9**, 18–34.

Rotter, J. B., & Rafferty, J. E. *Manual: The Rotter Incomplete Sentences Blank.* New York: Psychological Corporation, 1950.

Rybakow, T. *Atlas for experimental research on personality.* Moscow: University of Moscow, 1910.

Sacks, J. M. The relative effect upon projective responses of stimuli referring to the subject and of stimuli referring to other persons. *Journal of Consulting Psychology,* 1949, **13**, 12–20.

Sacks, J. M., & Levy, S. The sentence completion test. In L. E. Abt & L. Bellak (Eds.), *Projective psychology.* New York: Knopf, 1950. Pp. 357–402.

Sanders, J. L., Holtzman, W. H., & Swartz, J. D. Structural changes of the color variable in the Holtzman Inkblot Technique. *Journal of Projective Techniques and Personality Assessment,* 1968, **32**, 556–561.

Sanford, R. N. The effect of abstinence from food upon imaginal processes: A preliminary experiment. *Journal of Psychology,* 1936, **2**, 129–136.

Sarbin, T. R. Clinical psychology—Art or science. *Psychometrika,* 1941, **6**, 391–400.

Sargent, H. Projective methods: Their origins, theory, and application in personality research. *Psychological Bulletin,* 1945, **42**, 257–293.

Sawyer, J. Measurement and prediction, clinical and statistical. *Psychological Bulletin,* 1966, **66**, 178–200.

Schafer, R. *Psychoanalytic interpretation in Rorschach testing.* New York: Grune & Stratton, 1954.

Schwartz, L. A. Social situation pictures in the psychiatric interview. *American Journal of Orthopsychiatry,* 1932, **2,** 124–133.

Shneidman, E. S. *Thematic test analysis.* New York: Grune & Stratton, 1951.

Shneidman, E. S. *The Make a Picture Story Test.* New York: Psychological Corporation, 1952.

Shneidman, E. S. Projective techniques. In B. Wolman (Ed.), *Handbook of clinical psychology.* New York: McGraw-Hill, 1965. Pp. 498–521.

Smith, J., & Coleman, J. The relationship between manifestations of hostility in projective techniques and overt behavior. *Journal of Projective Techniques,* 1956, **20,** 326–334.

Souelem, O. Mental patients' attitudes toward mental hospitals. *Journal of Clinical Psychology,* 1955, **11,** 181–185.

Spiegelman, M. A note on the use of Fine's scoring system with the MAPS tests of children. *Journal of Projective Techniques,* 1956, **20,** 442–444.

Stein, M. I. The use of the Sentence Completion test for the diagnosis of personality. *Journal of Clinical Psychology,* 1947, **3,** 46–56.

Stein, M. I. *The Thematic Apperception Test.* Reading, Mass.: Addison-Wesley, 1948.

Stone, H. Relationship of hostile aggressive behavior to aggressive content of the Rorschach and Thematic Apperception Test. Unpublished doctoral dissertation, University of California at Los Angeles, 1953.

Stone, H. K., & Dellis, N. P. An exploratory investigation into the levels hypothesis. *Journal of Projective Techniques,* 1960, **24,** 333–340.

Strizver, G. L. Thematic sexual and guilt responses as related to stimulus relevance and experimentally induced drive and inhibition. In S. Epstein (Ed.), *The influence of drive and conflict upon apperception.* Washington, D.C.: National Institute of Mental Health, 1961. Pp. 10–11.

Sundberg, N. D. The practice of psychological testing in clinical services in the United States. *American Psychologist,* 1961, **16,** 79–83.

Swensen, C. H. Empirical evaluations of human figure drawings. *Psychological Bulletin,* 1957, **54,** 431–466.

Swensen, C. H. Empirical evaluations of human figure drawings: 1957–1966. *Psychological Bulletin,* 1968, **70,** 20–44.

Symonds, P. M. *The dynamics of human adjustment.* New York: Appleton-Century-Crofts, 1946.

Symonds, P. M. *Adolescent fantasy: An investigation of the picture story method of personality study.* New York: Columbia University Press, 1949.

Tendler, A. D. A preliminary report on a test for emotional insight. *Journal of Applied Psychology,* 1930, **14,** 123–136.

Thompson, C. E. *Thematic Apperception Test: Thompson modification.* Cambridge, Mass.: Harvard University Press, 1949.

Thorpe, J. S., & Swartz, J. D. Perceptual organization: A developmental analysis by means of the Holtzman Inkblot Technique. *Journal of Projective Techniques and Personality Assessment,* 1966, **30**, 447–451.

Tomkins, S. S. *The Thematic Apperception Test: The theory and technique of interpretation.* New York: Grune & Stratton, 1947.

Tulchin, S. H. The pre-Rorschach use of inkblot tests. *Rorschach Research Exchange,* 1940, **4**, 1–7.

Veroff, J. Development and validation of a projective measure of power motivation. In J. W. Atkinson (Ed.), *Motives in fantasy, action, and society.* Princeton, N.J.: Van Nostrand, 1958. Pp. 105–116.

Wagner, M. E., & Shubert, H. *DAP quality scale for late adolescents and young adults.* Kenmore, N.Y.: Delaware Letter Shop, 1955.

Walker, R. G. A comparison of clinical manifestations of hostility with Rorschach and MAPS performance. *Journal of Projective Techniques,* 1951, **15**, 444–460.

Weiner, I. B. *Psychodiagnosis in schizophrenia.* New York: Wiley, 1966.

Weiner, I. B. Does psychodiagnosis have a future? *Journal of Personality Assessment,* 1972, **36**, 534–546.

Weisskopf, E., & Dieppa, J. Experimentally induced faking of TAT responses. *Journal of Consulting Psychology,* 1951, **15**, 469–474.

Weisskopf-Joelson, E., & Wexner, L. B. Projection as a function of situational and figural similarity. *Journal of Projective Techniques and Personality Assessment,* 1970, **34**, 328–331.

Wheeler, D. R. Imaginal productivity tests: Beta inkblot test. In H. A. Murray (Ed.), *Explorations in personality.* New York: Oxford University Press, 1938. Pp. 111–150.

Wheeler, W. M. An analysis of Rorschach indices of male homosexuality. *Journal of Projective Techniques.* 1949, **13**, 97–126.

Whipple, G. M. *Manual of mental and physical tests.* Baltimore: Warwick & York, 1910.

Wiggins, J. S. *Personality and prediction: Principles of personality assessment.* Reading, Mass.: Addison-Wesley, 1973.

Wiggins, J. S., Renner, K. E., Clore, J. L., & Rose, R. J. *The psychology of personality.* Reading, Mass.: Addison-Wesley, 1971.

Witkin, H. A., Dyk, R. B., Faterson, H. F., Goodenough, D. R., & Karp, S. A. *Psychological differentiation: Studies of development.* New York: Wiley, 1962.

Wyatt, F. The scoring and analysis of the Thematic Apperception Test. *Journal of Psychology,* 1947, **24**, 319–330.

Zigler, E., & Phillips, L. Psychiatric diagnosis: A critique. *Journal of Abnormal and Social Psychology,* 1960, **63**, 607–618.

Zubin, J. *Manual of Projective and cognate techniques.* Madison, Wis.: College Typing Company, 1948.

Zubin, J. Failures of the Rorschach technique. *Journal of Projective Techniques,* 1954, **18,** 303–315.

Zubin, J. Discussion of symposium on newer approaches to personality assessment. *Journal of Personality Assessment,* 1972, **36,** 427–434.

Zubin, J., Eron, L. D., & Schumer, F. *An experimental approach to projective techniques.* New York: Wiley, 1965.

Zulliger, H. *Der Behn-Rorschach Test.* Bern: Hans Huber, 1952.

CHAPTER 3

Measures of Intelligence and Conceptual Thinking

GEORGE FRANK

Psychologists have devoted considerable attention to the potential utility of measures of intelligence and conceptual thinking, and the extensive literature on each of these kinds of measures may seem to merit separate chapters in this handbook. It may furthermore seem to some readers that the wedding of intelligence and conceptual thinking into a single chapter is arbitrary or forced. However, as will be elaborated in the discussion that follows, there is good reason to view intelligence and concept formation as two closely related facets of the more basic psychological process of thinking, and accordingly to consider them in a single, shared context.

The first section of the chapter is concerned with the definition, dimensions, and measurement of intelligence and with the utility of intelligence test data. The second section considers the nature and measurement of conceptual thinking and the utility of data derived from tests of conceptual thinking. Concluding sections then address (a) major unresolved issues in the measurement of intelligence and concept formation and (b) future lines of theory and research that might enhance the utility of assessments of cognitive processes.

THE DEFINITION OF INTELLIGENCE

Despite the extent to which "intelligence" has become a common term in psychology and in the English language, it has yet to be defined satisfactorily or to achieve any consensual meaning as a theoretical construct. Contrary to an assertion by Burt (1972) that the term was coined by Herbert Spencer, the Oxford dictionary indicates that "intelligence" was introduced into the English language in the fourteenth century; it is derived from the Latin *inter legere,* meaning to bring together, and its general English meaning is "the faculty of understanding." There the clarity surrounding the term ends, for what appears to be a perfectly reasonable definition has not characterized the thinking in psychology at all. Instead, there are probably almost as many definitions of the term "intelligence" as there are individuals who have struggled to elaborate its meaning and measurement.

Some psychologists have remained close to the dictionary definition of the term. Thus Pieron (1926) defined intelligence as the capacity to understand easily, and McNemar (1964) maintained that the concept encompasses the fact that individuals differ in their ability to learn, to comprehend, and to understand. Other psychologists have attempted to define intelligence in terms of the psychological processes involved in it. According to Binet (Binet & Simon, 1905), for example, intelligence comprises such factors as judgment, comprehension, and reasoning. In a similar vein, Peterson (1922) offered the following definition of intelligence:

> Intelligence refers . . . to one's ability to be affected by a wide range of circumstances and to delay reaction to them while the significant elements are selected out and weighed with respect to their bearing on the attainment of any particular end . . . . That person is most intelligent who, with a given amount of experience and maturing, is most apt to perceive significant relations and to react discriminatively to them as distinct from the numerous irrelevant elements in situations met [p. 388]

Writing from a phenomenological point of view, Combs (1952) offered an approach to intelligence focused on the effectiveness of perceptual processes:

> By the term *intelligence* we ordinarily refer to the effectiveness of the individual behavior. In a personal frame of reference the individual's behavior is described in terms of the perceptions that he can make in his own unique perceptual field . . . the precision and effectiveness of the individual's behavior will be dependent upon the scope and clarity of his personal field of awareness. Intelligence, then, from a perceptual point of view becomes a function of the factors which limit the scope and clarity of an individual's phenomenal field [p. 662]

A final example of a definition of intelligence in terms of psychological processes can be taken from Freeman (1925):

> Intelligence may be regarded as the capacity for successful adjustment by means of those traits which we ordinarily call intellectual. These traits involve such capacities as quickness of learning, quickness of apprehension, the ability to solve new problems, and the ability to perform tasks generally recognized as presenting intellectual difficulty because they involve ingenuity, originality, the grasp of complicated relationships, or the recognition of remote association [p. 258]

Another group of definitions of intelligence has focused less on psychological processes than on more specific aspects of what intelligence permits an individual to do. Thus Binet (Binet & Simon, 1908) defines intelligence as the capacity to learn, Terman (see Thorndike et al., 1921) as the ability to engage in abstract thinking, Haggerty (see Thorndike et al., 1921) as the ability to deal with novelty, Garrett (1946) as the capacity to utilize symbols, and Thurstone (1923, 1924; see also Thorndike et al., 1921) as the capacity to entertain hypotheses that permit trial-and-error behavior. Stern (1914) equates intelligence with the capacity for adaptation, and Fischer (1969) more recently notes that "Intelligence refers to the effectiveness, relative to age peers, of the individual's approach to situations in which competence is highly regarded by the culture" (p. 669). Finally of note is a statement by Wechsler (1939) that "Intelligence is the aggregate of global capacity of the individual to act purposefully, to think rationally, and to deal effectively with his environment" (p. 3).

In reaction to the conceptual confusion created by these varying kinds of definition, some psychologists have attempted to construct comprehensive definitions of intelligence that, by covering all possible aspects of intelligent behavior, can arrive at the "truth" of the matter. Pieron (1926), for example, wrote that intelligent behavior ". . . implies the play of the whole ensemble of the mental processes, but with a certain harmony, a certain equilibrium of the various functions which . . . participate in unequal and moreover various degrees according to the individual" (p. 54). Stoddard (1941) offered the following comprehensive definition:

> Intelligence is the ability to understand activities that are characterized by (1) difficulty, (2) complexity, (3) abstractness, (4) economy, (5) adaptiveness to a goal, (6) social value, and (7) the emergence of originals, and to maintain such activities under conditions that demand a concentration of energy and a resistance to emotional factors [p. 255]

As a final example of comprehensive definitions of intelligence, Piaget (1950) has suggested that intelligence involves the capacity for adaptation, via the assimilation of increasing amounts of abilities, and that it implies (a) increasingly higher (i.e., more complex) levels of cognitive organization, (b) a capacity to invent trial-and-error behavior, and (c) the capacity to anticipate consequences (i.e., means-end associations).

A different reaction to the conceptual morass in attempts to define intelligence has been to define it operationally. For example, Stockton (1921) defined intelligence as " . . . the ability to influence . . . [one's] destiny through the intentional utilization of an inner, active, nonpredictable, selective factor to effect a specific purpose through intentional choice based on similarities" (p. 22). Subsequently, Thurstone and Thorndike became the two most prominent exponents of the operational approach to defining intelligence. According to Thurstone (1923), intelligence "consists in carrying on the trial and error process among reactions that are as yet incomplete and approximate" (p. 78). Writing more explicitly, but not with much more clarity, Thurstone (1924) added: "Intelligence is defined . . . as the capacity to live a trial-and-error existence with alternatives that are as yet only incomplete conduct. . . The degree of intelligence is measured by the incompleteness of the alternatives which participate in the trial-and-error life of the actor" (p. xv).

As for Thorndike, he is often credited with having offered the most patently operational definition of intelligence that appears in the literature, namely, that intelligence is what intelligence tests measure. However, I have been unable to locate such a comment in Thorndike's writings; the closest he comes to such a statement is in commenting that tests measure only what they correlate with (Thorndike, 1919b), that intelligence is "the ability to succeed with intellectual tasks" (Thorndike et al., 1926), and that "An intelligence test . . . is an instrument to measure the amount of intelligence shown by a human being or lower animal" (Thorndike, 1929). Although Thorndike *may* at some time have stated that intelligence is what intelligence tests measure, my reading of the literature indicates that it was Spearman who wrote concerning intelligence that " . . . the word might be expressly reserved to denote without prejudice whatever these tests may some day, after full investigation, show themselves to measure" (Spearman, 1923, p. 22).

This brief overview of approaches to the definition of intelligence should be sufficient to convince the reader that the situation is characterized much more by confusion than by agreement. Similar pictures of the uncertain nature of intelligence have been painted in literature surveys by Thorndike et al. (1926), Peterson (1925), Edwards (1928) (who listed 17 definitions that had been offered to *that* date), Spearman (1939), Cattell (1943), Garrett (1946), Miles (1957), Tuddenham (1963), and Bouchard (1968). Multiple definitions abound, each based on its own "compelling" logic but none offering clarity or understanding. As can be seen from the examples cited above, some definitions have reached the heights of solipsism (e.g., Freeman: intelligence is what we refer to as intellectual); others the heights of comprehensiveness (e.g., Stoddard); and others the heights of operationalism (e.g., Spearman: intelligence permits one to do certain things). But neither these nor any other definitions have reached the heights of explanatory power.

It is furthermore apparent that, in their attempts to define the term "intelligence" psychologists have confounded what intelligence *is* with the processes it involves, such as judgment, reasoning, memory, and attention, and with the nature of intelligent behavior, with how intelligence is manifest. It is perhaps with unknowing wisdom that Rapaport, in a chapter titled "The Nature of Intelligence" in *Diagnostic Psychological Testing*

(Rapaport et al., 1945), did not even define the term. As Weisman (1968) suggests, it may even be that, beyond seeking to determine whether intelligence tests measure what an individual has learned, the search for a meaning of the term "intelligence" is a waste of time. Such pragmatism places us exactly where Thurstone (1924) was about 50 years ago:

> There is considerable difference of opinion as to what intelligence really is, but we can still use the term as long as it is demonstrably satisfactory for definite practical ends. We use electricity for practical purposes even though we have been uncertain as to its ultimate nature, and it is so with the intelligence tests. We use the tests and leave it for separate inquiry to determine the ultimate nature of intelligence [p. xiv]

THE MANY DIMENSIONS OF INTELLIGENCE

The wealth of ideas expressed on the definition of intelligence and the multiplicity of definitions that have been offered have led me to two conclusions. First, everyone who has attempted to define the term "intelligence" has touched a portion of the elephant, as it were, mentioning a part of the totality but not the totality of the nature of intelligence. Second, there *is* such a phenomenon as intelligence, the essence of which is captured by the aforementioned dictionary definition of it as the capacity to understand, but intelligence has many different dimensions, or what Guilford (1959) chooses to refer to as the "three faces of intellect."

Whatever intelligence is, it is clear from numerous factor analytic studies of intellectual processes that intelligent behavior is multidimensional. Of particular note in this regard are contributions by Thurstone (1936a, 1938, 1940), Thurstone and Thurstone (1941), French (1951), Guilford (1956), Green et al. (1953), Hertzka et al. (1954), Guilford et al. (1954), Wilson et al. (1954), Kettner et al. (1956, 1959), Holzinger and Harman (1938), Kaiser (1960), Rimoldi (1951), Woodrow (1939), Wrigley et al. (1958), and Zimmerman (1953). These studies provide solid empirical support for Guilford's view that there are many faces of intellect.

Particularly significant among factor analytic studies of intellectual functioning has been the work of Thurstone in isolating nine factors that he refers to as "primary mental abilities." These primary mental abilities are: capacity for verbal relations (V), word fluency (W), ability to entertain relations in the spatial dimension (S), perceptual ability (P), ability to manipulate numbers (N), memory (M), general reasoning ability (R), inductive reasoning (I), deductive reasoning (D).

Factor analyses of Thurstone's data by Zimmerman (1953) and Wrigley,

Saunders, and Neuhaus (1958), as well as analyses of data from tasks and tests other than those used by Thurstone in the factor-analytic studies referred to above, have confirmed the validity of these nine factors and also refined them. For example, it has been demonstrated that the perceptual factor is made up of at least two dimensions, ability and speed.

The demonstrable dimensionality of intelligence raises a question in its own right: "Is there one such thing as intelligence and just different ways of assessing it, or is there such a thing as intelligence of which there are many different dimensions?" This question underlies a classic controversy in psychology between those who believe intelligence is comprised primarily of a general (g) factor and those who believe it consists primarily of specific (s) factors. Binet, for one, believed there was a general factor of intelligence to which certain other factors were related, and Spearman (1904, 1923; see also Hart & Spearman, 1912) formalized this notion into what he called the two-factor theory of intelligence. In his psychometric studies, and particularly in his use of factor analysis, Spearman found that performance on intellectual tasks factored out into a large general factor (which subsequently came to be known as "Spearman's g") and several specific (s) factors.

On the other side of the argument, Thorndike (1913, 1919, a, b, 1920, 1924; see also Atkins et al., 1902; Thorndike et al., 1926) maintained that there was no such thing as general intelligence (g) but only a variety of intellectual functions (s). After about 70 years this controversy has yet to be resolved, and the experimental literature includes support for both positions. Among studies lending support to the Binet-Spearman formulation regarding g are those by Alexander (1935), Banks (1949), Blakey (1941), Brown (1932), Brown and Stephenson (1933), Burt (1911, 1954, 1955), Burt and John (1942), Cattell (1963), Cohen (1952a, 1952b, 1957a), Davey (1926), Eysenck and Halstead (1945), Moursy (1952), Oates (1928), Vernon (1950), and Wilson (1931). Among studies not finding a factor of g in their psychometric analysis of test data are those reported by Bernstein (1924), Blakey (1940), Carroll (1941), French (1951), Hertzka et al. (1954), Holzinger and Harman (1938), Jones (1949), Kaiser (1960), Kettner et al. (1956, 1959), McCall (1916), McCulloch (1935), Morris (1939), Rimoldi (1948, 1951), Thurstone (1936, 1938, 1940), Wilson et al. (1954), Woodrow (1939), Wrigley et al. (1958), and Zimmerman (1953).

This listing of studies is intended to guide the reader who may be interested in pursuing further this particular psychometric issue and not to imply that the issue can be resolved by adding up the number of studies on each side of the argument. As useful as the technique of factor analysis may be, its outcomes vary with the nature of the data fed into it, the kind of correlation used, the point at which simple structure is determined, hence the number of factors extracted, the manner in which the factors are extracted, whether or not rotation is performed and if so how, and even the names given the factors. Accordingly, the presence or absence of g in a particular factor-analytic study of intellectual test performance may well be an artifact of the data analysis. To make matters even more complicated, there is reason to think that, even if there is a g factor, not all tests in a battery will be equally saturated with it (see Cohen, 1952a, 1952b, 1957a; Davey, 1926; Lienart & Crott, 1964).

As one more aspect of the dimensionality of intelligence, is there no such thing as intelligence but just so many primary mental abilities? Or is there no such thing as intelligence but only intelligent behavior? Pieron (1926) has written in this regard that " . . . intelligence does not exist; it is only an effect, a functional resultant under certain defined conditions, a behavior-value" (p. 59). With equal conviction Chein (1945) contends, "No psychologist has ever observed *intelligence;* many have observed intelligent behavior" (p. 111) and, "Intelligence is an attribute of behavior, not an attribute of a person" (p. 120).

In summary, the material reviewed in this discussion of the definition and dimensions of intelligence raises more questions than it answers. Given available knowledge to date, it is illusory for psychologists to believe they know what intelligence is; any such comfortable position would be naive. Yet the definition of intelligence cannot be brushed aside as an academic or semantic issue; it makes a difference as to what we can expect from the data from measures of intelligence and what we can expect to be able to do with these data. To put it more emphatically, the definition of the term "intelligence" is the axis on which the understanding of psychological work related to intelligence revolves. However, all that can be stated with clarity in this regard is that there is no clarity about what the correct definition of intelligence is.

This state of affairs allows three options to the psychologist who gives serious consideration to the nature of intelligence. For one, he can throw up his hands in dismay and cease any further deliberation on the subject. For a second, he can conclude with Thurstone that there is such a phenomenon as intelligence about which the "truth" will someday be known and that for the moment, in the absence of perfect understanding and without being able to define it, we can nevertheless hypothesize that intelligence exists and that we can see and measure its effects. For a third option, he can concur with the behavioristic notion that there is no such thing as intelligence, but only intelligent behavior, and adopt the operational credo that intelligence is what intelligence tests measure. The first option would of course obviate the remainder of this chapter, and the third implies that we are dealing with some mysterious force which can influence behavior but cannot be measured in its own right. Accordingly, the following discussion of the measurement of intelligence reflects the second option and presumes that there is such a phenomenon as intelligence that can be examined psychometrically.

THE MEASUREMENT OF INTELLIGENCE: THE BINET AND WECHSLER SCALES

It is not always recognized that the so-called testing movement, which represented the beginnings of applied psychology, hence of clinical psychology, had its roots in experimental psychology. Although the participants in the Boulder conference on training in clinical psychology felt it necessary to urge that the work of the clinician be embedded in general psychology (thus implying that it was not), the first applied psychologists *were* experimental psychologists, and the methods they used were, in large measure, adaptations of methods that were common in the psychology laboratory of the day. It is also interesting to note, however, that applied psychology was not a natural outgrowth of the development of psychology; as indicated in the following brief history, it was foisted upon psychology by the demands of educators.

The aim of the early psychologists, such as Wundt and those who worked in his laboratory, was the development of general laws of psychological functioning. The focus was on sensorimotor behavior and the explication of the nature of experience. Thus, although Wundt defined psychology as the science of the study of experience, he did not consider the so-called higher mental processes, that is, processes other than sensation, perception, and reaction times, as within the province of psychology.

Yet it was in Wundt's very laboratory that James McKeen Cattell and Ebbinghaus followed Galton in studying individual differences and began to explore memory and the associational process. Galton (1870) had in fact begun the study of intelligence even prior to the development of Wundt's laboratory in 1879, and by the 1880s (Galton, 1883) he was deeply into the systematic exploration of individual differences in the higher mental processes of reasoning, judgment, and thinking. Of further historical note, it was Cattell (1890) who coined the term test to differentiate a "test" from an "experiment."

Alfred Binet is commonly identified as the father of intelligence testing, although it is not entirely correct to do so. Binet (Binet & Henri, 1895) described in 1895 his notion that measures of traditional psychological functions could be used to assess intelligence, but it was not until 1905 (Binet, 1905) that he developed an actual test for this purpose. However, in 1893 Gilbert at Yale had begun to explore and standardize the differential performance of children on measures of sensory discrimination (see Petersen, 1925). Moreover, Ebbinghaus in the early 1890s had constructed a test of intelligence, consisting of calculation, memory for digits, and sentence completion tasks, in response to a request from educators in Breslau for assistance in evaluating the scholastic aptitude of that city's school children.

It is not known whether the city fathers of Paris knew of these developments in America and Germany but, at any rate, Binet notes in 1905 that he was appointed a member of a commission whose task was to study the use of a psychological examination to help rate the scholastic aptitude of students in the public educational system of Paris. It was in this same way that Witmer (1896), who is credited with establishing the first psychological clinic in the United States, began his applied work. The common denominator among Ebbinghaus, Binet, and Witmer is that they were experimental psychologists who, in resonse to requests from educators, attempted to apply the methods of their experimental laboratory work to the solution of a practical problem. And so applied psychology, which Binet called "individual psychology," Stern "differential psychology," and Witmer "clinical psychology," was born. For many years to come, virtually up until World War II, clinical psychology and testing—specifically intelligence testing and, perhaps even more specifically, the uses of the Binet—were synonymous.

Buros (1972), in the *Mental Measurements Yearbook,* lists 121 tests of intelligence. These include a panorama of means of assessing intelligence, among them handwriting (Binet & Henri, 1895), facial expression (Pintner, 1918), voice (Michael & Crawford, 1927), drawing of the human figure (Goodenough, 1926), and a range from very brief assessments (Kent, 1932) to more lengthy tasks, some involving language and others involving sensorimotor behavior—a cafeteria of intelligence tests to statisfy one's palate, a test for all reasons. No attempt is made to cover all these tests here. Rather, the following discussion focuses on the most frequently used and commonly known tests of intelligence, those developed by Binet and Wechsler. The formats of these two scales stand as paradigms for the two major trends in the testing of intelligence, the developmental system and the point system; as such, they provide an excellent basis for confronting certain generic issues in intelligence testing.

To describe these two systems briefly, in the point system used by Wechsler the final total score for a subject is obtained by summing his performance on all subtests and relating this sum to a normal curve distribution for scores on the total test. The end result is an IQ score which represents a point in the distribution of total points one can obtain on the test. Although Binet also began in this way, he ultimately formulated a developmental scale which evaluates an individual's performance relative to the performance of other individual's of the same chronological age, and in which I Q represents a ratio of the subject's mental age to his chronological age.

The Binet Test

Binet began exploring intelligence by observing the sensorimotor and ideational development of his two children (see Varon, 1935), and his early formulation of intelligence (in 1883) was influenced by British associationism. As psychology expanded its methods of exploration, Binet expanded his, and in the 1890s we find him exploring a variety of mental activities, including attention, memory, perception, comprehension, suggestibility, and sensory discrimination. Binet was also interested in imagination, the development of moral ideas, and aesthetic appreciation, and he began to conceptualize intelligence not just in terms of simple associational theory or individual differences in sensorimotor behavior, but in terms of cognitive functions. Indeed, when Binet first speculated on the development of a test of intelligence (Binet & Henri, 1895), he recommended the assessment of individual differences in all of these facets of behavior.

In 1904 Binet was appointed by the Minister of Public Instruction of Paris as one of the members of a commission whose task was to find a way to identify children who would not be able to profit from regular instruction. In this role Binet was but following in the tradition of other Frenchmen, such as Pinel, Esquirol, and Seguin, who already had begun to attempt to classify the nature and degree of intellectual difficulties and to explore the possibility of making this differentiation on the basis of mental, rather than solely sensorimotor, functions.

The first form of the test Binet developed (in 1905) was little more than a standardized interview for assessing intelligence, and it differed from a clinical interview only in that the 30 questions he used were given a formal score. The original Binet scale, then, was a point scale: the 30 questions were scored either pass or fail, and a total score was derived. The functions tapped by this first test and the items included were sensorimotor behavior (ability to follow an object with the eyes, grasping objects placed in the visual field, and manipulation of objects toward some end—unwrapping a piece of candy, drawing, and imitation of behavior); sensory discrimination (comparative estimation of length and weight); memory (repetition of numbers, repetition of sentences, remembering elements in a picture presented and then removed, memory for designs, and memory for comparative weight); and simple comprehension (recognition of familiar objects, execution of simple commands, and susceptibility to being influenced by an absurd idea, such as being asked to give the examiner something that actually is not present).

Binet (Binet & Simon, 1916) had noted early in his work that the idea of grading answers to questions according to mental age had already been introduced into educational measurement in France by his predecessors, but it was not until 1908 that, in a revision of his test, he arranged the items according to mental age. Although in the 1908 scale the items were now arranged according to the age level at which they could generally be passed, there were not the same number of tasks at each level, nor were the same number of functions sampled at each level. In a further revision of the scale in 1911, Binet equalized the number of tasks at each level and rearranged the placement of the tasks according to a more refined measure of their difficulty than he had used earlier. He also added some tasks and eliminated others, and he provided a more thorough standardization which extended the age levels covered by the scale. Whereas the 1905 scale was standardized on 50 children aged 3–11, with 10 children at each year level, the standardization group for the 1908 scale consisted of 203 children from the ages of 3 to 12, and the 1911 revision extended the scale to adults as well as children.

These early revisions by Binet have been incorporated in all subsequent revisions of his scale, including revisions introduced by Kuhlman (1912, 1922), Terman (1916, 1917), Terman and Childs (1912), Terman and Merrill (1937), Terman et al. (1915), Herring (1922, 1924), and McNemar (1942). The Herring and McNemar revisions included two alternate forms of the test intended to facilitate retest assessment of changes in intellectual performance over time.

Despite these revisions, many criticisms were persistently leveled against the Binet scale by such writers as Ayers (1911), Cattell (1937), Goddard (1911, a, b), Kuhlman (1911a, 1911b), Krugman (1939), Peterson (1925), Terman (1911, 1913, 1916, 1917, 1918, Terman & Childs, 1912), Wallin (1929), and Wright (1939). These criticisms included the following: the standardization remained inadequate; there were an inadequate number of tests at each age level; tests were wrongly placed in the scale as regards mental age; items were wrongly placed within each subtest according to difficulty; within each age level the tests were not of equal difficulty; there were needs to broaden the factors assessed by the scale and to extend the test downward to infancy and upward to adults; the scale was too easy at the lower age levels and too difficult at the upper age levels; and some tests should be eliminated altogether.

Moreover, the tests in the scale seemed too heavily influenced by scholastic experience and by the variety of cultural stimulation available at different socioeconomic levels, and they appeared too heavily weighted with memory and verbal material (Cattell, 1937). Indeed, from an early comparison of his own results with those from the use of his scale in Belgium, Binet himself became aware of the influence of socioeconomic level on intelligence test performance. The subjects in the Belgium study were middle- and upper-class students in a private school, whereas the subjects in his own studies were drawn from the Paris public school system. The enhancing influence of socioeconomic level on intelligence test performance was noted by other early writers (e.g., Yerkes & Anderson, 1915) and was subsequently found to be a consistent effect, as reviewed by Neff (1938).

Factor-analytic studies of the Binet test by Burt and John (1942), Guilford (1956), Jones (1954), and Wright (1939) noted that, in the language of Thurstone's primary mental abilities, it tapped the following functions: verbal relations (V), ability to visualize spatial relations (S), ability for perceptual relations (P), memory (M), general reasoning ability (R), inductive reasoning (I), word fluency, (W), and the capacity for conceptual relations.

It was found, however, that each factor was not represented by an equal number of tests, which confirmed the widespread impression that the scale was tapping various functions unevenly. An even more serious criticism of the psychometric structure of the scale emerged from factor-analytic studies of the subtests at various age levels. These studies demonstrated that the same subtests varied in terms of their loading on g from year to year (McNemar, 1942) and, furthermore, that somewhat different factors are tapped by the tests at different age levels. For example, at age 7 the factors assessed are V, R, N, and M; at age 9, V, R, S, and M; at age 11, V, S, and M; and at age 13, V, R, S, M, and visualization (Jones, 1949).

From a practical point of view, probably the most telling criticism of the Binet was the fact that, beyond a certain point (about age 12), it is heavily loaded with tasks involving language and language development. The need during World War I to assess the intellectual performance of soldiers, many of whom came from backgrounds that did not place heavy emphasis on verbal ability (e.g., rural communities), followed after the war by the need to assess non-English-speaking emigrees from Europe, led to an urgency to develop other tests not predicated on the ability to utilize language and linguistic constructs. Thus was born the era of the so-called performance test during which much use was made of such measures as the formboard, originally developed by Seguin (1866), pictures with missing parts to be filled in (Healy, 1914), object assembly tasks (Knox, 1914), picture assembly and various learning tasks (Pintner, 1919), mazes (Porteus, 1915), block design (Kohs, 1923), and various reasoning tasks presented pictorially, including the Progressive Matrices (Raven, 1938).

From 1914 on many scales grouping a variety of performance tasks were developed to rival the Binet as *the* test of intelligence, including the Pintner-Paterson Scale (1917), the Army Performance Scale (Yoakum & Yerkes, 1920), and scales by Knox (1914), Pintner (1919), Thorndike (1919), and Arthur (1933). In addition to the Binet, with its emphasis on verbal material, and these many nonverbal tests and scales, there were also syntheses of both approaches. These syntheses consisted of omnibus tests which tried to combine the assessment of intelligence by both language and nonlanguage tasks (e.g., Healy & Fernald, 1911; Arthur, 1933). The persistent attempt to develop an omnibus test of intelligence to replace the Binet, as also discussed by Terman and Chamberlain (1918) and Thurstone (1921), was an important factor leading to the test developed by Wechsler (1939).

The Wechsler Test

In light of the above discussion, the test developed by David Wechsler, then Chief Psychologist at New York City's Bellevue Hospital, can be seen in its proper context in the testing movement. As previously noted, the Binet was a test designed primarily for children, and from the middle years of childhood on it is weighted unequally with verbal tasks, despite Binet's effort to assess intelligence via tasks involving both language and performance skills. Moreover, although Binet had intended to develop a scale that would enable an analysis of intellectual functioning developmentally, psychometric studies indicated that the difficulty of achieving this end had surpassed his expectations. Indeed, in commenting about the attributes of a meaningful intelligence test and summarizing some of the reactions of the field up until that time, Conrad (1931) called for a point scale which would eliminate the influence of prior learning, present the subtests in standard scores, and comprise an equal number of verbal and nonverbal tasks.

Yerkes and Bridges (1914) had previously tried to reorganize the material of the Binet so that it would constitute a point scale with a zero point of measurement and with its material organized according to common function, not age level. Their efforts were not particularly successful, however, and it became clear that what was needed was not a reorganization of the Binet, but an entirely new set of tasks, differently constructed. From this need the Wechsler arose.

The Wechsler scale has come to be the most well known and widely used point scale for measuring intelligence. Nevertheless, its construction consisted of little more than the gathering together first of 10 and later of 11 tests previously found in other scales and the grouping of these tests so as to provide an equal number of language and nonlanguage tasks. Although these tasks were not of equal length, Wechsler provided for translation of raw scores on them into standard scores, which permitted comparisons to be made of differential subtest performance. As Wechsler (1939) notes, "Our aim was not to produce a set of brand new tests but to select from whatever source available, such a combination of them as would best meet the requirements of an effective adult scale" (p. 76). The bases on which subtests were chosen were that they should (a) lend themselves to a point scale evaluation; (b) measure not only reasoning ability but also ability to handle practical situations; (c) stand up as measures of intelligence on the basis of experience and not just psychometrically; and (d) discriminate well among subjects.

In the actual construction of his scale, Wechsler borrowed from the Binet subtests he labeled Comprehension (C), Arithmetic (A), Digit Span (D), Similarities (S), Picture Completion (PC), and Vocabulary (V). From the tests developed for use in differentiation of army recruits he borrowed Information (I), Picture Arrangement (PA), and Digit Symbol ($DSym$) subtests. And from the Pintner-Paterson (1917) test he borrowed Block Design (BD) and Object Assembly (OA) subtests. The Wechsler scale thus yielded a summary score, or Full Scale IQ, which was computed on the basis of all the subtests, as well as partial IQ scores for the verbal (Verbal IQ) and nonverbal (Performance IQ) tasks taken separately.

Whereas on developmental scales such as the Binet mental age is computed on the basis of the number of tests passed at each age level, and presumably reflects the subject's comparative performance with respect to individuals of his or her own age and thus the general age level at which the person is functioning intellectually, the Wechsler IQ is derived from a summation of the number of points achieved in doing the various tasks. As is characteristic of point scales, then, this total number of points earned is then assigned to a position along a continuum reflecting the number of people who perform at various numerical levels. The scores that would be earned by the population at large are presumed to be normally distributed, with the mean standard score set at 100 and the standard deviation at 10. In other words, it is expected that approximately two-thirds of subjects will fall within one standard deviation of the mean (IQ 90–110) and 95% of subjects within two standard deviations of the mean (IQ 80–120). As each individual performs on the Wechsler, the sum of the points earned on the various subtests, translated into standard scores, is evaluated with respect to its deviation from the mean to determine the subject's IQ score.

For point scales as well as developmental scales of intelligence, the reliability of the IQ obtained depends significantly on the adequacy of the test's standardization. In this regard, Wechsler attempted to account for differential age-level performance by providing tables of standard scores for different age levels to be used in deriving the IQ score. Nevertheless, the original Wechsler scale was plagued by numerous standardization problems, and in response to these problems Wechsler (1955) revised the first version of his scale, known as the Wechsler-Bellevue (W-B), into the Wechlser Adult Intelligence Scale (WAIS). Compared to the W-B, the WAIS is standardized on a more comprehensive sample which more closely approximates the socioeconomic distribution of individuals in the United States, and the material within the subtests is better organized according to degree of difficulty. Additionally, Wechsler (1949) developed a form of his test for children, the Wechsler Intelligence Scale for Children (WISC), and he subsequently extended this test downward into the Wechsler Preschool and Primary Scale of Intelligence (WPPSI; Wechsler, 1967). The reader interested in a summary of research with the WISC is referred to Littell (1960).

The test Wechsler developed appears to obviate many of the psychometric criticisms aimed at the Binet, namely, that it is primarily for children, that it is weighted more heavily with verbal than nonverbal tasks, and that it samples various psychological functions unequally. However, because face validity is not tantamount to actual validity, it is appropriate next to examine how the Wechsler scale has fared in psychometric studies, especially those involving factor analysis.

With one exception (Davis, 1956), factor-analytic studies have generally supported Wechsler's differentiation of the subtests in his scale into tasks that involve primarily language and the utilization of verbal symbols and tasks that do not (e.g., Hammer, 1949; Maxwell, 1960). This differentiation holds up in the Wechsler performance of children (Balinsky, 1941; Cohen, 1959; Maxwell, 1959), elderly subjects (Balinsky, 1941; Berger et al., 1964; Birren, 1952; Maxwell, 1961; Riegel & Riegel, 1962), and various groups of psychiatric patients (Cohen, 1952b, 1957a & b; Frank, 1956; Russell, 1972). However, these factor-analytic studies have not demonstrated that the Wechsler subtests are factorially pure, that is, that the different psychological functions postulated by Wechsler and later by Rapaport et al. (1945) as being tapped by each subtest are in fact tapped by that subtest. Moreover, although research does confirm the validity of distinguishing between verbal and nonverbal tasks, the verbal and performance factors are found not always to be composed of the same subtests.

Table 1 identifies the Wechsler subtests that have loaded highly on Verbal, Performance, and Memory factors in several different factor-analytic studies of the scale. These studies demonstrate remarkable consistency of subtest loading on Verbal and Performance factors, although some variations do occur. For example, the Verbal factor may or may not include Vocabulary (V) and sometimes includes Arithmetic (A), and the

Table 1.   Variation in the Factor Structure of the Wechsler from Study to Study

Investigator	Factor Structure		
	Verbal	Performance	Memory
Berger et al. (1964)	C, I, S, V	OA, BD	A, D
Birren (1952)	C, I, S, V	OA, BD, PC, PA, DSym	A, D, BD, DSym
Cohen (1952b)	C, I, S, V	OA, BD, PC, PA	A, D, DSym
Hammer (1949)	C, I, S, V	OA, BD, PC	D, DSym
Maxwell (1959)	C, OA, BD, Coding, PIQ	OA, BD	[a]
Maxwell (1960)	[b]	OA, BD, PC, PA	[a]
Maxwell (1961)	C, S, A	OA, BD, DSym	[a]
Riegel & Riegel (1962)	C, I, S, V	OA, BD, PC	[a]

[a] No Memory factor was found.
[b] No Verbal factor was found.

Performance factor regularly includes Object Assembly (OA) and Block Design (BD) but not always Picture Completion (PC), Picture Arrangement (PA), and Digit Symbol (DSym). The Memory factor, which has also been labeled "freedom from distractibility" (Cohen, 1952a), consistently includes Arithmetic (A) and Digits (D), as might be expected, but on occasion also includes Digit Symbol (DSym) and Block Design (BD). Special note should be made of the study by Maxwell (1959) included in Table 1, since his results are strikingly incongruent with those of other investigators. Maxwell's unusual results may be derived from the particular way in which he rotated his data to produce factor structures, and they may also reflect in part the fact that his subjects were children (the Coding subtest he lists is the WISC equivalent of the WAIS DSymb), whereas the other studies summarized in the table used adult subjects.

The importance of these variations in factor structure is difficult to assess. They might indicate merely that the factors are not unidimensional and that apparent relationships among subtests in any particular study depend on the particular dimensions of the subtests touched on by the method of data analysis used. However, it might be that the structure of intellectual functioning is not uniform across all people and that there are systematic individual differences in how subtests of various kinds load on factors of intellectual ability. Some research by Cohen (1952a, 1957a) tends to support this latter hypothesis, although factor-analytic studies comparing the performance of different psychiatric groups have not revealed them to produce different factor structures with regard to Wechsler performance (Cohen, 1952b; Frank, 1956). Hence the question remains whether the differences in the factor structure of the Wechsler that sometimes emerge reflect on the factorial structure of the subtests, and perhaps on individual differences in this regard, or whether they are artifactual consequences of different ways of analyzing the data. Wherever the truth lies, it does seem clear that it is currently unwarranted to accept uncritically certain aspects of the rationale regarding the nature of the psychological functions involved in the subtests of the Wechsler.

For this reason it is relevant to consider further the manner in which methods of data analysis can produce artifacts which obscure the essential nature and consistency of such tests as the Wechsler. A case in point is the previously mentioned study by Davis (1956), which produced results significantly different from those of other studies exploring the Wechsler factor structure. Davis extracted the following six factors and patterns of factor loading: Verbal Comprehension (*I, V, S*) Visualization (*BD, PC, OA*); Numerical Facility (*DSym, A*); Mechanical Knowledge (*BD, A, D*); Fluency of Ideation (*C, D, DSym*); Perceptual Speed (*OA, BD, DSym*). In addition, three of the subtests—*I, PA,* and *S*—factored out as each being a function of a relatively strong desire of some unique psychological faculty.

Davis' study merits comment because the nine factors that emerged from it diverge so much in number and content from the factors found in most other studies. What is most important to consider is the effect that different statistical methods can have on the results of factor analytic studies. As noted earlier, the number and structure of the factors that emerge out of any factor analytic study are not fixed, and many aspects of rotation and determination of simple structure determine both the number of factors that will be extracted and their content. Whereas most factor analysts perform a limited number of rotations, manipulating the organization of the data only until they achieve a configuration that reflects a good fit, Davis in his study conducted *101* rotations. This aspect of his methodology alone could account for the difference between his results and those of other investigators. Indeed, the results of Davis' study are so inconsistent with other data that it is difficult not to conclude that his extraction of nine Wechsler factors, as compared to the three factors regularly extracted by others, represents an artifact of his methodology.

In view of some of the previously mentioned criticisms of the Binet, it is next important to consider the factorial structure of the Wechsler across different age levels. Table 2 summarizes data from a study by Birren (1952) in which the performances of individuals at six different age levels were compared. It can be seen from the table that the factors look somewhat different at different ages. Some subtests are consistently loaded on one factor or another, such as *I* and *C* on the Verbal factor and *OA* and *BD* on the Performance factor, whereas other subtests move in and out the factors

Table 2. Factor Structure of the Wechsler at Six Age Levels

	Factor Structure	
Age	Verbal	Performance
9	I, C, A, D	
12	I, C, A, D, DSym	OA, BD, DSym
15	I, C, A, PA	OA, BD, PA, PC, DSym
25–29	I, C, DSym	OA, BD, PC
35–44	I, C, A, D, PC	OA, BD, PA, PC, A
50–59		OA, BD, PA, PC, DSym

depending on the age group. Moreover, a specific Performance factor does not appear at age 9, and a specific Verbal factor does not appear at age 50–59. In both cases the "missing" factor is included in a g factor which appears only in the lower (9) and upper (50–59) ages. Some other factors have been identified only with specific age groups. These include a factor of Perception of Social Relations (C, PA, PC, D), which was found at age 12 but not at the other ages; a factor Balinsky (1941) calls Awareness (I, OA, BD) and a Reasoning factor of relatively similar structure (I, C, A, PA, PC), both of which occurred at age 15; and a somewhat differently composed Reasoning factor (I, C, A, PA, DSym, BD), which appeared at ages 25–29 and 50–59.

In other studies of factorial structure across age groups, Cohen (1959) found some variation in factor structure among groups of children aged 7½, 10½, and 13½. Additionally, the loading of the subtests on g varied with the age of his subjects. Maxwell (1961), drawing similar comparisons among groups of subjects aged 60–64, 65–69, 70–74, and 75 or older, also found differences in factor structure related to age. Finally, Cohen (1957b) reports differential loadings of each subtest on g for adults at several different age levels.

These findings of differences in factor structure associated with age might initially appear to reflect some psychometric weaknesses of the Wechsler, as they did in the case of the Binet. However, it needs to be recognized that these differences may reflect the nature of developmental changes in cognitive functioning, in which case the validity of the Wechsler is supported rather than challenged by its ability to parallel them. Data consistent with this view are presented with respect to cognitive development in general by Bruner, Olver, and Greenfield (1956) and Elkind and Flavell (1969), and with respect to developmental analyses of other tests by Asch (1936), Bayley (1933, 1955), Burt (1954), Garrett, Bryan, and

Perl (1935), Hofstaetter (1954), Sontag, Baker, and Nelson (1958), Thurstone (1936), and Wooley (1925).

As regards the matter of retest reliability, concern with the consistency of the performance of any individual from one testing to another goes back to some of the earliest preoccupations in the testing movement (see Downey, 1918; English & Killian, 1939; Nemzek, 1933). The data with regard to the Wechsler indicate good reliability for its summary measures, in the high .80's and low .90's for Verbal, Performance, and Full Scale IQs (Bayley, 1955; Derner, Aborn, & Cantor, 1950; Rabin, 1944; Webb & DeHaan, 1951). Reliability of the individual subtests, as indicated in Table 3, is less consistent, however. Whether because of the variable perfor-

Table 3. Reliability Coefficients for the Subtests of the Wechsler

Subtest	Derner et al. (1950)	Webb & DeHaan (1951)
V	.88	.94
I	.86	.82
C	.74	.53
S	.71	.74
A	.62	.82
D	.67	.44
BD	.84	.76
OA	.69	.46
PA	.64	.29
PC	.83	.42
DSym	.80	[a]

[a] DSym not given.

mance of individual subjects or because of the lack of internal homogeneity within the subtests, reliability coefficients vary from subtest to subtest and also change from one study to the next.

It is interesting to note at this point the extent to which the tests developed by Binet and Wechsler correlate with each other. Considering the differences in the composition of the two instruments, correlations between the Binet and Wechsler tests are surprisingly high, ranging from the .60's (e.g., Anderson et al., 1942) to the .80's (e.g., Gianell & Freeburne, 1963; Mitchell, 1942; Sartain, 1946). Correlations of the Wechsler with other tests of intelligence, such as the Army General Classification Test, ACE, CAVD, Otis, and Raven Progressive Matrices, vary in the same range (see Wechsler, 1958, p. 105). With respect to the assessment of children. the WISC also correlates with the Binet in the .80's (Barclay & Carolan, 1966), but the WPSSI correlates only in the .40's with the Binet (Ruschival & Way, 1971).

A closing word in this section is indicated with regard to shortened forms of such tests as the Binet and Wechsler. If the purpose of an assessment is to determine an individual's global level of functioning, as expressed in a number, then it seems justified to take the quickest route to this end, and thereby make the most efficient use of the time and energy of both the person taking the test and the one administering it. As a result of observations that an individual's performance on Binet Vocabulary correlates in the .90's with his total score (Lawrence, 1911; Terman, 1918), a short form of the Binet was devised early in its history by Doll (1917). Likewise, short forms of the Wechsler began to be devised as early as 1943, by Rabin. However, if the psychologist wishes to do more than just derive a number, but rather to examine an individual's intellectual performance with regard to various psychological functions, short forms will not serve his purpose. Not only do short forms not permit any extensive exploration of intellectual functioning but they have also been found to have low reliability (e.g., Bersoff, 1971; Luzki et al., 1970). In the end, then, the short form may not be a shortcut after all (Levy, 1968).

THE UTILITY OF INTELLIGENCE TEST DATA

With the nature and composition of omnibus tests of intelligence in mind, the next question to ask is how useful these measures are. In other words, what do such measures as the Binet and Wechsler enable us to do with the data we obtain from them? In this section the utility of intelligence tests is assessed with regard to their relationship to academic performance and to clinical application.

Academic Performance

If there is any utility that tests of intelligence should demonstrate, relationship to performance in school seems to be an area in which expectations can justifiably be high. Assessing capacity to perform in school is after all what Binet, Ebbinghaus, and Witmer set out to do when they initiated their experiments in testing. However, Binet himself commented that, although intelligence could be defined from a scholastic point of view as the capacity to learn, one should nevertheless differentiate between intelligence and scholastic aptitude (Binet & Simon, 1908).

In his own work Binet found only a fair relationship between measured intellectual level and scholastic performance. For example, of 24 students who tested significantly above their age level, Binet found that one was *behind* his grade level in school and 16 others were just at the grade level appropriate to their age, whereas only 7 (less than one-third of the group) were ahead of the grade level appropriate to their chronological age. Additionally, of 30 students who tested significantly below their grade level, Binet found that 14 were significantly behind in actual grade level but that 16 were at the grade level appropriate to their chronological age. Finally, of 47 students who tested at their age level, 9 were significantly behind in actual grade level, 5 were significantly ahead, and 33 were at their appropriate grade level. For the total group, then almost 30% were *not* functioning academically as one might predict from the overall intellectual measure (Binet & Simon, 1916).

This pattern of results has generally been characteristic of studies that followed Binet's work. Whether with regard to the Binet (Goddard, 1911a; Terman et al., 1915), the Wechsler (Conry & Plant, 1965; Duffy et al., 1972; Plant & Lynd, 1959; Wall et al., 1962), or a wide variety of other tests of intelligence (Allen,1944; Ames, 1943; Barton et al., 1972; Bridges, 1922; Chappell, 1955; Colvin, 1921; Edwards & Kirby, 1964; Humphreys, 1968; Keys, 1940; Lennon, 1950; Lunneborg & Lunneborg, 1967; MacPhail, 1943; Pintner, 1923), the same modest relationship to academic performance, comprising correlations between .30 and .60, is consistently found. Also consistently found in these studies is that, of the factors assessed by omnibus tests of intelligence, the verbal factor correlates best with academic performance (Ames & Walker, 1964; Lennon, 1950; McCall, 1916; Shaw, 1949; Stroud, et al. 1957).

As noted by Thornton (1941), Coleman and Cureton (1954), and others who have considered this issue, the closer the test material is to the "target" data of academic performance, the better is the prediction that can be achieved. Consistently with this postulate, tests of academic aptitude and level of previous actual academic achievement both predict future academic achievement to a much higher degree than overall measures of intelligence (Cobb, 1972; Cicerelli, 1965; La Haderne, 1968; Meyers et al., 1968; Oates, 1924; Robeck & Wilson, 1964). Furthermore, in this regard tests of intelligence have been found at best a modest (in the .60's) correlation with tests of such academic abilities as reading, arithmetic, and general language skill (Adams, 1944; Butsch, 1939; Franz et al., 1958; French et al., 1952; Harris, 1940; Henderson, 1957; Holland & Astin, 1962; Holland & Nichols, 1964; Humphreys, 1968; Jones & Siegel, 1962; Klugh & Bierly, 1959; Mann, 1961; McQuary, 1953; Michael & Jones, 1963; Michael et al., 1962; Pierson, 1947; Remmers et al., 1949; Richards, 1957; Scannell, 1960; Vick & Horaday, 1962; Worrell, 1959).

To summarize the available data, from the earliest research (e.g., Jordan 1923) it has been found that IQ correlates poorly (.17 to .22) with tests of learning, fairly well (.45 to .49) with grades, and modestly well (.60 to .70) with teacher estimates of students' intelligence. As compared to IQ, teacher ratings are significantly better in predicting academic performance (Ball, 1938; Holland, 1959; Thorndike, 1920), and previous grades are the best of all known predictors of future grades.

Clinical Use of Intelligence Test Data

In his early work Binet (Binet & Henri, 1895) articulated the notion that the data derived from a test of intelligence could also be utilized to explore nonintellective, personality characteristics of the individual. "Individual psychology," as he entitled his mode of approaching the data of psychology to differentiate it from the general psychology of his day, was focused on the study of individual differences in mental functioning. Binet accordingly directed attention to the *patterning* of intellectual functioning, that is, to the fact that various psychological processes arrange themselves in different configurations in different individuals and that these differences can be studied systematically. It was also Binet who commented that personality differences are reflected in the patterning of the higher mental processes, that is, in the thought processes underlying judgment, reasoning, and abstract thinking.

Binet's notions in this regard were echoed by other psychologists who were in the forefront of the testing movement (e.g., Hart & Spearman, 1914; Terman, 1916; Thorndike et al., 1921; Wechsler, 1943). Subsequent research by Webb (1915), Rawlings (1921), Brown (1923, 1924), Tendler (1923), and Alexander (1935) seemed to confirm Binet's hypothesis that the answers to questions from an intelligence test yield more data than just level of intelligence and that, in some instances, these data identify personality traits and motivational dispositions. More recent research has lent additional support to the validity of this thesis (see Eysenck, 1967; Eysenck & White, 1964; Frank, 1970).

The assumption that general personality traits could be reflected in intelligence test performance led to a subsequent hypothesis that pathological personality characteristics could also be "read" from intellectual functioning. Here again it was Binet (Binet & Henri, 1895; Binet & Simon, 1905) who articulated the thesis, to be echoed in other early formulations (e.g., Hart & Spearman, 1914; Wylie, 1902), and early research supported his view (Babcock, 1930; Hunt, 1936; Pressey, 1917; Pressey & Cole, 1918; Rawlings, 1921; Roe & Shakow, 1942).

Because both the notion that personality factors influence intellectual functioning and its corollary, that specific personality factors in psychopathology also differentially influence intellectual functioning, seemed to have merit, logically and empirically, much energy was invested in the use of the Binet in clinical assessment. Among other considerations such a notion freed the psychologist from experiencing himself merely as a psychometrician and allowed him to share with psychiatrists the exploration of the influence personality abnormalities have on thinking. Subsequently, however, a thorough review of the research with the Binet by Harris and Shakow (1937) failed to confirm that individuals from specific clinical groups could be identified by unique performance on this test of intelligence.

Nevertheless, the hypothesis regarding potential clinical uses of measures of intellectual functioning was so compelling that psychologists, rather than give up the notion, blamed their test. Because the structure of the Binet was found not to permit systematic exploration of the various psychological processes presumably involved in performance on an omnibus test of intelligence, the lack of research support for its clinical applications was attributed to this shortcoming of the instrument. As noted previously, it was partly in response to this psychometric limitation of the Binet that Wechsler developed his test and, when Wechsler presented his test of intelligence to the psychological community, hope was rekindled. Specifically, it was anticipated that the new instrument, which purported to allow systematic exploration and comparative analysis of the various psychological functions involved in intelligence, would generate research support for the hypothesis that personality characteristics, both normal and pathological, would be systematically reflected in a measure of intellectual functioning.

In the first presentation of his test, Wechsler (1939) referred to an earlier book by Wells (*Mental Tests in Clinical Practice,* 1927) in which the performance of psychiatric groups on specific intellectual tasks had been noted, but he made little mention of using the data derivable from his new scale in clinical assessments. In the second edition of his book (Wechsler, 1941) he considered somewhat more extensively the performance of psychiatric patients on the Wechsler, primarily as a reflection of his 2 years' experience in using the test at Bellevue Hospital and of some early research support in this regard. Rabin had conducted a study comparing the performance of schizophrenics with nonpsychotic individuals, which he had presented at the 1941 meeting of the, then, Eastern Section of the American Psychological Association, and Levi, a staff psychologist at Bellevue Hospital, had been conducting research on the performance of psychopaths. The presentation of clinical data in Wechsler's second edition is still qualitative and imprecise but, by the time of the third edition (Wechsler, 1944), there is a significant attempt at specificity in the clinical formulations, now based on many studies by Wechsler himself and by others.

This early research, as carried on by Wechsler (1943), Roe and Shakow (1942), Machover (1943), Rapaport et al. (1945), Schafer (1946, 1948a, 1948b, 1949), Reichard and Schafer (1943), and Schafer and Rapaport (1944), was conducted in the expectation that specific psychological functions tapped by a test of intelligence would be found to be differentially affected by patterns of psychopathology. Accordingly, influenced by some earlier formulations in this regard (Pressey, 1917; Pressey & Cole, 1918), studies of test scatter and patterns among different psychiatric groups poured forth, and the search pressed on for an empirical confirmation of the existence of specific patterns of performance on the Wechsler by specific psychiatric groups (e.g., Rabin, 1941, 1942, 1944).

However reasonable this expectation may appear to be, over the years it has not been supported by research with psychiatric groups. As reviewed by Rabin (1945), Rabin and Guertin (1951), Guertin, Frank, and Rabin (1956), Guertin et al. (1962, 1966, 1971), and Frank (1970), the weight of empirical evidence fails to confirm that specific psychiatric groups can be differentiated on the basis of their patterns of performance across the subtests of the Wechsler. However, although not supporting differential diagnostic use of the *quantitative* configuration of an individual's pattern of performance across the subtests of the Wechsler, available research indicates that psychopathology influences subtest performance in certain *qualitative* ways.

In particular, research beginning with studies by Magaret and Wright (1943) and Rabin (1944) consistently indicates that individuals diagnosed as schizophrenic show a significant degree of both intertest and intratest scatter, even though this scatter does not always result in the same pattern of subtest performance. Intertest scatter refers to the extent to which a subject's subtest performances vary around some criterion, such as his mean performance on all subtests, his mean performance on either the verbal or the performance subtests taken separately, or, because it has been found to be so highly correlated with Full Scale IQ and to hold up well even under the pressure of psychopathology (Babcock, 1930), his Vocabulary score. Intratest scatter refers to the extent to which a subject's pattern of successes and failures on the items of a particular subtest varies without relationship to the relative difficulty of the items, but occurs randomly within the subtest.

In addition to the contribution that scatter can accordingly make in identifying schizophrenic disturbance, there is evidence to indicate that aspects of a subject's mode of thinking and speaking in responding to the various subtest questions can differentiate among the intelligence test performance of schizophrenic, paranoid, obsessive, hysterical, and character-disordered individuals. Illustrative research in this regard, involving systematic exploration of qualitative manifestations on the Wechsler of schizophrenic thought disorder, is reported by Feifel (1949), Moran (1953), Moran et al. (1954), and Hunt et al. (1960).

These few examples notwithstanding, a retrospective look at research with the Wechsler indicates how naive it was to assume that, even if personality factors do influence performance on a task assessing intellectual functioning, parceling out the effect of level of intelligence leaves only the impact of personality factors for the clinician to examine. On the contrary, research demonstrates that such nonpersonality factors as age, sex, educational level, and socioeconomic status influence patterns of subtest performance and degree of scatter on omnibus measures of intelligence, and this knowledge has been available, although too frequently ignored, since the earliest days of the testing movement (see Burt, 1911; Stern, 1914).

It is also known now that the subject's relationship to the examiner and his attitudes toward the test and toward being tested significantly influence his performance on intellectual tasks. For this reason, some efforts have been made to develop automated procedures for administering these kinds of measures (e.g., Elwood, 1969; Elwood & Griffin, 1972).

In addition to overlooking these external sources of influence on intellectual task performance, clinicians pursuing differential diagnostic applications of the Wechsler have also frequently failed to appreciate psychometric considerations bearing on their work. For example, the expectation that useful diagnostic information could be derived from subtest scatter and patterning involves several unjustified assumptions. First, it assumes homogeneity of variance, that is, that the subtests are related relatively equally to overall intelligence; in fact, Wechsler's own data indicated that the various subtests correlate differently with the Full Scale IQ.

Second, most of the research on intratest scatter assumes that the items within each subtest are arranged according to difficulty, so that intratest scatter has clinical significance; in fact, because the items have been found not to be perfectly arranged according to difficulty, intratest scatter can occur simply as a function of the nature of the test. Third, research of this kind assumes that all items discriminate equally well, which is not necessarily the case. Fourth, this work assumes that performance on each subtest is a function solely of the particular psychological process Wechsler suggests it is, which is hardly tenable in light of the factor-analytic studies indicating that the subtests are multivariate and not univariate.

So it must be acknowledged that clinicians working with measures of intelligence have tended to be psychometrically unsophisticated. Their clinical experience has told them that schizophrenics, obsessives, hysterics, depressives, paranoids, and other diagnostic groups of individuals think and perceive the world differently, and that these differences should be reflected in a test that assesses thinking and perception. However, despite clinicans' ability to observe clear differences in psychological functioning among different psychiatric groups, their expectation that the Wechsler subtests would form into unique configurations for each group overestimated the cognitive uniqueness of diagnostic groups and underestimated the effects of psychometric considerations (including the nature and structure of the subtests, the relationship of individual test items to other items in the same subtest, and the relationship of the subtests to each other and to the overall measure) on the patterning of performance.

Intelligence, whatever it may be and however it might be measured, whether verbally or nonverbally, simply or comprehensively, must be regarded as a very complex phenomenon and its measurement as a complex event. Once the psychological complexity of human behavior and the psychometric complexity of the tests we use are grasped, it becomes understandable why the rather simplistically formulated hypotheses regarding the performance of individuals on measures of intelligence, as reviewed in this section, have by and large not been substantiated by research. The implications of this conclusion and recommended directions for future work in intelligence testing are considered further in the final section of the chapter. Next, however, attention is given to parallel issues concerning measures of conceptual thinking.

THE NATURE OF CONCEPTUAL THINKING

It is appropriate to begin this section by offering some further rationale for the decision indicated at the beginning of the chapter to include the topic of conceptual thinking. First, both classic psychometricians (Binet & Simon, 1905; Burt, 1911; Spearman, 1904; Thurstone, 1924; Thurstone & Thurstone, 1941) and cognitive theorists (e.g., Bruner, 1964; Piaget, 1950) have consistently spoken of intelligence and conceptual thinking interchangeably and translated the language of one into the language of the other. Second, this historical precedent is buttressed by the fact that the processes involved in forming a concept, namely, selective attention, selective perception, memory, reasoning, judgment, and understanding, are clearly the very same processes that are involved in intellectual functioning. It is because the same processes are involed in both intelligence and concept formation that it is natural to discuss them in the same context.

According to the dictionary, the term "concept" refers to an idea, a thought, or a generalized class of objects. Conceptual thinking therefore has to do with the process of the formation of ideas and classes of objects or, as defined by Reichard and Rapaport (1943), "concept formation is the seeing of the common essential factor in a variety of things."

The study of conceptual thinking has a history as long as study of intelligence, with the formal study of thinking going back to Galton (1870) and Kulpe (about 1900, at the University of Wurzburg). Several prominent psychologists did their doctoral research in this area during the first third of the present century. Clark Hull at the University of Wisconsin in 1918 (Hull, 1920) and Raymond Cattell at the University of London in 1929 (Cattell, 1930) both presented dissertations on the nature and development of concepts, as did English in 1922 at Yale, Smoke in 1931 at Ohio State University, and Wild in 1926 at the University of London. Studies by Moore (1910), Fisher (1916), and Gengerelli (1927) round out some of the other early research in this area, a review of which is provided by Vinacke (1951).

Thus considerable research is available on the process of the development of concepts in general, beginning with publications by Fisher (1916), English (1922), and Smoke (1932), and more recently on the development of concepts ontogenetically (Colby & Robertson, 1942; Maltz, 1963; Richards, 1941; Sigel, 1953; Welch, 1940a, 1940b; Welch & Long, 1940a, 1940b, 1943; White 1971). The data from these and other studies indicate that the development of concept formation is predicated on the development of the capacity for reasoning (see also Huttenlocher, 1964); that conceptual thinking develops from the simple to the more complex and from the concrete to the more abstract (see also Moursy, 1952; Rapaport et al., 1945; Schafer, 1948b; Wertham & Golden, 1941; Wideman, 1955); and that the meaning of concepts can change with age, so that a concept can have one meaning at one age level and another meaning later on.

Moreover, the research in this area indicates that it is not accurate to speak of conceptual thinking as a unitary process. First, it is possible to differentiate, as Aristotle did, between the form and the content of thinking. The form of thinking refers to its structure, that is, to the relationship of words and ideas to each other as reflected in such dimensions as logicality and communicability. The content of thinking refers to that which is to be communicated, its nature and complexity.

Second, it has become clear that there are different *levels* of conceptualizing, which means simply that the objects of the world can be grouped according to various principles. For example, a concept may refer to the fact that the objects included in it share some physical dimension (e.g., color, form, substance of which they are made), a functional relationship (can be used in a common task), or an abstract relationship (e.g., are not based on common physical or functional properties but belong in some general class of objects which share many common properties simultaneously, such as furniture, fruit, or animals). Level of abstraction therefore refers to the degree to which a concept remains close to (i.e., is defined by) concrete aspects of the phenomena involved, such as shape, substance, or use on the one hand, or to the degree to which the idea transcends concrete considerations on the other hand.

In turning next to the measurement of conceptual thinking, let it be agreed that the meaning of the term "concept formation" has to do with the process of thinking that enables a person to bring disparate stimuli together in some fashion.

THE MEASUREMENT OF CONCEPTUAL THINKING

As noted previously, the early work of psychology, exemplified by the research in Wundt's laboratory in Leipzig, dealt with psychophysiology and the laws of sensation. Gradually, however, the issues being explored broadened to include perception, memory (Ebbinghaus), and feeling (Kulpe). It was Kulpe, one of Wundt's students, who about 1900 decided that thinking was a legitimate area of study in psychology, and Titchener, another of Wundt's students, published in 1909 a book entitled *The Experimental Psychology of the Thought-Processes*. The work of Kulpe and his students at Wurzburg provided the basis for much of the dynamic research that followed on thinking and abstraction. Particularly important in this regard was Ach, one of Kulpe's students, who in the early 1920s developed the methodology later to be used in the assessment of concept formation by Gelb and Goldstein (about 1924), Lowenfeld (about 1929), and Vigotsky (about 1930). Ach's work also constituted the basis for some of the experimental work in gestalt psychology (see Zaslow, 1950). As in the case of intelligence, then, the study of thinking has its roots squarely in experimental psychology.

Also as in the case of intelligence tests, there are far more measures of concept formation than can be described or even listed within the confines of this chapter; Buros (1972) is again the best source for a comprehensive listing of such measures. Some of these measures explore concept formation through the presentation of verbal stimuli to the subject, and others through the presentation of perceptual stimuli. Inasmuch as the perceptual mode has been utilized more frequently and in a greater variety of ways than the verbal mode in these measures, the following discussion refers to three of the major perceptual tests in this area: the Lowenfeld Mosaic Test, the Vigotsky Test, and the Object Sorting Test.

The Lowenfeld Mosaic Test was developed by Margaret Lowenfeld in 1929 (see Lowenfeld, 1949). The materials for this test consist of 456 pieces of plastic which vary in shape (squares, diamonds, and triangles) and in color (white, black, red, yellow, blue, and green). The instructions to the subject are simply to make a design from these pieces, which he feels is "nice." Lowenfeld's original scoring of the subject's performance was based on the quality of the conceptual categories underlying his design, that is, the degree to which the design was organized or not, the complexity of the dimensions used, and the level of abstraction involved. Scoring methods more comprehensive and precise than those originally used by Lowenfeld were subsequently offered for her test by Wertham and Golden (1941) and Wideman (1955).

The Vigotsky Test (Vigotsky, 1934) consists of 22 wooden blocks of varying color, shape, height, and size, and each of these dimensions is represented by a nonsense syllable printed on the block. Like the Lowenfeld, the Vigotsky requires the subject to put the pieces of the test together in some way, and scoring is based in part on the kinds of conceptual categories he employs in doing so. Additionally on the Vigotsky, attention is paid to whether the subject can gain insight as to the meaning of the nonsense syllables on the blocks, which constitute in a sense the "hidden agenda" of the test.

With the exception of the challenge to the subject of recognizing the nonsense syllable representative of the geometric dimensions of the Vigotsky stimuli, the tests developed by Lowenfeld and Vigotsky are very similar. Both sets of test stimuli present the subject with geometric forms which, except for the dimension of color, may be grouped on the basis of a limited number of geometric dimensions. In other words, the concepts that can be formed in response to these two measures are limited by the physical dimensions that define the test stimuli.

A much broader range of possible concepts is sampled by the Object Sorting Test developed by Gelb and Goldstein (see Goldstein & Scheerer 1941; Rapaport et al., 1945, Chapter III). The Object Sorting Test comprises a variety of toy and real objects, including tools, eating utensils, playthings, smoking material, and food. The objects lend themselves to a wide variety of groupings, such as by substance (e.g., wood, metal, rubber) or by use (e.g., to play with, to eat with, to make things with). As such, the stimuli of the Object Sorting Test embrace virtually all the dimensions that can be involved in developing concepts—substance, color, shape, use, class, and any combination thereof.

The procedure in administering the Object Sorting Test is as follows. The subject is shown all the objects and told what they are. Then a stimulus object is drawn from the total sample (first by the subject himself, and then by the examiner), and the subject is asked to sort together all the objects in the total sample that he thinks are related in some way to the stimulus object. In a second phase of the administration the subject is shown a grouping of the objects, as already sorted by the examiner, and asked to determine the reason why the grouped objects might be considered to go together. Both the subject's sorting and his view of the examiner's sorting can be evaluated in terms of the breadth of the concepts he employs (number of items used), their level of abstraction (concrete, functional, abstract), and their quality of abstraction (degree of appropriateness and realisticness).

Perceptual tasks such as the Lowenfeld, Vigotsky, and Object Sorting Tests have the merit for assessment purposes of inviting the subject to present a concrete expression of his thinking right before the examiner's eyes. Of these three tests, the Object Sorting Test is particularly rich with respect to the variety and levels of concepts that can be produced in response to it and the breadth of dimensions of concept formation that can accordingly be tapped with it. Verbal measures of concept formation, which have included definition of words, identifying similarities and differences between the meaning of words, and interpretation of proverbs (e.g., Benjamin, 1951), as valid as they may be for assessing conceptual thinking, pale in comparison to the richness that can be derived from such perceptual measures as the Object Sorting Test.

THE UTILITY OF DATA FROM TESTS OF CONCEPTUAL THINKING

In parallel with the attempted applications of intelligence tests, measures of conceptual thinking have been frequently used to assess academic ability and clinical status. With regard to academic ability, it should be noted first that only fair success has been achieved in efforts to estimate level of intelligence from tests of concept formation. For example, judgments of intellectual functioning from performance on the Lowenfeld Mosaic Test have been found to correlate with measured IQ between .13 and .73 in some cases (Woolf & Gerson, 1953) and about the .40's in other cases (Robertson, 1957). Working with the Object Sorting Test, Silverstein (1960) found correlations with IQ of .40 for abstract definitions and $-.38$ for concrete definitions. As might be expected, then, neither these measures nor verbal measures of concept formation have been found to have a significant relationship to academic potential or achievement (Ames, 1963; Bernreuter & Goodman, 1941; Ellison & Edgerton, 1941; Goodman, 1944; Michael et al., 1964; Mukherjee, 1965; Yum, 1941).

The possible clinical significance of individual differences in thinking has been discussed with particular clarity by Rapaport (Rapaport, Menninger, & Schafer, 1946). Drawing on earlier contributions by several distinguished psychiatrists on the nature of thought disorder (Bleuler, in 1911: 1950; Bychowski, 1935; Kraepelin, 1902; Meyer, 1906; Sullivan, 1925; White, 1926), and on the then emerging ideas of psychoanalytic ego psychology, Rapaport assigned the highest level of priority in psychiatry to the study of thinking: "The mediating processes through which personality structure or dynamics express themselves in symptoms or behavior are thought processes. . . . When we study a patient, whether we interview or test him, we are dealing with the products of his thought processes" (Rapaport, 1967d, p. 432). In this same vein, Rapaport argued that the intensive, extensive, and relatively objective study of thinking was the unique contribution the clinical psychologists could make to the diagnostic process (Rapaport et al., 1945).

Two other statements by Rapaport reflecting his view of psychodiagnostic testing are relevant to note. In 1947 he wrote:

> What we see most immediately reflected in all our tests is the thought organization of the subjects. Whatever else we infer from the tests is read from the peculiarities of the subject's thought organization indicating his type of control of impulses or the encroachment of impulses on this thought organization. Thus, a theory of psychological testing implies a fundamental theory of thought organization [Rapaport, 1967b, p. 265]

And in 1950 he commented, "The essentials of the theory of psychodiagnostic testing rest upon the rationale of the process underlying test performance, that is, broadly speaking, upon the general theory of thought processes" (Rapaport, 1967c, p. 345).

Rapaport (1967c) takes pains to differentiate the form or structure of thinking from its content, and clinical observations seem consistently to have supported his expectations that differences in personality are reflected in differential structuring of the thought process. In particular, different clinical groups have been found to evince characteristic qualities of thinking, including the ruminative intellectualizing of the obsessive, the blandness of the hysteric, the ideational lethargy of the depressive, the autism of the schizophrenic, and the concreteness of the cerebrally impaired.

It has been an especially common clinical finding that schizophrenic and cerebrally impaired persons, as compared to patients in other diagnostic categories, have some degree of difficulty in forming abstract concepts. Because both groups share this impairment in abstract thinking, it was suggested many years ago that schizophrenic individuals suffer from some sort of brain dysfunction, and much research was done in the 1930s to examine this hypothesis (e.g., Bolles, 1937; Bolles & Goldstein, 1938; Bolles, Rosen, & Landis, 1938; Cameron, 1938a, 1938b, 1939a, 1939b; Goldstein, 1939; Hanfmann, 1939; Kasanin & Hanfmann, 1938a, 1938b, 1939). These studies demonstrated that, although on clinical examination schizophrenic and cerebrally impaired subjects appear to share difficulties in abstract thinking, more refined assessment of thought processes through psychological tests can identify differences in the nature of the abstracting difficulties they experience.

Helpful in understanding this difference has been the later delineation by McGaughran (1954) of two dimensions of conceptual thinking, the level of abstraction (whether concrete or abstract) and the quality of communicability (whether a thought is understandable and communicative, hence public, or whether it is autistic and noncommunicative, hence private). On close examination the thinking of the cerebrally impaired individual tends to be concrete and public; that is, it is of a low level of abstraction but understandable by most people. The thinking of the schizophrenic individual, however, tends to be either concrete or abstract but to be private; that is, the conceptualization (level and/or content) does not communicate effectively to others.

Rapaport et al. (1945) observe further in this regard that the thinking of the schizophrenic can be based either on a concrete idea, in which case it can be labeled *concretistic,* or an abstract idea, in which case it is referred to as *syncretistic.* A concretistic idea is a concept based on some physical or functional aspect of the phenomenon, but with a strange, or autistic, twist: "Things are considered as belonging together because of nonessentials, concrete features possessed by them (e.g., an orange and a banana are similar because both have peels)" (Reichard & Rapaport, 1943, p. 103). A syncretistic idea is a concept whose base is an idea that is not just abstract, but overly abstract, or what Cameron (1939a) refers to as *over-inclusive;* it includes so many phenomena in the world that it does not make any real differentiation (e.g., they are all made by man).

The reason for elaborating this particular area of investigation is that, unfortunately, much of the research on the clinical use of data from tests of concept formation over the past 40 years has focused almost exclusively on illuminating the nature of the thought processes in schizophrenic or cerebrally impaired individuals. Illustrative research in this regard is reported for verbal measures of concept formation by Benjamin (1951), Cameron (1938a, 1938b), Feifel (1949), Hunt et al. (1960), Moran (1953), and Moran et al. (1954); for the Vigotsky by Vigotsky (1934), Cameron (1939a), and Kasanin and Hanfmann (1938a, 1939b); for the Lowenfeld Mosaic Test by Maher and Martin (1954); and for the Object Sorting Test by Bolles and Goldstein (1938), Bolles et al. (1938), Goldstein (1939), Goldstein and Scheerer (1941), Hanfmann (1939), Lovibond (1954), McGaughran and Moran (1956, 1957), Morikawa (1969), and Payne et al. (1959).

In limited instances clinical applications of measures of concept formation have been explored from a broader perspective than is represented by the focus simply on schizophrenia or cerebral impairment. Noteworthy in this regard are broadly based studies of concept formation by Gardner et al. (1960), Gollin and Rosenberg (1956), and Sigel et al. (1967), and work with the Lowenfeld Mosaic by Diamond and Schmale (1944), Kerr (1939), Reiman (1950), and Rioch (1954). With the Mosaic in particular, efforts have been made to develop norms for the performance of children (Ames, 1964; Ames & Ilg, 1962; Ames, Ilg, & August, 1964) and to explore the functioning of neurotics (Colm, 1948; Himmelweit & Eysenck, 1944–1946) and mental defectives (McCulloch & Girdner, 1949; Shotwell & Lawrence, 1951).

By and large, however, it is clear that much more research is necessary on relating concept formation to personality in general and to more specific categories of psychological disturbance, such as the distinctions between paranoid and nonparanoid schizophrenia, process and reactive forms of disturbance, and the many varieties of neurosis (see Payne, 1961). Although having almost as long a history of clinical and research investigation, the study of conceptual thinking seems to lack the scientific drama found in the study of intelligence. This state of affairs is probably due to the fact that the study of conceptual thinking has not produced a test from which one can derive a number or some evaluative measurement presumably useful in a great variety of practical situations. As an important case in point, the clinician interested in developing new skills or sharpening existing skills in the assessment of intellectual functioning can turn to such recent major publications as Matarazzo's (1972) fifth edition of Wechsler's *Measurement and Appraisal of Adult Intelligence,* Zimmerman & Woo-Sam's (1973) *Clinical Interpretation of the Wechsler Adult Intelligence Scale* and Sattler's (1974) *Assessment of Children's Intelligence;* except for Rapaport et al. (1945), there are no comparable comprehensive texts from which one can learn clinical procedures for the assessment of conceptual thinking.

It is probably also relevant that the study of conceptual thinking has not generated the kinds of sweeping controversy associated with the nature and measurement of intelligence. Consider, for example, current issues concerning whether intelligence is inherited and, if so, to what extent; whether intelligence can be augmented or raised by various kinds of life experiences; and whether the intellectually well-endowed are superior to the less well endowed and should "rule" or receive other special considerations. No such compelling issues surround and invigorate the study of conceptual thinking.

UNRESOLVED ISSUES

This concluding section summarizes some of the important ideas, findings, and unresolved issues relating first to the testing of intelligence and then to the testing of conceptual thinking.

The Testing of Intelligence

It is above all apparent with regard to intelligence testing that a major resolved issue is the definition of the term "intelligence." As noted earlier, the conceptual contortions in which psychologists have engaged in attempts to define the term meaningfully or operationally have yet to yield an adequate definition. For the time being, it seems best to satisfy any needs for defining intelligence with the dictionary definition, namely, that it comprises the capacity to understand, so long as it is also recognized that this capacity has many dimensions, involves many psychological processes, and is influenced by many factors.

For example, it must be recognized that intelligence has many components, as defined by Thurstone's primary mental abilities, and that an individual may approach the attempt to understand either deductively or inductively. It must be recognized that the capacity to think intelligently involves such processes as memory, attention, judgment, and reasoning, and that it is influenced by mood, general personality integration, attitude, and motivational factors.

It must be recognized that a person's facility with language and prior learning significantly affect efforts to measure his intelligence via verbal tasks, and that the outcome of efforts to measure intelligence through nonverbal or performance tasks is significantly determined by speed and dexterity of motor coordination. Moreover, recognizing that verbal tests of intelligence are at least in part a function of scholastic learning and facility with language implies that they are also a function of socioeconomic level and cultural learning and stimulation (see Bayley & Schafer, 1960, 1964; Beckwith, 1971a, 1971b; Bee et al., 1969; Bosco, 1972; Ermalinski & Ruscelli, 1971; Golden & Birns, 1968; Golden et al., 1971; Jones, 1972; Kamii & Radin, 1967; Lewin & Goldberg, 1969; Moss, 1967; Moss et al., 1969; Pavenstadt, 1965; Radin, 1972; Rubinstein, 1967; Tulkin & Kagan, 1972).

As one extension of these issues, it is necessary for the clinician to struggle with the fact that performance on many tests of intelligence is a function of speed of response as well as quality of response. Because portions of many of these tests are timed, they are not *power* tests, that is, tests measuring *how much* a person can do, but *speed* tests, measuring *how fast* he can do it. Does intelligence imply rapidity of comprehension, as Thorndike (1925) and Freeman (1928) considered? Perhaps. But sometimes speed of response can be a function of need for achievement, and at other times it can certainly relate to other motivational variables that have little or no bearing on intelligence.

And what of the brief test of intelligence? A brief test is obviously economical in terms of time, particularly if what is being sought is an overall score such as an IQ or a mental age. If no more than this is needed, testing could be limited to the two tasks that seem to correlate most highly with overall IQ, Vocabulary and Block Design, one a verbal measure and the other nonverbal.

Economy aside, how informative *is* an overall measure of intellectual functioning, whether a mental age or an IQ? With respect to the mental age score, as derived from the Binet, it was assmed that an individual's measured performance would or would not be commensurate with the average intellectual functioning of people at a particular level of psychological development. As noted early, that assumption was undone by accumulating evidence that the Binet does not sample the same psychological processes at each mental age, that those it does sample are not sampled equally, and that the composition of intelligence, that is, the hierarchical organization and configuration of processes considered to constitute intelligence, differs from one age level to the next.

It is therefore not surprising that predictions of subsequent intelligence from test scores at an earlier age have not been particularly successful, except with regard to gross differentiations (Anderson, 1939; Escalona & Moriarity, 1961; Wooley, 1925). Furthermore, because different kinds of cognitive skills are required for successful academic performance at different grade levels, prediction of subsequent academic performance from overall mental age scores has been particularly difficult (Duffy et al., 1972). An additional problem with the mental age concept in general has been that the curve of its development flattens out somewhere between the ages 14 and 17. Hence, taken literally, any mental age data do not seem to be meaningful beyond this chronological age range; the normal adult is assumed by such data to have mental age between 14 and 17.

The Wechsler makes no assumptions about mental age level, hence does not suffer limitations related to the meaning of this concept. But how much sense does it make to say, as one does with the Wechsler test, that intelligence is the sum of different psychological processes and that an individual's level of intelligence equals the sum of his or her performance on 11 subtests each presumably measuring a different function? Even if it is granted that all the subtests are loaded with g, available data indicate that they are loaded unevenly and unequally with g and that they correlate differently with Full Scale IQ (Wechsler, 1958). Since the overall score on both the Binet and Wechsler tests is derived from summing scores from different subtests, one wonders what such arbitrary summing means. Is it a matter of adding apples and oranges to arrive at pieces of fruit, or is it a less justifiable and more arbitrary combination of disparate events that should be kept separate?

These concerns invoke again the question of just how much information an overall measure of intelligence conveys. It is clear that any overall measure, whether an IQ or a mental age score, can be composed of performance on a wide variety of tasks. This means that the same resulting IQ or mental age figure can mean something entirely different where, for example, the figure is derived from the performance of an individual with a narrow range of ability (i.e., one whose scores on the subtests hover closely around a given central tendency), or where the summation masks a wide distribution of subtest scores. What sense, then, does it make to compare the IQs of two individuals, even if both are the same number? The nonspecific informational value of summated overall mental age and IQ scores was noted many years ago by Mateer (1918) and Thorndike (1925), among others; unfortunately, their insights have little modified the behavior of psychologists in having recourse to such overall measures.

To reconfront the issue of what use can be made of the data from tests of intelligence, it is necessary to keep in mind the evidence that, from the earliest work of Binet, overall measures of intellectual functioning seem to have had little relationship to academic performance. The early psychologists recognized that scores predict best for those "target" situations in which the functions being tapped are identical or similar to those involved in the predictor tasks from which the scores are derived (see Thorndike et al., 1921). The farther away the data in a test are from the situation to which prediction is being attempted, the poorer the prediction. This important consideration in psychological assessment is elaborated by Goldfried in Chapter 5 of this book (see pp. 295–301). In the present context it implies that overall measures of intelligence, since they do not correlate highly with performance on academic tasks, are not closely enough related to them in terms of the functions tapped to be used to assess scholastic potential or in academic evaluations. Rather, it seems more meaningful and potentially helpful to use measures of academic ability and scholastic achievement to assess and predict academic performance.

Similarly conservative conclusions must be drawn with regard to the use of data from tests of intelligence in clinical evaluation. As noted in the earlier discussion of research in this area, neither the Binet nor the Wechsler has fared well in the assessment of psychopathology. First, Kraepelin's notion that a unique configuration of psychological processes characterizes each separate psychiatric state has not been confirmed (see Frank, 1975). Accordingly, it is no surprise that the elaborate speculations of Wechsler and Rapaport concerning expected subtest patterning on the Wechsler for each psychiatric category have not been validated by the research.

Second, it now appears to have been psychologically naive to assume that even if personality factors, normal or abnormal, do influence performance on tests of intelligence, that these factors will be the only ones that influence the test results. The research mentioned earlier on the Wechsler, for example, demonstrates that a subject's age, sex, education, socioeconomic status, and level of intelligence affect performance, as does the subject's attitude toward being tested and the examiner's attitude toward the subject.

Third, the efforts to use patterns of subtest performance in clinical evaluation have been compromised by several previously noted psychometric considerations bearing on the nature and interrelationships of the subtests. These include the facts that all the subtests do not measure overall intelligence (i.e., correlate with Full Scale IQ) equally, they do not correlate equally with each other, and they are not composed of items arranged in hierarchic difficulty (hence have inherent sources of scatter). Since intertest and intratest scatter have thus proved to be at least partly a function of many nonintellectual, nonpersonality, and test factors, the expectation that there would be an isomorphic relationship between personality on the one hand and pattern and scatter of intelligence test performance on the other has turned out to be ill-founded.

The question remains, then, what use *can* be made of the data from tests of intelligence. Surely the day of what Thurstone (1921) referred to as the omnibus test of intelligence should be over. Such measures attempt to do too much without accomplishing their task well, as is evident from the less than modest relationships the mental age and IQ scores they yield have with scholastic and personality variables. Of what value is it to know a person's performance on an intelligence test, that is, to have a mental age or IQ, if that datum does not say much more about the individual than what score he achieved on the test? The point has already been made that, to achieve desirable similarity between the predictor variable and the target situation, scholastic tests should be used for scholastic prediction and personality tests in the assessment of personality (see also Thornton, 1941; Coleman & Cureton, 1954). Where some assessment of intelligence *is* needed, as in estimating the presence of mental retardation, it should be obtained as efficiently as possible, which can be done with the use of Vocabulary and Block Design alone.

Hence I recommend that psychologists not waste time administering in their entirety such omnibus tests as the Binet and the Wechsler. There are more efficient ways of estimating intelligence, and there are much better ways of predicting academic performance and of assessing normal and abnormal personality functioning. However, this is not to say that some of the specific ways in which parts of these intelligence tests sample aspects of the thinking process cannot be adapted for purposes of examining personality style. Yet these possibilities lead away from traditional and widely used intelligence tests such as the Binet and the Wechsler and toward more specifically tailored measures of concept formation and cognitive style.

The Testing of Conceptual Thinking

The material reviewed in this chapter has identified two potentially useful perceptual measures of conceptual thinking, the Lowenfeld Mosaic test and the Object Sorting Test. Both of these measures explore concept formation with stimuli that present the subject with a variety of dimensions, and in my clinical work I have been particularly impressed with the meaningful way in which conceptual level can be assessed with the Object Sorting Test and the clarity and vividness with which it reflects the thinking process. Perhaps the additional dimension of the geometric forms provided by the Lowenfeld Mosaic Test is yet to be fully appreciated. It may be in this regard that combination of the relatively meaningful stimuli of the Object Sorting Test with the relatively nonmeaningful stimuli of the Lowenfeld Mosaic Test, into some kind of integrated measure, would permit an especially fruitful exploration of conceptualization.

Verbal measures of concept formation still lack the systematic design and research base of the more prominent perceptual measures. Similarities and proverbs tasks, for example, could benefit from the development of more intensive and extensive modes of scoring to parallel what has been done with the Object Sorting Test. Efforts in this direction seem to be worthwhile. Although traditional psychiatric categories have not been found to embody unique configurations of psychological processes, different personality types *do* appear to be characterized by different and somewhat unique modes of thinking. With a focus on modes of thinking, then, rather than on psychological processes more broadly defined, clinical psychologists might profit considerably from improving their capacity to assess thinking through both verbal and perceptual measures. With this goal in mind, it is also possible to increase the utility of such tests as the Wechsler through refined application of some of its subtests. Relevant in this regard are qualitative analyses of verbalizations on some of the Wechsler subtests initiated by Feifel (1949), Moran (1953), Moran et al. (1954), Hunt and Arnhoff (1955), and Hunt, Walker, and Jones (1960).

Thus, despite the somewhat pessimistic tone of this chapter and the somewhat dated quality of much of the available research, tests of thinking and concept formation may yet be an area in which clinical investigators can profitably invest their time and energy. To me the most exciting development in psychology is the current emphasis on the brain as a complex data processing structure, with one of the most important facets of understanding and predicting behavior being knowledge of how the individual makes meaning out of the world. This approach views the way in which people process information as the most meaningful dimension of the human condition to explore (e.g., Fulkerson, 1965; Hunt, 1961; Lindsay & Norman, 1972). The study of thinking is thus placed in the forefront of psychological research, and it becomes increasingly meaningful to speak of *intellectual style* (see Sigel, 1963; Stern, 1914); of *perceptual style,* as has been investigated for example with respect to field dependence-independence (Witkin et al. 1954, 1962), leveling and sharpening (Holzman & Klein, 1954), and expansive and restrictive style (Miller & Kemp, 1962); of *conceptual style,* as discussed by Hanfmann (1941), Sigel et al. (1967) and Wallach and Kogan (1965) and explored for such dimensions as narrow and broad conceptualization (Rokeach, 1951) and repression-sensitization (Byrne, 1961); and *cognitive style* (see Gardner, 1953; Gardner et al., 1959; Rapaport, 1967e; Kagan & Kogan, 1970).

CONCLUSIONS

The facts and ideas considered in this chapter point to the following conclusions:

1. Whatever our tests of intelligence are measuring, we do not have a concept to describe the phenomenon adequately or to everyone's satisfaction.

2. Whatever we are measuring with our tests of general or overall intelligence does not seem to have a significant relationship to performance in certain situations in which a significant relationship might be expected, as

in school, and we have consequently been asking our tests to perform a function for which they are ill-suited.

3. Rather than continue to invoke a specific construct for which there seems to be no satisfactory definition, namely, intelligence, we should concentrate our attention on the cognitive processes involved in what we may generally refer to as intelligence or intelligent behavior.

4. The processes to which we *are* referring when we attempt to describe a person as intelligent are the ways in which that individual makes meaning out of his world or, in other words, the ways in which he processes data.

5. What has customarily been construed as level of intelligence refers to the amount of data an individual is capable of processing at any given moment and over the course of his life; to the complexity of the data he can process; and to the degree of relatedness of these data, along the concrete-abstract dimension, to the actual phenomena they represent.

6. The quality of the data processing of which an individual is capable accounts for his ability to comprehend relationships among various items of data, and his degree of comprehension comprises both breadth (the number of different kinds of stimuli he is capable of processing) and depth (the number of stimuli in a class that can be subsumed under the concepts he forms).

7. The quality of an individual's data processing capabilities is in turn an important dimension of a person which can help us understand his capacity to form concepts; to see relationships among ideas, objects, and events; and to use data processing to learn from his experience and modify his behavior adaptively.

8. The manner of an individual's data processing, that is, the amount, complexity, and kind of data he can process with ease, might better be described as cognitive style rather than level of intelligence.

9. As a by-product of replacing what has customarily been referred to as intelligence with the concept of data processing, the same construct can be utilized to explain both how an individual makes meaning out the world and how he makes meaning out of the data that represent his own person, that is, the self-concept. In this way the data processing formulation provides a conceptual bridge between aspects of intelligence and personality, which has important implications for future lines of theory and research.

Having elaborated the current state of affairs and derived recommendations for translating the assessment of intelligence and conceptual thinking into both more general and more precise concern with cognitive functioning and cognitive style, we must acknowledge that the effort brings us back to a phase of development of ideas in psychology of about 30 years ago. This orientation was referred to by Heidbreder (1945) as a dynamic theory of cognition and has roots going back at least to the seminal writings of Kurt Lewin (1935). Also noteworthy are two decades of research exploring the relationship of personality and cognition, which culminated in major compendia on this topic by Bruner and Krech (1949) and Blake and Ramsey (1951). The following brief excerpts from Rapaport and Scheerer, two of the most able exponents of these earlier efforts toward a dynamic theory of cognition, summarize this approach:

> . . . A theory of cognition that is broad enough to have clinical relevance must account (a) for man's ways of gaining information about his environment as well as about his needs and other motivations; and (b) for man's ways of organizing the information he has obtained so that it will serve him in controlling and/or fulfilling his needs, and in coping with the environment [Rapaport, 1967e, p. 632]

> . . . Every performance is the expression of the organism's activity as a whole, and not a segmental response to a specific stimulus . . . in a given situation, the entire organism deals with that situation by structuring it in terms of a definite figure-ground pattern and activity with reference to that pattern . . . not only the thought processes should bear the stamp of the person's organizational matrix, but perception, feelings, and motor-acts as well. On second thought, these apparently different processes may actually be one unitary performance in which not true separation exists, but, instead, one definite pattern, in which emoting, thinking, and perceiving articulate in a configurational dynamic relation to each other [Scheerer, 1946, pp. 653–655]

> . . . Cognitive theory can conceptualize personality functioning as a total activity that always encompasses emoting, thinking, and perceiving, which are distinguishable but not separable part-processes in a functioning whole. . . . When applied to personality functioning, this orientation would result in an analysis of behavior in which so-called "motivational factors" will be found to be, more often than not, embedded in and determined by the cognitive matrix [Scheerer, 1953, p. 5]

This chapter began by struggling with the ideas of intelligence and concept formation, their individual meaning, and their measurement; it ends by seeing these two phenomena as but two facets of the more basic psychological process of thinking. Echoing Rapaport (1967b), one can suggest that what the psychologist assesses with all his tests is the thinking of a person and its vicissitudes. Proceeding on such an assumption, psychologists could not only learn to approach their tests as opportunities to sample this important aspect of a person, but could also be encouraged to develop tests that assess aspects of cognition more comprehensively and effectively than is possible with available instruments.

The conclusion that future progress in the assessment of intelligence and conceptual thinking lies in returning to ideas developed 30 years ago should not be interpreted as reactionary or iconoclastic. Reviewing the premises and methods in this area of assessment has convinced me that hypotheses and tests alike have been largely ill-formed. As has been the case in other areas of clinical psychology, there has been a tendency in intellectual and conceptual assessment to formulate epistemologically limited hypotheses and then, equipped with notions that frequently have no more than face validity, to dash off into the applied realm. Although imposing in bulk, much of the work on intelligence and conceptual thinking appears in retrospect to have been guided by premature convictions. We have consequently deluded ourselves in this area into believing that we knew what had to be known while, from a psychological and psychometric point of view, it seems that we did not. The return to 30 years ago, then, to nascent formulations of a dynamic theory of cognition, means that we need to think through again the techniques and purposes of assessing conceptual processes and perhaps go off into directions other than the ones we have been pursuing.

REFERENCES

Adams, W. M. Prediction of scholastic success in colleges of law: II. An investigation of pre-law grades and other indices of law school aptitude. *Educational and Psychological Measurement,* 1944, **4,** 13–20.

Alexander, W. P. Intelligence, concrete and abstract: A study in differential traits. *British Journal of Psychology,* 1935 (Monogr. Suppl. 19).

Allen, M. M. Relationship between Kuhlmann-Anderson Intelligence Tests in grade 1 and academic achievement in grades 3 and 4. *Educational and Psychological Measurement,* 1944, **4,** 161–168.

Ames, L. B. Usefulness of the Lowenfeld Mosaic Test in predicting school readiness in kindergarten and primary school pupils. *Journal of Genetic Psychology,* 1963, **103,** 75–91.

Ames, L. B. Age changes in children's Mosaic responses from five to ten years. *Genetic Psychology Monographs,* 1964, **69,** 195–245.

Ames, L. B., & Ilg, F. L. *Mosaic patterns of American children.* New York: Hoeber-Harper, 1962.

Ames, L. B., & Walker, R. N. Prediction of later reading ability from kindergarten Rorschach and IQ scores. *Journal of Educational Psychology,* 1964, **55,** 309–313.

Ames, L. B., Ilg, F. L., & August, J. The Lowenfeld Mosaic Test: Norms for five-to-ten-year-old American public school children and comparative study of three groups. *Genetic Psychology Monographs,* 1964, **70,** 57–95.

Ames, V. Factors related to high-school achievement. *Journal of Educational Psychology,* 1943, **34,** 229–236.

Anderson, E. A., Anderson, S. F., Ferguson, C., Gray, J., Hittinger, J., McKinstry, E., Motter, M. E., & Vick, G. Wilson College Studies in Psychology: I. A comparison of the Wechsler-Bellevue, revised Stanford-

Binet, and American Council on Education Tests at the college level. *Journal of Psychology*, 1942, **14**, 317–326.

Anderson, L. D. The predictive value of infancy tests in relation to intelligence at 5 years. *Child Development*, 1939, **10**, 203–212.

Arthur, G. *A point scale of performance tests*. New York: Commonwealth Fund, 1933.

Asch, S. E. A study of change in mental organization. *Archives of Psychology*, 1936, No. 195.

Atkins, H. A., Thorndike, E. L., & Hubbell, E. A. Correlations among perceptive and associative processes. *Psychological Review*, 1902, **9**, 374–382.

Ayres, L. P. The Binet-Simon measuring scale for intelligence: Some criticisms and suggestions. *Psychological Clinic*, 1911, **5**, 187–196.

Babcock, H. An experiment in the measurement of mental deterioration. *Archives of Psychology*, 1930, **18**, No. 117.

Balinsky, B. An analysis of the mental factors of various age groups from nine to sixty. *Genetic Psychology Monographs*, 1941, **23**, 191–234.

Ball, R. S. The predictability of occupational level from intelligence. *Journal of Psychology*, 1938, **2**, 184–186.

Banks, C. Factor analysis of assessment for army recruits. *British Journal of Psychology, Statistical Section*, 1949, **2**, 76–89.

Barclay, A., & Carolan, P. A comparative study of the Wechsler Intelligence Scale for Children and the Stanford-Binet Intelligence Scale, Form L-M. *Journal of Consulting Psychology*, 1966, **30**, 563.

Barton, K., Dielman, T. E., & Cattell, R. B. Personality and IQ measures as predictors of school achievement. *Journal of Educational Psychology*, 1972, **63**, 398–404.

Bayley, N. Mental growth during the first three years: A developmental study of sixty-one children by repeated tests. *Genetic Psychology Monographs*, 1933, **14**(1).

Bayley, N. On the growth of intelligence. *American Psychologist*, 1955, **10**, 805–818.

Bayley, N., & Schaefer, E. S. Relationships between socio-economic variables and the behavior of mothers toward young children. *Journal of Genetic Psychology*, 1960, **96**, 61–77.

Bayley, N., & Schaefer, E. S. Correlation of maternal and child behavior with the development of mental abilities: Data from the Berkeley Growth Study. *Monographs of the Society for Research in Child Development*, 1964, **29**(6), No. 97.

Beckwith, L. Relationship between attributes of mothers and their infants' IQ scores. *Child Development*, 1971, **42**, 1083–1097. (a)

Beckwith, L. Relationships between infants' vocalizations and their mothers' behaviors. *Merrill-Palmer Quarterly of Behavior and Development*, 1971, **17**, 211–226. (b)

Bee, H. L., Van Egeren, P. F., Streissguth, A. P., Nyman, B. A., & Leckie, M. S. Social class differences in maternal teaching strategies and speech patterns. *Child Development*, 1969, **1**, 726–734.

Benjamin, J. D. A method for distinguishing and evaluating formal thinking disorders in schizophrenia. In J. Kasanin (Ed.), *Language and thought in schizophrenia.* Berkeley: University of California Press, 1944. Pp. 65–90.

Berger, L., Bernstein, A., Klein, E., Cohen, J., & Lucas, G. Effects of aging and pathology on the factorial structure of intelligence. *Journal of Consulting Psychology*, 1964, **28**, 199–207.

Bernstein, E. Quickness and intelligence: An enquiry concerning the existence of a general speed factor. *British Journal of Psychology*, 1924 (Monogr. Suppl. 7).

Bernreuter, R. G., & Goodman, C. H. A study of the Thurstone Primary Mental Abilities Tests applied to freshmen engineering students. *Journal of Educational Psychology*, 1941, **32**, 55–60.

Bersoff, D. N. Short forms of individual intelligence tests for children: Review and critique. *Journal of School Psychology*, 1971, **9**, 310–320.

Binet, A. A propos la mesure de l'intelligence. *L'Annee Psychologique*, 1905, **11**, 69–82.

Binet, A., & Henri, V. La psychologie indiviuelle. *L'Annee Psychologique*, 1895, **2**, 411–465.

Binet, A., & Simon, T. Methodes nouvelles pour le diagnostic du niveau intellectual des anormaux. *L'Annee Psychologique*, 1905, **11**, 193–244.

Binet, A., & Simon, T. Le development de l'intelligence chez les enfants. *L'Annee Psychologique*, 1908, **14**, 1–94.

Binet, A., & Simon, T. *The development of intelligence in children.* Baltimore: Williams & Wilkins, 1916.

Birren, J. E. A factorial analysis of the Wechsler Bellevue Scale given to an elderly population. *Journal of Consulting Psychology*, 1952, **16**, 399–405.

Blake, R. R., & Ramsey, G. V. (Eds.) *Perception—An approach to personality.* New York: Ronald Press, 1951.

Blakey, R. A re-analysis of a test of the theory of two factors. *Psychometrika*, 1940, **5**, 121–136.

Blakey, R. A factor analysis of a non-verbal reasoning test. *Educational and Psychological Measurement*, 1941, **1**, 187–198.

Bleuler, E. *Dementia praecox or the group of schizophrenias.* New York: International Universities Press, 1950.

Bolles, M. M. The basis of pertinence: A study of the test performance of aments, dements and normal children of the same mental age. *Archives of Psychology*, 1937, No. 212.

Bolles, M., & Goldstein, K. A study of the impairment of "abstract behavior" in schizophrenic patients. *Psychiatric Quarterly*, 1938, **12**, 42–65.

Bolles, M. M., Rosen, G. P., & Landis, C. Psychological performance tests as prognostic agents for the efficacy of insulin therapy in schizophrenia. *Psychiatric Quarterly*, 1938, **12**, 733–737.

Bosco, J. The visual information processing speed of lower- and middle-class children. *Child Development*, 1972, **43**, 1418–1422.

Bouchard, T. J. Current conceptions of intelligence and their implications for assessment. In P. McReynolds (Ed.), *Advances in psychological assessment*. Vol. I. Palo Alto, Calif.: Science and Behavior Books, 1968. Pp. 14–33.

Bridges, J. W. The value of intelligence test in universities. *School and Society*, 1922, **15**, 295–303.

Brown, W. M. Character traits as factors in intelligence test performance. *Archives of Psychology*, 1923, No. 65.

Brown, W. M. A study of the caution factor and its importance in intelligence test performance. *American Journal of Psychology*, 1924, **35**, 368–386.

Brown, W. The mathematical and experimental evidence for the existence of a central intellective factor. *British Journal of Psychology*, 1932, **23**, 171–179.

Brown, W., & Stephenson, W. A test of the theory of two factors. *British Journal of Psychology*, 1933, **23**, 352–370.

Bruner, J. S. The course of cognitive growth. *American Psychologist*, 1964, **19**, 1–15.

Bruner, J. S., & Krech, D. (Eds.) *Perception and personality*. Durham, N.C.: Duke University Press, 1949.

Bruner, J. S., Olver, R. R., & Greenfield, P. M. *Studies in cognitive growth*. New York: John Wiley & Sons, 1956.

Burks, B. S. When does a test measure the same function at all levels? *Journal of Educational Psychology*, 1930, **21**, 616–620.

Buros, O. K. (Ed.) *The seventh mental measurements yearbook*. Highland Park, N.J.: Gryphon Press, 1972.

Burt, C. Experimental tests of higher mental processes and their relation to general intelligence. *Journal of Experimental Pedagogy*, 1911, **1**, 93–112.

Burt, C. The differentiation of intellectual ability. *British Journal of Educational Psychology*, 1954, **24**, 76–90.

Burt, C. The evidence for the concept of intelligence. *British Journal of Educational Psychology*, 1955, **25**, 158–177.

Burt, C. Inheritance of general intelligence. *American Psychologist*, 1972, **27**, 175–190.

Burt, C., & John, E. A factorial analysis of Terman Binet tests. *British Journal of Educational Psychology*, 1942, **12**, 117–127, 156–161.

Butsch, R. L. C. Improving the prediction of academic success through differential weighting. *Journal of Educational Psychology*, 1939, **30**, 401–420.

Bychowski, G. Certain problems of schizophrenia in the light of cerebral pathology. *Journal of Nervous and Mental Disease*, 1935, **81**, 280–298.

Byrne, D. The Repression-Sensitization Scale; Rationale, reliability and validity. *Journal of Personality*, 1961, **29**, 334–349.

Cameron, N. Reasoning, regression and communication in schizophrenics. *Psychological Monographs*, 1938, **50**(221). (a)

Cameron, N. A study of thinking in senile deterioration and schizophrenic disorganization. *American Journal of Psychology*, 1938, **51**, 650–664. (b)

Cameron, N. Deterioration and regression in schizophrenic thinking. *Journal of Abnormal Psychology*, 1939, **34**, 265–270. (a)

Cameron, N. Schizophrenic thinking in a problem-solving situation. *Journal of Mental Science*, 1939, **85**, 1012–1035. (b)

Carroll, J. B. A factor analysis of verbal abilities. *Psychometrika*, 1941, **6**, 279–307.

Cattell, J. McK. Mental tests and measurements. *Mind*, 1890, **15**, 373–380.

Cattell, R. B. The subjective character of cognition and the pre-sensational development of perception. *British Journal of Psychology*, 1930 (Monogr. Suppl. 14).

Cattell, R. B. Measurement versus intuition in applied psychology. *Character and Personality*, 1937, **6**, 114–131.

Cattell, R. B. The measurement of adult intelligence. *Psychological Bulletin*, 1943, **40**, 153–193.

Cattell, R. B. Theory of fluid and crystallized intelligence: A critical experiment. *Journal of Educational Psychology*, 1963, **54**, 1–22.

Chappell, T. L. Note on the validity of the Army General Classification Test as a predictor of academic achievement. *Journal of Educational Psychology*, 1955, **46**, 53–55.

Chein, I. On the nature of intelligence. *Journal of General Psychology*, 1945, **32**, 111–126.

Cicirelli, V. G. Form of the relationship between creativity, IQ, and academic achievement. *Journal of Educational Psychology*, 1965, **56**, 303–308.

Cobb, J. A. Relationship of discrete classroom behaviors to fourth-grade academic achievement. *Journal of Educational Psychology*, 1972, **63**, 74–80.

Cohen, J. A factor-analytically based rationale for the Wechsler-Bellevue. *Journal of Consulting Psychology*, 1952, **16**, 272–277. (a)

Cohen, J. Factors underlying Wechsler-Bellevue performance of three neuropsychiatric groups. *Journal of Abnormal and Social Psychology*, 1952, **47**, 359–365. (b)

Cohen, J. A factor-analytically based rationale for the Wechsler Adult Intelligence Scale. *Journal of Consulting Psychology*, 1957, **21**, 451–457. (a)

Cohen, J. The factorial structure of the WAIS between early adulthood and old age. *Journal of Consulting Psychology*, 1957, **21**, 283–290. (b)

Cohen, J. The factorial structure of the WISC at ages 7-6, 10-6, and 13-6. *Journal of Consulting Psychology*, 1959, **23**, 285–299.

Colby, M. G., & Robertson, J. B. Genetic studies in abstraction. *Journal of Comparative Psychology*, 1942, **33**, 385–401.

Coleman, W., & Cureton, E. E. Intelligence and achievement: The "jangle fallacy" again. *Educational and Psychological Measurement*, 1954, **14**, 347–351.

Colm, H. The value of projective methods in the psychological examination of children: The Mosaic Test in conjunction with the Rorschach and Binet tests. *Rorschach Research Exchange*, 1948, **12**, 216–237.

Colvin, S. S. The use of intelligence tests. *Educational Review*, 1921, **62**, 134–148.

Combs, A. W. Intelligence from a perceptual point of view. *Journal of Abnormal and Social Psychology*, 1952, **47**, 662–673.

Conrad, H. S. The measurement of adult intelligence, and the requisites of a general intelligence test. *Journal of Social Psychology*, 1931, **2**, 72–86.

Conry, R., & Plant, W. T. WAIS and group test predictions of an academic success. Criterion: High school and college. *Educational and Psychological Measurement*, 1965, **25**, 493–500.

Davey, C. M. A comparison of group verbal and pictorial tests of intelligence. *American Journal of Psychology*, 1926, **17**, 27–48.

Davis, P. C. A factor analysis of the Wechsler-Bellevue Scale. *Educational and Psychological Measurement*, 1956, **16**, 127–146.

Derner, G. F., Aborn, M., & Canter, A. H. The reliability of the Wechsler-Bellevue subtests and scales. *Journal of Consulting Psychology*, 1950, **14**, 172–179.

Diamond, B., & Schmale, H. The Mosaic Test: I. An evaluation of its clinical application. *American Journal of Orthopsychiatry*, 1944, **14**, 237–250.

Doll, E. A. A brief Binet-Simon Scale. *Psychological Clinic*, 1917, **11**, 197–211.

Downey, J. E. The constancy of the I.Q. *Journal of Delinquency*, 1918, **3**, 122–131.

Duffy, O. B., Clair, T. N., Egeland, B., & Dinello, M. Relationship of intelligence, visual-motor skills, and psycholinguistic abilities with achievement in the third, fourth, and fifth grades: A follow-up study. *Journal of Educational Psychology*, 1972, **63**, 358–362.

Edwards, A. J., & Kirby, M. E. Predictive efficacy of intelligence test scores: Intelligence quotients obtained in grade one and achievement test scores obtained in grade three. *Educational and Psychological Measurement*, 1964, **24**, 941–946.

Edwards, A. S. Intelligence as the capacity for variability or versatility of response. *Psychological Review*, 1928, **35**, 198–210.

Elkind, D., & Flavell, J. H. (Eds.), *Studies in cognitive development*. London: Oxford Press, 1969.

Ellison, M. L., & Edgerton, H. A. The Thurstone Primary Mental Abilities Tests and college marks. *Educational and Psychological Measurement*, 1941, **1**, 399–406.

Elwood, D. L. Automation of psychological testing. *American Psychologist*, 1969, **24**, 287–289.

Elwood, D. L., & Griffin, H. R. Individual intelligence testing without the examiner: Reliability of an automated method. *Journal of Consulting and Clinical Psychology*, 1972, **38**, 9–14.

English, H. B. An experimental study of certain initial phases of the process of abstraction. *American Journal of Psychology,* 1922, **33,** 305–350.

English, H. B., & Killian, C. D. The constancy of the I.Q. at different age levels. *Journal of Consulting Psychology,* 1939, **3,** 30–32.

Ermalinski, R., & Ruscelli, V. Incorporation of values by lower and middle socioeconomic class preschool boys. *Child Development,* 1971, **42,** 629–632.

Escalona, S. K., & Moriarty, A. Prediction of schoolage intelligence from infant tests. *Child Development,* 1961, **32,** 597–605.

Eysenck, H. J. Intelligence assessment: A theoretical and experimental approach. *British Journal of Educational Psychology,* 1967, **37,** 81–98.

Eysenck, H. J., & Halstead, H. The memory function. I. A factorial study of fifteen clinical tests. *American Journal of Psychiatry,* 1945, **102,** 174–180.

Eysenck, H. J., & White, P. O. Personality and the measurement of intelligence. *British Journal of Educational Psychology,* 1964, **34,** 197–202.

Feifel, H. Qualitative differences in the vocabulary responses of normals and abnormals. *Genetic Psychology Monographs,* 1949, **39,** 151–204.

Fischer, C. T. Intelligence defined as effectiveness of approach. *Journal of Consulting and Clinical Psychology,* 1969, **33,** 668–674.

Fisher, S. C. The process of generalizing abstraction; and its product, the general concept. *Psychological Monographs,* 1916, **21**(2).

Frank, G. H. The Wechsler-Bellevue and psychiatric diagnosis: A factor analytic approach. *Journal of Consulting Psychology,* 1956, **20,** 67–69.

Frank, G. H. The measurement of personality from the Wechsler tests. In B. Mahrer (Ed.), *Progress in experimental personality research.* New York: Academic Press, 1970. Pp. 169–194.

Frank, G. *Psychiatric diagnosis: A review of research.* London: Pergamon Press, 1975.

Franz, G., Davis, J. A., & Garcia, D. Prediction of grades from pre-admissions indices in Georgia tax-supported colleges. *Educational and Psychological Measurement,* 1958, **18,** 841–844.

Freeman, F. N. What is intelligence? *School Review,* 1925, **33,** 253–263.

Freeman, F. S. Power and speed: Their influence upon intelligence test scores. *Journal of Applied Psychology,* 1928, **12,** 631–635.

French, J. W. The description of aptitude and achievement tests in terms of rotated factors. *Psychometric Monographs,* 1951, No. 5.

French, J. W., Tucker, L. R., Newman, S. H., & Bobbitt, J. M. A factor analysis of aptitude and achievement entrance tests and course grades at the United States Coast Guard Academy. *Journal of Educational Psychology,* 1952, **43,** 65–80.

Fulkerson, S. C. Some implications of the new cognitive theory for projective tests. *Journal of Consulting Psychology,* 1965, **29,** 191–197.

Galton, F. *Hereditary genius: An inquiry into its laws and consequences.* New York: D. Appleton, 1870.

Galton, F. *Inquiries into human faculty and its development.* London: Macmillan, 1883.

Gardner, R., Holzman, P. S., Klein, G. S., Linton, H., & Spence, D. S. Cognitive control: A study of individual consistencies in cognitive behavior. *Psychological Issues,* 1959, **1**(4).

Gardner, R. W. Cognitive styles in categorizing behavior. *Journal of Personality,* 1953, **22**, 214–233.

Gardner, R. W., Jackson, D. N., & Messick, S. J. Personality organization in cognitive controls and intellectual abilities. *Psychological Issues,* 1960, **2**, (8).

Garrett, H. E. A developmental theory of intelligence. *American Psychologist,* 1946, **1**, 372–378.

Garrett, H. E., Bryan, A. I., & Perl, R. E. The age factor in mental organization. *Archives of Psychology,* 1935, No. 176.

Gengerelli, J. A. Mutual interference in the evolution of concepts. *American Journal of Psychology,* 1927, **38**, 639–646.

Giannell, A. S., & Freeburne, C. M. The comparative validity of the WAIS and the Stanford-Binet with college freshmen. *Educational and Psychological Measurement,* 1963, **23**, 557–567.

Goddard, H. H. Two thousand normal children measured by the Binet measuring scale of intelligence. *Pediatric Seminary,* 1911, **18**, 232–259. (a)

Goddard, H. H. *The Binet-Simon Measuring Scale for Intelligence.* (Rev. Ed.) Vineland, N.J.: Training School, 1911. (b)

Golden, M., & Birns, B. Social class and cognitive development in infancy. *Merrill-Palmer Quarterly of Behavior and Development,* 1968, **14**, 139–149.

Golden, M., Birns, B., Bridger, W., & Moss, A. Social-class differentiation in cognitive development among black preschool children. *Child Development,* 1971, **42**, 37–45.

Goldstein, K. The significance of special mental tests for diagnosis and prognosis in schizophrenia. *American Journal of Psychiatry,* 1939, **96**, 575–588.

Goldstein, K., & Scheerer, M. Abstract and concrete behavior. *Psychological Monographs,* 1941, **53**(239).

Gollin, E. S., & Rosenberg, S. Concept formation and impressions of personality. *Journal of Abnormal and Social Psychology,* 1956, **52**, 39–42.

Goodman, C. H. Prediction of College success by means of Thurstone's Primary Abilities Tests. *Educational and Psychological Measurement,* 1944, **4**, 125–140.

Goodenough, F. L. *Measurement of intelligence by drawings.* Yonkers, N.Y.: World Book, 1926.

Green, R. F., Guilford, J. P., Christensen, P. R., & Comrey, A. L. A factor-analytic study of reasoning abilities. *Psychometrika,* 1953, **18**, 135–160.

Guertin, W. H., Frank, G. H., & Rabin, A. I. Research with the Wechsler-Bellevue Intelligence Scale: 1950–1955. *Psychological Bulletin,* 1956, **53**, 235–257.

Guertin, W. H., Ladd, C. E., Frank, G. H., Rabin, A. I., & Hiester, D. S. Research with the Wechsler Intelligence Scales for Adults: 1960–1965. *Psychological Bulletin,* 1966, **66**, 385–409.

Guertin, W. H., Ladd, C. E., Frank, G. H., Rabin, A. I., & Hiester, D. S. Research with the Wechsler Intelligence Scales for Adults: 1965–1970. *Psychological Record,* 1971, **21**, 289–339.

Guertin, W. H., Rabin, A. I., Frank, G. H., & Ladd, C. E. Research with the Wechsler Intelligence Scales for Adults: 1955–60. *Psychological Bulletin,* 1962, **59**, 1–26.

Guilford, J. P. The structure of intellect. *Psychological Bulletin,* 1956, **53**, 267–293.

Guilford, J. P. Three faces of intellect. *American Psychologist,* 1959, **14**, 469–479.

Guilford, J. P., Christensen, P. R., Kettner, N. W., Green, R. F., & Hertzka, A. F. A factor-analytic study of Navy reasoning tests with the Air Force Aircrew Classification Battery. *Educational and Psychological Measurement,* 1954, **14**, 301–325.

Hammer, A. G. A factorial analysis of the Bellevue Intelligence Tests. *Australian Journal of Psychology,* 1949, **1**, 108–114.

Hanfmann, E. Analysis of thinking disorder in a case of schizophrenia. *Archives of Neurology and Psychiatry,* 1939, **41**, 568–579.

Hanfmann, E. A study of personal patterns in an intellectual performance. *Character and Personality,* 1941, **9**, 315–325.

Harris, A. J., & Shakow, D. The clinical significance of numerical measures of scatter on the Stanford-Binet. *Psychological Bulletin,* 1937, **34**, 134–150.

Harris, D. Factors affecting college grades: A review of the literature, 1930–1937. *Psychological Bulletin,* 1940, **37**, 125–166.

Hart, B., & Spearman, C. General ability, its existence and nature. *British Journal of Psychology,* 1912, **5**, 51–84.

Hart, B., & Spearman, C. Mental tests of dementia. *Journal of Abnormal Psychology,* 1914, **9**, 217–264.

Healy, W. A pictorial completion test. *Psychological Review,* 1914, **21**, 189–203.

Healy, W., & Fernald, G. M. Tests for practical mental classification. *Psychological Monographs,* 1911, **13**(54).

Heidbreder, E. Toward a dynamic psychology of cognition. *Psychological Review,* 1945, **52**, 1–22.

Henderson, H. L. Predictors of freshman grades in a Long Island college. *Educational and Psychological Measurement,* 1957, **17**, 623–627.

Herring, J. P. *Herring revision of the Binet-Simon tests.* Yonkers, N.Y.: World Book, 1922.

Herring, J. P. Herring revision of the Binet-Simon tests. *Journal of Educational Psychology,* 1924, **15**, 172–179.

Hertzka, A. F., Guilford, J. P., Christensen, P. R., & Berger, R. M. A factor-analytic study of evaluative abilities. *Educational and Psychological Measurement,* 1954, **14**, 581–597.

Himmelweit, H., & Eysenck, H. An experimental analysis of the Mosaic Projection Test. *British Journal of Medical Psychology,* 1944–46, **20,** 283–294.

Hofstaetter, P. R. The changing composition of "intelligence": A study in T-technique. *Journal of Genetic Psychology,* 1954, **85,** 159–164.

Holland, J. L. A theory of vocational choice. *Journal of Counseling Psychology,* 1959, **6,** 35–44.

Holland, J. L., & Astin, A. W. The prediction of the academic, artistic, scientific, and social achievement of undergraduates of superior scholastic aptitude. *Journal of Educational Psychology,* 1962, **53,** 132–143.

Holland, J. L., & Nichols, R. C. Prediction of academic and extra-curricular achievement in college. *Journal of Educational Psychology,* 1964, **55,** 55–65.

Holzinger, K. J., & Harmon, H. H. Comparison of two factorial analyses. *Psychometrika,* 1938, **3,** 45–60.

Holzman, P. S., & Klein, G. S. Cognitive system principles of leveling and sharpening: Individual differences in assimilation effects in visual time error. *Journal of Psychology,* 1954, **37,** 105–122.

Hull, C. L. Quantitative aspects of the evolution of concepts: An experimental study. *Psychological Monographs,* 1920, **28**(123).

Humphreys, L. G. The fleeting nature of the prediction of college academic success. *Journal of Educational Psychology,* 1968, **59,** 375–380.

Hunt, J. McV. Psychological experiments with disordered persons. *Psychological Bulletin,* 1936, **33,** 1–58.

Hunt, J. McV. *Intelligence and experience.* New York: Ronald Press, 1961.

Hunt, W. A., & Arnhoff, F. N. Some standardized scales for disorganization in schizophrenic thinking. *Journal of Consulting Psychology,* 1955, **15,** 171–174.

Hunt, W. A., Walker, R. E., & Jones, N. F. The validity of clinical ratings for estimating severity of schizophrenia. *Journal of Clinical Psychology,* 1960, **16,** 391–393.

Huttenlocher, J. Development of formal reasoning on concept formation problems. *Child Development,* 1964, **35,** 1233–1242.

Jones, H. E., & Conrad, H. S. The growth and decline of intelligence. *Genetic Psychology Monographs,* 1933, **13**(3).

Jones, L. V. A factor analysis of the Stanford-Binet at four age levels. *Psychometrika,* 1949, **14,** 299–331.

Jones, L. V. Primary abilities in the Stanford-Binet, age 13. *Journal of Genetic Psychology,* 1954, **84,** 125–147.

Jones, P. A. Home environment and the development of verbal ability. *Child Development,* 1972, **43,** 1081–1086.

Jones, R. L., & Siegel, L. The individual high school as a predictor of college academic performance. *Educational and Psychological Measurement,* 1962, **22,** 785–789.

Jordan, A. M. The validation of intelligence tests. *Journal of Educational Psychology,* 1923, **14,** 348–366.

Kagan, J., & Kogan, N. Individual variations in cognitive processes. In P. H. Mussen (Ed.), *Carmichael's manual of child psychology*. Vol. 1. New York: Wiley, 1970. Pp. 1273–1365.

Kaiser, H. F. Varimax solution for primary mental abilities. *Psychometrika*, 1960, **25**, 153–158.

Kamii, C. K., & Radin, N. L. Class differences in the socialization practices of Negro mothers. *Journal of Marriage and the Family*, 1967, **29**, 302–310.

Kasanin, J., & Hanfmann, E. An experimental study of concept formation in schizophrenia. *American Journal of Psychology*, 1938, **95**, 35–92. (a)

Kasanin, J., & Hanfmann, E. Disturbances in concept formation in schizophrenia. *Archives of Neurology and Psychiatry*, 1938, **40**, 1276–1282. (b)

Kasanin, J., & Hanfmann, E. An experimental study of concept formation in schizophrenia. I. Quantitative analysis of the results. *American Journal of Psychiatry*, 1939, **95**, 35–92.

Kent, G. H. Oral test for emergency use in clinics. *Mental Measurement Monographs*, 1932, No. 9.

Kerr, M. The validity of the Mosaic Test. *American Journal of Orthopsychiatry*, 1939, **9**, 232–236.

Kettner, N. W., Guilford, J. P., & Christensen, P. R. A factor-analytic investigation of the factor called general reasoning. *Educational and Psychological Measurement*, 1956, **16**, 438–453.

Kettner, N. W., Guilford, J. P., & Christensen, P. R. A factor-analytic study across the domains of reasoning, creativity, and evaluation. *Psychological Monographs*, 1959, Whole No. 479.

Keys, N. The value of group test IQ's for prediction of progress beyond high school. *Journal of Educational Psychology*, 1940, **31**, 81–93.

Klugh, H. E., & Bierley, R. The School and College Abilities Test and high school grades as predictors of college achievement. *Educational and Psychological Measurement*, 1959, **19**, 625–626.

Knox, H. A. A scale based on the work at Ellis Island for estimating mental defect. *Journal of the American Medical Association*, 1914, **62**, 741–747.

Kohs, S. C. *Intelligence measurement*. New York: Macmillan, 1923.

Kraepelin, E. *Clinical psychiatry*. New York: Macmillan, 1902.

Krugman, M. Some impressions of the revised Stanford-Binet Scale. *Journal of Educational Psychology*, 1939, **30**, 594–603.

Kuhlman, F. The present status of the Binet and Simon tests of the intelligence of children. *Journal of Psycho-Asthenics*, 1911, **16**, 113–139. (a)

Kuhlman, F. The Binet and Simon tests of intelligence in grading feeble-minded children. *Journal of Psycho-Asthenics*, 1911, **16**, 173–193. (b)

Kuhlmann, F. A revision of the Binet-Simon system for measuring the intelligence of children. *Journal of Psycho-Asthenics*, 1912 (Monogr. Suppl.).

Kuhlmann, F. *A handbook of mental tests*. Baltimore: Warwick & York, 1922.

LaHaderne, H. M. Attitudinal and intellectual correlates of attention: A study of four sixth-grade classrooms. *Journal of Educational Psychology*, 1968, **59**, 320–324.

Lawrence, I. A study of the Binet definition tests. *Psychological Clinic*, 1911, **5**, 207–216.

Lennon, R. T. The relation between intelligence and achievement test results for a group of communities. *Journal of Educational Psychology*, 1950, **41**, 301–308.

Levy, P. Short-form tests: A methodological review. *Psychological Bulletin*, 1968, **69**, 410–416.

Lewin, K. *A dynamic theory of personality*. New York: McGraw-Hill, 1935.

Lewin, M., & Goldberg, S. Perceptual-cognitive development in infancy: Mothers' behaviors. *Merrill-Palmer Quarterly of Behavior and Development*, 1969, **15**, 81–100.

Lienart, G. A., & Crott, H. W. Studies on the factor structure of intelligence in children, adolescents, and adults. *Vita Humana*, 1964, **7**, 147–163.

Lindsay, P. H., & Norman, D. A. *Human information processing*. New York: Academic Press, 1972.

Littell, W. M. The Wechsler Intelligence Scale for Children: Review of a decade of research. *Psychological Bulletin*, 1960, **57**, 132–156.

Lorr, M., & Meister, R. K. The concept of scatter in the light of mental test theory. *Educational and Psychological Measurement*, 1941, **1**, 303–308.

Lovibond, S. H. The Object Sorting Test and conceptual thinking in schizophrenia. *Australian Journal of Psychology*, 1954, **6**, 52–70.

Lowenfeld, M. The Mosaic Test. *American Journal of Orthopsychiatry*, 1949, **19**, 537–550.

Lunneborg, C. E., & Lunneborg, P. W. Pattern prediction of academic success. *Educational and Psychological Measurement*, 1967, **27**, 945–952.

Luzki, M. B., Schultz, W., Laywell, H. R., & Dawes, R. M. Long search for a short WAIS: Stop looking. *Journal of Consulting Psychology*, 1970, **34**, 425–431.

Machover, S. *Cultural and racial variations in patterns of intellect: Performance of negro and white criminals on the Bellevue Adult Intelligence Scale*. New York: Teachers College, Columbia University, 1943.

MacPhail, A. H. Ten years of intelligence testing. *Educational and Psychological Measurement*, 1943, **3**, 157–165.

Magaret, A., & Wright, C. Limitations in the use of intelligence test performance to detect mental disturbance. *Journal of Applied Psychology*, 1943, **27**, 387–398.

Maher, B., & Martin, A. Mosaic patterns in cerebroarteriosclerosis. *Journal of Consulting Psychology*, 1954, **18**, 40–42.

Maltz, H. E. Ontogenetic change in the meaning of concepts as measured by the semantic differential. *Child Development*, 1963, **34**, 667–674.

Mann, M. J. The prediction of achievement in a liberal arts college. *Educational and Psychological Measurement*, 1961, **21**, 481–483.

Masling, J. The influence of situational and interpersonal variables in projective testing. *Psychological Bulletin*, 1960, **57**, 65–85.

Matarazzo, J. D. *Wechsler's measurement and appraisal of adult intelligence.* (5th ed.) Baltimore: Williams & Wilkins, 1972.

Mateer, F. The diagnostic fallibility of intelligence ratios. *Pedagogical Seminary*, 1918, **25**, 369–392.

Maxwell, A. E. A factor analysis of the Wechsler Intelligence Scale for children. *British Journal of Educational Psychology*, 1959, **29**, 237–241.

Maxwell, A. E. Obtaining factor scores on the Wechsler Adult Intelligence Scale. *Journal of Mental Science*, 1960, **106**, 1060–1062.

Maxwell, A. E. Trends in cognitive ability in the older age ranges. *Journal of Abnormal and Social Psychology*, 1961, **63**, 449–452.

Mayman, M., Schafer, R., & Rapaport, D. Interpretation of the Wechsler-Bellevue Intelligence Scale in personality appraisal. In H. H. Anderson & G. L. Anderson (Eds.), *An introduction to projective techniques.* New York: Prentice-Hall, 1954. Pp. 541–580.

McCall, W. A. *Correlation of some psychological and educational measurements.* New York: Teachers College Columbia University Contributions to Education, 1916.

McCulloch, T. L. A study of the cognitive abilities of the white rat with special reference to Spearman's theory of two factors. *Contributions to Psychological Theory*, 1935, **1**(3).

McCulloch, T., & Girdner, J. Use of the Lowenfeld Mosaic Test with mental defectives. *American Journal of Mental Deficiency*, 1949, **53**, 486–496.

McGaughran, L. S. Predicting language behavior from object sorting. *Journal of Abnormal and Social Psychology*, 1954, **49**, 183–195.

McGaughran, L. S., & Moran, L. J. "Conceptual level" vs. "conceptual area" analysis of object-sorting behavior of schizophrenic and nonpsychiatric groups. *Journal of Abnormal and Social Psychology*, 1956, **52**, 43–50.

McGaughran, L. S., & Moran, L. J. Differences between schizophrenic and brain-damaged groups on conceptual aspects of object sorting. *Journal of Abnormal and Social Psychology*, 1957, **54**, 44–49.

McNemar, Q. *The revision of the Stanford-Binet Scale.* Boston: Houghton-Mifflin, 1942.

McNemar, Q. Lost: Our intelligence? Why? *American Psychologist*, 1964, **19**, 871–882.

McQuary, J. P. Some relationships between non-intellectual characteristics and academic achievement. *Journal of Educational Psychology*, 1953, **44**, 215–228.

Meyer, A. The relation of emotional and intellectual functions in paranoia and in obsession. *Psychological Bulletin,* 1906, **3**, 255–274.

Meyers, C. E., Atwell, A. A., & Orpet, R. E. Prediction of fifth grade achievement from kindergarten test and rating data. *Educational and Psychological Measurement,* 1968, **28**, 457–463.

Michael, W., & Crawford, C. C. An experiment in judging intelligence by the voice. *Journal of Educational Psychology,* 1927, **18**, 107–114.

Michael, W. B., & Jones, R. A. Stability of predictive validities of high school grades and of scores on the Scholastic Aptitude Test of the College Entrance Examination Board for liberal arts students. *Educational and Psychological Measurement,* 1963, **23**, 375–378.

Michael, W. B., Baker, D., & Jones, R. A. A note concerning the predictive validities of seleted cognitive and non-cognitive measures for freshman students in a liberal arts college. *Educational and Psychological Measurement,* 1964, **24**, 373–375.

Michael, W. B., Jones, R. A., Cox, A., Gershon, A., Hoover, M., Katz, K., & Smith, D. High school record and college board scores as predictors of success in a liberal arts program during the freshman year of college. *Educational and Psychological Measurement,* 1962, **22**, 399–400.

Miles, T. R. On defining intelligence. *British Journal of Educational Psychology,* 1957, **27**, 153–165.

Miller, A., & Kemp, E. Personality style and perceptual reactivity to the immediate environment. *Journal of Abnormal and Social Psychology,* 1962, **65**, 333–337.

Mitchell, M. Performance of mental hospital patients on the Wechsler-Bellevue and the revised Stanford-Binet Form L. *Journal of Educational Psychology,* 1942, **33**, 538–544.

Moore, T. V. The process of abstraction: An experimental study. *University of California Publications in Psychology,* 1910, **1**(2).

Moran, L. J. Vocabulary knowledge and usage among normal and schizophrenic subjects. *Psychological Monographs,* 1953, **67**(370).

Moran, L. J., Moran, F. A., & Blake, R. R. An investigation of the vocabulary performance of schizophrenics: II. Conceptual level of definition. *Journal of Abnormal and Social Psychology,* 1954, **49**, 183–195.

Morikawa, S. A study on concept formation in schizophrenics. *Japanese Journal of Clinical Psychology,* 1967, **6**, 21–29.

Morris, C. M. A critical analysis of certain performance tests. *Journal of Genetic Psychology,* 1939, **54**, 95–105.

Moss, H. A. Sex, age, and state as determinants of mother-infant reaction. *Merrill-Palmer Quarterly of Behavior and Development,* 1967, **13**, 19–36.

Moss, H. A., Robson, K. S., & Pederson, F. Determinants of maternal stimulation of infants and consequences of treatment for later reactions to strangers. *Developmental Psychology,* 1969, **1**, 239–246.

Moursey, E. M. The hierarchical organization of cognitive levels. *British Journal of Psychology, Statistical Section,* 1952, **5,** 151–180.

Mukherjee, B. N. The prediction of grades in introductory psychology from tests of Primary Mental Abilities. *Educational and Psychological Measurement,* 1965, **25,** 557–564.

Nemzek, C. L. The constancy of the I.Q. *Psychological Bulletin,* 1933, **30,** 143–168.

Oates, D. W. The nature and validity of subjective estimates of intelligence. *Forum of Education,* 1924, **2,** 103–121.

Oates, D. W. A statistical and psychological investigation of intelligence tests. *Forum of Education,* 1928, **6,** 38–62.

Pavenstadt, E. A comparison of the child rearing environment of upper-lower and very low-lower class families. *American Journal of Orthopsychiatry,* 1965, **35,** 89–98.

Payne, R. W. Cognitive abnormalities. In H. J. Eysenck (Ed.), *Handbook of abnormal psychology,* New York: Basic Books, 1961. Pp. 193–261.

Payne, R. W., Mattussek, P., & George, E. J. An experimental study of schizophrenic thought disorder. *Journal of Mental Science,* 1959, **105,** 627–652.

Peterson, J. Intelligence and learning. *Psychological Review,* 1922, **29,** 366–389.

Peterson, J. *Early conceptions and tests of intelligence.* Yonkers, N.Y.: World Book, 1925.

Piaget, J. *The psychology of intelligence.* London: Routledge & Kegan Paul, 1950.

Pieron, H. The problem of intelligence. *Pedagogical Seminary,* 1926, **33,** 50–60.

Pierson, G. A. School marks and success in engineering. *Educational and Psychological Measurement,* 1947, **7,** 612–617.

Pintner, R. Intelligence as estimated from photographs. *Psychological Review,* 1918, **25,** 286–296.

Pintner, R. A non-language group intelligence test. *Journal of Applied Psychology,* 1919, **3,** 199–214.

Pintner, R. *Intelligence testing: Methods and results,* New York: Holt, 1923.

Pintner, R., & Paterson, D. C. *A scale of performance tests.* New York: Appleton-Century, 1917.

Plant, W. T., & Lynd, C. A validity study and a college freshman norm group for the Wechsler Adult Intelligence Scale. *Personnel and Guidance Journal,* 1959, **37,** 578–580.

Porteus, S. D. Mental tests for feebleminded: A new series. *Journal of Psycho-Asthenics,* 1915, **19,** 200–213.

Pressey, S. L. Distinctive features in psychological test measurement made upon dementia praecox and chronic alcoholic patients. *Journal of Abnormal Psychology,* 1917, **12,** 130–139.

Pressey, S. L., & Cole, L. W. Irregularity in a psychological examination as a measure of mental deterioration. *Journal of Abnormal Psychology,* 1918, **13,** 285–294.

Rabin, A. I. Test-score patterns in schizophrenic and non-psychotic states. *Journal of Psychology,* 1941, **12,** 91–100.

Rabin, A. I. Differentiating psychometric patterns in schizophrenia and manic-depressive psychoses. *Journal of Abnormal and Social Psychology,* 1942, **37,** 270–272.

Rabin, A. I. A short form of the Wechsler-Bellevue Test. *Journal of Applied Psychology,* 1943, **27,** 320–324.

Rabin, A. I. Fluctuations in mental level of schizophrenic patients. *Psychiatric Quarterly,* 1944, **18,** 78–92.

Rabin, A. I. The use of the Wechsler-Bellevue Scales with normal and abnormal persons. *Psychological Bulletin,* 1945, **42,** 410–422.

Rabin, A. I., & Guertin, W. H. Research with the Wechsler-Bellevue Test: 1945–1950. *Psychological Bulletin,* 1951, **48,** 211–248.

Radin, N. Three degrees of maternal involvement in a preschool program: Impact on mothers and children. *Child Development,* 1972, **43,** 1355–1364.

Rapaport, D. (1946) Principles underlying non-projective tests of personality. In *The collected papers of David Rapaport.* New York: Basic Books, 1967. Pp. 221–229. (a)

Rapaport, D. (1947) Psychological testing: Its practical and its heuristic significance. In *The collected papers of David Rapaport.* New York: Basic Books, 1967. Pp. 261–275. (b)

Rapaport, D. (1950) The theoretical implications of diagnostic testing procedures. In *The collected papers of David Rapaport.* New York: Basic Books, 1967. Pp. 334–356. (c)

Rapaport, D. (1951) On the organization of thought processes. In *The collected papers of David Rapaport.* New York: Basic Books, 1967. Pp. 432–439. (d)

Rapaport, D. (1955) Cognitive structures. In *The collected papers of David Rapaport.* New York: Basic Books, 1967. Pp. 631–664. (e)

Rapaport, D., Gill, M., & Schafer, R. *Diagnostic psychological testing.* Vol. 1. Chicago: Yearbook Publishers, 1945.

Rapaport, D., Menninger, K. A., & Schafer, R. (1946) The new role of psychological testing in psychiatry. In *The collected papers of David Rapaport.* New York: Basic Books, 1967. Pp. 245–250.

Raven, J. C. *Progressive Matrices: A perceptual test of intelligence.* London: Lewis, 1938.

Rawlings, E. The intellectual status of patients with paranoid dementia praecox: Its relation to organic changes. *Archives of Neurology and Psychiatry,* 1921, **5,** 283–295.

Reichard, S., & Rapaport, D. The role of testing concept formation in clinical psychological work. *Bulletin of the Menninger Clinic,* 1943, **7,** 99–105.

Reichard, S., & Schafer, R. The clinical significance of the scatter on the Bellevue Scale. *Bulletin of the Menninger Clinic*, 1943, **7**, 93–98.

Reichard, S., Schneider, M., & Rapaport, D. Development of concept formation in children. *American Journal of Orthopsychiatry*, 1944, **14**, 156–167.

Reiman, G. The Mosaic Test: Its applicability and ability. *American Journal of Orthopsychiatry*, 1950, **20**, 600–615.

Remmers, H. H., Elliott, D. N., & Gage, N. L. Curricular differences in predicting scholastic achievement: Application to counseling. *Journal of Educational Psychology*, 1949, **40**, 385–394.

Richards, J. M. The prediction of academic achievement in a Protestant theological seminary. *Educational and Psychological Measurement*, 1957, **17**, 628–630.

Richards, T. W. Genetic emergence of factor specificity. *Psychometrika*, 1941, **6**, 37–41.

Riegel, R. M., & Riegel, K. F. A comparison and reinterpretation of factor structures of the W-B, the WAIS, and the HAWIE on aged persons. *Journal of Consulting Psychology*, 1962, **26**, 31–37.

Rimoldi, H. J. A. Study of some factors related to intelligence. *Psychometrika*, 1948, **13**, 27–46.

Rimoldi, H. J. A. The central intellective factor. *Psychometrika*, 1951, **16**, 75–101.

Rioch, M. The Mosaic Test as a diagnostic instrument and as a technique for illustrating intellectual organization. *Journal of Projective Techniques*, 1954, **18**, 89–94.

Robeck, M. C., & Wilson, J. A. R. Comparison of Binet and the kindergarten evaluation of learning potential. *Educational and Psychological Measurement*, 1964, **24**, 393–397.

Robertson, M. H. Scoring intelligence on the Lowenfeld Mosaic Test. *Journal of Consulting Psychology*, 1957, **21**, 418.

Roe, A., & Shakow, D. Intelligence in mental disorder. *Annals of the New York Academy of Sciences*, 1942, **42**, 361–490.

Rokeach, M. A method for studying individual differences in "narrow-mindedness." *Journal of Personality*, 1951, **2**, 219–233.

Rubinstein, J. Maternal attentiveness and subsequent exploratory behavior in the infant. *Child Development*, 1967, **38**, 1089–1100.

Ruschival, M. L., & Way, J. G. The WPPSI and the Stanford-Binet: A validity and reliability study using gifted preschool children. *Journal of Consulting and Clinical Psychology*, 1971, **37**, 163.

Russell, E. W. WAIS factor analysis with brain-damaged subjects using criterion measures. *Journal of Consulting and Clinical Psychology*, 1972, **39**, 133–139.

Sartain, A. Q. A comparison of the new revised Stanford-Binet, the Bellevue

Scale, and certain group tests of intelligence. *Journal of Social Psychology,* 1946, **23**, 237–239.

Sattler, J. M. *Assessment of children's intelligence.* Philadelphia: Saunders, 1974.

Scannell, D. P. Prediction of college success from elementary and secondary school performance. *Journal of Educational Psychology,* 1960, **51**, 130–134.

Schafer, R. The expression of personality and maladjustment in intelligence test results. *Annals of the New York Academy of Sciences,* 1946, **46**, 609–623.

Schafer, R. On the objective and subjective aspects of diagnostic testing. *Journal of Consulting Psychology,* 1948, **12**, 4–7. (a)

Schafer, R. *The clinical application of psychological tests.* New York: International Universities Press, 1948. (b)

Schafer, R. Psychological tests in clinical research. *Journal of Consulting Psychology,* 1949, **13**, 328–334.

Schafer, R., & Rapaport, D. The scatter: In diagnostic intelligence testing. *Character and Personality,* 1944, **12**, 275–284.

Scheerer, M. Problems of performance analysis in the study of personality. *Annals of the New York Academy of Sciences,* 1946, **46**, 653–678.

Scheerer, M. Personality functioning and cognitive psychology. *Journal of Personality,* 1953, **22**, 1–16.

Seguin, E. *Idiocy and its treatment by the physiological method.* Albany, N.Y.: Brandow, 1866.

Shaw, D. C. A study of the relationships between Thurstone Primary Mental Abilities and high school achievement. *Journal of Educational Psychology,* 1949, **40**, 239–249.

Shotwell, A., & Lawrence, E. Mosaic patterns of institutionalized mental defectives. *American Journal of Mental Deficiency,* 1951, **56**, 161–168.

Sigel, I. E. Developmental trends in the abstraction ability of children. *Child Development,* 1953, **24**, 131–144.

Sigel, I. E. How intelligence tests limit understanding of intelligence. *Merrill-Palmer Quarterly,* 1963, **9**, 39–56.

Sigel, I., Jarman, P., & Hanesian, H. Styles of categorization and their intellectual and personality correlates in young children. *Human Development,* 1967, **10**, 1–17.

Smoke, K. L. An objective study of concept formation. *Psychological Monographs,* 1932, No. 191.

Sontag, L. W., Baker, C. T., & Nelson, V. L. Mental growth and personality development: A longitudinal study. *Monograph of the Society for Child Development,* 1958, **23**(68).

Spearman, C. "General intelligence," objectively determined and measured. *American Journal of Psychology,* 1904, **15**, 201–293.

Spearman, C. *The nature of 'intelligence' and the principle of cognition.* London: Macmillan, 1923.

Spearman, C. "Intelligence" tests. *Eugenics Review,* 1939, **30,** 249–254.

Stern, W. The psychological method of testing intelligence. *Educational Psychology Monographs,* 1914, No. 13.

Stockton, J. L. The definition of intelligence in relation to modern methods of mental measurement. *Psychological Monographs,* 1921, **30** Whole No. 137.

Stoddard, G. D. On the meaning of intelligence. *Psychological Review,* 1941, **48,** 250–260.

Storch, A. The primitive archaic forms of inner experiences and thought in schizophrenia. *Nervous and Mental Disease Monographs,* 1924, No. 36.

Stroud, J. B., Blommers, P., & Lauber, M. Correlational analysis of WISC and achievement tests. *Journal of Educational Psychology,* 1957, **48,** 18–26.

Stutsman, R. *Mental measurement of preschool children: With a guide for the administration of the Merrill-Palmer Scale of Mental Tests.* Yonkers, N.Y.: World Book, 1931.

Sullivan, H. S. Peculiarity of thought in schizophrenia. *American Journal of Psychiatry,* 1925, **5,** 21–86.

Tendler, A. D. The mental status of psychoneurotics. *Archives of Psychology,* 1923, No. 60.

Terman, L. M. The Binet-Simon Scale for measuring intelligence. *Psychological Clinic,* 1911, **5,** 199–206.

Terman, L. M. Suggestions for revising, extending and supplementing the Binet intelligence tests. *Journal of Psycho-Asthenics,* 1913, **18,** 20–33.

Terman, L. M. *The measurement of intelligence.* Boston: Houghton, 1916.

Terman, L. M. *The Stanford revision and extension of the Binet-Simon Scale for measuring intelligence.* Baltimore: Warwick & York, 1917.

Terman, L. M. The vocabulary test as a measure of intelligence. *Journal of Educational Psychology,* 1918, **9,** 452–466.

Terman, L. M., & Chamberlain, M. B. Twenty-three serial tests of intelligence and their inter-correlation. *Journal of Applied Psychology,* 1918, **2,** 341–354.

Terman, L. M., & Childs, H. G. A tentative revision and extension of the Binet-Simon Scale of intelligence. *Journal of Educational Psychology,* 1912, **3,** 277–289.

Terman, L. M., Lyman, G., Ordahl, G., Ordahl, L., Galbreath, N., & Talbert, W. The Stanford revision of the Binet-Simon Scale and some results from its application to 1000 non-selected children. *Journal of Educational Psychology,* 1915, **6,** 551–562.

Terman, L. M., & Merrill, M. A. *Measuring intelligence.* Boston: Houghton Mifflin, 1937.

Thorndike, E. L. *Educational psychology.* New York: Columbia University Press, 1913.

Thorndike, E. L. A standard group examination of intelligence independent of language. *Journal of Applied Psychology,* 1919, **3,** 13–32. (a)

Thorndike, E. L. Tests of intelligence; reliability, significance, susceptibility to special training and adaptation to the general nature of the task. *School and Society*, 1919, **9**, 189–195. (b)

Thorndike, E. L. Intelligence and its uses. *Harper's Magazine*, 1920, **140**, 227–253.

Thorndike, E. L. Measurement of intelligence: I. The present status. *Psychological Review*, 1924, **31**, 219–252.

Thorndike, E. L. The improvement of mental measurements. *Journal of Educational Research*, 1925, **11**, 1–11.

Thorndike, E. L. Intelligence tests. *Encyclopedia Britannica*, 1929, **12**, 460–461.

Thorndike, E. L., Bregman, E. O., Cobb, C. V., & Woodyard, E. *The measurement of intelligence*. New York: Teachers College Bureau of Publications, Columbia University, 1926.

Thorndike, E. L., Terman, L. M., Freeman, F. N., Colvin, S. S., Pintner, R., Ruml, B., Pressey, S. L., Henmon, A. C., Peterson, J., Thurstone, L. L., Woodrow, H., Dearborn, W. F., & Haggerty, M. E. Intelligence and its measurement: A symposium. *Journal of Educational Psychology*, 1921, **12**, 123–147, 195–216.

Thornton, G. R. The use of tests of persistence in the prediction of scholastic achievement. *Journal of Educational Psychology*, 1941, **32**, 266–274.

Thurstone, L. L. A cycle-omnibus intelligence test for college students. *Journal of Educational Research*, 1921, **4**, 265–278.

Thurstone, L. L. The nature of intelligence. *Psychological Bulletin*, 1923, **20**, 78–79.

Thurstone, L. L. *The nature of intelligence*. New York: Harcourt, Brace, 1924.

Thurstone, L. L. The factorial isolation of primary abilities. *Psychometrika*, 1936, **1**, 175–182. (a)

Thurstone, L. L. A new conception of intelligence. *Educational Record*, 1936, **17**, 441–450. (b)

Thurstone, L. L. Primary mental abilities. *Psychometric Monographs*, 1938, No. 1.

Thurstone, L. L. Experimental study of simple structure. *Psychometrika*, 1940, **5**, 153–168.

Thurstone, L. L., & Thurstone, T. G. Factorial studies of intelligence. *Psychometric Monographs*, 1941, No. 2.

Tuddenham, R. D. The nature and measurement of intelligence. In L. Postman (Ed.), *Psychology in the making*. New York: Knopf, 1963. Pp. 469–525.

Tulkin, S. R., & Kagan, J. Mother-child interaction in the first year of life. *Child Development*, 1972, **43**, 31–41.

Varon, E. J. The development of Alfred Binet's psychology. *Psychological Monographs*, 1935, **46**(207).

Vernon, P. E. The American *vs.* the German methods of approach to the study of temperament and personality. *British Journal of Psychology*, 1933, **24**, 156–177.

Vick, M. C., & Hornaday, J. A. Predicting grade point average at a small southern college. *Educational and Psychological Measurement*, 1962, **22,** 795–799.

Vigotsky, L. S. Thought in schizophrenia. *Archives of Neurology and Psychiatry*, 1934, **31,** 1063–1077.

Vinacke, W. E. The investigation of concept formation. *Psychological Bulletin*, 1951, **48,** 1–31.

Wall, H. W., Marks, E., Ford, D. H., & Zeigler, M. L. Estimates of the concurrent validity of the W.A.I.S. and normative distributions for college freshmen. *Personnel and Guidance Journal*, 1962, **40,** 717–722.

Wallach, M. A., & Kogan, N. *Modes of thinking in young children.* New York: Rinehart, 1965.

Wallin, J. E. W. A statistical study of the individual tests in ages VIII and IX in the Stanford-Binet Scale. *Mental Measurement Monographs*, 1929, No. 6.

Webb, E. Character and intelligence. *British Journal of Psychology*, 1915 (Monogr. Suppl. 3).

Webb, W. B., & De Haan, H. Wechsler-Bellevue split-half reliabilities in normals and schizophrenics. *Journal of Consulting Psychology*, 1951, **15,** 68–71.

Wechsler, D. *The measurement of adult intelligence.* Baltimore: Williams & Wilkins, 1939.

Wechsler, D. *The measurement of adult intelligence.* (2nd ed.) Baltimore: Williams & Wilkins, 1941.

Wechsler, D. Non-intellective factors in general intelligence. *Journal of Abnormal and Social Psychology*, 1943, **38,** 101–103.

Wechsler, D. *The measurement of adult intelligence.* (3rd ed.) Baltimore: Williams & Wilkins, 1944.

Wechsler, D. *Wechsler Intelligence Scale for Children.* New York: Psychological Corporation, 1949.

Wechsler, D. Cognitive, conative, and non-intellectual intelligence. *American Psychologist*, 1950, **5,** 78–83.

Wechsler, D. *Manual for the Wechsler Adult Intelligence Scale.* New York: Psychological Corporation, 1955.

Wechsler, D. *The measurement and appraisal of adult intelligence.* (4th ed.) Baltimore: Williams & Wilkins, 1958.

Wechsler, D. *Manual for the Wechsler Preschool and Primary Scale of Intelligence.* New York: Psychological Corporation, 1967.

Weisman, A. G. Intelligent testing. *American Psychologist*, 1968, **23,** 267–274.

Welch, L. The genetic development of the association structure of abstract thinking. *Journal of Genetic Psychology*, 1940, **56,** 175–206. (a)

Welch, L. A preliminary investigation of some aspects of the hierarchical development of concepts. *Journal of General Psychology*, 1940, **22,** 359–378. (b)

Welch, L., & Long, L. The higher structural phases of concept formation of children. *Journal of Psychology,* 1940, **9,** 59–95. (a)

Welch, L., & Long, L. A further investigation of the higher structural phases of concept formation. *Journal of Psychology,* 1940, **10,** 211–220. (b)

Welch, L., & Long, L. Comparison of the reasoning ability of two age groups. *Journal of Genetic Psychology,* 1943, **62,** 63–76.

Wells, F. L. *Mental tests in clinical practice.* New York: World Book, 1927.

Wertham, F., & Golden, I. A differential diagnostic method of interpreting Mosaics and colored block designs. *American Journal of Psychiatry,* 1941, **98,** 124–131.

White, K. M. Conceptual style and conceptual ability in kindergarten through the eighth grade. *Child Development,* 1971, **42,** 1652–1656.

White, W. A. The language of schizophrenia. *Archives of Neurology and Psychiatry,* 1926, **16,** 395–413.

Wideman, H. Development and initial validation of an objective scoring method for the Lowenfeld Mosaic Test. *Journal of Projective Techniques,* 1955, **19,** 177–191.

Wilson, J. H. On the nature of intelligence. *Journal of Educational Psychology,* 1931, **22,** 20–34.

Wilson, R. C., Guilford, J. P., Christensen, P. R., & Lewis, D. J. A factor-analytic study of creative-thinking abilities. *Psychometrika,* 1954, **19,** 297–311.

Witkin, H. A., Dyk, R. B., Faterson, H. F., Goodenough, D. R., & Karp, S. A. *Psychological differentiation.* New York: Wiley, 1962.

Witkin, H. A., Lewis, H. B., Hertzman, M., Machover, K., Meissner, P. B., & Wapner, S. *Personality through perception.* New York: Harper, 1954.

Witmer, L. Practical work in psychology. *Pediatrics,* 1896, **2,** 462–471.

Woodrow, H. The common factors in fifty-two mental tests. *Psychometrika,* 1939, **4,** 99–108.

Wooley, H. T. The validity of standard of mental measurement in young children. *School and Society,* 1925, **21,** 476–482.

Woolf, H., & Gerson, E. Some approaches to the problem of evaluation of mental ability with the Mosaic Test. *American Journal of Orthopsychiatry,* 1953, **23,** 732–739.

Worrell, L. Level of aspiration and academic success. *Journal of Educational Psychology,* 1959, **50,** 47–54.

Wright, R. E. A factor analysis of the original Stanford-Binet Scale. *Psychometrika,* 1939, **4,** 209–220.

Wrigley, C., Saunders, D. R., & Neuhaus, J. O. Applications of the quartimax method of rotation to Thurstone's primary mental abilities study. *Psychometrika,* 1958, **23,** 151–170.

Wylie, A. R. T. On some recent work in mental pathology. *Journal of Psycho-Asthenics,* 1902, **7,** 1–5.

Yerkes, R. M., & Anderson, H. M. The importance of social status as indicated by the results of the Point-Scale method of measuring mental capacity. *Journal of Educational Psychology,* 1915, **6,** 137–150.

Yerkes, R. M., & Bridges, J. W. The Point Scale: A new method for measuring mental capacity. *Boston Medical and Surgical Journal,* 1914, **171,** 857–866.

Yoakum, C. S., & Yerkes, R. M. *Army mental tests,* New York: Holt, 1920.

Yum, K. S. Primary mental abilities and scholastic achievements in the divisional studies at the University of Chicago. *Journal of Applied Psychology,* 1941, **25,** 712–720.

Zaslow, R. W. A new approach to the problem of conceptual thinking in schizophrenia. *Journal of Consulting Psychology,* 1950, **14,** 335–339.

Zimmerman, I. L., & Woo-Sam, J. M. *Clinical interpretation of the Wechsler Adult Intelligence Scale.* New York: Grune & Stratton, 1973.

Zimmerman, W. S. A revised orthogonal rotational solution for Thurstone's original Primary Mental Abilities Test battery. *Psychometrika,* 1953, **18,** 77–93.

CHAPTER 4

Personality Inventories

MALCOLM D. GYNTHER AND RUTH A. GYNTHER[1]

Personality develops in an interpersonal context. Whether this construct is defined in terms of the mutual relations between id, ego, and superego (Freud, 1933), or of being able to predict what a person will do in a given situation (Cattell, 1950), or of what lies behind specific acts and within the individual (Allport, 1937), it is clear that from the layman's point of view that personality is "what makes Johnny run" (or cheat or steal or create). People are probably more interested in understanding other people (and themselves) than they are in anything else. Crises on the local and international scene come and go, but concerns about getting along with one's wife, outwitting or otherwise adapting to one's boss or supervisor, and keeping up with one's children are perennial. Courses that offer to teach one how to win friends and influence people are always popular, and books that offer solutions to interpersonal dilemmas (e.g., Ginott's *Between Parent and Child*) frequently become best sellers.

One often hears someone refer to another as "having a terrific personality," or as "not having much personality," or simply as "having a rotten personality." Sometimes there is consensus, and sometimes objections are made to the generalization offered. Nonetheless, one has the impression that the layman has a handle on personality description. Furthermore, one often hears comments to the effect that "Joe will come to a bad

[1]The first draft of this chapter was written while the senior author was at St. Louis University and the junior author at the University of Missouri at St. Louis. The writers thank Delbert Garnes, Jerome Holliday, Tim Jovick, Larry Nieters, Vicki Pickering, and Gordon Williams for their assistance in reviewing the literature. Gratitude is also expressed to Raymond B. Cattell, W. Grant Dahlstrom, Harrison G. Gough, and Douglas N. Jackson for their helpful suggestions concerning the reviews of the inventories with which they are associated. Finally, the constructive criticism of James N. Butcher, Milton E. Strauss, and Jerry S. Wiggins, each of whom read the entire manuscript, was much appreciated.

end," or "Mary has a bright future ahead of her," or "George is certain to make a pile of money." Here it appears that the layman also has the ability to predict future events, a goal that has tended to elude behavioral scientists.

What kinds of data is the layman working with? Are his generalizations and predictions accurate? What is it that professionals in this field are trying to accomplish over and above what everyone and his neighbor do every day?

It appears that the layman's concept of another's personality is primarily determined by the social stimulus value of that other person, that is, what impact he has and how he affects people who come in contact with him. First impressions seem to be formed very rapidly as we select friends, fall in love, choose candidates for political office, or size up customers. These judgments are, however, subject to many kinds of error. The observer may be influenced by hearsay and perceive the person as someone else has described him. He may produce a halo effect by finding one characteristic that turns him on or off and then generalize from this characteristic to other aspects of the person's behavior. He may use a stereotype based on characteristics believed to be universal in the group to which the person belongs. Furthermore, the person being judged may behave in such a way as to create a false impression. He may be putting his best foot forward. He may be making a deliberate effort to deceive by assuming a temporary role which is not characteristic of him. Or he may come from a background so different from that of the observer that he is hard to understand.

We should not conclude from this list of potential errors that the layman is bound to be wrong in his impressions or predictions. Every group or community seems to have its "wise old man" (or woman) who has great insight into the behavior of others. Taft (1955) concluded that accurate judgment occurs when the judge possesses appropriate judgmental norms, has high judging ability (a combination of general and social intelligence), and is motivated and free to make accurate judgments about the subject. More recent studies (e.g., Cline, 1964) provide modest but positive evidence for the generality of judgmental accuracy. For our purposes, the point is that none of the dimensions posited by Taft as related to making judgments of others excludes the possibility of laymen as experts. Indeed, there is a host of studies (e.g., Goldberg, 1959; Goldberg, 1965; Johnston & McNeal, 1967) suggesting that the amount of *professional* training and the experience of a judge are unrelated to his judgmental accuracy.

If, then, it may be conceded that certain laymen are good or even excellent judges of personality, what are professional personologists attempting to do? Hundreds or indeed thousands of individuals would not spend their careers in the fields of personality theory or assessment if there were satisfaction with the notion that wise old men or Delphic oracles could solve the perplexities of human nature. One clear distinction is that the professional is interested in quantification. Mathematical procedures underlie the advances made in the physical sciences; unless one can make explicit the bases of his predictions, the study of personality is apt to remain an art. Another feature likely to elude the layman is the need for systematic verification. Often dramatic predictive "hits"are remembered, but the many predictions not borne out are forgotten.

Generalization is also a goal of scientific endeavor. To be able to say something relevant about one individual is interesting, but not really adequate for developing "laws" of behavior. One needs to establish relationships that will hold, to a greater or lesser degree, for a class of individuals. Furthermore, methods or instruments for evaluating personality must be devised. There are so many occasions on which assessment is called for—in educational, clinical, business, industrial, legal, and research settings—that one cannot possibly solve the logistical problems of seeing that a few wise old men make contact with these hundreds of thousands or more potential clients per year. These instruments, hopefully, should possess qualities that enable those who use them to avoid the many errors characteristic of informal appraisals of personality (e.g., halo effect, stereotyping).

The material that follows attempts first to elucidate some principles of formal personality assessment, to describe how base rates and selection ratios affect decision making, and to indicate something of the nature of objective personality measurement. Then, following a historical sketch of the development of personality inventories, the chapter reviews several of the most important inventories available today. These reviews cover the aims of the test constructor, the strategy used to accomplish these goals, the resulting scales, the psychometric properties of the instrument, and the most salient research related to clinical interpretation of the scales or profiles. Brief evaluations of the current status of those inventories not given major coverage are also provided. A final section discusses several controversial issues in the area of objective personality assessment. The major purpose of this chapter is to give the reader a view of what psychologists are doing to bring order into a very complex area. Although some consideration is necessarily given to psychometric issues, the major focus is applied in keeping with the clinical orientation of this book.

BASIC STEPS IN ASSESSMENT: THE PREDICTION PARADIGM

This section outlines and illustrates briefly the basic steps in the prediction process. Although many earlier writers have described the process to a greater or lesser degree, we are following here the discussion presented in Wiggins' *Personality and Prediction* (1973), an excellent book which is highly recommended for a more extensive treatment of these and related issues. The following six steps constitute the basic prediction paradigm:

1. *Criterion analysis.* The criterion is that aspect of human behavior to be predicted in a given assessment problem. With its being stated boldly in that fashion, one might say, "Fine, let's get on with it." But closer examination reveals unexpected complexities. Suppose you are interested in predicting successful response to psychotherapy. By successful in this instance, you mean that the client will be able to handle his family, work, financial, and other responsibilities competently. But what exactly does that statement mean? Following therapy, the client may feel so liberated from his doubts and fears that he resigns from his safe, secure job to seek a more challenging one, or he may discover that his "old" wife is no longer compatible with his new "self"—are these behaviors classifiable under the heading of "family and work competency"? Perhaps these are academic questions, because *ultimate* criteria of this type are rarely employed in practice. Obviously one would have to spend years collecting the relevant data, and such time-consuming procedures are very expensive. Consequently, most assessment studies focus on *intermediate* criteria of performance presumed to be related to ultimate criteria. In our example, we might substitute "improvement" at the end of 30 weekly treatment sessions on whatever measures we are interested in for the more distant successful handling of real-life responsibilities. Other assessment studies might choose instead to focus on *immediate* criteria of performance. In the example used, that might be defined as the client's appearing for his first therapy session on time, being responsive verbally, seeming reluctant to leave, and asking to return the next week. Whether these particular indicators are relevant to the intermediate and ultimate criteria is a matter for conjecture, but the assessor should select immediate criteria he has reason to believe are relevant to more long-term values.

2. *Selection of instruments.* The next step in the process involves the selection of instruments to be used in the prediction of criterion scores. Ideally, the instrument should be relevant to the criterion, as in the "job sample" technique; if one wants to hire an automobile mechanic, that

individual might be asked to tune an engine to evaluate his proficiency. This approach is difficult to apply to personality assessment problems in which criteria are often complex or imprecisely defined. Great care should be taken to select or develop instruments that have predictive capability. Continuous evaluation to improve the instruments is essential. Considerations of convenience and economy often enter into the choice of instruments, but one must not allow these practical considerations to take precedence over criterion relevance. A short, inexpensive objective procedure that has no predictive power may be worse than previous highly informal unstructured interviewing, since some people (those who instituted it) insist on using the "numerical" results of the invalid procedure for decision making.

3. *Development of predictor battery.* After the instruments have been chosen, it is necessary to obtain empirical information concerning the relationships between predictors and criteria. Ideally, one gives the instruments to all candidates for the treatment in question and accepts all of them into the program, regardless of where their scores fall. Later, measures of response to treatment are obtained, and relations between predicted and actual criterion scores are computed. When the criterion standard is of an intermediate or ultimate nature, it is often not practical to wait until such measures become available. Under these conditions, the battery of instruments may be administered to patients currently in treatment on whom intermediate or ultimate criterion data already exist.

4. *Combination of data.* Predictor measures must be combined so as to yield the most accurate forecast of criterion scores. The multiple-regression model is often used for this purpose. The question of how much weight to give human (or more narrowly, clinical) judgment must also be considered.

5. *Cross-validation of predictor weights.* The multiple-regression equation derived for a given sample cannot be assumed to hold for other similar samples. A frequent solution to this problem is to divide randomly a group of patients for whom both predictor and criterion measures are available into a derivation sample and a cross-validation sample. A set of regression weights is determined for the derivation sample and then also used for prediction of the criterion in the cross-validation sample. The correlation between predicted and obtained scores in the cross-validation sample is then assumed to be a reasonably accurate estimate of the predictive validity of a fixed set of predictors. Although there are disagreements as to optimal cross-validation procedures, there is agreement that some kind of cross-validation is essential if one is to make accurate predictions.

6. *Application of predictor battery.* The final step of the prediction process involves the application of the assessment battery for purposes of

selection and/or classification. Testing under standard conditions, scoring of the inventories or tests, applying cross-validated regression weights to the test scores—all this is done to obtain a predicted criterion score for each subject. Individuals may then be rank-ordered in terms of their predicted criterion scores, which represent, let us say, their probable favorable response to parole. If the parole board wishes to achieve the best possible record, it may then select only those individuals in the top quartile of scores for release into the community. This latter point has to do with decision making, which, after all, is the overriding concern of personality assessment.

DISCRIMINATIVE EFFICIENCY OF PSYCHOLOGICAL TESTS: BASE RATES AND SELECTION RATIOS

Cronbach and Gleser's *Psychological Tests and Personnel Decisions* (1957) directed attention to the *outcomes* of decisions and their *consequences* for individuals and institutions, whereas traditional assessment psychologists have emphasized only measurement and prediction. The decision theory orientation raises questions about the classical procedures for determining the worth of a psychological test or assessment procedure. For example, the validity coefficient tells us the degree of association that exists between predicted and obtained criterion scores. However, from a practical standpoint the number of correct decisions resulting from use of a given cutoff score seems more important than knowledge of the validity coefficient. The following discussion represents only a small part of the area mapped out by Cronbach and Gleser. For a comprehensive view of this contribution, the interested reader should consult the original monograph (Cronbach & Gleser, 1957) or the revised edition (Cronbach & Gleser, 1965).

There are four possible outcomes of a prediction that, let us say, has to do with success in college (i.e., graduation). When success is predicted and success in fact occurs, the individuals so classified are called *valid positives*. When success is predicted and failure results, the individuals are referred to as *false positives*. When failure is predicted and failure occurs, the individuals are described as *valid negatives*. When failure is predicted, but success takes place, these individuals are known as *false negatives*. All these conditions involve cutoff scores on the predictor variable (e.g., an equation derived from the California Psychological Inventory) and cutoff classification on the criterion (in this instance, graduation versus failure to graduate from college). The extent to which a predictor score or set of scores is able to separate and classify outcomes accurately (valid positives and valid negatives) is referred to as the discriminative efficiency of the score or set of scores. The probability of occurrence of any of the subtypes mentioned above is determined by dividing the frequency of a given outcome by the total number of people in the sample.

Perhaps a simple illustration will elucidate the usefulness of this approach. Gynther and Mayer (1960) asked if a brief IQ test (the Kent EGY) could serve as a substitute for the WAIS, which takes about an hour to administer and about 15–20 minutes to score properly. The literature indicated that correlations of .60–.65 had been found between the two tests, but that information in no way answered the question. So both Wechslers and Kent-EGYs were given to 47 patients referred to a psychology service with a question of mental deficiency. They were classified as either defective or nondefective on the basis of cutoff scores established by the test constructors. The Wechsler classifications were considered the criterion measures and the Kent-EGY scores predictor variables. Analysis of the results by means of the usual fourfold contingency table showed that the Kent-EGY predicted mental deficiency correctly only 46% (13/28) of the time, while it identified nondefectives with 95% (18/19) accuracy. With respect to correct classification of all subjects, then, this test was accurate in 66% [(18 + 13)/47] of the cases. The original question can now be answered. If the Kent-EGY score is 19 or above, mental deficiency is essentially ruled out; if the score obtained is 18 or less, one must proceed with the WAIS to obtain an accurate "diagnosis."

Two other terms need to be mentioned: base rate and selection ratio. "Base rate," which refers to the proportion of actual positives (e.g., potential college graduates) that exist in the total sample, has been a very well-known term since Meehl and Rosen published an influential article on it in 1955. More generally, it refers to the frequency of occurrence of any event (e.g., suicide attempts) in a given sample. The term "selection ratio," which refers to the proportion of predicted positives *selected* in relation to the total number of subjects, has probably been more widely used in industrial or military circles than in clinical settings. A less technical definition of it has been given by Cronbach (1970); the selection ratio is the proportion of persons tested who are accepted.

A helpful example of the influence of the base rate can be drawn from Meehl and Rosen (1955). Men being inducted into the military service were given an inventory to detect "those men who would not complete basic training because of psychiatric disability or AWOL recidivism." All those given the inventory were allowed to undergo basic training regardless of their test scores. Samples of individuals who made a good adjustment (N = 415) and a poor adjustment (N = 89) to basic training were selected for a study of predictive validity. (Base rates for good and poor adjustment: 82 and 18%, respectively.) The most effective scale for screening out misfits picked up, at a given cutting point, 55% of the poor-adjustment group (valid positives) and 19% of the good-adjustment group (false positives). Meehl and Rosen asked, given these facts, how good this cutting score is for the purpose stated. They assumed that 5% of all inductees would fall into the poor-adjustment group and 95% would make a good adjustment. If one casts 10,000 cases into a fourfold contingency table (on the basis of the four percentages just given), it will be found that the cutting score is actually no good for screening out misfits. Only 275/2080, or 13%, of those predicted to make a poor adjustment would actually fall in that category. The decisions for 1805, or 87%, would be incorrect. [If one were to use the original base rates (i.e., 82 and 18%), decisions for "only" 62% of the predicted "poors" would be incorrect.]

Cronbach (1970, p. 540) has supplied an illustration which shows even more clearly than Meehl and Rosen's data how changes in the base rate influence the predictive accuracy of a cutoff score. In this case, the problem has to do with the number of patients coming to a clinic who are depressed. When that frequency (i.e., base rate) is 50%, use of a given cutting score on a psychological inventory correctly classifies 80% of these individuals. However, if only 20% are depressed, use of the same cutting score results in only 50% correct identification. If only 5% are depressed, use of this cutting score correctly identifies only 15–20% of these patients. Finally, if the base rate for depression is 2%, the cutting score accurately identifies less than 10% of the depressed patients. There are conditions under which the base rate is known to be less than 10% (e.g., suicide in psychiatric inpatients); the reader can imagine the probability of correct test predictions (and the tremendous number of false positives) likely to occur using a cutoff score obtained from any test with less than perfect validity.

As stated earlier, the concept of selection ratio has been applied more in industrial than clinical settings. Cronbach (1970) has said, "There are no quotas in clinical diagnosis; every person tested can be called 'normal' or every one called 'schizophrenic' if such uniform classification appears correct" (p. 446). However, it is possible to conceive of situations in which this concept might be relevant to the clinical or counseling psychologist, especially one who is interested in understanding outcomes of prediction. One might, for example, wish to consider assigning patients to treatment under conditions in which there are not enough therapists to handle every patient. Or one might wish to consider the relationship between test scores and admission to two kinds of colleges, the state university and a highly selective private university. Those in academic work certainly are familiar with differences between the number of applicants and the number of admissions to graduate school in psychology.

When most applicants for a position or treatment are accepted, the selection ratio is considered to be high. Such a ratio would be in effect in most state universities. When only a small fraction of applicants is accepted, the selection ratio is said to be low. At the present time, this type of ratio is characteristic of acceptances to graduate programs in clinical psychology.

Selection becomes increasingly efficient as the selection ratio becomes smaller. This is true even when the test being used possesses very modest validity. We are not referring to the *overall* proportion of correct decisions, but rather to the proportion of applicants selected who are subsequently judged to have performed well. This orientation ignores the outcome of rejection. In industrial settings, it may be appropriate to display little interest in the applicant who is not hired, but in clinical settings the proportion of false negatives who do not receive the required treatment is of great importance. If the selection ratio is set very low (e.g., 5%) for some specialized, expensive brain surgery, the vast majority of patients who could benefit from it will not receive it.

Base rates and selection ratios markedly affect the predictive power of cutoff scores derived from psychological tests. Indices developed under one set of circumstances cannot be expected to work equally well in other situations in which these parameters have different values. Individuals who are interested in developing new test indices or applying well-established ones cannot ignore the constraints these variables place on predictive accuracy.

THE NATURE OF OBJECTIVE PERSONALITY MEASURES

What kind of instrument might be used to carry out "objective personality assessment?" One often hears that projective tests such as the Rorschach are characterized by ambiguous stimuli (see Chapter 1), whereas objective measures such as the MMPI are noted for their unambiguous structured stimuli. However, if one were to give 20 students tracing paper and pencils and ask them to reproduce Card I of the Rorschach, it is likely that great correspondence would be found in the resulting drawings. As for structured inventories, they typically make use of statements containing such qualifiers as "usually," "sometimes," or "seldom," and

Simpson (1944) has shown that these adverbs are interpreted very differently by different people. For example, 25% of his subjects said they applied "usually" only to behaviors that occurred at least 90% of the time, whereas another 25% said that for them "usually" included frequencies of occurrence below 70%. Many other examples could be given to demonstrate that classification into "objective-projective" or "structured-unstructured" cannot be done on the basis of stimulus properties.

What *does* differentiate the two types of measurement techniques is the restriction placed on the response option. Objective personality measuring devices are commonly designed so that the subject must answer "true" or "false," whereas tests such as the Rorschach allow a multitude of responses. Wiggins (1973) emphasizes in this regard the nearly perfect scoring reliability that results from a true-false response option procedure. Subjects' test-taking attitudes and the examiner's set have also been considered as features distinguishing between structured and unstructured techniques. It would be difficult to improve on Kelly's (1958) comment: "When the subject is asked to guess what the examiner is thinking, we call it an objective test; when the examiner tries to guess what the subject is thinking, we call it a projective device" (p. 332).

Although graduate students frequently identify objective personality assessment courses as MMPI courses, the types of data available for this kind of assessment are far broader than even the self-report inventory approach in general. Cronbach (1970) proposes three general categories of objective personality assessment: observations in representative situations, reports from others and from the subject, and performance tests. Cattell (1946) has described the same basic sources of information somewhat differently, as life-record data (L data), questionnaire data (Q data), and objective test data (T data). L data are obtained from observations of subjects in everyday life situations, either by peers or trained observers, or from analysis of life-history documents or biographies. Q data are obtained from the self-reports of subjects. T data are obtained from subjects' behavioral responses (physiological, motoric, verbal) to a wide assortment of provocative physical, pictorial, or verbal stimuli. Performance tests are intended to obtain distortion-free information on overt behavior; it is assumed that the subject cannot perceive the relationship between his responses and the variable (e.g., persistence) being assessed. Cattell and Warburton (1967) have recently published a volume containing hundreds of examples of tests of this type.

Although other chapters of this book are concerned primarily with L data (Chapters 1 and 5) and T data (Chapters 2, 3, and 5), it may be appropriate to give some examples of the instruments being used in these areas. The life-history approach often takes the form of rating scales for evaluating the current mental status of psychiatric patients. Among the best known of these endeavors are the DIAGNO system (Spitzer & Endicott, 1969), the Inpatient Multidimensional Psychiatric Scale (Lorr & Klett, 1970), and the Brief Psychiatric Rating Scale (Overall & Gorham, 1962). As an illustration that L data need not take the form of rating scales, Overall's study (1971) of the relationship between marital status and psychopathology can be mentioned.

T data come in many forms. One of the longest, and most detailed analyses of such data in the literature has recently been presented by Cattell, Schmidt, and Bjerstedt (1972). Their monograph deals with Cattell's Objective-Analytic Personality Test Battery and examines the relationship between objective tests and clinical diagnoses. Another set of instruments that has also been investigated extensively is the Halstead Neuropsychological Test Battery. This battery has been used to differentiate among brain-damaged, schizophrenic, and medical patients (Levine & Feirstein, 1972) and to study in particular the cognitive functioning of neurological patients (Reitan & Boll, 1971). Other investigators have employed the Holtzman Inkblot Test (Overall & Gorham, 1972) and measures of digit copying and synonym learning (Kendrick, 1972) for similar purposes.

For extended general presentations of objective personality assessment, the reader is referred to the following texts: *Objective Personality Assessment* (Butcher, 1972), *Personality Measurement* (Kleinmuntz, 1967), and *Personality Assessment* (Lanyon & Goodstein, 1971). Goodstein and Lanyon (1971) have also edited *Readings in Personality Assessment*, which starts with selections from Galton and Jung and concludes with articles on such topics as computer interpretation of psychological tests. Two volumes of a series by McReynolds (1968, 1971), called *Advances in Psychological Assessment*, also contain many interesting and authoritative articles. As the major focus of this chapter is on self-report personality inventories (Q data), we now turn to that topic.

DEVELOPMENT OF PERSONALITY INVENTORIES: A HISTORICAL SKETCH

One writer traces the beginnings of assessment back to the Chinese civil service examinations of 4000 years ago (DuBois, 1970), while another (Hathaway, 1965) describes a biblical episode concerning a method of personnel selection. For our purposes, Galton appears to be a good starting point, inasmuch as he not only might be designated as the father of the scientific study of individual differences, but he also actually devised a questionnaire concerning imagery. Interest in individual differences can be traced from the writings of such men as J. McKeen Cattell and G. Stanley Hall, and the academic endeavors of these psychologists constitute one of two major influences leading to the development of personality inventories. The other major influence consisted of demands by society for help in dealing with such pressing problems as the education of slow learners and the classification and treatment of mental disorders, demands responded to by Binet, Kraepelin, Jung, and others.

These academic and pragmatic lines of investigation merged during World War I. Hundreds of thousands of men were being inducted into military service as rapidly as possible. Some evaluation of their emotional fitness for warfare was desired, but not enough qualified people were available for interviewing them all. Woodworth and Poffenberger responded to this need by developing the Personal Data Sheet (Woodworth, 1920), which is generally considered the first personality inventory. Psychiatric texts were examined for symptoms of psychological disturbance in order to develop a paper-and-pencil version of the psychiatric interview. The final scale (which was never actually used during the war) contained 116 items of the following kind: "Have you failed to get a square deal in life?" "Are you happy most of the time?" "Does the sight of blood make you sick or dizzy?" The respondent was to answer "yes" or "no" to each item. Recruits who reported many symptoms were to be detained for further questioning, and the Personal Data Sheet, by that criterion, seemed an impressive predictor of maladjustment. It should be stressed, however, that the item content of this inventory was chosen on the basis of face validity; that is, items were included if Woodworth thought they would elicit different responses from well-adjusted and poorly adjusted subjects.

Although many efforts were subsequently made to adapt Woodworth's questionnaire to groups such as school children, juvenile delinquents, and college students, the next substantive advance in item selection procedures for inventories was made by Strong (1927). The Strong Vocational Interest Blank was designed by means of an empirical approach to item selection. Unlike a priori or rational or face validity approaches, in which the test constructor tries to select items that *seem* adequately to sample the relevant domain, *criterion keying* (another term for the empirical strategy) is a technique that makes few theoretical assumptions about an item's proper inclusion in a personality test. Strong's procedure was to compare the responses given to test items by persons of one occupation with those given by people in general. For example, several thousand engineers took his test. He tabulated their answers item by item to determine on which items the difference in responses between engineers and people in general was statistically significant, and these items were retained for the engineer scoring key. A high score on this scale then led to two interrelated predictions: (a) this individual's pattern of interests is very similar to that of practicing engineers and, (b) hence he is more likely to enjoy a career in engineering than people with lower scores.

In the early 1930s two inventories that deserve comment were published. Bernreuter's Personality Inventory (1931) was notable in that it was one of the first adjustment questionnaires that was multidimensional (unlike the Personal Data Sheet, which yielded a single global measure of adjustment). Bernreuter combined items from earlier inventories measuring neurotic tendencies, ascendance-submission, and introversion-extroversion with his own Self-Sufficiency Scale. The other questionnaire, the Allport-Vernon Study of Values (1931), was novel in that it was the first popular inventory to be derived from theory, namely, Spranger's (1928) typology of the religious man, the aesthetic man, the economic man, and so forth, and it required forced-choice responding.

The next important historical development was the application of the external strategy to the construction of adjustment scales. The Humm-Wadsworth Temperament Schedule (1935) was probably the first of this type to be published (and to use psychiatric patients for criterion groups), although for various reasons it never was employed very much in clinical settings. One reason might be that the Minnesota Multiphasic Personality Inventory (MMPI) was "announced" in 1940 (Hathaway & McKinley, 1940) and published 3 years later (Hathaway & McKinley, 1943). This inventory became popular almost immediately, probably in large part as a result of the demand for assessment and classification associated with screening of personnel for military duty in World War II.

Several other trends emerged in the 1940s and 1950s, including (a) more concentrated efforts to develop inventories by factor analytic methods, (b) the use of criterion keying to develop an inventory to describe normal personalities, and (c) another application of the forced-choice method, this time derived from a different theory. Guilford and his associates published several inventories (STDCR, Guilford, 1940; GAMIN, Guilford & Martin, 1943; the Temperament Survey, Guilford & Zimmerman, 1949), all based on one version of the internal (i.e., factor-analytic) strategy of test construction. Basically, this is a statistical procedure for identifying clusters of items that are relatively highly correlated with each other. Cattell utilized a somewhat different approach from Guilford's in that he assembled personality trait names rather than inventory items. He published the Sixteen Personality Factor Questionnaire (16 PF) in 1949 and other inventories [e.g., the IPAT Anxiety Scale Questionnaire (Cattell & Scheier, 1963)] later. Eysenck, the third of the major figures associated with the factor-analytic approach, published the Maudsley Personality Inventory in 1959 and the Eysenck Personality Inventory 4 years later (Eysenck & Eysenck, 1963). Gough (1957) applied the empirical strategy to construction of the California Psychological Inventory (CPI), which was designed to tap important dimensions of normal functioning not being measured by any of the then existing adjustment inventories. The other well-known inventory published in the 1950s was the Edwards Personal Preference Schedule (EPPS) (Edwards, 1954). In some respects this inventory resembled the Study of Values, but Edwards derived his items from Murray's (1938) personality need theory.

We conclude this highly selective historical sketch by briefly describing three of the most recent inventories to appear on the scene: Edwards (1967) Personality Inventory (EPI), Jackson's (1967) Personality Research Form (PRF) and Jackson and Messick's not yet published Differential Personality Inventory (DPI). All three instruments were constructed using a mixed intuitive-internal strategy. Jackson in particular has been guided by the multitrait model (Campbell & Fiske, 1959), which emphasizes the necessity for demonstrating both convergent and discriminant validity of a personality scale.

The EPI is notable for including about 1200 items to measure 53 scales, which represents the farthest departure yet from Woodworth's simple global index of adjustment. This inventory no longer uses the forced-choice format of Edwards' earlier Personal Preference Schedule, but is administered with unusual instructions, that is, "Predict how people who know you best would mark each statement if they were asked to describe you." The PRF is the latest attempt to measure Murray's constructs. The inventory consist of 20 scales with such familiar names as Achievement, Affiliation, Aggression, and Autonomy. The DPI has appeared in certain research articles (e.g., Trott & Morf, 1972), but is not yet considered to be in final form (D. N. Jackson, Personal communication, January 1974). This questionnaire is definitely oriented toward the adjustment domain, in contrast to the EPI and the PRF. Maladjustment is fractionated into 28 components, including Cynicism, Impulsivity, Neurotic Disorganization, Psychotic Tendencies, Insomnia, and Sadism.

For the reader who wishes a comprehensive historical review of personality scales and inventories, Goldberg's (1971) article is recommended. We now turn to a brief discussion of the rationale used for selecting the inventories that receive fuller review in the remainder of this chapter.

CRITERIA FOR MAJOR REVIEWS

The principal criteria used for selecting personality inventories for discussion at length are (a) clinical (adjustment-maladjustment) emphasis, (b) multidimensionality (as opposed to single-scale approaches), (c) importance as determined by the amount of research activity, (d) importance as determined by degree of usage, and (e) exemplifying the different strategies of test construction. The first criterion excludes such excellent inventories as the Strong Vocational Interest Blank (Campbell, 1971), which at age 47 is probably more popular than ever before but is rarely used for clinical evaluation. The second criterion raises questions concerning the wisdom of including a questionnaire such as the EPI (Eysenck & Eysenck, 1963), which measures only two traits. The third criterion can be evaluated by examining the lists of references in the Character and Personality (Nonprojective) section of *The Seventh Mental Measurements Yearbook* (Buros, 1972). The top 10 in amount of research activity are the MMPI (Hathaway & McKinley, 1967) (first), the EPPS (Edwards, 1959), the CPI (Gough, 1969), the 16 PF (Cattell, Eber, & Tatsuoka, 1970), the Study of Values (Allport, Vernon, & Lindzey, 1970), the Adjective Check List (Gough & Heilbrun, 1965), the EPI (Eysenck & Eysenck, 1969), the Personal Orientation Inventory (Shostrom, 1966), the Tennessee Self-Concept Scale (Fitts, 1965), and the Omnibus Personality Inventory (OPI) (Heist & Yonge, 1968) (tenth). The MMPI has about 800 references listed for the approximately 6-7 years reviewed, which is more than twice the number of studies reported for the EPPS and 10 times the number reported for the OPI.

The best source for considering the fourth criterion is a recent survey of psychological test usage in the United States by Lubin, Wallis, and Paine (1971). These authors drew up a list of 149 tests and sent it to 551 mental health agencies in the United States. Usable responses were received from about half of the agencies, which included outpatient clinics, mental retardation schools and centers, state hospitals, counseling centers, and Veterans Administration stations. Several analyses were made of the results. The two most relevant for our purposes involve reports of tests used by 10% or more of the total sample and of testing practices of different psychological services. If only objective personality measures are considered, 10% or more use the MMPI (fifth of *all* tests in weighted scale rank), the EPPS (eighteenth), the CPI (thirty-third), the Mooney Problem Check List (thirty-fifth), the 16 PF (thirty-seventh), the Study of Values (thirty-eighth), the IPAT Anxiety Questionnaire (forty-eighth), the Guilford-Zimmerman Temperament Survey (fiftieth), Bell's Adjustment Inventory (sixty-first), and the California Test of Personality (sixty-fifth). Comparison of the use of two inventories, the MMPI and the EPPS, in what might be called counseling and clinical settings, is instructive. In state hospitals, VA stations, and outpatient clinics, the MMPI ranked fourth, first, and seventh, respectively, while the EPPS ranked sixty-sixth, twenty-fourth, and thirty-eighth. In the counseling centers the EPPS ranked third while the MMPI ranked fifth. In other words, the relatively high rank of the EPPS on the "10% or more" list is due almost entirely to its very frequent usage in counseling centers.

The final criterion has to do with strategy of scale construction. Our thought here was to attempt to include at least one example of each approach to inventory development if, in so doing, we could also reasonably satisfy the other criteria. There is some disagreement on what the strategies are. Goldberg (1974) has divided them into three categories: intuitive, intuitive-internal, and external. On other occasions, the same author (Goldberg, 1972b) has used the terms factor-analytic, contrasted-groups, rational, and theoretical. We find the latter set more meaningful, but this is probably a matter of taste. In any case, the inventories that best seemed to fufill the five criteria are the MMPI, the CPI, the 16 PF, and Jackson's PRF. The first two inventories named were developed primarily by the contrasted-groups strategy, the 16 PF was constructed by means of the factor-analytic strategy, and the PRF represents a sophisticated combination of rational and theoretical strategies.

THE MINNESOTA MULTIPHASIC PERSONALITY INVENTORY

Aims

This inventory was developed "as an aid in differential psychiatric diagnosis" (Hathaway & McKinley, 1940). Twenty-five years later Hathaway (1965) stated that the instrument was developed "as an objective aid in the routine psychiatric case work-up of adult patients and as a method for determining the severity of the conditions" (p. 463). Thus the inventory constructors had two purposes in mind, to assess type of maladjustment and degree of maladjustment.

Strategy of Test Construction

The method of contrasted groups was used. A set of 504 items derived from earlier inventories, clinical reports, psychiatric interviewing manuals, and various other sources was administered to normal subjects and carefully diagnosed psychiatric groups. The normal sample consisted of 724 visitors to University of Minnesota hospitals. Potential visitor subjects who said they themselves were currently under the care of a physician were excluded. This sample corresponded well in age, sex, and marital status to the overall Minnesota population. According to Dahlstrom, Welsh, and Dahlstrom (1972) a normal Minnesota adult, circa 1940, was "about thirty-five years old . . . married, lived in a small town or rural area . . . had eight years of general schooling, and worked at a skilled or semi-skilled trade (or was married to a man with such an occupational level)" (p. 8).

The psychiatric patients available to the test constructors numbered over 800, although far fewer than that number constituted the final criterion groups. For the derivation of the eight clinical scales of the instrument, the following kinds of criterion groups were used: (a) patients who showed an abnormal concern for their bodily functions; (b) patients who showed relatively uncomplicated depressive disorders; (c) patients who demonstrated conversion reactions; (d) cases in a psychiatric setting being studied at the request of courts because of delinquent actions (no capital offenders were included); (e) patients whose most prominent clinical features were ideas of reference, persecutory delusions, and grandiosity; (f) patients who showed obsessive ruminations, compulsive rituals, abnormal fears, and guilt feelings; (g) patients who displayed apathy, bizarre mentation, delusions and/or hallucinations, and autism; and (h) patients who showed overactivity, emotional excitement, and flight of ideas. For three other empirically derived scales, one used as a criterion group psychiatric patients whose profiles were all within normal limits on the clinical scales; a second used several criterion groups, including male sexual inverts relatively free from neurosis, normal males as distinguished from normal females, and feminine males identified by means of an attitude interest inventory (items added in this analysis brought the total up to 550); and the third used college students who scored high and low on a social introversion-extroversion inventory.

The typical item selection procedure involved contrasting the responses to the 504 items of the criterion groups listed above with the normative sample. Items that had true-false endorsement frequencies that differed at or beyond the .05 level of significance were retained for the final scales. In many cases derivation of the final scale actually progressed through several stages, so the outline just given is simpler than what actually occurred.

Although the MMPI has been described as the "prototypic example of empirical test construction in the realm of personality" (Wiggins, 1973, p. 389), it also includes two scales that were not derived by the method of contrasted groups. One of these scales, the Lie scale, might be described as rationally derived, in that it essentially duplicates items devised by Hartshorne and May (1928) for their studies of deceit in school children. The other scale, the Frequency scale, was statistically derived; its items were those answered by no more than 10% (and often less than 5%) of the normative sample in a particular direction.

Prior to presenting the scales that resulted from the analyses described above, we should point out that shifts in thinking about the meaning of MMPI scale scores and profiles had occurred by the time the current form of the inventory was published (Hathaway & McKinley, 1951). Meehl (cited by Cronbach, 1970) had the following to say in 1951:

> These days we are tending to start with the test, sort people on the basis of it, and then take a good look at the people to see what kind of people they are. This, of course, is different from the way in which the test was built . . . . The primary function of psychometrics is (not) . . . to prophesy what the psychiatrist is going to say about somebody [p. 534]

These remarks were based on nearly 10 years of research and clinical experience with the inventory and are included to show how and why the MMPI was transformed (by what has been called the "bootstraps effect") from a psychiatric inventory into a personality questionnaire.

The MMPI Scales

Table 1 gives the scales, number of items on the scales, and brief interpretations of high scale scores. The scales are listed by name (e.g., Schizophrenia), abbreviation (e.g., Sc), and number (e.g., 8) to reflect prevalent usage in the 1940s, the 1950s, and after 1960. Whereas scales once were referred to as "Depression" or "Paranoia," or as "D" or "Pa," one seldom hears any designation but "2" or "6" now. The word "classical" has been used to describe the interpretations of elevated scores given in the right-hand column of the table. Many more correlates are now available and are described later in this section; however, the table conveys the position taken before discouragement set in concerning precise delineation of psychiatric categories and prior to research on personological attributes of the scales. Profiles are typically referred to in terms of the two highest scale scores, that is 2-7 or 4-9. Sometimes 3-point high scores are used (e.g., 2-7-4).

Psychometric Properties

The method of item selection for the MMPI resulted in many items being included on more than one scale. For a summary of the amount and

Table 1.   Standard MMPI Scales

Scale Name	Scale Abbreviation	Scale Number	Number of Items	Classical Interpretation of Elevated Scores
Lie	L	—	15	Denial of common frailties
Frequency	F	—	64	Invalidity of profile
Correction	K	—	30	Defensive, evasive
Hypochondriasis	Hs	1	33	Emphasis on somatic complaints
Depression	D	2	60	Unhappy, depressed
Hysteria	Hy	3	60	Hysterical symptomatology
Psychopathic Deviancy	Pd	4	50	Lack of social conformity; often in trouble with law
Masculinity-Femininity	Mf	5	60	Effeminate (males); masculine orientation (females)
Paranoia	Pa	6	40	Suspicious
Psychasthenia	Pt	7	48	Worried, anxious
Schizophrenia	Sc	8	78	Withdrawn; bizarre mentation
Hypomania	Ma	9	46	Impulsive; expansive
Social Introversion-Extroversion	Si	0	70	Introverted, shy

direction of item overlap, the reader should see Dahlstrom, Welsh, and Dahlstrom (1972, p. 232). Their table indicates that some items appear on as many as six scales. Typically only a small fraction of the items identified with a scale appear only on that scale. Of the 78 items making up Scale 8, for example, only 16 are unique to that scale.

The True-False keying balance is also of interest. Examination of the basic scales shows that few of them have an approximately equal split of T-F answers. Scales L and K are the worst offenders; 100% of L's items are keyed False and 29 of K's 30 items are keyed False. Scales 7, 8, and 9 each have a T-F keying ratio of more than 3:1, whereas Scale 3's is less than 1:3. The only scales that one could call relatively well balanced are 4, 5 (for males and females), and 0.

Intercorrelations among the basic scales are reported in Dahlstrom and Welsh (1960, pp. 475–477). These correlations were obtained from eight different investigations using both normal and psychiatric patient subjects, and they indicate that several of the scales are highly interrelated. For example, the correlations between Scales 7 and 8 vary from .64 to .87

across the different samples, and three of the correlations between Scales 1 and 3 exceed .77. Some of the scales are negatively correlated with each other; for example, the values between Scales 2 and 9 vary from −.02 to −.63. In some cases the correlations are moderate (e.g., between Scales 4 and 9), and in other instances the relationships are minimal (e.g., between Scales 5 and 9). Generally speaking, the intercorrelations are positive and often significant, undoubtedly in part because of the item overlap.

Scales so obviously intercorrelated naturally draw the interest of factor-analytically oriented investigators, who ask whether the variance associated with the 10 or 13 scales can be explained more parsimoniously. Dahlstrom and Welsh (1960, pp. 84-85) have summarized the factor-analytic findings through 1959. The findings of Welsh (1956) are typical. His analyses disclosed that nearly all the variance across the scale scores can be identified by two factors, which he labeled A (anxiety) and R (repression). Other investigators have given these factors different labels, ranging from substantive (e.g., introversion) to stylistic (e.g., social desirability) designations. A more recent study by Block (1965), which attempted to control for various response biases, obtained factors called "ego resiliency" and "ego control." Although not everyone would agree on the meaning of the dimensions, there is consensus that two virtually independent factors account for most of the MMPI scale variance.

The final psychometric feature of the MMPI we wish to call attention to is the reliability of the scales (cf. Dahlstrom and Welsh, 1960, pp. 472–474). The short-term stability figures for psychiatric patients range from .52 to .93, with the median value being in the .80's. When there has been a long interval between testing (e.g., 4 years), the correlations drop considerably. For high school students, the long-term values ranged from .13 to .54 with a median in the high .30's. For college students somewhat more favorable results were obtained, consisting of long-term retest correlations from .16 to .73 with a median in the mid-.40's. Values for the longest interval (5–330 days) examined for psychiatric patients ranged from .37 to .83 with median values in the .60's. Since reliability coefficients limit validity coefficients, some writers have expressed concern about the size of these reliability figures. However, it is difficult to see how an inventory that, at least in part, measures mood can display the level of reliability coefficients found with intelligence tests.

As for split-half estimates of reliability, Dahlstrom and Welsh (1960) report several investigations with psychiatric patients but only one involving a normal group. The obtained coefficients over all samples ranged from −.05 to .96 with median values in the .70's. Many of the values would be considered unacceptable for inventories constructed by internal consistency analyses. Perhaps the reason that so few internal consistency studies of the MMPI have been done is that they do not make much sense. For example, in splitting the scale one might find nearly all the True-keyed statements in one half and nearly all the False-keyed statements in the other half.

Many psychometrically sophisticated psychologists have expressed dismay concerning the properties of the MMPI we have briefly reviewed above. The heterogeneity of the scales, the relatively high scale intercorrelations, the item overlap, the imbalance in T-F keying, and the moderate stability coefficients have all been criticized. However, the intent of the test constructors was to produce an instrument that could help make judgments and decisions. Hathaway (1972a, p. xiv) acknowledges the MMPI's "lack of constructural quality" but feels that it "affords some independent security for insecure personal judgments." In the next section we review the principal work that undergirds Hathaway's guarded optimism about the utility of the inventory.

Research on the Interpretation of Scales and Profiles

The MMPI has been investigated more thoroughly than any other personality inventory. According to Dahlstrom (1974), approximately 6000 studies will be cited in Volume 2 of his revised handbook on the instrument. Butcher's (1969) classified bibliography indicates that major attention has focused on psychometric characteristics and diagnosis of psychopathology. Other areas of research are more specific and include such diverse foci as aging, genetic studies, operant conditioning, profile similarity, and additional scale development. An attempt to review a representative sample of these studies or to concentrate on the most important among them might produce some worthwhile generalizations but would not serve the applied aims of this chapter. Hence the emphasis falls on empirical findings most relevant to the clinical interpretation of the MMPI.

Much of the early work investigated relationships between scale scores and either self-ratings or ratings by others (friends or experts). The investigators obtained correlates of high scale scores, low scale scores, and high-point scale scores by the method of contrasted groups. The distinction between the first and third of these terms is that "high" means that the scale score has a T value greater than 60, 65, or possibly 70, whereas "high-point" means that the scale so designated has the highest T score in the profile. These two kinds of high score definitions have been termed "nomothetic" and "idiographic," respectively; correlates arising from each method are presented in Chapters 6 and 7 of the revised handbook (Dahlstrom, Welsh, & Dahlstrom, 1972).

The problem with high scale analysis is that "high" is defined in different ways by different investigators. Therefore, the correlates obtained are not very useful for MMPI interpretation. High-point correlates, however, do have an immediate application, since anyone can look at an MMPI and reliably determine which is the peak score. Guthrie (1949), for example, found that medical patients with peak scores on Scale 1 presented a wide variety of symptoms and complaints, little manifest anxiety, and a marked tendency to consult with doctors frequently. Black (1953) found only one term significantly related to an MMPI peak score on Scale 2 in a group of college women: shy. However, ratings of these women by others significantly omitted such adjectives as cheerful, kind, energetic, relaxed, and self-confident and painted a general picture of self-depreciation and inadequacy. Guthrie's (1949) medical patients with high-point 2's showed a high incidence of depression with some physical symptoms.

Halbower (1955) selected profile types to be investigated on the basis of a survey of MMPIs of 113 Veterans Administration mental hygiene cases. He used the average category assigned to each Q-sort item by the patients' therapists to obtain a modal Q sorting for each of the MMPI profile types he investigated: 1-2/2-1's, 1-3/3-1's, 2-7/7-2's, and 8-7/7-8's. In addition to the profiles having the indicated scale scores as high points, numerous other selection criteria were imposed. For example, to be included in the 1-2/2-1 group, MMPIs had to have a 1-2-3 slope, with all three scales above a T score of 70; Scale 7 above 70; Scales 4, 6, and 9 below 70, preferably with Scale 9 a low point; Scale 8 less than 7 by three points, preferably below 70; F between 55 and 70 and equal to or greater than L and K; and the subtle score on Scale 3 less than 65. This type of procedure obviously has two consequences, namely, selected profiles are more homogeneous than a simple high-point grouping and many are eliminated because of lack of fit with the criteria.

Halbower's 1-2/2-1's presented themselves as organically sick. Complaints of pain, weakness, and easy fatiguability were prominent. They were passive-dependent and lacked insight into their own behavior. Halbower's 1-3/3-1's also manifested somatization or psychophysiological reactions. However, they were also described as self-centered, demanding, passively aggressive, and likely to lose their tempers under slight provocation. The 2-7/7-2 group demonstrated feelings of inferiority along with strong motivation for personal recognition. In contrast with the 1-2/2-1's and 1-3/3-1's, these patients did not rely on somatic complaints to reduce anxiety or use denial or projection to "solve" their problems. Halbower's 8-7/7-8's were described as worrying and overideational and as lacking in poise, self-confidence, and common sense.

Somatic symptoms did not provide them with relief from anxiety; in fact, they lacked any efficient defenses to protect themselves from environmental threats.

Meehl (1956), in a widely cited paper titled "Wanted—A Good Cookbook," stressed the need for a complete collection of test-defined code types with empirically derived descriptive data. It is generally agreed that the first real MMPI cookbook, in Meehl's terms, was produced by Marks and Seeman (1963).

Marks and Seeman examined hundreds of MMPIs obtained from psychiatric patients admitted to the University of Kansas Medical Center. Eventually 16 high-frequency code types, which accounted for 78% of the total sample, were selected. Two-point or 3-point high codes and many additional rules were used to specify each profile type. The primary source of descriptor data was a 108-item Q deck containing both descriptive and dynamic items. Professional staff familiar with the patient sorted each Q item into one of nine categories on the basis of how well it fit the patient's behavior. For each profile type the five patients whose descriptions were most similar were selected as a defining group. The mean placement of each Q item was then computed on the five patients in each of the 16 profile types. Demographic data and descriptive data from case histories, hospital records, and therapy notes were also analyzed and included in the correlates offered. Frequency of occurrence of descriptor data for a given code type was compared to base rates derived from the entire sample. Although males were included in the study, the profile-type descriptors are for women only. It should also be noted that the average amount of education for the final sample of 320 patients (20 per code type) was 13 years and the average IQ was 112. The patients were almost all voluntary admissions, preference having been given to those likely to benefit from short-term treatment.

So many differentiating correlates were found for each code type that it is not possible to illustrate the richness and complexity of this system in the limited space available. Perhaps an example would be helpful. Five "most descriptive" and five "least descriptive" Q-item characteristics are given for a profile that fit Marks and Seeman's 8-9/9-8 code type. The most descriptive characteristics are: genotype has schizoid features; delusional thinking is present; spends a good deal of time in personal fantasy and daydreams; tends to be ruminative and overideational; and utilizes regression as a defense mechanism. The least descriptive characteristics include: is normal, healthy, symptom-free; has the capacity for forming close interpersonal relationships; has a resilient ego-defense system; has a safe margin of integration; and would be organized and adaptive if under stress or trauma. Response to treatment, prognosis, school history, relations with father, and many other correlates are also given for this and the other 15 code types.

A psychologist in Idaho, Maine, or Texas who obtains a profile that fits one of Marks and Seeman's 16 code types should, in principle, be able to describe his patient in terms of the significant correlates given in the "cookbook." In practice, this has not worked very well. The code types, which accounted for about 80% of the derivation sample, have shown classification rates of only 15–28% in other samples (e.g., Gynther, Altman, Warbin, & Sletten, 1972; Pauker, 1966; Shultz, Gibeau, & Barry, 1968). The difficulty is caused by the numerous criteria used to define the code types, a point mentioned in connection with Halbower's study. Furthermore (and somewhat surprisingly considering the empirical nature of this enterprise), there have been very few attempts to cross-validate Marks and Seeman's findings.

Although over 10 years have passed since the publication of this milestone in cookbook construction, the writers know of only two efforts, one very limited, to check out the accuracy of these correlates in other settings. Gynther and Brilliant (1968) showed that diagnoses and certain demographic characteristics ascribed to the MMPI $K+$ profile did not hold up in a public mental health center. Palmer (1970), in a much more comprehensive study, examined the validity of all the code types developed by Marks and Seeman in 2119 subjects available to him. He secured sufficient "perfect matches" only for the 3-2-1, 4-8-2, 8-9, 2-8, and $K+$ code types. Of these, he found that the 3-2-1 code type had moderate, the 4-8-2 and 8-9 fair, and the 2-8 and $K+$ poor generalizability to his sample. A recent revision of the manual (Marks, Seeman, & Haller, 1974) provides empirical correlates of profile types among adolescents as well as adults, but does not resolve the question of generalizability of the adults' correlates.

The next effort to establish empirical correlates of MMPI code types was carried out by Gilberstadt and Duker (1965). These investigators selected profiles for detailed analysis not on the basis of high-frequency codes, but to represent cardinal types of disturbed patients with classical case history characteristics. As Wiggins (1973) said, "Although the Gilberstadt-Duker system is primarily actuarial in method, it is clearly clinical in spirit" (p. 113). The profiles used were those of males tested in a Veterans Administration Hospital setting. Specifications for defining the profiles were built up by reading many case records and gradually refining the rules on the basis of continuous input of this type. Nineteen profile types based on 266 cases were finally defined; the number of subjects representing each type ranged from 6 to 36, with a median of 11. The primary source of descriptors was a 131-item checklist from which three judges independently rated each case history record for the presence or absence of each item. An item was retained if two of the three judges agreed on its presence in the case history material. Comparisons were then made between the code type sample and a general abnormal (control) sample of 100 patients. Items that appeared significantly more often ($p \leq .05$) in the code type sample were listed as profile correlates.

As an illustration of the Gilberstadt and Duker findings, they list the following correlates as being significantly associated with the 4-3 code type: assaultive, father alcoholic, financial status poor, headache, heavy drinking, hostile, impulsive, moodiness, and suicide attempt. In addition to such correlates, diagnosis, alternative diagnoses, and other salient characteristics are listed for each profile.

Application of the Gilberstadt and Duker system to MMPIs obtained in other settings has unfortunately resulted in the same problems of limited applicability that have plagued the Marks and Seeman system. Whereas approximately 80% of the MMPIs in the Minneapolis Veterans Administration Hospital were classifiable into one of the 19 code types in the system, workers elsewhere have typically been able to classify only about 25% of their profiles. Validity generalization studies have also been rare. Fowler and Athey (1971) found good validity generalization for Gilberstadt and Duker's 1-2-3-4 code type, as did Palmer (1970). However, it is probably no coincidence that 1-2-3-4 is based on the largest derivation group (36 subjects) of any of the 19 code types. Less favorable were the validity generalization results for seven other Gilberstadt and Duker code types Palmer was able to test: 2-7-4 and 8-6 were classed as only moderate in generalizability; 2-7, 2-7-8, and 8-1-2-3 as fair; and 4 and 4-3 as poor.

Sines (1966) subsequently employed an interpretive approach quite different from the two just described. In an initial sample each MMPI profile was compared to every other profile, and a D^2 value, representing the sum of the squared differences between MMPI scale scores, was obtained. Following a series of steps too complicated to be briefly described, a prototype profile was derived. Profiles related to this precisely defined prototype, with D^2 values of 484 or less in relation to it, were classified as members of the code type.

Output data for Sines' actuarial system were gathered from the total contents of institutional records of about 80 patients. A final pool of approximately 2500 descriptors was obtained in this way, including such data as diagnosis, response to treatment, ward behavior, genotypic and phenotypic personality descriptions, demographic information, and miscellany relating to childhood, parents, spouse, and work history.

Although Sines' approach appears to be potentially very powerful, inasmuch as homogeneity of profiles is assured and the criteria are extremely comprehensive, only one code type, 4-3, has been extensively investigated thus far. Many correlates have been generated for this code type, most of which point to a hostile-aggressive behavior pattern. Validity generalization has been established by demonstrating that males with this code type in state hospital, prison, and medical center settings display essentially the same characteristics (Davis & Sines, 1971). Work by Persons and Marks (1971) also supports the generality of this particular predictor-criterion relationship. They found that male prisoner 4-3's committed significantly more violent acts than 4-2's, 4-9's, or 4-8's and significantly more violence than the base rate of inmates in general. One drawback of D^2-derived code types is that they may and often do contain profiles that ordinary coding practices would classify in a different category (e.g., a 3-4 or 4-2 may be properly classified in the 4-3 category). Hence it may be difficult for the clinician to determine whether his 4-3 qualifies as a Sines' 4-3.

Two other MMPI studies have been published that follow the empirical tradition pioneered by Guthrie (1949), Hathaway and Meehl (1952), Black (1953), and others. Both share one significant feature not included in any of the multicode studies reviewed (except Halbower's demonstration project), namely, replication was an intrinsic part of the design. Lewandowski and Graham (1972) randomly divided MMPI profiles of 588 hospitalized psychiatric patients into two subsamples. Profiles were classified according to 19 frequently occurring reciprocal two-point code types (i.e., 1-2/2-1). For each subsample, each code type was compared with all other profiles on 68 behavioral and demographic variables. Although more than 300 significant differences were found for the comparisons in each subsample, in only 66 instances were the same differences significant in both subsamples. This finding is very suggestive when one recalls that Marks and Seeman's and Gilberstadt and Duker's correlates are based on the derivation samples only.

As an example of Lewandowski and Graham's (1972) findings, correlates for their 2-3/3-2 code type included: has to be reminded what to do, more somatic concern, less conceptually disorganized, less unusual mannerisms and posturing, less suspicious, less hallucinatory behavior, and less unusual thought content. Although 588 MMPIs may seem a large number, replication procedures of this kind require even larger samples. For example, 10 of Lewandowski and Graham's 19 code types had fewer than 10 profiles in one or another of their samples, and 6 of these 10 had just one replicated descriptor or none at all.

Gynther, Altman, and Sletten (1973) carried out a similar study with much larger samples. They analyzed 16 two-point code types, plus a high F code type, which accounted for 76% of all MMPIs obtained from patients in several public mental health facilities. Positive cross-validating results were obtained for 11 code types, marginal results for three code types, and negative results for three code types. As an illustration of their findings, part of their interpretation of the $F > 25$ profile was:

This type of patient usually appears to be confused. . . . In an interview situation, patients . . . tend to be withdrawn and verbally unproductive. . . . Delusions of reference and hallucinations, particularly auditory hallucinations, may be present. . . . Despite the frequency of symptoms of confusion, organic diagnoses are not more common than for other patients. A diagnosis of alcoholism is relatively infrequent [p. 272]

Gynther et al. conducted several additional analyses of their data that suggested that (a) 3-point codes seem to have correlates essentially similar to those found for the parent 2-point codes; (b) absolute elevation seems to have little effect on correlates; (c) sex does not seem to affect code type correlates, although results for 2-4/4-2 were an exception to this generalization; (d) reciprocal code types have very similar correlates, although differential results for 2-8 and 8-2 were found; and (e) descriptors that apply to profiles given by whites do not seem to hold for blacks.

Two other developments, both unrelated to the actuarial studies, should be brought to the attention of the clinician who wishes to use the MMPI for applied purposes. One of these developments allows the psychologist to obtain additional information from the MMPI, while the other offers temptingly shorter versions of the inventory.

Wiggins (1969) was concerned with clarifying the *content* of the MMPI item pool. He developed 13 mutually exclusive scales that were " . . . internally consistent, moderately independent, and representative of the major substantive clusters of the MMPI" (p. 144). These scales are labeled Social Maladjustment, Depression, Feminine Interest, Poor Morale, Religious Fundamentalism, Authority Conflict, Psychoticism, Organic Symptoms, Family Problems, Manifest Hostility, Phobias, Hypomania, and Poor Health. Although some of these scales appear to be measuring much the same dimensions the standard scales measure, others clearly give new information. In our opinion, these scales can profitably be used to supplement interpretation of an MMPI profile.

For many years neophytes in MMPI administration have been told to give the first 375 items (plus the 7 additional K items) if giving the whole inventory was not feasible. This so-called abbreviated version simply amounted to omitting the unscored items and yielded full-scale scores (except for Scale 0). More recently, however, Kincannon (1968) has published a 71-item inventory called the Mini-Mult. This major modification was designed to be given orally and take not more than 10–15 minutes. Hugo (1971) developed a 174-item version of the MMPI for use with college students. Hugo's abbreviated MMPI includes scales 5 and 0, which are conspicuous by their absence from Kincannon's version. Most recently, Overall, Hunter, and Butcher (1973) have factored the first 168 items of the MMPI and concluded that their results justify using this modification of the MMPI as a screening instrument.

Comment

As we stated earlier, the psychometric properties of the MMPI have been criticized by many writers. Norman (1972) was emphatic in this regard:

> . . . The Multiphasic is a mess! Its original clinical criteria are anachronistic; its basic clinical scales are inefficient, redundant, and largely irrelevant for their present purposes; its administrative format and the repertoire of responses elicited are, respectively, inflexible and impoverished; and its methods for combining scale scores and for profile interpretation are unconscionably cumbersome and obtuse [p. 64]

Rodgers (1972), reviewing the MMPI in *The Seventh Mental Measurements Yearbook,* characterized the instrument as a "psychometric nightmare." Yet the same writer, in the following sentence, said ". . . it is well worth the investment of the professional psychologist to become proficient in its use" (p. 250).

Some might claim that what praise the MMPI receives is largely because it has no rival in the assessment of maladjustment. Yet that cannot be the explanation for, as we have seen, the MMPI has subtly shifted from being a psychiatric inventory to being a personality questionnaire, and there are many competing instruments in that field. Hathaway (1972b) states, "My chief defense of the MMPI would be the large amount of information provided at a low cost in professional time" (p. 22). Some might question the validity of that information, although many would probably agree that, at least in principle, actuarial studies such as those we have reviewed can eventually lead to accurate interpretations of all but the most exotic profiles.

Why do so many psychologists continue to use this obsolete instrument? Undoubtedly, inertia has something to do with it. Psychologists are notoriously unwilling to give up the old and familiar and try something new. Why? Because the "apperceptive mass" one has developed over years of reading the literature and looking at hundreds or thousands of profiles cannot be immediately transferred to another inventory, regardless of its claims to psychometric elegance. Then too, most MMPIers are on a partial reinforcement schedule. The occasional brilliant "hit" overshadows the more frequent partially correct interpretation and the occasional complete miss. And finally, practitioners are aware of the enormous quantity of research being done with this instrument and hope that when "all the blood is squeezed out of the psychometric turnip" (to use Meehl's colorful phrase), the validity of MMPI interpretations will be considerably higher than it is at present.

To paraphrase Hathaway (1965, 1972b), ghost measuring is a very difficult business.

THE CALIFORNIA PSYCHOLOGICAL INVENTORY (CPI)

Aims

The goal of the constructor of this inventory was to devise an instrument to diagnose and evaluate individuals, with emphasis on interpersonal behavior and dispositions relevant to social interactions: "The purpose of each scale is *to predict what an individual will do in a specified context, and/or to identify individuals who will be described in a certain way*" (Gough, 1968, p. 56). To achieve this end Gough selected "folk concepts," that is, attributes of interpersonal behavior found in all cultures and societies. Advantages of this approach, according to Gough, are that such folk-concept scales should be valid cross-culturally, readily comprehended by the user, and of value in forecasting longitudinal criteria as well as immediate and current behavior.

Strategy of Test Construction

The primary test construction strategy Gough employed was the method of contrasted groups, although four of the CPI scales were rationally derived and one was defined statistically. The external criteria used varied considerably from scale to scale. For two scales friends and acquaintances were asked to nominate members of their group who were high or low on the trait in question. The friends (judges) were provided with a written description of the behavior patterns considered to be relevant. The number of nominations received by each person in the group was tallied, and the group rank-ordered. Then responses to individual items of the inventory were correlated with these nominations. For several scales Gough used scores obtained on other tests or scales—IQ, California Fascism and Ethnocentrism, Sims score cards (social status)—to select criterion groups for subsequent item analysis. For other scales more objective criteria were used. One scale contrasted the responses of males to those of females, and the responses of homosexual to heterosexual males. Another scale was based on the number of extracurricular activities in which student subjects participated. Another scale was derived by contrasting the item responses of delinquents and nondelinquents. Two scales were constructed by using grade-point averages, one at the high-school level and the other at the college level. Two other scales were developed by comparing protocols obtained from psychiatric patients with responses of subjects trying to feign anxiety and distress, and protocols obtained from high school students responding either to standard or "fake good" instructions. The final scale derivation using the method of contrasted groups compared a group of 25 able young psychologists with subjects in other fields and training programs. Items that distinguished these groups were then correlated with instructors' ratings of the competence and potential of 50 psychology graduate students, and items correlating with this second criterion were retained.

Four of the scales were derived rationally to tap other dimensions Gough felt were important in social interactions, namely, poise, rigidity, a sense of personal worth, and freedom from impulsivity. Although there were some differences in the exact procedures used to derive these scales, internal consistency analyses were prominent in the construction design.

The remaining scale was developed by surveying response frequencies obtained in several samples. Those items answered in a particular way by 95% or more of all respondents comprise this scale.

The CPI Scales

The scales resulting from these many analyses are presented in Table 2. The scales are grouped in four classes, partially on the basis of factor analytic findings and partially because of interpretive considerations. According to Gough (1968), Class I scales pertain to "*interpersonal* effectiveness, style, and adequacy"; Class II scales emphasize "*intrapersonal* controls, values, styles and beliefs"; Class III scales "are of basic relevance to academic counseling and guidance"; and Class IV scales "reflect broad and far reaching attitudes toward life" [p. 76]. Although all the scales in the inventory have now been shown to have some personological meaning, it should be noted that *Wb, Gi,* and *Cm* were originally constructed as validity scales. Thus these scales now serve a dual purpose: in addition to saying something about an individual's intra- and interpersonal behavior, low scores on *Wb* and *Cm* and either very low or very high scores on *Gi* raise questions about the validity of the profile.

Table 2. CPI Scales

	Scale	Abbreviation	Number of Items
Class I	Dominance	Do	46
	Capacity for Status	Cs	32
	Sociability	Sy	36
	Social Presence	Sp	56
	Self-acceptance	Sa	34
	Sense of Well-being	Wb	44
Class II	Responsibility	Re	42
	Socialization	So	54
	Self-control	Sc	50
	Tolerance	To	32
	Good Impression	Gi	40
	Communality	Cm	28
Class III	Achievement via Conformance	Ac	38
	Achievement via Independence	Ai	32
	Intellectual Efficiency	Ie	52
Class IV	Psychological-mindedness	Py	22
	Flexibility	Fx	22
	Femininity	Fe	38

Psychometric Properties

Gough was an undergraduate at the University of Minnesota in the late 1930s and a graduate student in the late 1940s. As might be expected for a student at Minnesota at that time, he worked with the MMPI and developed some of his scales from MMPI items. For other scales, however, he found the MMPI item pool lacking in relevant questions, and he therefore turned to new items addressed more explicitly to interpersonal behavior and constructive achievement. The result is that approximately 178 of the 480 CPI items are virtually identical to MMPI items and 35 others are quite similar (see Megargee, 1972). Megargee also notes that "The proportion of MMPI items on the various CPI scales ranges from a low of 4% for the Communality (Cm) scale, to a high of 91% for the Well-Being (Wb) scale" (p. 25). Thorndike (1959) reacted to these similarities by calling the CPI "the sane man's MMPI," but he obviously failed to appreciate the remarkably different philosophies underlying construction of the two inventories.

Item overlap among the CPI scales is extensive, although less so than on such other inventories as the Strong Vocational Interest Blank. From 1 to 6 of Do's 46 items, for example, appear on every other scale except Cm and Fx. Thirteen of Sc's 50 items are members of Gi and 10, scored in the opposite direction, belong to Sp. The number of unique or pure items per scale ranges from lows of 2 out of 50 for *Sc*, 3 out of 34 for *Sa*, and 6 out of 56 for *Sp* to highs of 28 out of 28 for *Cm* and 22 out of 22 for *Fx*. Perhaps surprisingly, Rogers and Shure (1965) found that the factorial structure of the CPI was almost entirely unaffected by the item overlap problem.

T-F keying on the scales ranges from balanced to almost completely imbalanced. *Sa* and *Cm*, for example, are perfectly balanced. *Do, Sy, Sp, Re, So, Ie*, and *Fe* are reasonably well balanced. *Fx* (1T, 21F), *To* and *Ai* (both 3T, 29F), and *Wb* (5T, 39F) are least well balanced. Of the 18 scales, 14 have more False than True keyed responses, and the total item T-F ratio is approximately 1 : 2.

Gough's (1969) revised manual contains intercorrelation matrices, for males and females separately, for the 18 CPI scales. These values are based on more than 9000 subjects from many different sources. The correlations vary from $-.28$ to $+.78$, with the vast majority being positive. Some examples might be instructive. *Re* (females) correlates .60 with *Ac* and .58 with *To*, yet only .06 with *Sp* and .09 with *Sa*. *Py*'s correlations with the other scales are all low to moderate, whereas *Gi*'s correlations range from $-.13$ to .78. The scales with the lowest correlations with the other scales appear to be *Fx, Fe*, and *Cm*.

The intercorrelations just briefly described have stimulated a host of factor analytic studies. Megargee (1972) reported 20 such investigations and noted that nearly all were performed from 1960 to 1964. According to Gough, the best of these studies is one by Nichols and Schnell (1963), and Levin and Karni's (1970) demonstration of cross-cultural invariance of the CPI is also worth special study. In general the same basic factors, usually five in number, have been found. Factor 1, the largest factor, appears to be a measure of impulse management and socialization. *Sc* has shown loadings as high as .93 on this factor, and *Gi, Wb, To, Ac*, and *Re* also typically have high loadings on it. This factor resembles Gough's Class II (see Table 2), with the addition of *Wb* and *Ac*. Factor 2, the second largest factor extracted, appears to be a measure of interpersonal effectiveness (some psychologists refer to this cluster as a measure of extraversion). *Do, Cs, Sy, Sp*, and *Sa* all load highly on this factor. Clearly, these variables represent Gough's Class I, excluding *Wb*.

The other three factors account for considerably less variance than the first two factors. Factor 3 is usually defined by high loadings of *Ai* and *Fx*; sometimes secondary loadings of *To* and *Ie* are present. Each investigator has labeled this factor differently, but adaptive flexibility seems to be an important common feature. Factor 4 has high loadings of *Cm* and *So* and may be regarded as reflecting the internalization of conventional values. The label ''super-ego strength'' has also been applied to it (Mitchell &

Pierce-Jones, 1960). Factor 5 is invariably defined, when it appears, by a high loading of the *Fe* scale. Consequently, it has been labeled femininity.

Stability coefficients over 1–4 weeks have been shown to range from .49 to .87 for prisoners and .71 to .90 for first-year college women. In the former sample *Fx, Py,* and *Cm* were the only correlations below .70, and the median value was .80. In the latter study, which only included 11 scales, the median was .83. Test-retest reliability coefficients obtained from studies using a 1-year interval have ranged from .38 to .77 with a median value in the middle .60's. *Cm* and *Py* scores have appeared least stable, and *Wb* and *Ie* most stable. Internal consistency coefficients have also been calculated. Several sets are presented in Megargee's (1972) *Handbook.* KR-21 values computed on over 7500 high school students ranged from .22 to .94. The lowest coefficient was obtained for *Py*; only one other coefficient was less than .50. In fact, the median value was in the .70's. *Sc, Gi, Ie,* and *Wb* were among the scales with the highest coefficients. Split-half coefficients are also given for 500 men and women. Uncorrected values ranged from .45 to .77. As usual, *Py* was among the lowest coefficients.

Research on the Interpretation of Scales and Profiles

Before reporting research relevant to CPI interpretation, it is appropriate to give Gough's and Megargee's recommendations concerning the task of interpretation. Assuming the inventory is valid (i.e., by checking *Cm, Gi,* and *Wb* scores), the interpreter should consider overall profile height. Scores above the mean suggest positive adjustment, whereas those below the mean indicate problem areas. Next, one should look at the relative elevations of the different homogeneous groups of scales. Gough recommends examining the four classes of scales, as they are divided on the profile sheet, whereas Megargee suggests that the five factors discussed earlier be considered next. The next step is to look at the scores on the individual scales. Listing the highest and lowest scales is helpful. Finally, one integrates the data into "an overall CPI portrait. Here configural analysis of scale interactions is of primary importance" (Megargee, 1972, p. 145). The overall approach is obviously clinical, and Gough himself teaches students by engaging "in free wheeling clinical interpretations . . . specifying whenever possible the test cues to which he is responding" (Megargee, 1972, p. 129). Gough obviously feels that there is no substitute for the master interpreter, a position that is at some odds with Meehl's and Hathaway's hopes for an actuarially derived master cookbook.

Despite his emphasis on the subjective aspects of interpretation, Gough has carried out many studies to furnish empirical correlates of high and low scores on the various CPI scales. His primary technique for accomplishing this goal has been through comparison of Adjective Check List (ACL) (Gough & Heilbrun, 1965) and *Q*-sort (Block, 1961) findings with scale scores. A convenient method for making such comparisons is to correlate scale scores with the number of times an ACL item is checked by a panel of observers or with the mean placement a panel of observers gives to a *Q*-sort description. The aim of these analyses is to reveal what others tend to say about subjects with higher or lower scores on a certain scale or variable. The methodology is applicable not only to scale scores, but also to signs, clusters, and regression equations. For the rationale underlying these procedures, see Gough (1965).

This technique can be illustrated with reference to the derivation of correlates for the *Do* scale, for which 101 fraternity and 92 sorority members at the University of California served as subjects. Each subject was described on the ACL by five peers.

> If an adjective was checked by one observer, a score of one was assigned to the subject on that attribute; if three checked the word, the subject's score became three. If all five observers checked the word, and if in addition three of these observers double-checked the word (to indicate its centrality in characterizing the subject), then the score became eight . . . in the way indicated each student was given a score on each of the 300 descriptions in the Check List. . . . By correlating the . . . descriptions with the *Do* scale, for males and females separately, patterns of relationships were specified [Gough, 1968, p. 60]

High- and low-scoring *Do* males were described as ambitious, dominant, and forceful or apathetic, indifferent and interests narrow, respectively. Among females the high and low scorers were characterized as aggressive, bossy, and conceited, or as cautious, gentle, and inhibited, respectively. *Do* correlates for male and females thus appear to be somewhat different. As Gough (1968) pointed out "The high scoring female is equally strong, but more likely to be coercive" (p. 60).

Clusters of differentiating attributes have been derived for high and low scores for each of the 18 CPI scales and may be found in Gough (1968, 1969) or Megargee (1972). Space does not permit us to list all these correlates here, but perhaps one other set would be of interest. These are the descriptors derived for *Cm*, which, it is recalled, is a statistically derived validity scale. High and low male scorers on *Cm* have been characterized as cautious, conscientious, and deliberate, or as attractive, careless, and courageous, respectively. Female high scorers have been described as clear-thinking, confident, and energetic, and female low scorers as appreciative, artistic, and awkward.

These kinds of data obviously permit an interpreter to make numerous comments about a subject's CPI scale scores. Are there equivalent empirical data to assist with interpretation of the other elements—profile elevations, factors, homogeneous clusters, combination of scales—considered important by Gough and Megargee?

The answer is—some, but not as many as one might expect. Goodstein, Crites, Heilbrun, and Rempel (1961) compared overall CPI profile elevation of personal adjustment clients, vocational-educational clients, and nonclient controls and found a definite ordering of the groups in the expected direction, that is, the nonclients had higher average profiles than the second group, who in turn had higher average profiles than the first group. Enthusiasm for this type of analysis has undoubtedly been tempered, however, by indications that some scales have a curvilinear relation with behavior. For example, Megargee (1966) found that very high Sc scores are associated with episodic aggressive acts, whereas moderate elevations on this scale contraindicate such acting out.

Megargee (1972) has also provided adjectives presumably descriptive of high and low scorers on the several factors of the CPI, but it appears that these descriptions were obtained via inspection of the adjectives in the different scales making up the factors rather than by empirical analyses. Megargee (1972) states in this regard, "Some of the redundancy to be found in the factor 1 scales is evident in the adjectival descriptions. One would be hard put to differentiate from one another those individuals high on Re, So, and Sc" (p. 125). His specific comments about factor correlates are not reported here.

Concerning correlates of clusters or combination of CPI scales, Megargee (1972) remarks:

Scale configuration patterns are thus part of the psychological folklore, one step beyond the realm of well-validated test-behavior relationships . . . only a minuscule percentage of the 153 possible pairs of CPI scales has been investigated; no studies . . . have attempted systematic validation of triads or larger combinations of scales [p. 146]

In other words, studies such as those of Marks and Seeman (1963) and Gilberstadt and Duker (1965) with the MMPI have still to be done with the CPI.

However, most recent CPI investigations have featured the "combinations of scales" approach. For example, Gough (1968) obtained behavioral correlates for Do-Re and Ac-Ai interactions. His procedure was to select the 36 subjects, half male and half female, who were most extreme on the bisecting diagonal of the quadrant for a combination of two scales and then perform t tests of the mean scores on the ACL items for this subgroup versus the remainder of the sample. High Do–high Re students selected in this way were (to name 3 of 10 adjectives given) described as dominant, ambitious, and responsible; high *Do*–low *Re* students, however, were touchy, dominant, and aggressive. Low *Do*–high *Re* students were described as quiet, calm, and peaceable, whereas low *Do*–low *Re* students were irresponsible, suggestible, and careless. It appears that some of these quadrant correlates are predictable from what is known of the two scales taken alone, while others take on "added meaning."

Gough's analysis of the *Ac-Ai* interactions is also of interest. He found that college students who scored high on both scales were described as intelligent, rational, and realistic, whereas those who scored low on both scales were described as irresponsible, careless, and distrustful. The high *Ac*–low *Ai* combination elicited idealistic, cautious, and praising correlates, whereas the low *Ac*–high *Ai* group members were seen as spunky, reckless, and unexcitable. Domino (1968), studying these same four groups, obtained their grades for their previous four semesters' work and, on the basis of interviews with the instructors, classified the courses according to whether conformity or independence was rewarded. As expected, the high *Ac*–high *Ai* group had received the best grades and the low *Ac*–low *Ai* group the poorest grades of the four groups. Of greater interest, however, was the finding that the high *Ac*–low *Ai* group did relatively well in the courses requiring conformity and the low *Ac*–high *Ai* group did relatively well in the courses emphasizing independence.

In a later study with college students, Domino (1971) examined relationships between achievement orientation, teaching style, academic achievement, and expressed satisfaction with the scholastic environment. Four groups were used: high *Ai*'s exposed to an independent teaching style, high *Ai*'s with a conforming teaching style, high *Ac*'s exposed to an independent teaching style, and high *Ac*'s with a conforming teaching style. Although no significant teaching style main effects were found, interaction effects were striking. Students taught in a manner consonant with their achievement orientation obtained significantly higher scores on multiple-choice and essay examinations and rated teacher and course as more satisfactory than their peers taught in a dissonant manner. This finding suggests that students could be provided with the type of educational setting that would most effectively utilize their potential.

The power of scale interaction models has also been convincingly demonstrated by Block, von der Lippe, and Block (1973), who classified male and female subjects according to their scores on the *So* and *Fe* scales as sex-appropriate/socialized, sex-appropriate/unsocialized, sex-inappropriate/socialized and sex-inappropriate/unsocialized. Comparison of the target subgroups with the remaining subjects of the same sex revealed numerous differences in independently obtained personality descriptions, occupational commitments, and antecedent family characteristics. The findings are too complex to be briefly summarized; however, one conclusion of the authors seems particularly interesting, namely, that sex-role typing for men appears to expand the personal options available to them, whereas sex-role typing for women seems to restrict their alternatives.

A technique has also been devised to obtain what might be called very specialized CPI interpretations. What kind of women, for example, make good airline stewardesses? Those with a sexy, "fly me" air? Gough (1968) reported deriving a four-variable equation which correlated .40 with ratings of stewardess inflight performance. He then correlated the adjectival descriptions in the sample of 92 sorority women mentioned earlier with scores on the "airline stewardess" equation (which was $64.293 + .227\,So - 1.903\,Cm + 1.226\,Ac - .398\,Ai$). Adjectives used most frequently to describe college women with relatively high scores on the stewardess equation were modest, reserved, and feminine, whereas adjectives such as adventurous, pleasure-seeking, and uninhibited were associated with lower scores. Hence the "coffee, tea, or me" image of stewardesses is not consistent with the data.

A similar procedure was applied to performance among psychiatric residents by Gough, Fox, and Hall (1972), who derived a five-variable CPI equation on which scores correlated .32 with ratings of the residents' performance. The Sa, Py, and Fe scales were weighted positively on this equation, and Sp and Cs negatively. The authors then correlated scores on the equation with Adjective Check List descriptions of military officers and college males. High scorers in these two groups were seen as having both favorable and unfavorable and both attractive and unattractive personal qualities. The authors inferred from this finding that superior therapists may be complex individuals who are judged by others to be capable but not always as being likable. Low scorers lacked any descriptors suggesting sentience or the capacity for intuitive response to others.

Although they are not relevant to scale or profile interpretation for the individual client, any sketch of CPI findings is incomplete without reference to a vast number of studies concerned with predicting academic achievement. As Megargee (1972) has pointed out, "The CPI could not have come on stage at a more propitious time" (p. 161). Sputnik had just been launched by the U.S.S.R. and concern was great throughout the United States with locating intellectually talented, highly motivated young people. Research with the CPI was addressed to predicting achievement in secondary school and in college; achievement in student teaching, medicine, dentistry, police work, and military training; and success in leadership roles. Generally speaking, it proved possible to develop multiple-regression equations that could make significant and noteworthy improvements over more traditional techniques in selection and classification for such purposes.

Finally, we should note that the CPI, in keeping with Gough's folk-concept philosophy, has been applied to other cultures both more frequently and more successfully than any other personality inventory. Either the full inventory or selected scales have been evaluated in studies involving translations into Chinese (Mandarin and Cantonese), Ceylonese, Portuguese, Norwegian, Dutch, Italian, Polish, and French. The *So* scale, in particular, has been administered in the native language to offenders and nonoffenders in countries as diverse as Austria, Costa Rica, India, Israel, Japan, South Africa, and Taiwan. In every nation tested thus far, highly significant differences between delinquent and nondelinquent groups have been found. Furthermore, the mean raw scores for the groups have been remarkably similar in the different countries. The highest mean score obtained by any delinquent group is significantly lower than the lowest score obtained by any nondelinquent group and, even more important, the differences between groups have been large enough to be useful for decision-making purposes.

Comment

The CPI has stimulated widely disparate opinions among reviewers. Kelly (1965) and Goldberg (1972a) have praised the instrument, Cronbach (1959) has been essentially neutral, and Thorndike (1959) and Walsh (1972) have been negative in their assessment of its utility. One has the impression of a Rashomon-type situation, in which the eye of the beholder is more responsible for the reactions than what is beheld.

The most cogent recent criticism is that offered by Goldberg (1972a), who points out that

> Gough explicitly encourages test users to intuit personality traits "clinically" from various profile configurations—in spite of (a) a paucity of research on CPI profiles, (b) the failure of configural prediction schemes more generally, and (c) the model provided by Gough's own research, which has relied almost exclusively on linear regression equations [pp. 95–96]

Goldberg concludes, however, that "the knowledgeable practitioner should be able to provide more valid nontest predictions from the CPI than from most other comparable instruments on the market today" (p. 96).

The explanation for the apparent paradox in Goldberg's statements is that so much empirical research has been done with the CPI, and Gough and his co-workers have been so responsive to constructive criticism, that a user can readily evaluate the utility of the instrument in educational, clinical, and industrial settings. Also, the CPI's utility is constantly expanding as a result of Gough's belief that the worth of the instrument lies primarily in the context of application. Most of the early findings were based on high school or college subjects, but by now data from thousands of nonstudent subjects have been analyzed and published. Furthermore, whereas little was known until recently about performance of minority groups on the CPI, information of this kind is now becoming available (see Fenelon & Megargee, 1971; Mason, 1971).

The CPI was designed to be used with normal subjects and individuals with behavior problems. It is not the instrument of choice for appraising neurotic or psychotic disturbance since, although it may identify personality assets, it does not clarify diagnostic issues. However, some psychologists have begun giving both the MMPI and the CPI to psychiatric patients. The MMPI tells what is wrong and perhaps why, and the CPI looks into the future and says something about postrelease prospects, strengths on which a therapeutic program can build, and the like (H. G. Gough, personal communication, May 1974).

What kind of additional research is most needed by CPI users? In our opinion development of behavioral correlates of profile types should have first priority. Further accumulation of empirical data concerning relations between pairs of CPI scales and nontest findings also appears to have considerable practical utility. Continued exploration of the influence of demographic variables such as sex, age, and education on scale scores and profiles should also prove helpful.

When individuals are tested recommendations must be made on the basis of the results. If this is to be done most accurately, the interpreter cannot be confined to the test scores alone. As Gough (1968) has said, "Validity-in-use is not something that resides purely in the inventory itself; it is an outcome that derives from the interpreter's skill and insight in making manifest what is inherent in the instrument" (p. 55).

THE SIXTEEN PERSONALITY FACTOR QUESTIONNAIRE (16 PF)

Aims

Raymond B. Cattell (personal communication, May 1974) states his goal in personality research quite simply: "to define and measure objectively the basic components of personality demonstrated factor analytically to be unitary in nature." The 16 PF was devised as one of the measures of these basic components, and Cattell describes it as:

> . . . not a questionnaire composed of arbitrary scales, but one which consists of scales carefully oriented and groomed to basic concepts in human personality structure research. Its publication was undertaken to meet the demand of research psychologists for a personality measuring instrument duly validated with respect to the primary personality factors and rooted in basic concepts in general psychology [Cattell, Eber, & Tatsuoka, 1970, p. 13]

Strategy of Test Construction

In developing his concept of the "total personality," Cattell turned to what he designated the "language personality sphere," which "captures all the particularity of behavior accumulated in our speech and dictionaries" (Cattell, 1957, p. 71). Allport and Odbert had already cataloged all trait names appearing in an unabridged dictionary and reduced the list to 4504 "real traits." From this list Cattell culled 171 terms which he felt, on the basis of semantic meaning, represented "synonym groups." College students rated their acquaintances using these 171 terms, the results were intercorrelated, and on the basis of cluster analysis approximately 36 surface traits were identified. Thus surface traits are clusters of observable attributes which are encoded in the ordinary language of personality. These 36 dimensions plus others Cattell felt needed to be represented served as the basis for bipolar rating scales which were used in a series of peer-rating studies conducted in college, military, and clinical settings. Factorial study of these data led Cattell to conclude that there were approximately 15 distinct factors (plus intelligence) that accounted for the intercorrelations among rating variables, and he designated these the "primary personality factors."

Eighteen hundred items were then written representing (a) the surface trait variables identified by the rating method, (b) marker variables suggested by previous factorial studies of temperament, and (c) several areas of interest and values which were thought to represent general personality dimensions. A series of factor-analytic studies revealed at least 16 source traits in the questionnaire realm, four of which had not appeared in rater descriptions. Items for the 16 PF were selected that had high correlations with the source traits they were designed to measure, and the 1967–1968 edition contains only those items that continued to have significant validity for the factors after 10 successive factor analyses on different samples (Cattell, 1973a).

As this brief account indicates, trait definition via factor analysis is the most distinctive aspect of Cattell's theory of personality. Cattell is interested in factor analysis not as a technique for reducing a number of variables to a simpler mathematical form, but as a procedure that, when used properly, permits the direct identification and measurement of primary source traits that account for observable covariation among surface traits (Wiggins, 1973, pp. 496–498). Cattell rotates factors obliquely to a position uniquely defined by simple structure in the data itself and therefore having "general scientific meaningfulness." Incidentally, it should be noted that even if factoring is to orthogonal solutions, as in Guilford's analyses, the *scales* themselves come out substantially correlated, but not in the way that represents the natural complexity of human nature (Cattell, Eber, & Tatsuoka, 1970).

In addition to the 16 primary source traits it was designed to measure, the 16 PF can be scored for eight composite or second-stratum factors. (The two main Eysenck scales, E and N, are approaches to the first two of these higher-order factors.) These second-stratum factors may be viewed as organizers contributing to the primary factors and accounting for their intercorrelations (Cattell, Eber, & Tatsuoka, 1970, p. 112).

There are six forms of the 16 PF: Forms A and B for "newspaper literate" adults consisting of 187 items each; Forms C and D with a somewhat less demanding vocabulary and consisting of 105 items each; and Forms E and F,[2] which have 142 items with a very simple vocabulary and are intended for use with the educationally disadvantaged. Forms A through D use a three-choice response which includes an "in-between" alternative. Forms E and F have only two choices. A tape recording is available for the E form, so that it may be given orally. Cattell *strongly* recommends the use of more than one form in evaluating a subject, and for crucial assessments he advocates using four forms (e.g., A, B, C, and D) and breaking up the testing time (Cattell, Eber, & Tatsuoka, 1970, p. 3). There are four editions of the test, published between 1949 and 1969. Unfortunately, data in articles other than those of Cattell, Eber, and Tatsuoka are often reported without reference to the form and/or edition used.

Standardization data on the 16 PF are available for U.S. adults, university undergraduates, and high school seniors. Norms are provided for each of these groups for males alone, females alone, and the total male-female population. Significant differences between males and females on 12 of the 16 scales are noted, and age correction tables (recommended especially for research) are available for those scales that show a significant change with age.

---

[2] As of this writing (July 1974), Form F was still in the experimental stage.

All editions of Form A and the latest editions of the other forms have norms based on samples stratified according to geographic area, population density, age, family income, and (in the 1967–1968 edition) race in proportions indicated by the U.S. Census Bureau. More than 10,000 individuals were tested to establish the 1967–1968 norms for Forms A and B, and more than 5000 for Forms C and D.

The 16 PF Scales

The 16 primary factors of the 16 PF are shown in Table 3. Each factor is designated by a letter, and the high and low poles of each factor are designated by both a technical name and a popularly descriptive label. The alphabetical order is based on evidence of diminishing contribution to behavioral variance (Cattell, Eber, & Tatsuoka, 1970, p. 15). In several cases the technical terms are acronymic names given to factors in an attempt to increase precision and to distinguish them from surface traits of ordinary language. Nearly 100 research articles present evidence tied to these precise, technical designations on such matters as degree of inheritance of the traits, age curves, physiological correlates, achievement and clinical criteria. However, such terms as Premsia, Parmia, and Threctia make communication difficult with those not immersed in the system.

Although eight second-stratum factors may be scored from the 16 PF, only four are as yet considered sufficiently defined to be generally useful. The primary factors involved with Q_I, Extraversion, include Affectothymia (A), Dominance (E), Happy-Go-Lucky (F), Venturesomeness (H), and Group Adherence (Q_2-). Q_{II}, Anxiety, is made up of Low Ego Strength ($C-$), High Guilt Proneness (O), High Ergic Tension (Q_4), Suspiciousness (L), Shyness ($H-$), and Low Self-sentiment Integration (Q_3). This factor possesses high constancy of pattern across cultures (Cattell & Nichols, 1972). Q_{III}, Cortertia, is related to Reserve ($A-$), Tough-mindedness ($I-$), and Practicality ($M-$). Q_{IV}, Independence, involves Dominance (E), Suspiciousness (L), and Imaginativeness (M). This factor has shown considerable variability with respect to sex and culture; men score significantly higher on it than women, and both psychotics and neurotics score relatively low on it.

Psychometric Properties

In contrast to the MMPI and CPI, there is no item overlap among the 16 PF scales. Keying is balanced between responses "a" and "c", with the keyed response contributing 2 points to the scale raw score (except for scale B, Intelligence, where each keyed response is worth 1 point). The

Table 3. The 16 PF Factors

	Primaries	
Factor	Low Sten Score Description[a]	High Sten Score Description
A	Reserved, Sizothymia	Outgoing, Affectothymia
B	Dull, Low Intelligence	Bright, High Intelligence
C	Affected by Feelings, Lower Ego Strength	Emotionally Stable, Higher Ego Strength
E	Humble, Submissiveness	Assertive, Dominance
F	Sober, Desurgency	Happy-Go-Lucky, Surgency
G	Expedient, Weaker Super-ego Strength	Conscientious, Stronger Super-ego Strength
H	Shy, Threctia	Venturesome, Parmia
I	Tough-minded, Harria	Tender-minded, Premsia
L	Trusting, Alaxia	Suspicious, Protension
M	Practical, Praxernia	Imaginative, Autia
N	Forthright, Artlessness	Astute, Shrewdness
O	Self-assured, Untroubled Adequacy	Apprehensive, Guilt Proneness
Q_1	Conservative, Conservativism of Temperament	Experimenting, Radicalism
Q_2	Group Dependent, Group Adherence	Self-sufficient, Self-sufficiency
Q_3	Undisciplined Self-conflict, Low Self-sentiment Integration	Controlled, High Strength of Self-sentiment
Q_4	Relaxed, Low Ergic Tension	Tense, High Ergic Tension

	Secondaries	
Symbol	Technical Title	Popular Label
Q_I	Exvia-Invia	Extraversion-Introversion
Q_{II}	Adjustment-Anxiety	Low Anxiety–High Anxiety
Q_{III}	Pathemia-Cortertia	Sensitivity, Emotionalism Tough Poise
Q_{IV}	Subduedness-Independence	Dependence-Independence

[a] The second term given for each of the primaries is Cattell's technical term.

intermediate response, "b," contributes 1 point. In order to minimize distortion, items were chosen to be as neutral in social desirability as possible. Also of note, items that are not "face valid" were used whenever possible. Motivational Distortion scales are built into Forms C and D—the forms more commonly used in personnel selection—and involve items showing maximum shift from an anonymous to a job-seeking situation.

A test-retest study of 146 U.S. adults and undergraduates with an intervening time of 4–7 days produced correlations ranging from .65 on

Intelligence to .93 on Venturesomeness, with a median value of .87 for all scales. This study used the 1961 edition of forms A and B combined. The lower figure for Intelligence is explained in terms of subjects attempting to solve the intelligence items between sessions. The other factors that typically have low stability coefficients are Imaginativeness (*M*), Shrewdness (*N*), and Self-sentiment (Q_3). These factors, according to Cattell, Eber, and Tatsuoka (1970), seem relatively likely to fluctuate with psychological state and to be affected by conditions of test administration, as when rapport is not properly established or when the subject is not cooperative or is physically uncomfortable.

When the test-retest interval is extended to 2 months, the range of coefficients for Forms A plus B has been from .63 for Intelligence to .88 for Venturesomeness, with a median coefficient of .78. A 4-year between-testing interval produced stability coefficients for Form A ranging from .21 for females on Shrewdness (*N*) to .64 for females on Venturesomeness (*H*). It is suggested that in order to cancel out reversible state changes in evaluating a trait, one might retest two or three times over a month or so and average the results (Cattell, Eber, & Tatsuoka, 1970, p. 31).

Equivalency coefficients for Form A correlated with B (1967–1968 edition) ranged from .21 for Shrewdness (*N*) to .71 for Venturesomeness (*H*). The median value reflecting the degree to which these forms parallel each other over all scales was .51. The equivalency coefficient for C with D (1961–1962 edition) ranged from .16 for Shrewdness (*N*) and Suspiciousness (*L*) to .55 for Venturesomeness (*H*), with a median of .38. The Forms A and C combination correlated with Forms B and D yielded coefficients between .35 (Shrewdness—*N*) and .79 (Venturesomeness—*H*), with a median of .60.

Split-half correlations for the 16 PF have been deemphasized on the grounds that "the highest multiple-R validity is obtained by finding items which correlate consistently with the factor, but trivially with one another" (Cattell, Eber, & Tatsuoka, 1970, p. 32).

As already noted, the 16 PF factors are correlated with each other. The intercorrelation matrix provided in the Cattell et al. handbook indicates that the highest correlations (.70 to .75) exist among scales *C*− (Low Ego Strength), *O* (Guilt-proneness), and Q_4 (Tenseness), which make up the second-order factor Anxiety. The Intelligence scale (*B*) has very low correlations with other scales, as does *I* (Tender-minded). Approximately 20% of the intercorrelations are greater than ±.30.

Other researchers have subjected the 16 PF scales to factor analysis, frequently in conjunction with the MMPI, CPI, and EPPS scales. Kear-Colwell (1973) factor-analyzed the scores of 174 psychiatric hospital admissions on the 16 PF and the EPPS. He found second-order factors on the 16 PF that closely matched those reported by Cattell and Nichols (1972) and, as might be expected, he found only limited relationships between information provided by the 16 PF and results from the need-oriented EPPS. LaForge (1962) factor-analyzed the responses of 178 undergraduate students to the 16 PF and the MMPI. A large fraction of the variance on the 16 PF (excluding B) was derivable from four components which LaForge designated Anxiety, Extraversion, Unbroken Success, and Sensitivity. O'Dell and Karson (1969) also factored combined 16 PF and MMPI scales and reported the following factors: MMPI pathology, anxiety versus dynamic integration, exvia-invia, cortical alertness, and independence-dependence. In spite of investigators changing the original technically chosen names for them, there is very high convergence of findings on the patterns of these second-order factors.

Research on the Interpretation of Scales and Profiles

Cattell, Eber, and Tatsuoka (1970) provide two approaches to interpretation and diagnosis with the 16 PF: profile matching and criterion estimation using specification equations. As an example of the first of these approaches, the mean profile of neurotic subjects tested in the midwestern and eastern United States and in Canada, Australia, and Britain shows poor ego strength $(C-)$, lack of independence of mind and capacity to solve problems forcefully $(E-)$, greater than average inhibition $(F-)$, and below-average superego expression $(G-)$. The average neurotic also tends to be shy $(H-)$, overprotected $(I+)$, and dominated by high anxiety and a sense of guilty unworthiness $(Q_4$ and $O)$. With the use of formulas and tables the similarity between an individual subject's profile and such typical profiles can be determined, as a basis for drawing a diagnostic conclusion.

The second approach involves, for example, the application of a Neuroticism specification equation for which weights have been determined by comparing scores of consensually diagnosed neurotics with those of normal control subjects. The equation for Neuroticism is:

$$6.27 - .07B - .26C - .17E - .38F - .10G + .10H + .22I + .26 O - .09 Q_1 + .35 Q_4$$

The higher a profile's score on this equation, the more similar it is to profiles of neurotic individuals.

Mean profiles are provided by Cattell et al. (1970) for many different subject groups, including delinquents, attempted suicides, homosexuals, addicts, and patients with psychosomatic disorders. Profiles and specification equations are also presented for many different occupational groups, including academicians, accountants, artists, miners, policemen, social workers, and writers, and there are specification equations for variables relevant to educational and vocational guidance, such as freedom from accidents, salesmanship, teaching effectiveness, and creativity. For those wishing to use the 16 PF without mastering its considerable complexities, a computer interpretation is available.

Profiles and specification equations are provided for psychotics, but with cautions about their tentativeness. Significant mean differences have been found between the profiles of psychotic and normal subjects, with the psychotic typically demonstrating submissiveness, soberness, and threat responsiveness, as well as relatively poor performance on the Intelligence scale. Nevertheless, although the 16 PF is sensitive to pattern differences among varieties of neurotics, alcoholics, and sociopaths, as shown by published research on each, it was not designed to encompass the dimensions of psychosis and is thus unable to substantiate a psychotic diagnosis.

In order to encompass these diagnostic dimensions, Cattell and his associates (e.g., Cattell & Bolton, 1969; Delhees & Cattell, 1971a) have recently factor-analyzed the whole domain of psychotic pathological items and derived 12 factors additional to the 16 PF factors (which also are needed, however, in defining the psychotic personality). This work has resulted in Form A of the Clinical Analysis Questionnaire (CAQ) (Delhees & Cattell, 1971b), and Form B is under construction by Sells and Cattell. The CAQ appears to be a promising device for measuring traits that underlie deviant behavior patterns and for assisting clinicians in the task of differential diagnosis. The 12 new scales measure seven varieties of depression (hypochondriasis, suicidal disgust, brooding discontent, anxious depression, low energy, guilt and resentment, and bored depression), paranoia, psychopathic deviation, schizophrenia, psychasthenia, and general psychosis.

Profile matching and specification equations thus permit classification by the 16 PF, but what about behavioral correlates? The most extensive and systematic presentation of "natural history" and criterion associates appears in Cattell's recent compendium *Personality and Mood by Questionnaire* (1973b). There is empirical evidence, for example, that a high-*A* person is relatively likely to be a "joiner," to be generous in interpersonal relationships, to be unafraid of criticism, and to be casual in meeting obligations. Low *C* is the most general pathological indicator and tends to characterize neurotics, psychotics, alcoholics, and drug addicts; in neurotics it is associated with poor muscle tone and posture and a long history of symptoms which intensify under stress.

As further examples of 16 PF correlates, a change toward surgence

($F+$) might be found in successful psychotherapy and with mild intoxication. High F is associated with conversion hysteria and low F with headaches, worrying, irritability, depression, and phobias. Elected leaders are far higher than followers on surgency, but "effective" leaders show a much smaller difference. The high Q_3 score is more characteristic of the effective than the merely popular leader (Cattell & Stice, 1953). Factor G correlates negatively with delinquency and sociopathic behavior and positively with school and general achievement, and in group dynamic experiments G significantly distinguishes leaders from followers. Those who are chosen as leaders are also likely to be high on H. The high L person is unpopular in group dynamic experiments, and the high M individual tends to feel unaccepted but lacks concern. For more information regarding each of the factors the reader is referred to Chapter 9 in the handbook (Cattell, Eber, & Tatsuoka, 1970).

Although Cattell measures validity in terms of the extent to which the scales correlate with the factors, information such as the above helps throw light on the types of behaviors associated with the scales. Further understanding can be gained by examining their relationship to scales from other inventories. A study by Edwards and Abbott (1973b) found the following correlations between 16 PF and Edwards Personality Inventory scales: Venturesome (H) and Shy, $-.71$; Conscientious (G) and Plans and Organizes Things, .57; Tense (Q_4) and Becomes Angry, .55; Assertive (E) and Critical of Others, .51; Controlled (Q_3) and Virtuous, .46; and Tender-minded (I) and Has Cultural Interests, .43. This same study found that the 16 PF scale Tense had a high positive loading on the factor on which the CPI scale Sense of Well-Being had a high negative loading. Venturesome and the CPI Dominance scale both had high positive loadings on another factor, while Tender-minded and the CPI Femininity scale shared a factor. Conscientious showed a high positive loading on the same factor on which CPI Flexibility had a high negative loading.

Cattell and his associates are pursuing seven additional factors which have been replicated but have not shown the clarity of the 16 that appear on the inventory. Scales for these seven factors by Marshall and Cattell (1974) have been made available by the Institute for Personality and Ability Testing. The reader should also be aware of work being done to extend the measurement of these same personality factors to children and adolescents. The High School Personality Questionnaire, the Children's Personality Questionnaire, and the Early School Personality Questionnaire are now available in standardized form, and the Pre-School Questionnaire will soon be released.

Recent publications show that the 16 PF has been used to study the personality characteristics of diverse clinical types, creative scientists and writers, athletes, counselors and counselees, accident-prone drivers, and about 40 occupational groups. Dating preferences, marital stability, job promotions, and personality change with therapy, marriage, and chronic illness have also been investigated with this instrument. The vast majority of studies has used normals or individuals in counseling rather than the mentally ill.

Much cross-cultural work with the 16 PF is also taking place. Studies have been reported from Czechoslovakia, Iran, Italy, France, West Germany, Brazil, Mexico, Great Britain, New Zealand, Australia, and Canada. In some instances the translation or adaptation of the instrument has been checked for factor structure and in some cases it has not. Further cross-cultural results should be of considerable interest for a test that purports to measure basic dimensions of personality.

Comment

Cattell's personal contribution in the area of personality research has been unprecedented in terms of its scope and vigor. His theoretical conceptions and mathematical procedures as well as assessment techniques have provided significant stimulation to the field, and he has shown genius in perceiving unity in seemingly diverse areas. The 16 PF is unique among personality inventories in that it is but one part of an assessment program designed to explore relationships within the multivariate theoretical framework. Along with the High School Personality Questionnaire and other factorial inventories, it is squarely embedded in a general theory of personality structure.

Although this review has concentrated on the 16 PF, Cattell has also developed instruments for measuring ability (the Culture Fair Intelligence Scales 1, 2, and 3) and motivation (the Motivation Analysis Test and the School Motivation Analysis Test), and he has extensively researched relations between life history (L) and objective test (T) data and personality functioning. A recent study by Cattell, Pierson, Finkbeiner, Willes, Brim, and Robertson (1974) has answered the long-neglected issue of alignment of L- and Q-data factors by showing that the series of factors in the 16 PF correspond to the series of factors from ratings of behavior *in situ*. Cattell's chief current enthusiasm is for T data, which he feels avoid the distortion problem inherent in the questionnaire approach. He would like to see psychologists provided with the materials and skills needed to put these objective performance tests into widespread use. Yet because the questionnaire is familiar and easy to administer, it is likely to remain an important instrument within Cattell's system as well as in personality assessment in general.

Despite the years of sophisticated effort put into its development, the 16 PF has not been used as widely as might be warranted. Almost certainly the main reason that Cattell's work has not received acclaim in proportion to its volume and elegance is that psychologists who do not understand factor analysis—and this is perhaps the majority—tend to be defensive about this approach or to think of factors merely as "mathematical abstractions."

The 16 PF has also been the target of much criticism, especially revolving around its low interform reliabilities and the fact that validity of the scales with regard to significant external criteria has not been systematically presented. We agree with Wiggins (1973): "Cattell (1957) seems to assume, and properly so, that his own contributions as a theoretician and psychometrician should be directed toward test development and that the application of such tests should fall within the province of the practitioners of educational, industrial, and clinical assessment" (p. 505). We urge practitioners to accept this challenge so that evaluation of the practical utility of the multivariate-trait model can be achieved.

THE PERSONALITY RESEARCH FORM (PRF)

Aims

The goals in constructing the PRF were "to develop sets of personality scales and an item pool which might be useful in personality research" and "to provide an instrument for measuring broadly relevant personality traits in settings such as schools and colleges, clinics and guidance centers, and in business and industry" (Jackson, 1967a, p. 4).

Strategy of Test Construction

The methodology used to construct the PRF was a mixed intuitive-internal strategy. Prior to describing the procedures employed, it is important to recognize Jackson's guiding principles, which were (a) the importance of psychological theory, (b) the necessity for suppressing response style variance, (c) the importance of scale homogeneity as well as generalizability, and (d) the importance of enhancing convergent and discriminant validity from the beginning of the test construction program (see Jackson, 1970, for further details). Murray's (1938) need system was selected as the theoretical substructure for the instrument, since these variables give comprehensive coverage of the domain of needs, states, and dispositions and have been defined carefully and researched extensively.

The first step in scale construction was a careful study of Murray's 20 traits. Mutually exclusive, specific definitions of each trait were developed. The next task—according to Jackson, the most difficult of all—was to create an item pool. About 3000 items, over 100 for each trait, were written. These items had to be relatively short and free of ambiguity, and also conceptually linked to the relevant trait and conceptually distinct from each irrelevant trait. Following critical review by two or more judges, these items were administered to over 1000 college students. Biserial correlations were computed between each item and (a) the provisional scale of which it was a member, (b) related scales, and (c) a large set of items scaled for desirability (the provisional Desirability scale). Items that showed endorsement rates of less than 5% or over 95% were eliminated, as were items showing higher correlations with the Desirability scale or related scales than with the scale to which they were assigned.

In order to maximize content saturation and keep desirability variance within manageable limits, items were next ranked in terms of the magnitude of the Differential Reliability Index within each scale. The Differential Reliability Index for each item was calculated by obtaining the square root of the difference between an item's squared biserial correlation with its own scale and its squared biserial correlation with desirability. No absolute value was required. If desirability variance was quite low, an item of moderately high content saturation might be considered satisfactory. If desirability variance was relatively high, however, correlation with content would have to be very high for the item to be retained. Items that survived these hurdles were assigned to parallel forms by pairing items in terms of similarity of endorsement proportions and item-scale correlations and reassigning each member of the paired items to alternate forms until these forms were maximally similar in summary statistics. Finally, each scale was reviewed to evaluate the generalizability and representativeness of its content. As Jackson (1967a) said, "An exhibition scale containing a majority of items solely concerned with interest in public speaking . . . may not adequately reflect the broader construct of exhibition" (p. 17).

The description given above outlines what is clearly an elaborate series of sequential strategies faithfully based on the principles enunciated earlier. Validity scales for the PRF were conceived somewhat differently.

The emphasis here was on assessment of general styles of responding, rather than on specific content dimensions. Means for detecting nonpurposeful responding and the tendency to respond desirably or undesirably were considered essential. To identify nonpurposeful responding, items were written which, although neither bizarre nor particularly undesirable, would be highly unlikely to be endorsed (e.g., "I learned to repair watches in Switzerland"). Sixty-five provisional items were given to over 300 subjects, and those were retained that correlated higher with this Infrequency scale than with any of the other scales, including Desirability. The scale to measure desirability was developed by selecting about 60 items from each extreme of the distribution of Desirability scale values, eliminating those showing substantial content homogeneity, and giving the remaining 107 items to over 300 college students. The responses were subjected to the same item analysis routine used with content scales, except that desirability was not suppressed. The surviving items for Desirability were then assigned to one of the two parallel forms of the inventory.

The PRF is available in four formats, two 300-item parallel forms and two 440-item parallel forms. Forms A and B are divided into fifteen 20-item scales, while Forms AA and BB contain the same scales plus seven different 20-item scales. The PRF is also available in a new format, Form E, which is comprised of all 22 scales with 16 items for each. Form E was based on a new item analysis and includes the best items from Forms AA and BB, selected on the basis of high content saturation and mutual minimum redundancy. In the following section the scales included on the longer forms are labeled and briefly defined.

The PRF Scales

Table 4 provides the names of the PRF scales and 2 of the 15 defining trait adjectives given for each scale in the manual (Jackson, 1967a). Although the definitions are unipolar, it should be pointed out that all these dimensions were conceived as bipolar. For every scale, half of the items were written in terms of one pole of the dimension and half in terms of the other. As Jackson (1967a) notes, "Rather than calling one scale Dominance, it would have been equally correct to label it Submissiveness" (p. 11). Thus low scores as well as high scores on PRF scales are interpretable in terms of personality characteristics.

Psychometric Properties

As in the 16 PF, there is no item overlap among PRF scales, and response keying is balanced. Each scale contains 10 items keyed True and 10 items

Table 4. PRF Scales

Scale	Abbreviation	Two Trait Adjectives
Abasement	*Ab*	Self-blaming, humble
Achievement	*Ac*	Industrious, ambitious
Affiliation	*Af*	Warm, cooperative
Aggression	*Ag*	Aggressive, irritable
Autonomy	*Au*	Self-reliant, individualistic
Change	*Ch*	Unpredictable, vacillating
Cognitive Structure	*Cs*	Perfectionistic, rigid
Defendence	*De*	Defensive, touchy
Dominance	*Do*	Domineering, persuasive
Endurance	*En*	Steadfast, jealous
Exhibition	*Ex*	Spellbinding, ostentatious
Harmavoidance	*Ha*	Fearful, cautious
Impulsivity	*Im*	Reckless, excitable
Nurturance	*Nu*	Comforting, charitable
Order	*Or*	Neat, methodical
Play	*Pl*	Playful, carefree
Sentience	*Se*	Aware, sensuous
Social Recognition	*Sr*	Approval seeking, courteous
Succorance	*Su*	Trusting, dependent
Understanding	*Un*	Curious, reflective
Desirability[a]	*Dy*	—
Infrequency[a]	*In*	—

[a]Validity scales.

keyed False. Questions could be raised concerning the rational or intuitive selection of items, but Jackson (1970) has provided a persuasive argument in defense of his procedure in this regard. The argument draws attention to studies in which judges (given descriptions of hypothetical people) were asked to rate the probability that these people would endorse certain personality items. Multidimensional successive intervals scaling was then applied to appraise the degree to which each item was considered relevant to a hypothetical item universe. For further details, see Jackson (1970, pp. 68–71).

Intercorrelations among the basic scales for Form A are reported in the manual (Jackson, 1967a). These correlations, which are based on the normative sample of 1029 males and 1002 females, range from +.64 to −.63. Achievement and Endurance are highly positively correlated in both samples, as are Cognitive Structure and Order. Succorance and Autonomy are highly negatively related in both samples. However, these examples are exceptions. Only 15 out of the 462 correlations are as large as ±.50. The vast majority of the values are between ±.30. Lack of item overlap, plus suppression of a desirability factor, no doubt accounts for the relative independence of the scales from each other. As Jackson pointed out, desirability variance can be totally eliminated from content scale scores on the longer PRF forms by partial regression techniques.

Jackson (1970) also reports factor-analytic findings for the PRF. Traditional linear components factor analysis was rejected because of interactions between trait and method factors, and a new technique called multimethod factor analysis, which considers only trait variance, was developed. Variance unique to a single method is eliminated with this procedure, which Jackson and Guthrie (1968) used to factor correlations between PRF scales, self-ratings, and peer behavior ratings. Eighteen factors appeared for the 20 PRF content scales. The factor loadings provided strong evidence for convergent and discriminative properties of the PRF scales. As an example, Dominance as measured by self-ratings, peer ratings, and PRF scores loaded .76, .64, and .60 on Factor II, respectively; equivalent correlations for Abasement on the same factor were −.52, −.38, and −.56, respectively.

Other studies have used more traditional factor analytic procedures to describe the inventory's structure. Stricker (1974), for example, found six oblique factors (conscientiousness, hostility, ascendance, dependence, imagination, and carefreeness) in a principal axis analysis of the content scales. Stricker also found that response bias measures were only moderately related to the PRF scales and did not define any of the factors.

Two studies of PRF test-retest reliability have been undertaken. Bentler (1964) administered Form AA to college students on two occasions 1 week apart. Stability coefficients for the 20 content scales ranged from .69 for Change to .90 for Harmavoidance. Most correlations were in the .80's. The stability coefficient for Infrequency was only .46, but this kind of result seems unavoidable for scales with very small means and markedly skewed distributions. The other study evaluated parallel form reliability over two testing sessions separated by 2 weeks. In this instance values reflect not only stability but also degree of similarity between forms. Subjects took either Form AA or BB first, then the other long form on the second occasion. Corrected odd-even reliability coefficients of Form AA content scales ranged from .48 for Defendence to .86 for Dominance and Order, with a median value in the mid .70's. Infrequency, again, had the lowest coefficient, .33. No long-term test-retest studies have been reported in the literature.

Internal consistency estimates are also reported in the manual (Jackson, 1967a). For the original item pool, KR-20 coefficients for the content scales ranged from .80 for Defendence to .94 for six of the scales. The median value was .925, which is remarkably high for any test and almost unbelievable for personality scales. The KR-20 estimates for the final 20 item scales are naturally not as high as for the 100+ item original scales. In a sample of 202 subjects, Form AA scale coefficients, excluding Infrequency, ranged from .54 for Change to .85 for Dominance and Order, with a median in the low .70's.

Research Related to Interpretation

The PRF was developed much more recently than the MMPI, CPI, or 16 PF, and Jackson's major concern appears to have been to construct the best possible inventory on the basis of current psychometric knowledge. Any practical utility of the instrument, one gathers, was a hoped-for by-product of the construction program. If this evaluation is correct, one might not expect an immediate focus on applied concerns. Examination of the studies conducted by Jackson and others from 1965 to 1970 tends to confirm this impression. Several studies (e.g., Braun & Asta, 1969; Braun & Costantini, 1970; Hoffman, 1968) are concerned with the effects of "fake good" or "fake bad" instructions on PRF performance. Other authors (e.g., Acker, 1967; Bither, 1969; Kusyszyn & Greenwood, 1970) have used from two to eight PRF scales to examine postulated relationships between variables such as need achievement and academic performance, decision making and needs for exhibition and dominance, and defensiveness and a tendency to distort responses to personality items in a favorable direction.

A few studies, although primarily concerned with construct validation, do contain material of interest to applied psychologists. The manual (Jackson, 1967a), for example, reports correlations of the PRF with 37 occupational scales from the Strong Vocational Interest Blank and also with the CPI scales. Careful perusal of these tables helps to clarify what the PRF scales are measuring. To give a few examples, PRF Achievement correlates .62 with CPI Achievement via Conformance, but only .27 with Achievement via Independence. PRF Exhibition correlates .69 with CPI Self-acceptance, .68 with Social Presence, and .67 with Sociability. The highest correlation reported is .78 for PRF Dominance and CPI Dominance, which demonstrates good convergent validity. PRF Cognitive Structure, which is unlikely to be familiar to most psychologists, correlates $-.70$ with CPI Flexibility and $-.48$ with Capacity for Status. Turning to the PRF-SVIB correlations, some interesting relationships emerge. Clinical Psychologist correlates .40 with Exhibition, whereas Experimental Psychologist correlates $-.37$ with this scale. Biological Scientist correlates .49 with Understanding, whereas Banker correlates $-.51$ with the same scale. Banker also correlates .36 with Harmavoidance, whereas Army Officer correlates $-.38$. Engineer correlates .32

with Endurance, whereas Real Estate Sales correlates $-.35$. Most of these correlations make intuitive sense and add additional meaning to scores on both instruments.

Edwards and Abbott (1973a) compared scores on the Edwards Personality Inventory (EPI), the EPPS, and PRF. Fairly large correlations were found between the PRF and EPI scales. PRF scales having the highest correlation with an EPI scale were Achievement with Is a Hard Worker (.74), Affiliation with Makes Friends Easily (.70), Aggression with Critical of Others (.64), Cognitive Structure with Plans and Organizes Things (.66), Dominance with Assumes Responsibility (.80), Exhibition with Enjoys Being the Center of Attention (.69), Nurturance with Helps Others (.64), Order with Plans and Organizes Things (.70), and Succorance with Dependent (.73). These relations offer evidence that traits with similar names on the different inventories appear to be measuring the same substantive dimensions.

Trott and Morf (1972) compared college students' responses to the PRF and MMPI by means of multimethod factor analysis. Several interesting relationships emerged. One factor, for example, included MMPI F (loaded $-.68$) and PRF Achievement (loaded .80) as salient variables. The authors suggested that the negative pole of this factor might reflect a genuine and pathological inability to marshal resources to compete effectively. Another factor included MMPI Scale 3 (Hy) (.79) and PRF Harmavoidance (.42) and Understanding ($-.38$). The caution, fearfulness, lack of curiosity and of reflective thought indicated by the PRF variables were considered to be consistent with the clinical description of the hysterical personality. Another factor, which was interpreted as reflecting difficulty in the control of hostile impulses, included PRF Aggression (.43) and MMPI K ($-.68$). The authors concluded that high scores on many PRF scales, especially Dominance and Affiliation, are contraindications of pathology and, more broadly, that psychopathological behavior is intimately linked with interpersonal behavior in general.

The major evidence for external validity of the scales is based on comparisons of PRF scores with behavior ratings of the various traits (see Jackson, 1967a, pp. 23–24). Judges were asked to rate on a 9-point scale the degree to which each trait was present or absent. Pooled ratings of peers served as the principal criterion measures, although comparisons of PRF scores and self-ratings were also done. Validity coefficients were based on cross-validational data with no cases excluded. The values ranged from .16 to .64 with a median of .27 to .30. All these values were probably attenuated by the very small number of judges used. If one considers only the 14 content scales included in the shorter PRF forms, the results were more impressive. These validity coefficients ranged from

.16 to .64 with a median of .36–.38. The highest coefficients were found for Order and Harmavoidance; the lowest for Understanding, Cognitive Structure and Abasement.

Kusyszyn (1968) also used this same procedure to establish the validity of eight of the PRF scales (*Ac*, *Ag*, *Au*, *Ex*, *Im*, *Nu*, *Or*, and *Pl*). Subjects were members of fraternities. Coefficients ranged from .24 for Autonomy to .58 for Play for the total sample. For that portion of the sample who shared common living quarters and would be expected to be better acquainted, the coefficients ranged from .35 to .71, with a median of .47. These data suggest that PRF scales do in fact measure those traits whose labels they bear, although it is clear that an interpreter of the PRF should place more confidence on results associated with some scales (e.g., Order) than on data obtained from others (e.g., Abasement).

The most recent research has been directed toward an explication of relationships between nontest data and PRF scores. A sampling of many studies indicates that the following groups have been used as subjects: alcoholics (Gross & Nerviano, 1973), Antarctic explorers (Butcher & Ryan, 1974), child aides (Sandler, 1972), depressives (Hoffman, 1970), nonprofessional health workers (Dorr, Cowen, Sandler, & Pratt, 1973), and student activists (Pierce & Schwartz, 1971). Relations between PRF scores and cigarette consumption (Ahmed, 1972), A-B therapist types (Berzins, Dove, & Ross, 1972), changes in alcoholics after treatment (Hoffman, 1971), existential anxiety (Good & Good, 1974), proximity preferences (Sewell & Heisler, 1973), and product usage patterns (Worthing, Venkatesan, & Smith, 1973) have also been examined. Results have demonstrated the usefulness of the PRF for personality research. However, no studies of external correlates of PRF scales in the manner of Marks with the MMPI and Gough with the CPI have been undertaken to date. Hence the clinician who feels most comfortable interpreting scales for which he has a variety of empirical correlates may conclude that the data he needs are not yet available for the PRF.

Comment

The highly sophisticated development of the PRF has been generally rewarded by laudatory reviews. Anastasi (1972), for example, states "Technically the PRF appears to be exemplary" (p. 298), and Kelly (1972) calls the inventory an "extremely promising" device which is "a welcome contribution to the field of personality assessment" (p. 301). However, not everyone has been satisfied. Wessler and Loevinger (1972) state, "Although Jackson invokes Loevinger's notion of the structural aspect of construct validity, he has not adopted its central tenet" (p. 303) and, further, ''The acid test of a personality inventory, as Jackson says, lies in the Campbell-Fiske notion of convergent and discriminant validity, and it is to these ideas that he has done most violence'' (p. 304). Wiggins (1972) has pointed out what appears to be the key issue: ''Whether these scale construction efforts, and particularly the attention paid to substantive considerations, will guarantee significant incremental validities in applied settings is another question'' (p. 303).

The PRF is ''unquestionably the best example of a large-scale personality inventory developed under the construct point of view'' (Wiggins, 1973, p. 409). Yet, about 7 years after publication, insufficient evidence has been accumulated to assert that an inventory developed in this manner is superior with regard to empirical validity to inventories developed from different orientations (e.g., MMPI). The PRF and its adherents are not to blame for this state of affairs; rather, it appears that it takes an inventory as long as human beings to mature (in the sense of reaching full development). The PRF will come of age in 1988.

In the meantime, we hope that greater efforts will be made to provide data to aid in profile interpretation. It is tempting to assume that scales that have been carefully constructed to measure achievement and affiliation do indeed measure those dimensions and no others. However, experience with other inventories (e.g., MMPI, CPI) suggests that a scale may have other correlates than those that were built into it, and that the relative elevation of other scales may influence the meaning of a score on a given scale. Clarification of the effects of age, race, intelligence, and other demographic factors on PRF scores could extend the applicability of the inventory beyond college students.

Whether this inventory will supercede the EPPS in counseling centers is unclear at this point. The popularity of a psychological test or inventory seems to be unrelated to the elegance of its construction or its psychometric properties. If Jackson and his students continue to bring this inventory to psychologists' attention through vigorous research efforts *and* demonstrate its clinical utility, odds are good that the PRF will be accepted with enthusiasm.

OTHER WELL-KNOWN PERSONALITY INVENTORIES

Allport-Vernon-Lindzey Study of Values

For an instrument nearing 45 years of age, the Study of Values shows remarkable vigor. Examination of *The Seventh Mental Measurements Yearbook* (1972) indicates that this questionnaire acquired 188 new research citations between 1963 and 1970. Nearly half of these articles compare different groups' values or evaluate the values of a particular population. Approximately one-quarter of the articles use the Study of Values as an adjunct to other instruments in exploring topics such as creativity, critical thinking, and halo effects. About one-sixth of the articles explore relationships between values and such behaviors as smoking, dropping out of school, and conformity. The remaining small fraction of studies considers value changes over time (or associated with treatment) or use the Study of Values for assessment, evaluation, or selection (especially of counselors and therapists).

The Study of Values has an appearance and scoring system different from any other inventory. There are 45 questions and 120 answers. The first section includes 30 questions, each with two choices [e.g., Assuming that you have sufficient ability, would you prefer to be (a) a banker or (b) a politician]. Agreement with one or the other or a slight preference for one over the other can be indicated by distributing 3 points in different ways. The second section contains 15 questions, each having four answers. The answers are to be ranked as to preference (4 for most preferred to 1 for least preferred). Scores for the different categories are added, corrected by adding up to 4 or subtracting up to 5 points, and then plotted on a profile.

This brief but complicated procedure was designed to measure the relative prominence of six basic interests or motives: theoretical, economic, aesthetic, social, political, and religious. This typology was proposed by Spranger (1928), who believed that personalities are best known in terms of values or evaluative attitudes. The major interests of the different types are discovery of truth, what is practical or useful, form and harmony, altruistic love, power, and mystic unity, respectively. Many reviewers have noted the absence of hedonistic or malevolent types in this list of interests.

Intercorrelations between the values range from −.48 to .27. Generally, the correlations are relatively low and suggest that relatively different types are being measured. Although the manual (Allport, Vernon, & Lindzey, 1970) implies that the six types represent six factors, Sciortino (1970) found that aesthetic, social, and religious factors accounted for nearly all the variance. Split-half reliabilities for the six values varies from .84 to .95. Stability coefficients for 1 month and 2 months in two small samples varied from .77 to .93. The case for validity presented in the manual rests primarily on scores obtained from various groups: "Common experience leads us to expect that women will on the average be more *religious, social* and *aesthetic* than men," and "We . . . expect students of engineering by and large to stand relatively high in *theoretical* and *economic* values" (Allport, Vernon, & Lindzey, 1970, p. 13). The tables show that 500 engineering students obtained their highest mean score on Theoretical and their second highest mean score on Economic; 180 art and design students obtained their highest mean score on Aesthetic; and 61 Air Force officers obtained their highest mean score on Political. These findings are all consistent with the authors' expectations, but we are more interested in analyses that would provide information concerning false positives, valid positives, and so on.

The 1970 version of the manual was apparently published to include normative data collected from 12,616 high school students in 1968. Means and standard deviations for the six values had previously been available only from students at the college or postgraduate level and from a miscellaneous assortment of occupational groups (scoutmasters, clergymen, dietitians, etc.). Sex differences in scores are clearly discernible in the collegiate and high school norms. Effects associated with age, ethnicity, nationality, and religion are alluded to in the manual, but are not described.

Allport, Vernon, and Lindzey (1970) state, "Marriage counselors, especially among the clergy, have found the test helpful in preparing and counseling prospective marriage partners," and "Personnel managers frequently find that the results of the scale are helpful in the hiring and placement of special classes of employees" (p. 16). Although studies have suggested that this inventory may help identify creative architects (Hall & MacKinnon, 1969), potential therapists (Liberty, Doughtie, & Embree, 1965), and effective rehabilitation counselors (Luzzi, 1970), the lack of external behavioral correlates for the scales or profiles is disturbing. Significant differences between group means do not ordinarily permit one to interpret the inventory performance of individuals with any confidence. Furthermore, what do you tell a prospective bride after you tell her that her aesthetic values are higher than her theoretical values?

Edwards Personal Preference Schedule (EPPS)

According to the manual (Edwards, 1959), the EPPS was designed to "provide quick and convenient measures of a number of relatively independent *normal* personality variables" (p. 5). Since these variables were taken from Murray's list of manifest needs, which Jackson's (1967) Personality Research Form also used, they are not enumerated here. The other major goal of the inventory constructor was to minimize the influence of social desirability on subjects' responses to the statements. Edwards' procedure in this regard was to scale items for social desirability and then pair statements of comparable social desirability. The client is instructed to select whichever of the paired statements is more characteristic of what he likes or how he feels.

The main group for whom the EPPS was developed consisted of high school graduates with some college experience. Normative data were also collected for a large sample of adults who were household heads. Percentile values for scores on all 15 needs are given in the manual for these two groups. Norms for high school students are also available from the publisher. Concerning usage, the manual (1959) states, "The EPPS can add a good deal to the vocational and educational counseling of college students" and "The EPPS is particularly useful in stimulating conversations about the degree and kind of interpersonal relations desired in social contacts . . . ." (p. 18).

If one considers Edwards' distinguished reputation in the area of statistics and psychometric theory, the negative reviews of this instrument come somewhat as a surprise. Radcliffe (1965) concludes, "There is nothing to suggest that the counselor will find the Edwards Personal Preference Schedule particularly useful . . ." (p. 200), and Stricker (1965) concludes that "a decade of research into the validity of the EPPS offers little justification for assuming that its scales measure the constructs that they are intended to reflect or that . . . the scales are useful in predicting socially important variables" (p. 206). Heilbrun (1972) has essentially agreed with these comments and pointed out that a new manual is long overdue.

What are all these writers basing their criticism on? Scale reliabilities are satisfactory (ranging from .60 to .87 for split-half coefficients and from .74 to .88 for short-term stability coefficients), norms are based on stable samples, and intercorrelations between the variables are rather low (ranging from $-.34$ to .46). Some research (e.g., Feldman & Corah, 1960) has raised doubts that social desirability is effectively controlled, and it has been demonstrated that the EPPS can be consciously faked in order to create a particular impression (Dicken, 1959). The major problem, however, has to do with validity, for which the manual gives extremely scanty information. Correlations between the EPPS and the Guilford-Martin Personnel Inventory and the Taylor Manifest Anxiety Scale are presented, and these coefficients are interpreted as falling in the expected directions. However, Edwards proposes that a common factor of social desirability might partially account for the significant relationships found. When subjects were asked to rank themselves on the 15 personality variables and these rankings were compared with rankings based on EPPS scores, some agreed very well but others not at all. Self Q sorts of the EPPS statements have also been correlated with EPPS scores with comparable results. These findings constitute the total "evidence" for validity presented.

It is somehow refreshing to note that critical reviews and a paucity of nontest correlates have not prevented psychologists from using this instrument extensively for counseling and research. The MMPI is the only personality inventory that has been researched more frequently in the past 6–7 years, and only the Strong VIB is used more often in counseling centers. A plausible reason for this continuing attraction may be that the concept "needs" is as strongly associated with the EPPS as the concept "values" is with the Allport-Vernon-Lindzey inventory. New rivals (e.g., the PRF) no doubt find this kind of "paired-associates learning" difficult to overcome.

What kinds of research is the EPPS being used for now? Apparently comparison of groups remains very popular. Examination of the reference list in *The Seventh Mental Measurements Yearbook* (1972) reveals the following: counseled versus uncounseled students, law- and non-law-oriented students, smokers and nonsmokers, high- and low-authoritarian student teachers, Mennonites and non-Mennonites, ROTC and non-ROTC undergraduates, honors and nonhonors students, and so on. Determination of the relative strength of needs in a given group has also been frequently undertaken. The yearbook indicates such studies of champion-level female fencers, medical students, male psychiatric nursing assistants, handicapped employees in industry, typewriting and shorthand teachers, and beginning adult singers. The EPPS bibliography additionally reveals that it has been very popular for master's and doctor's theses.

The EPPS has served a useful purpose, especially in calling attention to the role of the social desirability response set in personality inventories. Apparently it will continue to be widely used, until another need-measuring instrument with better evidence of external validity makes its presence known to psychologists. One has the impression that Edwards himself has lost interest in the inventory, since repeated requests to update the manual have been ignored and a new 53-scale inventory (with a T-F response format) has recently appeared bearing his name.

Eysenck Personality Inventory (EPI)

This questionnaire is a modification and improvement of the earlier Maudsley Personality Inventory (Eysenck, 1959). Both instruments were devised to link personality dimensions with the main body of experimental and theoretical psychology. On the basis of numerous factor-analytic investigations of different sets of items, as well as theoretical considerations, Eysenck concluded that nearly all the variance in the personality domain could be accounted for by two factors, namely, neuroticism-stability (N) and introversion-extroversion (E). Eysenck and Eysenck (1963) state that " the N factor is closely related to the inherited degree of lability of the autonomic nervous system, while the *E* factor is closely related to the degree of excitation and inhibition prevalent in the central nervous system'' (p. 13). As one might expect, the EPI has often been used in laboratory investigations, especially in the area of conditioning.

This questionnaire is among the briefest of those instruments purporting to measure personality (as opposed to scales designed to measure a single trait). Parallel forms, each consisting of 57 items, are available. Each dimension is measured by 24 questions to which the respondent answers "yes" or "no." The additional 9 items form a Lie scale to detect subjects showing a desirability response set. *E* and *N* are conceptualized as uncorrelated and independent dimensions of personality, and the near-zero correlations reported in the manual are consistent with this hypothesis. Test-retest correlations over a 1-year period generally run in the .80's (i.e., for normal English subjects). Split-half reliability (Form A versus Form B) has ranged from .75 to .91 in studies with normal, neurotic, and psychotic subjects. Validity has been established by studies comparing self-ratings of introversion-extroversion with *E* scores and by studies comparing subjects nominated by judges as extreme on the extraversion or neuroticism dimensions with *E* and *N* scores.

The reader may wonder why such a theoretically based and laboratory-oriented inventory is being discussed in a chapter with an applied focus. Eysenck and Eysenck (1963) provide the rationale for its inclusion: "In the area of therapeutic treatment of behavior disorders the Eysenck Personality Inventory can play a major part in diagnosis" (p. 22). Later the same authors (1963) stated, "Choice of treatment is largely dependent upon the precise position of the patient in the two-dimensional framework provided by the EPI" (p. 22). Apparently these claims are based on findings that dysthymic neurotics (anxiety reactions, phobics, depressives, obsessive-compulsives) score high on *N* and low on *E*, whereas psychopaths score high on *N* and also high on *E*. Eysenck and Eysenck interpret these findings as follows. "In short, the neurotic introvert might be characterized as being *oversocialized* and the neurotic extrovert as being *undersocialized*" (p. 7). Different kinds of treatment may indeed be recommended for over- and undersocialized individuals. The treatment implications of the findings for schizophrenics is unclear, however, since this group's location in *E-N* space is far removed from neurotics and prisoners and closest to English students. A recent publication (Eysenck & Eysenck, 1972) suggests that a psychoticism dimension will probably be included in the next revision of the EPI.

Researchers have administered the EPI to various clinical groups. McKerracher and Watson (1968) showed that Eysenck's description of psychopathic disorder (high *N*, high *E*) was evidenced by 41% of the females but only 16% of the males in a criminal population. In another study (Verghese & Abraham, 1972) no differences were found in E scores of schizophrenics, neurotics, and a normal control group, but N scores effectively discriminated the normals from the psychiatric patients and the schizophrenics from the neurotics. Platman and Plutchik (1970) showed that the EPI discriminates poorly between a manic state and the normal state, but that it is a useful indicator of depressive mood.

The manual (Eysenck & Eysenck, 1963) gives norms based on U.S. college students and means and standard deviations for a variety of English normal and abnormal samples. One would apparently have to develop local norms to interpret findings of U.S. psychiatric groups. Age, sex, and class effects have also been reported: E and N decline with advancing age, women score higher on N and lower on E than men, and working-class groups obtain higher N scores than middle-class groups. Additionally, Lowe and Hildman (1972) recently demonstrated significant differences between E and N scores of black and white college students. Further information concerning the theoretical background and experimental validation of the E and N concepts may be found in Eysenck and Eysenck (1969).

The EPI can be strongly recommended for research use, but claims for clinical utility may be questioned by those accustomed to the more familiar terminology and multidimensional aspect of the MMPI. Most EPI work has focused on demonstrations of construct validity, which of course is in keeping with the test constructor's aim and philosophy. However, a paucity of external validity data, especially nontest correlates of factor scores or of locations in bivariate space, is apt to limit practitioners' interest in using this inventory.

CONTROVERSIAL TOPICS

Mastery of the area of personality assessment by inventories requires not only an appreciation of the background and context of application and of the strengths and weaknesses of the principal assessment devices, but also knowledge of problems that have not yet been resolved. Nine controversial issues have come to our attention in preparing this chapter. Unfortunately, space limitations do not permit us to present each topic in the detail it merits. Hence those controversial topics that have been discussed most frequently elsewhere are simply labeled and briefly described, and key references are also given to assist the reader in obtaining more detailed information about them. Topics that are likely to be less familiar to the reader are covered fairly extensively.

Clinical versus statistical prediction deserves the honor of being the first controversial topic to be mentioned. Meehl's (1954) monograph raised the question of whether human judgment or an actuarial table serves better as a prediction method in personality assessment. Recommended reading on this topic includes contributions by Meehl (1957, 1965), Holt (1958, 1970), Gough (1962), Sawyer (1966), Goldberg (1968a), and Sines (1970). A second controversial topic can be labeled "faking, styles, sets, and content." The question here is, are inventories actually measuring the traits or dimensions they were designed to evaluate or are they measuring subjects' tendencies to acquiesce or give socially desirable responses? From the vast literature concerned with this question, the reader would profit from examining Cronbach (1950), Jackson and Messick (1962), Edwards and Walsh (1964), Berg (1955), Norman (1963), Goldberg and Slovic (1967), Block (1965), Edwards (1970), Rorer (1965), and Jackson (1967b). A third controversial issue can be summarized by the phrase "situational specificity and the trait approach." Here the question is, does the situation determine one's behavior or does a person behave in essentially the same way whenever the opportunity to display a certain trait arises? For further information on this matter the reader is referred to Kanfer and Saslow (1965), Mischel (1968), Peterson (1968), Passini and Norman (1966), Norman and Goldberg (1966), Cattell (1963), and Endler and Hunt (1969).

A fourth and related topic is frequently known as "traits versus states." A trait theorist may consider day-to-day variation in aggressive or affiliative tendencies as error variance, but state theorists consider these variations critical to an understanding of the person. For more details on this difference in view see Thorne (1967), Spielberger (1966, 1972), Zuckerman and Lubin (1965), and Cronbach (1970). A fifth important issue relates to invasion of privacy and might legitimately involve "objectionability of MMPI items" as a major subcategory. This topic can be defined very broadly, but in the context of personality measurement it is often narrowly defined by such questions as, does the MMPI ask people to reveal facts about themselves under a kind of pressure that violates the concept of freedom in our society? Relevant sources on this question are Nettler (1959), Gross (1962), Packard (1964), Hathaway (1964), and Brayfield (1965). Concerning the more factual issue of what exactly do people object to about the MMPI, the reader should consult Butcher and Tellegen (1966), Rankin (1968), Walker (1967), Simmons (1968), and Hoerl (1971).

A sixth controversial topic has been described by Wiggins (1973) as "automated clinical interpretation." At issue here are commercial interpretive systems which send a report for a fee to those who submit MMPIs (or in some cases CPIs and 16 PFs) to them. These systems are all nonactuarial, in contrast with the actuarial programs reviewed in the MMPI section. For further details on the matter of automated clinical interpretation in personality assessment, the reader should consult Eichman (1972), Manning (1971), Fowler (1967, 1969, 1972), Finney (1965, 1967), Pearson and Swenson (1967), Dunlop (1966), Caldwell (1970), Eber (1964), and Hedlund, Morgan, and Master (1972). Three other controversial topics are treated next in some detail.

Clinical Judgment: Linear, Configural, or Illusory?

How do clinicians combine assessment and life history data to arrive at predictions of patient behavior? Often what Meehl (1960) has referred to as the "cognitive activity of the clinician" is characterized as an art, so complex and inaccessible that it cannot be verbalized. The arcane body of knowledge accumulated in this manner is usually supported primarily by consensual validation. Clearly, this type of folklore is difficult to prove or disprove, since hypotheses are not sufficiently articulated to be experimentally testable. Chapman and Chapman (1971), however, have performed a series of ingenious experiments which cast new light on this murky area. In one study they presented naive subjects with a series of human figure drawings, each of which was arbitrarily paired with contrived statements about the symptoms of an alleged patient who had drawn it. The drawings and symptom statements were paired so as to avoid any relationship between the occurrence of a symptom and any drawing characteristic viewed as its correlate in conventional clinical practice. These conventional correlates were ascertained by asking practicing clinicians to list drawing characteristics they had observed to be associated with the six contrived symptoms (e.g., "He is worried about how manly he is").

The naive subjects in the Chapman and Chapman study regarded each drawing characteristic as systematically occurring with one symptom more than with any of the others, and these subjects agreed on which symptom belonged with each drawing characteristic. Since there was no connection in fact between the drawings and the symptoms paired with them, the authors labeled this phenomenon "illusory correlation." Since the clinicians as well as the naive subjects demonstrated considerable agreement concerning the drawing-symptom relationships, the suggestion emerged that many clinical inferences may derive from illusory correlations based on high-strength associative connections (e.g., suspiciousness-eye; intelligence-head) rather than on sound validity data. In a second study, using 20 Rorschach content signs of male homosexuality, the Chapmans found that the five most popular but apparently *invalid* signs had a stronger associative connection to male homosexuality in the minds of the clinicians they sampled than either of two unpopular but apparently *valid* signs. For further details of these fascinating experiments, see Chapman and Chapman (1971).

A more well-known and less pejorative descriptor for clinicians' judgmental activities than "artistic" is "configural." Kleinmuntz (1963), for example, asked an expert MMPI interpreter to "think aloud" into a tape recorder as he placed 126 profiles obtained from college students into adjusted and maladjusted categories. Approximately 60 hours of tape-recorded material were compiled, and content analysis of this material suggested that the expert's verbalizations could be summarized by 16 sequential rules. Meehl and Dahlstrom (1960) collected 861 MMPIs from male psychiatric patients who had received a primary diagnosis of either psychosis or neurosis. They then developed an elaborate sequential strategy for differentiating these two types of profiles (see Dahlstrom, Welsh, & Dahlstrom, 1972, pp. 417–419). These highly configural rules achieved a validity coefficient of .39, correctly classified 66% of all cases, and indentified correctly 74% of predicted cases when an indeterminate category was permitted.

Goldberg (1965) utilized the data collected by Meehl to assess the predictive validity of 65 diagnostic signs on the MMPI. The signs ranged from single scale scores through linear combinations of scale scores to highly configural rules. The signs were derived from the published literature, from suggestions of experts, and from analysis of the derivation sample itself. Validity coefficients and percentage of correct identifications, with and without an indeterminate category, were computed for each of the diagnostic signs. The most satisfactory predictor was a simple, unweighted linear composite of five MMPI scales. This sign ($[L + Pa + Sc]$ $- [Hy + Pt]$) achieved a validity coefficient of .44 and correctly classified 70% of all cases as neurotic or psychotic (74% when an indeterminate category was allowed). Comparison of these results with those obtained by the configural Meehl-Dahlstrom rules indicates that this linear rule does at least as well, if not better, than the complex sequential strategy, which presumably reflects expert clinical cognitive activity.

Hoffman (1960) explored whether a linear model might be applied to clinical judgment. Two judges were asked to predict "intelligence" from profiles of nine cues for 100 subjects. These cues consisted of percentile scores on such dimensions as study habits and emotional anxiety. For each judge a multiple correlation was calculated between the cue values and the intelligence predictions. The estimated coefficients were 1.00 for one judge and .91 for the other judge. Thus the linear model (i.e., multiple correlation) reproduced the behavior of these judges with almost complete certainty. It is interesting to note that the judge whose behavior was perfectly predictable by the linear equation described his cue utilization as highly configural.

In another investigation of linear versus configural representation of clinical judgment, Wiggins and Hoffman (1968) reanalyzed the data previously used by Meehl and Dahlstrom (1960) and Goldberg (1965). Judges were 29 clinicians with varying degrees of experience in MMPI interpretation. Three models of these clinicians' judgments were compared: linear, quadratic, and sign. The linear model was the standard multiple-regression equation, and the other two models were configural. The quadratic model included linear terms, nonlinear terms, and interactive terms, whereas the sign model involved a combination of 70 clinical signs reported by clinicians as being relevant to the psychosis-neurosis discrimination. Data analysis by rigorous cross-validational procedures yielded the following results. The sign model predicted 13 of the clinical judges best, the linear model 12, the quadratic model 3, and the sign and linear model predicted 1 judge equally well. These findings seem to offer at least partial support for the contention that clinical judgment is configural in nature. However, one might ask how well these configural models can be represented by the simple linear model. Goldberg (1968b) commented, "The most overwhelming finding from this study was how much of the variance in clinicians' judgments could be represented by the linear model" (p. 490). The interpretation of the data seems to depend on one's theoretical predilections.

Whether clinicians' judgments are configural or linear, the possibility of simulating them by a computer program exists. The question then arises, Will the program outperform the clinician on whose judgments the program was based? Two studies have considered this problem. Kleinmuntz (1963) compared the predictive accuracy of the expert MMPI clinician with that of the computer program (generated by the expert clinician). A comparison of correlations of predictions with an adjusted-maladjusted criterion showed that the computer was superior to the clinician in all instances. Since the clinician in the study was originally selected as most expert among the 10 who originally undertook the task, one could infer that the computer program outperformed all these clinicians in assessing adjustment from MMPI data. In the second study relevant to this issue, Goldberg (1970) once again utilized the Meehl-Dahlstrom data. He constructed a linear model for each of 29 clinical judges by regressing the MMPI scale scores on their judgments across all 861 profiles. When the validity of the clinical judges was compared with the corresponding validity of the models of these judges, it was found that the model was more accurate than the man in 25 out of 29 comparisons.

The average validity of clinical predictions for the 29 judges was .28, and the average validity for the 29 models was .31. The figures do not demonstrate that the models significantly improve on clinical prediction, but they do show that the models represent a satisfactory substitute. And it should be stressed that the models can be automated, whereas the human judges cannot.

The reader might conclude that the clinician should be relieved of all responsibilities involving prediction. However, Wiggins (1973) puts this state of affairs into perspective: "When criterion information does not exist and there is a clinical judge with experience in the task, capture his policy (by linear regression techniques) and use the model instead of the man. (This frees a staff member for other duties or allows the short-term employment of an outside consultant)" (p. 221).

Generalizability of MMPI Interpretations: Limiting Factors

How do changes in the frame of reference affect interpretation of MMPI profiles? Suppose one has two profiles obtained from male subjects, each with an *Mf* T score of 75. In one case the profile has been obtained from a student engaged in ministerial studies, and in the other case from a truck driver with an eighth-grade education. Should one draw the same conclusion in both cases? Or take a somewhat more complex situation. Again, we have two profiles from males, this time with peak T scores between 70 and 80 on scales 6 (*Pa*) and 8 (*Sc*). One profile was obtained from a 35-year-old white mental hospital patient, the other from a 16-year-old black in trouble with the law. Is the same interpretation applicable to both cases?

The questions posed above could be framed more generally, namely, does "blind" analysis of the MMPI lead to valid conclusions? Our response would be an unqualified "no."[3] Sometimes analyses that are ostensibly "blind" are presented for teaching purposes. For example, Dahlstrom's (Baughman, 1972, pp. 368–371) interpretation of "Pete Rogers' " MMPI is so described. However, in an accompanying footnote we read that Dahlstrom "had not met Pete and had no information about him *except his age, sex, and educational and marital status*" (italics added). It is also clear from the report that Dahlstrom knew Pete was a senior in college at the time of testing. Hence his analysis was far from blind, if by "blind" one means having no information other than the profile itself (and sex of subject, since that is part of the MMPI

---

[3]Exner expresses a similar view with regard to the interpretation of projective test data in Chapter 2 (see pp. 98–99).

profile form). Hospitalized/nonhospitalized, married/single, youthful/ elderly, poorly educated/highly educated, and other life history variables all may be related to how one performs on personality inventories. The purpose of the following discussion is to present the interrelations that have been found between certain demographic factors and responses to the MMPI. MMPI research is used to illustrate these limitations on generalizability, because more relevant studies have been done with this instrument than with any other personality inventory. However, research carried out with other psychological instruments indicates that none is free of such limitations.

Age. Dahlstrom and Welsh (1960) reported six studies that investigated the relations between age and MMPI scale scores. However, of these, only studies by Aaronson (1958) and Calden and Hokanson (1959) used relatively unrestricted age ranges. Aaronson analyzed the relative frequencies of different profile peaks in atlas cases (Hathaway & Meehl, 1951) and found that peaks of Scales 1 (*Hs*) and 2 (*D*) are more common, and peaks of Scales 4 (*Pd*) and 8 (*Sc*) less common, in older than in younger subjects. Calden and Hokanson found that the scores for Scales 1, 2, and 0 (*Si*) increased as a function of age in a sample of male tuberculosis patients. All six studies found that Scale 2 scores increased with advancing age and, in four of these investigations, Scale 1 followed the same pattern.

Gynther and Shimkunas (1966) examined the relationship between age and MMPI scale scores with intelligence controlled in white hospitalized psychiatric patients of both sexes. Their major findings were that T scores on Scales *F*, 4, 6, 8, and 9 varied as a function of age, but that Scale 2 T scores were not related to age, in contrast with earlier findings. However, peak analysis showed that older patients more often have Scale 2 peaks. This apparently contradictory finding resulted from decreases in T scores on the other scales, rather than increases in Scale 2 scores. Thumin (1969) found that age was negatively related to scale scores on *F*, 7, and 8 among a group of male job applicants who were 19 to 56 years old.

Webb (1970) investigated the relative occurrence of all 45 possible 2-point code combinations in a representative nationwide sample of over 12,000 psychiatric outpatients. He found that age differences were significantly related to 2-point code frequency in 19 of the codes for male patients and 18 of the codes for female patients. Illustrative findings were that 1-3/3-1's are much more frequently found with older patients and 4-8/8-4's with younger patients. Other evidence (e.g., Devries, 1966; Pearson, Swenson, & Rome, 1965) could be brought to bear on this issue, but the major point seems clear: There are distinctive interrelationships between age and MMPI performance.

Sex. Male-female response to the MMPI was sufficiently different to require the test constructors to assign different T scores to the same raw scores on all the basic clinical scales except 4, 6, and 9. Despite these corrections, profile differences associated with sex have consistently been demonstrated. Aaronson (1958), for example, showed for the cases in Hathaway and Meehl's atlas (1951) that Scales 1 and 7 were more frequently the high point for male patients, whereas Scales 3 and 6 were more frequently the high point for female patients. Webb (1970) also investigated the relationships involving this variable, using the very large sample described in the preceding paragraph. He found that on 36 of the 45 two-point codes, sex differences were significant. Although there were approximately equal numbers of males and females in the sample, males produced more than 15 times as many 2-5/5-2's, 5-7/7-5's and 5-8/8-5's as females did. Obviously, response to the MMPI covaries with the sex of the subject.

Race. Dahlstrom and Welsh (1960) reported a total of four studies considering interrelations between race and MMPI scale scores. All these studies found that blacks obtained higher scores than whites on Scales 8 and/or 9; however, none used samples that would be considered representative of normal blacks. More recently, Gynther (1972) reviewed the results of the 15 to 20 MMPI comparisons of blacks and whites then available and concluded that blacks, whether male or female, normal or institutionalized, young or old, obtain higher scores than whites on Scales *F*, 8 and 9. Might these higher scores lead to interpretative errors? Two studies have addressed this question. Gynther, Fowler, and Erdberg (1971) found that a respected automated computer service characterized nearly 90% of a rural, isolated black sample as resembling psychiatric patients. All these individuals were functioning normally according to their peers and had no history of time spent in mental hospitals or penitentiaries. The second study (Strauss, Gynther, and Wallhermfechtel, 1974) compared MMPI "diagnoses" with psychiatric diagnoses for black and white psychiatric patients. It was hypothesized that there would be less predictor-criterion agreement for black patients, and a higher rate of misclassification was in fact demonstrated by each of the three methods of analysis employed. An implication of these findings is that, if the MMPI were used to diagnose all patients, blacks would receive less adequate treatment than whites because their problems and symptoms would be less often understood.

Have any empirical correlates of blacks' profiles been established? Gynther, Altman, and Warbin (1973a) compared descriptors for highly elevated profiles obtained from black and white psychiatric patients with those for less elevated profiles in two independent samples. Cross-validated findings for the white sample included a meaningful cluster of descriptors; for the black sample, not one descriptor was replicated. Two conclusions are warranted: similar profiles given by blacks and whites do not have the same interpretive significance, and blacks with high-ranging profiles are seen as no different on mental status examination from blacks who do not obtain high-ranging profiles. Another study (Gynther, Altman, and Warbin, 1973b), which compared blacks and whites on the more familiar 4-9/9-4 code type, also failed to disclose any replicated correlates for the black sample.

A high-priority task for MMPI researchers is to establish empirical correlates for MMPIs obtained by blacks and other minority groups. Information acquired to date indicates that the use of traditional interpretations can no longer be justified. For this reason, the fact that none of the automated clinical interpretive services includes race as a parameter in their statement libraries is very disturbing. The individual clinician, who cannot wait for research to answer his decision-making problems, might be well advised to start collecting local data concerning relationships between profiles and behavior. A facetious answer to the earlier question of how to interpret the MMPI of a 16-year-old black male in trouble with the law is "cautiously, very cautiously."

Intelligence, Education, and Socioeconomic Status. Dahlstrom and Welsh (1960) stated that the variables of intelligence, education, and socioeconomic status are so interrelated that distinctive relationships are difficult to separate. Perlman (1950) analyzed the original Minnesota normative data and found that lower-class subjects obtained significantly higher scores than middle- or upper-class subjects on Scales 1, 7, and 8. Nelson (1952) found that low-status Veterans Administration patients obtained higher scores on Scales *L,* 1, 3, and 6, whereas the high-status group obtained higher scores on Scale 5. Nelson (1952) also found that intelligence was negatively related to Scale *L.* Thumin (1969) obtained the same results with a normal sample, with the effects of age and education partialed out. Applezweig (1953) demonstrated that Scale *F* was negatively related to intelligence, a result which was later confirmed by Gynther and Shimkunas (1965). Scale *K* has been shown to be positively related to intelligence (Williams & Lawrence, 1954). Among the clinical scales, the only consistently positive correlations with intelligence have been with Scale 5, but only for males. Results with education are similar. Early work (Brehm, 1954; Gough, 1954) disclosed positive relations between years of education and Scale *K* and 5 scores and negative relations between education and Scale *F* scores. More recently, Thumin (1969) found that education was positively related to Scales *L, K,* and 9, but negatively to Scale 0, with age and intelligence partialed out. Dahlstrom and Welsh's (1960) comment about interrelatedness is clearly correct. However, that there are covariations between MMPI performance and this cluster of variables is also obvious.

Place of Residence. Webb (1971) investigated the frequency of high-point codes for males and females separately in five regions of the United States: Northeast, Southeast, Midwest/Great Lakes, Southwest, and Far West. Results disclosed no significant difference among high-code distributions for males or females. Erdberg (1969), however, found striking differences associated with rural-urban residence. Urban subjects obtained significantly higher scale scores than rural subjects. The conclusion that city living leads to emotional disturbance is unwarranted, but we appear to have yet another demographic variable related to response to the MMPI.

The object of this section has been to draw attention to a problem often not sufficiently emphasized, namely, the marked covariation between demographic variables and MMPI performance. Interpreters must carefully consider the attributes of the person who has taken the MMPI or some other inventory; if they ignore variables other than sex, gross interpretive errors may occur. For the clinician, a satisfactory solution is difficult to imagine. To keep the possible interrelations of all these variables in mind when looking at an MMPI profile is an intimidating and frustrating requirement. Since computers could successfully process this information, we hope that individuals connected with such enterprises will attempt to expand their programs to include these variables.

The Barnum Effect

Why do so many people buy astrology books and read the daily horoscopes found in many newspapers? No evidence exists to show that the moment of birth determines personality, yet predictions based on this "system" are accepted as facts by some and as likely probabilities by others. Perhaps you can "fool some of the people all of the time," but what is there about the predictions that reinforces individuals' horoscope-reading (and horoscope-accepting) behavior?

Forer (1949) was one of the first psychologists to examine this problem empirically. He found that, if individuals are given generalized descriptions of themselves, most believe that these descriptions size them up pretty well. Examples of such descriptions are, "Under stressful circumstances, you occasionally experience some feelings of self doubt," and "Although you have considerable affection for your parents, there have been times when you disagreed with them." These statements are modified from examples given in psychology tests, but can the reader distinguish them from "If you show more devotion to the one you love, you will have better rapport . . . ," which was found in the horoscope section of a metropolitan newspaper? These examples have one thing in common, namely, that they are true of virtually anyone. Hence they give the illusion of accuracy when applied to the individual case.

Apparently Patterson (1951) was the first to apply the term "Barnum effect" to this phenomenon. No doubt he derived this phrase from Barnum's famous dictum: "There's a fool born every minute." Since Patterson's manuscript was unpublished, Meehl's (1956) MPA presidential address and ensuing articles are usually credited with bringing this problem to the attention of psychologists in general. Meehl (1956) suggested that the term might help to

. . . stigmatize those pseudo-successful clinical procedures in which patient descriptions from tests are made to fit the patient largely or wholly by virtue of their triviality; and in which any nontrivial, but perhaps erroneous, inferences are hidden in a context of assertions or denials which carry high confidence simply because of the population base rates [p. 266]

These comments, incidentally, were made in the context of Meehl's plea for a "good cookbook" (i.e., actuarially derived predictor-criterion relationships).

Several investigators (e.g., Stagner, 1958) have demonstrated that persons tend overwhelmingly to rate generalized descriptions as accurate sketches of their own personalities. Sundberg (1955) found no difference in perceived accuracy between real and Barnum reports. The usual procedure in such studies is to ask subjects to take personalty inventories for which interpretations will be furnished as soon as the psychologist has had time to analyze the individual responses and/or profiles. Some days later the subjects are given typed reports in sealed envelopes, which they are asked to read and rate for accuracy. Unknown to the subjects, all the presumably individualized reports are identical.

More recently, O'Dell (1972) has extended the findings in this area by giving subjects Barnum, real, and "prosecuting-attorney" interpretations derived from 16 PF inventories and asking them which they liked best and which described them most accurately. The "prosecuting-attorney" version (Tallent, 1958) is a variant of the Barnum report. High base rate statements are used, but they are saturated with clinical jargon (e.g., "The amount of libidinal energy used in maintaining defenses reduces his ability to function at times"). O'Dell (1972) assumed that the Barnum statements would be best liked, since they contain statements that are subtly flattering or at least not negative in tone, whereas the real interpretation ". . . takes a rather definite, and hence negative, stand in its statements" (p. 270). The results, however, indicated no difference in liking between Barnum and real reports, although the Barnum reports were perceived as being far more accurate than the real reports. O'Dell also assumed that the "prosecuting-attorney" reports would not be liked as well or considered as accurate as the other reports, and his data confirmed both of these expectations. On the basis of his findings O'Dell appropriately warns against validation of test reports by means of indices of user acceptance, inasmuch as users appear to be more impressed by elegantly worded Barnum statements than by statements with established external validity.

The final studies to be reviewed were carried out by Snyder and Larson (1972) and Snyder (1974). In the first of these studies subjects who were told that a general personality interpretation was "for you" found it more accurate than did subjects who were told that the interpretation was "for people generally." If one relates this information to the topic mentioned at the beginning of this section, the implication is that people find individualized horoscopes more believable than those published in the newspapers. Snyder and Larson (1972) also showed that higher external locus of control (Rotter, 1966) correlated positively with acceptance; that is, people who believe their life is governed by fate are more apt to accept a Barnum report as self-descriptive than those who feel they control their own destiny.

In Snyder's (1974) second study the findings showed that highest acceptance of an interpretation resulted when subjects were told that it was based on a projective test they had taken, second highest acceptance when the interpretation was allegedly based on an interview in which they had participated, third highest when subjects were informed that the interpretation derived from their responses on an objective personality test, and lowest acceptance when they were told that the interpretation was "generally true of people." Snyder speculates that these results parallel the relative mystique associated with the different assessment procedures. That is, people believe they are revealing themselves in ways they do not understand in responding to projective techniques, whereas they are relatively familiar with personality inventories and can control their responses to the "objective" items. This hypothesis has some face validity, when one thinks of the mystique associated with palmistry, fortune telling with Tarot cards, and tea-leaf reading.

This review demonstrates how readily people accept reports based on psychological tests and inventories, as well as those proffered by astrologers. However, the danger is not restricted to consumers of reports. Constructors of interpretation programs may be very successful by using nothing but Barnum phrases and sentences in their statement library. As

O'Dell (1972) states, ''This should be regarded as a serious potential trap
. . .'' We cannot expect to be saved from ourselves by subjects' relative
sophistication with regard to objective personality inventories. A closer
look at Snyder's (1974) results shows that this differential receptivity does
not protect the subject from acceptance of inventory data (mean of 4.1 for
acceptance versus projective technique's mean of 4.5 on a 5-point scale).
Prediction needs to be something more than merely accurate. We can be
accurate nearly all of the time, if we say a psychiatric patient is ''anxious.'' We need to discover meaningful ways in which one person differs
from another not simply for purposes of classification, but so that individuals can be assigned to particular treatments ''. . . to help people live
happier lives'' (Cronbach, 1970).

CONCLUDING REMARKS

Many people have labored in the field of personality assessment since
Woodworth published his inventory about 55 years ago. Hundreds of
questionnaires have been constructed and tens of thousands of studies
have investigated their reliability, validity, and utility. Different strategies
have been used to construct these inventories, and their proponents have
produced theoretical frameworks and/or empirical data to demonstrate
the superiority of one approach over the others. Yet what little evidence
is available (e. g., Hase & Goldberg, 1967) suggests that the different
methods are equally effective with regard to predictive validity and,
furthermore, that their average cross-validity coefficients account for
only a small portion of the variance. Hase and Goldberg found that scales
constructed by the contrasted-group method possess moderate validity
for the entire range of criteria against which they have been compared,
whereas scales constructed by factor-analytic, theoretical, and rational
approaches have done either very well or very poorly. In Cronbach and
Gleser's (1965) terms, inventories such as the MMPI and CPI would be
considered to have ''broad band-moderate fidelity,'' whereas inventories
such as the 16 PF and PRF would be designated as having ''narrow band-
high fidelity.''

High fidelity suggests validity coefficients large enough to account for
most of the variance in a measurement situation. However, in the area of
personality assessment by inventories, .60 appears to be the upper limit
for obtained validities. Can anything be done to obtain more powerful
predictive devices? In the first place, the influence of the situation should
be taken into account. Although this position has been argued most
strongly by behavioral analysts (see Chapter 5), the work of Endler and
Hunt (1969) indicates that situational variables can be built into inven-

tories. Second, fluctuations in mood, as well as stable dispositions, should be measured systematically by multidimensional inventories. Spielberger's investigations of anxiety (e.g., Spielberger, Auerbach, Wadsworth, Dunn, and Taulbee, 1973) indicate that state-trait measures provide more information than either state or trait measures alone. Third, trait measures should be validated against criteria based on multiple acts, not single behaviors (see Fishbein & Ajzen, 1974). Jaccard (1974), for example, found correlations in the .20's between trait measures of dominance and individual dominant behaviors, but correlations near .60 between these trait measures and the sum of multiple acts. Finally, individual predictions should be based, as far as possible, on data collected from relevant reference groups. Since this orientation requires numerous decision-making rules, programming and interpretation by computer seem highly desirable, if not mandatory.

A real challenge for the would-be innovative inventory constructor is posed by the findings of Mehrabian (1972), which demonstrated that nearly all the impact of a message reaches a listener through nonverbal means. Mehrabian also showed that, if there is a discrepancy between vocal information and verbal content, the vocal message is what is perceived. Since all self-report inventories rely exclusively on responses to verbal content for personality description, disagreements between these self-descriptions and judges' ratings may reflect the absence in the materials available of what has determined the feelings of the judge for the subject. Predictive validities may also have been attenuated by failure to consider those nonverbal communications by which an individual influences significant others positively or negatively. A task for the future, then, is to construct a questionnaire to measure those aspects of nonverbal behavior that determine how one is viewed by others.

One can be both optimistic and pessimistic concerning personality assessment by inventories. Comparison of the recently devised inventories with those published several decades ago shows numerous advances in psychometric sophistication. Also, many of the problems in this area of work appear to have been well delineated, even if definitive solutions to all of them are not yet available. Nevertheless, progress, as measured by such criteria as increases in predictive validities, is agonizingly slow; and theory seems to lag behind practice. However, the myriad issues, variables, and complexities in this field should not blind us to the fact that present questionnaires, in the hands of qualified users, make valuable social and personal contributions. If better inventories can be developed or better understanding of our current inventories can be achieved, the value of the enterprise can be further extended. Sound knowledge of personality-treatment interactions will permit us to "shift from a selection model or a prediction model to an allocation model, and use test procedures to pick the educational, therapeutic or other approach that promises best results for the individual" (Cronbach, 1970, p. xxix). In the final analysis, that is what personality measurement is all about.

REFERENCES

Aaronson, B. S. Age and sex influence on MMPI profile peak distributions in an abnormal population. *Journal of Consulting Psychology*, 1958, **22**, 203–206.

Acker, M. B. The relation of achievement need, time perspective, and field articulation to academic performance. Unpublished doctoral dissertation, University of California, 1967.

Ahmed, S. A. Prediction of cigarette consumption level with personality and socioeconomic variables. *Journal of Applied Psychology*, 1972, **56**, 437–438.

Allport, G. W. *Personality: A psychological interpretation*. New York: Holt, Rinehart & Winston, 1937.

Allport, G. W., & Vernon, P. E. *Study of Values*. Boston: Houghton-Miffllin, 1931.

Allport, G. W., Vernon, P. E., & Lindzey, G. *Study of Values* (revised manual). Boston: Houghton-Mifflin, 1970.

Anastasi, A. Personality Research Form. In O. K. Buros (Ed.), *The seventh mental measurements yearbook*, Vol. 1. Highland Park, N.J.: Gryphon Press, 1972. Pp. 297–298.

Applezweig, M. H. Educational levels and Minnesota Multiphasic profiles. *Journal of Clinical Psychology*, 1953, **9**, 340–344.

Baughman, E. E. *Personality: The psychological study of the individual*. Englewood Cliffs, N.J.: Prentice-Hall, 1972.

Bentler, P. M. Response variability: Fact or artifact? Unpublished doctoral dissertation, Stanford University, 1964.

Berg, I. A. Response bias and personality: The deviation hypothesis. *Journal of Psychology*, 1955, **40**, 61–71.

Bernreuter, R. G. *The Personality Inventory*. Palo Alto, Calif.: Consulting Psychologists Press, 1931.

Berzins, J. I., Dove, J. L., & Ross, W. F. Cross-validational studies of the personality correlates of the A-B therapist "type" distinction among professionals and nonprofessionals. *Journal of Consulting and Clinical Psychology*, 1972, **39**, 388–395.

Bither, S. W. A study of the relationship among personalities in groups and group task performance. Unpublished doctoral dissertation, University of Washington, 1969.

Black, J. D. The interpretation of MMPI profiles of college women. *Dissertation Abstracts*, 1953, **13**, 870–871.

Block, J. *The Q-sort method in personality assessment and psychiatric research.* Springfield, Ill.: Charles C Thomas, 1961.

Block, J. *The challenge of response sets: Unconfounding meaning, acquiescence, and social desirability in the MMPI.* New York: Appleton-Century-Crofts, 1965.

Block, J., von der Lippe, A., & Block, J. H. Sex-role and socialization patterns: Some personality concomitants and environmental antecedents. *Journal of Consulting and Clinical Psychology,* 1973, **41**, 321–341.

Braun, J. R., & Asta, P. Changes in Personality Research Form scores (PRF, Form A) produced by faking instructions. *Journal of Clinical Psychology,* 1969, **25**, 429–430.

Braun, J. R., & Costantini, A. Faking and faking detection on the Personality Research Form, AA. *Journal of Clinical Psychology,* 1970, **26**, 516–518.

Brayfield, A. H. (Ed.) Special issue: Testing and public policy. *American Psychologist,* 1965, **20**, 857–1005.

Brehm, M. L. An examination of MMPI results and delinquency data for college and non-college groups. Unpublished manuscript, 1954.

Buros, O. K. (Ed.) *The seventh mental measurements yearbook.* Highland Park, N.J.: Gryphon Press, 1972.

Butcher, J. N. (Ed.) *MMPI: Research developments and clinical applications.* New York: McGraw-Hill, 1969.

Butcher, J. N. (Ed.) *Objective personality assessment: Changing perspectives.* New York: Academic Press, 1972.

Butcher, J. N., & Ryan, M. Personality stability and adjustment to an extreme environment. *Journal of Applied Psychology,* 1974, **59**, 107–109.

Butcher, J. N., & Tellegen, A. Objections to MMPI items. *Journal of Consulting Psychology,* 1966, **30**, 527–534.

Calden, G., & Hokanson, J. E. The influence of age on MMPI responses. *Journal of Clinical Psychology,* 1959, **15**, 194–195.

Caldwell, A. B. Recent advances in automated interpretation of the MMPI. Paper presented at the Fifth Annual MMPI Symposium, Mexico City, Mexico, February 1970.

Campbell, D. P. *Handbook for the Strong Vocational Interest Blank.* Stanford, Calif.: Stanford University Press, 1971.

Campbell, D. T., & Fiske, D. W. Convergent and discriminant validation by the multitrait-multimethod matrix. *Psychological Bulletin,* 1959, **56**, 81–105.

Cattell, R. B. *The description and measurement of personality.* Yonkers-on-Hudson, N.Y.: World Book, 1946.

Cattell, R. B. *Manual for forms A and B: Sixteen Personality Factor Questionnaire.* Champaign, Ill.: Institute for Personality and Ability Testing, 1949.

Cattell, R. B. *Personality: A systematic theoretical and factual study.* New York: McGraw-Hill, 1950.

Cattell, R. B. *Personality and motivation, structure and measurement.* Yonkers-on-Hudson, N.Y.: World Book, 1957.

Cattell, R. B. Personality, role, mood, and situation perception: A unifying theory of modulators. *Psychological Review*, 1963, **70**, 1–18.

Cattell, R. B. Personality pinned down. *Psychology Today*, 1973, **7**, 40–46. (a)

Cattell, R. B. *Personality and mood by questionnaire.* San Francisco: Jossey-Bass, 1973. (b)

Cattell, R. B., & Bolton, L. S. What pathological dimensions lie beyond the normal dimensions of the 16 PF? A comparison of MMPI and 16 PF factor domains. *Journal of Consulting and Clinical Psychology*, 1969, **33**, 18–29.

Cattell, R. B., Eber, H. W., & Tatsuoka, M. M. *Handbook for the Sixteen Personality Factor Questionnaire (16 PF).* Champaign, Ill.: Institute for Personality and Ability Testing, 1970.

Cattell, R. B., & Nichols, K. E. An improved definition, from 10 researchers, of second-order personality factors in Q data (with cross-cultural checks). *Journal of Social Psychology*, 1972, **86**, 187–203.

Cattell, R. B., Pierson, G., Finkbeiner, C., Willes, P., Brim, B., & Robertson, J. Proof of alignment of personality source trait factors in questionnaires and observer ratings: The theory of instrument-free-patterns. Advance Publication No. 38. Boulder, Colo.: Institute for Research on Morality and Self-Realization, 1974.

Cattell, R. B., & Scheier, I. H. *The IPAT Anxiety Scale Questionnaire: Manual* (2nd ed.) Champaign, Ill.: Institute for Personality and Ability Testing, 1963.

Cattell, R. B., Schmidt, L. R., & Bjersted, A. Clinical diagnosis by the Objective-Analytic Personality Batteries. *Journal of Clinical Psychology*, 1972, **28**, 239–312.

Cattell, R. B., & Stice, G. F. The psychodynamics of small groups. Final report on research project NR-172-369, Contract ZN 80 nr-79600. Human Relations Branch Office of Naval Research, 1953.

Cattell, R. B., & Warburton, F. W. *Objective personality and motivation tests: A theoretical introduction and practical compendium.* Urbana, Ill.: University of Illinois Press, 1967.

Chapman, L. J., & Chapman, J. P. Associatively based illusory correlation as a source of psychodiagnostic folklore. In L. D. Goodstein & R. I. Lanyon (Eds.), *Readings in Personality Assessment.* New York: Wiley, 1971.

Cline, V. B. Interpersonal perception. In B. A. Maher (Ed.), *Progress in experimental personality research*, Vol. 1. New York: Academic Press, 1964. Pp. 221–284.

Cronbach, L. J. Further evidence on response sets and test design. *Educational and Psychological Measurement*, 1950, **10**, 3–31.

Cronbach, L. J. California Psychological Inventory. In O. K. Buros (Ed.), *The fifth mental measurements yearbook*. Highland Park, N.J.: Gryphon Press, 1959. Pp. 96–99.

Cronbach, L. J. *Essentials of psychological testing* (3rd ed.). New York: Harper & Row, 1970.

Cronbach, L. J., & Gleser, G. C. *Psychological tests and personnel decisions*. Urbana, Ill.: University of Illinois Press, 1957.

Cronbach, L. J., & Gleser, G. C. *Psychological tests and personnel decisions*. (2nd ed.). Urbana, Ill.: University of Illinois Press, 1965.

Dahlstrom, W. G. MMPI Handbook, Volume II: A sneak preview. Invited presentation at the Ninth Annual MMPI Symposium, Los Angeles, California, February 1974.

Dahlstrom, W. G., & Welsh, G. S. *An MMPI handbook: A guide to use in clinical practice and research*. Minneapolis: University of Minnesota Press, 1960.

Dahlstrom, W. G., Welsh, G. S., & Dahlstrom, L. E. *An MMPI Handbook*. Vol. I: *Clinical Interpretation*. (Rev. ed.) Minneapolis: University of Minnesota Press, 1972.

Davis, K. R., & Sines, J. O. An antisocial behavior pattern associated with a specific MMPI profile. *Journal of Consulting and Clinical Psychology*, 1971, **36**, 229–234.

Delhees, K. H., & Cattell, R. B. The dimensions of pathology: Proof of their projection beyond the normal 16 PF source traits. *Personality*, 1971, **2**, 149–173. (a)

Delhees, K. H., & Cattell, R. B. *Manual for the Clinical Analysis Questionnaire (CAQ)*. Champaign, Ill.: Institute for Personality and Ability Testing, 1971. (b)

Devries, A. G. Demographic variables and MMPI responses. *Journal of Clinical Psychology*, 1966, **22**, 450–452.

Dicken, C. F. Simulated patterns on the Edwards Personal Preference Schedule. *Journal of Applied Psychology*, 1959, **43**, 372-378.

Domino, G. Differential prediction of academic achievement in conforming and independent settings. *Journal of Educational Psychology*, 1968, **59**, 256–260.

Domino, G. Interactive effects of achievement orientation and teaching style on academic achievement. *Journal of Educational Psychology*, 1971, **62**, 427–431.

Dorr, D., Cowen, E., Sandler, I., & Pratt, D. M. Dimensionality of a test battery for nonprofessional health workers. *Journal of Consulting and Clinical Psychology*, 1973, **41**, 181–185.

DuBois, P. H. *A history of psychological testing*. Boston: Allyn & Bacon, 1970.

Dunlop, E. *Essentials of the automated MMPI*. Glendale, Calif.: Institute of Clinical Analysis, 1966.

Eber, H. W. Computer reporting of 16 PF data. Paper presented at the American Psychological Association meetings, Los Angeles, September 1964.

Edwards, A. L. *Manual for the Edwards Personal Preference Schedule*. New York: Psychological Corporation, 1954.

Edwards, A. L. *Edwards Personal Preference Schedule*. New York: Psychological Corporation, 1959.

Edwards, A. L. *Edwards Personality Inventory: Manual*. Chicago: Science Research Associates, 1967.

Edwards, A. L. *The measurement of personality traits by scales and inventories*. New York: Holt, Rinehart & Winston, 1970.

Edwards, A. L., & Abbott, R. D. Relationships among the Edwards Personality Inventory scales, the Edwards Personal Preference Schedule, and the Personality Research Form scales. *Journal of Consulting and Clinical Psychology*, 1973, **40**, 27–32. (a)

Edwards, A. L., & Abbott, R. D. Relationships between the EPI scales and the 16 PF, CPI, and EPPS scales. *Educational and Psychological Measurement*, 1973, **33**, 231–238. (b)

Edwards, A. L., & Walsh, J. N. Response sets in standard and experimental personality scales. *American Educational Research Journal*, 1964, **1**, 52–61.

Eichman, W. J. (Re Minnesota Multiphasic Personality Inventory) Computerized scoring and interpreting services. In O. K. Buros (Ed.), *The seventh mental measurements yearbook*. Vol. 1. Highland Park, N.J.: Gryphon Press, 1972. Pp. 250–266.

Endler, N. S., & Hunt, J. McV. Generalizability of contributions from sources of variance in the S-R inventories of anxiousness. *Journal of Personality*, 1969, **37**, 1–24.

Erdberg, S. P. MMPI differences associated with sex, race, and residence in a southern sample. Unpublished Ph.D. dissertation, University of Alabama, 1969.

Eysenck, H. J. *Maudsley Personality Inventory*. London: University of London Press, 1959.

Eysenck, H. J., & Eysenck, S. B. G. *Eysenck Personality Inventory*. San Diego: Educational and Industrial Testing Service, 1963.

Eysenck, H. J., & Eysenck, S. B. G. *Eysenck Personality Inventory* (revised manual). San Diego: Educational and Industrial Testing Service, 1969.

Eysenck, S. B. G., & Eysenck, H. J. The questionnaire measurement of psychoticism. *Psychological Medicine*, 1972, **2**, 50–55.

Feldman, M. J., & Corah, N. L. Social desirability and the forced choice method. *Journal of Consulting Psychology*, 1960, **24**, 480–482.

Fenelon, J. R., & Megargee, E. I. The influence of race on the manifestation of leadership. *Journal of Applied Psychology*, 1971, **55**, 353–358.

Finney, J. C. Purposes and usefulness of the Kentucky program for the automatic interpretation of the MMPI. Paper presented at the American Psychological Association meetings, Chicago, September 1965.

Finney, J. C. Methodological problems in programmed composition of psychological test reports. *Behavioral Science*, 1967, **12**, 142–152.

Fishbein, M., & Ajzen, I. Attitudes toward objects as predictors of single and multiple behavioral criteria. *Psychological Review*, 1974, **81**, 59–74.

Fitts, W. H. *Tennessee Self Concept Scale manual.* Nashville, Tenn.: Counselor Recordings and Tests, 1965.

Forer, B. R. The fallacy of personal validation: A classroom demonstration of gullibility. *Journal of Abnormal and Social Psychology*, 1949, **44**, 118–123.

Fowler, R. D., Jr. Computer interpretation of personality tests: The automated psychologist. *Comprehensive Psychiatry*, 1967, **6**, 455–467.

Fowler, R. D., Jr. Automated interpretation of personality test data. In J. N. Butcher (Ed.), *MMPI: Research developments and clinical applications.* McGraw-Hill, 1969. Pp. 105–126.

Fowler, R. D., Jr. Automated psychological test interpretation: The status in 1972. *Psychiatric Annals*, 1972, **2**, 10–28.

Fowler, R. D., Jr., & Athey, E. B. A cross-validation of Gilberstadt and Duker's 1-2-3-4 profile type. *Journal of Clinical Psychology*, 1971, **27**, 238–240.

Freud, S. (1933) *New introductory lectures on psychoanalysis. Standard Edition*, Vol. XXII. London: Hogarth Press, 1964. Pp. 7–182.

Gilberstadt, H., & Duker, J. *A handbook for clinical and actuarial MMPI interpretation.* Philadelphia: Saunders, 1965.

Goldberg, L. R. The effectiveness of clinicians' judgments: The diagnosis of organic brain damage from the Bender-Gestalt Test. *Journal of Consulting Psychology*, 1959, **23**, 25–33.

Goldberg, L. R. Diagnosticians versus diagnostic signs: The diagnosis of psychosis versus neurosis from the MMPI. *Psychological Monographs*, 1965, **79**(9, Whole No. 602).

Goldberg, L. R. Seer over sign: The first "good" example? *Journal of Experimental Research in Personality*, 1968, **3**, 168–171. (a)

Goldberg, L. R. Simple models or simple processes? Some research on clinical judgments. *American Psychologist*, 1968, **23**, 483–496. (b)

Goldberg, L. R. Man versus model of man: A rationale plus evidence for a method of improving on clinical inferences. *Psychological Bulletin*, 1970, **73**, 422–432.

Goldberg, L. R. A historical survey of personality scales and inventories. In P. McReynolds (Ed.), *Advances in psychological assessment,* Vol. II. Palo Alto, Calif.: Science and Behavior Books, 1971. Pp. 293–336.

Goldberg, L. R. California Psychological Inventory. In O. K. Buros (Ed.), *The seventh mental measurements yearbook.* Vol. 1. Highland Park, N.J.: Gryphon Press, 1972. Pp. 94–96. (a)

Goldberg, L. R. Parameters of personality inventory construction and utilization: A comparison of prediction strategies and tactics. *Multivariate Behavioral Research Monographs*, 1972, 7(2). (b)

Goldberg, L. R. Objective diagnostic tests and measures. *Annual Review of Psychology*, 1974, **25**, 343–366.

Goldberg, L. R., & Slovic, P. Importance of test item content: An analysis of a corollary of the deviation hypothesis. *Journal of Counseling Psychology*, 1967, **14**, 462–472.

Good, L., & Good, K. A preliminary measure of existential anxiety. *Psychological Reports*, 1974, **34**, 72–74.

Goodstein, L. D., Crites, J. O., Heilbrun, A. B., Jr., & Rempel, P. P. The use of the California Psychological Inventory in a university counseling service. *Journal of Counseling Psychology*, 1961, **8**, 147–153.

Goodstein, L. D., & Lanyon, R. I. (Eds.). *Readings in personality assessment.* New York: Wiley, 1971.

Gough, H. G. Some personality differences between high ability high school students who do, and do not, go to college. *American Psychologist*, 1954, **9**, 559.

Gough, H. G. *California Psychological Inventory manual.* Palo Alto, Calif.: Consulting Psychologists Press, 1957.

Gough, H. G. Clinical versus statistical prediction in psychology. In L. Postman (Ed.), *Psychology in the Making.* New York: Knopf, 1962. Pp. 526–584.

Gough, H. G. Conceptual analysis of psychological test scores and other diagnostic variables. *Journal of Abnormal Psychology*, 1965, **70**, 294–302.

Gough, H. G. An interpreter's syllabus for the California Psychological Inventory. In P. McReynolds (Ed.), *Advances in psychological assessment*, Vol. 1. Palo Alto, Calif.: Science and Behavior Books, 1968. Pp. 55–79.

Gough, H. G. *California Psychological Inventory* (revised manual). Palo Alto, Calif.: Consulting Psychologists Press, 1969.

Gough, H. G., Fox, R. E., & Hall, W. B. Personality inventory assessment of psychiatric residents. *Journal of Counseling Psychology*, 1972, **19**, 269–274.

Gough, H. G., & Heilbrun, A. B. *The Adjective Check List Manual.* Palo Alto, Calif.: Consulting Psychologists Press, 1965.

Gross, M. L. *The brainwatchers.* New York: Random House, 1962.

Gross, W. F., & Nerviano, V. J. The use of the Personality Research Form with alcoholics: Effects of age and IQ. *Journal of Clinical Psychology*, 1973, **29**, 378–379.

Guilford, J. P. *An inventory of factors STDCR.* Beverly Hills, Calif.: Sheridan Supply, 1940.

Guilford, J. P., & Martin, H. G. *The Guilford-Martin inventory of factors GAMIN: Manual of directions and norms.* Beverly Hills, Calif.: Sheridan Supply, 1943.

Guilford, J. P., & Zimmerman, W. S. *The Guilford Temperament Survey: Manual of instructions and interpretations.* Beverly Hills, Calif.: Sheridan Supply, 1949.

Guthrie, G. M. A study of the personality characteristics associated with the disorders encountered by an internist. Unpublished Ph.D. dissertation, University of Minnesota, 1949.

Gynther, M. D. White norms and black MMPIs: A prescription for discrimination? *Psychological Bulletin*, 1972, **78**, 386–402.

Gynther, M. D., Altman, H., & Warbin, R. W. The interpretation of uninterpretable MMPI profiles. *Journal of Consulting and Clinical Psychology*, 1973, **40**, 78–83. (a)

Gynther, M. D., Altman, H., & Warbin, R. W. Behavioral correlates for the MMPI 4-9/9-4 code type: A case of the emperor's new clothes? *Journal of Consulting and Clinical Psychology*, 1973, **40**, 259–263. (b)

Gynther, M. D., Altman, H., & Sletten, I. W. Replicated correlates of MMPI two-point code types: The Missouri actuarial system. *Journal of Clinical Psychology*, 1973, **29**, 263–289.

Gynther, M. D., Altman, H., Warbin, R. W., & Sletten, I. W. A new actuarial system for MMPI interpretation: Rationale and methodology. *Journal of Clinical Psychology*, 1972, **28**, 173–179.

Gynther, M. D., & Brilliant, P. J. The MMPI *K*+ profile: A reexamination. *Journal of Consulting and Clinical Psychology*, 1968, **32**, 616–617.

Gynther, M. D., Fowler, R. D., & Erdberg, P. False positives galore: The application of standard MMPI criteria to a rural, isolated, Negro sample. *Journal of Clinical Psychology*, 1971, **27**, 234–237.

Gynther, M. D., & Mayer, A. D. The prediction of mental deficiency by means of the Kent-EGY. *American Journal of Mental Deficiency*, 1960, **64**, 988–990.

Gynther, M. D., & Shimkunas, A. M. Age, intelligence, and MMPI *F* scores. *Journal of Consulting Psychology*, 1965, **29**, 383–388.

Gynther, M. D., & Shimkunas, A. M. Age and MMPI performance. *Journal of Consulting Psychology*, 1966, **30**, 118–121.

Halbower, C. C. A comparison of actuarial versus clinical prediction to classes discriminated by MMPI. Unpublished Ph.D. dissertation, University of Minnesota, 1955.

Hall, W. B., & MacKinnon, D. W. Personality inventory correlates of creativity among architects. *Journal of Applied Psychology*, 1969, **53**, 322–326.

Hartshorne, H., & May, M. A. *Studies in deceit.* New York: Macmillan, 1928.

Hase, H. D., & Goldberg, L. R. The comparative validity of different strategies of deriving personality inventory scales. *Psychological Bulletin*, 1967, **67**, 231–248.

Hathaway, S. R. MMPI: Professional use by professional people. *American Psychologist*, 1964, **19**, 204–210.

Hathaway, S. R. Personality inventories. In B. B. Wolman (Ed.), *Handbook of clinical psychology*. New York: McGraw-Hill, 1965. Pp. 451-476.

Hathaway, S. R. Foreword to new edition. In W. G. Dahlstrom, G. S. Welsh, & L. E. Dahlstrom, *An MMPI handbook*. Vol. I. *Clinical Interpretation* (Rev. ed.). Minneapolis: University of Minnesota Press, 1972. Pp. xiii–xiv. (a)

Hathaway, S. R. Where have we gone wrong? The mystery of the missing progress. In J. N. Butcher (Ed.), *Objective personality assessment: Changing perspectives*. New York: Academic Press, 1972. Pp. 21–43. (b)

Hathaway, S. R., & McKinley, J. C. A multiphasic personality schedule (Minnesota): I. Construction of the schedule. *Journal of Psychology*, 1940, **10**, 249–254.

Hathaway, S. R., & McKinley, J. C. *Manual for the Minnesota Multiphasic Personality Inventory*. New York: Psychological Corporation, 1943.

Hathaway, S. R., & McKinley, J. C. *Minnesota Multiphasic Personality Inventory: Manual* (Rev. ed.). New York: Psychological Corporation, 1951.

Hathaway, S. R., & McKinley, J. C. *Minnesota Multiphasic Personality Inventory* (revised manual). New York: Psychological Corporation, 1967.

Hathaway, S. R., & Meehl, P. E. *An atlas for the clinical use of the MMPI*. Minneapolis: University of Minnesota Press, 1951.

Hathaway, S. R., & Meehl, P. E. Adjective check list correlates of MMPI scores. Unpublished materials, 1952.

Hedlund, J. L., Morgan, D. W., & Master, F. D. The Mayo Clinic automated MMPI program: Cross validation with psychiatric patients in an army hospital. *Journal of Clinical Psychology*, 1972, **28**, 505–510.

Heilbrun, A. B., Jr. Edwards Personal Preference Schedule. In O. K. Buros (Ed.), *The seventh mental measurements yearbook*. Highland Park, N.J.: Gryphon Press, 1972. Pp. 148–149.

Heist, P., & Yonge, G. *Omnibus Personality Inventory manual*. New York: Psychological Corporation, 1968.

Hoerl, J. B. Objections to selected MMPI items as a function of sex, internal versus external locus of control and procedures for objecting. Unpublished Ph.D. dissertation, St. Louis University, 1971.

Hoffman, H. Performance on the Personality Research Form under desirable and undesirable instructions: Personality disorders. *Psychological Reports*, 1968, **23**, 507–510.

Hoffman, H. Personality patterns of depression and its relation to acquiescence. *Psychological Reports*, 1970, **26**, 459–464.

Hoffman, H. Personality changes of hospitalized alcoholics after treatment. *Psychological Reports*, 1971, **29**, 948–950.

Hoffman, P. J. The paramorphic representation of clinical judgment. *Psychological Bulletin*, 1960, **57**, 116–131.

Holt, R. R. Clinical and statistical prediction: A reformulation and some new data. *Journal of Abnormal and Social Psychology*, 1958, **56**, 1–12.

Holt, R. R. Yet another look at clinical and statistical prediction: Or, is clinical psychology worthwhile? *American Psychologist*, 1970, **25**, 337–349.

Hugo, J. A., II. Abbreviation of the Minnesota Multiphasic Personality Inventory through multiple regression. Unpublished Ph.D. dissertation, University of Alabama, 1971.

Humm, D. G., & Wadsworth, G. W. The Humm-Wadsworth Temperament Scale. *American Journal of Psychiatry*, 1935, **92**, 163–200.

Jaccard, J. J. Predicting social behavior from personality traits. *Journal of Research in Personality*, 1974, **7**, 358–367.

Jackson, D. N. *Personality Research Form manual*. Goshen, N.Y.: Research Psychologists Press, 1967. (a)

Jackson, D. N. A review of J. Block, "The challenge of response sets." *Educational and Psychological Measurement*, 1967, **27**, 207–219. (b)

Jackson, D. N. A sequential system for personality scale development. In C. D. Spielberger (Ed.), *Current topics in clinical and community psychology*, Vol. 2. New York: Academic Press, 1970. Pp. 61–96.

Jackson, D. N., & Guthrie, G. M. A multitrait-multimethod evaluation of the Personality Research Form. *Proceedings of the 76th Annual Convention, American Psychological Association*, 1968, **3**, 177–178.

Jackson, D. N., & Messick, S. Response styles on the MMPI: Comparison of clinical and normal samples. *Journal of Abnormal and Social Psychology*, 1962, **65**, 285–299.

Johnston, R., & McNeal, B. F. Statistical versus clinical prediction: Length of neuropsychiatric hospital stay. *Journal of Abnormal Psychology*, 1967, **72**, 335–340.

Kanfer, F. H., & Saslow, G. Behavioral analysis: An alternative to diagnostic classification. *Archives of General Psychiatry*, 1965, **12**, 529–538.

Kear-Colwell, J. J. The factor structure of the 16 PF and the Edwards Personal Preference Schedule in acute psychiatric patients. *Journal of Clinical Psychology*, 1973, **29**, 225–228.

Kelly, E. L. California Psychological Inventory. In O. K. Buros (Ed.), *The sixth mental measurements yearbook*. Highland Park, N.J.: Gryphon Press, 1965. Pp. 168–170.

Kelly, E. L. Personality Research Form. In O. K. Buros (Ed.), *The seventh mental measurements yearbook*, Vol. 1. Highland Park, N.J.: Gryphon Press, 1972. Pp. 298–301.

Kelly, G. A. The theory and technique of assessment. *Annual Review of Psychology*, 1958, **9**, 323–352.

Kendrick, D. C. The Kendrick battery of tests: Theoretical assumptions and clinical uses. *British Journal of Social and Clinical Psychology*, 1972, **11**, 373–386.

Kincannon, J. C. Prediction of the standard MMPI scale scores from 71 items: The Mini-Mult. *Journal of Consulting and Clinical Psychology*, 1968, **32**, 319–325.

Kleinmuntz, B. MMPI decision rules for the identification of college maladjustment: A digital computer approach. *Psychological Monographs*, 1963, **77**(14, Whole No. 477).

Kleinmuntz, B. *Personality measurement: An introduction*. Homewood, Ill.: Dorsey Press, 1967.

Kusyszyn, I. Comparison of judgmental methods with endorsements in the assessment of personality traits. *Journal of Applied Psychology*, 1968, **52**, 227–233.

Kusyszyn, I., & Greenwood, D. E. Marlowe-Crowne defensiveness and personality scale faking. *Proceedings of the 78th Annual Convention, American Psychological Association*, 1970, **5**, 343–344.

LaForge, R. A correlational study of two personality tests: The MMPI and Cattell 16 PF. *Journal of Consulting Psychology*, 1962, **26**, 402–411.

Lanyon, R. I., & Goodstein, L. D. *Personality assessment*. New York: Wiley, 1971.

Levin, J., & Karni, E. S. Cross-cultural structural stability of the California Psychological Inventory. *Journal of Cross-Cultural Psychology*, 1970, **1**, 253–260.

Levine, J., & Feirstein, A. Differences in test performance between brain-damaged, schizophrenic, and medical patients. *Journal of Consulting and Clinical Psychology*, 1972, **39**, 508–511.

Lewandowski, D., & Graham, J. R. Empirical correlates of frequently occurring two-point MMPI code types: A replicated study. *Journal of Consulting and Clinical Psychology*, 1972, **39**, 467–472.

Liberty, P. G., Jr., Doughtie, E. B., Jr., & Embree, R. B., Jr. Value and trait comparisons of clinical and counseling students: An exploratory study. *Psychological Reports*, 1965, **17**, 157–158.

Lorr, M., & Klett, C. J. Life history differentia of five acute psychotic types. In M. Roff & D. F. Ricks (Eds.), *Life history research in psychopathology*. Minneapolis: University of Minnesota Press, 1970. Pp. 147–157.

Lubin, B., Wallis, R. R., & Paine, C. Patterns of psychological test usage in the United States: 1935–1969. *Professional Psychology*, 1971, **2**, 70–74.

Luzzi, M. H. A study of the relationship of self-acceptance and social value to effectiveness of male rehabilitation counselor trainees. Unpublished doctoral dissertation, Boston University, 1970.

Manning, H. M. Programmed interpretation of the MMPI. *Journal of Personality Assessment*, 1971, **35**, 162–176.

Marks, P. A., & Seeman, W. *The actuarial description of personality: An atlas for use with the MMPI*. Baltimore: Williams & Wilkins, 1963.

Marks, P. A., Seeman, W., & Haller, D. L. *The actuarial use of the MMPI with adolescents and adults.* Baltimore: Williams & Wilkins, 1974.

Marshall, D., & Cattell, R. B. *The seven factor supplement to the 16 PF Test.* Champaign, Ill.: Institute for Personality and Ability Testing, 1974.

Mason, E. P. Stability of differences in personality characteristics of junior high school students from American Indian, Mexican, and Anglo ethnic backgrounds. *Psychology in the Schools*, 1971, **8**, 86–89.

McKerracher, D. W., & Watson, R. A. The Eysenck Personality Inventory in male and female subnormal psychopaths in a special security hospital. *British Journal of Social and Clinical Psychology*, 1968, **7**, 295–302.

McReynolds, P. (Ed.), *Advances in psychological assessment.* Vol. I. Palo Alto, Calif.: Science and Behavior Books, 1968.

McReynolds, P. (Ed.), *Advances in psychological assessment.* Vol. II. Palo Alto, Calif.: Science and Behavior Books, 1971.

Meehl, P. E. *Clinical versus statistical prediction: A theoretical analysis and a review of the evidence.* Minneapolis: University of Minnesota Press, 1954.

Meehl, P. E. Wanted—A good cookbook. *American Psychologist*, 1956, **11**, 263–272.

Meehl, P. E. When shall we use our heads instead of the formula? *Journal of Counseling Psychology*, 1957, **4**, 268–273.

Meehl, P. E. The cognitive activity of the clinician. *American Psychologist*, 1960, **15**, 19–27.

Meehl, P. E. Seer over sign: The first good example. *Journal of Experimental Research in Personality*, 1965, **1**, 27–32.

Meehl, P. E., & Dahlstrom, W. G. Objective configural rules for discriminating psychotic from neurotic MMPI profiles. *Journal of Consulting Psychology*, 1960, **24**, 375–387.

Meehl, P. E., & Rosen, A. Antecedent probability and the efficiency of psychometric signs, patterns or cutting scores. *Psychological Bulletin*, 1955, **52**, 194–216.

Megargee, E. I. Undercontrolled and overcontrolled personality types in extreme anti-social aggression. *Psychological Monographs*, 1966, **80**(3, Whole No. 611).

Megargee, E. I. *The California Psychological Inventory handbook.* San Francisco: Jossey-Bass, 1972.

Mehrabian, A. *Nonverbal communication.* Chicago: Aldine-Atherton, 1972.

Mischel, W. *Personality and assessment.* New York: Wiley, 1968.

Mitchell, J. V., Jr., & Pierce-Jones, J. A factor analysis of Gough's California Psychological Inventory. *Journal of Consulting Psychology*, 1960, **24**, 453–456.

Murray, H. A. *Explorations in personality.* New York: Oxford University Press, 1938.

Nelson, S. E. The development of an indirect, objective measure of social status and its relationship to certain psychiatric syndromes. Unpublished Ph.D. dissertation, University of Minnesota, 1952.

Nettler, G. Test burning in Texas. *American Psychologist*, 1959, **14**, 682–683.

Nichols, R. C., & Schnell, R. R. Factor scales for the California Psychological Inventory. *Journal of Consulting Psychology*, 1963, **27**, 228–235.

Norman, W. T. Relative importance of test item content. *Journal of Consulting Psychology*, 1963, **27**, 166–174.

Norman, W. T. Psychometric considerations for a revision of the MMPI. In J. N. Butcher (Ed.), *Objective personality assessment: Changing perspectives*. New York: Academic Press, 1972. Pp. 59–83.

Norman, W. T., & Goldberg, L. R. Raters, ratees, and randomness in personality structure. *Journal of Personality and Social Psychology*, 1966, **4**, 681–691.

O'Dell, J. W. P. T. Barnum explores the computer. *Journal of Consulting and Clinical Psychology*, 1972, **38**, 270–273.

O'Dell, J. W., & Karson, S. Some relationships between the MMPI and 16 PF. *Journal of Clinical Psychology*, 1969, **25**, 279–283.

Overall, J. E. Associations between marital history and the nature of manifest psychopathology. *Journal of Abnormal Psychology*, 1971, **78**, 213–221.

Overall, J. E., & Gorham, D. R. The brief psychiatric rating scale. *Psychological Reports*, 1962, **10**, 799–812.

Overall, J. E., & Gorham, D. R. Organicity versus old age in objective and projective test performance. *Journal of Consulting and Clinical Psychology*, 1972, **39**, 98–105.

Overall, J. E., Hunter, S., & Butcher, J. N. Factor structure of the MMPI-168 in a psychiatric population. *Journal of Consulting and Clinical Psychology*, 1973, **41**, 284–286.

Packard, V. *The naked society*. New York: McKay, 1964.

Palmer, W. H. Actuarial MMPI interpretation: A replication and extension. Unpublished Ph.D. dissertation, University of Alabama, 1970.

Passini, F. T., & Norman, W. T. A universal conception of personality structure. *Journal of Personality and Social Psychology*, 1966, **4**, 44–49.

Patterson, D. G. Character reading at sight of Mr. X according to the system of Mr. P. T. Barnum. Unpublished manuscript, University of Minnesota, 1951.

Pauker, J. D. Identification of MMPI profile types in a female, inpatient, psychiatric setting using the Marks and Seeman rules. *Journal of Consulting Psychology*, 1966, **30**, 90.

Pearson, J. S., & Swenson, W. M. *A user's guide to the Mayo Clinic automated MMPI program*. New York: Psychological Corporation, 1967.

Pearson, J. S., Swenson, W. M., & Rome, H. P. Age and sex differences related to MMPI response frequency in 25,000 medical patients. *American Journal of Psychiatry*, 1965, **121**, 988–995.

Perlman, M. Social class membership and test-taking attitude. Unpublished master's thesis, University of Chicago, 1950.

Persons, R. W., & Marks, P. A. The violent 4-3 MMPI personality type. *Journal of Consulting and Clinical Psychology*, 1971, **36**, 189–196.

Peterson, D. R. *The clinical study of social behavior.* New York: Appleton-Century-Crofts, 1968.

Pierce, R. A., & Schwartz, A. J. Personality styles of student activists. *Journal of Psychology*, 1971, **79**, 221–231.

Platman, S. R., & Plutchik, R. Eysenck Personality Inventory as a mood test with manic-depressive patients. *Psychological Reports*, 1970, **27**, 947–952.

Radcliffe, J. A. Edwards Personal Preference Schedule. In O. K. Buros (Ed.), *The sixth mental measurements yearbook.* Highland Park, N.J.: Gryphon Press, 1965. Pp. 195–200.

Rankin, R. J. Analysis of items perceived as objectionable in the MMPI. *Perceptual and Motor Skills*, 1968, **27**, 627–633.

Reitan, R. M., & Boll, T. J. Intellectual and cognitive functions in Parkinson's disease. *Journal of Consulting and Clinical Psychology*, 1971, **37**, 364–369.

Rodgers, D. A. Minnesota Multiphasic Personality Inventory. In O. K. Buros (Ed.), *The seventh mental measurements yearbook.* Vol. 1. Highland Park, N.J.: The Gryphon Press, 1972. Pp. 243–250.

Rogers, M. S., & Shure, G. H. An empirical evaluation of the effect of item overlap on factorial stability. *Journal of Psychology*, 1965, **60**, 221–233.

Rorer, L. G. The great response style myth. *Psychological Bulletin*, 1965, **63**, 129–156.

Rotter, J. B. Generalized expectancies for internal *versus* external control of reinforcement. *Psychological Monographs*, 1966, **80**(1, Whole No. 609).

Sandler, I. N. Characteristics of women working as child aides in a school based preventive mental health program. *Journal of Consulting and Clinical Psychology*, 1972, **39**, 56–61.

Sawyer, J. Measurement *and* prediction, clinical *and* statistical. *Psychological Bulletin*, 1966, **66**, 178–200.

Sciortino, R. Allport-Vernon-Lindzey Study of Values: I. Factor structure for a combined sample of male and female college students. *Psychological Reports*, 1970, **27**, 955–958.

Sewell, A., & Heisler, J. Personality correlates of proximity preferences. *Journal of Psychology*, 1973, **85**, 151–155.

Shostrom, E. L. *Manual for the Personal Orientation Inventory.* San Diego: Educational and Industrial Testing Service, 1966.

Shultz, T. D., Gibeau, P. J., & Barry, S. M. Utility of MMPI "cookbooks." *Journal of Clinical Psychology*, 1968, **24**, 430–433.

Simmons, D. D. Invasion of privacy and judged benefit of personality-test inquiry. *Journal of General Psychology*, 1968, **79**, 177–181.

Simpson, R. H. The specific meanings of certain terms indicating different degrees of frequency. *Quarterly Journal of Speech*, 1944, **30**, 328–330.

Sines, J. O. Actuarial methods in personality assessment. In B. A. Maher (Ed.), *Progress in experimental personality research*. New York: Academic Press, 1966. Pp. 133–193.

Sines, J. O. Actuarial versus clinical prediction in psychopathology. *British Journal of Psychiatry*, 1970, **116**, 129–144.

Snyder, C. R. Acceptance of personality interpretations as a function of assessment procedures. *Journal of Consulting and Clinical Psychology*, 1974, **42**, 150.

Snyder, C. R., & Larson, G. R. A further look at student acceptance of general personality interpretations. *Journal of Consulting and Clinical Psychology*, 1972, **38**, 384–388.

Spielberger, C. D. Theory and research on anxiety. In C. D. Spielberger (Ed.), *Anxiety and behavior*. New York: Academic Press, 1966. Pp. 3–20.

Spielberger, C. D. Anxiety as an emotional state. In C. D. Spielberger (Ed.), *Anxiety: Current trends in theory and research*. New York: Academic Press, 1972. Pp. 23–49.

Spielberger, C. D., Auerbach, S. M., Wadsworth, A. P., Dunn, T. M., & Taulbee, E. S. Emotional reactions to surgery. *Journal of Consulting and Clinical Psychology*, 1973, **40**, 33–38.

Spitzer, R. L., & Endicott, J. DIAGNO II: Further developments in a computer program for psychiatric diagnosis. *American Journal of Psychiatry*, 1969, **125**, 12–21.

Spranger, E. *Types of men*. (Trans. by P. J. W. Pigors). Halle: Niemeyer, 1928.

Stagner, R. The gullibility of personnel managers. *Personnel Psychology*, 1958, **11**, 347–352.

Strauss, M. E., Gynther, M. D., & Wallhermfechtel, J. Differential misdiagnosis of blacks and whites by the MMPI. *Journal of Personality Assessment*, 1974, **38**, 55–60.

Stricker, L. J. Edwards Personal Preference Schedule. In O. K. Buros (Ed.), *The sixth mental measurements yearbook*. Highland Park, N.J.: Gryphon Press, 1965. Pp. 200–207.

Stricker, L. J. Personality Research Form: Factor structure and response style involvement. *Journal of Consulting and Clinical Psychology*, 1974, **42**, 529–537.

Strong, E. K., Jr. A vocational interest test. *Educational Record*, 1927, **8**, 107–121.

Sundberg, N. D. The acceptability of "fake" versus "bona fide" personality test interpretations. *Journal of Abnormal and Social Psychology*, 1955, **50**, 145–147.

Taft, R. The ability to judge people. *Psychological Bulletin*, 1955, **52**, 1–23.

Tallent, N. On individualizing the psychiatrist's clinical interpretation. *Journal of Clinical Psychology*, 1958, **14**, 242–244.

Thorndike, R. L. California Psychological Inventory. In O. K. Buros (Ed.), *The fifth mental measurements yearbook*. Highland Park, N.J.: Gryphon Press, 1959. P. 99.

Thorne, F. C. *Integrative psychology: A systematic clinical viewpoint*. Brandon, Vt.: Clinical Psychology Publishing, 1967.

Thumin, F. J. MMPI scores as related to age, education and intelligence among male job applicants. *Journal of Applied Psychology*, 1969, **53**, 404–407.

Trott, D. M., & Morf, M. E. A multimethod factor analysis of the Differential Personality Inventory, Personality Research Form, and Minnesota Multiphasic Personality Inventory. *Journal of Counseling Psychology*, 1972, **19**, 94–103.

Walker, C. E. The effect of eliminating offensive items on the reliability and validity of the MMPI. *Journal of Clinical Psychology*, 1967, **23**, 263–266.

Walsh, J. A. California Psychological Inventory. In O. K. Buros (Ed.), *The seventh mental measurements yearbook*. Vol. 1. Highland Park, N.J.: Gryphon Press, 1972. Pp. 96–97.

Webb, J. T. The relation of MMPI two-point codes to age, sex, and education level in a representative nationwide sample of psychiatric outpatients. Paper presented at Southeastern Psychological Association meetings, Louisville, Ky., April 1970.

Webb, J. T. Regional and sex differences in MMPI scale high-point frequencies of psychiatric patients. *Journal of Clinical Psychology*, 1971, **27**, 483–486.

Welsh, G. S. Factor dimensions A and R. In G. S. Welsh and W. G. Dahlstrom (Eds.), *Basic readings on the MMPI in psychology and medicine*. Minneapolis: University of Minnesota Press, 1956.

Wessler, R., & Loevinger, J. Personality Research Form. In O. K. Buros (Ed.), *The seventh mental measurements yearbook*, Vol. I. Highland Park, N.J.: Gryphon Press, 1972. Pp. 303–305.

Wiggins, J. S. Content dimensions in the MMPI. In J. N. Butcher (Ed.), *MMPI: Research developments and clinical applications*. New York: McGraw-Hill, 1969, Pp. 127–180.

Wiggins, J. S. Personality Research Form. In O. K. Buros (Ed.), *The seventh mental measurements yearbook*, Vol. I. Highland Park, N.J.: Gryphon Press, 1972. Pp. 301–303.

Wiggins, J. S. *Personality and prediction: Principles of personality assessment*. Reading, Mass.: Addison-Wesley, 1973.

Wiggins, N., & Hoffman, P. J. Three models of clinical judgment. *Journal of Abnormal Psychology*, 1968, **73**, 70–77.

Williams, H. L., & Lawrence, J. F. Comparison of the Rorschach and MMPI by means of factor analysis. *Journal of Consulting Psychology*, 1954, **18**, 193–197.

Woodworth, R. S. *Personal Data Sheet*. Chicago: Stoelting, 1920.

Worthing, P., Venkatesan, M., & Smith, S. Personality and product use revisited: An exploration with the Personality Research Form. *Journal of Applied Psychology*, 1973, **57**, 179–183.

Zuckerman, M., & Lubin, B. *Manual for the Multiple Affect Adjective Check List*. San Diego, Calif.: Educational and Industrial Testing Service, 1965.

CHAPTER 5

Behavioral Assessment

MARVIN R. GOLDFRIED[1]

The field of personality assessment is forever changing. One of the clearest barometers of its progress over the years is the ever-changing title of the journal specifically devoted to assessment. This journal was initially founded in 1936, at which time it was entitled *Rorschach Research Exchange*. In 1947, as various other projective techniques were included within the clinician's standard test battery, the expanded scope of personality assessment was reflected in a title change to *Rorschach Research Exchange and Journal of Projective Techniques*. The name was again changed in 1950 to *Journal of Projective Techniques*, indicating the relatively less dominant role played by the Rorschach in clinical assessment. The search for greater objectivity led many clinicians and researchers toward nonprojective assessment procedures, such as those described in the previous chapter, and in 1963 the title was changed to *Journal of Projective Techniques and Personality Assessment*. Over the years the disappointing research findings on the validity of projective techniques caused the projective movement to wane in popularity, and in 1971 this was reflected in the journal's present title, *Journal of Personality Assessment*. Whether a new title will be forthcoming is not immediately clear. What is clear, however, is that the field is making room for a very definite trend toward behavioral assessment.

The emerging interest in behavioral assessment has been an obvious by-product of the growing popularity of behavior therapy techniques. For reasons that become increasingly apparent throughout the remainder of this chapter, most of the traditionally available personality assessment methods are of little utility to the behaviorally oriented clinician. As a result, a different paradigm for assessment has been developed, and work is currently in progress on this new approach.

[1]Preparation of this chapter was facilitated in part by Grant MH24327 from the National Institute of Mental Health.

Exactly what is this "new" approach, and how is it different from what has traditionally been used? Which specific methods qualify as behavioral assessment procedures, and which do not? How is behavioral assessment related to behavior therapy? And where does the field of behavioral assessment have to go in the future in order to establish itself firmly within the general scope of clinical psychology? The remainder of this chapter attempts to address itself to these questions.

THE DISTINCTION BETWEEN BEHAVIORAL AND TRADITIONAL ASSESSMENT

Although there are numerous differences between the behavioral and traditional approaches to personality assessment, most of these differences are closely tied to the underlying assumptions that each approach adheres to in attempting to understand human functioning. Obviously, it is an oversimplification to categorize under one heading the wide variety of nonbehavioral personality theories in existence. Despite their diversity, however, most nonbehavioral theories share a common assumption, in that they conceive of personality as consisting of certain relatively stable and interrelated motives, characteristics, and dynamics which underlie and are responsible for a person's overt actions. In order to understand fully why an individual behaves the way he does, then, one needs to obtain a comprehensive understanding of the underlying dynamics. From this vantage point, simply to observe and tally overt behavior in various life situations is inadequate, in that the essence of personality is deeper and more inferential than what may be directly observed. Instead, the assessment frequently focuses on the structural or dynamic components assumed to make up personality structure. This may be done by means of paper-and-pencil questionnaires (see Chapter 4) or by projective tests (see Chapter 2) which presumably enhance the tendency of individuals to manifest underlying personality characteristics.

When behavior therapists and behavioral assessors talk about personality, they do so in a very different way. As Goldfried and Kent (1972) have observed, "personality may be construed as an intervening variable that is defined according to the likelihood of an individual manifesting certain behavioral tendencies in the variety of situations that comprise his day-to-day living" (p. 412). What this means is that personality is a more-or-less shorthand term for summarizing the sum total of an individual in his social environment. An individual does not have a personality, but rather the concept personality is an abstraction one may make after observing a person interacting in a comprehensive sampling of situations. Similarly, an individual cannot undergo a personality change, but only a behavior change; once behavior has changed, however, the individual's personality may be conceptualized differently.

From within a behavioral framework, it is perhaps most useful to view an individual's personality as one would any other set of abilities (see Wallace, 1966). A secretary may show varying degrees of competence, depending on his or her ability to carry out various tasks, such as typing, shorthand, answering the telephone, making appointments, and whatever else may exist within the particular "role" of secretary. A football player's ability is determined by his effectiveness in the sum total of activities in which he is required to function. And a human being's interpersonal ability can similarly be described in reference to the various skills associated with functioning in various life situations.

These different conceptions of personality associated with traditional and behavioral viewpoints have important implications for test construction. From within the more traditional framework, the nature of the situation in which the individual is functioning is of less interest in the assessment than are underlying motives, dynamics, or structural components. From within a behavioral orientation, the abilities conception of personality carries with it the implication that comprehensive and carefully sampled task requirements be reflected within one's personality measure. Thus the *content validity* of the test becomes particularly crucial, as one must obtain a representative sample of those situations in which a particular behavior of interest is likely to manifest itself. When the APA *Standards for Educational and Psychological Tests* (1974) speaks of content validity as a requirement for proficiency tests but not tests of personality, it is clearly referring to more traditional conceptions of personality.

The basic difference between traditional and behavioral assessment procedures is best reflected in a distinction originally made by Goodenough in 1949, when she drew the comparison between a "sign" and "sample" approach to the interpretation of tests. When test responses are viewed as a sample, one assumes that they parallel the way in which a person is likely to behave in a nontest situation. Thus, if a person responds aggressively on a test, one assumes that this aggression also occurs in other situations as well. When test responses are viewed as signs, an inference is made that the performance is an indirect or symbolic manifestation of some other characteristic. An example is a predominance of Vista responses on the Rorschach, in which the individual reports that his percepts are viewed as if they were seen from a distance. In interpreting such a response, one does not typically conclude that the individual is in great need of optometric care, but rather that such responses presumably indicate the person's ability for self-evaluation and insight. For the most part, traditional assessment has employed a sign as opposed to sample approach to test interpretation. In the case of behavioral assessment, only the sample approach makes sense.

Goldfried and Kent (1972) drew a direct comparison between traditional and behavioral orientations toward assessment, with specific focus on the assumptions associated with each of these approaches. This comparison is depicted graphically in Figure 1. What this figure basically

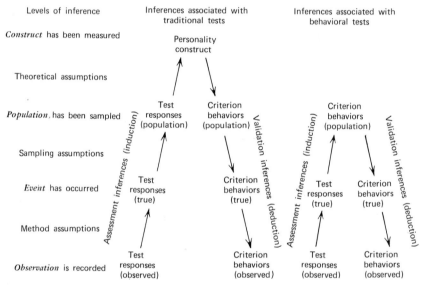

Fig. 1. Levels of inference in traditional and behavioral tests. (From Goldfried and Kent, 1972, p. 416. Copyright 1972 by the American Psychological Association. Reprinted by permission.)

attempts to illustrate are the implicit assumptions associated with drawing conclusions from one's assessment procedures, as well as the assumptions involved in validating the accuracy of this conclusion. The arrows pointing upward reflect those inferences or lines of inductive reasoning from one's testing, whereas the arrows pointing downward depict the implicit assumptions entailed when one deduces how a person is likely to behave in a nontest or real-life situation.

The levels of assumptions associated with the assessment and prediction process are arranged graphically according to the degree to which inferences depart from what is directly observable. At the most basic level, there exists what is referred to in the figure as *method* assumptions. When an individual responds to a test in a given way, one hopefully has obtained a "true" response, minimally affected by unwanted sources of error, such as unreliability of scoring or the reactivity of the measurement process itself. Similarly, in selecting certain criterion behaviors to be used in confirming the accuracy of one's deductions, it is assumed that the method associated with establishing the criterion (e.g., judges' ratings) reflects the true state of affairs, in the sense of being minimally influenced by method variance.

Following the assumption that the observation is an accurate reflection of some event, one then makes an inference as to the extent to which this event (or these events) is an accurate *sample* of some larger population of events. In making an inference from the test, there exists the implicit assumption that the test response is part of a hypothetical population of many such responses, which conceivably could be elicited if the test were increased in length. In a similar vein, in deciding which specific behavior will constitute the criterion during the validation process, one typically selects criterion behaviors from a larger pool of behaviors assumed to reflect the characteristic one is interested in assessing.

The third level depicted in the figure—which is involved only in the case of traditional tests—is associated with inferring a given *personality construct* from a population of test responses, and entails assumptions of a theoretical nature. Thus, after one assumes that the test responses elicited on the test are a good sampling of the potential of possible test responses, the task then involves interpreting what these test responses reflect about the individual's personality. Once certain personality characteristics have been induced from the testing, this personality description is then used to deduce how these characteristics or traits are likely to manifest themselves in nontest settings.

This schematic comparison of traditional and behavioral test behaviors is admittedly abstract. Hopefully, a concrete example will serve to illustrate the similarities and differences. Assume, for example, that one wishes to assess the extent to which an individual is capable of expressing his feelings openly with members of the opposite sex. In using a traditional test of personality, the method assumptions refer to the belief that the test scores—such as Form Dominance on the Rorschach or Social Introversion on the MMPI—are only minimally affected by artifacts associated with the measurement and scoring process itself. At the next level of inference, one must assume that the testing procedure has accurately sampled from the population of potential responses presumably indicative of the personality characteristics associated with emotional expressiveness. At the final level of inference, some interpretation needs to be made regarding the precise nature of the personality characteristics or construct manifested by the test responses themselves.

When inducing personality constructs associated with emotional expressiveness in heterosexual situations, one's assumptions can be based on a relatively formalized theory of personality. An interpretation of the TAT, for example, may draw on Murray's (1938) theory of personality and infer emotional expressiveness on the basis of how certain needs (e.g., nurturance and succorance) are reflected in the subject's stories. The theoretical assumptions can also be less formal and more intuitive in nature, as is the case in which one infers emotional reactivity on the Rorschach based on the extent to which form is dominant or subordinate when color responses are reported by the subject. Finally, a strictly empirical approach to interpretation may be used, as in the case of the MMPI.

The particular construct believed to be related to emotional expressiveness is likely to vary from theory to theory. Once the construct is integrated within a broader theoretical framework, variations may exist regarding exactly what deductions are made about how emotional expressiveness manifests itself in real-life situations. Given the deduction of a population of criterion behaviors, one must then sample the particular behaviors that will define the criterion (e.g., expression of positive feelings toward a loved one), and then decide on the specific method by which these criterion behaviors may be observed (e.g., direct observation, ratings of acquaintances).

This description of the way in which traditional tests are used in making predictions is, in fact, oversimplified. It is rare that a single type of test response is used to infer a personality construct. The more typical practice is to use several types of test responses as they manifest themselves within a battery of tests in order to induce a personality construct. Additional inferences surrounding the implications of a given personality construct are also likely to draw on the tester's own clinical experiences.

In attempting to assess emotional expressiveness in heterosexual situations by means of a behavioral test, the procedure consists of providing the subject with the opportunity to respond to a sample of heterosexual situations in which emotional expressiveness is called for. The precise way in which these interactions are simulated (e.g., paper and pencil, role playing, contrived situations, naturalistic observation) carries with it certain method assumptions, whereby one assumes that the person's true response is uncontaminated by the methodology. The second level of inference involves sampling assumptions, in the sense that one must be satisfied that the interactions one has measured reflect a representative sampling of the population of possible interactions of an emotionally expressive nature. In referring again to Figure 1, it becomes apparent that the assessment inferences do not continue beyond this point, and that the emotional expressiveness sampled provides a sufficient basis for making various predictions or deductions as to how the individual is likely to behave in real-life heterosexual situations. In following the behavioral-analytic model (Goldfried & D'Zurilla, 1969) as outlined later in this chapter, behavioral tests may essentially be developed "backward" on the basis of what one initially establishes as relevant criterion behaviors.

The basic point being made in comparing traditional and behavioral tests is not necessarily that behavioral assessment procedures have been found to be superior. Although indirect evidence does exist regarding the potentially greater predictive accuracy of behavioral tests (see Goldfried & Kent, 1972), no direct comparative prediction studies have been carried out as yet. What *is* being suggested is that the assumptions underlying behavioral assessment are fewer and more clearly delineated, and therefore more readily accessible to empirical confirmation. When the predictive efficiency of a test is less accurate than one might desire, one or more of the underlying assumptions associated with the prediction process is likely to be at fault. Not only do behavioral measures involve fewer assumptions, but whatever assumptions do exist can more readily be tested empirically, and any necessary modifications be made toward the goal of enhancing its predictive ability.

METHODS OF BEHAVIORAL ASSESSMENT

There is a variety of different approaches one may employ in sampling an individual's response to certain life situations. Behavioral assessment has made use of (a) direct observation in naturalistic settings, (b) the observation of responses to situations that have been contrived by the assessor, (c) responses that manifest themselves in role-playing situations, and (d) the individual's own self-report of behavior. There are also assessment procedures that have developed from other theoretical orientations, but which nevertheless may be viewed as consistent with a behavioral viewpoint. Each of these different approaches to assessment is discussed below.

Observations in Naturalistic Settings

In attempting to implement the criterion sampling orientation to behavioral assessment described in the previous section, it follows logically that behavioral assessors would have turned to the use of direct observation in naturalistic settings. Not only can such observation allow one to measure the various dimensions of the behavior of interest (e.g., frequency, strength, pervasiveness), but it can also provide a good opportunity to understand those variables that may be currently maintaining the behavior.

Naturalistic observation is hardly an invention of behavior therapists. Psychologists, anthropologists, and sociologists have made use of such procedures since long before the current behavioral orientation came into being. For example, Barker and Wright (1951) emphasized the importance of observing the "stream of behavior" in its appropriate ecological setting. They illustrated this approach to observation dramatically in their book *One Boy's Day*, in which they provide a detailed account of the activities of a 7-year-old boy whom observers literally followed around for an entire day. Any such attempt to observe the natural stream of behavior represents an admirable, if not staggering, undertaking, as is attested by the fact that Barker and Wright's observational data for a single day encompass an entire book.

Largely as a function of practical considerations, behaviorally oriented assessors have typically been more goal-oriented in making their observations than were Barker and Wright. Thus, depending on the particular purpose of the assessment, behavioral codes are customarily devised which outline the categories of behavior to be attended to during the observation procedure. Different codes have been devised by investigators to observe behavior as it occurs in various settings, such as in schools, homes, and hospitals. These observations are typically carried out at specified periods of time and are tailored to the particular subject population being assessed.

An early attempt to employ behavioral observations within the school setting is described by O'Leary and Becker (1967). The main goal of their observation was to evaluate the effect of a token reinforcement program with a class consisting of disruptive children. Teams of trained observers recorded the incidence of various behavioral categories for specific time periods, typically lasting 1½ hours each. The observer sat toward the rear of the classroom and attempted to be as unobtrusive as possible. Included among the categories within the behavioral code were such behaviors as making disruptive noises, speaking without raising one's hand, and pushing. Based on extensive research and continual revisions, the code has been refined and updated (O'Leary & O'Leary, 1972) for future applications.

An observation code has also been developed for the assessment of positively reinforcing behaviors (Bersoff & Moyer, 1973). Included among the 10 behavioral categories in this code are positive reactions (e.g., administration of concrete rewards, verbal or nonverbal praise, attention, physical contact), behaviors that presumably are neutral with respect to their reinforcement qualities (e.g., asking questions), and responses of an aversive nature (e.g., admonishment, nonverbal disapproval).

The use of behavioral observation codes involving frequency counts of various categories of behavior has provided researchers and clinicians with an invaluable approach for evaluating the effectiveness of various therapeutic intervention programs. Despite the obvious utility of such behavioral codes, one may nonetheless raise questions as to the relevance of data that they may ignore. Of particular importance is the likelihood that an individual behaving in a given way is probably reacting to some antecedent event in his environment, and that there also may be certain environmental consequences of the behavior being observed.

Toward the goal of evaluating the antecedent and/or consequent occurrences that may maintain any particular behavior, Patterson, Ray, Shaw, and Cobb (1969) developed an observational code to evaluate the interaction between an individual and significant others in his environment. The observations specifically focus on predelinquent boys, particularly as they interact with members of their families within the home setting. The code essentially attempts to take the complex stream of behavior and break it down into categories focusing on various aspects of the child's behavior (e.g., yelling, talking, teasing, hitting, crying) and the way in which other members of the family react to him (e.g., positive physical contact, ignoring, disapproval). The behavioral code is utilized by trained observers who go directly to the home and record the family interactions on a time-sampling basis.

A code for assessing the interaction among adults has been developed by Lewinsohn and Shaffer (1971), who focused specifically on the observation of depressed individuals. Here too, observers go directly into the home and time-sample the interaction among family members at mealtime. Although the distinction at times may be difficult to make, Lewinsohn and Shaffer's code attempts to classify an individual's behavior as being either an "action" or a "reaction" to another family member's behavior. Among the class of "actions" are such categories as criticism, information request, statement of personal problem, and complaint. The "reactions," which are presumed to have the potential of maintaining a given behavior, may be either "positive" or "negative." Among the positive categories are approval, laughter, and interest; the negative reactions comprise such responses as disagreement, criticism, punishment, and ignoring.

A method of coding the verbal and nonverbal interplay between husband and wife developed by Gottman (1974) has been applied both to directly observed interactions and to typed transcripts. Gottman codes three aspects of each verbal message: the content (e.g., statements of opinion, problem-solving statements, feedback statements, commands, questions); the affective component (positive, negative, or neutral); and the implications for the relationship (e.g., puts partner down, puts self down, puts partner up, puts self up). The code was developed specifically for use in an ongoing research program on marital counseling.

Within the context of observations in hospital settings, Paul and his associates (Mariotto & Paul, 1974; Paul, Tobias, & Holly, 1972) developed a time-sample behavioral checklist for use with chronic psychiatric patients. Among the behaviors recorded by trained observers are such categories as verbalized delusions or hallucinations, repetitive and stereotypic movements, grimacing or frowning without apparent stimulus, physical assault, blank staring, and various other forms of appropriate behavior. Interobserver reliability is high for this checklist, with coefficients typically in the .90's.

Although it might appear at first blush that direct naturalistic observation is the procedure par excellence for carrying out a behavioral assessment, there nonetheless are certain methodological problems associated with this approach. As described in Figure 1, the legitimacy of certain method and sampling assumptions must be confirmed in order to insure the accuracy of a behavioral assessment procedure. Although there has been a considerable amount of research focusing on method assumptions in naturalistic observations, relatively little attention has been paid to the question of the representativeness of the behaviors sampled. In the case of the time-sample behavioral checklist developed by Paul for use with psychiatric patients, this is not too much of an issue, as the observations are carried out for 2-second intervals during each of the patient's waking hours. Where the issue of sampling assumptions does come into play, however, is with codes in which the observations are made only during certain times and places. The question becomes the legitimacy of generalizing from what is observed to some larger class of behaviors or interactions. As yet, no research efforts have been directed toward this most important issue.

One of the method assumptions associated with naturalistic observations is the extent to which the observers actually interfere with or influence the phenomena they are attempting to assess. This has been labeled the *reactivity* problem within behavioral observation methods. In studying this problem, Purcell and Brady (1966) attempted to determine the extent to which being monitored by a miniature wireless radio transmitter would alter the verbal behavior of a group of adolescents. The subjects were monitored 1 hour per day for a total of 10 successive days, and they seemed to behave more naturally after the first few days. However, the indications that their behavior became more natural were based on somewhat weak criteria, such as the decrease in the number of references made to the transmitter, the amount of talking done, and impressionistic reports of the subjects themselves.

The reactivity issue was followed up by Moos (1968), who studied the effect of wearing a radio transmitter on a group of psychiatric patients observed both when they were wearing the transmitter and when the transmitter was absent. His findings indicated that the effect of being monitored by the radio transmitter was small and, when it did occur, it occurred for more disturbed patients. He also found an interaction between individual differences and the location of the setting in which the observation was taking place. One limitation to keep in mind in interpreting these data, however, is that what was really determined was not simply the effect of being observed, but rather patients' reactions to wearing a transmitter when they knew they were otherwise being observed. In other words, there was no "pure" measure of the patients' behavioral tendencies. The same interpretative limitation applies in a more recent study by Johnson and Bolstad (1974), who found that tape-recorded family interactions were no different when observers were present or absent.

The problem of reactivity is obviously a complex issue, and one that is not easy to study. The nature of the reactivity that may exist probably depends on the subject's knowledge of what aspect of his behavior is being observed. There is ample research evidence to indicate that, when a person is made to be self-conscious about certain aspects of his behavior by means of self-monitoring, there is a clear effect on the frequency of this behavior (Kazdin, 1974a). However, if a person is told that he is being observed by someone, but is not informed as to what aspects of his behavior are being noted, then the effects are likely to be a more general self-consciousness, and perhaps an attempt to second-guess what the observer is looking for.

With the exception of the ethically questionable procedure of observing individuals without their knowledge, the possibility of reactivity remains a methodological issue toward which a behavioral assessor must attend. Thus, observers are usually instructed to remain as unobtrusive as possible (e.g., "become part of the furniture"). One should also allow for a period of acclimation, to let subjects become accustomed to the presence of observers, and this initial period of observation should not be used as part of the actual baseline against which any behavior change is compared.

Another potential difficulty in satisfying method assumptions has to do with the observer himself and the extent to which any source of bias may be associated with the observation process. In this regard, unreliability among independent observers may be a function of either differential expectancies about what is supposed to be occurring and/or idiosyncratic interpretations of the behavior code.

Researchers in the area of behavioral observation have been concerned about the findings of Rosenthal (1966) and others that, under certain circumstances, there may exist an experimenter or observer effect. The question here is whether any intial hypotheses or expectations regarding what is "supposed to be seen" can influence the observation process itself. Some data by Kent, O'Leary, Diament, and Dietz (1974) suggest that, to the extent to which one uses a behaviorally anchored observational code, biases resulting from differential expectancy can be kept to a minimum. Their study used the code described in O'Leary and O'Leary (1972), and they experimentally manipulated observers' expectations regarding the type of change likely to occur. In one condition the observers were told that the therapeutic treatment procedures received by the children they were observing was expected to produce a decrease in disruptive behavior. In the second condition the observers were told that no behavior change was anticipated. In reality, both groups of observers viewed the same videotapes, which in fact showed no change in the frequency of disruptive behavior from baseline to treatment phase. The study did not find any differences in the *use of the behavioral code* as a function of differential expectations; in contrast, the overall, more *impressionistic judgments* of change in the two conditions were significantly influenced by initial expectations. The influence on global impression is particularly striking, especially since these observers had just completed carrying out concrete and detailed observations providing information contrary to their overall impressions.

A follow-up study by O'Leary, Kent, and Kanowitz (1975) found that it *was* possible to influence the observer so that a biased observation would emerge even with the use of a concrete behavioral code. The observers were informed that the children they would be rating on the videotapes were participating in a token reinforcement program in which two specific disruptive classes of behavior were being modified while two others were not being treated. As was the case in the previous study, the tapes revealed no actual behavior change whatsoever. Each time the observers coded the behavior and turned in their data, the experimenter provided them with differential feedback. If the data submitted were consistent with what was initially stated as an anticipated predicted change, the experimenter would offer positive feedback (e.g., "These tokens are really reducing the level of vocalization"). If no change from baseline was manifested in the observation, but one was actually "predicted," the experimenter would say such things as "We really ought to be picking up some decreases in the rate of playing by now." The results of this study revealed that, with observers receiving this differential feedback, they eventually presented the "expected" results.

In dealing with the expectancy issue, then, every attempt should be made to have the behavioral categories be as concrete and operationally defined as possible. Observers should not be informed of the changes expected, and, if possible, they should be kept "blind" as to experimental or therapeutic manipulations applied to the individuals being observed. Further, the observational data should not be inspected in any detail while the study is under way, so as to avoid any inadvertent reinforcement for what the observer has recorded.

A related methodological problem is the extent to which independent observers can reliably utilize a given behavioral code. Although it seems evident that potential sources of unreliability are reduced when one utilizes a coding system focusing on specific behaviors, it should also be pointed out that most behavioral codes nonetheless require a certain amount of interpretation. For example, if one is attempting to observe the incidence with which a child in a classroom is engaging in "off-task" behavior (e.g., not doing his work), some problems of interpretation may arise. Such a category represents a large behavior class, under which a wide variety of specific behaviors may fall, and the observer needs to be familiar with potential specific behaviors that would be scored in this category, and to be able to differentiate them from "on-task" behaviors. There are times, however, when a judgment about a specific behavior may be most difficult to make. What of a child who is supposed to be doing his arithmetic assignment in class but spends periods of time toying with his pencil? Should this be considered as an instance of off-task behavior? Or is this recurrent behavior something the child engages in when he pauses to concentrate on a problem? For each particular observational code, the specificity of guidelines for resolving such ambiguities can have substantial bearing on observer reliability.

A typical finding reported for each of the behavioral observational codes described above has been that interobserver reliability is in fact quite good. But what has emerged in looking at this issue more closely is that a kind of reactivity exists when observers realize that *their* behavior is being observed. This effect was dramatically demonstrated in a study by Reid (1970), who trained and examined the performance of observers in the use of a behavioral code and then had them apply the code in observations of behavior they viewed on videotape recordings. Before viewing the videotapes, the observers were led to believe that no reliability check would be made and that they would be the only ones doing the rating. The results indicated that, in comparison to a reliability coefficient of .76 when the observers thought their reliability was being evaluated, there was a sharp drop to a coefficient of .51 once the raters felt they were completely on their own.

Elaborating this phenomena are some findings by Romanczyk, Kent, Diament, and O'Leary (1973), who not only confirmed Reid's finding that interobserver reliability was higher when the observers felt their accuracy was being evaluated, but additionally found that interobserver agreement could be increased further by providing the raters with information as to exactly who was going to be checking their reliability. In other words, it was possible for the observers to modify their interpretation of the code so as to be more consistent with the criteria employed by the specific person doing the reliability check.

Another potential source of unreliability that sometimes goes unnoticed is the "drift" problem (O'Leary & Kent, 1973). A typical procedure in the application of behavioral codes involves the use of teams of observers. Following the observation periods, the teams often have the opportunity to compare their observations more closely and discuss among themselves any potential sources of unreliability. As a result of working together, various ambiguities in the use of a code are clarified. Although this at first does not seem to be an undesirable practice, the problem arises when each team begins to develop its own idiosyncratic interpretation of the code. It is not readily apparent, as the reliability checks made between pairs of observers lead one to conclude that interobserver agreement is good. However, even though teams of observers are in fact reliably applying the behavioral code, they may drift away from each other with regard to what they are actually observing. To the extent that such drift occurs, the different teams of observers are unwittingly utilizing different behavioral codes.

As in the case of the expectancy problem, unreliability among observers may be kept to a minimum by clarifying any ambiguities inherent in the behavioral code. Further, a more extensive training period can be utilized, the reliability of observers can be constantly monitored, and teams of observers can be continually rotated so as to avoid any potential drift.

One final point might be made in this discussion of observations in naturalistic settings. From a practical point of view, it may not always be feasible to have trained observers readily available. In fact, much of what has been described thus far is much more likely to be carried out within the context of a research program than in routine clinical work. The reason for this should be obvious, in that the systematic implementation of many of these observation procedures can be very costly. As a practical compromise, behavioral observations have been carried out by individuals typically present in the subject's naturalistic environment, such as friends, spouses, parents, teachers, nurses, and other significant individuals. Although the nature of their observations are not likely to be as detailed or precise as those of more highly trained observers, there is a definite advantage in obtaining information from individuals who have occasion to view the subject over relatively long periods of time, in a wide variety of situations, and with minimal likelihood of reactivity. Among the various behavior checklists that have been employed are those that utilize the observations of psychiatric nurses (Honigfeld, Gillis & Klett, 1966), classmates (Wiggins & Winder, 1961), and teachers (Ross, Lacey, & Parton, 1965).

Situation Tests

A basic limitation associated with observations in naturalistic settings is that one typically has little control over the situation to which the subject or client must respond. Although every attempt is made to standardize the setting in which the observation is to take place—such as carrying out home observations during dinner time—little can be done to control exactly what goes on during this time and place. Thus, depending on what may be said or done to the person being observed, his behavior can vary greatly. As a way of circumventing these shortcomings, behavioral assessors have made use of various situation tests.

Although situation tests have been used for assessment purposes in the past (e.g., OSS Assessment Staff, 1948), their use by behavioral assessors has focused specifically on confronting the subject with situations likely to elicit the type of behavior toward which the assessment is specifically directed. Not only is the individual's behavior objectively observed in such situations but, whenever relevant, subjective and physiological measures of anxiety are employed as well.

One frequently-employed situation test was dervised by Paul (1966) in conjunction with an outcome study on the effectiveness of systematic desensitization in treating speech anxiety. The situation test, which was used as a measure of improvement, required subjects to present a

4-minute speech before a live audience. Immediately before giving the talk, they were administered self-report and physiological measures of anxiety. During the speech itself, trained observers in the audience recorded various overt signs of axiety, coding such behaviors as extraneous hand movements, hand tremors, pacing, and absence of eye contact. This type of situation test has proved useful in a variety of other clinical outcome studies (e.g., Goldfried & Trier, 1974; Meichenbaum, Gilmore, & Fedoravicius, 1971).

Situation tests have also been employed for the assessment of interpersonal anxiety (Borkovec, Fleischmann, & Caputo, 1973; Borkovec, Stone, O'Brien, & Kaloupek, 1974; Kanter, 1975). In these assessments the subject is required to maintain a brief conversation with one or two trained confederates of the experimenter, the interaction is videotaped, and the subject's performance is evaluated in terms of behavioral, subjective report, and physiological indices of anxiety. Research on this procedure has demonstrated that the interaction situation is capable of eliciting emotional arousal in individuals for whom interpersonal anxiety is a problem.

The interpersonal skills of chronic psychiatric patients has been assessed by means of the Minimal Social Behavior Scale, a procedure originally developed by Farina, Arenberg, and Guskin (1957). The scale is applied within a stardardized interview situation requiring the interviewer to do various things (e.g., drop a pencil on the floor) or ask various questions (e.g., "How are you today?"). The scale comprises 32 different items, each of which is scored as eliciting either an appropriate or an inappropriate response. The scoring criteria are clearly spelled out, and the interrater reliability is high. Although one may legitimately raise the question whether or not the behavior observed within the context of the particular interview setting is a representative sample of the patient's behavior in all situations, the scale has nonetheless been shown to be sensitive to behavior change following drug treatment and to be able to discriminate among patients at varying levels of functioning (Farina et al., 1957; Ulmer & Timmons, 1966).

Numerous attempts have been made to assess assertive behavior by means of controlled situation tests (Kazdin, 1974b; McFall & Lillesand, 1971; McFall & Marston, 1970; McFall & Twentyman, 1973). Subjects were called on the telephone, and some unreasonable request was made of them. This request, which varied from study to study, entailed either purchasing a subscription to several magazines or lending one's lecture notes immediately prior to a final examination. The subject's response was unobtrusively recorded and later evaluated by judges for its assertiveness. In most of these studies, however, the assessment procedure failed to discriminate between individuals who were otherwise found to have changed as a function of assertion training.

Although it is certainly possible that the inability to obtain positive results could have resulted from the failure to sample adequately from situations in which the subject actually achieved behavior change, positive results found in one instance by McFall and Twentyman (1973) suggest that the methodology may have been at fault. Instead of making a single unreasonable request during the telephone conversation, they presented the subject with a series of seven increasingly unreasonable requests. The telephone calls were made less than a week before a scheduled final examination, and began by simply asking the subject to spend a few minutes discussing the lecture material. The subject was then confronted with a series of more and more outlandish requests, which culminated in asking him to lend out his lecture notes for two full days prior to the examination. By extending the nature of the interaction in this manner, the assessment procedure was found to be more sensitive in detecting changes resulting from assertion training.

Situation tests have also been employed to observe the way in which parents interact with their children. This is frequently done behind a one-way mirror, with the situation constructed in such a way as to sample the type of instances in which the child's problematic behaviors typically occur. For example, if the child's primary problem consists of having difficulty in working independently, one might set up a section of the room where he is asked to carry out various homework problems while his mother is involved in some other task in another section of the room. The behavior of both parent and child can then be observed, providing data useful toward a functional analysis of the child's difficulties.

This observation procedure is nicely illustrated in a study by Wahler, Winkel, Peterson, and Morrison (1965), in which mother and child were observed in a playroom located behind a one-way mirror. The child's primary difficulty was that he was overly demanding, as manifested by such statements as "You go over there, and I'll stay here," "Now we'll play this," and "No, that's wrong! Do it this way!" Following a baseline period, the mother was told to reinforce cooperative statements positively, and to ignore any demanding statements. Depending on the child's actual behavior, the observer would signal the mother by means of signal lights present in the playroom. As a result of such differential reinforcement, dramatic decreases were observed in the child's demanding behavior. Not only does this approach demonstrate the way in which a situation test may be contrived so as to depict a typical parent-child interaction, but it also illustrates the very close interplay between behavioral assessment and behavior therapy.

One additional example of a situation test should be discussed, not only because it represents one of the more frequently used behavioral assessment procedures but also because it may serve to illustrate some of the potential methdological problems inherent in situation tests. The assessment procedure is the Behavioral Avoidance Test (BAT), which is used as a means of evaluating the strength of fears and phobias. Although the exact procedures have varied somewhat from study to study (see Bernstein & Nietzel, 1973), the test basically requires that the individual enter a room in which the feared object is present (e.g., a snake in a cage), walk closer to the object, look at it, touch it, and if possible hold it. In addition to evaluating the closeness with which the subject is willing to approach the object, subjective, physiological, and overt behavioral indices of anxiety may be assessed as well. In addition to various small-animal phobias (e.g., snakes, rats, spiders, dogs), more clinically relevant fears have also been assessed by means of the BAT, such as enclosed places and heights.

For several years, behavioral assessors utilizing the BAT in their research have assumed that the measure provided them with a completely accurate assessment of an individual's phobia. More recent tests of the method assumptions underlying this procedure, however, have revealed that this may not always be the case. When an individual enters an assessment session, whether for research or clinical purposes, there are certain socially defined characteristics of the situation which can influence the nature of his or her response. An illustration of such so-called "demand characteristics" of situations was first demonstrated by Orne (1962), who showed that the very fact of a subject's participating in an experiment was reactive, causing him to behave in ways that were perhaps atypical for him. In one experiment, for example, Orne had a group of subjects enter a room, and gave them the tedious task of adding up columns of figures on a sheet of paper, after which they were instructed to tear the paper into small pieces, throw them in the air, and begin with a new list of figures. Subjects continued to persist at this task for long periods of time, simply because it was the thing to do in this situation.

In the case of the BAT, research evidence is accumulating to the effect that, here too, a subjects' perception of the demand characteristics of the assessment can greatly influence the extent to which they will approach the feared object or stay in the phobic situation. A study by Miller and Bernstein (1972), for example, divided a group of claustrophobic subjects into two experimental conditions, after which they were individually put in a small, dark chamber. Under a low-demand condition subjects were told that they could leave the room at any point by simply signaling, whereas under a high-demand condition they were encouraged to stay in the room regardless of how anxious they might be. Following this experimental procedure, the conditions were reversed, so that subjects who were initially in a low-demand group were now in a high-demand group, and vice versa. The findings clearly demonstrated the very powerful effect the demand characteristic instructions had on the subjects' behavior, in that subjects under low-demand instructions behaved more phobically than those under the high-demand condition. This was true when a comparison was made between groups of subjects and also when the instructions were changed for each subject individually. A second finding of some interest was that the experimental instructions, although they had a clear effect on the subjects' behavior, had no impact on their anxiety reactions as measured by either subjective report or physiological measures.

Further investigation of the effect of demand characteristics in using the BAT to assess small-animal phobias has similarly revealed that changing the subjects' perception of the task requirements can significantly influence their willingness to approach caged rats (Smith, Diener, & Beaman, 1974) and snakes (Bernstein & Neitzel, 1973). The Smith et al. study additionally confirmed the finding noted by Miller and Bernstein (1972) that, although the demand characteristics of the situation can significantly alter approach behavior, they have relatively little impact on subjective and physiological indices of anxiety.

In evaluating the BAT in light of the research findings on demand characteristics, as well as with the hindsight that the early users of this assessment procedure obviously did not have, it is not at all surprising to expect subjects to have their approach behavior influenced by factors unrelated to their actual phobia. All of us are aware of instances in which otherwise fearful individuals have been able to do things "on a dare," on in which people have displayed unusual acts of courage despite the high level of anxiety they might have been experiencing at the time.

The nature of the demand characteristics one chooses to convey in administering the BAT should probably vary as a function of the experimenter's or clinician's purpose for the assessment. If one wishes to screen out all but the most phobic of individuals, then the demand characteristics for approaching the feared objects should be set as high as possible. If, however, one wishes to predict how the individual is likely to respond in the more naturalistic context—such as when one is out in the woods and notices a snake climbing down a tree—then the BAT should be contrived so as to parallel more accurately the real-life situation. The exact way in which this parallel may be implemented and validated constitutes a challenge to the ingenuity of behavioral assessors.

One of the problems associated with the assessment of phobic behavior is that it is comprised of an operant as well as a respondent, the implication of which is that it can at times be influenced by external contingencies. The fact that demand characteristics are not necessarily an issue in all situation tests, however, is clearly illustrated in a study by Borkovec, Stone, O'Brien, and Kaloupek (1974). Borkovec et al. found that instructions to behave "in a relaxed, nonanxious manner" had no influence on subjects' performances in a situation test of heterosexual anxiety. In comparison with the assessment of phobic behavior, this situation test focused solely on anxiety, as measured by self-report, behavior signs, and physiological indices. In all likelihood, the potential influence of demand characteristics on situation tests probably depends on the extent to which the behavior being measured is under the subject's voluntary control.

In concluding this discussion of situation tests, there is a possible methodological issue inherent in all of them which has yet to be investigated, namely, the *difficulty level* of the task presented to the subject. Take, for example, the use of a situation test for assessing public-speaking anxiety. Although practical limitations obviously limit what can actually be implemented, one can easily think of a wide variety of situations in which to place the speech-anxious individual. Audiences may vary in their size and composition, the length of the speech can be short or long, the preparation period can be extensive or minimal, the topic can be familiar or strange, and numerous other variations may be introduced to vary the aversiveness of the situation.

What most users of situation tests have not addressed themselves to is just how difficult the task should be for the subject. To take the extremes, it is obvious that speaking to two individuals for a brief period of time about a topic with which one is familiar is likely to elicit less anxiety than speaking at length to a group of several hundred about an unfamiliar topic. In using a situation test to assess change in clinical outcome studies, there probably exists some interaction between the effectiveness of one's treatment procedure and the difficulty level reflected in the test situation. More powerful and extensive therapeutic interventions are likely to have more of an impact on higher levels of anxiety, whereas briefer and less effective therapies will probably reflect changes at lower levels only. Thus, depending on how one constructs the situation test in such research, the experimental findings are likely to vary. Perhaps this is why the only situation test of assertive behavior that has proved to discriminate among treatment procedures is the one used by McFall and Twentyman (1973), in which the telephone conversation was comprised of a series of gradually increasing unreasonable requests. What may be called for in the use of the situation tests in the future, then, might be to incorporate a series of increasingly more difficult tasks which are presented to the subject, thereby providing a potentially more sensitive measure of behavior change.

Role Playing

Although there are similarities between certain situation tests as described above and a role-playing approach to assessment, the primary distinction between the two is that the situation test focuses on placing the subject in the real-life situation, whereas role playing emphasizes that the subject react "as if" the event were occurring to him in real life. Although the line between the two at times may be a fine one, it is probably wise to maintain this distinction until it has been demonstrated empirically that the differences between the two procedures are nonfunctional.

The use of role playing for assessment purposes was described several years ago in a report by Rotter and Wickens (1948), whose stated rationale for the procedure is quite consistent with a behavioral orientation to assessment. They suggested that sampling behavioral interactions has considerable potential for providing the assessor with useful information, primarily because of the extent to which it parallels criterion behavior. Rotter and Wickens were interested mainly in demonstrating the feasibility of conducting such an assessment, and they consequently report no validity data for their procedure. Subjects in their study were required to respond to various simulated situations, and their behavior in these instances was rated by judges according to the degree to which "social aggressiveness" was reflected. Their report is important in that it offers an early statement of the potential utility of this procedure.

Another early use of role playing as an assessment device is reported in a study by Stanton and Litwak (1955), who provided validity data of a most encouraging sort. Using foster parents and college students as their subject populations, they attempted to assess "interpersonal competence." Subjects were presented with three situations—meeting a troubled friend, handling an interfering parent, and criticizing an old employee—and their responses were rated for competence with the aid of a behavior checklist. Highly significant correlations were found between ratings of the subjects' behavior during role-playing situations and evaluations of them obtained from individuals who knew them well. For the foster parents a correlation of .82 was found with social workers' ratings; in the case of students, friends' ratings correlated .93 with the scores obtained from the role-playing assessment. Not unexpected, but nonetheless providing discriminant validity, was the finding that criterion ratings provided by individuals who did not know the subjects well did not correlate nearly as well with the role-playing assessment. Moreover, when the role playing was compared with an assessment based on 12 hours of intensive interviews, the role playing was found to fare considerably better in matching the ratings of well-acquainted individuals.

In recent years, role playing has gained in popularity among behavioral assessors as a means of evaluating the effectiveness of various therapeutic procedures. One of the initial uses of role playing in this context is described by Rehm and Marston (1958), who developed a procedure for assessing heterosexual anxiety in males. In an attempt to standardize and make the procedure otherwise more practically feasible, a series of 10 social situations was presented orally on audiotape. Each situation begins with a description of the context, after which there is a comment by a female requiring some response on the part of the subject.

For example, one situation starts with the narrator describing a scene in the college cafeteria in which the subject is walking out when he suddenly is approached by a female. At this point in the tape, a female voice states, "I think you left this book." For each of these situations the subject is asked to imagine that it is actually occurring to him at the moment and to respond as he would in real life. The response is recorded on a separate tape recorder and evaluated later for such characteristics as anxiety, adequacy of response, length of response, and delay before responding. In comparison to subjects not volunteering for a therapy program focusing on heterosexual anxiety, role-playing scores for those participating in the clinical research were found by Rehm and Marston to be significantly different. Performance on the role-playing assessment was furthermore found to change as a function of the therapeutic intervention.

A role-playing assessment procedure similar to that used by Rehm and Marston was investigated by Arkowitz, Lichtenstein, McGovern, and Hines (1975), who compared the performance of high versus low socially competent males as determined independently on the basis of their frequency of dating and their subjective comfort, social skills, and general satisfaction in their heterosexual behaviors. Two role-playing situations were studied, one conducted *in vivo* with a female confederate and the other involving a role-played telephone conversation. In the face-to-face situation subjects were asked to imagine that they had just met this female and were attempting to get to know her better. In the telephone conversation the subject was instructed to ask the female confederate for a date. The primary finding was that the low socially competent individuals displayed a lower rate of verbal activity than the high socially competent subjects in each of these role-played situations.

A face-to-face role-played interaction for assessing social skills in males has also been developed by Mac Donald and her colleagues (Mac Donald, Lindquist, Kramer, Mc Grath, & Rhyne, 1975; Rhyne, Mac Donald, Mc Grath, Lindquist, & Kramer, 1973). The role-playing procedure involves three separate 4-minute encounters with female confederates trained to follow a predetermined script. The subject's interpersonal skills are evaluated on the basis of two separate criteria, one involving the rated social adequacy of their responses and the other concerned with observable behavioral signs of anxiety. The interrater agreement for both the social skills and anxiety indicators was found to be high, and the validity of the assessment procedure was confirmed by two different lines of evidence. First, the skill score was found to distinguish between males who did and did not qualify for a treatment program designed to focus on facilitating social adequacy. Second, expected changes were found to occur on the measure as a function of therapeutic intervention.

In a comprehensive program designed to assess and facilitate interpersonal skills among psychiatric inpatients, Goldsmith (1973) employed the behavioral-analytic model (Goldfried & D'Zurilla, 1969) in developing a role-playing assessment procedure. Twenty-five separate situations were sampled from various aspects of the patients' typical day-to-day interactions, each of which was then presented to them on audiotape with instructions to respond as they would in a real-life situation. The subjects' responses to each situation were rated on the basis of certain predetermined and reliably applied criteria for interpersonal effectiveness. Goldsmith found that, as a result of a behavior training program designed to facilitate interpersonal skills, scores of these patients on the role-playing assessment procedures showed significant improvement. No change was found for control subjects who had been assigned to attention-placebo or no-contact conditions.

Another related problem area that has been assessed by means of role-playing procedures has involved assertive behavior. The initial work in this area was reported by Mc Fall and Marston (1970), who sampled several situations representative of instances in which college students might be required to assert themselves. These included such situations as being interrupted by a friend while attempting to study, having one's laundry lost by the cleaners, and being asked to work by an employer at a time that would be inconvenient. Following the methodology originally devised by Rehm and Marston (1968), the situations were presented to subjects on audiotapes, and their responses were recorded on a second tape recorder. In this particular study the subjects responses were not scored; instead, independent judges carried out a paired comparison between subjects' behavior before and after assertion training. These judges' ratings, which were completely blind as to which interaction was obtained before and which after therapy, revealed significant improvement in role-played assertive behavior.

A later report by McFall and Lillesand (1971) indicated that, when assertiveness was rated on the basis of a 5-point scale, interrater reliability was in the .90's. McFall and Lillesand also report some experimentation with a modification of the role-played assessment procedure. Rather than presenting the situation and asking the subject to give his typical response, the interaction was extended so as to parallel more closely what might occur in a real-life situation. Specifically, if the subject was successful in refusing the unreasonable request, the taped confederate would press him further for a total of five "pushes." This variation in the assessment procedure also revealed changes reflecting the effects of assertion training.

A series of studies on the role-playing assessment of assertive behavior within a population of psychiatric patients has also been carried out by Eisler and his associates (Eisler, Hersen, & Agras, 1973a; Eisler, Hersen, & Agras, 1973b; Eisler, Hersen & Miller, 1973; Eisler, Miller, & Hersen, 1973; Hersen, Eisler, Miller, Johnson, & Pinkston, 1973). The role-playing assessment procedure consisted of 14 situations in which a male psychiatric patient was required to interact with a female confederate in such standard impositions as having someone cut ahead in line, having one's reserved seat taken at a ball game, having a steak delivered overcooked at a restaurant, and having a service station carry out extensive repairs on one's car without previous approval. Unlike most role-playing measures of assertive training, the Eisler interaction is carried out *in vivo,* and the ratings of assertiveness are based on videotape recordings of the interaction. The reliability of ratings is generally high for both an overall rating of assertiveness and ratings of several behavioral components. Among those components that have been found to improve as a result of assertion training are duration of reply, affective quality of response, loudness of response, and content of assertive reply (Eisler, Hersen, & Miller, 1973).

In what probably constitutes the most well-conceived and psychometrically sophisticated of attempts to develop a behavioral assessment procedure, MacDonald (1974) devised a measure of assertive behavior for college women. In comparison to the work on the assessment of assertive behavior conducted by most previous investigators, Mac-Donald's approach in sampling situations and likely responses to them was empirically based and far more comprehensive. Using the general behavioral-analytic guidelines outlined by Goldfried and D'Zurilla (1969), she began with a pool of over 800 items derived from the self-observations of college women and pared them down to 52 frequently occurring and unambiguous situations. For each situation the range of potential responses was sampled (consisting of 50 to 56 responses per situation) and then evaluated with regard to their assertiveness. The format of the measure involves a taped presentation of each of the 52 situations, with the subject's response to each item scored for latency, duration, and assertiveness of content. The validity data reported by MacDonald thus far are encouraging.

Although much of the recent work on the use of role playing as an assessment procedure is promising, relatively little attention has been paid to any potential methodological problems that may serve to attenuate its effectiveness, such as the failure to satisfy both method and sampling assumptions (see Figure 1). Among the method assumptions that need to be satisfied is the extent to which the behavior of the confederate can be appropriately standardized. This can be done by providing the confederate with detailed guidelines and adequate training, or more simply by presenting a tape-recorded stimulus situation.

Although most users of role-playing assessment report good interrater reliability, virtually no attempt has been made to control the possibility of a "halo effect" occurring. That a halo effect may be an issue is reflected in the study by Rotter and Wickens (1948). They found that, when a given subject's role-played responses to two separate situations were rated by the same judges, the average interrater reliability of the subject's behavior in these two situations was .78. However, when different judges were used to rate the subjects' behavior in the two separate situations, the average correlations were only .55. The erroneously imposed cross-situational consistency may very well have accounted for the spuriously higher correlation obtained originally. As discussed in conjunction with behavioral observation in naturalistic settings, there are numerous potential sources of bias when one sets out to observe and code human behavior. Thus the issues of observer expectancies, continual monitoring of reliability, and the possibility of drift among pairs of observers need to be attended to in the coding of role-playing interactions as well.

The question of demand characteristics has yet to be a topic of empirical investigation in the use of role-playing assessment. Are sub-jects truly "in role" during the assessment procedure, or are they somehow responding to some unique aspects of the demand characteris-tics within the assessment setting? Is it easier or more difficult for subjects to behave as they typically would when the stimulus situation is presented on audiotape as compared to an *in vivo* interaction? Are there any individual differences associated with subjects' abilities to immerse themselves naturally in the role-playing interaction? These are but some of the questions related to method assumptions that need to be answered.

With regard to the question of sampling assumptions, most developers of role-playing assessment procedures have used only a few situations, selected more or less on an a prori basis. The notable exceptions have been the procedures outlined by Mac Donald (1974) and Goldsmith (1973), who conducted an empirically based situational analysis. Unless one assumes cross-situational consistency with whatever variable one is assessing (e.g., social skills, assertiveness), some form of empirical sampling is essential if one wishes to generalize the finding of the assessment.

Self-Report

In using self-report procedures, behavioral assessors have focused on the report of specific behavioral interactions, on subjective reports of emotional response, and on perceptions of environmental settings. Each of these areas of assessment is described below.

Self-Report of Overt Behavior. The behavioral characteristic that has been the focus of most self-report measures of overt behavior is assert-iveness. For example, Wolpe and Lazarus (1966) describe a series of 30 questions that they recommend be asked of clients in assessing the extent to which they may be inhibited in expressing their opinion in interpersonal situations. More recent questionnaires, based in part on the questions described by Wolpe and Lazarus, have been reported by Rathus (1973) and Galassi, DeLo, Galassi, and Bastien (1974). Although the formats of these two more recent questionnaires are slightly different—Rathus presents 30 true-false questions rated on a 6-point scale, whereas Galassi et al. use 50 items and a 5-point scale—the assessment inventories are more similar than they are different. In fact, some of the items are virtually identical. Both questionnaires are simi-larly limited in the sense that they fail to satisfy the sampling assump-tions essential in the development of behavioral assessment procedures.

For the most part, the items in these inventories were taken from previous questionnaires or were determined on an a priori basis. In using these inventories, the general trait of assertiveness is assumed, and no subscales reflecting different aspects of one's interactions (e.g., with friends, strangers, authority figures) are available.

A more sophisticated approach to the development of a measure of assertiveness may be seen in the work of Mc Fall and Lillesand (1971), whose focus was specifically on the ability of college students to refuse unreasonable requests. Their Conflict Resolution Inventory consists of 35 items, each of each is specific to a particular situation in which some unreasonable request might be made of the subject. For example, one such item is: "You are in the thick of studying for exams when a person whom you know only slightly comes into your room and says, 'I'm tired of studying. Mind if I come in and take a break for awhile?' " For each item, subjects are to indicate the likelihood that they would refuse each of the requests and how comfortable they would feel about either refusing or giving in. Unlike the developers of the other assertiveness questionnaires described above, Mc Fall and Lilles and derived their items empirically on the basis of extensive pilot work, in which the sample of college students used in generating the initial item pool was similar to the subject population toward whom the assessment measure was later to be applied. The Conflict Resolution Inventory has been found to be useful as a dependent variable in clinical outcome studies (Mc Fall & Lillesand, 1971; Mc Fall & Twentyman, 1973), in which change was found to occur as a function of assertion training.

Self-Report of Emotion. Although the assessment of overt behavior—whether via self-reports of behavior, naturalistic observation, situation tests, or role playing—holds considerable promise, there is more to human functioning than a person's overt behavior can reveal. In fact, several reports indicate that even when demand characteristics influence an individual's performance on a behavioral avoidance test, subjective reports of anxiety remain unaffected (Miller & Bernstein, 1972; Smith et al., 1974). Furthermore, there are instances, as in an outcome study on agrophobia reported by Jacks (1972), in which subjective reports of anxiety may be more sensitive to differential change than is approach behavior.

A measure frequently used by behavioral assessors in the self-report of anxiety is the Fear Survey Schedule (Geer, 1965). The schedule consists of a series of 51 potentially anxiety-arousing situations and objects (e.g., snakes, being alone, looking foolish), which subjects are asked to rate for the degree of fear they typically elicit in them. The

Schedule is at best a gross screening device and should probably be viewed as nothing more than that. Although some researchers have attempted to carry out extensive factor analyses of the schedule to determine the potential dimensions of fear, such research activities are of dubious value, especially as no attempt had originally been made to sample representatively the full range of fears and phobias typically present in most individual's lives.

Although several attempts have been made to use the Fear Survey Schedule to predict subjects' reactions to a behavioral avoidance task, the data on its predictive efficiency have been mixed. In viewing these conflicting findings, it is important to keep in mind that these two measures of fear are of a very different form, in the sense that one is primarily verbal and the other more behaviorally observable. Moreover, these two measures appear to be focusing on different aspects of anxiety. In the case of the Fear Survey Schedule, subjects are asked to state how afraid they would feel when in the presence of certain situations or objects. When subjects are placed in the behavioral avoidance task, the primary measure consists of the extent to which they will approach the fearful object. As noted earlier, there are often situations in which the demand characteristics or task requirements are such that individuals, despite their feelings of fear and trepidation, will approach a fearful object or remain in anxiety-producing circumstances.

In the context of some of his research on the way in which demand characteristics affect performance on the behavioral avoidance test, Bernstein (1973) demonstrated that the Fear Survey Schedule could differentially predict approach behavior, depending on the situational context in which the behavioral avoidance test was carried out. When the test was carried out in a clinic context, subjects' initial reports on the Fear Survey Schedule were predictive of their actions. However, the verbal reports of subjects who participated in the avoidance test conducted in a laboratory setting had no relationship to their likelihood of approaching a feared object.

Whatever assets the Fear Survey Schedule may have as a relatively quick and easily administered screening device, there are nonetheless certain limitations which severely restrict its utility. Perhaps the most telling of these is the fact that subjects are required to indicate their degree of fear about situations or objects that are described in only general and very vague terms (e. g., being criticized). The specific nature of the situation (e. g., who is doing the criticizing, what the criticism is about) is left unspecified. Furthermore, the nature of the person's anxiety response (e. g., sweaty palms, increased heart rate, desire to run away) is not assessed by the questionnaire.

A commonly used self-report measure of anxiety that takes into account the nature of the situation, as well as each of the possible components of the anxiety response, is described by Endler, Hunt, and Rosenstein (1962). Their assessment procedure, called the S-R Inventory of Anxiousness, consists of a series of potentially anxiety-arousing situations which are briefly described in writing, after which there are a series of rating scales reflecting varying ways in which a person might become anxious. For example, one such situation is, "You are about to take an important final examination," for which the subject is asked to indicate the extent to which his "heart beats faster," he "gets an uneasy feeling," his "emotions disrupt action," and several other reactions indicative of anxiety.

The S-R Inventory is important for its utility as a dependent measure and also as a vehicle for studying the question of cross-situational behavioral consistency. In keeping with the behavioral orientation to assessment, which emphasizes the importance of the situation to which an individual reacts, research with the S-R Inventory is useful in learning more about the extent to which individual differences and consistencies may manifest themselves in various types of situations.

Both the Fear Survey Schedule and the S-R Inventory ask subjects to indicate their typical reaction. In a sense these self-reports are hypothetical, since they are based on the subjects' *recollections* of how they reacted in the past to certain types of situations. Consistent with the overall philosophy that behavioral assessment should focus directly on criterion behavior, it seems only reasonable that behavioral assessors have also made attempts to elicit self-reports of emotional reactivity during the time the individual is actually *in* certain situations, rather than recollecting them. Among the several available subjective measures of situational state anxiety are Spielberger, Gorsuch, and Lushene's (1970) State-Trait Anxiety Inventory and Zuckerman and Lubin's (1965) Multiple Affect Adjective Checklist. The former measures involve a series of descriptive statements, such as, "I am tense," "I am jittery," and "I feel calm," which the subject is asked to rate on a 4-point scale for its accuracy as a self-descriptive statement. In the case of the Multiple Affect Adjective Checklist, feelings of depression and hostility are assessed, as well as those of anxiety. For both of these measures appropriate changes are frequently found in response to various kinds of experimental manipulations, such as those intended to elicit or reduce stress.

In using any self-report measure, one must recognize the possibility that subjects are reporting what they assume the examiner wants to hear. In some respects such subject behavior may relate to the issue of demand characteristics discussed above in conjunction with behavioral avoidance tests. Husek and Alexander (1963) focused on this issue and devised a measure of state anxiety, called the Anxiety Differential, which is minimally susceptible to response bias. This measure is modeled after the semantic differential (Osgood, Suci, & Tannenbaum, 1957) and consists of a series of words and 7-point bipolar adjectival rating scales. Sample items include "TODAY: Straight . . . Twisted; HANDS: Wet . . . Dry; SCREW: Nice . . . Awful." The "appropriate" way of responding to each of these items is not immediately apparent and is consequently not susceptible to the influence of situational demand characteristics. However, research with the Anxiety Differential has shown it to be sensitive to both increases and decreases in emotional state brought about by various experimental and therapeutic manipulations.

In addition to focusing on various negative emotional states, behavioral assessors have also developed self-report measures to assess positive feelings. For example, Cautela and Kastenbaum (1967) developed a Reinforcement Survey Schedule which in part parallels the Fear Survey Schedule. Various objects and situations are presented in questionnaire form, and subjects are asked to indicate the extent to which they hold a personal preference for each of them. This measure suffers from numerous problems, not the least of which is the fact that the items themselves were not empirically derived from a pool of potentially reinforcing events of objects.

In contrast, the Pleasant Events Schedule constructed by MacPhillmay and Lewinsohn (1972) includes items generated from an actual situational analysis. College students were asked to specify "events, experiences, or activities which you find pleasant, rewarding, or fun," and the net result of this sampling was a series of 320 items of both a social and nonsocial type. In responding to the Pleasant Events Schedule, subjects are asked to indicate not only how often each of these various events might have occurred within the past month, but also how pleasant and enjoyable they were. If for some reason subjects have not experienced any particular event, they are simply asked to estimate how enjoyable it might have been it if had occurred. This more sophisticated approach to the assessment of potential reinforcers has been found to be useful in research in the area of depression (Lewinsohn & Graf, 1973; Lewinsohn & Libet, 1972).

Self-Report of Environment. Consistent with the behavioral assessor's interest in the nature of the social environment with which individuals must interact, there is a growing interest in what has been referred to as "social ecology" (Insel & Moos, 1974; Moos, 1973). Moos and his colleagues have been actively involved in developing questionnaires for assessing the social psychological impact made by various environments, including psychiatric wards, community-oriented psychiatric treatment programs, correctional institutions, military basic training companies, university student residences, junior and senior high school classrooms, work environments, and social, therapeutic, and decision-making groups. The questionnaires focus on the individual's perception of various aspects of his social environment and include items such as, "On this ward everyone knows who's in charge," "Members are expected to take leadership here," and "Members here follow a regular schedule every day."

In assessments of the impact made by varying environmental settings, three dimensions appear to be common across several diverse environmental contexts: the nature and intensity of interpersonal relationships (e.g., peer cohesion, spontaneity); personal development opportunities (e.g., competition, intellectuality); and the stability and responsivity of the social system to change (e. g., order and organization, innovation). In much the same way as the assessment of behavioral characteristics within an individual has relevance for behavioral change, so the various environmental assessment questionnaires have implications for the modification of social environments (Moos, 1974).

Other Assessment Procedures

Several other approaches to assessment have been employed by behaviorally oriented clinicians and researchers, as well as certain assessment procedures not typically aligned with the behavioral approach but which nonetheless are somewhat consistent with this orientation. For example, in the measurement of anxiety behavioral assessment has frequently focused on physiological reactivity, including heart rate, blood pressure, muscle tension, and galvanic skin response. Although similar physiological responses have also been found to accompany increased sexual arousal, physiological technology has approached the point where methods are available for a more direct assessment of sexual arousal (Goldfried & Sprafkin, 1974). For males the penile plethysmograph has been shown to be a sensitive measure of extent of erection. In the assessment of sexual responsivity in females, recent advances have been made with an insertion device placed directly in the vagina to measure blood flow changes accompanying sexual arousal (Geer, Morokoff, & Greenwood, 1974).

Other measures used by behavioral assessors in clinical outcome research include various paper-and-pencil questionnaires focusing on anxiety in specific classes of situations. Included among these are measures of social anxiety (Watson & Friend, 1969), public-speaking anxiety (Paul, 1966), and test anxiety (Alpert & Haber, 1960).

Although the sample-sign distinction was used earlier in this chapter as a means of differentiating between behavioral and traditional assessment procedures, it should be emphasized that there are instances in which sample approaches have been used within the context of more traditional assessment. Even in the case of the Rorschach, for example, it may be argued that the testing situation provides much the same function as a structured interview (Goldfried, Stricker, & Weiner, 1971), in that the subject's verbal and nonverbal responses to the test and the testing situation can be observed and interpreted as samples of the individual's behavior. This is clearly a legitimate interpretation, provided one's inferences regarding generalizability are made with caution.

As far as the interpretation of the subject's response to the Rorschach itself is concerned, there are even scoring systems that make explicit use of the sample approach. One such system, developed by Friedman (1953), is used to assess the developmental level of perceptual organization. In the Friedman system the subject's percepts are interpreted as a sample of perceptual-cognitive behavior and are ordered along a scale of organization and integration. If one is interested in assessing where any given subject is with regard to level of perceptual organization, then a strong case can be made for the use of the Rorschach as one of the more direct assessment procedures. Not only does this approach make sense on an a priori basis, but it also has been found to be one of the most valid uses of the Rorschach (Goldfried et al., 1971).

There are other measuring instruments available which bear great similarity to behavioral assessment procedures but which have certain inherent limitations. An excellent case in point is the Rosenzweig Picture Frustration Study (Anderson & Anderson, 1951). This test consists of a series of frustrating stimulus situations presented in cartoon form, for which the subject is asked to supply the central character's likely reaction to the frustration. Certain situations depicted in the Rosenzweig closely resemble situations employed in the role-playing and self-report measures of assertiveness described above. For example, there is one scene of two people sitting in a theater with their view obstructed by a hat worn by a woman in front of them. Although Rosenzweig's theoretical rationale for the test is clearly psychodynamic in nature, the form of his measure can readily be reinterpreted along behavioral lines. A severe limitation inherent in this measure, however, is the fact that some of the situations included are rather unique, such as instances in which a passing automobile splashes water on one's clothing, or in which a visitor drops a valuable vase in one's home. Although one may readily interpret a subject's response to these frustrating situations as a behavior sample, the atypical nature of the situations makes it most difficult to generalize from them to real-life settings.

There is still another assessment procedure that is frequently employed by traditionally oriented clinicians, but may also be used by the behaviorally oriented assessor, namely, the interview. In fact, interview procedures are among the most frequently used assessment methods employed by behavior therapists in routine clinical work. Because of its frequent application in the clinical situation, this approach to assessment is discussed in conjunction with the section that follows.

BEHAVIORAL ASSESSMENT AND BEHAVIOR THERAPY

If one interprets behavior therapy in its broadest sense as involving the application of what we know about psychology in general to problems that may manifest themselves within the clinical setting (Davison & Goldfried, 1973), it follows that the number and variety of behavior therapy procedures available to the clinician will be large and forever changing. This is clearly a double-edged sword which provides one with several potentially effective treatment methods, but also with the dilemma of which to use in any given case. With this in mind, Goldfried and Pomeranz (1968) have argued that "assessment procedures represent a *most crucial and significant* step in the effective application of behavior therapy" (p. 76).

Exactly what should the behavioral assessor look for? How does he employ the interview to obtain relevant information? And how does the information obtained become organized so as to have implications for the treatment plan? These issues are touched on below.

A Behavioral Analysis of the Problem

One of the initial tasks of the behavioral assessor in the clinical setting is to take what the client may have presented as a very general problem or set of problems and define it in concrete and operational terms. Individuals seeking professional help sometimes talk in abstractions, frequently complaining, "Things are not right," or "I don't seem to have any direction," or "The joy of life is just not there." The task for the behavioral assessor, then, is to find out more precisely what the person may be doing or not doing that is resulting in such vaguely described feeling states.

What one is confronted with in the clinical interaction may be understood by conceptualizing the client's current status as entailing numerous dependent and independent variables. In the most general sense, when a person comes in with a problem, the behavioral assessor assumes that this presenting problem represents a dependent variable. The behavioral assessor's task is to look for the independent variable or variables that may be maintaining this problem behavior, and therapeutically manipulate them to produce behavior change. Within this context the term "manipulate" is used in a non-Machiavellian sense to refer generally to whatever therapeutic procedures are employed.

Behavior therapists have frequently been faulted for dealing with symptoms and failing to acknowledge the potential operation of "underlying causes." However, the attempt to obtain a parsimonious understanding of behavior in no way implies that behavioral assessment need be superficial. For example, take the case of a man whose presenting problem is that he and his wife have frequent fights. Although there might be an initial temptation to instigate and reinforce directly cooperative or affectionate behavior between the couple, such a procedure might be clinically naive under certain circumstances. A possible reason why the man frequently argues with his wife may be that he drinks heavily and his drinking makes him aggressive. And the reason he drinks so much may be because he is very anxious. And the reason he is so anxious may be because he finds himself under continual pressure at work. And the reason he is under such pressure may be because he expects too much of himself and others. The question here becomes, "What variable should one focus on in order to decrease the fighting behavior?" A related question is where to stop in this search for underlying causes.

From within the behavioral orientation, the guideline employed is that one stops looking when it seems likely that the variable being explored is no longer operating. Take an example of an individual with unrealistic standards for perfection for himself and others. Why is he that way? In all likelihood he has modeled such standards from significant figures during his early social learning experiences. However, one cannot go back and change past interactions, but must instead work with what exists at present. Thus, in this example one would probably want to focus on the person's unrealistically high standards as they currently manifest themselves, with the assumption that the other problematic behaviors in his life are maladaptive consequences of his distorted expectations and attitudes.

In focusing on the types of variables one attends to in a behavioral assessment, the acronym SORC has frequently been employed. This indicates the focus on *S*ituational antecedents, *O*rganismic variables, *R*esponse dimensions, and *C*onsequences.

In evaluating the *situational antecedents* of behavior, the behavioral assessor differs most radically from those using a more traditional approach to assessment. For example, focus is placed on obtaining a detailed account of the specific situations likely to make an individual anxious. This information is useful not only for assessment purposes, but also for its implications for therapeutic intervention, such as in the case of systematic desensitization. In addition to identifying the situations that elicit various forms of emotional response, the situational antecedents that are assessed can also be discriminative, in that they serve as cues for the person to behave in different ways. Here the distinction being made is between respondents and operants. In the case of operants, knowledge of the specific nature of the discriminative stimuli as well as of the problematic responses can have implications for treatment. For example, with a child showing certain behavior problems, simple knowledge that he behaves appropriately in school but is a problem at home requires further clarification, with the assessment focusing on exactly what happens at home and at school that serves as cues for appropriate and inappropriate behaviors.

Among those *organismic* variables involved in a behavioral assessment are such aspects of an individual's physiological makeup as general energy or activity level, hormonal and chemical imbalance, and any psychoactive drugs present within one's system, all of which can serve as important determinants of behavior. Also included among relevant organismic variables are cognitive factors. Except when one is working with young children, mental retardates, or back-ward schizophrenics, the failure to attend to mediating cognitive processes can easily lead one to overlook what may be an essential determinant of maladaptive functioning. Based on early learning experiences, individuals develop various "cognitive sets" about the world around them, some of which may be distorted and serve to mediate various maladaptive responses and emotional reactions. Thus, if an individual walks around with the expectation that large classes of situations are potentially "dangerous," the emotional reaction that creates the problem may be a direct and appropriate reaction to what essentially is a distorted perception. In such instances the important maintaining variable may be the distortion, which should eventually be the direct target of the therapeutic intervention (Ellis, 1962; Goldfried, Decenteceo, & Weinberg, 1974; Goldfried & Goldfried, 1975).

In focusing on *response* variables, we are referring to what is often synonymous with behavioral assessment, namely, the sampling of various behaviors. The dimensions one focuses on in looking directly at behavioral tendencies include frequency, strength, duration, and latency of response. In assessing any response category, one frequently makes the distinction between respondents and operants, the former referring to some emotional reaction and the latter to some voluntary behavior. In some cases this distinction may not be clear-cut, as in the case of an individual who shows some reluctance to go out and find a job. Although he may be truly fearful of seeking employment, his inertia may also be reinforced by various fringe benefits, such as unemployment checks and the attention and sympathy of others.

The fourth class of variables involves the *consequences* of certain behaviors, which are important because of the well-established principles that so much of what we do—whether it be deviant or adaptive—is maintained by its consequences (Skinner, 1953). Even when a given course of action has a mixed payoff, in the sense of having both positive and negative consequences, the fact that the behavior continues to persist is frequently explained by the immediate positive, as opposed to long-range negative, consequences that ensue. Thus the drug user has obvious pleasurable sensations after a fix, but experiences numerous long-term consequences because of his involvement with drugs.

In observing the consequences of certain behaviors, it is apparent that there are certain settings that may inadvertently reinforce behaviors that it also labels as maladaptive. As Goffman (1961) and Rosenhan (1973) have vividly described, there are numerous instances in which psychiatric hospitals force dependence on patients and then interpret this dependence as being indicative of their disturbance. Wherever maladaptive behavior exists by virtue of conflicting incentives in the environment, the appropriate direction to take therapeutically is toward environmental and not individual modification.

In focusing on each of the SORC variables, it should be apparent that the analysis of problem behaviors in such terms has clear implications for therapeutic intervention. As has been argued by Kanfer and Saslow (1965), this is in sharp contrast to the more traditional, Kraepelinian nosological system. Alternate classification systems have been suggested by Staats (1963) and have been elaborated on by Bandura (1968) and Goldfried and Sprafkin (1974). This alternate approach to classification categorizes behavior according to the variables likely to be maintaining it. Thus the potential determinants in need of therapeutic manipulation included any possible difficulties associated with the stimulus antecedents; potentially unrealistically high standards for self-reinforcement; the absence of certain behaviors within an individual's response repertoire; the presence of behavioral tendencies that turn out to be aversive to others; and potential difficulties with reinforcers, including the inability of certain consequences to serve as reinforcers, the inappropriateness of one's incentive system, the absence of reinforcers in one's environment, and confusion in one's environmental milieu as to what behaviors in fact receive reinforcement.

Additional Variables in Need of Assessment

In addition to conducting an evaluation of those variables required for a behavioral analysis of the presenting problem, the behaviorally oriented clinician focuses on several other variables that similarly have implications for the implementation of appropriate treatment procedures.

Prior to actually initiating any therapeutic intervention program, the behavior therapist frequently focuses on the client's expectations for improvement. As suggested by Goldstein (1962), positive expectations of at least a moderate nature are required in order to ensure therapeutic success. In instances in which the client may show a certain amount of skepticism regarding the likelihood of changing, the behavior therapist would be wise to work directly on such skepticism and attempt to modify it. In order to enhance the credibility of the treatment approach, one may describe the success achieved with previous clients having similar problems. Another possible approach might involve the therapist's attempt to foster change in some readily modifiable aspect of the client's behavior. For example, one might decide to begin relaxation training with a client relatively early in the treatment, primarily because its therapeutic effects tend to be obvious and relatively easily obtainable.

The client's expectancies about the nature of the therapeutic relationship should also be assessed. Individuals vary considerably with regard to the amount of control and guidance they wish from the therapist, ranging from some who feel they must be in complete control of the change process to others who figuratively throw themselves at the therapist's feet. Depending on the client's expectancies, the behavior therapist must adapt the presentation of the treatment procedure so as to avoid appearing overly manipulative to the one type of client or doubting and incompetent to the other type.

As noted earlier in this chapter, a large measure of what is involved in behavioral assessment and behavior therapy deals with specific events. Significantly in this regard, there are individual differences among clients in their ability to focus on specific instances and concrete events. Ironically, relatively psychologically sophisticated individuals tend to talk about their problems in highly abstract terms, which means they may be less in tune with a behavioral orientation then less sophisticated people, who tend more often to relate in great detail "who said and did what to whom." To the extent that the initial assessment reveals that the client has difficulty communicating in sufficient detail to provide a clear picture of the problem, guidance and training are required to change the individual's style of communication within the therapeutic interaction.

There are other types of behavioral tendencies that may hinder treatment. For example, individuals who tend to procrastinate or give up easily may be reluctant to initiate and follow through on various between-session homework assignments (e.g., relaxation training, self-monitoring). Even if these tendencies are not presenting problems, their existence should be a target for modification, if for no other reason than to help facilitate a treatment plan directed to other problems. Another frequently encountered hindrance in behavior therapy is the tendency for certain individuals to have very high standards for self-reinforcement. These characteristics have the potential for interfering with the treatment procedure to the extent that such individuals become discouraged with the gradual nature of behavior change process.

There are certain other client characteristics which, whether adaptive or maladaptive, can facilitate behavior change. For example, some individuals are very adept at self-observation and enjoy keeping detailed diaries of their day-to-day interactions. Such tendencies can be capitalized on and put to very good therapeutic use. An example of what might otherwise be classified as maladaptive behavior but which can nonetheless be useful therapeutically is seen in the overly dependent client. Dependent individuals are relatively willing to respond to the therapist's instigation to try out new behaviors, and they are likewise particularly receptive to therapist reinforcement for having done so. This type of responsiveness is particularly important, as much of the change that occurs in behavior therapy depends on between-session activities. It should be strongly emphasized, however, that the client's dependency should be employed therapeutically only during the early stages of behavior change, with the eventual goal clearly being to enable the person to function completely independent of the therapist and his influence (see Goldfried & Merbaum, 1973).

A final point might be made with regard to treatment priorities. Except in very rare instances, most clients come to therapy with more than one presenting problem. For those problems construed as being relatively independent—in the sense of one not being functionally tied to each other—some decision must be made regarding how to best spend one's therapeutic sessions and how much focus to place on each of these problems for homework assignments between sessions. Although the client's own preferences should be taken into consideration, the therapist must independently assess the entire life situation and attempt to evaluate the possible consequences of each presenting problem.

As a rule of thumb, one might ask the following question about each presenting problem: What are the consequences of my *not* doing anything therapeutically to handle this particular problem? Depending on the severity of the consequences associated with ignoring—at least temporarily—each of the different presenting problems, one can obtain a clearer picture as to what is most important. Thus, in working within a university clinic setting, for example, failure to focus on study problems when they present themselves along with other difficulties may mean the student will drop out of school and be lost as a client. In the case of a client who is severely depressed and also phobic about being alone, the possible consequences of not dealing with the depression include suicidal behavior and hospitalization, whereas the phobia can temporarily be dealt with by making certain that others are in the client's presence.

The Intake Evaluation

For the most part, the frequent use of interview procedures by behavior therapists is based on practical considerations. Direct observation by trained assistants and/or recourse to simulated and role-playing assessment may not always be feasible. In contrast to the use of interview procedures by clinicians of other orientations, behavior therapists focus on the specific SORC variables described above. Yet, despite some of the differences associated with the general guidelines of the interview as carried out by the behavioral assessor, the interview techniques themselves bear great similarity to those employed by clinicians from other orientations. In fact, Sullivan's (1954) *The Psychiatric Interview* can offer the behavioral assessor numerous guidelines for effectively conducting the interview. Additional behavioral interview techniques may be found in Storrow (1967) and Peterson (1968).

After one or more initial interview sessions, the task of the behavioral assessor becomes one of collating the information that has been obtained—whether by means of interview procedures or any other behavioral assessment method available—and organizing this information in such a way as to arrive at a preliminary behavioral analysis of the presenting problems, and at some decision regarding appropriate treatment procedures.

Although clinical report writing has received much attention in the literature, the guidelines for what to include and what to omit are frequently poorly spelled out. Human beings can be incredibly complex—even when viewed from a behavioral orientation—and numerous decisions must be made concerning inclusions and omissions from a clinical report about a person and his life situation. Unfortunately, there are instances in which such decisions are not intelligently made. As Storrow (1967) has observed:

Case reports . . . [typically] contain massive collections of useful as well as useless information, with the useful usually so well buried that it, too, becomes useless. I have long suffered from an acute boredom syndrome from reading too many such reports. They read like poorly written biographies, full of information that has no bearing on the problem at hand. I usually find I can't even *remember* all the data, much less utilize it to make predictions and treatment plans [p. 41].

In order to help focus assessment reports on information likely to be relevant to subsequent treatment procedures, Pomeranz and Goldfried (1970) have described a behaviorally oriented intake report format. The format, an outline of which follows, should be viewed as a general guideline, with the clear recognition that not all aspects of the outline are necessarily relevant to each case at hand.

I. *Behavior during interview and physical description.* The behavioral assessor includes here any observations construed as providing relevant samples of the client's behavior, whether it be specific to the therapeutic interaction or indicative of a more general behavioral tendency. Further, to the extent that the person's physical appearance may be typical or atypical of those in his social milieu, one may raise hypotheses (i.e., leads for further assessment) regarding the likelihood of the client's having a positive or negative impact on others.

II. *Presenting problem*

A. *Nature of problem(s).* Included here is a statement of the problem as described by the client himself. This may involve one or more possible difficulties, and they may need to be reconstrued by the behavioral assessor in conceptual terms different from those used by the client.

B. *Historical setting events.* Although behavioral assessors and behavior therapists make few attempts to deal with historical material, this in no way implies that such information is always irrelevant. The need for such data is particularly important when the client's presenting problems are vague or when the behavioral assessor has difficulty in conceptualizing them in functional terms. Thus by learning more about the person's past (e.g., overly perfectionistic parent), one may make inferences as to the likely consequences of such early social learning experiences. Such added information can often help to clarify the nature of the presenting complaints.

C. *Current situational determinants.* Inasmuch as the report is often written after just a few assessment sessions, sufficient information may not yet be available regarding the specific nature of those situations that either elicit respondents or serve as discriminative stimuli for operants. Consequently, the information included here might entail general classes of situations, each of which has to be followed up as the treatment progresses.

D. *Relevant organismic variables.* In addition to any physiological states that may account for the client's problem, information bearing on the client's labeling processes should be included here as well. Such covert self-statements may serve as an actual determinant of the problem (e.g., "I must be perfect in everything I do"), or they may consist of a more secondary attribution which is applied to the problem behavior itself (e.g., "My heart is beating faster because I am about to have a heart attack").

E. *Dimensions of problem(s).* The problematic response is analyzed here in terms of duration, pervasiveness, magnitude, and frequency of occurrence.

F. *Consequences of problem(s).* The information included here can refer either to potentially reinforcing consequences in the individual's environment (e.g., the reaction of others) or to the impact the problem has on various aspects of the person's current functioning (e.g., ability to maintain friendships, job status).

III. *Other problems.* Included here are any problems that emerged as a function of the assessment procedure, but were not stated by the client as being the original reason for having the therapeutic contact. Whether or not such problems constitute a target for modification depends on the client's own preferences, as well as the therapist's deliberations regarding treatment priorities.

IV. *Personal assets.* The information included in this category involves not only the positive attributes the individual may have (e.g., intelligence, attractive physical appearance), but also any interests or personal preferences that may serve as potential reinforcers in his life. Any aspect of the environment that has a potential for being therapeutically useful (e.g., a cooperative spouse) can also be included here as well.

V. *Target(s) for modification.* In many respects this section provides a culmination of the behavioral assessment procedures, in that it specifies exactly what variables are in need of modification, be they situational antecedents, organismic variables, components of the problem behavior itself, and/or consequent reinforcers. If possible, some ordering of priorities should be indicated.

VI. *Recommended treatment(s).* The therapeutic intervention procedures for modification of the targets indicated above are described here.

VII. *Motivation for treatment.* Based on the client's perception of the severity of the problem, his verbal commitment, past attempts at behavior change, and any other relevant indices, some general classification of motivation (e.g., high, medium, or low) should be indicated.

VIII. *Prognosis.* As much as possible, some indication as to the likelihood of the success of therapy should be indicated (e.g., very poor, fair, good, or very good). This may be based on such issues as the duration of the problem, past success with similar kinds of problems, relevant client variables, and so forth.

IX. *Priority of treatment.* This category is of particular use within a clinic setting, where requests for treatment typically outweigh the available therapeutic time. A simple low, medium, or high priority rating may be given, based on an evaluation of the possible consequences of *not* treating a given client.

X. *Expectancies.* Expectancies regarding the client's perception of the likelihood of change, as well as his view of the nature of the therapeutic relationship, should be included here.

XI. *Other comments.* In this category can be placed any information not readily included above. Thus one may indicate here any leads, hunches, or areas to follow up in subsequent interviews.

FUTURE DIRECTIONS

The field of behavioral assessment is undoubtedly here to stay, and all indications are that it will be the object of increased research and clinical activities. Along with its rapid growth rate have come numerous problems, however, such as how best to convey the ever-changing body of knowledge within a graduate course in behavioral assessment (Evans & Nelson, 1974), and how to guide the growth of behavioral assessment in such a way that it is likely to be methodologically sophisticated and clinically useful.

Despite the advances that have been made to date, there exist numerous vacuums within the field. As a result, there is a danger that poorly conceived procedures may proliferate and, because they fill a need at the time, establish themselves within the scope of behavioral assessment. This is reminiscent of what happened in the development of both projective techniques and measures of intelligence: Tests that were developed on idiosyncratic hunches became established and sometimes firmly entrenched within the clinician's test battery (see Chapters 1, 2 and 3).

Once a test is reported in the literature—whether it be behavioral, projective, or anything else—it seems to develop a momentum of its own, regardless of what a sophisticated methodological analysis of the procedure may reveal, to say nothing of disappointing validity data.

This is not to say that research on the development of new assessment procedures is not called for. Quite the contrary. Perhaps one of the greatest needs that exists at present is for behavioral assessment procedures of a more standardized nature. Although various methods of behavioral assessment are used in clinical practice, they tend to vary from therapist to therapist. In the research context, even when the methodology used for assessing a given target behavior is similar from study to study, there nonetheless exist procedural variations which make interpretations difficult (see Bernstein & Nietzel, 1973; Jeger & Goldfried, in press).

As was described at the outset of this chapter, the assumptions associated with behavioral assessment deal not only with issues of method variance, but also with careful criterion sampling of the behavior of interest. Very recently, problems associated with method assumptions have come under closer research scrutiny (Goldfried & Sprafkin, 1974; Johnson & Bolstad, 1973; Lipinski & Nelson, 1974; O'Leary & Kent, 1973). In their haste to fill the need for measures, however, not all behavioral assessors have taken care to attend to sampling assumptions. In the development of standardized behavioral assessment procedures, the guidelines outlined by Goldfried and D'Zurilla (1969) in conducting such a criterion sampling can help to direct future research efforts, as they have in the work of Goldsmith (1973) and MacDonald (1974).

In their description of the behavioral-analytic model for test construction, Goldfried and D'Zurilla suggest that four steps be taken: (a) a situational analysis, (b) a response enumeration, (c) a response evaluation, and (d) the development of the measurement format. In the situational analysis, what is required is some sort of empirical sampling of the various situations with which the individual is likely to interact on a day-to-day basis. During the response enumeration, a sampling of the possible responses to each of the situations derived from the situational analysis is determined. What emerges is a comprehensive sampling of potentially important situations within a particular environmental setting, as well as the likely responses to each of these situations. During the response evaluation, those individuals in the environment who typically evaluate the effectiveness of this class of behavior are used to carry out such an evaluation on the environment-behavior units that have been sampled. The net result of this entire process provides one with an empirically derived criterion analysis, a test item pool for incorporation in one's measure, and a set of evaluative criteria which might be used for scoring purposes. Having carried out the construction procedure thus far, the assessor must decide on a method of simulating situations and eliciting responses; depending on the nature of the behavior being evaluated, this method may involve one or more of the various methods of behavioral assessment described in this chapter.

REFERENCES

Alpert, R., & Haber, R. N. Anxiety in academic achievement situations. *Journal of Abnormal and Social Psychology*, 1960, **61**, 207–215.

American Psychological Association. *Standards for educational and psychological tests*. Washington, D.C.: American Psychological Association, 1974.

Anderson, G. L., & Anderson, H. L. (Eds.) *An introduction to projective techniques*. Englewood Cliffs, N.J.: Prentice-Hall, 1951.

Arkowitz, H., Lichtenstein, E., McGovern, K., & Hines, P. The behavioral assessment of social competence in males. *Behavior Therapy*, 1975, **6**, 3–13.

Bandura, A. A social learning interpretation of psychological dysfunctions. In P. London & D. Rosenhan (Eds.), *Foundations of abnormal psychology*. New York: Holt, Rinehart & Winston, 1968. Pp. 293–344.

Barker, R. G., & Wright, H. F. *One boy's day*. New York: Harper & Row, 1951.

Bernstein, D. Behavioral fear assessment: Anxiety or artifact? In H. Adams & P. Unikel (Eds.), *Issues and trends in behavior therapy*. Springfield, Ill.: Charles C Thomas, 1973.

Bernstein, D. A., & Nietzel, M. T. Procedural variation in behavioral avoidance tests. *Journal of Consulting and Clinical Psychology*, 1973, **41**, 165–174.

Bersoff, D. N., & Moyer, D. Positive reinforcement observation schedule (PROS): Development and use. Paper presented at the annual meeting of the American Psychological Association, Montreal, August 1973.

Borkovec, T. D., Fleischmann, D. J., & Caputo, J. A. The measurement of anxiety in an analogue social situation. *Journal of Consulting and Clinical Psychology*, 1973, **41**, 157–161.

Borkovec, T. D., Stone, N. M., O'Brien, G. T., & Kaloupek, D. G. Evaluation of a clinically relevant target behavior for analog outcome research. *Behavior Therapy*, 1974, **5**, 503–513.

Cautela, J. R., & Kastenbaum, R. A. A reinforcement survey schedule for use in therapy, training, and research. *Psychological Reports*, 1967, **20**, 1115–1130.

Davison, G. C., & Goldfried, M. R. Postdoctoral training in clinical behavior therapy. In I. B. Weiner (Ed.), *Postdoctoral education in clinical psychology*. Topeka, Kans.: Menninger Foundation, 1973. Pp. 80–88.

Eisler, R. M., Hersen, M., & Agras, W. S. Videotape: A method for the controlled observation of non-verbal interpersonal behavior. *Behavior Therapy*, 1973, **4**, 420–425. (a)

Eisler, R. M., Hersen, M., & Agras, W. S. Effects of videotape and instructional feedback on non-verbal marital interactions: An analogue study. *Behavior Therapy*, 1973, **5**, 551–558. (b)

Eisler, R. M., Hersen, M., & Miller, P. M. Effects of modeling on components of assertive behavior. *Journal of Behavior Therapy and Experimental Psychiatry*, 1973, **4**, 1–6.

Eisler, R. M., Miller, P. M., & Hersen, M. Components of assertive behavior. *Journal of Clinical Psychology*, 1973, **24**, 295–299.

Ellis, A. *Reason and emotion in psychotherapy*. New York: Lyle Stuart, 1962.

Endler, N. S., Hunt, J. McV., & Rosenstein, A. J. An S-R inventory of anxiousness. *Psychological Monographs*, 1962, **76**, 1–33.

Evans, I. M., & Nelson, R. A curriculum for the teaching of behavior assessment. *American Psychologist*, 1974, **29**, 598–606.

Farina, A., Arenberg, D., & Guskin, S. A scale for measuring minimal social behavior. *Journal of Consulting Psychology*, 1957, **21**, 265–268.

Friedman, H. Perceptual regression in schizophrenia: An hypothesis suggested by use of the Rorschach test. *Journal of Projective Techniques*, 1953, **17**, 171–185.

Galassi, J. P., DeLo, J. S., Galassi, M. D., & Bastien, S. The college self-expression scale: A measure of assertiveness. *Behavior Therapy*, 1974, **5**, 165–171.

Geer, J. H. The development of a scale to measure fear. *Behavior Research and Therapy*, 1965, **3**, 45–53.

Geer, J. H., Morokoff, P., & Greenwood, P. Sexual arousal in women: The development of a measurement device for vaginal blood volume. *Archives of Sexual Behavior*, 1974, **3**, 559–564.

Goffman, E. *Asylums*. Garden City, N.Y.: Doubleday, 1961.

Goldfried, M. R., Decenteceo, E. T., & Weinberg, L. Systematic rational restructuring as a self-control technique. *Behavior Therapy*, 1974, **5**, 247–254.

Goldfried, M. R., & D'Zurilla, T. J. A behavioral-analytic model for assessing competence. In C. D. Spielberger (Ed.), *Current topics in clinical and community psychology*, New York: Academic Press, 1969. Pp. 151–196.

Goldfried, M. R., & Goldfried, A. P. Cognitive change methods. In F. H. Kanfer & A. P. Goldstein (Eds.), *Helping people change*. Elmsford, N.Y.: Pergamon Press, 1975. Pp. 89–116.

Goldfried, M. R., & Kent, R. N. Traditional vs. behavioral assessment: A comparison of methodological and theoretical assumptions. *Psychological Bulletin*, 1972, **77**, 409–420.

Goldfried, M. R., & Merbaum, M. (Eds.) *Behavior change through self-control*. New York: Holt, Rinehart & Winston, 1973.

Goldfried, M. R., & Pomeranz, D. M. Role of assessment in behavior modification. *Psychological Reports,* 1968, **23,** 75–87.

Goldfried, M. R., and Sprafkin, J. N. *Behavioral personality assessment.* Morristown, N.J.: General Learning Press, 1974.

Goldfried, M. R., Stricker, G., & Weiner, I. B. *Rorschach handbook of clinical and research applications.* Englewood Cliffs, N.J.: Prentice-Hall, 1971.

Goldfried, M. R., & Trier, C. S. Effectiveness of relaxation as an active coping skill. *Journal of Abnormal Psychology,* 1974, **83,** 348–355.

Goldsmith, J. B. Systematic development and evaluation of a behavioral program for training psychiatric inpatients in interpersonal skills. Unpublished doctoral dissertation, University of Wisconsin, 1973.

Goodenough, F. L. *Mental testing.* New York: Rinehart, 1949.

Gottman, J. Couples interaction scoring system (CISS): Instructions for use of CISS. Unpublished manuscript, Indiana University, 1974.

Hersen, M., Eisler, R. M., Miller, P. M., Johnson, M. B., & Pinkston, S. G. Effects of practice instructions and modeling on components of assertive behavior. *Behaviour Research and Therapy, 1973,* **11,** 443–451.

Honigfeld, G., Gillis, R. D., & Klett, C. J. Nosie-30: A treatment-sensitive ward behavior scale. *Psychological Reports,* 1966, **19,** 180–182.

Husek, T., & Alexander, S. The effectiveness of the anxiety differential in examination stress situations. *Education and Psychological Measurement,* 1963, **23,** 309–318.

Insel, P. M., & Moos, R. H. Psychological environments: Expanding the scope of human ecology. *American Psychologist,* 1974, **29,** 179–188.

Jacks, R. N. Systematic desensitization versus a self-control technique for the reduction of acrophobia. Unpublished doctoral dissertation, Stanford University, 1972.

Jeger, A. M., & Goldfried, M. R. A comparison of situation tests of speech anxiety. *Behavior Therapy,* in press.

Johnson, S. M., & Bolstad, O. D. Methodological issues in naturalistic observation: Some problems and solutions for field research. In L. A. Hamerlynck, L. C. Handy, & E. J. Mash (Eds.), *Behavior change: Methodology, concepts and practice.* Champaign, Ill.: Research Press, 1973. Pp. 7–67.

Johnson, S. M., & Bolstad, O. D. Reactivity to home observation: A comparison of audio recorded behavior with observers present or absent. Unpublished manuscript, University of Oregon, 1974.

Kanfer, F. H., & Saslow, G. Behavioral analysis: An alternative to diagnostic classification. *Archives of General Psychiatry,* 1965, **12,** 529–538.

Kanter, N. J. Comparison of self-control desensitization and systematic rational restructuring in the reduction of interpersonal anxiety. Unpublished doctoral dissertation, State University of New York at Stony Brook, 1975.

Kazdin, A. E. Self-monitoring and behavior change. In M. J. Mahoney & C. E. Thoresen (Eds.), *Self-control: Power to the person.* Monterey, Calif.: Brooks/Cole, 1974. (a) Pp. 218–246.

Kazdin, A. E. Effects of covert modeling and model reinforcement on assertive behavior. *Journal of Abnormal Psychology*, 1974, **83,** 240–252. (b).

Kent, R. N., O'Leary, K. D., Diament, C., & Dietz, A. Expectation biases in observational evaluation of therapy change. *Journal of Consulting and Clinical Psychology*, 1974, **42,** 774–780.

Lewinsohn, P. M., & Graf, M. Pleasant activities and depression. *Journal of Consulting and Clinical Psychology*, 1973, **41,** 261–268.

Lewinsohn, P. M., & Libet, J. Pleasant events, activity schedules, and depressions. *Journal of Abnormal Psychology*, 1972, **79,** 291–295.

Lewinsohn, P. M., & Shaffer, M. Use of home observations as an integral part of the treatment of depression: Preliminary report and case studies. *Journal of Consulting and Clinical Psychology*, 1971, **37,** 87–94.

Lipinski, D., & Nelson, R. Problems in the use of naturalistic observation as a means of behavioral assessment. *Behavior Therapy*, 1974, **5,** 341–351.

MacDonald, M. L. A behavioral assessment methodology applied to the measurement of assertion. Unpublished doctoral dissertation, University of Illinois, 1974.

MacDonald, M. L., Lindquist, C. U., Kramer, J. A., McGrath, R. A., & Rhyne, L. L. Social skills training: The effect of behavior rehearsal in groups on dating skills. *Journal of Counseling Psychology*, 1975, **22,** 224–230.

MacPhillamy, D. J., & Lewinsohn, P. M. Measuring reinforcing events. *Proceedings of the 80th Annual Convention, American Psychological Association*, 1972.

Mariotto, M. J., & Paul, G. L. A multimethod validation of the inpatient multidimensional psychiatric scale with chronically institutionalized patients. *Journal of Consulting and Clinical Psychology*, 1974, **42,** 497–508.

McFall, R. M., & Lillesand, D. V. Behavior rehearsal with modeling and coaching in assertive training. *Journal of Abnormal Psychology*, 1971, **77,** 313–323.

McFall, R. M., & Marston, A. An experimental investigation of behavior rehearsal in assertive training. *Journal of Abnormal Psychology*, 1970, **76,** 295–303.

McFall, R. M., & Twentyman, C. T. Four experiments on the relative contributions of rehearsal modeling, and coaching on assertion training. *Journal of Abnormal Psychology*, 1973, **81,** 199–218.

Meichenbaum, D. H., Gilmore, J. B., & Fedoravicious, A. Group insight versus group desensitization in treating speech anxiety. *Journal of Consulting and Clinical Psychology*, 1971, **36,** 410–421.

Miller, B., & Bernstein, D. Instructional demand in a behavioral avoidance test for claustrophobic fears. *Journal of Abnormal Psychology*, 1972, **80,** 206–210.

Moos, R. H. Behavioral effects of being observed: Reactions to a wireless radio transmitter. *Journal of Consulting and Clinical Psychology*, 1968, **32,** 383–388.

Moos, R. H. Conceptualizations of human environments. *American Psychologist*, 1973, **28**, 652–665.

Moors, R. H. *Evaluating treatment environments: A social ecological approach.* New York: Wiley, 1974.

Murray, H. A. *Explorations in personality.* New York: Oxford University Press, 1938.

Office of Strategic Services Assessment Staff. *Assessment of men.* New York: Rinehart, 1948.

O'Leary, K. D., & Becker, W. C. Behavior modification of an adjustment class: A token reinforcement program. *Exceptional Children,* 1967, **33**, 637–642.

O'Leary, K. D., & Kent, R. Behavior modification for social action: Research tactics and problems. In L. A. Hamerlynck, L. C. Handy, & E. J. Mash (Eds.), *Critical issues in research and practice.* Champaign, Ill.: Research Press, 1973. Pp. 69–96.

O'Leary, K. D., Kent, R. N., & Kanowitz, J. Shaping data collection congruent with experimental hypothesis. *Journal of Applied Behavior Analysis,* 1975, **8**, 43–51.

O'Leary, K. D., & O'Leary, S. G. (Eds.), *Classroom management.* Elmsford, N.Y.: Pergamon Press, 1972.

Orne, M. T. On the social psychology of the psychological experiment: With particular reference to demand characteristics and their implication. *American Psychologist,* 1962, **17**, 776–783.

Osgood, C. E., Suci, G. J., & Tannenbaum, P. H. *The measurement of meaning.* Urbana: University of Illinois Press, 1957.

Patterson, G. R., Ray, R. S., Shaw, D. A., & Cobb, J. Manual for coding of family interactions, 1969. Available from ASIS/NAPS, c/o Microfiche Publications, 305 E. 46th Street, New York, N.Y. 10017. Document #01234.

Paul, G. L. *Insight vs. desensitization in psychotherapy.* Stanford, Calif.: Stanford University Press, 1966.

Paul, G. L., Tobias, L. L., & Holly, B. L. Maintenance psychotropic drugs in the presence of active treatment programs: A "triple-blind" withdrawal study with long-term mental patients. *Archives of General Psychiatry,* 1972, **27**, 106–115.

Peterson, D. R. *The clinical study of social behavior.* New York: Appleton-Century-Crofts, 1968.

Pomeranz, D. M., & Goldfried, M. R. An intake report outline for behavior modification. *Psychological Reports,* 1970, **26**, 447–450.

Purcell, K., & Brady, K. Adaptation to the invasion of privacy: Monitoring behavior with a miniature radio transmitter. *Merrill-Palmer Quarterly of Behavior and Development,* 1966, **12**, 242–254.

Rathus, S. A. A 30-item schedule for assessing assertive behavior. *Behavior Therapy,* 1973, **4**, 398–406.

Rehm, L. P., & Marston, A. R. Reduction of social anxiety through modification of self-reinforcement: An instigation therapy technique. *Journal of Consulting and Clinical Psychology,* 1968, **32,** 565–574.

Reid, J. B. Reliability assessment of observation data: A possible methodological problem. *Child Development,* 1970, **41,** 1143–1150.

Rhyne, L. D., MacDonald, M. L., McGrath, R. A., Lindquist, C. U., & Kramer, J. A. The RPDI: An instrument for the measurement of male social dating skills. Unpublished manuscript, University of Illinois, 1973.

Romanczyk, R. G., Kent, R. N., Diament, C., & O'Leary, K. D. Measuring the reliability of observational data: A reactive process. *Journal of Applied Behavior Analysis,* 1973, **6,** 175–184.

Rosenhan, D. L. On being sane in insane places. *Science,* 1973, **179,** 250–258

Rosenthal, R. *Experimenter effects in behavioral research.* New York: Appleton-Century-Crofts, 1966.

Ross, A. O., Lacey, H. M., & Parton, D. A. The development of a behavior checklist for boys. *Child Development,* 1965, **36,** 1013–1027.

Rotter, J. B., & Wickens, D. D. The consistency and generality of ratings of "social aggressiveness" made from observations of role playing situations. *Journal of Consulting Psychology,* 1948, **12,** 234–239.

Skinner, B. F. *Science and human behavior.* New York: Macmillan, 1953.

Smith, R. E., Diener, E., & Beaman, A. L. Demand characteristics and the behavioral avoidance measure of fear in behavior therapy analogue research. *Behavior Therapy,* 1974, **5,** 172–182.

Spielberger, C. D., Gorsuch, R. L., & Lushene, R. E. *The state-trait anxiety inventory (STAI) test manual for form X.* Palo Alto, Calif.: Consulting Psychologists Press, 1970.

Staats, A. W. (with contributions by C. K. Staats). *Complex human behavior.* New York: Holt, Rinehart & Winston, 1963.

Stanton, H. R., & Litwak, E. Toward the development of a short form test of interpersonal competence. *American Sociological Review,* 1955, **20,** 668–674.

Storrow, H. A. *Introduction to scientific psychiatry.* New York: Appleton-Century-Crofts, 1967.

Sullivan, H. S. *The psychiatric interview.* New York: Norton, 1954.

Ulmer, R. A., & Timmons, E. O. An application and modification of the minimal social behavior scale (MSBS): A short objective, empirical, reliable measure of personality functioning. *Journal of Consulting Psychology,* 1966, **30,** 1–7.

Wahler, R. G., Winkel, G. H., Peterson, R. F., & Morrison, C. C. Mothers as behavior therapists for their own children. *Behaviour Research and Therapy,* 1965, **3,** 113–124.

Wallace, J. What units shall we employ? Allport's question revisited. *Journal of Consulting Psychology,* 1967, **31,** 56–64.

Watson, D., & Friend, R. Measurement of social-evaluative anxiety. *Journal of Consulting and Clinical Psychology,* 1969, **33,** 448–457.

Wiggins, J. S., & Winder, C. L. The peer nomination inventory: An empirical derived sociometric measure of adjustment in preadolescent boys. *Psychological Reports,* 1961, **9,** 643–677.

Wolpe, J., & Lazarus, A. A. *Behavior therapy techniques.* New York: Pergamon Press, 1966.

Zuckerman, M., & Lubin, B. *Manual for the multiple affect adjective checklist.* San Diego, Calif.: Educational and Industrial Testing Service, 1965.

PART TWO

Methods of Intervention

CHAPTER 6

Individual Psychotherapy

IRVING B. WEINER

The second half of this handbook is devoted to five methods of intervention by which clinicians attempt to meet the psychological needs of people who seek their help: individual psychotherapy, group therapy, family therapy, behavior modification, and crisis intervention. This chapter, while addressed primarily to individual psychotherapy, introduces the reader to the broad area of psychotherapy theory, research, and practice by (a) defining the nature of psychotherapy; (b) describing the major theories of psychotherapy; (c) identifying the general and specific factors that promote behavior change in psychotherapy; (d) outlining the course of psychotherapy in the initial, middle, and final phases of treatment; and (e) commenting briefly on trends in psychotherapy research, particularly with respect to treatment outcome.

THE NATURE OF PSYCHOTHERAPY

Like styles of putting among golfers, psychotherapy embraces almost as many definitions as there are people who write about it. Wolberg (1967, pp. 7–10) lists 26 different definitions of psychotherapy, only 9 of which are common to another list of 31 definitions provided by Reisman (1971, pp. 11–18). To comprehend the essential nature of psychotherapy, it is helpful to begin by sorting out the implications of these various definitions and then to consider the appropriate *goals* of psychotherapy, the distinction between *uncovering and supportive approaches* in psychotherapy, and the complementary role of *strategy and tactics* in working toward the treatment goals.

Definitions of Psychotherapy

In an important volume entitled *Toward the Integration of Psychotherapy,* Reisman (1971) has recently brought some order to the myriad definitions of psychotherapy and proposed an integrated definition that is both more precise and more comprehensive than its predecessors. In his analysis and synthesis of the literature Reisman weighs the advantages and disadvantages of psychotherapy definitions classified according to the following four types.

1. *Psychotherapy defined by its goals.* Definitions of this type view psychotherapy as a treatment method intended to alleviate psychological disorder:

> The art of treating mental diseases or disorders [Hinsie & Campbell, 1960]
> . . . A method of treatment which aims to help the impaired individual by influencing his emotional processes, his evaluation of himself and of others, his evaluation of and his manner of coping with the problems of life [Maslow & Mittelman, 1951, p. 179]

These definitions call attention to a key and generally acknowledged characteristic of psychotherapy, namely, the wish of the therapist to be of help to his patient. However, definitions of this type have two significant shortcomings. First, they describe what psychotherapy is intended to do, not what is consists of, so that judgments about whether psychotherapy is taking place must be based on the therapist's intent rather than on his actual behavior. Second, they are so broad as to include many forms of treatment that may be *psychotherapeutic* but are not usually regarded as constituting *psychotherapy,* such as drug therapy, shock therapy, psychosurgery, and recreational therapy.

2. *Psychotherapy defined by its procedures.* These definitions regard psychotherapy as the use of psychological measures, usually in the form of some kind of verbal communication, to modify personality maladjustments:

> Psychotherapy may be defined as the treatment of emotional and personality problems and disorders by psychological means [Noyes & Kolb, 1963, p. 500]
> The generic term for any type of treatment which is based primarily upon verbal or nonverbal communication [Deutsch & Fishman, 1963]

Definitions of this type identify another widely agreed on feature of psychotherapy, namely, the use of psychological procedures to communicate a message. Defining psychotherapy in this way is more precise than emphasizing the goals of psychotherapy independently of the methods used to achieve these goals. However, unspecified phrases such as "psychological means" and "verbal communication" give little inkling as to the nature of the means to be used or the messages to be communicated in psychotherapy, and they also fail to exclude methods of communicating with people that may benefit them psychologically but are not usually considered psychotherapy, such as giving advice.

3. *Psychotherapy defined by its practitioners.* In this approach to definition psychotherapy is considered to be what psychotherapists do:

> . . . The term [psychotherapy] should be reserved for treatment by a professionally trained person [English & English, 1958]
>
> . . . Psychotherapy is a form of help-giving in which a trained, socially sanctioned healer tries to relieve a sufferer's distress by facilitating certain changes in his feelings, attitudes, and behavior [Frank, 1961, p. 114]

By specifying psychotherapy as a trained professional's use of psychological procedures to help disturbed people, these definitions improve on the imprecision of definitions based only on the goals or procedures of the treatment. However, restricting the label *psychotherapy* to the behavior of a trained psychotherapist means that identical behavior would not be called psychotherapy if it were performed by someone else. Leaving aside ethical and legal considerations in restricting the practice of psychotherapy to trained professionals, definitions tied to who is performing certain behaviors rather than to what these behaviors consist of contribute little to identifying the essential nature of psychotherapy.

4. *Psychotherapy defined by the relationship.* These definitions conceive of psychotherapy as a special kind of interpersonal relationship in which unique types of social learning, emotion-arousing interactions, and growth experience take place:

> The therapeutic process occurs as a unique growth experience, created by one person seeking and needing help from another who accepts the responsibility of offering it [Allen, 1942, p. 45]
>
> Psychotherapy is a process in which changes in an individual's behavior are achieved as a result of experiences in a relationship with a person trained in understanding behavior [Stein, 1961, p. 7]
>
> . . . The relearning or new learning that the patient is able to accomplish through talk with the therapist and through the ensuing personal relation [White, 1964, pp. 283–284.]

These definitions highlight another generally acknowledged aspect of psychotherapy, that it is an interpersonal relationship in which one person respects and addresses the capacity of the other to work toward finding a fuller and more rewarding life for himself. Yet definitions of psychotherapy in terms of the relationship identify only the hoped-for effects of the treatment process, such as "social learning" or "a growth experience,'' and do not indicate how the therapist acts to achieve these effects. Furthermore, to define psychotherapy as a relationship in which learning and growth occur implies that without learning and growth there has been no psychotherapy. This confusion of the treatment (psychotherapy) with its effects (learning and growth) places psychotherapy in the awkward position of being judged as taking place only when it proves successful. Since psychotherapy may in fact be more or less successful (see Bergin, 1966; Truax & Wargo, 1966; Wolman, 1972), it is clearly preferable to define psychotherapy in terms of the work of the therapist rather than the response of the patient.

Although each of these four approaches to defining psychotherapy is flawed in some respect, together they identify several characteristics common to all instances of what is usually regarded as psychotherapy. These include (a) the use of psychological measures to assist people who are experiencing emotional problems in living, (b) the wish of the therapist to be of help to his patient, (c) an attitude of respect by the therapist for the personal integrity of the patient, and (d) reliance on an understanding of the patient to guide the conduct of the treatment. Following Reisman (1971, pp. 135–136), then, psychotherapy can be defined as *the communication of person-related understanding, respect, and a wish to be of help.* In addition to integrating previous definitions, this view of the nature of psychotherapy clarifies further two important issues touched on above, the distinction between *psychotherapy* and what may be psychotherapeutic, and the bearing of a professional relationship on the likelihood that psychotherapy will occur.

Distinguishing Psychotherapy from What May Be Psychotherapeutic. As just defined, psychotherapy comprises treatment approaches in which the therapist attempts to enhance his patient's understanding of himself, and it includes such work with groups and families as well as with individuals. However, psychotherapy does not include treatment methods in which the therapist seeks to do something to or for his patient rather than engage him in a quest for increased self-understanding. Thus prescribing drugs or electric shock, arranging for directed recreational activities, and offering sound advice may each be psychotherapeutic, by relieving the patient's emotional distress or increasing his life satisfaction, but they do not constitute psychotherapy.

Likewise, behavior modification in its traditional forms of systematic desensitization, operant conditioning, and aversive training does not constitute psychotherapy, even though it has considerable potential for promoting positive behavior change. Behavioral, somatic, recreational, and advice-giving treatment methods should of course be based on some understanding of the patient's needs and problems, and the therapist conducting these treatments implicitly conveys by his actions that he has arrived at such an understanding. In psychotherapy, however, the therapist not only arrives at and implies an understanding of his patient, but utilizes *explicit communication* of this understanding as the central feature of his method.

This distinction between psychotherapy and the broader category of what may be psychotherapeutic can contribute significantly to advances in practice and research. To learn and apply principles for the effective conduct of psychotherapy, the therapist must be able to distinguish between when he is providing psychotherapy and when he is employing other procedures that should be guided by other or more general clinical considerations. To design and conduct useful research on psychotherapy, the researcher must be able to define in a precise and replicable fashion the kinds of clinical interactions that should be the subject of his investigations. Unless such distinctions are made, neither clinical nor experimental findings can systematically shape knowledge about psychotherapy.

The Bearing of a Professional Relationship on the Likelihood That Psychotherapy Will Occur. When psychotherapy is defined as the communication of understanding, respect, and a wish to be of help, it is possible to conceive of its occurring in many different kinds of interpersonal relationships, and even occurring inadvertently. For several reasons, however, the behaviors that constitute psychotherapy are much more likely to occur in the context of a professional relationship designed to provide psychotherapy than in any other kind of relationship.

First, the likelihood that understanding, respect, and a wish to be of help will be communicated in a relationship between two people is considerably enhanced if one of them is a professional trained in the understanding of human behavior and consciously intent on applying his training for the benefit of the other. Although a naturally intuitive person may be keenly sensitive to the thoughts and feelings of others, he cannot be expected to translate his sensitivity into the communication of understanding as frequently as someone trained in and dedicated to doing so.

Second, a professional psychotherapy relationship is designed primarily for the benefit of the patient and does not depend on the therapist's receiving any equal share of understanding, respect, and help. Whereas most other kinds of interpersonal relationships must be sustained by mutual need gratification, a professional psychotherapy relationship is based on one person (the therapist) single-mindedly serving the psychological needs of another (the patient), without seeking to gratify any needs of his own other than to be an effective psychotherapist.

Third, a professional psychotherapy relationship involves arrangements and commitments that increase the prospects for understanding to be communicated in a systematic fashion. The participants meet on a regularly scheduled basis for a specified length of time, and neither their intercurrent personal affairs nor their feelings about each other are ordinarily allowed to disrupt their work together. Moreover, the psychotherapy relationship continues as long as it serves the needs of the patient and, unlike other kinds of interpersonal relationships, it is not broken off during transient periods of waning enthusiasm.

Goals of Psychotherapy

People seek psychotherapy primarily for three reasons. Some are troubled by distressing symptoms, such as anxiety, depression, phobias, or difficulty in thinking clearly. Some experience certain problems in living, such as work inhibition, school failure, marital discord, or social withdrawal. And some are generally dissatisfied with themselves for failing to become the kind of person they would like to be. These reasons why people come to psychotherapy identify what the goals of the treatment should be, namely, to relieve emotional distress, to promote solutions to problems in living, and to minimize conflicts and concerns that limit a person's realization of his potential for productive work and rewarding interpersonal relationships.

Because psychotherapy is defined in part by the explicit communication of understanding, it is sometimes assumed that the goal of the treatment is insight, which consists of the patient's being able to understand his thoughts, feelings, and actions. However, any such assumption incorrectly equates the methods of psychotherapy with its goals. Effective communication by the therapist should increase a patient's ability to understand himself, but this increased insight is not an end in itself. Insight in psychotherapy is only a means to the end of achieving the behavior changes sought by the patient. Psychotherapy without behavior change, whether in the form of symptom relief, problem resolution, or progress toward a more rewarding life-style, has not achieved its goals. Whenever a patient remains unwilling or unable to translate increased understanding of himself into desired behavior change, further or more incisive treatment is required.

However, even with desired behavior change as a guide, it is easier to enumerate the goals of psychotherapy than it is to identify when they have been achieved. How fully should psychotherapy relieve emotional distress, for example? How thoroughly should it resolve conflicts and concerns? How perfectly should it promote solutions to problems? How extensively should it enhance life satisfaction? The constraints of reality recommend modest rather than ambitious answers to these questions. Biogenetic and sociocultural factors limit the degree to which people can alter their personality or redirect their way of living. Moreover, behavior patterns that are ideal at one point in a person's life can become less adaptive and less self-fulfilling as his capacities and circumstances change.

Hence psychotherapy cannot be expected to achieve complete cures or perfect resolutions, nor can increments in self-understanding be expected to provide indefinite insulation against psychological difficulties. Working toward such utopian goals is more than likely to result in what Freud (1937) aptly labeled "analysis interminable." To avoid interminable treatment, psychotherapy should be regarded as a helping procedure, not a curative one, and as a means of facilitating progress toward desired behavior change, rather than as a route to total and permanent change. Thus psychotherapy should end when a patient has made substantial progress toward achieving the goals with which he entered treatment, and when he appears unlikely to make sufficient further progress to justify the time, effort, and expense that such progress would require.

Uncovering and Supportive Approaches in Psychotherapy

The distinction between uncovering and supportive approaches in psychotherapy is essential in selecting the most appropriate procedures for working with a particular patient at a particular time. *Uncovering* approaches, which are also referred to as *insight-oriented* or *reconstructive* psychotherapy, concentrate on promoting behavior change by examining the origins of an individual's personality style and helping him modify personality characteristics that are contributing to his psychological difficulties. Supportive approaches, which are also called *limited-insight* or *educative* psychotherapy, promote behavior change by examining a person's psychological difficulties and helping him bring his existing personality characteristics more effectively to bear in resolving them.

To illustrate this difference between uncovering and supportive approaches, suppose a male patient has been performing poorly in his work, and suppose further that a characterological preoccupation with details appears responsible in part for this problem. Uncovering psychotherapy for this man would focus on the origins and manifestations of his apparently obsessive-compulsive personality style. By becoming more fully aware of this feature of his personality, especially in relation to his inefficient functioning on the job, the patient would gain increased capacity to modify it. The resulting reduction in his compulsivity would alleviate both the work problem for which he sought help and any other problems caused by his preoccupation with detail.

Supportive psychotherapy for this same man would focus on the nature of his work, on the ways in which his organization and execution of tasks assigned to him had proved inefficient, and on alternative means of planning and carrying out his assignments so as to reduce or eliminate his inefficiency. In this approach the same amount and kind of attention would be paid as in an uncovering approach to helping him understand the relationship between his personality style, his preoccupation with details, and his poor work performance. However, instead of exploring and seeking to modify the personality style underlying his preoccupation, as would be done in uncovering psychotherapy, a supportive approach would avoid probing the patient's personality style and instead work toward more effective functioning within it. Thus this patient could be helped to weigh the component parts of a task assigned to him, in an obsessive-compulsive fashion, and then to use his judgment about their relative importance to guide him in concentrating on the more important parts of the task and minimizing distraction by less important details.

As this illustration hopefully makes clear, supportive psychotherapy is concerned primarily with helping the patient understand the *what* and the *how* of his psychological problems, whereas uncovering psychotherapy is concerned primarily with helping him understand the *why*. Uncovering psychotherapy seeks to help the patient understand why he became the kind of person he is, whereas supportive psychotherapy focuses on helping him understand how being the kind of person he is has contributed to the difficulties that brought him into treatment. Supportive psychotherapy is at times confused with the general meaning of being supportive, such that advice, reassurance, sympathy, and even lending a patient money are regarded as constituting supportive psychotherapy. However, in as much as supportive as well as uncovering psychotherapy utilizes communication of understanding as the primary modality of the treatment, it should be distinguished from supportive procedures that, although they may be psychotherapeutic, are not addressed to communicating understanding.

Because uncovering and supportive approaches in psychotherapy differ mainly in the kinds and extent of understanding they seek to communicate, they represent degrees of emphasis rather than mutually exclusive types of treatment. Psychotherapy addressed to modifying personality characteristics inevitably gives some consideration to how certain problems can be resolved within the framework of existing personality characteristics. Likewise, psychotherapy focused on bringing existing personality characteristics more effectively to bear on current problems almost always devotes some attention to understanding the origin of these personality characteristics. In actual practice, then, psychotherapy for the individual patient tends to be primarily uncovering or primarily supportive in nature, and not exclusively one or the other.

Finally in this regard, it is important to dispel some lingering myths that uncovering psychotherapy, because it aims at personality modification, is generally preferable to and better than supportive psychotherapy. What is preferable in psychotherapy is what best meets the patient's needs and most fully helps him achieve desired behavior change. Depending on the nature of a patient's problem, the extent and kinds of changes he seeks, the flexibility of his personality style, and the amount of effort he is able and willing to devote to psychotherapy, either a primarily uncovering or a primarily supportive approach may best serve his needs (see Dewald, 1971, Chapter 8; Wolberg, 1967, Chapter 13).

Strategy and Tactics in Psychotherapy

To conduct psychotherapy in a manner that consistently meets the needs of his patient, a psychotherapist must operate with a keen sense of strategy and tactics. *Strategy* refers to what the therapist tries to accomplish at a given point, whereas *tactics* refers to the particular means by which he attempts to accomplish it. For example, a therapist whose strategy is to learn more about a patient's mother without asking any direct or specific questions that would curb the patient's spontaneity may select for his tactics an indirect observation ("You haven't said much about what your mother is like") or a general request for information ("Tell me about your mother"). As another example, a therapist may feel at a particular point that he should help the patient recognize his obvious avoidance of sexual matters (the strategy), but that he needs to approach this topic gradually (the tactics), beginning with, "I get the feeling there are some things you are finding it hard to talk about today."

Like uncovering and supportive approaches, strategy and tactics play complementary roles in effective psychotherapy. The most perceptive strategies go for naught unless they are joined with tactics for implementing them; the most brilliant tactics serve little purpose unless they are guided by strategies for where and when they should be employed. The good strategist who lacks tactical sense often knows what should be done but not how to do it; the good tactician who lacks a grasp of strategy is prone to doing the right thing but at the wrong time. The strategist may be acutely aware of how psychotherapy is proceeding and what directions it ought to take, but be unable to do or say what is necessary to move it in these directions; the tactician may respond brilliantly to his patient on an occasional basis, but be unable to help the patient progress in any systematic fashion toward the goals of the treatment.

The distinction between strategy and tactics in psychotherapy has important implications for theory and research as well as for practice. As discussed next, several different theories of psychotherapy have emerged out of different ways of conceptualizing personality functioning and behavior change. Yet the differences among these theories reside primarily in the strategies they emphasize, that is, in what the treatment aims to accomplish at various points, whereas there is evidence to suggest that the tactics employed by experienced practitioners representing various theories of schools of psychotherapy, that is, what they actually say to their patients, have much in common.

THEORIES OF PSYCHOTHERAPY

Clinicians with different views on the origins of psychological disturbance and on the therapist's role in helping to alleviate it have developed many different theories or schools of psychotherapy. As among the classical philosophers, there has been some historical tendency for each "new" view of psychotherapy to be promulgated as if it constituted a radical departure from all previous views and provided a necessary corrective to errors of the past. In reality, however, even the most seemingly divergent schools of psychotherapy share many common threads in the goals they pursue and the methods they employ.

The following discussion summarizes several prominent theories of psychotherapy and comments on their historical significance. For a more extensive and detailed analysis of systems of psychotherapy than is possible in this brief overview, the reader is referred to contributions by Corsini (1973), Ford and Urban (1963), Harper (1959), Heine (1971), Stein (1961), and Wolberg (1967, Chapters 9–11).

Classical Psychoanalysis: Freud

Classical psychoanalysis, which was the first formal theory of psychotherapy to be elucidated, emerged from Sigmund Freud's efforts to treat patients troubled by anxiety, conversion, and phobic symptoms. Freud's collaboration with Josef Breuer led to the publication of *Studies on Hysteria* (Breuer & Freud, 1893–1895), in which Freud's chapter on psychotherapy is generally regarded as marking the inception of the psychoanalytic method. Here Freud explicated the two key features of his treatment approach: *free association,* which consists of having the patient express whatever thoughts and feelings come into his mind, without exercising any censorship or making any prior judgments as to their relevance, importance, logicality, or propriety; and *interpretation,* a process by which the therapist points out to the patient aspects of his personality and previous experience that influence his behavior without his being aware of them.

Whereas these basic elements of the psychoanalytic method were derived from clinical experience, Freud subsequently elaborated them in terms of his theories of personality development, neurotic symptom formation, and the topography and structure of the mental apparatus. Because he believed that personality was shaped for better or worse by conflicts arising during the early years of life, Freud stressed that the way to resolution of adult problems lay through genetic reconstruction and resolution of the "infantile neurosis." In the treatment these conflicts from the early formative years are reactivated in the patient's relationship to the therapist. By experiencing a regressive "transference neurosis" in his analysis the patient can be helped to relive his infantile neurosis and bring it to a more adaptive resolution.

With regard to symptom formation, Freud attributed neurosis to repressed or warded-off impulses that press for discharge through numerous "derivatives," including neurotic symptoms, dreams, and such "everyday psychopathology" as slips of the tongue and convenient forgetting. In Freud's topographic terms, the psychoanalytic method seeks to bring these unconscious impulses into conscious awareness; in the language of his later structural theory, "Where id was, there shall ego be" (1933, p. 80). To this end derivatives, along with transference phenomena and childhood recollections, are utilized heavily to uncover the early origins of the patient's psychological difficulties and to bring them into his awareness. Current situations and reality factors, however, are prevented as much as possible from intruding on the recognition and analysis of derivatives.

Unfortunately, matters of psychoanalytic technique never received Freud's concentrated attention following the *Studies on Hysteria.* Of considerable value, however, are several papers in which he made specific rcommendations for conducting various aspects of the treatment (Freud, 1904, 1910, 1912, 1913, 1915). For additional reading on classical psychoanalysis, comprehensive texts by Glover (1955), Greenson (1967), Kubie (1950), Menninger and Holzman (1973), Nunberg (1932), and Saul (1973) are recommended.

The Early Dissenters: Jung, Adler, and Rank

Freud's early circle of followers included three who came to disagree with him about the origins of neurosis. Their dissenting views have exerted broad influence on current concepts of psychotherapy, sometimes with and sometimes without adequate appreciation of where these concepts originated.

Jung's Analytic Psychology. Gustav Jung (1911, 1923, 1933) became less interested in early childhood conflicts as the source of neurotic problems than in the challenges to individual personality growth posed by the primordial experience of mankind. In a highly abstract and somewhat mystical fashion, Jung postulated that each person has both a "personal unconscious," which is similar to the unconscious as described by Freud, and a "collective unconscious," which consists of various inborn images or "archetypes" based on the shared experience of the human race. Neurosis, according to Jung, represents a person's struggle to free himself from the interference of these archetypes with his progress toward personality integration and fulfillment of his human potential. In this sense neurosis signified for Jung not so much illness as a striving toward psychological maturity.

The task of the Jungian analyst, as in classical psychoanalysis, is to utilize interpretation to help the patient become aware of his unconscious, but in both its personal and collective aspects. Because of the nature of the collective unconscious, there is a particular focus on the symbolic meaning of dreams, myths, and folklore as a means of bringing an individual into contact with the deposit of the racial past. The therapist's role is conceived as an active effort to guide the patient into a productive relationship with elements of his unconscious and thereby to liberate the creative, growth-promoting forces within his personality. To this end, directed focusing of the interviews rather than free association, and an exchange of ideas at the level of a real relationship between patient and therapist rather than the development of a transference neurosis, characterize the treatment method.

Jung's voluminous writings pay relatively little attention to psychotherapy, and current literature written outside a specific Jungian framework rarely alludes to his contributions in this area. As the preceding capsule of his views should make clear, however, Jung anticipated several central features in subsequent theories of psychotherapy, including the individual's innate potential for positive personality growth and the utility of an active, focused, and realistic patient-therapist relationship. For the interested reader, summaries of Jung's psychology have been published by Ellenberger (1970, Chapter 9), Jacobi (1963), Progoff (1969), and Wheelright (1956).

Adler's Individual Psychology. Alfred Adler (1907, 1924, 1933) believed that the primary source of neurosis lay not in repressed impulses pressing for discharge, but in maladaptive efforts to compensate for feelings of inferiority. Feelings of inferiority develop in all people, says Adler, either in relation to some real or perceived "organ inferiority" or as a result of the early life experience of being relatively small, weak, and helpless. Each individual strives in his own way to overcome his feelings of inferiority and achieve power, and the various attitudes, aspirations, and behavior patterns he employs toward this end, including such "guiding fictions" as a sense of superiority, constitute his "life-style." The more an individual's life-style is bound up with struggles for power, at the expense of "social feelings," the more likely he is to engage in neurotic and maladaptive patterns of behavior.

The focus of Adlerian psychotherapy is on exploring the nature of the patient's life-style and guiding him into more effective ways of functioning, with particular attention to replacing his struggles for power with social interests. Although interpretation is the main therapist tool for this purpose, the subjects selected for interpretation differ markedly from those selected in a Freudian genetic reconstruction or a Jungian elaboration of symbolic meaning. Adler stressed analysis of the patient's current concerns and future goals rather than his past conflicts, and he recommended a pragmatic, problem-solving approach addressed to the patient's actual daily behavior rather than to any highly inferential significance of this behavior. Adlerian therapy can best be characterized as an educational process in which the therapist tries to influence the patient to surrender his neurotic strivings, to form more positive attitudes toward himself and others, and to adopt more effective and socially acceptable patterns of living.

Even more so than Jung, Adler anticipated numerous subsequent developments in psychotherapy for which he rarely receives credit. His emphasis on the patient's characterological style as expressed in current adjustment difficulties became central features of the later neo-Freudian and ego-analytic approaches to psychotherapy, and his preference for an active, problem-solving therapist role is reflected in most directive and counseling approaches to psychotherapy. For an integrated summary of Adler's views on personality development and psychotherapy, the reader is referred to Ellenberger (1970, Chapter 8) and to an excellent book by Ansbacher and Ansbacher (1956).

Rank's Will Therapy. Otto Rank (1929, 1945) concluded from his clinical work that the most important single event influencing personality development is the trauma of birth. According to Rank, the traumatic experience of being born generates in every person a lifelong conflict between forces pushing for *reunification* and forces pushing for *separation*. Reunification means a return to the womb and has implications for a submissive, dependent, and conforming pattern of behavior. Separation means having sufficient *will* to establish one's existence independent of his uterine origins and has implications for an assertive, individualistic, and self-determining life-style. The more fully an individual is able to overcome his birth trauma and develop a will for separation, the less prone he is to neurotic behavior, which represents inadequate development of self-defining and self-directing patterns of thought.

Although the highly abstract and speculative nature of Rank's theorizing about personality development is reminiscent of Jung's mysticism, the treatment approach he developed had much more in common with Adler's pragmatism than with either Freud's or Jung's attention to probing the unconscious. Rank viewed the therapist's role as helping the patient come to regard himself as a worthwhile person capable of directing his own life and making sound decisions about how to behave. Furthermore, he postulated that the treatment relationship provides the primary vehicle for achieving these ends.

Rather than being led through a content-oriented review of his past traumatic experiences, then, the patient in Rankian therapy is encouraged to focus on his current reaction patterns, to strengthen and assert his will in relation to the therapist, and to determine for himself how his strengthened will can best be exercised in the future. As an important aspect of promoting the patient's movement toward separation and individuation, the treatment relationship itself is defined as finite, and a specific time limit is set for its duration.

These recommendations for the conduct of psychotherapy have had a far more significant and lasting impact than the theoretical notions from which Rank derived them. His focus on an essentially nondirective approach in which the patient works toward self-determination has become a central feature of client-centered and humanistic psychotherapies as currently practiced, and his use of a finite treatment relationship to foster individuation is reflected in considerable current interest in short-term psychotherapy (e.g., Bellak & Small, 1965; Phillips & Wiener, 1966; Sifneos, 1972; Wolberg, 1965) and in the effective utilization of time-limited psychotherapy (see Mann, 1973; Muench, 1965). Also of note is the subsequent influence of Rank's approach on the development of the "functional" school of social casework, through the writings of Jessie Taft (1933, 1948), and on psychotherapeutic work with children, through the work of Frederick Allen (1942).

The Neo-Freudians: Horney, Fromm, and Sullivan

Subsequent to the major contributions of Freud and the early dissenters, a distinguished group of clinicians often referred to as "neo-Freudians" took issue with the view that personality evolves from balances struck between basic drives and adaptive strivings within the individual. The neo-Freudians argued instead that man is a social being shaped primarily by his cultural and interpersonal environment, and that personality accordingly evolves from the manner in which each individual learns to adapt to his sociocultural context. In this frame of reference psychological disturbance results from faulty learning and consists of a characterologically maladaptive style of interacting with the environment.

Neo-Freudian psychotherapy employs a free-associational, insight-oriented approach that differs from classical psychoanalysis mainly in the kinds of insights that are emphasized. Although unconscious conflicts are elicited and explored, the focus is less on conflicts between impulses pressing for discharge and efforts to repress these impulses than it is on conflicts between inconsistent ways of attempting to relate to the environment in an anxiety-free and productive manner. Likewise, although the patient-therapist relationship is analyzed extensively, the relationship is used not to foster a transference neurosis from which early experiences can be reconstructed, but to identify and modify maladaptive ways in which the patient currently deals with the people in his life.

Among the neo-Freudians Karen Horney (1937, 1939, 1945) and Erich Fromm (1941, 1947, 1955) stand out for their rich discussions of character types. Horney postulated that childhood experiences of rejection and disapproval produce a "basic anxiety" that motivates efforts to escape from it. These escape efforts lead to the emergence of three kinds of neurotic character types: the *compliant* type, who moves excessively toward others; the *aggressive* type, who moves excessively against others; and the *detached* type, who moves excessively away from others. According to Horney, psychotherapy should concentrate on helping the patient to recognize the ineffectiveness of his characterological style of interacting with people and to alter his patterns of "thinking, feeling, valuing, and acting," so that he can achieve greater "responsibility, inner dependence, spontaneity of feeling, and wholeheartedness."

Fromm stressed in his basic writings the manner in which environmental restrictions, primarily in the form of institutional authority, can suppress and eventually eliminate creative aspects of the self. Not only to retain the security of infantile emotional ties, in the sense emphasized by Rank and Horney, but also to fit himself to the demands of his social, political, and economic environments, the individual may become motivated to escape the dangerous freedom of being himself. Instead of developing into an independent and productive person, then, the individual will cling to irrational authority and relate to his social group through such nonactualizing character styles as the "receptive orientation," the "exploitative orientation," the "hoarding orientation," and the "marketing orientation." Psychotherapy in Fromm's opinion should therefore focus on helping the patient to distinguish between rational and irrational authority and to replace all other characterological orientations with a "productive orientation," which allows a person "to utilize his powers and to realize the potentialities inherent in him."

Harry Stack Sullivan (1953, 1954, 1956), the founder of the "interpersonal" school of psychiatry, is the best known and most influential of the neo-Freudians. His impact derives from the sensitivity reflected in his writings, the systematic detail with which he elaborated his theories of personality structure and development, and the wide range of his attention to clinical problems. Central to Sullivan's approach are the postulates (a) that interpersonal relationships during the developmental years pose a successive series of threats to an individual's security and (b) that people learn from their experience various "security operations" for coping comfortably with the "significant others" in their lives.

Since in Sullivan's view the interpersonal context is the essence of the human condition, the nature of a person's security operations define his character style, and the effectiveness of these operations determines whether or not he encounters psychological problems in living. Psychotherapy then becomes an interpersonal experience in which the therapist, acting as a "participant observer," engages the patient in examining his difficulties in relation to people. The treatment relationship is used to facilitate identifying and correcting the patient's tendencies to misperceive or misinterpret the behavior of others ("parataxic distortions").

In addition to his contributions to theories of personality and psychotherapy, Sullivan innovated the application of psychodynamic concepts to the treatment of schizophrenic patients. A significant body of literature concerning the practice of psychotherapy with schizophrenics, including the work of Frieda Fromm-Reichmann (1950, 1969) and Harold Searles (1965), has emerged within the Sullivanian framework. Also of note was Sullivan's flexibility in such respects as having the patient sit face to face with the therapist, rather than recline on a couch in the classical psychoanalytic fashion, which anticipated the prevailing mode in most current psychotherapies.

Ego-Analytic Approaches

Ego-analytic approaches to psychotherapy evolved gradually within the mainstream of psychoanalysis, independently of any spirit of dissent or intent to establish a new school of thought. From the writings of such theorists as Anna Freud (1936), Heinz Hartmann (1939), Ernst Kris (1950), Rudolph Loewenstein (1953), David Rapaport (1950, 1951, 1953), and Erik Erikson (1950, 1956) emerged a psychoanalytic ego psychology generally considered the most important single development in psychoanalysis from Freud's basic contributions to the present time (see Hofling & Meyers, 1972). Psychoanalytic ego psychology differs from classical psychoanalysis primarily in the emphasis it places on adaptive rather than instinctual strivings in people, in the importance it assigns to environmental influences as well as inner impulses in molding and modifying behavior, and in the attention it devotes to the lifelong cycle of personality development rather than to any crystallization of personality determined by early life experiences.

Ego-analytic psychotherapy, which is also commonly referred to as psychoanalytically oriented or dynamic psychotherapy, employs the exploratory and interpretive procedures of classical psychoanalysis but attempts neither a reconstruction of infantile experiences nor the fostering of a regressive transference neurosis. Rather, the treatment seeks to expand the patient's awareness of and conscious control over whatever intrapsychic, interpersonal, or environmental events are currently creating psychological difficulties for him. In many respects psychodynamic psychotherapy differs from psychoanalysis more in degree—that is, in how intensive the uncovering process is—than in kind, and it also has many links with the neo-Freudian focus on characterological coping styles.

Because the ego-analytic approach incorporates the thinking of many able clinicians, without being tied to the theoretical eccentricities or idiosyncratic terminology of any one systematizer, and because it relates closely to widely employed psychodynamic conceptualizations of psychopathology and personality development, it is among the most commonly applied psychotherapies in current clinical practice. From a long list of books concerned with the theory and methods of dynamic psychotherapy, those by Blanck and Blanck (1974), Chessick (1973), Dewald (1971), Langs (1973, 1974), and Weiner (1975) are especially recommended for further reading.

Client-Centered Therapy

Client-centered therapy, as formulated by Carl Rogers (1942, 1951, 1961), rests on the premise that all people have inborn capacities for purposive, goal-directed behavior and, if free from disadvantageous learning conditions, will develop into kind, friendly, self-accepting, and socialized human beings. In an atmosphere antithetical to personal growth, however, faulty learning can cause people to become hateful, self-centered, ineffective, and antagonistic to others. Therapy should aim to correct such faulty learning by providing the client an opportunity to expand his awareness of and liking for himself.

Central to Rogers' approach was the conviction that a person's behavior can be understood only from his own subjective point of view and can be changed only through his own determination to change. Hence the task of the client-centered therapist is not to offer direction or make interpretations, but to create an accepting, nonthreatening atmosphere in which the client can examine and reconsider his ways of thinking and feeling. By listening in a friendly and empathic manner, reflecting the feeling tone of the client's remarks, and encouraging the client to manage his own affairs, the therapist makes it possible for him to grow through the relationship, to form a more positive view of himself, and to direct himself toward more rewarding and self-actualizing patterns of behavior.

The client-centered approach has had an enormous impact on the field of psychotherapy, far beyond the number of clinicians who specifically employ it. Perhaps most importantly, Rogers' emphasis on the therapist as someone who creates an atmosphere in which the client can seek his own solutions, rather than as someone who suggests solutions through interpretation, directed increased attention to the role of therapist dimensions in psychotherapy. Whereas much had been said previously about *what the therapist should do,* before Rogers little consideration had been given to *how he should be.* Now it has been demonstrated that success in psychotherapy depends in part on the therapist's being able to display certain personal qualities in the treatment relationship, and this advance in knowledge can be directly credited to Rogers' influence.

Rogers also contributed to advancing knowledge in the field by encouraging his colleagues to formulate testable hypotheses about psychotherapy and to conduct research on the validity of these hypotheses. Empirical studies of client-centered therapy constituted the first systematic effort to bring the methods of behavioral science to bear on understanding psychotherapy, and investigations conducted within the client-centered framework account for a large portion of the psychotherapy research literature. Additionally, the example set by client-centered researchers has had a salutary effect on the entire field, stimulating empirical studies within and across many theoretical contexts.

Like psychoanalytic psychotherapy, client-centered therapy has evolved into varying degrees of classicism and revisionism. Rogers himself has modified many of his views over the course of a long and prolific career. Furthermore, just as Freud was followed by a neo-Freudian generation, important contributions to theory and practice in psychotherapy have been made by clinicians who could appropriately be called "neo-Rogerians." For overviews of current thinking on the client-centered approach, the reader is referred to edited volumes by Hart and Tomlinson (1970) and Wexler and Rice (1974).

Humanistic Psychotherapy

Humanistic psychotherapy is in many respects an outgrowth of the client-centered method, although it reflects a humanistic psychology that has in its own right entered the mainstream of approaches to conceptualizing human behavior. As expressed in the writings of Bugental (1965), Buhler (1971), Buhler and Allen (1971), Jourard (1964, 1971), and Maslow (1962), humanistic psychology is concerned above all with the uniqueness and wholeness of each individual person. Humanism is an idiographic psychology, and as such it rejects efforts to group people according to shared personality traits or diagnostic labels. Instead, humanism attends to the process by which an individual comes to experience and enjoy himself "as the sole member of his class." Difficulties in experiencing oneself, inability to find pleasure and fulfillment in one's activities, and failure to make meaningful contact with others are viewed as the basic problems in living for which psychotherapy may be indicated.

Treatment within the humanistic framework is essentially an experiential process in which the patient, through an open relationship with the therapist, increases his awareness of himself and his capacity to relate himself both to other people and to his own needs, talents, and future prospects. As in client-centered therapy, the solutions to the patient's difficulties remain entirely in his hands, and his destiny remains his alone to determine. In addition, however, humanistic therapists may employ various active techniques intended to promote the patient's openness to his experience and his ability to share intimate experiences with others. Of particular note in this regard is having the therapist disclose his own feelings and experiences as a means of encouraging the patient to do likewise (see Jourard, 1971, Chapters 7–9).

Existential Analysis

As exemplified in the writings of Rollo May (1958, 1969), Medard Boss (1963), and Victor Frankl (1965, 1966), existential psychotherapy has its roots less in theories of personality development than in the philosophy of Kierkegaard, Husserl, and Heidegger. Existentially oriented clinicians are concerned not so much with psychological disturbance and its amelioration as with the conditions of man's existence, or his *being in the world*. Because of the nature of the world, especially in modern times when existence seems so precarious, anxiety about survival interferes with finding purpose and meaning in life and discourages people from committing themselves to each other and to productive pursuits. The challenge for man is to exercise his freedom to choose a rewarding way of being and thereby to undertake commitments both to intimate interpersonal relationships and creative endeavors.

The role of the therapist in the existential approach is to provide the patient an encounter in which he can first come into closer contact with what he is experiencing and then create for himself some positive values and aspirations that will give purpose and meaning to his existence. As in humanistic psychotherapy, the therapist's wish to have the patient find his own solutions to life's problems does not restrict him to a passive role in the treatment. Rather, the therapist employs various procedures, including mutual self-revelations, to expand the patient's experiencing of himself.

Gestalt Therapy

Gestalt therapy is the most recent treatment approach to exert a significant impact on the field of psychotherapy and to attract a substantial number of adherents. Introduced by Fritz Perls in 1951 (Perls, Hefferline, & Goodman, 1951), it received little attention in the literature until the more recent appearance of books by Perls (1969), Fagan and Shepherd (1970), and Polster and Polster (1973). The basic tenets of gestalt theory are that man structures his experience as a whole, integrated organism, not in cognitive or affective fragments; that individual experience consists of "gestalts," which are configurations of "figures" (what is being attended to) and "grounds" (what is being ignored or overlooked); and that the individual must have sufficient initiative to close some gestalts and break others up, in order to maintain flexible and adaptive contact with his own needs and with his environment. Inability to close or to shift gestalts produces personality fragmentation, limited awareness of one's experience, and deficiencies in responsibility, authenticity, and self-regulation.

The gestalt therapist seeks to redress such personality limitations by enhancing the individual's capacity to communicate with himself and others. The treatment approach is very active and, in common with Rogerian, humanistic, and existential approaches, it focuses more on experiencing and affective expression than on a cognitive analysis of behavior. Moreso than in these other approaches, however, the gestalt method utilizes a variety of specific and graded exercises in experiencing and self-expression, prescribed by the therapist in a hierarchal fashion, to promote progress toward the goals of the treatment.

Comment

This brief summary of approaches to psychotherapy identifies two basic respects in which they apparently differ. First, some approaches advocate a relatively passive role for the therapist, in which his main task is to interpret or reflect the patient's remarks, whereas other approaches encourage a more active therapist role in which he directs associations, discloses aspects of his own experience, or employs specific training exercises. Second, some approaches regard the therapist's technical procedures as the agent of change in psychotherapy, whereas other approaches stress the atmosphere and the interpersonal relationship provided by the therapist as the major impetus to change.

Both of these dimensions of psychotherapy can be objectively measured and are therefore suitable for attempting to categorize treatment approaches. However, any effort in this direction quickly turns up as many exceptions as neat categories. For example, it is not uncommon for psychoanalytic and psychodynamic approaches to be classified as relatively therapist-passive and technique-oriented methods, and for client-centered and experiential approaches (humanistic, existential, and gestalt) to be classified as relatively therapist-active and relationship-oriented methods. Yet included in the psychoanalytic and psychodynamic framework are Adler's active problem-solving approach, Rank's explicit utilization of the treatment relationship, and Sullivan's emphasis on the therapist's being a participant observer. Included in the client-centered and experiential framework are Rogers' recommendation for relatively passive, nondirective therapist behavior and the gestalt therapist's use of prescribed exercises that constitute a highly specific technical procedure.

Moreover, the active-passive and technique-relationship dimensions themselves generate much ambiguity. In a presumably passive approach such as psychoanalysis, for example, the therapist's interpretations intrude very actively and with considerable impact on the patient's consciousness; in contrast, the unstructured opportunities for personal growth provided in the presumably active experiential approaches constitute a passive, nonintrusive therapist stance. Furthermore, technique-oriented therapists regularly acknowledge that the effectiveness of their procedures depends on the support of an open and trusting patient-therapist relationship, and relationship-oriented therapists devote much attention to the techniques for establishing and sustaining a treatment relationship from which the patient can derive benefit.

In short, then, approaches to psychotherapy begin to converge when attention shifts from their terminology and personality theories to their aims and methods in the treatment. First, all of them are actively concerned with exerting a beneficial influence on the patient's life, whether through interpretations or through providing a growth experience, and all of them rely on both technical procedures and relationship variables to promote progress toward their aims. Second, although interpretive approaches are sometimes viewed as being primarily cognitive in their orientation and experiential approaches as being primarily affective, all approaches seek to bring the patient into more effective contact with both his thoughts and his feelings. Finally, it should be apparent from the previous summary that all approaches, regardless of the language in which they express their goals, seek through psychotherapy to expand the patient's self-awareness, to increase his capacity to understand and control his behavior, and to promote his finding for himself a rewarding and self-fulfilling way of life.

Consistent with these convergences, research suggests that experienced therapists of different theoretical persuasions display many similarities in their treatment tactics, that is, in what they actually say to their patients (Fiedler, 1950; Strupp, 1955a, 1955b, 1958; Wrenn, 1960). This is not to overlook that therapists of different schools may employ mutually exclusive technical procedures, such as the use of a couch by a psychoanalyst and of systematic self-disclosure by a humanistic psychotherapist, neither of which the other would be likely to do. In terms of the verbal messages used to communicate understanding, respect, and a wish to be of help, however, the tactical similarities among skillful and experienced psychotherapists appear to transcend many of their differences in underlying theory.

Finally in this regard it should be noted that, despite occasional partisan claims to the contrary, outcome research to date provides no evidence that any one type of psychotherapy is more effective than another, nor is there any evidence that types of psychotherapy differ in the kinds of personality change they produce (see Luborsky & Spence, 1971). Hence there is no justification for propounding one method of psychotherapy as pure truth and deprecating other methods as ill-conceived. Some early words of Freud (1904) remain apt in this respect: "There are many ways and means of practicing psychotherapy. All that lead to recovery are good" (p. 259).

GENERAL AND SPECIFIC FACTORS PROMOTING CHANGE IN PSYCHOTHERAPY

As the preceding discussion implies, it is generally recognized that behavior change in psychotherapy is promoted by both general and specific factors in the treatment situation (see Strupp, 1970, 1972, 1973). *General factors* refer to aspects of the psychotherapy relationship, whereas *specific factors* refer to technical procedures employed within this relationship. In the actual conduct of psychotherapy, these general (relationship) and specific (technique) factors are intertwined rather than discrete. A helpful psychotherapy relationship comes into being only when the therapist employs adequate procedures for establishing it, and technical procedures promote progress only when they are employed in the context of a good treatment relationship. Nevertheless, distinguishing between the general and specific factors that promote change in psychotherapy provides a useful perspective on divergent lines of psychotherapy research and helps to identify the kinds of activity in which a therapist must learn to engage.

General Factors Promoting Change

The general factors that promote behavior change in psychotherapy comprise four aspects of the treatment relationship, each of which has important implications for effective conduct of the treatment: (a) opportunity for catharsis, (b) expectation of change, (c) attention from the therapist, and (d) reinforcement effects.

Opportunity for Catharsis. It is a common experience for people to feel better on getting worrisome concerns off their chest, and for clearer perspectives on a vexing problem to emerge from talking it out. Psychotherapy, by encouraging the patient to express himself, provides such a cathartic opportunity to find relief from distress and routes to improved problem solving. Prior to formulating his psychoanalytic method, Freud emphasized catharsis as the primary means of alleviating his patients' symptoms. To this end he employed exhortation, insistence, hypnosis, and even pressing with his hand on the patient's forehead as techniques for inducing the patient to unburden himself and thereby find relief: "The patient only gets free from the hysterical symptom by reproducing the pathogenic impressions that caused it and by giving utterance to them with an expression of affect, and thus the therapeutic task consists soley in inducing him to do so" (Breuer & Freud, 1893–1895, p. 283).

Freud soon abandoned the cathartic method in favor of the free-associative and interpretive methods of psychoanalysis, because he found people limited in how extensively they could report their difficulties and benefit just from doing so. Nevertheless, the limitations of catharsis as a total treatment procedure do not negate its potential for contributing to the the helping process in psychotherapy. As testimony to the value of catharsis, Stollak and Guerney (1964) found beneficial introspection to occur in a sample of patients who came regularly for sessions in which they simply talked into a tape recorder, without a therapist's even being in the room (see also Meltzoff & Kornreich, 1970, pp. 288–293). Although these patients would presumably have derived even more benefit from a traditional psychotherapy relationship, in which other aspects of the treatment situation that promote change could have been combined with the opportunity for catharsis, the data indicate that catharsis alone can account for some of the effects of psychotherapy.

Expectation of Change. It is a well-established fact that what people experience as happening can be influenced by what they expect to happen. This phenomenon has had a long history of application in medical practice in the form of *placebo* treatment, which involves the judicious use of nonactive substances or benign procedures accompanied by firm assurances that symptom relief will ensue (see Shapiro, 1971). The potency of placebo treatment is sufficiently well documented for it to have become a standard feature of studies on the effectiveness of psychoactive drugs. In these studies a control group is administered placebo in the same manner as the experimental group is administered the drug being assessed, since only in this way can it be determined whether changes induced by the drug relate to its psychopharmacological properties or merely to expectations of change induced by receiving medication.

In psychotherapy expectation of change comes from several sources, including (a) preconceived notions a patient brings to therapy about the benefits he will derive from it, (b) the professional status of the therapist or his reputation for helping people, (c) information the therapist may provide about the potential of psychotherapy to promote behavior change, (d) the promise of good results implicit in the therapist's recommending a course of treatment and arranging to provide it, and (e) the anticipation of future gains that is fostered by initial gains in the treatment. Regardless of whatever else about psychotherapy proves helpful to him, a patient who benefits from psychotherapy probably owes some part of his improvement to his own hopeful expectations.

Experimental studies of expectancy effects in psychotherapy, which were stimulated primarily by the work of Jerome Frank (1959, 1961; see also Rosenthal & Frank, 1956) and Arnold Goldstein (1960, 1962a, 1962b), appear to document that patients who receive instructions intended to instill high expectancy of gain from psychotherapy are more likely to continue in and benefit from treatment than subjects who receive low-expectancy instructions. However, there is some question whether or not such instructions need to include specific assurances that the patient will soon begin to feel and function better. Research by Heilbrun (1972), Hohen-Saric et al. (1964), and Sloane et al. (1970), for example, suggests that simply preparing the patient with explanations of how psychotherapy works, what his role in it will be, and what he can expect from the therapist contributes as much to subsequent improvement as does combining such explanations with specific assurances.

If confirmed, this finding would indicate that sufficient expectation of change to support effective psychotherapy can be instilled just by recommending, explaining, and arranging to provide the treatment, without having to make promises about its outcome. Because promises of outcome have the disadvantage of exposing the patient to premature discouragement if he fails to progress as rapidly as he was led to expect he would, it would be important to know that no positive benefits are sacrificed by omitting them.

It should also be noted that recent reviews of the research on expectancy effects raise questions about the adequacy of these studies (see Wilkins, 1973). In some studies patient reports have been used as measures of outcome, in some the therapists have been aware of the hypothesis under investigation, and in others expectancy states have been defined after the fact, that is, in terms of their effects rather than the procedures used to instill them. The extent to which research on expectancy effects has been compromised by such possible methodological limitations remains a subject for further investigation.

Attention from the Therapist. Psychotherapy provides a patient an opportunity to meet regularly with another person who listens to what he says, respects his dignity, and conscientiously attempts to understand and be helpful. To be accepted as a person worthy of respect and to receive the undivided attention of a trained professional who is bringing his every skill to bear in one's behalf inevitably contribute to a person's feeling better about himself and about what the future holds for him. Accordingly, attention from the therapist promotes change in psychotherapy partly by enhancing a patient's expectations of change. Beyond whatever expectations it fosters, however, the experience of being accorded dignity, respect, and an unswerving professional effort serves to increase a person's feelings of self-worth and self-confidence and thereby to facilitate his achieving positive behavior change.

The significant role of the therapist's attention to his patient in promoting behavior change was first elaborated by Rogers (1942, 1951) in his previously described formulations of client-centered therapy. Rogers (1974) has recently restated the basic tenets of his approach with a clear emphasis on the importance of the climate the therapist creates:

> It was the gradually formed and tested hypothesis that the individual has within himself vast resources for self-understanding, for altering his self-concept, his attitudes, and his self-directed behavior—and that these resources can be tapped if only a definable climate of facilitative psychological attitudes can be provided [p. 116]

In research stimulated by Rogers' views on the treatment relationship, the therapist's attention to his patient has frequently been translated into measures of *empathy, warmth,* and *genuiness.* Therapist *empathy* is the means by which the therapist conveys to the patient that he is being listened to and understood. It consists of demonstrating sensitivity to the patient's needs, appreciation for the distress he feels, and comprehension of the difficulties that brought him for help. Empathy does not mean being curious or intrusive, nor does it mean being generally intuitive about the motives that influence human behavior. Rather, empathy means commenting accurately on the specific hopes, fears, conflicts, and concerns influencing the patient as a unique individual.

Therapist *warmth* is the means by which the therapist creates an atmosphere in which his patient can feel safe, secure, and respected as a person. It consists of valuing the patient as an individual in his own right, accepting whatever he says or does as worthy of being understood, refraining from passing judgment on his actions or assuming responsibility for his decisions, maintaining a consistently friendly, receptive, and nondominating attitude, and conveying a strong sense of caring and commitment. Being warm does not mean sparing the patient's feelings by avoiding critical examination of features of his behavior that appear self-defeating or incongruent with his talents and aspirations. It means that, in conducting such potentially painful aspects of the treatment, the therapist takes care not to denigrate the patient's worth as a person or his right to lead any kind of life he chooses for himself.

Therapist *genuineness* is the means by which the therapist facilitates his patient's talking in a open, truthful, and nodefensive manner. It consists of engaging the patient in a direct personal encounter in which the therapist is a truthful and authentic person who says only what he believes and does only what is comfortable and natural for him to do. Genuineness does not mean participating with the patient in a mutual sharing of opinions, recollections, and concerns, except in so far as there are specific reasons for doing so. Rather, genuineness means that whatever the therapist chooses to disclose represents a real aspect of himself, and however he chooses to express himself is congruent with his personality style.

As summarized by Swenson (1971), Truax and Carkhuff (1967), and Truax and Mitchell (1971), accumulating research evidence points to a positive relationship between successful outcome in psychotherapy and the extent to which therapist empathy, warmth, and genuineness characterize the treatment relationship. Some concerns have been raised about the adequacy of the scales so far designed to measure these complex qualities of therapist behavior (see Bordin, 1974, pp. 128–131; Chinsky & Rappaport, 1970), and considerable validating research remains to be done in this area. Yet no one currently contributing to the psychotherapy literature seriously questions that a treatment climate of caring, commitment, trust, respect, and understanding contributes to positive behavior change.

Reinforcement Effects. A psychotherapist is constantly engaged in responding to his patient's statements or actions. He may respond by sitting silently and without facial expression. He may respond with some bodily communication, such as smiling or frowning, nodding his head or shaking it from side to side, and leaning forward in his chair toward the patient or sitting back in it away from him. He may respond with brief utterances intended to help the patient continue talking, such as "Mm-hmm," "Uh-huh," "I see," "Go on," or "And then?" Or he may respond with substantive comments or questions addressed to what the patient has been saying or doing. All these responses, by virtue of their timing and the feeling tone they convey, influence patient behavior through reinforcement effects.

With respect to timing, first of all, active responsiveness of any kind suggests that what the patient is saying at the moment is of interest to the therapist and of some importance, whereas passive responsiveness, that is, not saying or doing anything, conveys disinterest and unimportance. Accordingly, what the therapist responds to actively tends to be discussed and thought about further by the patient, thereby increasing the likelihood of related behavior change, whereas what he ignores tends to receive reduced attention from the patient and not to become involved in behavior change.

Regarding feeling tone, second, a therapist cannot avoid having his responses convey positive or negative attitudes, no matter how noncommittal he intends them to be, and thereby positively or negatively reinforce aspects of his patient's behavior. In positive terms, for example, "I see" can communicate "You're absolutely right"; "Mm-hmm" can mean "I approve"; and "Go on" may say "I really care." By virtue of the reinforcement effects they create, such messages participate in behavior change by influencing what the patient chooses to talk about and which aspects of himself he considers modifying.

Research on the reinforcing effects of therapist behavior developed from some innovative work by Greenspoon (1955) on verbal conditioning. In Greenspoon's initial study subjects were asked to say all the words they could think of, and the experimenter responded with "Mm-hmm" whenever a plural noun was verbalized. Over time subjects were found gradually to increase the frequency with which they gave plural nouns. Subsequent studies have demonstrated that many features of what people say and how they say it can similarly be influenced by verbal reinforcers.

In an actual interview situation, for example, Williams and Blanton (1968) found that subjects who received verbal reinforcement for statements expressing feeling made an increasing percentage of feeling statements in later interviews, whereas subjects who received reinforcement for statements without feeling content expressed feelings with decreasing frequency. Similarly, verbal reinforcement of statements containing positive references to oneself can increase the rate with which positive self-references are made (Ince, 1969). Additional research on verbal conditioning is reviewed by Greenspoon (1962), Kanfer (1968), Krasner (1958), Salzinger (1959), and Williams (1964), and studies relating such reinforcement effects to behavior in psychotherapy interviews are summarized by Krasner (1962, 1965), Matarazzo and Wiens (1972), and Matarazzo et al. (1965, 1968).

The Complementarity of General and Specific Factors Promoting Change

The preceding discussion of factors in the psychotherapy relationship that can promote behavior change identifies the kind of atmosphere therapists should seek to create: an atmosphere in which the patient feels safe and secure, expresses himself freely and openly, believes he is respected and understood, and anticipates deriving some benefit from the treatment procedures. As noted on page 355, however, the beneficial properties of such an atmosphere depend for their existence on the therapist's skill in blending the ingredients of a good treatment relationship. Once established, an atmosphere conducive to change also supports various technical procedures that promote faster and fuller progress than reliance on the relationship alone.

Thus the general and specific factors promoting change in psychotherapy are without question complementary. Relationship factors in psychotherapy owe their effectiveness to the skill of the therapist in establishing and sustaining them, and only when a sound treatment relationship is augmented by techniques for promoting the patient's understanding and control of his behavior does psychotherapy progress maximally toward its goals.

The complementarity of general and specific factors promoting change contradicts two notions about the treatment relationship in psychotherapy that occasionally appear in the literature. First, it is sometimes maintained that, since a human relationship is the essence of psychotherapy, anyone with mature interpersonal skills who wants to help someone else can do so as effectively as a trained professional. Second, it is sometimes argued that effective use of catharsis, expectancy, therapist attention, and reinforcement is sufficient to accomplish all the possible ends of psychotherapy, independently of the specific content of what the patient talks about or the therapist says in response.

Regarding the human relationship, it is tempting to conclude that, if behavior change can be promoted just by listening to someone talk, encouraging him to expect change, treating him with empathy, warmth, and genuineness, and reinforcing the positive things he says and does, then anyone who is a decent, caring, sensitive person can function well as a psychotherapist without professional education and training. But what are the best means of helping someone talk freely about himself? How should the therapist act so as to foster expectation of change? When should the therapist make some special effort to display empathy, when should he attempt to convey warmth, and when should he emphasize his genuineness? How can empathy, warmth, and genuineness be most clearly expressed? What items in the patient's comments or actions should be reinforced, and what are the most effective means of reinforcing them?

It is the professional clinician's training and experience in psychotherapy that provide him answers to these questions, that teach him how to translate his interpersonal skills into specific words and deeds that are timed, phrased, and modulated so as to foster a helpful treatment relationship. Research findings in this regard confirm that the amount of empathy, warmth, and genuineness therapists are capable of expressing to their patients is directly related to the amount of training and experience they have had (Beery, 1970; Perlman, 1973).

Additionally, numerous studies comparing relatively experienced and inexperienced therapists indicate that experienced therapists have fewer dropouts among the patients they take into treatment (Baum et al., 1966; McNair et al., 1963), help their patients achieve more personality change (Barrett-Lennard, 1962), and bring more of their patients to a successful termination point (Myers & Auld, 1955). Only in exceptional circumstances is an untrained individual likely to establish and sustain a treatment relationship in which the general factors promoting change are brought to bear as effectively as in a relationship conducted by a professional therapist with experience and training in facilitating behavior change.

As for the effects of the treatment relationship, the documented potential of catharsis, expectancy, therapist attention, and reinforcement to foster behavior change has tempted some clinicians to conclude that these relationship factors can produce all the possible and necessary changes in psychotherapy. However, even though a good working relationship is essential to progress in psychotherapy, the extent and durability of any improvement a patient makes is limited unless he has acquired some understanding of the problems that brought him for help and of the basis on which he may have resolved them.

The importance of the patient's having an opportunity to profit not only from generally beneficial aspects of the treatment relationship but also from specific information provided to him by the therapist about his problems is endorsed by most clinicians, including many who have been influential primarily for their attention to relationship factors. Rogers (1974), for example, notes: "I had learned through hard and frustrating experiences that simply to listen understandingly to a client and *to attempt to convey that understanding* [italics added] were potent forces for individual therapeutic change" (p. 116). Frank (1971) includes among the features of the psychotherapy situation that contribute to its success the "provision of new information concerning the nature and sources of the patient's problems and possible alternative ways of dealing with them" (p. 356).

Schofield (1964, 1970), who argues that some people with psychological concerns can benefit merely from the opportunity for a sympathetic friendship, nevertheless urges trained psychotherapists not to devote their professional time to providing such friendships, because of ''the large number of persons with emotional or psychological disorders who require specific treatment over and above the meliorating effects of a relationship'' (1970, p. 218). And even in the context of behavior modification, which places considerable emphasis on reinforcement procedures for effecting behavior change, recent work emphasizes that cognitive mediation of these changes increases the patient's future capacity to think through and regulate his own behavior (see Goldfried & Merbaum, 1973).

Thus there is broad consensus that effective psychotherapy requires the therapist to be technically skilled both in nurturing a helpful treatment relationship and in communicating useful information to the patient about himself. If it is assumed that the therapist comprehends the meaning of his patient's behavior and has a treatment strategy in mind, every tactical decision he makes about precisely when to share his understanding and how to implement his strategy will call on his technical skill. Although it is conceivable that a therapist with limited skill might by hunch or happenstance say or do just the right thing at the right time to sustain a treatment relationship and expand his patient's self-awareness, there is little likelihood of his doing so on any but an occasional or irregular basis. However, the greater the technical skill a therapist has acquired from his training and experience, the more frequently and systematically he is likely to respond to his patient in ways that expand the patient's self-knowledge and sustain the treatment relationship.

Specific Factors Promoting Change

The specific factors promoting change in psychotherapy comprise technical procedures employed by the therapist to engage and sustain the patient's involved participation in the treatment and to increase his ability to understand and control his behavior. The technical procedures used in all forms of psychotherapy derive mainly from the two cornerstones of Freud's psychoanalytic method, free association and interpretation.

With respect to free association, psychotherapy can promote behavior change only if the therapist can induce his patient to express himself. Unless the patient reveals his thoughts and feelings, there is little basis from which the therapist can gain an understanding of the problems he is trying to help resolve. To generate adequate information with which to work, the therapist must command a repertoire of procedures for motivating his patient to talk, for aiding him to recall and report experiences both close to and remote from his prior awareness, and for helping him continue to express himself even when it becomes painful or embarrassing for him to do so. The more skillful the therapist's techniques in this regard, the more information will become available for pursuing the goals of the treatment.

With respect to interpretation, the effectiveness of psychotherapy depends on how well the therapist can combine his skills in eliciting information from his patient with skills in formulating useful responses to this information, especially responses that expand the patient's self-awareness. This is not to suggest that every response of the therapist constitutes an interpretation, even though such a view is occasionally advanced in the literature. Although every therapist response has the potential for influencing how a patient thinks and feels, interpretations differ from four other kinds of intervention in the nature of the impact they are likely to have. Hence it is helpful to distinguish among the following five kinds of therapist intervention:

1. *Questions.* Direct questioning ("What kind of person is your father?" "How do you feel about that?" "What happened next?") serves to elicit information and to help a patient continue talking. Although questions focus the patient's attention on certain subjects, they communicate little new information to him and thus have minimal impact on his progress in the treatment.

2. *Clarifications.* Clarifications convey the possible significance of certain subjects by directing the patient's further attention to them ("Perhaps you could go over that experience again and fill in some more of the details") or by recapitulating his remarks ("If I follow you correctly, you think that your feeling uncomfortable around women has to do with sexual fantasies you have"). Although helpful by virtue of the emphasis they create, clarifications go little further than questions in presenting the patient with new ideas or possibilities about himself.

3. *Exclamations.* Exclamations include various noncommittal therapist utterances intended to facilitate the patient's talking, such as "Mm-hmm" or "I see." As noted previously, such exclamations can exert potent reinforcement effects on what a patient chooses to think or talk about, hence on the areas in which his attitudes and behavior are likely to undergo change. Like questions and clarifications, however, they do not provide the patient substantive information or specifically influence the content of his self-reflections.

4. *Confrontations.* Confrontations are statements that call the patient's attention to factual aspects of his behavior that have escaped his notice but can readily be made apparent to him. Confrontations may be addressed to what the patient is saying ("You've described your hus-

band physically, but you haven't said anything about what he's like as a person"); or to what he is doing ("You've been drumming your fingers on the desk for the last 5 minutes or so, since you began talking about your boss"); or to his recollections ("The feelings you just described as having toward your father are the same kind of feelings you've been having about me"). In contrast to questions, clarifications, and exclamations, confrontations *do* present the patient with information beyond what he is already fully aware of. Unlike interpretations, however, they refer to obvious facts rather than to hypotheses or alternatives, and their accuracy requires no documentation.

5. *Interpretations.* Interpretations suggest some previously unrecognized meaning of or connection between a patient's thoughts, feelings, and actions. Although interpretations may prove congruent with a patient's experiencing of himself, and hopefully do, they are never obvious facts requiring no further documentation. Rather, they constitute possibilities or alternative hypotheses for exploration, and they should accordingly be phrased in the language of conjecture and probability ("Could it be that your disinterest in studying relates to some reluctance you have to graduate and complete your career as a student?"; "From what we've learned, it seems likely that your dissatisfaction with yourself has little to do with what you're like as a person, but has to do with an image you've carried around since childhood of being bad and unworthy").

What is unique about interpretations, then, is that they communicate new self-knowledge to the patient that he can use to restructure his ways of looking at and feeling about himself, and from which he can identify more rewarding and self-fulfilling ways of behaving. Questions, clarification, exclamations, and confrontations contribute to the interpretive process by helping the patient talk and by preparing him in gradual stages to understand and consider interpretations when they are finally offered. As just noted, however, these other interventions lack the impact of interpretations because they do not provide the patient new information about himself.

Research by Garduk and Haggard (1972) lends empirical support to this distinction between interpretations and other interventions. Analyzing the content of psychotherapy interviews, Garduk and Haggard found that patients spend more time thinking about interpretive than noninterpretive statements, apparently as a function of the greater impact they have, and give more indications of understanding and insight (e.g., "I see what you mean"; "I never realized that about myself before, but it's clear to me now") in response to interpretations than in response to other kinds of therapist response.

THE COURSE OF PSYCHOTHERAPY[1]

Psychotherapy proceeds through three continuous but nevertheless distinct phases. The *initial* phase of the treatment consists of evaluating a patient who has come for help, assessing the appropriateness of psychotherapy to meet his needs, and arranging an appropriate contract for the conduct of the treatment. The *middle* phase, which is usually by far the longest part of the treatment, involves the communication of understanding through interpretation and the resolution of such phenomena of the psychotherapy process as resistance, transference, and countertransference. The *final* phase of psychotherapy is devoted to consolidating the patient's gains in the treatment and arranging for termination of the treatment contract. An overview of these three phases of psychotherapy summarizes the typical course of the treatment and provides some basic guidelines for the therapist's activity in conducting it.

The Initial Phase: Evaluation, Assessment, and the Treatment Contract

Psychotherapy begins with a series of interviews in which the therapist accomplishes three tasks. First, he evaluates the patient's personality functioning and the nature of the problems for which he has sought help. Second, he assesses the patient's capability for participating in and benefiting from psychotherapy. Third, he arranges a treatment contract in which patient and therapist agree to the means and objectives of their ensuing work together. Although evaluation, assessment, and the formation of a treatment contract involve many of the same kinds of information about the patient, they direct the therapist's attention to separate sets of issues.

Evaluating the Patient. Adequate evaluation of the patient consists of ascertaining the nature and background of the patient's presenting problem and arriving at some understanding of him as a person, including his characterological style of coping with his experience, his attitudes toward the important people in his life, and the developmental events that have most significantly influenced him. This evaluation should yield *clinical* and *dynamic* working formulations of the patient and his needs. The clinical formulation denotes the patient's primary symptoms (e.g., anxiety reaction), his characterological style (e.g., passive-aggressive personality), and

---

[1]This brief outline of the course of psychotherapy is drawn from the author's recent book, *Principles of Psychotherapy* (Weiner, 1975). For elaboration of the outline, including references to relevant research and detailed guidelines for the conduct of psychotherapy, the reader is referred to the full-length text.

the extent of his personality resources and limitations. The dynamic formulation identifies the major sources of conflict and concern that appear to be causing the patient problems in living or dissatisfaction with himself.

Methods of obtaining such information from a person who seeks psychotherapy are elaborated in the previous five chapters of this book and need not be considered further here. However, it should be stressed that preliminary diagnostic information is *essential* to responsible planning in psychotherapy. Psychotherapy is but one among many potentially psychotherapeutic treatment methods; it embraces various different approaches, and each of these approaches can in turn be tailored to the particular problems and concerns of the individual patient.

Hence there is no justification for assuming equipotentiality among people seeking help for psychological difficulties. Some are served best by treatment approaches other than psychotherapy, some are suitable for primarily uncovering and others for primarily supportive psychotherapy, and, whatever approach is employed, the individual patient benefits most if the treatment he receives is focused on the particular issues underlying his need for help. Adequate selection among these alternatives is possible only in the presence of sufficient diagnostic information to guide treatment planning.

The necessity of a working formulation to guide differential treatment planning does not mean that a detailed diagnostic case study must be made prior to establishing a treatment contract. Indeed, there may be some disadvantage in pursuing an extensive case history in the initial phase of treatment. Acting as a diagnostician can cast the therapist in the role of someone who is more interested in obtaining information than in understanding it, and pressing for detailed information may limit the spontaneity with which the information can emerge in subsequent psychotherapy. What is needed initially is just enough information to support tentative formulations from which the appropriateness of psychotherapy can be adequately assessed.

Assessing the Appropriateness of Psychotherapy. Assessing the appropriateness of psychotherapy involves determining whether a person who appears in need of psychological help is capable of participating in and benefiting from this form of treatment. Considerable attention has been devoted in the literature to identifying characteristics of the so-called "good candidate" for psychotherapy. However, current research indicates that successful outcomes in psychotherapy depend less on the characteristics of the patient than on the way in which the therapist conducts the treatment, particularly with respect to how genuinely he can feel respect for the patient and how fully he can empathize with his thoughts and feelings. The responsible clinician should avoid selecting patients to fit a particular treatment approach and should concentrate instead on selecting a treatment approach geared to the needs of the particular patient.

Nevertheless, as I have elaborated elsewhere (Weiner, 1975, Chapter 2), available data suggest that at least three patient characteristics generally increase the likelihood of being able to participate in and benefit from psychotherapy. First, the patient should be motivated to receive psychotherapy and have some expectation that it will be helpful to him. Motivation for psychotherapy consists of sufficient felt distress about his problems to induce the patient to persevere in the treatment even when the work of the therapy becomes difficult or distressing for him. Regarding expectation, it has already been noted that a patient's belief in the potential of the treatment to benefit him constitutes a general factor promoting favorable outcome in psychotherapy.

Second, despite the level of his felt distress, the patient should demonstrate reasonably well-integrated personality functioning. Generally speaking, the more consistently a person has been able to engage in goal-directed behavior and the more successfully he has met previous life challenges, the better his prospects are for persevering and progressing in psychotherapy.

Third, the patient should have some capacity to express and reflect on his experiences. As a verbal treatment method that revolves around what the patient says, psychotherapy has little potential for benefiting people who are unwilling or unable to talk about themselves. In this regard, it is sometimes suggested that working-class and disadvantaged minority-group patients are poor candidates for psychotherapy because they are not oriented toward verbal self-expression. However, there is good reason to wonder whether many negative outcomes with such patients are due to incapacity or reluctance on their part to participate in verbal psychotherapy, or reflect instead the inability of many advantaged, middle-class therapists to communicate effectively with them. Accumulating research points toward the second of these alternatives. Specifically, these studies suggest that verbal psychotherapy can be highly successful with working-class and minority-group patients if the therapist is able to grasp the sociocultural context of their problems and convey empathy and respect to them (see Fisher & Cohen, 1972; Gould, 1967; Lerner & Fiske, 1973; Lorion, 1973; Minuchin et al., 1967).

Arranging the Treatment Contract. When the therapist concludes from this evaluation and assessment that psychotherapy is indicated and appropriate, his next task is to arrange an explicit treatment contract with the patient. The first step in arranging this contract is obtaining the patient's agreement to undertake psychotherapy. To provide a basis for such agreement, the therapist needs to summarize his impressions of the patient's difficulties, specifically recommend psychotherapy as a means of attempting to ameliorate these difficulties, and explain briefly how psychotherapy works to accomplish its aims.

No assumptions should be made about what the patient already wants or knows in these respects. To begin psychotherapy without inviting the patient to accept or reject a specific recommendation for treatment is an affront to his dignity, no matter how obvious his wishes in the matter seem to be. To ask him to decide about undertaking psychotherapy without first providing him some explanation of the treatment process may deny him the opportunity to give his informed consent, even if he has appeared to be psychologically sophisticated. In either case the therapist risks conveying a lack of respect that may detract from the effectiveness of the treatment relationship.

Following agreement to undertake psychotherapy, the second step in formulating a treatment contract is to discuss the goals of the therapy and the procedures that will be employed in pursuing them. Although the treatment goals usually have become apparent during the evaluation of the patient's reasons for seeking help, the treatment contract should include an explicit review of the objectives of the treatment. Such an explicit listing of objectives, whether they consist of symptom relief, resolution of life problems, or modification of personality characteristics, serves better than any presumed goals to guide the focus of the treatment and help monitor its progress.

As for the procedures to be employed, the patient should be informed about what his role and the role of the therapist will be in the treatment sessions. Although the kinds of information given in this regard may vary with the particular treatment approach to be used, by and large some relatively brief indication of the patient's primary responsibility for expressing himself and the therapist's primary responsibility for communicating understanding suffice: "Your job will be to talk about yourself as freely as you can, and my job will be to listen, to help you talk, and to help you learn more about yourself from what you're able to say."

The third step in formulating a treatment contract consists of making specific arrangements for the time, place, and fee for sessions, and the frequency with which they will be held. The elements of advantageous planning in these respects are beyond the scope of this chapter and are discussed in the psychotherapy textbooks recommended on page 349. However, given the importance noted above of avoiding assumptions in the treatment contract, it can be emphasized that no feature of the specific arrangements for psychotherapy should either be legislated or left to chance. Rather, the therapist should complete arrangements for the treatment through a series of recommendations the patient fully understands and can accept, reject, or counter with an alternative suggestion (e.g., "Could I come at one o'clock rather than two, so I could make it part of my lunch hour?").

The Middle Phase: Interpretation, Resistance, Transference, and Countertransference

The middle phase of psychotherapy involves the major work of the treatment, namely, the effort to expand the patient's ability to understand and control his behavior. During the evaluation interviews the general factors promoting change in psychotherapy, especially those deriving from the treatment relationship, may already have increased the patient's sense of well-being and perhaps even relieved some of his symptoms. However, it is not until the patient has formally agreed to a treatment contract that the therapist has the right to proceed with various technical procedures for the communication of understanding, and it is at this point that the middle phase of treatment begins.

As indicated in the preceding section, the major technique for the communication of understanding in psychotherapy is *interpretation*. The impact of the therapist's interpretive stance invariably produces periods of *resistance* by the patient, which consist of intercurrent interferences with the communication process and which must be relieved or circumvented if the treatment is to progress. Additionally, the communication process is complicated by the intrusion of irrational feelings and attitudes the patient and therapist form toward one another, called *transference* and *countertransference,* and these aspects of the treatment relationship must also be resolved in order for therapy to reach a successful conclusion.

Interpretation. As already defined, interpretations are statements that bring to a patient's attention aspects of himself and his behavior that he has not previously been aware of. To make effective use of interpretation, the therapist needs to decide *what* to interpret, *when* to interpret it, and *how* best to construct the interpretive sequence.

Regarding decisions about what to interpret, interpretations should be selectively addressed to features of the patient's thoughts, feelings, or actions that seem distressing to him or that reflect distorted, unrealistic, inconsistent, or ineffective means of coping with his experience. Rather than being spread in shotgun fashion over every facet of a patient's behavior, in other words, interpretations should be reserved for what appears to be causing him trouble in his life.

In addition to being selectively focused on content related to the patient's difficulties, interpretations should suggest connections or relationships close to his awareness, so that he can sense their plausibility. Interpretations addressed to aspects of the patient's thoughts, feelings, and actions of which he is not even remotely aware are more likely to create dissonance than to provide a logical next step in the self-exploratory process. Accordingly, a sound general principle of psychotherapy is to interpret near the surface of the patient's awareness. As a corollary principle, deeply unconscious concerns should not be interpreted until the uncovering effects of the treatment have brought them close to conscious awareness.

Knowing when to offer interpretations is a matter of good *timing* and proper *dosage*. The best time for a patient to receive an interpretation is when he is approaching awareness of the particular connection or explanation it suggests and when he seems both open to new ideas and enthusiastic about the treatment process. It the patient does not appear to be in a receptive frame of mind, then interpretations should be reserved for another time, except for interpretations addressed specifically to his inability or unwillingness to come to grips with some new information about himself. Additionally, the therapist should offer interpretations only when he is reasonably sure they are accurate and can be documented in reference to matters previously discussed in the therapy. Interpretations that lack congruence with a patient's experiencing of himself and cannot be supported with evidence from prior interviews add little to the patient's self-knowledge and give him cause to question the therapist's empathic capacity.

Proper dosage consists of offering interpretations only as frequently as the patient is able to think them through. Because they provide new information, interpretations require some reflection on the patient's part, and bombarding him with interpretations more rapidly than he can integrate them can create an information overload. It is important in this regard not to "save" interpretations for the end of a session, as a culmination of the interview, since the patient is then deprived of an adequate opportunity to explore with the therapist either the basis of the interpretation or its implications for his behavior.

Constructing an interpretive sequence involves using a graded series of interventions to pave the way for each interpretation to be made. For example, the therapist might begin an interpretive sequence with a clarification ("As I hear you, then, you found yourself saying something insulting when you really wanted to become more friendly"); continue with a confrontation ("We've seen several times now when you were on the verge of getting closer to someone and then spoiled things for yourself by saying or doing something offensive''); and conclude with an interpretation (''It's as if you have some underlying fear of getting close to others, so that you have to prevent it from happening'').

This example illustrates several characteristic features of the interpretive process. The sequence moves with deliberation, sticking close to the data and allowing the patient opportunities along the way to demur or ask about the nature of the evidence. The conclusion of the sequence is expressed conjecturally (''It's as if . . . ''), which is appropriate to the fact that interpretations are no more than alternative hypotheses until the patient confirms them. And the interpretation itself, if accepted, can be used as a confrontation (''We've learned that you have some underlying fears of getting close to people'') in a subsequent interpretive sequence that takes the exploratory process one step further, as to an interpretation concerning the origin of the patient's fears of personal intimacy. The dramatic revelation that cuts immediately to the nub of the patient's problems, eliminates his neurosis, and earns his undying gratitude exists only in fictionalized versions of uncovering psychotherapy. In reality, this treatment method is a painstaking process in which learning derives from the gradual accrual of new information and progress is measured in hard-won increments of self-understanding.

Resistance. Resistance consists of a temporary inability or unwillingness on the part of the patient to adhere to the terms of the treatment contract. As such, resistance originates in four kinds of motivation that run counter to the patient's conscious wish to participate in and benefit from psychotherapy.

First, a patient may be reluctant to give up his present life patterns, no matter how much difficulty they are causing him, or he may become uneasy about accommodating to the new life patterns that are emerging out of the therapy, no matter how potentially rewarding they promise to be. In these circumstances *resistance to change* is likely to develop.

Second, a patient may have preferred styles of coping with cognitive and affective experience that oppose the demands of psychotherapy for integrated coping with both kinds of experience. In this situation a *characterological resistance* to the treatment process may become manifest.

Third, because psychotherapy inevitably confronts people with aspects of themselves and their experiences that may be painful, depressing, or embarrassing for them to think or talk about, it produces in all patients periods of *resistance to content.*

Fourth, virtually all patients develop thoughts and feelings about their therapist that at times command more of their attention in the treatment sessions than the problems for which they are seeking help. At these times *transference resistance* is being expressed.

Whatever its origins, resistance leads to certain characteristic treatment behaviors from which the therapist can identify its presence. A resisting patient may reduce the amount of time he spends in psychotherapy by skipping, canceling, or coming late for his sessions. He may limit the amount and range of his conversation in the sessions by falling silent, by concentrating on certain aspects of his experience (such as past events) and ignoring others (such as what is happening currently), or by engaging in superficial and mundane conversation that has little to do with his problems. At other times, resistance may be expressed through efforts to ward off the impact of psychotherapy. In these instances the patient may seek to make the therapist more of a personal friend than a helping professional, or he may take some precipitous action as a replacement for discussing alternative possibilities with the therapist, or he may develop a "flight into health," which consists of a sudden and unjustified feeling that all is well and psychotherapy is no longer needed.

Although these patterns of resistance interfere with communication in psychotherapy and may lead to premature termination of the treatment relationship, resistance behavior can also yield valuable information about the patient's personality style and the sources of his anxiety. By addressing timely interpretations to the circumstances that elicit resistance and the manner in which it is expressed, the therapist can both minimize the interference it causes and help the patient learn more about himself.

Transference. The psychotherapy relationship includes three concurrent levels of interaction between patient and therapist. First, there is a *real* relationship between them, which consists of the patient's factual knowledge about his therapist, including such matters as his or her sex, approximate age, overt physical characteristics, and manner of dress; of practical discussions concerning such matters as a necessary change in appointment time; and of exchanging such social amenities as "Hello," "Goodbye," and "Merry Christmas."

Second, there is a *working alliance* between them, which consists of their commitments to the treatment contract and to the roles prescribed by it. Because the working alliance is conceived and implemented on a realistic basis, it may appear to constitute part of the real relationship between patient and therapist. However, by virtue of the asymmetric interpretive relationship it creates, in which the patient is to express himself without restraint and the therapist is to listen and comment, the working alliance differs sharply from the kinds of interpersonal relationships people usually establish in real life, outside of an arrangement for psychotherapy.

Third, patients in psychotherapy develop a *transference relationship* to their therapist, which consists of positive or negative feelings and attitudes originally held toward other people in their life and now transferred without justification in reality to the person of the therapist. When transference feelings and attitudes arise, they may be expressed either in veiled or direct form. In relatively veiled form, transference may appear in such behavior as the patient's sitting closer to or farther away from the therapist during sessions, asking for more frequent and longer interviews or to reduce the amount of contact with the therapist, or trying to impress the therapist with his personal attributes or to convey disdain for what the therapist may think of him.

Expressed more directly, transference may take the form of favorable or unfavorable comments about the therapist's profession ("Some of my friends have been telling me that psychotherapy didn't help them a bit"), about his trappings ("I wish your office wasn't so hard to get to"), or about his person ("That's a handsome tie you're wearing"). Even more directly, a patient may specifically express such feelings toward the therapist as love, hate, admiration, anger, envy, or sexual attraction. Although these feelings may have some elements of reality in them, as transference they have more to do with how the patient has felt or feels about others than with any cause the therapist has given him to feel that way about him.

Whenever a patient is experiencing or expressing transference feelings, his attention is being diverted from the problems in his life for which he has sought help. Hence transference always constitutes a resistance to the treatment process. Like resistance, then, transference both interferes with communication in psychotherapy and provides a source of important information about the patient, particularly with respect to his interpersonal attitudes and his characteristic styles of expressing these attitudes. Whether transference phenomena are used to reconstruct earlier experiences or to identify maladaptive patterns of coping with current experience, they facilitate progress toward increased self-understanding when they are correctly identified and interpreted.

The interpretation of transference begins with helping the patient recognize that the feelings and attitudes he experiences toward the therapist are not justified in reality and must reflect interpersonal dispositions he has brought with him into the treatment situation. The patient can then draw on his transference experience in relation to the therapist to trace these feelings and attitudes to their true origins, whether in anger toward a rejecting mother, generalized resentment of authority figures, or whatever. In this way he can gain increased understanding and control over the extent to which his previous experiences exert a maladaptive influence on his current interpersonal behavior.

Countertransference. Therapists are also subject to inappropriate personal reactions in the treatment relationship, known as countertransference. Countertransference can result either from generalized attitudes the therapist has toward certain kinds of people (e.g., enormous admiration for creative artists or limited patience with passive-aggressive individuals) or from discussions in the treatment that touch on areas in which the therapist himself has unresolved conflicts. However they originate, inappropriate reactions of the therapist to his patient can undermine the working alliance if their manifestations are not promptly recognized and controlled.

The manifestations of countertransference, like those of transference, may be more or less direct. In overt countertransference the therapist openly experiences positive or negative feelings toward his patient that cannot be justified in light of the treatment contract. The treatment contract calls on the therapist to respect the patient, not to judge him, and to understand his behavior, not react to it. This means, for example, that distaste for a patient who brutalizes his children or anger in response to a patient who is being insulting, although justifiable in a real interpersonal context, are inappropriate to the treatment situation and constitute countertransference. The therapist's task is to explore with the patient the origins and self-defeating consequences of such brutal or insulting behavior, not to respond in terms of his personal feelings about it.

The therapist's personal feelings may at times sensitize him to implications of a patient's behavior and even prove useful to mention ("You're making me angry, and we have to wonder why you're apparently trying to provoke me"). However, personal values and sensitivities cannot be allowed to direct the therapist away from his primary responsibility, which is meeting the patient's needs, not seeing to his own.

In its less overt forms countertransference reactions can subtly influence a therapist's behavior without his immediately being aware of them. The therapist may find himself looking forward eagerly to a patient's next visit—or "forget" to inform the patient of a necessary cancelation. He may become inattentive or drowsy in sessions with a patient, or allow the sessions to run overtime. He may attack the patient with an overzealous series of anxiety-provoking interpretations or spare his feelings by withholding appropriate interpretations. He may encounter a patient in his own dreams and fantasies, in either a pleasant or unpleasant context. These and similar phenomena identify counter-transference reactions, positive or negative as their content suggests. When present, they should alert the therapist to the possibility that his conduct of the treatment is being inappropriately influenced by his personal needs and should be modified accordingly.

The Final Phase: Termination

As the interpretive process continues, the patient in psychotherapy gradually increases his knowledge of himself and his behavior. However, as implied early in this chapter, the insight produced by interpretation does not automatically unlock an individual's self-actualizing potential and effect positive behavior change. A patient's initial comprehension of previously unrecognized aspects of himself is only a first step in the process of behavior change. To be effective, interpretations must be thoroughly *worked through,* which means that they must be reassessed in a variety of contexts for the consistency with which they can account for perplexing or maladaptive thoughts, feelings, and actions.

Not until an interpretation has been extensively cross-validated in recurrent experiences is a patient ready to begin modifying his behavior in light of it. "If my feeling that other people are better than I am is *really* something I've been carrying around from childhood and has no basis in what I'm like as an adult," the patient may come to say to himself, "it should be safe for me at least to experiment with being more assertive." When such a point is reached, behavior change starts to follow in the wake of enhanced self-understanding, tentatively at first but with gradually increasing regularity and decreasing self-consciousness, until the desired behavior change becomes a natural and integrated feature of the person's life-style.

When a patient has made substantial progress toward integrating desired behavior change, psychotherapy enters its final phase. As also mentioned earlier, "substantial progress" does not necessarily mean that all the objectives with which the treatment began have been fully and permanently realized. Rather, termination can appropriately be considered when it seems to both the patient and the therapist that a satisfactory amount of progress has been made, and that a point of diminishing returns has been reached that would make further gains more costly in time and effort than appears justified.

Once a patient has made substantial progress toward the goals of the treatment and reached a point of diminishing returns, two other considerations help determine when psychotherapy should be terminated.

First, any lingering transference elements in the treatment relationship must be resolved, so that patient and therapist can complete their work together primarily on the level of the real relationship. A patient who leaves psychotherapy harboring unexpressed feelings toward his therapist may continue to be troubled by them, just as he was troubled by other unfinished psychological business when he entered the treatment. To avoid merely exchanging one set of problems for another, the therapist should work through all aspects of the transference relationship before the treatment is stopped.

Second, the patient should appear capable of continuing on his own to engage in the kinds of self-observation that he has profited from in the treatment. Successful completion of therapy does not innoculate the patient against future psychological distress when new or recurrent difficulties arise. However, psychotherapy should provide the successfully treated patient with a reservoir of techniques to draw on for evaluating and dealing constructively with new problems as they arise. Hence when an improved patient whose transference reactions have been worked through begins to use his sessions less for discussing unsolved problems than for recounting problem situations that he has already brought to a satisfactory resolution by himself, the time has come to consider terminating the treatment contract.

TRENDS IN PSYCHOTHERAPY RESEARCH

It is the ethical responsibility of clinicians who practice psychotherapy to keep abreast of progress in psychotherapy research. This chapter accordingly concludes with some comments on trends in psychotherapy research and some recommendations for further reading in this area.

Psychotherapy research literature is about evenly divided between attention to *method* and *substance*. Attention to method focuses on the manner in which psychotherapy research should be done, whereas attention to substance concerns the findings that emerge from such research. Psychotherapy research can be categorized further according to whether it addresses *outcome* or *process* aspects of the treatment situation. Outcome research is concerned with the effectiveness of psychotherapy and with identifying variables related to the amount and kinds of personality change that take place as a result of the treatment. Process research is concerned with events occurring within the treatment situation, that is, with the influence of one set of patient-therapist behaviors (e.g., therapist warmth) on another set of patient-therapist behaviors (e.g., patient openness).

With this distinction in mind, it is possible to catalog the relatively short history of psychotherapy research by its shifting emphasis from outcome to process studies and back again. Empirical work in the field emerged out of the natural interest of clinicians in whether their efforts to help people were achieving this desired end, and research accordingly began with efforts simply to tabulate numbers of successful and unsuccessful outcomes. When early studies of this kind came under the scrutiny of sophisticated investigators, however, they were found to suffer numerous methodological limitations that consigned outcome research to a dark age.

Particularly important in this regard were shortcomings in the criteria of success and failure used in the early outcome work. Many of the studies relied on *phenomenological* criteria consisting of patient reports of whether they considered their therapy to have benefited them; such self-reports were appropriately criticized as being open to many sources of bias and distortion, hence unreliable. Other studies used *intratherapy* criteria consisting of measures or ratings of behavior change within the therapy interviews; these measures and ratings were justly criticized as being unvalidated with respect to behavior change occurring outside the therapy. In a then very influential summary of these criticisms, Zax and Klein (1960) concluded that the only adequate basis for evaluating treatment outcome would be external measures of patient behavior or, more specifically, systematic assessment of the patient's pretherapy and posttherapy behavior in his real-life activities. The difficulty of mounting studies that could sample a patient's behavior at home, at work, and in social situations both before and after psychotherapy cast a pall on outcome research for several years to come.

Concurrently with discouragement about the obstacles to doing adequate outcome research, some creative advances in methodology stimulated considerable interest in process studies of psychotherapy. The publication by Rogers and Dymond of *Psychotherapy and Personality Change* (1954) and preliminary reports from the University of Michigan Psychotherapy Research Project (Bordin, 1954, 1959; Harway et al., 1955; Speisman, 1959) presented researchers with intriguing illustrations of how tape-recorded interviews could be used in combination with other kinds of patient and therapist data to study not only changes in patient status over time, but also such complex dimensions of psychotherapy as resistance and depth of interpretation.

Process research tapping many different features of the patient-therapist interaction continues to the present time to figure prominently in the psychotherapy literature (see Kiesler, 1973; Marsden, 1971; Truax

& Mitchell, 1971). However, following papers by Bergin (1963) and Strupp (1963), which "revisited" problems in psychotherapy outcome research, outcome studies experienced a renaissance that has brought them back into equal prominence with studies of process. Several factors account for this renewed interest in outcome research. First, process studies have been found to pose their own share of methodological difficulties, particularly with respect to developing adequate measures of patient and therapist interview behaviors (see Kiesler, 1973). These methodological difficulties have led some researchers to redirect their interest toward extratherapy criteria of behavior change, especially criteria that can be objectively measured, and thus to seek better ways of conducting outcome research rather than to abandon it as a hopeless pursuit.

Second, advances in personality and behavioral assessment have answered many of the criticisms reviewed by Zax and Klein. New assessment techniques have been developed that are more suitable for evaluating psychotherapy outcome than the phenomenological methods previously found unreliable, and recent research has demonstrated reasonable validity for several intratherapy measures in representing extratherapy behavior. As summarized by Bergin (1971, pp. 259–263), several kinds of outcome criteria have now proved useful or promising for measuring the effects of therapeutic interventions, including structured assessment interviews, peer ratings, patient self-ratings and self-concept measures, behavioral assessment inventories, and such traditional psychodiagnostic measures as the MMPI and the TAT.

Third, influenced by process research on the interaction of patient and therapist variables, outcome research has in recent years become increasingly sophisticated and meaningful. Previous attention simply to whether psychotherapy works has been replaced with more specific interest in the particular circumstances under which a particular form of psychotherapy provided by a particular kind of therapist produces certain kinds of change in a particular kind of patient.

For further reading on the methodological challenges of designing adequate outcome and process studies of psychotherapy, the reader is referred to valuable contributions by Bordin (1965, 1974), Goldstein, Heller, and Sechrest (1966, Chapter 2), Gottschalk and Auerbach (1966), Keisler (1966a, 1966b, 1971), Meltzoff and Kornreich (1970, Chapters 1–2), and Strupp and Bergin (1969). Regarding the significant new substantive trends in psychotherapy research, it is relevant to close this chapter with a brief review of the history of outcome studies and their major implications to date.

Outcome Research in Psychotherapy

The modern history of outcome research in psychotherapy dates from Eysenck's publication in 1961 of *The Effects of Psychotherapy* (see also Eysenck, 1965, 1966), in which he concluded from an exhaustive search of the literature that the effects of psychotherapy are "small or nonexistent." Furthermore, said Eysenck, psychotherapy at best produces no advantage over everyday events in a person's life ("spontaneous remission") in alleviating neurotic disturbance. Eysenck's devastating-critique stimulated numerous rejoinders, the impact of which has been to affirm the potential effectiveness of psychotherapy and to sharpen thinking about many issues of research design in outcome studies.

For example, by simply averaging percentages of success and failure over all available reports of treatment outcome, Eysenck gave equal weight to the results achieved by experienced and inexperienced therapists, both of whom are represented in the literature. Yet as documented earlier in this chapter, experienced therapists are better able than inexperienced therapists to keep their patients in treatment and achieve successful termination. To judge psychotherapy even in part from the accomplishments of inexperienced therapists is to underestimate its potential effectiveness. A treatment method should be evaluated according to the results it achieves in the hands of practitioners skilled and experienced in employing it. For this reason, prior outcome studies need to be reviewed more selectively than Eysenck did, and future studies should be designed with careful attention to the qualifications of the participating therapists.

As a second example, Eysenck's conclusion that psychotherapy offers no advantage over spontaneous remission has been found to involve some unwarranted assumptions about the natural course of psychological disturbance. As reviewed by Subotnik (1972), there is no adequate evidence that improvement occurs in neurotically disturbed individuals simply as a matter of the passage of time. When Eysenck cites as large a percentage figure for spontaneous remission as he does for success in psychotherapy, Subotnik concludes, he is "grinding disparate reports and surveys into a statistical sausage, concealing more than it reveals" (p. 33).

Among the major weaknesses of studies purporting to demonstrate a substantial spontaneous remission effect has been the nature of the criterion groups used. Typically these studies have compared patients placed on a waiting list for treatment (the "untreated" group) with patients begun in therapy immediately following an evaluation period (the "treated" group). Such a research design takes no account of the hopeful expectations that can be created by being placed on a waiting list to receive psychotherapy, nor does it allow for the beneficial impact of whatever evaluation procedures the patient participates in prior to being accepted for the waiting list. Hence it is very doubtful whether a waiting-list patient can be considered untreated for purposes of serving as a control subject in studies of the effects of psychotherapy (see Goldstein, 1960, 1962a).

As a third example, summing indiscriminately over available outcome reports involves other unwarranted assumptions about the homogeneity of numerous variables in the treatment situation. In reality, some kinds of patients and patient problems are more amenable to psychotherapy than others, which means that the implications of success and failure in psychotherapy depend to some extent on the patient's initial prospects for benefiting from psychotherapy. Likewise, some treatment approaches are more attuned than others to the needs and capacities of a particular patient, which means that the efficacy of psychotherapy as a treatment method should be assessed according to the success or failure of approaches independently judged to have been well-tailored for the individual patient. Finally, there is mounting evidence that interactions between various personality attributes of the patient and the therapist have as much or more bearing on the outcome of psychotherapy than the characteristics of the patient or of the treatment approach employed.

For a thorough review of outcome research the reader is referred to contributions by Bergin (1971), Luborsky et al. (1971), and Meltzoff and Kornreich (1970, Chapters 3–7). Bergin, who provides a particularly incisive refutation of Eysenck's position, provides a reanalysis of available data that indicates a 65% average improvement rate with psychotherapy and only a 30% likelihood of improvement without treatment among neurotic adults. Here and in the earlier monograph with Strupp (Strupp & Bergin, 1969), Bergin additionally elaborates on the importance of designing future outcome research to account for the interaction effects now known to influence success or failure in psychotherapy.

With respect to this interaction, reference was made earlier to evidence that certain patient characteristics, such as motivation and capacity for self-expression, and certain therapist characteristics, such as the capacity to display warmth and genuineness, enhance the prospects for successful outcome in psychotherapy. A further body of research suggests that these characteristics are *dyadic* rather than *static* variables or, in other words, that the "match" between patient and therapist on various personality dimensions affects the extent to which they are able to display in each other's presence the characteristics contributing to good outcome. For example, one current line of investigation indicates that relatively intuitive therapists who are oriented primarily toward establishing a meaningful patient-therapist relationship (called "A-type" therapists) communicate more effectively with schizophrenic patients than do relatively intellectual therapists who are oriented primarily toward helping their patients achieve insight into their difficulties (called "B-type" therapists); B-type therapists, however, appear more effective than A-type therapists in work with neurotic patients (see Berzins, Dove, & Ross, 1972; Carson, 1967; Razin, 1971).

As noted above, these research developments are redirecting outcome studies from the simplistic question of whether psychotherapy works to the more complex and meaningful question of under what kinds of circumstances does what type of psychotherapy approach provided by what kinds of therapists prove beneficial for what kinds of patients. In addition, questions are now being raised about the circumstances in which apparent failure in psychotherapy can be transformed into successful treatment by changing the therapist or the approach being used. It is the pursuit of these questions and the application of the answers to clinical practice that hold the key to future advances in psychotherapy.

REFERENCES

Adler, A. (1907) *Study of organic inferiority and its psychical compensation.* New York: Nervous and Mental Diseases Publishing Company 1917.

Adler, A. (1924) *The practice and theory of individual psychology.* New York: Harcourt, Brace & World, 1927.

Adler, A. (1933) *Social interest: A challenge of mankind.* London: Faber & Faber, 1938.

Allen, F. H. *Psychotherapy with children.* New York: Norton, 1942.

Ansbacher, H. L., & Ansbacher, R. R. *The individual psychology of Alfred Adler.* New York: Basic Books, 1956.

Barrett-Lennard, G. T. Dimensions of therapist response as causal factors in therapeutic change. *Psychological Monographs,* 1962, **76**(Whole No. 562).

Baum, O.E., Felzer, D. B., D'Zmura, T. L., & Shumaker, E. Psychotherapy, dropouts and lower socioeconomic patients. *American Journal of Orthopsychiatry,* 1966, **36**, 629–635.

Beery, J. W. Therapists' responses as a function of level of therapist experience and attitude of the patient. *Journal of Consulting and Clinical Psychology,* 1970, **34**, 239–243.

Bellak, L., & Small, L. *Emergency psychotherapy and brief psychotherapy.* New York: Grune & Stratton, 1965.

Bergin, A. E. The effects of psychotherapy: Negative results revisited. *Journal of Counseling Psychology,* 1963, **10,** 244–250.

Bergin, A. E. Some implications of psychotherapy research for therapeutic practice. *Journal of Abnormal Psychology,* 1966, **71,** 235–246.

Bergin, A. E. The evaluation of therapeutic outcomes. In A. E. Bergin & S. L. Garfield (Eds.), *Handbook of psychotherapy and behavior change.* New York: Wiley, 1971. Pp. 217–270.

Berzins, J. I., Dove, J. L., & Ross, W. F. Cross-validational studies of the personality correlates of the A-B therapist "type" distinction among professionals and non-professionals. *Journal of Consulting and Clinical Psychology,* 1972, **39,** 388–395.

Blanck, G., & Blanck, R. *Ego psychology: Theory and practice.* New York: Columbia University Press, 1974.

Bordin, E. S. Simplification as a strategy for research. *Journal of Consulting Psychology,* 1965, **29,** 493–503.

Bordin, E. S. *Strategies in psychotherapy research.* New York: Wiley, 1974.

Bordin, E. S., Cutler, R. L., Dittmann, A. T., Harway, N. I., Raush, H. L., & Rigler, D. Measurement problems in process research in psychotherapy. *Journal of Consulting Psychology,* 1955, **19,** 9–15.

Boss, M. *Psychoanalysis and daseinanalysis.* New York: Basic Books, 1963.

Breuer, J., & Freud, S. (1893–1895) Studies on hysteria. *Standard Edition,* Vol. II. London: Hogarth Press, 1955. Pp. 1–319.

Bugental, J. F. T. *The search for authenticity.* New York: Holt, Rinehart & Winston, 1965.

Buhler, C. Basic theoretical concepts of humanistic psychology. *American Psychologist,* 1971, **26,** 378–386.

Buhler, C. & Allen, M. *Introduction into humanistic psychology.* Belmont, Calif.: Brooks/Cole, 1971.

Carson, R. C. A and B therapist "types": A possible critical variable in psychotherapy. *Journal of Nervous and Mental Disease,* 1967, **144,** 47–54.

Chessick, R. D. *Technique and practice of intensive psychotherapy.* New York: Jason Aronson, 1973.

Chinsky, J. M., & Rappaport, J. Brief critique of the meaning and reliability of "Accurate Empathy" ratings. *Psychological Bulletin,* 1970, **73,** 379–382.

Corsini, R. J. *Current psychotherapies.* Itasca, Ill.: Peacock, 1973.

Deutsch, A., & Fishman, H. (Eds.) *The encyclopedia of mental health.* New York: Encyclopedia of Mental Health, 1963.

Dewald, P. A. *Psychotherapy: A dynamic approach* (2nd ed.) New York: Basic Books, 1971.

Ellenberger, H. F. *The discovery of the unconscious: The history and evolution of dynamic psychiatry.* New York: Basic Books, 1970.

English, H. B., & English, A. C. *A comprehensive dictionary of psychological and psychoanalytical terms.* New York: Longmans, Green, 1958.

Erikson, E. H. *Childhood and society.* New York: Norton, 1950.

Erikson, E. H. The problem of ego identity. *Journal of the American Psychoanalytic Association,* 1956, **4,** 56–121.

Eysenck, H. J. The effects of psychotherapy. In H. J. Eysenck (Ed.), *Handbook of abnormal psychology.* New York: Basic Books, 1961. Pp. 697–725.

Eysenck, H. J. The effects of psychotherapy. *International Journal of Psychiatry,* 1965, **1,** 97–178.

Eysenck, H. J. *The effects of psychotherapy.* New York: International Science Press, 1966.

Fagan, J., & Shepherd, I. L. (Eds.) *Gesalt therapy now.* Palo Alto, Calif.: Science and Behavior Books, 1970.

Fiedler, F. E. A comparison of therapeutic relationship in psychoanalytic, nondirective and Adlerian therapy. *Journal of Consulting Psychology,* 1950, **14,** 436–445.

Fisher, E. H., & Cohen, S. L. Demographic correlates of attitude toward seeking professional psychological help. *Journal of Consulting and Clinical Psychology,* 1972, **39,** 70–74.

Ford, D. H., & Urban, H. B. *Systems of psychotherapy: A comparative study.* New York: Wiley, 1963.

Frank, J. D. The dynamics of the psychotherapeutic relationship. *Psychiatry,* 1959, **22,** 17–39.

Frank, J. D. *Persuasion and healing.* Baltimore: Johns Hopkins University Press, 1961.

Frank, J. D. Therapeutic factors in psychotherapy. *American Journal of Psychotherapy,* 1971, **25,** 350–361.

Frankl, V. E. *The doctor and the soul: From psychotherapy to logotherapy.* New York: Knopf, 1965.

Frankl, V. E. Logotherapy and existential analysis: A review. *American Journal of Psychotherapy,* 1966, **20,** 252–260.

Freud, A. (1936) *The ego and the mechanisms of defence.* New York: International Universities Press, 1946.

Freud, S. (1904) On psychotherapy. *Standard Edition,* Vol. XI. London: Hogarth Press, 1953. Pp. 257–268.

Freud, S. (1910) "Wild" psycho-analysis. *Standard Edition,* Vol. XI. London: Hogarth Press, 1957. Pp. 221–227.

Freud, S. (1912) Recommendations to physicians practising psycho-analysis. *Standard Edition,* Vol. XII. London: Hogarth Press, 1958. Pp. 11–120.

Freud, S. (1913) On beginning the treatment (further recommendations on the technique of psycho-analysis I). *Standard Edition,* Vol. XII. London: Hogarth Press 1958. Pp. 123–144.

Freud, S. (1915) Observations on transference-love (further recommendations on the technique of psycho-analysis III), *Standard Edition,* Vol. XII. London: Hogarth Press, 1958. Pp. 159–171.

Freud, S. (1933) New introductory lectures on psycho-analysis. *Standard Edition,* Vol. XXII. London: Hogarth Press, 1964. Pp. 5–182.

Freud, S. (1937) Analysis terminable and interminable. *Standard Edition,* Vol. XXIII. London: Hogarth Press, 1964. Pp. 216–253.

Fromm, E. *Escape from freedom.* New York: Farrar & Rinehart, 1941.

Fromm, E. *Man for himself.* New York: Rinehart, 1947.

Fromm, E. *The sane society.* New York: Rinehart, 1955.

Fromm-Reichmann, F. *Principles of intensive psychotherapy.* Chicago: University of Chicago Press, 1950.

Fromm-Reichmann, F. *Psychoanalysis and psychotherapy.* Selected papers edited by D. M. Bullard. Chicago: University of Chicago Press, 1959.

Garduk, E. L., & Haggard, E. A. Immediate effects on patients of psychoanalytic interpretations. *Psychological Issues,* 1972, **7,** No. 4.

Glover, E. *The technique of psycho-analysis.* New York: International Universities Press, 1955.

Goldfried, M. R., & Merbaum, M. A perspective on self-control. In M. R. Goldfried & M. Merbaum (Eds.), *Behavior change through self-control.* New York: Holt, Rinehart & Winston, 1973. Pp. 3–34.

Goldstein, A. P. Patient's expectancies and non-specific therapy as a basis for (un)-spontaneous remission. *Journal of Clinical Psychology,* 1960, **16,** 399–403.

Goldstein, A. P. Patient expectancies in psychotherapy. *Psychiatry,* 1962, **25,** 72–79. (a)

Goldstein, A. P. *Therapist-patient expectancies in psychotherapy.* New York: Pergamon Press, 1962. (b)

Goldstein, A. P. *Structured learning therapy: Toward a psychotherapy for the poor.* New York: Academic Press, 1973.

Goldstein, A. P., Heller, K., & Sechrest, L. B. *Psychotherapy and the psychology of behavior change.* New York: Wiley, 1966.

Gottschalk, L. A., & Auerbach, A. H. *Methods of research in psychotherapy.* New York: Appleton-Century-Crofts, 1966.

Gould, R. E. Dr. Strangeclass or: How I stopped worrying about the theory and began treating the blue collar worker. *American Journal of Orthopsychiatry,* 1967, **37,** 78–86.

Greenson, R. R. *The technique and practice of psychoanalysis.* Vol. 1. New York: International Universities Press, 1967.

Greenspoon, J. The reinforcing effect of two spoken sounds on the frequency of two responses. *American Journal of Psychology,* 1955, **68,** 409–416.

Greenspoon, J. Verbal conditioning and clinical psychology. In A. J. Barchrach (Ed.), *Experimental foundations of clinical psychology*. New York: Basic Books, 1962. Pp. 510–553.

Harper, R. A. *Psychoanalysis and psychotherapy: 36 systems*. Englewood Cliffs, N.J.: Prentice-Hall, 1959.

Hart, J. T., & Tomlinson, T. M. (Eds.) *New directions in client-centered therapy*. Boston: Houghton-Mifflin, 1970.

Hartmann, H. (1939) *Ego psychology and the problem of adaptation*. New York: International Universities Press, 1958.

Harway, N. I., Dittmann, A. T., Raush, H. L., Bordin, E. S., & Rigler, D. The measurement of the depth of interpretation. *Journal of Consulting Psychology*, 1955, **23,** 379–386.

Heilbrun, A. B. Effects of briefing upon client satisfaction with the initial counseling contact. *Journal of Consulting and Clinical Psychology*, 1972, **38,** 50–56.

Heine, R. W. *Psychotherapy*. Englewood Cliffs, N.J.: Prentice-Hall, 1971.

Hinsie, L. E., & Campbell, R. J. *Psychiatric dictionary*. (3rd ed.) New York: Oxford University Press, 1960.

Hofling, C. K., & Meyers, R. W. Recent discoveries in psychoanalysis. *Archives of General Psychiatry*, 1972, **26,** 518–523.

Hohen-Saric, R., Frank, J. D., Imber, S. D., Mansh, E. H., Stone, A. R., & Battle, C. C. Systematic preparation of patients for psychotherapy. I. Effects on therapy behavior and outcome. *Journal of Psychiatric Research*, 1964, **2,** 267–281.

Horney, K. *New ways in psychoanalysis*. New York: Norton, 1939.

Horney, K. *The neurotic personality of our time*. New York: Norton, 1937.

Horney, K. *Our inner conflicts*. New York: Norton, 1945.

Ince, L. P. A behavioral approach to motivation in rehabilitation. *Psychological Record*, 1969, **19,** 105–111.

Jacobi, J. *Psychology of C. G. Jung*. New Haven: Yale University Press, 1963.

Jourard, S. M. *The transparent self: Self-disclosure and well-being*. Princeton, N.J.: Van Nostrand, 1964.

Jourard, S. M. *Self-disclosure: An experimental analysis of the transparent self*. New York: Wiley, 1971.

Jung, C. G. (1911) *Psychology of the unconscious*. New York: Moffat, Yard, 1916.

Jung, C. G. *Psychological types or the psychology of individuation*. New York: Harcourt, Brace, 1923.

Jung, C. G. *Mordern man in search of a soul*. New York: Harcourt, Brace, 1933.

Kanfer, F. H. Verbal conditioning: A review of its current status. In T. R. Dixon & D. L. Horton (Eds.), *Verbal behavior and general behavior theory*. Englewood Cliffs, N.J.: Prentice-Hall, 1968. Pp. 245–290.

Kiesler, D. J. Some myths of psychotherapy research and the search for a paradigm. *Pyschological Bulletin,* 1966, **65,** 110–136. (a)

Kiesler, D. J. Basic methodologic issues implicit in psychotherapy process research. *American Journal of Psychotherapy,* 1966, **20,** 135–155. (b)

Kiesler, D. J. Experimental designs in psychotherapy research. In A. E. Bergin & S. L. Garfield (Eds.), *Handbook of psychotherapy and behavior change.* New York: Wiley, 1971. Pp. 36–74.

Kiesler, D. J. *The process of psychotherapy: Empirical foundations and systems of analysis.* Chicago: Aldine, 1973.

Krasner, L. Studies of the conditioning of verbal behavior. *Psychological Bulletin,* 1958, **55,** 148–170.

Krasner, L. The therapist as a social reinforcement machine. In H. H. Strupp & L. Luborsky (Eds.), *Research in psychotherapy.* Vol. 2. Washington, D.C.: American Psychological Association, 1962. Pp.61–94.

Krasner, L. Verbal conditioning and psychotherapy. In L. Krasner & L. P. Ullmann (Eds.), *Research in behavior modification.* New York: Holt, Rinehart & Winston, 1965. Pp. 211–228.

Kris, E. On preconscious mental processes. *Psychoanalytic Quarterly,* 1950, **19,** 540–560.

Kubie, L. S. *Practical and theoretical aspects of psychoanalysis.* New York: International Universities Press, 1950.

Langs, R. *The technique of psychoanalytic psychotherapy.* Vol. 1. New York: Jason Aronson, 1973.

Langs, R. *The technique of psychoanalytic psychotherapy.* Vol. 2. New York: Jason Aronson, 1974.

Lerner, B., & Fiske, D. W. Client attributes and the eye of the beholder. *Journal of Consulting and Clinical Psychology,* 1973, **40,** 272–277.

Loewenstein, R. M. *Drives, affects and behavior.* New York: International Universities Press, 1953.

Lorion, R. P. Socioeconomic status and traditional treatment approaches reconsidered. *Psychological Bulletin,* 1973, **79,** 263–270.

Luborsky, L., Auerbach, A. H., Chandler, M., & Cohen, J. Factors influencing the outcome of psychotherapy: A review of quantitative research. *Psychological Bulletin,* 1971, **75,** 145–185.

Luborsky, L., & Spence, B. P. Quantitative research on psychoanalytic therapy. In A. E. Bergin & S. L. Garfield (Eds.), *Handbook of psychotherapy and behavior change.* New York: Wiley, 1971. Pp. 408–438.

McNair, D. M., Lorr, M., & Callahan, D. M. Patient and therapist influences on quitting psychotherapy. *Journal of Consulting Psychology,* 1963, **27,** 10–17.

Mann, J. *Time-limited psychotherapy.* Cambridge, Mass.: Harvard University Press, 1973.

Marsden, G. Content analysis studies of psychotherapy: 1954 through 1968. In A. E. Bergin & S. L. Garfield (Eds.), *Handbook of psychotherapy and behavior change*. New York: Wiley, 1971. Pp. 345–407.

Maslow, A. H. *Toward a psychology of being*. Princeton, N.J.: Van Nostrand, 1962.

Maslow, A. H., & Mittelman, B. *Principles of abnormal psychology*. New York: Harper, 1951.

Matarazzo, J. D., & Wiens, A. N. *The interview: Research on its anatomy and structure*. Chicago: Aldine-Atherton, 1972.

Matarazzo, J. D., Wiens, A. N., Matarazzo, R. G., & Saslow, G. Speech and silence behavior in clinical psychotherapy and its laboratory correlates. In J. M. Schlien (Ed.), *Research in psychotherapy*. Vol. III. Washington, D.C.: American Psychological Association, 1968. Pp. 347–394.

Matarazzo, J. D., Wiens, A. N., & Saslow, G. Studies in interview speech behavior. In L. Krasner & L. P. Ullman (Eds.), *Research in behavior modification*. New York: Holt, Rinehart & Winston, 1965. Pp. 179–210.

May, R. *Love and will*. New York: Norton, 1969.

May, R., Angel, E., & Ellenberger, H. F. (Eds.) *Existence: A new dimension in psychiatry and psychology*. New York: Basic Books, 1958.

Meltzoff, J., & Kornreich, M. *Research in psychotherapy*. New York: Atherton, 1970.

Menninger, K. A., & Holzman, P. S. *Theory of psychoanalytic technique*. (2nd ed.) New York: Basic Books, 1973.

Minuchin, S., Montalvo, B., Guerney, B. G., Rosman, G. L., & Schumer, F. *Families of the slums: An exploration of their structure and treatment*. New York: Basic Books, 1967.

Muench, G. A. An investigation of the efficacy of time-limited psychotherapy. *Journal of Counseling Psychology*, 1965, **12**, 249–299.

Myers, J. K., & Auld, F. Some variables related to outcome of psychotherapy. *Journal of Clinical Psychology*, 1955, **11**, 51–54.

Noyes, A. P., & Kolb, L. C. *Modern clinical psychiatry*. (6th ed.) Philadelphia: Saunders, 1963.

Nunberg, H. (1932) *Principles of psychoanalysis*. New York: International Universities Press, 1955.

Perlman, G. Change in "central therapeutic ingredients" of beginning psychotherapists. *Psychotherapy: Theory, Research and Practice*, 1973, **10**, 48–51.

Perls, F. *Gestalt therapy verbatim*. Lafayette, Calif.: Real People Press, 1969.

Perls, F., Hefferline, R., & Goodman, P. *Gestalt therapy*. New York: Julian Press, 1951.

Phillips, E. L., & Wiener, D. N. *Short-term psychotherapy and structured behavior change*. New York: McGraw-Hill, 1966.

Polster, E., & Polster, M. *Gestalt therapy integrated.* New York: Brunner/ Mazel, 1973.

Progoff, I. *Jung's psychology and its social meaning.* (Rev. ed.) New York: Julian Press, 1969.

Rank, O. *The trauma of birth.* New York: Harcourt, Brace, 1929.

Rank, O. *Will therapy and reality.* New York: Knopf, 1945.

Rapaport, D. On the psychoanalytic theory of thinking. *International Journal of Psycho-Analysis,* 1950, **31,** 161–170.

Rapaport, D. The autonomy of the ego. *Bulletin of the Menninger Clinic,* 1951, **15,** 113–123.

Rapaport, D. On the psychoanalytic theory of affects. *International Journal of Psycho-Analysis,* 1953, **34,** 177–198.

Razin, A. M. A-B variable in psychotherapy: A critical review. *Psychological Bulletin,* 1971, **75,** 1–21.

Reisman, J. M. *Toward the integration of psychotherapy.* New York: Wiley, 1971.

Rogers, C. R. *Counseling and psychotherapy.* Boston: Houghton-Mifflin, 1942.

Rogers, C. R. *Client-centered therapy.* Boston: Houghton-Mifflin, 1951.

Rogers, C. R. *On becoming a person: A therapist's view of psychotherapy.* Boston: Houghton-Mifflin, 1961.

Rogers, C. R. In retrospect: Forty-six years. *American Psychologist,* 1974, **29,** 115–123.

Rogers, C. R., & Dymond, R. R. (Eds.) *Psychotherapy and personality change.* Chicago: University of Chicago Press, 1954.

Rosenthal, D., & Frank, J. D. Psychotherapy and· the placebo effect. *Psychological Bulletin,* 1956, **53,** 294–302.

Salzinger, K. Experimental manipulation of verbal behavior: A review. *Journal of Genetic Psychology,* 1959, **61,** 65–94.

Saul, L. J. *Psychodynamically based psychotherapy.* New York: Jason Aronson, 1973.

Schofield, W. *Psychotherapy: The purchase of friendship.* Englewood Cliffs, N.J.: Prentice-Hall, 1964.

Schofield, W. The psychotherapist as friend. *Humanitas,* 1970, **6,** 221–223.

Searles, H. *Collected papers on schizophrenia and related subjects.* New York: International Universities Press, 1965.

Shapiro, A. K. Placebo effects in medicine, psychotherapy, and psychoanalysis. In A. E. Bergin & S. L. Garfield (Eds.), *Handbook of psychotherapy and behavior change.* New York: Wiley, 1971. Pp. 439–473.

Sifneos, P. E. *Short-term psychotherapy and emotional crisis.* Cambridge, Mass.: Harvard University Press, 1972.

Sloane, R. B., Cristol, A. H., Pepernik, M. C., & Staples, F. R. Role preparation and expectation of improvement in psychotherapy. *Journal of Nervous and Mental Disease*, 1970, **150**, 18–26.

Speisman, J. C. Depth of interpretation and verbal resistance in psychotherapy. *Journal of Consulting Psychology*, 1959, **23**, 93–99.

Stein, M. I. (Ed.) *Contemporary psychotherapies*. Glencoe, Ill.: Free Press, 1961.

Stollak, G. E., & Guerney, B., Jr. Exploration of personal problems by juvenile delinquents under conditions of minimal reinforcement. *Journal of Clinical Psychology*, 1964, **20**, 279-283.

Strupp, H. H. An objective comparison of Rogerian and psychoanalytic techniques. *Journal of Consulting Psychology*, 1955, **19**, 1–7. (a)

Strupp, H. H. Psychotherapeutic techniques, professional affiliation and experience level. *Journal of Consulting Psychology*, 1955, **19**, 97–102. (b)

Strupp, H. H. The performance of psychoanalytic and client-centered psychotherapists in an initial interview. *Journal of Consulting Psychology*, 1958, **14**, 219–226.

Strupp, H. H. The outcome problem in psychotherapy revisited. *Psychotherapy: Theory, Research and Practice*, 1963, **1**, 1–13.

Strupp, H. H. Specific vs. nonspecific factors in psychotherapy and the problem of control. *Archives of General Psychiatry*, 1970, **23**, 393–401.

Strupp, H. H. On the technology of psychotherapy. *Archives of General Psychiatry*, 1972, **26**, 270–278.

Strupp, H. H. On the basic ingredients of psychotherapy. *Journal of Consulting & Clinical Psychology*, 1973, **41**, 1–8.

Strupp, H. H., & Bergin, A. E. Some empirical and conceptual bases for coordinated research in psychotherapy: A critical review of issues, trends, and evidence. *International Journal of Psychiatry*, 1969, **7**, 18–90.

Subotnik, L. Spontaneous remission: Fact or artifact? *Psychological Bulletin*, 1972, **77**, 32–48.

Sullivan, H. S. *The interpersonal theory of psychiatry*. New York: Norton, 1953.

Sullivan, H. S. *The psychiatric interview*. New York: Norton, 1954.

Sullivan, H. S. *Clinical studies in psychiatry*. New York: Norton, 1956.

Swenson, C. H. Commitment and the personality of the successful therapist. *Psychotherapy: Theory, Research and Practice*, 1971, **8**, 31–36.

Taft, J. *The dynamics of therapy in a controlled relationship*. New York: Macmillan, 1933.

Taft, J. Family casework and counseling: A functional approach. Philadelphia: University of Pennsylvania Press, 1948.

Truax, C. B., & Carkhuff, R. R. *Toward effective counseling and psychotherapy*. Chicago: Aldine, 1967.

Truax, C. B., & Mitchell, K. M. Research on certain therapist interpersonal skills in relation to process and outcome. In A. E. Bergin & S. L. Garfield (Eds.), *Handbook of psychotherapy and behavior change.* New York: Wiley, 1971. Pp. 299–344.

Truax, C. B., & Wargo, D. G. Psychotherapeutic encounters that change behavior for better or for worse. *American Journal of Psychotherapy,* 1966, **20,** 499–520.

Weiner, I. B. *Principles of psychotherapy.* New York: Wiley, 1975.

Wexler, D. A., & Rice, L. N. (Eds.) *Innovations in client-centered therapy.* New York: Wiley, 1974.

Wheelright, J. Jung's psychological concepts. In F. Fromm-Reichmann & J. L. Moreno (Eds.), *Progress in psychotherapy.* Vol. 1. New York: Grune & Stratton, 1956.

White, R. W. *The abnormal personality.* New York: Ronald Press, 1964.

Wilkins, W. Expectancy of therapeutic gain: An empirical and conceptual critique. *Journal of Consulting and Clinical Psychology,* 1973, **40,** 69–77.

Williams, J. H. Conditioning of verbalization: A review. *Psychological Bulletin,* 1964, **62,** 383–393.

Williams, R. I., & Blanton, R. L. Verbal conditioning in a psychotherapeutic situation. *Behavior Research and Therapy,* 1968, **6,** 97–103.

Wolberg, L. R. *Short-term psychotherapy.* New York: Grune & Stratton, 1965.

Wolberg, L. R. *The technique of psychotherapy.* (2nd ed.) New York: Grune & Stratton, 1967.

Wolman, B. B. (Ed.) *Success and failure in psychoanalysis and psychotherapy.* New York: Macmillan, 1972.

Wrenn, R. L. Counselor orientation: theoretical or situational. *Journal of Counseling Psychology,* 1960, **7,** 40–45.

Zax, M., & Klein, A. Measurement of personality and behavior changes following psychotherapy. *Psychological Bulletin,* 1960, **57,** 435–448.

CHAPTER 7

Group Therapy

BERNARD LUBIN

This chapter presents an orientation to the field of group psychotherapy, a field in which there are exciting developments and rapid growth. Increases in the use of the group method for treatment purposes, in publications on group therapy, in training opportunities, and in research output have led to the questioning of many previously stated "self-evident" truths concerning group methods of intervention, and to the relaxation of previously narrowly drawn and fiercely held boundaries.

The history and development of group therapy is presented in the first section of the chapter, and the sections that follow discuss types of group therapy, intensive small-group experiences, research and training in group therapy, group therapy with specialized populations, and issues (trends and needs) in the area of group therapy. An attempt is made to indicate where the cutting edge of the group therapy field lies and the kinds of areas that invite eventual contributions from newcomers to it.

It had been suggested at times that the term "group psychotherapy" should be restricted to those forms of group work based primarily on a psychoanalytic approach involving the analysis of resistance and transference, and that it should be distinguished from "group therapy" or "group counseling" approaches, which deal less with historical-genetic material, are briefer in length, and are not concerned with "reconstructing personality" (see Slavson, 1964). However, in keeping with clear-cut trends in general practice, these various terms are used interchangeably here.

Three separate streams—group therapy, laboratory training, and encounter groups—each with a separate origin and development, are finding more and more points of convergence as group therapists explore the other two areas and adapt concepts and techniques from them into their practice of group therapy. Which ones are tributaries and which are the main flow may be debatable, but group therapy has unquestionably been effected by engagement with laboratory training and encounter groups. For many contemporary group therapists goals of practice include growth as well as psychological repair, and many therapists, regardless of their primary orientation, are showing an increased appreciation for the contributions of the group to the therapy process. Hence the following brief history of the development of group therapy is amplified in the later discussion of intensive small-group experiences.

THE HISTORY AND DEVELOPMENT OF GROUP PSYCHOTHERAPY

Group pyschotherapy can be traced back to classes for tubercular patients held by Joseph H. Pratt, a Boston internist, in 1905. Between then and World War II a literature large enough to justify a bibliographic summary (Corsini & Putzey, 1957) was produced. Only since World War II, however, has the use of group methods for therapeutic purposes and the published work in this area increased sharply.

Some indication of the growth in the use of group methods can be seen in the increase in the membership of the American Group Psychotherapy Association over the past 30 years, from fewer than 20 members in 1943 (Mullan & Rosenbaum, 1962) to just under 3000 in 1974. Publication trends show the same picture. The first year in which the total number of published writings in group therapy (books and articles) exceeded 100 items was 1947 (Corsini & Putzey, 1957). The total output reached 200 items in 1957, and over 400 publications on group therapy appeared in 1969. Comprehensive bibliographies of the group therapy literature from 1956 to the present are provided chronologically by Lubin and Lubin (1966), MacLellan and Levy (1966, 1967, 1968, 1969, 1970, 1971), Lubin, Sargent, and Lubin, (1972), Lubin and Lubin (1973), and Reddy and Lansky (1974).

Economics was prominent among the early reasons given for the growth in the use of groups for treatment and therapy; that is, more patients could receive professional assistance at less cost. More recently, on the basis of accumulating experience, group therapy has become accepted as the treatment of choice for certain psychological-behavioral conditions, independently of economic considerations, and as a suitable adjunct to other treatment programs for many other conditions (Anthony, 1972).

Dating the exact beginning of a historical movement such as group therapy is difficult and at best arbitrary. As one approach, it is possible to list those persons and events generally thought to have been influential in the development of group therapy. Some of the following early historical material is drawn from Rosenbaum and Berger (1963).

Joseph H. Pratt, as already noted, is generally credited with being the first person to practice a rudimentary form of group therapy. In his earlier writings Pratt was primarily concerned with describing his "class method" of instructing tuberculosis patients in methods of physical hygiene. By means of an inspirational approach involving lectures and group discussions he counteracted patients' depression about their condition and motivated them to provide better self-care. Through observations of their own work, some contact with psychiatrists, and their readings of the literature, Pratt and his co-workers became impressed with the important role that emotions played in their treatment program. They subsequently extended their "thought control class method" to diabetic and cardiac patients, and other physicians used the method with undernourished children, hypertensive adults, and patients with peptic ulcers (AGPA, 1971).

Lazell adapted the Pratt method (inspirational approach, exhortation, and supportive techniques) for use with psychiatric patients at St. Elizabeth's Hospital in 1921. Pratt's authoritarian-inspirational approach was also practiced in an extreme form by Cody Marsh, a minister who became a psychiatrist. Whereas Lazell used a lecture method, Marsh's approach to group work with psychotic patients was very active and included art classes and dance classes as well as talking.

During this early period neither psychology nor psychiatry showed much interest in the use of group methods of treatment. There were a few prominent exceptions, however. A form of "collective counseling" for neurotic patients, alcoholics, stammerers, and patients with sexual disturbances was practiced by several German and Austrian psychotherapists between 1900 and 1930. During this same period, Paul Schilder used a psychoanalytic frame of reference in working with outpatient groups at Bellevue Hospital.

From 1910 to 1914 Jacob L. Moreno experimented with group methods in Vienna, and in 1925 he introduced psychodrama to the United States. In addition to pyschodrama and sociodrama, Moreno's contributions to the field of group work include role playing and sociometry, a method for mapping the positive and negative affective ties that exist within a group. Moreno in 1932 was among the first to use the term "group therapy" in print. Another early group psychotherapist was Louis Wender, a psychoanalytically oriented clinician who began treating groups of hospitalized mental petients in 1929.

As noted by Rosenbaum (1965), important early contributions of Trigant Burrow to group therapy have been relatively ignored. Burrow, one of the first psychoanalysts to practice in the United States, employed the term "group analysis" in 1925. He argued against the tendency of psychoanalysis to deal primarily with the individual to the exclusion of social factors. His work took place in residential settings where therapists and patients lived together. Burrow is also credited with introducing the concepts "here and now" and "analysis of group tensions" (AGPA, 1971).

During the 1930s Slavson developed and conducted a program of activity group therapy for emotionally disturbed adolescents at the Jewish Board of Guardians. Patients were encouraged to work through their problems within a permissive but controlled play setting, and, although psychoanalytic concepts were used to study the patients' problems, interpretations were not made directly to them. The average activity group consisted of eight children of the same age and sex selected carefully in order to construct groups with a certain degree of socio-psychological balance. During this same period, in 1938, Alexander Wolf began a group of analysands and referred to his method as "the psychoanalysis of groups." Wolf is credited with innovating the method of "going around," in which each patient in turn is asked to talk about his problems.

The American Group Psychotherapy Association

Slavson is a particularly central figure in group therapy for his contributions to the development of the American Group Therapy Association and to the increase in the number of people using group treatment methods. He convened an interest group at the New York meetings of the American Orthopsychiatric Association in 1943, and it was this group that decided to form the American Group Therapy Association with Slavson as its first president. Slavson also served as the first editor of the association's journal, and the association operated from his office at the Jewish Board Of Guardians between 1943 and 1956. Because so few people were doing group therapy during that period, much effort was expended to promote the method through conferences, discussions, and publications.

The name of the organization was changed in 1952 from the American Group Therapy Association to the American Group Psychotherapy Association, "thus definitively acknowledging the Association's commitment to psychotherapy as contrasted to other uses of groups for helping people, which the previous title may have suggested, though not intended" (AGPA, 1971, p. 432). This represented a victory at that time for those who favored exclusion rather than inclusion. In more recent years the association seems to be developing a broader base, and the *International Journal of Group Psychotherapy*, the journal of the organization, reflects a more inclusive intellectual base than formerly. The association passed another milestone in 1968 when a previously unresolved question concerning its nature and purpose was settled by its assuming responsibility for certifying the competence of group therapy practitioners.

The Impact of World War II and Subsequent Growth

During and immediately after World War II the number of patients who needed psychological treatment or counseling, particularly in the armed forces, sharply increased. Necessity led to great expansion in training and treatment programs utilizing group methods. The Veterans Administration was an acknowledged leader in this upsurge, as the niceties of intellectual debate and interprofessional territorial struggles gave way to a pragmatic orientation which asked only, "How can we provide services to all those in need?" Group methods flourished; just about every school of psychotherapy began to practice its form of treatment in group settings, even though its theory and techniques had been developed for use in the dyadic situation. In most cases no attempt was made to articulate a more elaborate rationale for the use of these techniques in group settings.

The post-World War II years have seen additional professional organizational development, development of accreditation criteria, and professional development programs. There has also been an emergence of many types of group therapy and a number of categorization schemes attempting to classify these various types. Spotnitz (1972) provides a useful history of group therapy as seen through successive attempts to classify the types of group therapy influential in each period. It is obvious from the successive schema that some types of group therapy have not survived and that the classifications have shifted over the 25-year period from method-oriented to goal oriented classifications. During this period there seems to have been some tendency toward greater specificity in the statement of goals and methods and also, somewhat paradoxically, greater flexibility in attempting innovative methods in a greater variety of settings.

TYPES OF GROUP THERAPY

A brief description of some of the types of group therapy that have developed during the period following World War II is presented under two categories: (a) group psychotherapy with the focus on individuals, and (b) group psychotherapy with a group focus. These categories are analogous to an interesting attempt by Astrachan (1970) to apply a social systems model to therapeutic groups by noting who communicates with whom, whether member with therapist, group with therapist, or member with member.

Group Psychotherapy with the Focus on Individuals

As is true in the field of individual psychodynamic psychotherapy, considerable variability in practice obtains among analytically oriented group therapists. A major source of this variation involves the degree to which the group therapist incorporates group processes into his theory and interventions. Practice ranges from the literal translation of techniques developed for individual psychoanalysis into a group setting to experimentation with methods uniquely suited to working effectively with individuals being seen in groups rather than singly.

The previously mentioned work of Trigant Burrow, for example, was based on his familiarity with psychoanalysis, but involved methods bearing little resemblance to individual psychoanalytic therapy. To avoid confusion, he later changed the name of his method from "group analysis" to "phyloanalysis," by which he intended to indicate his interest in studying man's evolutionary status. The other major types of group therapy focused on individuals derive from the approaches of Slavson, Wolf, and Foulkes, from transactional analysis, and from behavior therapy.

Slavson's "Analytic Group Psychotherapy." Although Slavson was certainly aware of group processes, he emphasized in developing his approach to group therapy the analysis of the individual in the group setting. Accordingly, his analytic group therapy involves aspects of free association, interpreting resistance and transference, and working through, as described in the previous chapter. At the same time, Slavson introduced new notions concerning the variety of intermember effects and the influence of multiple transferences in group therapy, and he also acknowledged that the member-therapist transference is modified in the group setting (Slavson, 1964).

Wolf's "Psychoanalysis in Groups." Wolf took issue with the lingering antigroup bias of psychoanalysis by stating his belief that psychoanalysis could take place in groups as well as in the individual therapy situation (Wolf, 1968). Contrary to statements by many other psychoanalysts, Wolf maintained further that each member's identification with the group ego increases his anxiety tolerance and thereby enables deeper analytic exploration in many cases than is possible in individual psychoanalysis.

Specifically, Wolf believes that the following six parameters of a well-structured group make the therapeutic conditions more readily available to the patients than is the case in individual psychoanalysis: (a) the dimension of "multiple reactivity" among group members and between members and the therapist; (b) "hierarchical and peer vectors," which refer to authority and intimacy relationships among group members; (c) the opportunity to observe each patient's intercommunication patterns; (d) the "principle of shifting attention," which refers to the nonexclusive attention of the therapist to each patient and the patient's relief from sustained scrutiny; (e) the "principle of alternating roles," in that each patient is a "help giver" as well as "help receiver"; and (f) "forced interaction," or the pressure toward and expectation of maximal interaction.

Wolf also pioneered in proposing the "alternate meeting," a weekly meeting held in addition to the regular session but with the therapist absent. He saw the alternate meeting as important in precipitating early transference attitudes toward the therapist and thereby shortening the duration of therapy, in facilitating participation by reserved and shy patients, and in making it easier for patients to criticize the therapist. Further, since his method calls for discussing the alternate session in the regular session, discrepancies in behavior in the two settings can be highlighted.

Although Slavson and Wolf differ in several respects in the way in which they see the possibilities for conducting psychoanalysis in groups, they agree that the emphasis should be on individual analysis enhanced by the group setting, and not on the group and its dynamics. Both of them emphasize further that it is the therapist rather than the group, or the leader-member relationship rather than the peer relationships, that is the all-important treatment factor (Slavson, 1964; Wolf, 1968).

Foulkes. Although trained in psychoanalysis, the British psychiatrist Foulkes developed a system of group psychotherapy that is very different from those of Slavson and Wolf. The therapist (in this case "conductor") meets for an hour and a half with seven or eight patients, which is a format similar to Wolf's. In contrast to Wolf's leadership of the group, however, Foulkes' groups proceed without directions from the therapist, and spontaneous contributions of the members are treated by the group as free associations. The therapist functions as a participant-observer, interprets transferences and resistances, and notes the various relationships in the total group field. He is primarily responsible for developing and maintaining an analytic attitude and a therapeutic atmosphere in the group. Foulkes acknowledges that his conceptualization was influenced by Kurt Lewin's field theory and by gestalt psychology via Kurt Goldstein. Anthony (1972) characterizes Foulkes' emphasis as falling "on the interpersonal rather than on the group as a whole."

Transactional Analysis. Much of the early development of transactional analysis (TA) as a theory of personality and therapy took place at the San Francisco Social Psychiatry Seminars held in Eric Berne's office beginning in 1958. The title of the seminars was later changed to the San Francisco Transactional Analysis Seminars, and they are now known as the Eric Berne Seminars of San Francisco. TA has grown considerably in its organizational membership and general influence during the past 10 years. In 1964, the year of formation, membership in the International Transactional Analysis Association was 168; by 1974 membership had grown to 6500 (Calahan, 1974). Although influence is difficult to measure, there are also informal indications that some group therapists who do not practice TA have modified their techniques in response to considerations highlighted by the exposition of TA.

The structural analysis model of TA has become well known (Berne, 1961) and consists of three ego states: Parent, Adult, and Child. These ego states are not to be confused with the structural model of psychoanalysis, which comprises id, ego, and superego. The ego states with which TA is concerned can usually be directly inferred from such observable behavior as gestures, mannerisms, voice tone and quality, and the use of specific words.

The Parent ego state is divided into the Nurturant Parent and the Critical Parent. Cues diagnostic of the latter include pointing the finger and making moralizing ("You should . . .") or prejudicial ("They are all the same") statements. The Child ego state is observable in labile displays of feelings, as in laughing or crying, expansive behavior such as jumping and clapping, and use of such expressions as golly and gee. The Child ego state can be further subdivided into the Adapted Child (fashioned to parental demands), the Professor (a bright, inquisitive stance), and the Natural Child (the free emotive aspect of the personality). The Adult ego state is the nonfeeling aspect of the personality, which gathers data about the world through the senses and processes these data in a logical manner for the purpose of making predictions.

The analysis of *transactions*, which are defined as consisting of the stimuli and responses between specific ego states in two or more people, is a fundamental activity in TA, as the title of this form of therapy indicates. Transactions are classified as being simple (parallel or complementary), crossed, or ulterior. Communication continues as long as transactions are parallel or complementary, but is interrupted when transactions are crossed. Ulterior transactions are those that contain a psychological level different from the social level, and transactions of this kind produce a "game," which is a frequently used method of structuring time between individuals.

Berne also introduced the concept of "stroke economy," the intricacies of which have been developed further by other writers (Dusay & Steiner, 1971). According to this concept, all higher organisms have a need for stimulation, and this need is satisfied in the young organism by physical stroking. Later, praise and recognition become substitutes for physical stroking, so that much of interpersonal activity involves the psychological exchange of strokes. Other recurring concepts in the TA literature analysis are *positions* (postures toward self and others, e.g., "I'm okay—you're okay," "I'm not okay—you're okay," "I'm not okay—you're not okay"); *games* (an orderly series of transactions containing ulterior motives which serve as a mechanism for obtaining strokes and avoiding intimacy; and *scripts* (those life blueprints developed out of childhood decisions which control the major moves in a person's life).

The positive, action-oriented climate of transactional analysis theory and practice make it attractive to group therapists who are frustrated with the slowness and long-term aspects of group treatment by other means. Both the therapist and the patient seem to have greater control over moment-to-moment interpersonal events. The heavy emphasis placed on studying the options available to the person and considering consequences of behavior reinforces the notion of patient responsibility for his actions and feelings and provides a hopeful climate for change in patient behavior. Since both the patient and therapist conceptualize events within the same theoretical system, any elitist status of the therapist is eliminated and patients can continue to work on ongoing problems and situations between therapy sessions. The instructional aspect of the therapist's role is clearly legitimized, thus insuring that patient and therapist are using the same language. Some TA therapists who were trained initially with a psychoanalytic orientation appreciate TA's seeming conceptual simplicity and pragmatism. Even when concepts appear to be translations or paraphrases from other theoretical systems, they seem to take on more of a utilitarian ring in TA.

Transactional analysis has also drawn sharp criticism, however. It has been accused among other things of "trivializing" human experience by denying the tragic nature of man and by implying that complex, overlearned self-destructive tendencies can be unlearned with relative ease

(Todd, 1973). Other writers have objected to the popularization of TA theory, to the entrepreneurial zest of some of its practitioners, and to the strong use of suggestion made by the method.

The fact that TA has not produced a body of research makes it difficult to evaluate the theory and method in objective terms. Indeed, a straightforward comparative analysis of TA versus other types of group therapy with suitable control groups would be difficult to design, for some bias in favor of positive outcomes for TA would seem to be assured by the emphasis in TA on the contract, that is, on working with patients who have made a strong therapeutic work commitment. It would be necessary, therefore, to provide a means to insure a comparable level of patient commitment to the process in each of the other groups in a comparative study of treatment effectiveness.

Behavior Therapy in Groups. Behavior therapy attempts to apply the methods and findings of experimental psychology to behavior problems, specifically by drawing as appropriate on such learning procedures as extinction, generalization, and counterconditioning (see Chapter 9). Behavior therapy in groups follows the same general principles as behavior therapy in individual cases, but with added possibilities for the potentiating, intensifying, and clarifying influence of the group situation. Some behavior therapists such as Lazarus (1968) have specifically welcomed the additional nonspecific effects available in the group setting: "Group discussions provide a fertile terrain for discrimination learning. Individual therapy obviously imposes limitations upon the person to person exploration of certain specific behaviors (which include attitudes and belief)" (Lazarus, 1968, p. 150).

Lazarus (1968) also provides a broad statement of the goals of behavior therapy, namely, "to eliminate suffering by changing habits judged undesirable" (p. 152). Beyond this, the goals of the behavior therapist are compatible with therapists of almost all other theoretical orientations: to increase the individual's capacity for productive work, to increase his enjoyment of interpersonal relationships, to increase his enjoyment of sex, and to improve his ability to cope with the more usual of life's stresses.

Specificity in diagnosis and in treatment are obvious advantages of a method derived from experimental psychology. Lazarus, however, is quick to acknowledge the importance of nonspecific benefits patients derive from being members of a therapy group. Moreover, although he does not believe insight to be an effective agent of behavioral change, he states, "There is nothing in modern learning theory to justify withholding the combined advantages of interpretation and desensitization, or any other method or technique which seems to have beneficial effect" (Lazarus, 1968, p. 155). In a more recent work Lazarus (1971) presents an array of group procedures and suggestions which could as easily have been put forward by a humanistic encounter group leader as by a behavior therapist.

Goldstein and Wolpe (1972) list several advantages of the group over the individual situation in behavioral work. For behavioral analysis there is greater thoroughness in the group situation, that is, observations of the patient's behavior in relation to each group member are available in addition to those in relation to the therapist. In the realm of therapeutic interventions, there are several options that either do not exist in the individual situation or exist in attenuated form, such as feedback by therapist and group members, modeling by therapist and group members, behavioral rehearsal including role reversal, and group motivational factors and social reinforcement.

In some kinds of group behavior therapy, especially in the assertiveness training form of group desensitization, there is considerable contamination of learning with nonspecific effects. An anecdotal acount of an assertive training group provided by Lazarus (1968) in fact resembles sessions from several other theoretically varied intensive small group experiences in the diversity of procedures used. Needless to say, this loss in specificity among treatment approaches complicates the task of objectively evaluating their differential effectiveness.

Group Psychotherapy with the Focus on the Group

The theoretical positions mentioned thus far, despite differences in concepts and methods, are similar in that their major focus is on individual therapy in a group setting. The key therapeutic agent is believed to be the therapist, who initiates or guides patient change by means of his interventions or the reinforcement contingencies he arranges. The group setting functions as a catalyzing, potentiating, reinforcing medium in which the individual therapy takes place. Although a patient's relationships with other group members are brought into the discussion, this is done mainly to cast light on that patient's problems and his attempts to cope with them. Allowing for some variation in the behavior of group therapists who practice individual therapy in a group, it still seems accurate to state that the group as a group receives little or no direct attention from them. In contrast, the next three theorists to be presented—Bion, Ezriel, and Whitaker and Lieberman—attempt to make direct use of the group process at the molar level as a means of treating patient's problems.

Bion. Interestingly, it is not clear that Bion ever claimed to do group psychotherapy; although trained in psychoanalysis, Bion (1961) refers in his writings only to his "experiences in groups" with neurotic patients.

One of Bion's major contributions was to delineate the two levels of functioning in which all groups engage: the level of the "work group" and the level of the "basic assumption group." The work group has to do with those aspects of group functioning that are in operation as the group realistically attempts to work on its task. It is observable in the rational problem-solving, planning, and decision-making aspects of the group's work. According to Bion, groups also frequently function on another level, the basic assumptions level, which can be inferred from observable behavior. The basic assumptions are the tacit assumptions that are operative usually outside the awareness of group members and which are brought to awareness, as appropriate, by the group leaders.

Dependency, fight-flight, and *pairing* are the three basic assumptions about the group that can be deduced from the group member's behavior. The basic assumption *dependency group* assumes that the group has met for the purpose of achieving security through the protection of an omnipotent, omniscient leader. The leader's refusal to serve in this role leads to resentment and feelings of abandonment. The group sometimes attempts to manipulate the leader into this role by pushing one of its members forward in the sick role (Rioch, 1972). When frustrated by the leader's consistent refusal to gratify these group needs, the group usually finds a substitute leader among its members who serves briefly in this role and then is discarded.

The hypothesis involved in the basic assumption *fight-flight* group is that the survival of the group is at stake and that fighting or running away is the only means for insuring the group's survival. Individual survival definitely is a secondary consideration. The orientation is toward action, and the prized leader is one who will energize and guide the group for aggression or flight. The group mood is strongly hostile to the goal of self-study.

In the *pairing group* basic assumption it is as if the group believes that a pair of members will produce a creative act (a thought, a leader, a solution, etc.), which will deliver them from their problems. The group's mood is a hopeful one.

Bion's concepts are interesting as ways of understanding seemingly irrational aspects of group behavior. His concept of *valency* is the vehicle through which the contribution of individual behavior to group behavior can be understood. Valencies refer to the inclination of individuals to enter into various of the group's basic assumptions. Although each person has the capacity to enter into all three of the basic assumption groups, all people have more of a tendency to engage in some one of the three. Even though these valencies are thought to be fundamental personal tendencies and not greatly alterable, it is of use to individuals to learn from the group experience about the nature of their own valencies.

Ezriel. Whereas Bion described the emotional climate of a group in terms of the three basic assumption groups mentioned above, Ezriel attempted to understand group interaction as a manifestation of an unconscious, common group tension, which is the "common denominator" of the dominant unconscious fantasies of the group. The common group tension is related to by each group member in terms of his individual defensive style.

Therapist interpretations in Ezriel's approach are limited to the "here and now." It is believed that, if the interpretation is accurate, the patient will link up the interpretation with relevant historical material. When suitable clarity as to the nature of the common group tension has emerged, the group therapist characteristically makes an interpretation in terms of three levels: (a) the *required relationship* (the relationship sought with the therapist); (b) the *avoided relationship* (expression of feelings of anger, dependence, helplessness, and the like); and (c) the *calamitous relationship* (fear of embarrassment and/or rejection by the therapist). The patient seeks to develop an optimal relationship with the therapist (*required relationship*) and attempts to control those feelings (*avoided relationship*) that might create a *calamitous relationship*. The latter would prevent development of the *required relationship*. The therapist then describes each group member's contribution to the common group tension (Heath & Bacal, 1972).

Whitaker and Lieberman. Although more psychologically sophisticated, *Psychotherapy through the Group Process* (Whitaker & Lieberman, 1964) shows structural similarities to the formulations of Bion, and particularly Ezriel. The "group focal conflict" supplants the common group tension as the organizing principle for a variety of subsurface group forces both seeking and avoiding expression at any moment. An equilibrium exists between the relatively equal forces of the *disturbing motive* (e.g., resentment toward the therapist, wish to be the "favorite child") and the *reactive motive* (e.g., fear of appearing foolish).

The "group solution" represents a compromise between opposing motives and attempts in particular to reduce the reactive motives or fears. A secondary objective of a group solution is to satisfy as much as possible the disturbing motive or impulse. Group solutions are identified as "enabling" or "restrictive." Enabling solutions are those that alleviate anxiety but at the same time allow for some satisfaction, expression, or exploration of the disturbing motive. Restrictive solutions are also directed toward alleviating anxiety, but do so at the expense of satisfying, expressing, or exploring the disturbing motive. The equilibrium between the disturbing motive and the reactive motive constantly shifts, thus stimulating new group behavior and group solutions. A group's "culture" is defined by the nature of the aggregate of its solutions. Initially the group's culture is restrictive, but over time it tends to become more enabling and to permit the group to explore disturbing motives that earlier were defended against.

Therapy for the individual group member takes place as his "nuclear conflicts" (derivatives of his earlier experiences) are activated by group focal conflicts. The adequacy of the individual's habitual solutions is tested as he attempts to cope with the anxiety that is aroused. If his habitual solution is not successful, he usually will attempt to influence the group solution or will insulate himself psychologically from the group focal conflict. If a group's culture is dominated by enabling solutions, a group member is more likely to feel free to question his own solutions and to experiment with other solutions. Conditions for change include (a) the patient experiencing personal focal conflicts relevant to core nuclear conflicts, (b) the failure of the patient's maladaptive solutions to cope with anxiety generated in the group situation, and (c) the patient's experience that giving up his maladaptive solutions is potentially beneficial rather than catastrophic (Glassman, 1967).

Additional Categories

As mentioned earlier, the foregoing was not intended as an exhaustive listing of forms of group therapy. Two major omissions are gestalt group therapy and psychodrama, which were omitted because they did not fit neatly into the previously employed categories. Both are important, however, in becoming familiar with the history and current practice of group psychotherapy.

Gestalt Group Therapy. Gestalt group therapy, perhaps more than any other method, focuses with sustained intensity on the experience of individuals. The concept of the "hot seat," seemingly the ultimate in individual focus, was devised by the founder of gestalt therapy, Fritz Perls (1973). Gestalt therapy deals with "here and now" experiences in a fundamental sensory manner. In this sense gestalt therapy focuses keenly on the individual, and it has made a major contribution to general therapeutic practice by explicating the concept of responsibility in interpersonal relationships (Levitsky & Perls, 1969; Harman, 1974). The influence of gestalt therapy has gone far beyond the number of people who practice it, primarily as a result of its impact on group therapists of various persuasions who have attended gestalt group therapy workshops and seminars. It is generally the case that group therapists' attempts to achieve genuineness, to be more in touch with their experience, and to work toward a meaningful sense of responsibility have influenced their therapeutic work in important ways regardless of their fundamental orientation.

Psychodrama. Psychodrama is another method that has influenced the development and practice of group therapy out of proportion to the actual number of individuals who claim to practice it. Many group therapists have come to use such psychodramatic techniques as the alter ego, the double, and role reversal (see Moreno, 1946) when they deem them appropriate. Psychodrama's message about how important spontaneity and empathy training are for effective living, and therefore for progress in treatment groups, has permeated general group therapy practice. Psychodrama remains difficult to categorize, however; although much attention is given in each session to individuals, processes occurring within the group also play a prominent role in the method.

Therapeutic Factors

In the absence of definitive comparative data, a summary of alleged "therapeutic factors" is helpful in indicating a final respect in which the various types of group therapy appear to differ. Among types of group therapy focused on the individual, first of all, those with a psychoanalytic orientation emphasize the importance for successful outcome of the twin factors of (a) patient motivation and (b) therapist skill in the interpretation of transferences and resistances. Three very important "curative factors" said to reside in the behavior of the TA group therapist are "potency," "permission," and "protection" (Dusay & Steiner, 1971). In the behavioral group therapies the leader's arrangement of suitable reinforcement contingencies is seen to be the crucial change agent.

In those forms of group therapy that focus more upon the group, it is the group leader's skill in keeping the group at work while at the same time preventing its members from grasping at quick, anxiety-reducing solutions that appears to be considered most important for achieving the treatment goals. The leader's skill in these two respects increases the likelihood of the activation and exploration of individual patient problems.

Yalom (1970), writing from an eclectic orientation to group therapy, delineates the following 12 categories of "curative factors": altruism, group cohesiveness, universality, interpersonal learning ("input"), interpersonal learning ("output"), guidance, catharsis, identification, family reenactment, insight, instillation of hope, and existential factors [e.g., "recognizing that ultimately there is no escape from some of life's pain and death" (pp. 66–69)]. Although it may be too early to know which if any of these are necessary and sufficient conditions for patient improvement in group psychotherapy, an impressive amount of evidence is accumulating regarding the importance of the group therapist's accurate empathy, nonpossessive warmth, and genuineness (Truax, 1971).

Some of the "therapeutic factors" listed above can be understood as mechanisms through which behavior and attitude change are thought to take place. In connection with these "mechanisms" the potential of intermember and leader-member mutual influences to foster behavior and attitude change in the group situation has been recognized for some time (Scheidlinger, 1955; Frank, 1961). Formulations by Kelman (1963) provide a particularly useful way of conceptualizing the influence process that takes place in groups, regardless of the type of group. He posits three processes that underlie the acceptance of influence: compliance, identification, and internalization. Each process has its own antecedent conditions and its own consequents. This formulation cuts across various types of groups, including both therapy groups and the intensive small group experiences to be discussed next, and enables one to identify key factors in the social influence process.

INTENSIVE SMALL-GROUP EXPERIENCES

The current group therapy scene overlaps at several points between traditional group therapy and intensive small-group experiences. The latter has taken a different evolutionary route, however, which merits a brief review. As with the history of group therapy, the listing of starting points and contributors to the development of the intensive small-group experience is somewhat arbitrary. Rosenbaum and Berger (1963) present what seems to be a logical line of development, from Charles H. Cooley in the early 1900s through Mead, LeBon, Durkheim, Park, Zorbaugh and Thrasher, White, Mayo, and Sapir, and their contribution is recommended for further reading on these historical matters.

A name that is closely linked to the development of laboratory education, which is the generic form of the intensive small-group experience (Lubin & Eddy, 1970), is Kurt Lewin, a German gestalt psychologist whose research interests ranged over a wide spectrum. Together with two of his students, Ronald Lippitt and Ralph K. White, Lewin conducted classical experiments on the effects of leadership style (authoritarian, laisez faire, and democratic) on group structure, functioning, and climate (Lippitt & White, 1958). One of his abiding interests was the study of attitude and behavior change of individuals as a result of their participation in group discussions. His success in using group discussion and public commitment to change the food-purchasing habits of American housewives during World War II in the direction of less preferred meats is well known (Lewin, 1943).

These interests of Lewin, as well as his general dedication to action research and to developing effective means for resolving social tensions, led Frank Simpson, executive director of the Connecticut Interracial Commission, to ask him to assist in training group leaders (school teachers, businessmen, other community leaders) who would hopefully be instrumental in changing racial attitudes and working effectively with interracial tensions. The specific need was for a training conference to implement the newly enacted Connecticut Fair Employment Practices Act. In response to this request, Lewin in June of 1946 organized and conducted a workshop at New Britain, Connecticut. The workshop comprised three 10-person groups of participants led by Leland Bradford, Kenneth Benne, and Ronald Lippitt. The small discussion groups, which looked at "back home" problems of participants, were to be studied by Lewin and a small research staff, and each of the small groups accordingly contained a research observer. These observers—Morton Deutsch, Murray Horwitz, and Melvin Seeman—used pretested schedules, coded interactions, and behavioral sequences to record and report their group's process to the evening meeting of the training staff.

Participants who received permission to attend the evening staff meeting showed keen interest in the reports of individual, group, and leader interactions. Within a few days all the participants were attending the evening meeting on a voluntary basis and were permitted to interact around the observations. It was apparent to participants and staff that there was a high level of interest in acquiring objective observations of one's behavior and its effects on others and in learning about the formation and development of small groups.

The next year, 1947, Leland Bradford (National Education Association), Ronald Lippitt (Research Center for Group Dynamics), and Kenneth D. Benne (Columbia University) organized a 3-week summer session in Human Relations Training at Gould Academy in Bethel, Maine. This isolated "cultural island" was chosen for the training session in order to capitalize on Lewin's conviction that reducing or eliminating the usual situational forces that tend to resist change would increase the likelihood that change would take place. From these beginnings emerged significant current directions in the use of T groups and laboratory training.

The T Group

A major component of the 3-week session held in Bethel in 1947 was a "basic skills training group," which in 1949 came to be referred to more briefly as a "T group." This was a small discussion group which included a "trainer" who helped the group to evaluate and generalize from what it was learning from the observer's comments and the data supplied by participants.

It was an ebullient era. Creativity, drive, optimism, and energy led to the setting of an impossibly large and diverse range of objectives for the basic skills training group. As reported by Benne (1964), these objectives included (a) group members were to learn in a meaningful way sets of concepts, including concepts of planned change and associated skills, indices, and criteria of group development; (b) the group was to provide an opportunity for members to practice diagnostic action skills of the change agent, group leader, and member via skill practice and role playing; (c) the behavioral perspective was to shift from the interpersonal to the group to the intergroup and organizational levels; (d) opportunities were to be provided for generalization and plans for application to the back home situation; (e) members were to receive feedback about their relationship and communication style and its impact on other members and on the development of the group; (f) members were to develop a greater appreciation for democratic values; and (g) members were also to acquire trainer skills with which to help others function as change agents and group members.

It is important to notice that "personal growth" in a quasi-therapeutic sense is absent from this list of objectives, or present in embryonic form only. The emphasis was on experimental education, skill development, value exploration, and a posture of inquiry, with high value placed on the collection and evaluation of objective as well as subjective (feelings, perceptions, reactions) data.

The National Training Laboratories, now the NTL Institute for Applied Behavioral Science, was established as a branch of the National Education Association and was led from its inception in 1949 to 1970 by its director, Leland P. Bradford. In 1971 the NTL Institute became an independent nonprofit organization which provides training, consultation, and research in the applied behavioral sciences. The NTL Institute is recognized as the parent organization that has made major contributions to and has overseen the development of laboratory training, particularly, but not exclusively in the United States.

Benne (1964) delineates two phases in the evolution of the method. From 1949 through 1955 there were many attempts to experiment with training formats and technologies with which to implement learning objectives that did not seem to be squarely within the purview of the T group. The latter had emerged as a unique educational vehicle which was emotionally intense, somewhat antiintellectual in philosophy, and rejecting of discussions not concerned with immediate data ("the here and now"). As various kinds of special groups were formed in order to concentrate on these additional objectives, the T group was experienced at times as not sufficiently integrated into the rest of the design for conferences at the NTL. In the second phase, from 1956 to the present, attempts were made to reintegrate the T group and T-group-type experiences into laboratory designs for residential setting conferences.

Until 1962, the evolutionary routes of group psychotherapy and laboratory training clearly were traced from different points of origin, followed different courses, and sought to arrive at different destinations (objectives). The objectives of group psychotherapy were healing, repair, restoration of function, and alleviation of distress; the objectives of laboratory training were to provide a vehicle for experiential learning of group leadership and membership skills, and for greater understanding and effective ways of intervening in the field of forces at work in the formation, development, and functioning of small groups. Although it was noted even in the conference that preceded the first Human Relations Laboratory that participants seemed fascinated with the opportunity to receive direct feedback about the effects of their behavior and style, and even though intimacy was a definite phase of the development of each T group (Benne, 1964), this aspect of laboratory training received secondary billing for several years.

The Personal Development T Group

In 1962 three members of the NTL Institute's Western Training Laboratory, Irving R. Weschler, Fred Massarick, and Robert Tannenbaum, published what became the conceptual basis for a shift in emphasis from the group process T group to the T group with a personal-interpersonal focus. Weschler et al. (1962) referred to their method as "group therapy for normals."

The need for such an approach is detailed by these authors in terms of the "cultural neurosis" that afflicts everyone. For the "pseudohealthy" person "tensions below the surface debilitate realization of potential capacities, stunt creativity, infuse hostility into a vast range of human contact, and frequently generate hampering psychosomatic problems" (Weschler et al,. 1962, p. 34). A person who lives under conditions that alienate him so profoundly from others and from himself needs intensive small-group experiences that deal "with his tendency to control or be controlled by others, with his management of anger, with his ability to express and receive love or affection, with his feelings of loneliness, with his search for personal identity, [and] with his testing of his own adequacy. . . ." (p. 35).

These views represented a definite shift away from group process to a focus on the enhancement of individual development. Shortly after the development of the "self-in-process" model of the T group, residential laboratories conducted by the NTL Institute began to show greater differentiation than previously. The name of the Human Relations Laboratory was changed to the Human Interaction Laboratory, thus indicating a change in emphasis to include the interpersonal realm as well as group process. New offerings included a Personal Growth Laboratory and an Advanced Personal Growth Laboratory.

It is important to recognize that professionals as well as the public subsequently contributed to considerable terminological confusion by using such terms as group therapy, sensitivity training, marathon group, growth group, T group, laboratory training, and integrity group interchangeably (Lubin & Eddy, 1970). To achieve clarity of exposition and delineate the unique contribution of laboratory training, the term should be reserved for referring

> . . . to a range of experience-based learning activities in which participants are centrally involved in goal setting, observing, feeding back, analyzing data, planning action or change steps, evaluating, etc. Data which are within the learning situation itself provide the material for learning. The format may take a number of forms; the best known form, the "laboratory," has the character of a conference [Lubin & Eddy, 1970, p. 306]

Another description that clarifies the nature of the laboratory further states that it consists of

> . . . different groupings of participants with differing technologies of training in the service of various learning objectives. Staff members are in continuous communication in order to establish and maintain relationships among the parts of the laboratory experience. As the laboratory proceeds in time, participants are brought together in integrating sessions designed to help them relate the parts of their overall laboratory experience. Integration of learnings becomes a central concern for participants in work on problems of application of laboratory learnings in their home situations [Benne, 1964, pp. 108–109]

The notions of "conference" and "range of experience-based learning activities" imply various kinds of groupings (T group, general sessions for conceptual input, total conference exercises and simulations, intergroup sessions) arranged in such a manner as to potentiate and assist in the integration of different kinds of learning. Unfortunately, it is to just one of the components of the laboratory, albeit an important component—the T group—that many writers refer in discussing laboratory training, while ignoring the rest of the design. The situation is much like that of the symphony orchestra; the string section is important and colorful and can function independently of the rest of the orchestra; by separating this section from the rest, however, one loses depth and range, counterpoint, variety and contrast, a sense of shifting focus, blend and resolution, and so forth.

Laboratory Training and Stress

It has been said that small-group experiences produce excessively high levels of stress for the participants (Business Week, 1963; Kutash, 1971; Winthrop, 1971). As mentioned above, in these allegations laboratory training frequently is included under the general rubric of "sensitivity training" or "small groups." In point of fact, two types of data indicate that the probability of laboratory training producing psychological casualty is very small. The records of the NTL Institute for Applied Behavioral Science indicate that "of 14,200 participants in its summer and industrial programs between 1947 and 1968, for 33 (.2%) the experience was stressful enough to require them to leave the program prior to its completion" (NTL Institute News and Reports, 1969). These findings are supported by the outcome of a long-term study of an intensive program of laboratory training in the YMCA. Data collected in interviews from participants, their work supervisors, their trainers, and other group members indicate that in only 0.3% of the cases did a severe negative experience occur (Batchelder & Hardy, 1968, pp. 83–84).

Another line of investigation has produced the sobering finding that T groups, at their most stressful points, arouse significantly less anxiety, depression, and hostility (all of which are subjective indicators of stress) than do regularly scheduled college examinations (Lubin & Lubin, 1971).

Encounter Groups

In the same period during which the "Personal Development T Group" developed, another form of intensive small-group experience appeared initially at the Esalen Institute in Big Sur, California (Murphy, 1967), and then spread to various "growth centers" around the country. The "encounter group," as many of these offerings were called, varied in format, duration, and emphasis from leader to leader and from one growth center to the next. An emphasis on the nonverbal, on feelings, on physical contact, and on the use of fantasy techniques and movement are some of the parameters encounter groups have in common (Lubin & Eddy, 1970). In as much as Fritz Perls was the psychiatrist in residence at Big Sur, his orientation and philosophy had a strong influence on the development of encounter groups. Thus, despite considerable diversity in form and method, most encounter groups espouse concerns for genuineness, contact, personal growth, and game-free interaction. The absence of a parent organization to guide and supervise the overall development of the encounter group movement appears to have resulted in some excesses in its use, but it had also permitted a kind of freedom that has encouraged innovations in many dimensions of the encounter group experience (Stoller, 1972).

Participants in encounter groups report being captivated by the immediacy, vividness, sense of release, and experience of intimacy created by these experiences. Some writers speculate that the popularity of these short-lived groups stems mainly from the rare and welcome contrast they provide to the widespread alienation and mechanization of Western culture (Rogers, 1968; Yalom, 1970).

As suggested above, frequent concern has been expressed about the relative absence of standards for the practice of encounter group work and for the qualifications of its practitioners (Lakin, 1969; Lubin & Eddy, 1970[1]; Strassburger, 1971; Wysor, 1971). Much of this concern has arisen from the alleged psychonoxious aspects of the intensive encounter group experience. Lieberman, Yalom, and Miles (1973), in one of the more important contributions in this area, added weight to such concern by reporting a relationship between encounter group leader style and casualty rate in encounter groups. Evidence in this regard is still very meager, however, and the Lieberman et al. study has been questioned on methodological grounds (Schutz, 1974). Generally speaking, the encounter group movement has produced very little research to date. However, a considerable volume of research has been associated with the laboratory training area (Lubin & Eddy, 1970), and

[1]This concern refers to the specific field of encounter groups. A note regarding accreditation for practitioners of various forms of laboratory training appears on page 435.

Gibb (1974) summarizes the research in this field that appeared between 1947 and 1972.

RESEARCH IN GROUP THERAPY

Some therapists find the group situation with its multiple interactions so complex and tension producing that they avoid it and do only individual therapy (Bach, 1956). This complexity also confronts anyone who proposes to conduct meaningful research on group therapy. Conceptualization and design problems are more complex in group than in individual therapy research, because there is an additional class of variables that need to be considered (group variables) and because of an increased number of interactions among variables (patient variables, therapist variables, situational variables, and outcome variables) is possible. Consequently, it is not surprising that, despite an increase in the volume of group therapy research, it is difficult to compare the findings of various studies with each other or to see systematic progess in the accumulation of knowledge in this area.

Several reviewers have commented thoughtfully on the need to improve research efforts in group therapy (Goldstein, Heller, & Sechrest, 1966; Gundlach, 1967; Lewis & McCants, 1973; Psathas, 1967; Stollak, 1966; Yalom, 1970). In the past, wasted effort and conceptual confusion have resulted from what has been called the "uniformity myths." These myths refer to the tendency of earlier researchers to proceed as if they were attempting to evaluate "the effect of something called 'group psychotherapy' on somebody called 'patients,' 'outpatients,' or 'schizophrenics.' Group psychotherapy is not a homogeneous treatment condition; group psychotherapists differ from one another in a multitude of ways, and so do group therapy patients" (Lewis & McCants, 1973, p. 271). "Uniformity myths" are growing less apparent in the research literature, but by no means have they been demolished. There remains a pressing need for much greater specification of variables in future research.

Outcome of therapy is another concept that has been a candidate for the "uniformity myth" category. Outcome has been treated in the past as if everyone agreed as to what form of outcome should be measured, or that it made no difference how outcome was conceptualized as long as posttreatment measurements were made. To the contrary, the evidence suggests that improvement is not a unitary process and that changes in different outcome measures and criteria do not necessarily occur together (Kelman & Parloff, 1957). A more recent study (Kurtz & Grummon, 1972) has shown that six different measures of the same construct (therapist empathy) have different relationships to a process measure (depth of self-exploration) and to four different outcome measures.[2]

In this same vein, the importance of individualizing the goals of therapy and, accordingly, the assessment of outcome for each patient, has been mentioned by several reviewers (Lewis & McCants, 1973; Parloff, 1973; Yalom, 1970). Such an idiographic orientation to the measurement of outcome would be consistent with clinical practice, in which, for example, achieving a lower level of anxiety is the treatment goal for one patient, whereas achieving a higher level of anxiety is a treatment goal for another patient.

Two suggested solutions to the problems of conducting research in group therapy in the clinical setting are (a) designing laboratory analogs to group therapy and (b) extrapolating the findings of appropriate small-group research to group therapy. Heller (Goldstein et al., 1966) is a proponent of the analog approach, which is a method that has worked well in engineering and experimental medicine. Given adequate ingenuity of the researcher, knowledge of the processes and mechanisms of group therapy can potentially be advanced by this method. The important point in evaluating the adequacy of this approach of course is to determine that the major points in the analog are truly analogous to the clinical practice of group therapy.

Goldstein et al. (1966) strongly urge the group therapy researcher to look to the field of small-group research as a source of group relevant variables. They review several studies, make extrapolations from the field of small-group research, and state hypotheses for testing in the following areas: group composition and initial structure, group size, initiation into the therapy group, group therapist orientation, and group cohesiveness. The small-group approach also seems promising, although confidence in it must await more demonstrations that important small-group research findings can be replicated in the group therapy situation.

In turning from issues to substantive findings, self-disclosure and group composition are two areas in which several interesting studies on group therapy have been reported.

[2]The nature of outcome and process research in psychotherapy is elaborated in Chapter 6.

Self-Disclosure

Current concern about the issue of group therapist transparency has no doubt fueled the large number of articles that are appearing on self-disclosure (SD), although the obvious importance of SD as a patient variable has been known for many years. It is through SD that much of the interpersonal learning in group therapy takes place, that is, the "universality" of one's problems is established, and important data for the feedback process are made available.

The literature on SD is reviewed by Allen (1973), who draws from it some implications for group therapy practice. The relevance to group therapy of earlier findings on SD is not clear, as many of the studies are based on high school and college students who are unrepresentative of the population of group therapy patients in terms of psychopathology. Moreover, the findings derive from dyadic interactions rather than group situations, most of them have been concerned with nonthreatening, nonintimate disclosures. A comprehensive critique of the SD construct has recently been presented by Goodstein and Reinecker (1974), who discuss the philosophical background of the concept of SD, the content of what is disclosed, characteristics of the target of the disclosures, characteristics of the discloser, situational determinants of SD, and problems in the measurement of SD.

Block and Goodstein (1971), in an earlier critique of work by Jourard and Jaffe (1970) on SD, called particular attention to the potential complexity of the construct, and this complexity of SD has been further delineated by two recent studies. In the first of these studies, Simonson and Bahr (1974) examined relationships among three patterns of disclosure (no disclosure, disclosure of demographic information, and personal disclosure) and two levels of therapist affiliation (professional and paraprofessional). Professional therapist disclosure of personal information resulted in less attraction and disclosure from subjects than did professional therapist disclosure of demographic information. However, subjects displayed greater attraction and disclosure when exposed to personal disclosure by the paraprofessional therapist than when exposed to demographic disclosure by him.

In addition to suggesting the complexity of SD, the second study also has implications for its manipulability. In an investigation of the effect of an explict group contract on self-disclosure and group cohesiveness, Ribner (1974) found that "the contract (to disclose) served to increase significantly both the frequency and depth of self-disclosure but did not affect the level of intimacy of the topics discussed." He also concluded that "the contract [to disclose] significantly enhanced the cohesiveness of the groups (i.e., attraction to the group) but had the opposite effect on members' mutual liking" (p. 116).

Some findings on SD, if treated with caution, do seem to have implications for group therapy. The fact that SD is manipulable (Jourard & Friedman, 1970; Ribner, 1974) and tends to be reciprocal (Culbert, 1970) are cases in point. Also instructive is an apparent curvilinear relationship between SD and adjustment (Culbert, 1970; Jourard, 1964); that is, very high and very low SD seem to be associated with maladjustment. In selecting patients and composing groups, therefore, the principle of balance in SD tendency among patients seems to be worth considering.

Although the therapist variable has received relatively little study in the group therapy literature, it seems to be a potentially fruitful domain. SD tendency of the group therapist seems likely to be observable in his SD behavior, in the group therapy philosophy he espouses, in the way in which he structures the group, and in his style of interacting with patients. Continued study of consequences of various combinations of therapist-group SD should prove worthwhile.

Group Composition

Group composition is another area that has attracted a large volume of research interest. Reddy (in press), in a very useful review of the literature of group composition research, indicates that studies can be grouped into those concerned with the dimension of homogeneity-heterogeneity and those in the area of compatability-incompatability of needs. These two dimensions have frequently been confused. In summarizing the findings of several studies, Reddy states that "composition based upon the homogeneous-heterogeneous dimension influences the change process in groups [and]. . . heterogeneous composition leads . . . to a wider range of alternative behaviors and change" (p. 8).

The Fundamental Interpersonal Relationship Orientation (FIRO-B) inventory developed by Schutz (1958) is the major instrument used to study the effects of need compatability-incompatability. The basic social needs addressed by this instrument are inclusion, control, and affection. According to Schutz, these three needs are sufficient for prediction of interpersonal and group behavior. The self-report instrument (FIRO-B) measures two aspects of each of these three needs, the amount of the need the person desires, and the amount he expresses. The "fit" between the degree of a need one person wants and another person expresses defines the "interchange compatability" score, which has been found to be positively related to group goal achievement and satisfaction (Schutz, 1958). Focusing on the affection dimension, Reddy developed a model of interaction within the FIRO-B structure which, although developed for the T-group setting, might be usefully tested in the group therapy situation (Reddy, in press).

Homogeneity-heterogeneity, as mentioned earlier, is a special aspect of the group composition issue. Earlier discussions of this dimension led to many overgeneralizations concerning it (Frust, 1963), but subsequent research findings have fortunately been more specific and limited. Thus there is evidence that homogeneity tends in some cases to promote a feeling of security among group members, whereas heterogeneity seems to result in less security but more learning in the group (Harrison & Lubin, 1965).

Experience in therapy with special groups of people all having similar problems, such as alcoholics, drug addicts, and parents of children with problems, suggests that homogeneity of type of problem heightens the visibility of the problem as well as the characteristic defenses and life-styles of the patients. However, homogeneity seems to foster superficial, problem-focused discussions (Mullan & Rosenbaum, 1962; Powdermaker & Frank, 1953). Yalom's (1970) discussion of this issue is helpful. He asks, "Homogeneous for what? Heterogeneous for what?" (p. 193). He then supports Whitaker and Lieberman (1964) in indicating that the therapist might want to consider *both* homogeneity and heterogeneity in composing therapy groups, for example, heterogeneity in patients' areas of conflict and styles of coping, but homogeneity in patients' tolerance for anxiety.

Elsewhere it has been suggested that the complexity of the group therapy situation requires study by means of multivariate designs. Thus the interactions of therapist style, group composition, and stage of group development are likely to be rich exploratory domains for advancing knowledge of group therapy as a clinical and social psychological phenomenon, and also for improving the applied aspects of the method. As to the former, it might well be that absolute differences among patients on a variety of dimensions are less important than the therapist's manner of relating to these differences, for example, "leveling-sharpening" (Byrne, 1964). Effects of treatment on patients' moods and response tendencies, for example, have been shown to be a function of type of group therapy orientation and patients' pretreatment interpersonal styles (Glad & Glad, 1963; Glad, Ferguson, Hayne, & Glad, 1963; Glad, Glad, & Barnes, 1959). In regard to the applied considerations, "lack of readiness" seems to be a factor in some cases of individuals who drop out of group therapy during the early phases. Conceptualizing this problem as arising out of the interaction of several factors might alert the therapist to the need to provide protection and encouragement for those patients whose anxiety tolerance and self-disclosure tendencies are lower than those of the rest of the group.

TRAINING IN GROUP THERAPY

Discussions of training in group psychotherapy have centered around conceptual, skill, and personal considerations. Several writers agree on the importance of a strong didactic phase in group therapy training programs (Knopka, 1949; Slavson, 1947; Stein, 1963), although they differ somewhat in the material they recommend covering in didactic exercises. There are furthermore considerable differences in the suggested items included in various published reading lists for learning about group therapy, and several of these lists contain more books and articles drawn from the field of individual therapy than from group therapy. The key elements to consider in reviewing training methods in group therapy are cotherapy, training aids, experience as a patient, and continuing education.

Cotherapy

In many training settings the actual learning and practice of the skills of the group therapist take place by means of a tutorial model in which the student either serves as cotherapist with an experienced group therapist or conducts group therapy under the observation of an experienced group therapist who sits with the group or views the session through a one-way vision mirror. The discussion that follows the sessions may be used for the training of students other than the therapist, if they too have observed the session.

Most students serve at some time during their training in a cotherapy relationship (Berman, Messersmith, & Mullens, 1972; McGee & Shuman, 1970) and this technique appears to be a helpful vehicle for learning group therapy. The cotherapist role allows beginners initially to function mainly as observers with little responsibility for active participation. Later, as their learning progresses, they gradually increase their level of activity in the sessions. As developing but still inexperienced cotherapists become increasingly active, however, it is necessary to guard against their assuming roles that, although comfortable, might not be responsive to the changing needs of the patients, the group, or the cotherapy team.

Training Aids

Group therapists learn by means of the same mechanisms that group therapy patients learn, namely, by receiving feedback on the effects of their behavior and by practicing alternative behaviors. Given this premise, recordings, diaries, and rating scales are useful aids in the growth of the group therapist.

Recordings. The past few years have seen a growing use of audiovisual equipment as an adjunct to training in group therapy (Bodin, 1969; Sadock & Kaplan, 1971). An accurate account of patient and therapist behavior and of their verbal and nonverbal communication, as captured on videotape, is becoming an important part of supervisory training sessions (Berger, 1971). The learning potential of seeing one's behavior on videotape is considerable, and use of this training aid is recommended whenever feasible. In the absence of videotape equipment, audiotaping provides a less rich but still instructive replacement.

Diaries. A systematically kept diary as an adjunct to postsession group notes can document the self in process of the group therapist in the same manner as the group notes document the group in process. To be most useful as a training aid, the student group therapist's diary should contain technical questions about the tactics he is employing, thoughts and feelings he has in regard to his role and his own personal development, and goals and plans he has for modifying his behavior.

Rating Scales. Rating scales are a third means, along with recordings and diaries, of providing feedback regarding the behavior of the group therapist. Rating scales can aid both self-assessment and supervisor assessment processes, especially if at least some of them are constructed so as to be bipolar, for example, confronting-supportive, and descriptive rather than judgmental and evaluative. An additional suggestion is that some of the scales be constructed by the trainee in consultation with his supervisor, so as to indicate those dimensions on which the trainee believes feedback would be helpful.

Experience as a Patient

A survey of senior members of the American Group Psychotherapy Association who were involved in training group therapists revealed some differences in attitude concerning whether group therapists in training should have an experience as a patient in a group (Stein, 1963). Favorable respondents indicated that participation of the trainee in a group gives him some appreciation for how the patient feels in group therapy, helps him to discern the differences between individual and group therapy, and enables him to work through problems in relating to groups, authority figures, and peers.

Regardless of individual differences in viewpoint, however, centers that train group therapists seem to agree that an experiential dimension to the training program is essential: "Neither the seminar method nor individual supervision seem able to convey to the therapist more than an intellectual awareness of his patterns of operation in the group, especially since these patterns often are ego-syntonic in nature and, therefore, most difficult for the therapist to grasp fully" (Leichter, 1963, p. 74). To experience "how the patient feels in group therapy" is a salutary reason for expecting the student to have a group experience, but it is only a partial rationale for the experience. More important as a reason for the required group experience is the fact that it is useful for the group therapist to have an accurate picture of the effects of his behavior on individual group members and on the group—effects of his leadership style and his style of communicating, relating, managing conflict, dealing with feelings, working with negative affect and resistances, handling criticism and attack, dealing with depression and hope, and so on. The best opportunity for obtaining accurate information of this nature is participation in a small, agendaless group conducted by a leader who is trained both in clinical psychology and group dynamics.

An even more ideal training program envisions each student group therapist, in addition to other didactic and experimental sessions, being a member of two different experiential groups, one an encounter group and the other a T group. The encounter group experience would enable the student to deal directly and at some depth with such issues as dependency-autonomy, dominance-submission, and feelings about himself and his body. Some of these same issues would surface in varied forms in the T group, but there the student could explore in addition the self in relation to a range of group level phenomena: leadership, cohesion, norms, procedures, decision making, inclusion, and so forth. The two types of experience would be designed to supplement each other; thus to the impactful personal perspective a frame of reference would be added which alerts the student to alterable group properties that influence the quality and nature of the group experience. Each type of group experience then would become both a corrective and an extension for the other.

The similarities and differences between these two types of group experiences and their relevance for learning about group therapy merit further attention from group therapists concerned with training. Individual students tend to be attracted to one type of experience or the other, depending on its fit with their personal needs and the personal benefit they perceive in it. A balanced approach, however, should recognize that leadership styles and procedures appropriate for the group therapist may at times resemble those used by the leader of the encounter group or the T group, but also vary with respect to the objectives of the treatment, the nature of the patient population being seen, the setting in which the group therapy is taking place, and the phase the therapy is in (Schein & Bennis, 1965; Yalom, 1970). For additional discussions of the roles of supervision and experiential learning in training for group therapy, the reader is referred to contributions by Abels (1970), Gladfelter (1970), Glatzer (1971), Grossman and Karmiol (1973), Grotjahn (1970), Kadis (1971), Lanning (1971), MacLennan (1971), and Rockwell (1971).

Continuing Education

More than ever before, professionals are experiencing the need for and finding opportunities to participate in additional group therapy training at training institutes and seminars. Training institutes with offerings in group therapy are held in connection with the annual meetings of the American Psychological Association. In addition, periodic, brief, specialized sessions in group therapy are offered by various centers during the year. Information about these training sessions can be obtained by writing to the appropriate organization.[3-7] It may be that the intangible aspects of "hope" are most meaningfully communicated to patients when they sense that the group therapist has developmental expectations for himself as well as for his patients.

GROUP THERAPY WITH SPECIALIZED POPULATIONS

In this section the use of the group therapy method with the following specialized populations is surveyed: children and their parents, adolescents, the aged, physically ill patients, drug abusers, and alcoholics.

[3]American Group Psychotherapy Association, Inc., P.O. Box 230, 150 Christopher Street, New York, New York 10014.

[4]American Society of Group Psychotherapy and Psychodrama, Inc., Beacon House, Inc., 259 Wolcott Avenue, Beacon, New York, 12508.

[5]Gestalt Institute of Cleveland, Inc., 1291 Euclid Avenue, Cleveland, Ohio 44112.

[6]International Transactional Analysis Association, Inc., 3155 College Avenue, Berkeley, California 94705.

[7]International Association of Applied Social Scientists, Inc., Suite 300, 1755 Massachusetts Avenue, N.W., Washington, D.C. 20036.

Children and their Parents

Several considerations influence the form and orientation of group therapy conducted with children, mostly in relation to their immaturity. In particular, the short attention span of children, their incompletely developed capacity for dealing with verbal abstractions, and their natural proclivity to learn and develop through the various modalities involved in play have led to widespread use of group play-therapy methods. These methods differ from other group therapy methods in the extent to which the child's behavior, interactions, verbalizations, and productions are actively interpreted (Dana & Dana, 1969; Rhodes, 1973; Rose, 1972; Witenberg & Bruseloff, 1972). Children in play groups are encouraged to describe their phenomenological world, and in the process can be helped to explicate their difficulties by projecting their feelings and attitudes on a fantasy level onto toys and other materials. As the group therapy situation is analogous in some ways to the family, opportunities arise for the group therapist to provide interpretations and sometimes reassurance regarding feelings of jealousy, abandonment, affectional hunger, and the like (Witenberg & Bruseloff, 1972)

The child's real dependency situation also places constraints on the group therapy approach and requires that the group therapist have insight into the effects of his own parenting needs and tendencies. Typically, it is necessary for the group therapist to be nurturant at one time and to set firm limits at another time with the same child or with different children (Harper, 1973; Ginott, 1961; Gratton & Rizzo, 1969).

It is logical to involve parents in a therapeutic alliance wherever possible in the treatment of children. In some cases the behavior of parents is directly implicated in the difficulty the child is having, and individual therapy for one or both parents may be indicated. If the child's difficulties are thought to reflect complex interactions among parents and siblings, then the child's group therapy might be supplemented with family therapy (Westman et al., 1963; Woods, 1974).

Parent guidance groups, using a somewhat conventional educational format to present general principles of parenting, may also be useful. Parents in these groups are helped to personalize the concepts discussed and to achieve at least a beginning grasp of the consequences of their parenting styles. Sometimes parents are encouraged to mention specific problems they are having with their children and, as they share in the group problems and attempts to handle the problems, their anxiety and frustration frequently diminish.

Because of the importance of school in the social and educational development of children, it is not suprising that various attempts to assist children with behavioral-emotional problems take place in group situations in the school. The formats for these groups range from those that utilize conventional educational methods primarily to those that emphasize more clinical or psychotherapeutic approaches (Rhodes, 1973). Life-adjustment classes for children who have been referred by teachers because of disruptive behavior are an example of the former, whereas group therapy conducted by specially trained clinical personnel is an example of the latter. It should also be noted that behavior analysis and behavior modification methods employed in groups seem to be increasing in use, and that many of the same behavioral principles and methods utilized with adults seem to apply with children also (Goldstein & Wolpe, 1971; Lazarus, 1971).

Children's hospitals provide another important setting for the use of group psychotherapy, particularly to alleviate psychological and behavioral problems associated with surgery and its sequelae, asthma, phobias, homesickness, and other similar difficulties (Wohl, 1967). Clinicians working in day hospitals and day care centers, aware of children's educational as well as psychological needs, have contributed to the development of a variety of group activities having psychoeducational goals. Psychoeducational approaches have been used appropriately to address problems that are sometimes seen as psychopathology and sometimes as learning disabilities, but appear to embrace both kinds of causation (Kraft, 1971).

Adolescents

Similar to the case with children, particular aspects of adolescents' developmental state have influenced the format, methods, and nuances of group therapy with patients of this age. The adolescent has often been characterized as being no longer a child but not yet an adult (Kraft, 1971; Spotnitz, 1972). The existential task of the adolescent, as described by Rachman (1972), has much to do with a need to understand, modulate the effects of, and grow with the emergence of new biological, hormonally related, and culturally shaped impulses. Effective group work with adolescents requires the therapist to be familiar with these sources of developmental confusion and turmoil during the teenage years and to be able to distinguish them from serious psychopathology (Meeks, 1973; Spotnitz, 1972).

As with younger children, adolescent therapy groups are capable of evoking sibling rivalry and parent-child conflict situations which need to be worked through. Success in this regard seems to be related to the ability of the group therapist to maintain a nurturant motivational posture toward the adolescents and toward the group, while at the same time setting appropriate limits on both. Given the intermediate emotional developmental state of the adolescent, the group therapist must avoid either overindulging the "child" in him or expecting too much from the "adult" in him.

The proclivity of adolescents to redirect their emotional dependence away from adults and toward peers creates an important dynamic for the beneficial effects of group therapy with these clients (Berkovitz, 1972; Greene, 1972; MacLennan & Felsenfeld, 1970). Group therapists who are trained in and who make consistent use of group processes in their work thus have a particularly effective set of skills for utilizing adolescents' peer-group orientation to enhance their participation in and benefit from group therapy.

Because sexual and aggressive concerns and activity increase generally during adolescence, circumstances sometimes require special groupings that accentuate these issues for discussion. For example, groups of pregnant adolescent girls may work meaningfully together on such topics as sex, boy-girl relationships, and personal hygiene, in addition to exploring their shared concerns about pregnancy, delivery fears, relationships with parents, plans for the child, and so on. There are differences of opinion, however, concerning whether male and female adolescents can be treated better in separate or in combined groups. Having groups of just one sex helps to minimize sexual acting out. Having both sexes in the same group, however, although potentially more tumultuous, is more reality-based and probably more growth facilitating (Kraft, 1971).

As to general considerations in the treatment of adolescents, Spotnitz (1972) believes that patients can be divided into two different diagnostic groups having different treatment implications: (a) patients who are "emotionally overcharged" and vulnerable to developing high states of tension, and (b) those who exhibit high levels of "emotional hunger" and tendencies to relate to authority in childlike, dependent ways. The first group of patients requires a minimum of intervention on the part of the group therapist and a calm constructive environment; the second group needs a high level of communication with the therapist and seems to profit from a nurturant family situation. Based on this formulation, Spotnitz describes a novel method of treatment he has been using with "emotionally hungry" patients, which he calls "constructive emotional interchange." In this method, the usual attempt to enlist the cooperation of the parents to assist in the treatment of the adolescent is reversed; the adolescent is involved as the "therapist's assistant" in training his parents regarding his needs and in assisting them to develop more effective coping mechanisms for their own feelings.

The Aged

Group therapy with the aged has taken various forms as a reflection of the multiple service needs of these patients. As a result, the term "group therapy" has been used broadly to refer to such intervention modalities as group counseling, activity therapy, and social group work.

According to Linden (1956), "The complete series of steps in the development of the severe emotional disturbances which lead to physiological breakdown if unimpeded are as follows: (1) disillusionment, (2) partial neurotic surrender, (3) senescent melancholy, (4) attempted reorganization, (5) secondary surrender, (6) senescent decline, (7) emotional regression, and (8) combined physiological and psychological recession" (pp, 131–132). Hence, Linden continues, a treatment program for the aged should include the following components as a minimum: (a) environmental manipulation (surroundings that provide acceptance for the elderly); (b) activity (movement and moderate excitement); (c) resocialization opportunities (reversal of withdrawal tendencies); and (d) psychotherapy. Group therapy for these elderly patients can prove particularly useful, Linden concludes, in alleviating depressive moods, increasing alertness, reducing confusion, improving orientation, and promoting the exchange of concern and affection.

Families of the aged are also likely to benefit from the improved functioning these patients are able to realize through group therapy. Family members of elderly patients are frequently burdened with feelings of guilt related to self-accusations of abandonment or neglect of the patient. These painful feelings are usually reduced following apparent improvement in the mood of the aged patients, in the enjoyment they are finding in their relationships, and in their mental efficiency. As the complaints of the patients lessen, family members experience some release from a sense of futility and feelings of frustration.

Group therapy for the aged is being provided both in outpatient and in inpatient settings (Euster, 1971; Liederman, Green & Liederman, 1967; Wolff, 1962). Older people who are ambulatory and in relatively good physical and psychological condition receive outpatient group therapy conducted in such settings as community centers, day centers, social agencies, and senior citizens clubs (Liederman, et al., 1967), as well as in outpatient departments of general hospitals. In all these settings group therapy programs frequently include an educational as well as a treatment component (consumer purchasing information, self-protection strategies, social skills, etc.) (Conrad, 1974; Goldfarb, 1972).

The aged population in inpatient settings, especially state hospitals, includes many patients who have been in the hospital for many years with a diagnosis of schizophrenia or who entered the hospital with diagnosis of organic brain syndrome when they were already old. Thus group therapy with elderly patients in state hospitals needs to include among its objectives attempts to reverse or arrest the process of "institutionalitis" and consequent dependency and social withdrawal (Burnside, 1970, 1971; Manaster, 1972; McNiel & Verwoerdt, 1973). Concurrently with the recent movement to shift elderly patients where possible from state hospitals to community agencies such as nursing and boarding homes, group therapy programs are now developing in these newer settings also (Saul & Saul, 1974).

The student of group therapy should not overlook the potential opportunity for continued personal and professional growth provided by therapeutic work with the elderly. Many young group therapists have been reared in surroundings from which grandparents and elderly aunts and uncles has been removed years earlier either by reason of death or institutionalization. Children reared in such environments have missed an opportunity to live through and work through important relationships and their feelings about physical and psychological decline and death (Kubler-Ross, 1969). Opportunities available to the therapist to deepen his appreciation for the full cycle are to be valued.

Physically Ill Patients

It was mentioned earlier in the chapter that group therapy in the United States originated with the work of Pratt with tuberculosis patients in the early 1900s. Pratt's "class method" attempted to assist patients with attitudinal, emotional, and behavioral aspects of their illness. The field of psychosomatics has grown over the past few decades in both scope and conceptual sophistication. Earlier psychoanalytic contributions in this area promoted the concept of psychogenicity, which focused usefully on needs for psychological treatment of psychosomatic disorders but limited development in the field by suggesting greater specificity in the relationship between certain psychological concerns and certain physical illnesses than could be justified. Lipowski (1968) provides a well-reasoned review and critique of changes in psychosomatic concepts, and two of his concluding remarks indicate the degree to which the field has moved from overspecificity to a general and comprehensive position:

> Human health and disease are viewed as states without a sharp dividing line between them; they are determined by multiple factors: biological, psychological, social; any event at any level of organization of the human organism—from the symbolic to the molecular—may have repercussions at all other levels . . . Psychotherapy may be of value whenever psychological factors are recognized

as significantly contributing to the precipitation, maintenance, or exacerbation of any illness in a given person [p. 414]

Group therapy has been employed in treating a wide range of physical illnesses to reduce precipitating, concomitant, exacerbating, or subsequent anxiety and depression (Stein, 1971). Among the groups with whom the methods have been used are asthmatics (Groen & Pelser, 1960; Mascia & Teiter, 1971; Reckless, 1971; Reed, 1962; Wohl, 1963), parents of asthmatic children (Abramson & Peshkin, 1960), peptic ulcer patients (Fortin & Abse, 1956), diabetics (Frizzell, 1968), parents of diabetics (Hefferman, 1959), and cardiac and hypertensive illness patients (Adsett & Bruhn, 1968; Bilodeau & Hackett, 1971; Goldner & Kyle, 1960; Mone, 1970; Oradie & Waite, 1974; Titchener, Sheldon, & Ross, 1959). Helpful applications of group therapy have also been reported with brain-injured patients (Edwards, 1967), patients with multiple sclerosis (Whally & Strehl, 1969), cystic fibrosis patients (Farkas & Shwachman, 1973), adult male patients with cerebral palsy (Lubin & Slominski, 1960), and parents of cerebral-palsied children (Heisler, 1974). Patients on hemodialysis (Hollon, 1973), the deaf (Landau, 1968; Sarlin & Altshuler, 1968; Stinson, 1971), and obese patients (Holt & Winick, 1961; Lassiter & Willett, 1973; Penick, 1970; Slawson, 1965; Snow & Held, 1973) also have been treated with group methods. Finally of note are pregnancy, delivery, and abortion, all of which are experiences that at some time have been associated with anxiety, fear, guilt, and depression (Lubin, Gardiner, & Roth, 1975). Group therapy has been used with each of these conditions (Bernstein & Tinkham, 1971; Black, 1972; Coleman, 1971).

Drug Abuse

Comprehensive drug abuse treatment programs have tended to be of two kinds, total abstention programs or drug substitution programs. Total abstention programs have employed group psychotherapy to assist in reducing the addict's anxiety and thus his need for the narcotic, to help the addict to confront and change his stress-avoidant strategies, and to reduce his sense of alienation and loneliness (Kaufman, 1972; Ketai, 1973; Ross, McReynolds, & Berzins, 1974). Provision of emotional support during the period of abstinence is another important use for group therapy (Kaufman, 1972), which in abstinence-oriented programs has varied from brief, supportive meetings to intensive, time-extended sessions in total-control environments (Ross et al., 1974). Many of these groups are led by trained exaddicts who are thoroughly familiar with the nuances of the addict's life-style and defenses. Confrontive techniques originally developed at Synanon are used in many of these programs (Casriel, 1964).

The success of abstinence-oriented programs, as measured by the proportion of patients who remain in the program and abstain from the use of narcotics, has been less than hoped for (Binot, 1973; Ross et al., 1974). This has led to the search for and discovery of a substitute drug (methadone) that could block the addict's craving for heroin and thus bring his overall behavior under therapeutic guidance. Dole, Nyswander and Warner (1968), originators of the methadone maintenance program, reasoned that much of the heroin addict's difficulties were circular and stimulated by the buildup of a craving for the drug. The methadone program is controversial, as some claim that the addiction itself remains unchanged even though the addict's drug-associated behavior has been brought under control. Of note in the present context is that group therapy has played a role in the design of methadone maintenance programs for heroin addicts (La Rosa, Lipsius, & La Rosa, 1974; Willett, 1973).

Alcoholism

Alcoholism is a complex behavioral-emotional-physiological problem which in the recent past was viewed as an example of failure of will, slothfulness, and general moral inferiority. It is now seen as a debilitating condition causing widespread social and economic problems, and as a condition that can afflict people of any socieconomic level and of any ethnic, racial, or religious group. Also, it is a condition that if untreated usually is progressively deteriorating (Stein & Friedman, 1971).

A variety of group and group-related treatment programs has been reported in which group therapy for alcoholics has been used in conjunction with psychodrama (Cabrera, 1961; Weiner, 1966), individual psychotherapy (Preston, 1960), hypnosis (Paley, 1952), aversive drug therapy (Greenbaum, 1954), and crisis intervention (Chafetz & Blane, 1963). Anecdotal and quasi-evaluative studies report successful outcomes in the use of such group methods with alcoholic patients (Hartocollis & Sheafor, 1968; Pittman & Tate, 1969; Westfield, 1972).

The importance of relationship and communication factors in the continuance and exacerbation of the alcoholic's problems has led to the development of several concurrent group treatment programs for the spouses of alcoholics (Cadogan, 1973; Kotis, 1968; Smith, 1969). Wives and husbands of alcoholics have been found to need therapy for their own problems, not only because they may themselves have a drinking problem but also because they may have such characterological problems as oversubmissiveness or overdominance with attendant manifestations of anxiety and depression. In addition, the wife or husband of the alcoholic often needs support and other assistance in dealing with the vicissitudes of the spouse's condition. In those cases in which the stability of the marital relationship depends heavily on rather rigidly defined personality and/or role complementarity, change in the patient's behavior that implies change in the tenously balanced marital relationship can stimulate the spouse to attempt to reestablish the prior relationship. Group therapy for the spouse in such a case would reduce the need for this countertherapeutic response and would involve the spouse as a therapeutic agent for the patient.

Inasmuch as an alcoholic's treatment needs vary at different times, group treatment has been offered in general hospitals and state hospitals, in partial hospitalization contexts, in halfway houses, and in clinics and community mental health centers. An increasing number of business organizations is providing company facilities and resources for various treatment programs for employees with alcohol-related problems.

The complexity of the alcoholic's problems have resulted in the employment of group treatment methods varying considerably in format, intensity, and duration. As one example, the *orientation group* was devised to help alcoholics overcome their resistances to treatment, provide instruction on the objectives and procedures of group therapy, and to ease them into a treatment situation by making their entry less threatening. Institutions sometimes use the orientation group as a "holding" mechanism is order to initiate patients into the treatment environment before decisions about more definite treatment assignments are made (Lubin et al., 1973). As other examples, the *activity group* stresses pleasant group-centered projects (dance, music, recreational therapy, occupational therapy, work projects), whereas the *therapeutic group* represents an opportunity in addition to the activity group for patients to improve their socialization skills.

Alcoholics Anonymous is the best known of the peer-led self-help groups for alcoholics. The aspects of mutual support, avowal of the alcohol problem, and denial of psychological illness fostered by A.A. are well known, and many patients who have been helped by A.A. had previously failed to profit from more professional psychological methods. In general, the methods used in group therapy for alcoholics are similar to those used with other types of psychological problems. Steiner (1971), however, has classified different types of alcoholics in TA terms, explicated the games employed by alcoholics, and accordingly devised differential strategies for use in treatment.

Additional Special Groups

Therapy has been conducted with numerous other homogeneously composed groups of patients. Of particular interest for further reading are descriptions of group therapy with predelinquents, delinquents, and prison inmates provided in reports by Arnold and Stiles (1972), Baumgold (1970), Federn (1962), Hersko (1962), Kassoff (1958), McCarty (1972), O'Donnell (1973), Rappaport (1971), and Slaikeu (1973). Also of note are reports of group therapy with marital couples by Cochrane (1973), Gurman (1973), Leichter (1973), Burns (1972), Nadeau (1972), Glendening and Wilson (1972), Hardcastle (1972), Wadeson (1972), Kohn (1971), Lindenauer (1971), McClellan and Stieper (1971), and Olsen (1971).

In the use of group therapy with groups of people who have similar special problems of the kinds mentioned in this section, it is well to remember that the act of composing homogeneous groups may influence the group therapist to spotlight the "common problem" and not attend sufficiently to the patients' individual growth and learning needs. As mentioned earlier, however, emphasizing the shared problems increases the sense of "universality" (Yalom, 1970), increases group cohesion, and makes the "problems" more visible. A challenge to the group therapist, then, is to remain aware of and to relate to the full range of intragroup differences while working with the general and unique properties and developments in the homogeneous group.

ISSUES, TRENDS, AND NEEDS

Several issues currently being discussed and debated among group therapists are either explicitly stated or implied in the earlier discussions in the sections on types of group therapy and intensive small-group experiences. Salient among these issues are genetic-historical insight versus learning from interactional feedback, leader centrality, high versus low structure, the therapist's social role, group leader accreditation, and the extension of group therapy services to underinvolved populations.

Genetic-Historical Insight versus Learning from Interactional Feedback

The strong psychoanalytic influence on psychotherapy practice until a decade ago, and the relative paucity of empirical studies of "what is

therapeutic" and how learning takes place during group therapy, prolonged an overreliance on the importance of genetic-historical insight as
a "curative factor" (Winer, 1974). The success of the application of
learning theory principles (Lazarus, 1968) and the widespread enthusiasm for the small-group movement (Bradford et al., 1964) during
the past decade have reduced the reliance now placed on genetic-
historical insight in bringing about behavior change. The nature of this
issue certainly lends itself to empirical study, however, rather than to
conclusions based on belief or enthusiasm, and much group therapy
investigative work remains to be done in this regard.

Change toward a more interactive focus in group psychotherapy on
what is therapeutic seems to have been influenced primarily by two
factors: movement away from a structural and toward an interpersonal
emphasis in psychotherapy by such influential neo-Freudian analysts as
Horney (1950) and Sullivan (1955), and the growing number of group
therapists who have acquired experience as participants in and leaders
of brief intensive small groups. These group therapists have been impressed by the apparent impact of behaviorally based feedback on behavior
change. Major advantages of interpersonal feedback in a supportive climate as a precursor of change are its immediacy and the fact that the
protagonist is given specific behavioral change cues.

In actual practice, most group therapists seem to work in their
sessions both with aspects of the patient's past life as it seems relevant
in the present and aspects of his current interpersonal behavior. They
differ of course in the relative emphasis, timing, and prominence they
give to these two factors.

Leader Centrality

The theoretical positions of some of the previously presented schools of
group therapy have relevance for the degree of centrality of the group
therapist's position and for the rate and nature of his activity. The
psychoanalytic and TA positions are quite clear in emphasizing that the
group therapist is one of the central agents in the change process. Those
theorists who rely more on "psychotherapy through the group process,"
however, such as Whitaker & Lieberman (1964), see the therapist's role
as more of a facilitator than a teacher or purveyor of psychological
insights.

These considerations are related to the issue of leader structuring
versus working with the commmon group tension (Bion, 1961; Ezriel,
1950; Foulkes, 1965). Obviously, if a therapist seeks to discover common group themes and concerns, he is likely to regulate his own

activity so as to facilitate the emergence of this material. In some cases, this might mean relatively little verbal participation by the group therapist. In other words, then, the degree and type of activity engaged in by a group therapist is likely to be related to his theory of *change*, that is, the way in which he believes change to occur and what he believes the primary agents of change to be.

Those theorists who hold an eclectic view of the nature of the "curative factors" in group therapy and are willing to acknowledge and work with "nonspecific effects" (Fish, 1973) vary their behavior in terms of their judgment of the needs of individual patients and/or group conditions. A therapist who subscribes to Yalom's (1970, pp. 66–69) previously mentioned list of curative factors, for example, shows considerable variation in his behavior both within and across sessions.

The therapist's personality and needs certainly influence his choice of style and theory of group therapy (Bach, 1956). The activity-passivity dimension of the group therapist's personality can affect his behavior in at least two ways: the general rate of his activity and, in so far as there is likely to be correlation between the general trait of activity-passivity and an activist orientation to change situations, his selection of techniques.

In addition to the variables of therapist personality and attitude, therapist participation in small, intensive, group experiences has stimulated a great deal of experimentation with format and activities. Cases in point are the extension of the length of the session (Mintz, 1969), physically touching patients (O'Hearne & Glad, 1968), and using structured experiences (Pfeiffer & Jones, 1969), which are innovations intended to intensify the group experience and shorten the length of the treatment.

High versus Low Structure

How much structure and patient preparation should be provided prior to the beginning of group psychotherapy? Group therapists differ on this issue. Those with a more psychoanalytic orientation seem to believe that patient selection, the admonition to "speak spontaneously," and the obvious role differential of therapist and patient are sufficient to launch and maintain the treatment process. Group therapists with a more activist orientation and those who work more in the ego-psychology domain tend to face the therapeutic task as an educational procedure which includes thorough initial orientation (Rabin, 1970), perhaps including viewing a film for induction into the role of a group therapy patient (Logue, Peterson & Miller, 1969; Strupp & Bloxom, 1973), setting of a therapeutic contract (Mallucio & Marlow, 1974), assigning homework and extragroup tasks, periodic review of progress toward patients' personal goals, and so on. The philosophy is more in keeping with a consumer model in which the patient's wishes regarding treatment are given credence (Berne, 1961; Hornstra et al., 1972).

Therapist's Social Role

Another issue on which group therapists differ is one that has current sociopolitical significance—the issue of the adjustment of the individual to society's norms versus the facilitation of individual development even if it means a challenge to social norms. Should the group therapist facilitate the raising to awareness and discussion of racist-sexist-ageist issues or should he view these as individual and group resistances when they occur? Or should the group therapist be an advocate of the individual even though the client's behavior challenges social norms? (Fried, 1974; Franks & Vasanti, 1974; Steiner, 1971).

Group Leader Accreditation

As noted previously, professional organizations have been devoting attention to the task of devising standards of practice and standards for the training of practitioners. Specifically, criteria and procedures for accreditation within their own fields have been developed by the American Group Psychotherapy Association, the American Society of Group Psychotherapy and Psychodrama, the Gestalt Institute of Cleveland, and the International Transactional Analysis Association. Most recently, the International Association of Applied Social Scientists was formed in 1971 as a nonprofit professional organization in order to accredit practitioners of group methods deriving from the laboratory training model. Accreditation is based on demonstrated conceptual and behavioral competence and is evaluated by regional peer review panels. Currently, accreditation is available in the following areas: Laboratory Educator, Organization Development Consultant, and Personal Growth Group Consultant (*APA Monitor*, 1971).

Extension of Group Therapy Services to
Underinvolved Populations

In addition to the substantive research needs mentioned earlier, there is an urgent need to develop effective methods for providing group therapy–type services to populations who have been relatively neglected up to now (e.g., children and the aged; see Lubin & Lubin, 1973), who typically are late to apply for such services (Lubin et al., 1973), or who do not continue in programs once they have begun them. The experience of public mental health facilities, including comprehensive community mental health centers, with the dropout problem among lower socioeconomic class patients has been distressing (Reissman, Cohen & Pearl, 1964), and Cobb's (1971) survey of the literature on outpatient services for lower socioeconomic patients at community mental health centers found very few attempts to develop and evaluate novel programs. Exploration of adaptations and modifications to existing programs to make them more suitable for those who typically do not regularly attend therapy programs should receive some impetus from the work of Warren and Rice (1972), who demonstrated that by careful planning and slight modification of the general routine, the therapy attrition of low-prognosis patients can be reduced, their total therapy involvement lengthened, and their general improvement enhanced.

SUMMARY AND CONCLUSIONS

In this concluding section, major points from the preceding pages are presented together with some summary statements. Group therapy is going through an exciting period in its history. A variety of approaches and techniques from parallel developing intensive small-group fields (laboratory training and encounter groups) are being employed by group therapists of various theoretical persuasions. Professional organizations are beginning to turn their attention to such important issues as certification of practitioners and educating the public regarding the effectiveness and limitations of the various group methods. Publication, another index of a field's vitality, shows a consistent increase in the area of group therapy.

What are the "curative factors" in group therapy? Various ones have been put forward and, not unexpectedly, the factors mentioned are consistent with the individual or group focus of the proponent's theory. Psychoanalytically oriented theories posit patient motivation and therapist analysis of transference and resistance as all-important. For the practitioner of transactional analysis, patient-therapist change contracts and therapist potency, protection, and permission are the crucial factors. The behavior group therapist attempts to diagnose and manage suitable reinforcement contingencies for individual behavior within the group setting. Those theorists who focus on the group see one of the major functions of the group therapist to be guiding the group away from premature anxiety-reducing solutions produced by immediate authority and peer relationship problems.

The recent research literature indicates an attempt to come to grips with the complexity of the group therapy situation by achieving greater specificity in the manipulation of patient, therapist, group, situational, and outcome variables, and by using multivariate designs. Extrapolating the findings of suitable small-group research to the group therapy field and studying group therapy by means of analog research are two additional methods that have been suggested, and SD and group composition are two substantive areas that have received recent research interest.

The components of many group therapy training programs include a didactic phase plus readings and an apprenticeship arrangement (cotherapy). There is an increasing tendency for training centers also to include an experiential phase for the student group therapist. The use of recordings (videotape and audiotape), diaries kept by trainees, and rating scales to be used for feedback regarding the performance of student group therapists are recommended. In addition, considering the need for group therapists to be knowledgeable about and skilled in influencing group forces, and also to continue their own growth in such areas as authority relationships, feelings of affection, hostile feelings, and the like, it is suggested that the training program include experience in a group process seminar and in an encounter group. In order to supplement a possible pendulum swing in the direction of too much influence from brief intensive group experiences, group therapists should be aware of the need to acquire experience with people who are under considerable stress and the need for experience in working with the same groups over a period of a year or more.

The continued development of group therapy requires freedom for group therapists to try new methods. However, ethical considerations and the continued development of group therapy also require that the *safety* as well as the *effectiveness* of these newer methods be determined. Despite the exploratory use of various methods by some group therapists, most group therapy is still conducted in a small, circular group within a discussion format. As an "educational" or "reeducative" technique, patients in group therapy might benefit from experimentation with a wide range of educational formats and electronic aids.

REFERENCES

Abels, P. A. On the nature of supervision: The medium is the group. *Child Welfare*, 1970, **49**, 304–311.

Abramson, H., & Peshkin, M. Psychosomatic group therapy with parents of children with intractable asthma. *Annals of Allergies,* 1960, **18,** 87–91.

Adsett, C. C., & Bruhn, J. G. Short-term group psychotherapy for postmyocardial infarction patients and their wives. *Canadian Medical Association Journal,* 1968, **99,** 577–584.

Allen, J. G. Implications of research in self-disclosure for group psychotherapy. *International Journal of Group Psychotherapy,* 1973, **23,** 306–321.

American Group Psychotherapy Association. Committee on History. A brief history of the American Group Psychotherapy Association 1943–1968. *International Journal of Group Psychotherapy,* 1971, **21,** 406–435.

American Psychological Association. New professional association formed; Focus: certification and public education. *APA Monitor,* 1971, **2**(11), 7.

Anthony, E. J. Comparison between individual and group psychotherapy. In H. I. Kaplan & B. J. Sadock (Eds.), *The evolution of group therapy.* New York: Jason Aronson, 1972, Pp. 83–96.

Arnold, W. R., & Stiles, B. A summary of increasing use of group methods in correctional institutions. *International Journal of Group Psychotherapy,* 1972, **22,** 77–92.

Astrachan, B. M. Towards a social systems model of therapeutic groups. *Archives of General Psychiatry,* 1970, **5,** 110–119.

Ayllon, T. Intensive treatment of psychotic behavior by stimulus satiation and food reinforcement. *Behavior Research and Therapy,* 1963, **1,** 53–61.

Bach, G. R. Current trends in group psychotherapy. In D. Brower & L. E. Abt (Eds.), *Progress in clinical psychology.* Vol. II. New York: Grune & Stratton, 1956, Pp. 114–145.

Batchelder, R. L., & Hardy, J. M. *Using sensitivity training and the laboratory method: An organizational case study in the development of human resources.* New York: Association Press, 1968.

Baumgold, J. Prison notes. *Voices: Art and Science of Psychotherapy,* 1970, **6,** 37–41.

Benne, K. D. History of the T-Group in the laboratory setting. In L. P. Bradford, J. R. Gibb, & K. D. Benne (Eds.), *T-Group theory and laboratory method: Innovation in re-education.* New York: Wiley, 1964. Pp. 80–135.

Berger, M. *Videotape techniques in psychiatric training and treatment.* New York: Brunner/Mazel, 1971.

Berger, M. M., & Berger, L. F. Psychogeriatric group approaches. In H. I. Kaplan & B. J. Sadock (Eds.), *Comprehensive group psychotherapy.* Baltimore: Williams & Wilkins, 1971. Pp. 726–736.

Berkovitz, I. H. (Ed.) *Adolescents grow in groups: Clinical experiences in adolescent group psychotherapy.* New York: Brunner/Mazel, 1972.

Berman, A. L., Messersmith, C. E., & Mullens, B. N. Profile of group-therapy practice in university counseling centers. *Journal of Counseling Psychology,* 1972, **19,** 353–354.

Berne, E. *Transactional analysis in psychotherapy.* New York: Grove Press, 1961.

Bernestein, N. R., & Tinkham, C. B. Group therapy following abortion. *Journal of Nervous and Mental Disease,* 1971, **152,** 303–314.

Bilodeau, C. B., & Hackett, T. P. Issues raised in a group setting by patients recovering from myocardial infarction. *American Journal of Psychiatry,* 1971, **128,** 105–110.

Binot, E. Group therapy for hospitalized drug addicts: Review of four years of experience. *Toxicomanies,* 1973, **5,** 31–45.

Bion, W. R. *Experiences in groups.* London: Tavistock, 1961.

Black, S. Group therapy for pregnant and nonpregnant adolescents. *Child Welfare,* 1972, **51,** 514–518.

Block, E. L., & Goodstein, L. D. Comment on "Influence of an interviewer's disclosure on the self-disclosing behavior of interviewees." *Journal of Counseling Psychology,* 1971, **18,** 595–597.

Bodin, A. M. Videotape applications in training family therapists. *Journal of Nervous and Mental Disease,* 1969, **148,** 251–261.

Bradford, L. P., Gibb, J. R., & Benne, K. D. (Eds.). *T-Group theory and laboratory method: Innovation in re-education.* New York: Wiley, 1964.

Burns, C. W. Effectiveness of the basic encounter group in marriage counseling. *Dissertation Abstracts International,* 1972, 1281B.

Burnside, I. M. Loss: A constant theme in group work with the aged. *Hospital and Community Psychiatry,* 1970, **21,** 175–177.

Burnside, I. M. Long-term group work with hospitalized aged. *Gerontologist,* 1971, **11,** 213–218.

Business Week. Yourself as others see you. March 16, 1963, p. 160.

Byrne, D. Repression-sensitization as a dimension of personality. In B. A. Maher (Ed.), *Progress in experimental personality research.* New York: Academic Press, 1964. Pp. 169–220.

Cabrera, F. J. Group psychotherapy and psychodrama for alcoholic patients in a state hospital rehabilitation program. *Group Psychotherapy,* 1961, **14,** 151–159.

Cadogan, D. A. Marital group therapy in the treatment of alcoholism. *Quarterly Journal of Studies in Alcohol,* 1973, **34,** 1187–1194.

Calahan, S. Personal communication, 1974.

Casriel, D. *So fair a house: The story of Synanon.* Englewood Cliffs, N.J.: Prentice-Hall, 1964.

Chafetz, M., & Blane, H. T. Alcohol-crisis treatment approach and establishment of treatment relations with alcoholics. *Psychological Reports,* 1963, **12,** 862.

Cobb, C.W. Community mental health services and the lower socio-economic classes: A summary of research literature on outpatient treatment (1963–1969). *American Journal of Orthopsychiatry,* 1971, **42,** 404–414.

Cochrane, N. Some reflections on the unsuccesful treatment of a group of married couples. *British Journal of Psychiatry*, 1973, **123**, 395–401.

Coleman, A. Psychology of a first baby group. *International Journal of Group Psychotherapy*, 1971, **21**, 74–83.

Conrad, W. K. A group therapy program with older adults in a high-risk neighborhood setting. *International Journal of Group Psychotherapy*, 1974, **24**, 358.

Corsini, R. J., & Putzey, L. J. *Bibliography of group psychotherapy 1906–1956*. Psychodrama and Group Psychotherapy Monographs, No. 29. New York: Beacon House, 1957.

Culbert, S. A. The interpersonal process of self-disclosure: It takes two to see one. In R. T. Golembewski & A. Blumberg (Eds.), *Sensitivity training and the laboratory approach*. Itasca, Ill.: Peacock, 1970.

Dana, R. H., & Dana, J. M. Systematic observation of children's behavior in group therapy. *Psychological Reports*, 1969, **24**, 134.

Davidson, G. C. A social learning therapy program with an autistic child. *Behavior Research and Therapy*, 1964, **2**, 149–160.

Dole, V. P., Nyswander, M., & Warner, A. Successful treatment of 750 criminal addicts. *Journal of the American Medical Association*, 1968, **206**, 2708.

Dusay, J. M., & Steiner, C. Transactional analysis in groups. In H. I. Kaplan & B. J. Sadock (Eds.), *Comprehensive group psychotherapy*. Baltimore: Williams & Wilkins, 1971. Pp. 198–240.

Edwards, S. L. Group work with brain damaged patients. *Hospital and Community Psychiatry*, 1967, **18**, 267–270.

Euster, G. L. A system of groups in institutions for the aged. *Social Casework*, 1971, **52**, 523–529.

Ezriel, H. A psycho-analytic approach to group treatment. *British Journal of Medical Psychology*, 1950, **23**, 59–74.

Farkas, A., & Shwachman, H. Psychological adaption to chronic illness: A group discussion with cystic fibrosis patients. *American Journal of Orthopsychiatry*, 1973, **43**, 259–260.

Federn, B. Limited goals in short-term group psychotherapy with institutionalized delinquent adolescent boys. *International Journal of Group Psychotherapy*, 1962, **12**, 503.

Fish, J. M. *Placebo therapy*. San Francisco: Jossey-Bass, 1973.

Fortin, J., & Abse, D. Group psychotherapy with peptic ulcer: A preliminary report. *International Journal of Group Psychotherapy*, 1956, **6**, 383–391.

Foulkes, S. H. *Therapeutic group analysis*. New York: International Universities Press, 1965.

Frank, J. D. *Persuasion and healing: A comparative study of psychotherapy*. Johns Hopkins University Press, 1961.

Franks, V. & Vasanti, B. *Women in therapy: New psychotherapies for changing society*. New York: Brunner/Mazel, 1974.

Fried, E. Does woman's new self-concept call for new approaches in psychotherapy? *International Journal of Group Psychotherapy,* 1974, **24,** 265–272.

Frizzell, M. K. Group therapy for diabetic mental patients. *Hospital and Community Psychiatry,* 1968, **19,** 287–298.

Frust, W. Homogeneous versus heterogeneous groups. In M. Rosenberg & M. Berger (Eds.), *Group psychotherapy and group function.* New York: Basic Books, 1963. Pp. 407–410.

Gibb, J. R. The message from research. In J. W. Pfeiffer & J. E. Jones (Eds.), *The 1974 annual handbook for group facilitators.* La Jolla, Calif.: University Associates, 1974.

Ginott, H. *Group psychotherapy with children.* New York: McGraw-Hill, 1961.

Glad, D. D., Ferguson, R., Hayne, M., & Glad, V. B. Schizophrenic factor reactions to four group psychotherapy methods. *International Journal of Group Psychotherapy,* 1963, **13,** 196–210.

Glad, D. D., & Glad, V. B. *Interpersonality synopsis.* New York: Libra, 1963.

Glad, D. D., Glad, V. B., & Barnes, R. H. *Operational values in psychotherapy.* New York: Oxford University Press, 1959.

Gladfelter, J. H. Videotape supervision of co-therapists. *Journal of Group Psychoanalysis and Process,* 1970, **2,** 45–46.

Glassman, S. Group psychotherapy. Unpublished manuscript, Ft. Logan Mental Health Center, Denver, Colorado, 1967.

Glatzer, H. T. Analytic supervision in group psychotherapy. *International Journal of Group Psychotherapy,* 1971, **21,** 436–443.

Glendening, S. E., & Wilson, A. J., III. Experiments in group premarital counseling. *Social Casework,* 1972, **53,** 551–562.

Goldfarb, A. L. Group therapy with the old and aged. In H. I. Kaplan & B. J. Sadock (Eds.), *Group treatment of mental illness.* New York: Dutton, 1972.

Goldner, R., & Kyle, E. A group approach to the cardiac patient. *Social Casework,* 1960, **41,** 346.

Goldstein, A. P., Heller, K., & Sechrest, L. B. *Psychotherapy and the psychology of behavior change.* New York: Wiley, 1966.

Goldstein, A., & Wolpe, J. Behavior therapy in groups. In H. I. Kaplan & B. J. Sadock (Eds.), *New models for group therapy.* New York: Dutton, 1972.

Goodstein, L. D., & Reinecker, V. M. Factors affecting self-disclosure: A review of the literature. In B. Maher (Ed.), *Progress in experimental personality research.* Vol. 7. New York: Academic Press, 1974. Pp. 49–77.

Gratton, L., & Rizzo, A. E. Group therapy with young psychotic children. *International Journal of Group Psychotherapy,* 1969, **19,** 63–71.

Greenbaum, H. Group psychotherapy with alcoholics in conjunction with antibuse treatment. *International Journal of Group Psychotherapy,* 1954, **4,** 30.

Greene, R. J., & Crowder, D. L. Group therapy with adolescents. *Journal of Contemporary Psychotherapy,* 1972, **5,** 55–61.

Groen, J., & Pelser, H. Experiences with and results of group psychotherapy in patients with bronchial asthma. *Journal of Psychosomatic Research*, 1960, **4**, 191–205.

Grossman, W. K., & Karmiol, E. Group psychotherapy supervision and its effects on resident training. *American Journal of Psychiatry*, 1973, **130**, 920–921.

Grotjahn, M. The analytic group experience in the training of therapists. *Voices: Art and Science of Psychotherapy*, 1970, **5**, 108–109.

Gundlach, R. H. Overview of outcome studies in group psychotherapy. *International Journal of Group Psychotherapy*, 1967, **177**, 196–210.

Gurman, A. S. The effects and effectiveness of marital therapy: A review of outcome research. *Family Process*, 1973, **12**, 145–170.

Guthrie, E. R. *The psychology of learning*. New York: Harper, 1952.

Hardcastle, D. R. Measuring effectiveness in group marital counseling. *Family Coordinator*, 1972, **21**, 213–218.

Harman, R. L. Goals of Gestalt therapy. *Professional Psychology*, 1974, **5**, 178–184.

Harper, J. Embracement and enticement: A therapeutic nursery group for autistic children. *Slow Learning Child*, 1973, **20**, 173–176.

Harrison, R. L., & Lubin, B. Interpersonal perception and interpersonal behavior in training groups: A study in group composition. *Journal of Applied Behavioral Sciences*, 1965, **1**, 13–16.

Hartocollis, P., & Sheafor, D. Group psychotherapy with alcoholics: A critical review. *Psychiatric Digest*, 1968, **29**, 15–22.

Heath, E. S., & Bacal, H. A. A method of group psychotherapy at the Tavistock Clinic. In C. J. Sager & H. S. Kaplan (Eds.), *Progress in group and family therapy*. New York: Brunner/Mazel, 1972. Pp. 33–46.

Hefferman, A. An experiment in group therapy with mothers of diabetic children. *Acta Psychotherapy*, 1959, 7(Suppl.), 155.

Heisler, V. Dynamic group psychotherapy with parents of cerebral palsied children. *Rehabilitation Literature*, 1974, **35**, 329–330.

Hersko, M. Group therapy with delinquency girls. *American Journal of Orthopsychiatry*, 1962, **32**, 169–175.

Hill, M. J., & Blane, H. T. Evaluation of psychotherapy with alcoholics: A critical review. *Quarterly Journal of Studies in Alcohol*, 1967, **28**, 76.

Hollon, T. H. Modified group therapy in the treatment of patients on chronic hemodialysis. *American Journal of Psychotherapy*, 1973, **26**, 501–510.

Holt, H., & Winick, C. Group psychotherapy with obese women. *Archives of General Psychiatry*, 1961, **5**, 156.

Horney, K. *Neurosis and human growth*. New York: Norton, 1950.

Hornstra, R. K., Lubin, B., Lewis, R. V., & Willis, B. S. Worlds apart: Patients and professionals. *Archives of General Psychiatry*, 1972, 553–557.

Jourard, S. M. *The transparent self: Self-disclosure and well-being*. Princeton, N.J.: Van Nostrand, 1964.

Jourard, S. M., & Friedman, R. Experimenter-subject "distance" and self-disclosure. *Journal of Personality and Social Psychology,* 1970, **15,** 278–282.

Jourard, S. M., & Jaffe, P. E. Influence of an interviewer's disclosure on the self-disclosing behavior of interviewees. *Journal of Counseling Psychology,* 1970, **17,** 252–257.

Kadis, A. L. A new group supervisory technique for group therapists. *Voices: The Art and Science of Psychotherapy,* 1971, **7,** 31–32.

Kassoff, A. L. Advantage of multiple therapists in a group of severely acting-out adolescent boys. *International Journal of Group Psychotherapy,* 1958, **8,** 70–75.

Kaufman, E. A psychiatrist views an addict self-help program. *American Journal of Psychiatry,* 1972, **128,** 846–852.

Kelman, H. C. The role of the group in the induction of therapeutic change. *International Journal of Group Psychotherapy,* 1963, **13,** 399–432.

Kelman, H. D., & Parloff, M. B. Interrelations among three criteria of improvement in group therapy: Comfort, effectiveness, and self-awareness. *Journal of Abnormal and Social Psychology,* 1957, **54,** 281–288.

Ketai, R. Peer-observed psychotherapy with institutionalized narcotic addicts. *Archives of General Psychiatry,* 1973, **29,** 51–53.

Knopka, G. Knowledge and skill in the group therapist. *American Journal of Orthopsychiatry,* 1949, **19,** 56–60.

Kohn, R. Treatment of married couples in a group. *Group Process,* 1971, **4,** 96–105.

Kotis, J. P. Initial sessions of group counseling with alcoholics and their spouses. *Social Casework,* 1968, **49,** 228–232.

Kraft, I. A. Child and adolescent group psychotherapy. In H. I. Kaplan & B. J. Sadock (Eds.), *Comprehensive group psychotherapy,* Baltimore: Williams & Wilkins, 1971. Pp. 534–565.

Kubler-Ross, E. *On death and dying.* New York: McMillan, 1969.

Kurtz, R. R., & Grummon, D. L. Different approaches to the measurement of therapist empathy and their relationship to therapy outcomes. *Journal of Consulting and Clinical Psychology,* 1972, **39,** 106–115.

Kutash, S. B. Values and dangers in group process experiences. *Group Process,* 1971, **3,** 7–11.

Lakin, M. Some ethical issues in sensitivity training. *American Psychologist,* 1969, **24,** 923–128.

Landau, M. E. Group psychotherapy with deaf retardates. *International Journal of Group Psychotherapy,* 1968, **18,** 345–351.

Lanning, W. L. A study of the relation between group and individual supervision and three relationship measures. *Journal of Counseling Psychology,* 1971, **18,** 401–416.

La Rosa, J. C., Lipsius, S. H., & La Rosa, J. H. Experiences with a combination of group therapy and methadone maintenance in the treatment of heroin addiction. *International Journal of the Addictions,* 1974, **9,** 605.

Lassiter, R. E., & Willett, A. B. Interaction of group therapists in the multidisciplinary team treatment of obesity. *International Journal of Group Psychotherapy*, 1973, **23**, 82–92.

Lazarus, A. A. Behavior therapy in groups. In G. M. Gazda (Ed.), *Basic approaches to group psychotherapy and group counseling*. Springfield, Ill.: Charles C Thomas, 1968. Pp. 149–175.

Lazarus, A. A. *Behavior therapy and beyond*. New York: McGraw-Hill, 1971.

Leichter, E. Use of group dynamics in the training and supervision of group therapists in a social agency. *International Journal of Group Psychotherapy*, 1963, **13**, 74–79.

Leichter, E. Treatment of married couples groups. *Family Coordinator*, 1973, **22**, 31–42.

Levitsky, A., & Perls, F. The rules and games of Gestalt therapy. In H. M. Ruitenbeek (Ed.), *Group therapy today: Styles, methods, and techniques*. New York: Atherton Press, 1969. Pp. 221–230.

Lewin, K. Forces behind food habits and methods of change. *Bulletin of the National Research Council*, 1943, **108**, 35–65.

Lewis, P., & McCants, J. Some current issues in group psychotherapy research. *International Journal of Group Psychotherapy*, 1973, **23**, 268–291.

Lieberman, M. A., Yalom, I. D., & Miles, M. B. *Encounter groups: First facts*. New York: Basic Books, 1973.

Liederman, P. C., Green, R., & Liederman, B. R. Outpatient group therapy with geriatric patients. *Geriatrics*, 1967, **22**, 148–153.

Linden, M. E. *Geriatrics in the field of group psychotherapy*. New York: International Universities Press, 1956.

Lindenauer, G. G. Marriage education in a group therapy setting. *Journal of Emotional Education*, 1971, **11**, 165–177.

Lipowski, Z. J. Review of consulation in psychiatry and psychosomatic medicine. III. Theoretical issues. *Psychosomatic Medicine*, 1968, **30**, 395–422.

Lippitt, R., & White, R. K. An experimental study of leadership and group life. In E. E. Maccoby, T. M. Newcomb, & E. E. Hartley (Eds.), *Readings in social psychology*. New York: Holt, 1958. Pp. 496–511.

Logue, P. E., Peterson, L., & Miller, C. An orientation vidoe tape for psychiatric patients. *Mental Hygiene*, 1969, **53**, 301–302.

Lubin, B., & Eddy, W. B. The laboratory training model: Rationale, method, and some thoughts for the future. *International Journal of Group Psychotherapy*, 1970, **20**, 305–339.

Lubin, B., Gardiner, S., & Roth, A. Mood and symptoms during pregnancy. *Psychosomatic Medicine*, 1975, **37**, 136–146.

Lubin, B., Hornstra, R. K., Lewis, R. V., & Bechtel, B. S. Correlates of initial treatment assignment in a community mental health center. *Archives of General Psychiatry*, 1973, **29**, 497–500.

Lubin, B., & Lubin, A. W. *Group psychotherapy: A bibliography of the litera-*

ture from 1956 through 1964. East Lansing, Mich.: Michigan State University Press, 1966.

Lubin, B., & Lubin, A. W. Laboratory training stress compared to college examination stress. *Journal of Applied Behavioral Science,* 1971, **7,** 502–597.

Lubin, B., & Lubin, A. W. The group psychotherapy literature: 1972. *International Journal of Group Psychotherapy,* 1973, **23,** 474–513.

Lubin, B., Sargent, C. W., & Lubin. A. W. The group psychotherapy literature: 1971. *International Journal of Group Psychotherapy.* 1972, **22,** 492–529.

Lubin, B., & Slominski, A. A counseling program with adult male cerebral palsied patients. *Cerebral Palsy Review,* 1960, **21,** 3–5.

MacLennan, B. W. Simulated situations in group psychotherapy training. *International Journal of Group Psychotherapy,* 1971, **21,** 330–332.

MacLennan, B. W., & Felsenfeld, N. *Group counseling and psychotherapy with adolescents.* New York: Columbia University Press, 1970.

MacLennan, B. W., & Levy, N. The group psychotherapy literature: 1965. *International Journal of Group Psychotherapy,* 1966, **16,** 233–241.

MacLennan, B. W., & Levy, N. The group psychotherapy literature: 1966. *International Journal of Group Psychotherapy,* 1967, **17,** 387–398.

MacLennan, B. W., & Levy, N. The group psychotherapy literature: 1967. *International Journal of Group Psychotherapy,* 1968, **18,** 393–408.

MacLennan, B. W., & Levy, N. The group psychotherapy literature: 1968. *International Journal of Group Psychotherapy,* 1969, **19,** 382–408.

MacLennan, B. W., & Levy, N. The group psychotherapy literature: 1969. *International Journal of Group Psychotherapy,* 1970, **20,** 280–411.

MacLennan, B. W., & Levy, N. The group psychotherapy literature: 1970. *International Journal of Group Psychotherapy,* 1971, **21,** 345–380.

McCarty, P. T. Effects of sub-professional group counseling with probationers and parolees. *Dissertation Abstracts International,* 1972, 5550A.

McClellan, T. A., & Stieper, D. R. A structured approach to group marriage counseling. *Mental Hygiene,* 1971, **55,** 77–84.

McGee, T. F., & Schuman, B. N. The nature of the co-therapy relationship. *International Journal of Group Psychotherapy,* 1970, **21,** 25–36.

McNiel, J. N., & Verwoerdt, A. Group treatment program combines with work project on geriatric unit of state hospital. *Psychiatric Digest,* 1973, **34,** 11–17.

Mallucio, A. N., & Marlow, W. D. The case for the contract. *Social Work,* 1974, **19,** 28–36.

Manaster, A. Therapy with the "senile" geriatric patient. *International Journal of Group Psychotherapy,* 1972, **22,** 250–257.

Mascia, A. V., & Teiter, S. R. Group therapy in rehabilitation of severe chronic asthmatic children. *Annals of Children,* 1971, **29,** 223.

Meeks, J. E. Structuring the early phase of group psychotherapy with adolescents. *International Journal of Child Psychotherapy,* 1973, **2,** 391–405.

Milberg, I. Group psychotherapy in the treatment of some neurodermatoses. *International Journal of Group Psychotherapy,* 1956, **6,** 53–76.

Mintz, E. E. Time-extended marathon groups. In H. M. Ruitenbeek (Ed.), *Group therapy today: Styles, methods, and techniques.* New York: Atherton Press, 1969. Pp. 310–320.

Mone, L. C. Short-term group psychotherapy with the post-cardiac patients. Paper presented at the 27th Annual Conference of the American Group Psychotherapy Association, New Orleans, January 1970.

Moreno, L. *Psychodrama: Foundations of psychotherapy.* Vol. II. New York: Beacon House, 1946.

Mullan, H., & Rosenbaum, M. *Group psychotherapy.* New York: Free Press, 1962.

Murphy, M. Esalen's where it's at. *Psychology Today,* 1967, **1,** 34–39.

Nadeau, H. G. An examination of some effects of the marital enrichment group. *Dissertation Abstracts International,* 1972, 5453B.

National Training Laboratories Institute. *News and Reports,* 1969, **3**(4), 1.

O'Donnell, C. R. Predicting success in a group treatment program for delinquent males. *Proceedings of the 81st Annual Convention of the American Psychological Association,* Montreal, 1973, **8,** 951–952.

O'Hearne, J. J., & Glad, D. D. The case for interaction. In a panel, Roles of insight and interaction. Paper presented at meetings of the American Group Psychotherapy Association, Chicago, January 1968.

Oradie, D. M., & Waite, N. S. Group psychotherapy with stroke patients during the immediate recovery phase. *American Journal of Orthopsychiatry,* 1974, **44,** 386–395.

Paley, A. Hypnotherapy in the treatment of alcoholism. *Bulletin of the Menninger Clinic,* 1952, **16,** 14.

Parloff, M. B. Some current issues in group psychotherapy research: Discussion. *International Journal of Group Psychotherapy,* 1973, **23,** 282–288.

Penick, S. B. Group treatment of obesity in a day hospital. Paper presented at the 27th Annual Conference of the American Group Psychotherapy Association, New Orleans, January 1970.

Perls, F. *The gestalt approach and eye witness to therapy.* Palo Alto, Calif.: Science and Behavior Books, 1973.

Pfeiffer, J. W., & Jones, J. E. (Eds.), *Handbook of structured experiences for human relations training,* Vol. I. La Jolla, Calif.: University Associates, 1969.

Pittman, D. J., & Tate, R. L. A comparison of two treatment programs for alcoholics. *Quarterly Journal of Studies of Alcohol,* 1969, **30,** 388–389.

Powdermaker, F. B., & Frank, J. D. *Group psychotherapy: Studies in methodology of research and therapy.* Cambridge, Mass.: Harvard University Press, 1953.

Preston, F. B. Combines individual joint and group therapy in the treatment of alcoholism. *Mental Hygiene,* 1960, **44,** 522.

Psathas, G. Overview of process studies in group psychotherapy. *International Journal of Group Psychotherapy*, 1967, **17**, 225–235.

Rabin, H. N. Preparing patients for group therapy. *International Journal of Group Psychotherapy*, 1970, **20**, 135–145.

Rachman, A. W. Group psychotherapy in treating the adolescent identity crisis. *International Journal of Child Psychotherapy*, 1972, **1**, 97–119.

Rappaport, R. G. Group therapy in prison. *International Journal of Group Psychotherapy*, 1971, **21**, 489–496.

Reckless, J. B. A behavioral treatment of bronchial asthma in modified group therapy. *Psychosomatics*, 1971, **12**, 168–173.

Reddy, W. B. Interpersonal affection and change in sensitivity training: A composition model. In C. Cooper (Ed.), *Theories of group processes*. New York: Wiley, in press.

Reddy, W. B., & Lansky, L. M. The group psychotherapy literature: 1973. *International Journal of Group Psychotherapy*, 1974, **24**, 477–517.

Reed, J. Group therapy with asthmatic patients. *Geriatrics*, 1962, **17**, 823.

Reissman, F., Cohen, J., & Pearl, A. (Eds.), *Mental health of the poor*. New York: Free Press, 1964.

Rhodes, S. L. Short-term groups of latency-age children in a school setting. *International Journal of Group Psychotherapy*, 1973, **23**, 204–216.

Ribner, N. G. Effects of explicit group contract on self-disclosure and group cohesiveness. *Journal of Counseling Psychology*, 1974, **21**, 116–120.

Rioch, M. J. The work of Wilfred Bion on groups. In C. J. Sager & H. S. Kaplan (Eds.), *Progress in group and family therapy*. New York: Brunner/Mazel, 1972. Pp. 18–32.

Rockwell, D. Some observations on "living in." *Psychiatry*, 1971, **34**, 214–223.

Rogers, C. R. Interpersonal relationships: Year 2000. *Journal of Applied Behavioral Science*, 1968, **4**, 265–280.

Rose, S. D. *Treating children in groups*. San Francisco: Jossey-Bass, 1972.

Rosenbaum, M. Group psychotherapy and psychodrama. In B. B. Wolman (Ed.), *Handbook of clinical psychology*. New York: McGraw-Hill, 1965. Pp. 1254–1274.

Rosenbaum, M., & Berger, M. (Eds.) *Group psychotherapy and group function*. New York: Basic Books, 1963.

Ross, W. F., McReynolds, W. T., & Berzins, J. I. Effectiveness of marathon group psychotherapy with hospitalized female narcotic addicts. *Psychological Reports*, 1974, **34**, 611–616.

Sadock, B. J., & Kaplan, H. I. Training and standards in group psychotherapy. In B. J. Sadock & H. I. Kaplan (Eds.), *Comprehensive group psychotherapy*. Baltimore: Williams & Wilkins, 1971. Pp. 774–798.

Sarlin, M. B., & Altshuler, K. Z. Group psychotherapy with deaf adolescents in a school setting. *International Journal of Group Psychotherapy*, 1968, **18**, 337–344.

Saul, S. R., & Saul, S. Group psychotherapy in a propietary nursing home. *Gerontologist*, 1974, **14**, 446–450.

Scheidlinger, S. The relationship of group therapy to other group influence attempts. *Mental Hygiene*, 1955, **39**, 367–390.

Schein, E. H., & Bennis, W. G. *Personal and organizational change through group methods: The laboratory approach*. New York: Wiley, 1965.

Schultz, W. C. *FIRO-B: A three dimensional theory of interpersonal behavior*. New York: Holt, Rinehart & Winston, 1958.

Schutz, W. C. Not encounter and certainly not facts: A review of "Encounter groups: First facts" by Lieberman, M. A., Yalom, I. D., & Miles, M. B. In J. W. Pfeiffer & J. E. Jones (Eds.), *The 1974 annual handbook for group facilitators*, San Diego, Calif.: University Associates, 1974.

Shoemaker, R. J., Guy, W. B., & McLaughlin, J. T. Usefulness of group therapy in management of atopic eczema. *Pennsylvania Medical Journal*, 1955, **58**, 603.

Simonson, N. R., & Bahr, S. Self-disclosure by the professional and paraprofessional therapist. *Journal of Consulting and Clinical Psychology*, 1974, **42**, 359–363.

Slaikeu, K. A. Evaluation studies on group treatment of juvenile and group offenders in correctional institutions. A review of the literature. *Journal of Research in Crime and Delinquency*, 1973, **10**, 87–100.

Slavson, S. R. Qualification and training of group therapists. *Mental Hygiene*, 1947, **31**, 386–396.

Slavson, S. R. *A textbook in analytic group psychotherapy*. New York: International Universities Press, 1964.

Slawson, P. F. Group psychotherapy with obese women. *Psychosomatics*, 1965, **6**, 206–209.

Smith, C. G. Alcoholics: Their treatment and their wives. *British Journal of Psychiatry*, 1969, **115**, 1039–1042.

Snow, D. L., & Held, M. L. Group psychotherapy with obese adolescent females. *Adolescence*, 1973, **8**, 407–414.

Spotnitz, H. Constructive emotional interchange in adolescence. In C. J. Sager & H. S. Kaplan (Eds.), *Progress in group and family therapy*. New York: Brunner/Mazel, 1972, pp. 737–747.

Spotnitz, H. Comparison of different types of group psychotherapy. In H. I. Kaplan & B. J. Sadock (Eds.), *The evolution of group therapy*. New York: Jason Aronson, 1972. Pp. 51–82.

Stein, A. The training of the group psychotherapist. In N. Rosenbaum & M. Berger (Eds.), *Group psychotherapy and group function*. New York: Basic Books, 1963. Pp. 558–576.

Stinson, M. Group communication for the deaf. *Journal of Rehabilitation*, 1971, **37**, 42–44.

Stollak, G. E., Guerney, B. G., Jr., & Rothberg, M. *Psychotherapy research: Selected readings*. Chicago: Rand-McNally, 1966.

Stollar, F. H. Marathon groups: Toward a conceptual model. In L. N. Solomon & B. Berson (Eds.), *New perspectives on encounter groups*. San Francisco, Calif.: Jossey-Bass, 1972.

Strassburger, F. Ethical guidelines for encounter groups. *APA Monitor*, 1971, **2**(7), 3, 32.

Strupp, H. H., & Bloxom, A. L. Preparing lower-class patients for group psychotherapy: Development and evaluation of a role-induction film. *Journal of Consulting and Clinical Psychology*, 1973, **41**, 373–384.

Sullivan, H. S. *Conceptions of modern psychiatry*. London: Tavistock, 1955.

Titchener, J. L., Sheldon, M. B., & Ross, W. D. Changes in blood pressure of hypertensive patients with and without group psychotherapy. *Journal of Psychosomatic Research*, 1959, **4**, 10–12.

Todd, R. I am nobody—Who are you? *The Atlantic Monthly*, 1973, **232**, No. 5, 108–114.

Truax, C. B. Perceived therapeutic conditions and client outcome. *Comparative Group Studies*, 1971, **2**, 301–310.

Truax, C. B. Degrees of negative transference occuring in group psychotherapy and client outcome in juvenile delinquents. *Journal of Clinical Psychology*, 1971, **27**, 132–136.

Wadeson, H. Conjoint marital art therapy techniques. *Psychiatry*, 1972, **35**, 89–98.

Warren, N. C., & Rice, L. N. Structuring and stabilizing of psychotherapy for low-prognosis clients. *Journal of Consulting and Clinical Psychology*, 1972, **39**, 173–181.

Weber, L., & Hill, T. A therapy group of juvenile delinquent boys. *Psychiatric Forum*, 1973, **3**, 25–33.

Weiner, H. B. An overview of the use of psychodrama and group psychotherapy in the treatment of alcoholism in the United States and abroad. *Group Psychotherapy*, 1966, **19**, 159–165.

Weschler, I., Massarik, F., & Tannernbaum, R. The self in process: A sensitivity training emphasis. In I. Weschler & E. Schein (Eds.), *Issues in human relations training*. Selected Readings Series, No. 5. Washington, D.C.: National Training Laboratories, 1962.

Westfield, D. R. Two year's experience of group methods in the treatment of male alcoholics in a Scottish mental hospital. *British Journal of Addiction*, 1972, **67**, 267–276.

Westman, J. C., Kansky, E. W., Erikson, M. E. Arthur, B., & Vroom, A. L. Parallel group psychotherapy with the parents of emotionally disturbed children. *International Journal of Group Psychotherapy*, 1963, **13**, 52.

Whally, M., & Strehl, C. Evaluation of the three year group therapy program for multiple sclerosis patients. *International Journal of Group Psychotherapy*, 1969, **13**, 328–353.

Whitaker, D. S., & Lieberman, M. A. *Psychotherapy through the group process*. New York: Atherton Press, 1964.

Willett, E. A. Group therapy in a methadone treatment program: An evaluation of changes in interpersonal behavior. *International Journal of Addiction*, 1973, **8**, 33–39.

Winer, M. F. Genetic versus interpersonal insight. *International Journal of Group Psychotherapy*, 1974, **24**, 230–237.

Winthrop, H. Abuses of sensitivity training on the American campus. *Bulletin of the Menninger Clinic*, **35**, 28–41.

Witenberg, M. J., & Bruseloff, P. A therapeutic nursery group in a day care center. *International Journal of Child Psychiatry*, 1972, **1**, 7–16.

Wohl, T. The role of group psychotherapy for mothers in a rehabilitative approach to juvenile interactable asthma. *Mental Hygiene*, 1963, **47**, 151.

Wohl, T. H. The group approach to the asthmatic child and family. *Journal of Asthma Research*, 1967, **4**, 237.

Wolf, A. Psychoanalysis in groups. In G. M. Gazda (Ed.), *Basic approaches to group psychotherapy and group counseling*. Springfield, Ill.: Charles C Thomas, 1968. Pp. 80–108.

Wolff, K. Group psychotherapy with geriatric patients in a psychiatric hospital: Six year study. *Journal of the American Geriatric Society*, 1962, **10**, 1077–1080.

Wolpe, J. *Psychotherapy by reciprocal inhibition*. Standford, Calif.: Stanford University Press, 1958.

Woods, T. L. A group method of engaging parents at a child psychiatry clinic. *Child Welfare*, 1974, **53**, 394–401.

Wysor, B. Encounter games: A dangerous new trend. *Harpers Bazaar*, 1971, **104**, 60–61.

Yalom, I. D. *The theory and practice of group psychotherapy*. New York: Basic Books, 1970.

Yong, J. Advantages of group therapy in relation to individual therapy for juvenile delinquents. *Corrective Psychiatry and Journal of Social Therapy*, 1971, **2**, 34–40.

CHAPTER 8

Family Therapy

RONALD E. FOX

Family therapy is a method of psychological treatment aimed at improving the functioning of the family as a system through appraisal of the family as a unit and through interventions calculated to bring about changes in the family's interpersonal relationships. This chapter traces the development of family therapy, discusses methods of assessing families, and reviews current theories and techniques of family intervention. The chapter concludes with consideration of the results of family therapy, of ethical issues involved in this treatment method, and of approaches in training.

THE DEVELOPMENT OF FAMILY THERAPY

The development of family therapy, both as a method for alleviating emotional distress and as a conceptual tool for understanding psychopathology, is a relatively recent phenomenon. The technique was initiated independently by several clinicians in various regions of the United States in the 1950s, each working without prior knowledge of the others' endeavors.

One can only guess as to the historical and social forces that gave rise to the idea of studying and treating families instead of individuals, but the following general trends are worth considering in this regard: increasing sophistication in the conceptualization of individual psychotherapy; the child guidance movement of the 1930s and 1940s; the emergence of group therapy; the emergence of marriage counseling as a profession; intensified research efforts to understand such intractable clinical problems as schizophrenia; and serendipitous influences. Several of these sources of influence are also mentioned in reviews by Haley (1959), Jackson and Satir (1961), and Parloff (1961).

To elaborate, *individual psychotherapy* in the early 1950s was heavily dominated by psychoanalytic theories and techniques. The primary emphasis was on the individual patient and his symptoms, and therapeutic efforts were directed at helping the patient achieve insight into his unconscious defenses and motivations. In achieving such insight, much time was spent in helping the patient to understand that many of his current methods of relating to others (including the therapist) could be seen as repetitions of patterns he had established in his family of origin. What was important was not so much what the patient's family had actually been like, but rather how he had perceived them. The basic idea was that the patient as a child had been involved in an interpersonal field (family) which had led to the development of a mental disturbance. Actual therapeutic contact with the patient's family was discouraged out of fear that the patient-therapist transference relationship would be disrupted.

Over time, however, it became increasingly evident that the patient's current family, and not only his family of origin, was an important mediating factor in the success of the analytic undertaking. Family members seemed able to potentiate or to prevent efforts of the patient to change even after very thorough analysis. It was also commonly observed that individual patients often made dramatic changes after major shifts in the structure of the family, and that these changes frequently could not be linked to the results of individual psychotherapy. The need for rapid treatment of psychiatric casualties during World War II had also helped clinicians to see that an understanding of the individual's milieu, as well as of his inner conflicts, was essential in quickly restoring him to optimal functioning. It was considerations such as these, as well as the desire to prevent the occurrence of later problems in the children of identified patients, that led one psychoanalyst, Nathan Ackerman (1958), to establish the first family mental health clinic in the United States and thus extend the scope of therapeutic interventions.

Other individual psychotherapists were heavily influenced by clinicians such as Sullivan, Fromm, Erikson, and Horney, who emphasized the interpersonal nature of neurotic behaviors. For Sullivan it was the interpersonal pressures and the need to respond to, control, and mediate their effects, rather than intrapsychic conflict, that were the most crucial for an understanding of emotional disturbances. From this viewpoint it was but a short conceptual step to the study and treatment of the family unit. Neurosis was no longer something that resided within the individual like a germ or infection; it was also part of an interpersonal process, and it therefore involved forces outside the patient as well. Several of the early innovators in family therapy were heavily influenced by Sullivan, Don Jackson being a prominent example.

The *child guidance movement* in this country was a major phenomenon in the mental health field in the 1930s and 1940s. As increasing attention was paid to the emotional problems of children, the influence of the parents in the etiology and amelioration of these problems became evident. At first it was primarily the mother who was the focus of attention, partly because of her greater availability and partly because of the assumed importance of the early mother-child relationship on the child's subsequent emotional development. Gradually it was discovered that children also had fathers who had significant effects on them. When it was observed over and over that parents often seemed to involve their children in their own emotional problems, that they often resisted what clinicians felt were growthful changes in the child, and that they frequently removed the child from treatment just when the therapist felt that real progress was underway, clinics began to involve the parents in the treatment process. Although this step initially was taken more to help the parents understand the child (and not interfere with the treatment) than to help the parents themselves, it was at least no longer being denied that patients have families. The typical treatment format was for a therapist to work with the child (the primary patient) and for a social worker to interview the parent(s). It became obvious, as information and experience accumulated, that each person in the system contributed to the problem. To assign each of these people an individual therapist proved so costly that sooner or later the idea that one therapist could work with all of the family together was bound to come up.

The emergence of *marriage counseling* as a profession in some ways parallels the family therapy movement and is an offshoot of it. In other ways, it is an independent field of endeavor with its own historical roots. In any event, the cross-fertilization between family therapy and marriage counseling has been evident in the literature (see Green, 1965). A prominent example, to cite just one of many, is in the area of the role of sexuality in family and marital life. Marriage counselors were among the first to point out the damaging effects of misconceptions about sex on marriages and to cite the need for better understanding of normal sexual behavior patterns. Some of the techniques they developed for treating sexual difficulties were later utilized by family therapists. Conversely, family therapists' findings concerning the importance of family interaction styles in understanding how individual problems are developed and maintained have been drawn on by marriage counselors. See Kaplan (1974), Masters and Johnson (1970), and Vincent (1973) for excellent examples of the blending of sexual counseling and family therapy techniques. As marriage counselors accumulated experience with couples, the contribution of marital problems to the development of individual symptoms, and vice versa, became obvious. Thus an understanding of the entire family unit became of increasing importance.

Group therapy as a method of intervention gained in popularity during and after World War II as the demand for mental health services rapidly outstripped society's ability to produce practitioners. By its emphasis on the significance of the peer group and the interpersonal milieu, this movement helped create the *Zeitgeist* that gave rise to family therapy. In the 1940s and 1950s there were several reports of group therapy with schizophrenic patients and their parents (see Ross, 1948, for an early example). The superficial similarities between group and family therapy are obvious. Indeed, Midelfort (1957), who was one of the first family therapists, says that "Family therapy is an example of group therapy. . . ." Yet there are also important differences between group and family therapy, as noted by Handlon & Parloff (1962):

1.   The group members do not have a prior history together, whereas family members do.
2.   Group members typically do not have a future together once therapy is terminated, whereas family members do.
3.   Group members are not involved in an ongoing day-to-day relationship with each other, but family members are.
4.   The group is an artificial unit created by the therapist. The family is a socially and legally sanctioned natural grouping which the therapist must take as a given.
5.   The group must develop communication styles, and rules for obtaining need satisfaction while avoiding hurt. The family comes with a history of fixed modes of interaction.

Although group therapy is therefore not a generic form of treatment of which family therapy is a specific class, the willingness to look at the phenomena of groups in clinical settings helped create an atmosphere in which the idea of family treatment was likely to emerge. In addition, as clinicians became more familiar with the idea of sitting with several patients at once, reluctance about meeting with the whole family was easier to overcome. This latter point should not be underemphasized, as anyone familiar with the fervor with which the sanctity, inviolability, and absolute necessity of an exclusive therapist-patient relationship was once defended can well understand. Brodey (1963) poetically described another source of such reluctance: "Why has family therapy been/avoided/in the past?/ Remember it's man's first institution/ . . . .It's too damn close/to home!"

Efforts to understand and resolve *perplexing clinical problems,* such as schizophrenia, also led many investigators to the utilization of family assessment and treatment techniques. The most influential studies in this area were conducted by several investigators who worked with limited knowledge of each other but who came to common conclusions regarding the importance of understanding the schizophrenic's family in order to understand fully the schizophrenic process. These efforts each had their own historical antecedents, which have been adequately summarized elsewhere (Zuk & Rubinstein, 1965). Their historical progression is described by Haley (1959):

> A transition would seem to have taken place in the study of schizophrenia; from the early idea that the difficulty in these families was caused by a schizophrenic member, to the idea that they contained a pathogenic mother, to the discovery that the father was inadequate, to the current emphasis upon all three family members involved in a pathological system of interaction.

One of the research teams whose conceptualizations, theories, and treatment techniques have enjoyed widespread popularity comprises the Palo Alto group: Gregory Bateson, Don Jackson, Jay Haley and, later, Virginia Satir and others. Bateson and his colleagues began their study of schizophrenia because of a prior interest in communication patterns. In the course of their studies they brought together a schizophrenic patient and his parents to try to find out why the patient became more severely disturbed after spending only a few minutes with his family on visiting days. "It was an information-gathering session, not a family treatment interview. Yet what we observed so changed our views about treating schizophrenics that by the beginning of the next year we had started a systematic program of treating families of schizophrenics" (Haley, 1971). Since this group began their investigations with an interest in communication, it is perhaps not too surprising that the theory of schizophrenia they developed placed primary emphasis on the causal nature of family patterns of communication. Despite their possibly limited focus, their "double-bind" theory of schizophrenia (Bateson et al., 1956) has proved a highly useful one in stimulating subsequent research, theoretical developments, and treatment approaches.

Another research team, headed by Theodore Lidz, began by studying the intrafamilial environment of 14 families with a schizophrenic member. They came to view the primary etiological factor as a pathological marital relationship. In such families the marriage partners fail to meet each other's emotional needs, which in turn paves the way for one parent or the other to form a pathological alliance with the child (Lidz et al., 1957a, 1957b).

Murray Bowen (1959, 1960) began some other studies of schizophrenia by focusing on female patients and their mothers. After failing in his efforts to affect the schizophrenic process significantly by working with such dyads, he arranged for several schizophrenic patients and their parents to live in a hospital ward for periods of up to 2½ years. The direct observations of these whole families led to the clear-cut finding that the entire unit was in serious turmoil. Like Lidz, Bowen came to view a pathological marital relationship in parents of schizophrenics as an important etiological factor in the disorder, but he used different terms to characterize the observed types of marital disharmonies.

Lyman Wynne and his colleagues (Wynne et al., 1958) studied the families of hospitalized schizophrenics through the use of concurrent interviews. They concluded that pathological relationships in the family as a whole were the major causative factors in schizophrenia. Unlike the Bateson group, which focused primarily on disturbed communication patterns, Wynne's emphasis was more "broad-gauged," and made use of psychoanalytic concepts such as identification and internalization:

> The fragmentation of experience, the identity diffusion, the disturbed modes of perception and communication, and certain other characteristics of the acute reactive schizophrenic's structure are to a significant extent derived, by process of internalization, from characteristics of the family social organization [p. 215].

The theories of these investigators have been the subject of several critical reviews (Beels & Ferber, 1969; Mishler & Waxler, 1966; Zuk & Rubenstein, 1965). It is clear that, as in the story of the blind men describing an elephant from what each can discern by touching, each theorist seems to be holding a different animal. But, in spite of differences in descriptive terms, in assumptions about schizophrenia, in relative emphasis on communication or affective tone, and in the importance attached to social roles or to personality dynamics, there are common themes in this work: (a) the parents of schizophrenics are seen as immature people, anxious and conflicted, who tend to use primitive mechanisms of defense; (b) marital relationships are unsatisfactory; (c) family roles are rigid; (d) ways of meeting each others' needs are disturbed; (e) there is chronic family disequilibrium; (f) the child who became schizophrenic was typically weak, sick, or in need of special care to begin with; and (g) the process is transactional in nature. That is, the pathological influence was no longer being viewed as a unidirectional one with the schizophrenic as an innocent victim. Rather, the child and the parents are seen as engaging in a reciprocal process in which each is both acting on and being acted on by others (Mishler & Waxler, 1966).

The implications of the above observations went beyond the original aim of understanding schizophrenia. First, schizophrenic pathology (and, by implication, other pathological states) was found to occur in a context of intense family relationships which enhanced, maintained, and gave rise to symptomatic behavior in one or more family members and subclinical symptoms in others. Improvement in one often led to disruption of equilibrium in another, which led to resistance by the entire unit. Second, the unit of study and intervention in schizophrenia (and probably other syndromes) had to be extended beyond the identified patient. Third, in families, as in chemistry, the whole is greater than the sum of the parts. Pathology in interaction can only be discovered (or changed) by observing interaction directly. Transactions cannot be reconstructed on the basis of the individual dynamics of the several family members. Fourth, more complex models of causation are called for than was previously believed. Schizophrenia is not caused by a schizophrenogenic mother or a passive father, but by the nature of the parents' relationship with each other, which in turn is a result of the relationship each had with his or her parents. This leads to a three-generation model of schizophrenia which may apply to other syndromes as well. Fifth, the concept of the schizophrenic as a passive victim was altered. Far from being helpless, the schizophrenic, when observed with his family, was seen to be enormously powerful in controlling his destiny. There appeared to be some compliance on the patient's part to fit into a particular family role and thus obtain certain rewards. "The patient may believe, consciously or unconsciously, that no other role in life could give him equal satisfaction" (Zuk & Rubinstein, 1965).

Serendipity also played a prominent role in the development of family therapy. Bateson, Bowen, Lidz, and others began their studies in an effort to learn more about schizophrenia. In the process they learned much about families, saw new possibilities for the understanding of psychopathology, and developed new treatment approaches. Bell (1961) gives an amusing account of how he "accidentally" began doing family therapy. A visiting clinician from England mentioned to Bell that at his clinic in England they had begun a "new" approach involving therapy with whole families and were pleased with the results. Excited by the possibilities of such an approach, Bell began treating family units at the National Institute of Mental Health and was an influential figure in supporting and encouraging other early family therapists in the United States.

Later, when Bell was in Europe, he took occasion to look up his English colleague and report on how well the family therapy idea was flourishing. To his amazement, Bell found that he had misunderstood what his colleague had meant by treating families. What had been meant was collateral sessions with other family members while the primary patient was in session with his therapist. Since this was an old model of treatment in the United States, particularly in child guidance clinics, Bell had incorrectly concluded that his English colleague was talking about something different. Perhaps it is not too speculative to say that Bell was part of a social-professional-intellectual climate in which a different way of thinking could take root and flourish. In the 1950s family therapy was an idea whose time had come, and widely scattered clinicians suddenly "discovered" that patients had fathers, siblings, and grandparents as well as mothers.

Since the family approach developed from the work of several investigators with different backgrounds and different intellectual predecessors, the field has always shown a healthy diversity. In family therapy there is little in the way of orthodoxy either to provide security for the neophyte or to limit experimentation. Even in what to call this approach there is diversity. The terms used may be descriptive of a specialized form of family therapy (e.g., multiple-impact family therapy described by MacGregor et al., 1964), but this is not always the case. "Conjoint family therapy" (a term first used by Jackson, 1959) refers to joint interviews of members of the family and the identified patient. "Family group therapy" sometimes refers to joint interviews with several families together (also called multiple family therapy by Laquer et al., 1964), while at other times it is simply another name for what Jackson calls conjoint family therapy (Grosser & Paul, 1964). "Experimental family therapy" is used by Kempler (1965) to emphasize the here-and-now nature of his approach, whereas "psychoanalytic family therapy" refers to the theoretical orientation of the therapist (Grotjahn, 1965).

Diversity also exists in deciding which members of a family should be seen in order to call the effort family therapy. Satir (1965) states flatly that "treating the family as a unit means having all family members present at the same time in the same place with a single therapist or with male and female co-therapists." Wynne (1971) draws the distinction between family therapy as an orientation and family therapy as a method of treatment. In the former, a therapist may see only one member of a family at a time, while giving special attention to the family system, and thus treat the system indirectly. Wynne prefers to reserve the term "family therapy" to "the special circumstance when two or more family members actually meet together (conjointly) with the therapist." Others are more flexible on this point. Jackson (1961) says:

> Any combination of the basic group's members may be seen as outside necessity . . . dictates, or if the therapist feels it technically wise. We used to be fairly rigid about meeting only if all members could be present. Now, although the general emphasis remains on the whole group, there is variation on this among our several therapists.

Bowen (1966) goes even further. After assessing the family system, he may work exclusively with one family member who is helped to make changes which will then force complementary changes in other members of the family group. From his orientation, "a theoretical system that 'thinks' in terms of family and works toward improving the family system *is* family psychotherapy.

My viewpoint is closer to Bowen's than Satir's. If the family is functioning as an integrated transactional system, and if the therapist understands that system, then he can cause changes in the system by facilitating change in any of its component parts. Practically speaking, some persons are more capable of change than others. In my own work, I try to determine which person(s) is capable of change and which of the possible changes is likely to be most beneficial and least harmful to the family as a whole. Once this is determined, I proceed. With Bowen, I agree that the more family members there are who are willing and able to change, the greater the likelihood of a positive outcome and the shorter the treatment is likely to be. Beels and Ferber (1969) summarize current opinion on this point as follows:

> . . . family therapy's attention is devoted towards a family group, but the whole group does not need to be present at any one time. The *interest* and *allegiance* of the therapist is towards the whole family, and this interest and allegiance defines family therapy, not the number of people in the room.

Besides differences on preferred labels for family therapy and degrees of flexibility with respect to which members are seen when, experts also differ on several other variables, including (a) their extent of reliance on psychoanalytic concepts, (b) their conceptualization of pathology (e.g., disturbed communication versus shared unconscious fantasies), (c) their goals (e.g., changing how people communicate versus increasing insight), and (d) the implications they assign to the family therapy approach [e.g., simply another therapeutic technique versus "a new orientation to the human condition" (Framo, 1973)].

After observing several therapists interacting with families, Beels and Ferber (1969) developed a classification system based on how each relates to a family. One group was labeled *conductors* because of their tendency to be very active and directive. Conductors promote interaction "by establishing a star-shaped verbal communication pattern with themselves at the center." Rather than focusing on family members talking with each other, the therapist disrupts old patterns by forcing most of the communication to come through him, and he can thus model and insist on clear, open, unambiguous messages. Examples of therapists using this method of interacting are Ackerman, Satir, and Minuchin.

The second broad type of therapists was labeled *reactors*. Reactors tend to be less directive than conductors and to focus more on reacting to whatever the family presents. A subgroup, called *analysts,* makes use of analytic concepts and is likely to use cotherapists, to express concern about the pitfalls for the therapist, and to emphasize the therapist's need for help when he becomes entangled in the family system. Therapists grouped in this category included Whitaker and Wynne. A second subgroup of reactors was called *system purists.* Therapists such as Jackson, Haley, and Zuk were seen as prime examples of clinicians who emphasize changing communication patterns, express little or no regard for their families' gaining insight, and are more likely than others to use paradoxical prescriptions for behaviors calculated to force change by unbalancing the homeostatic system.

In spite of such differences among themselves, family therapists have succeeded in calling attention to the functioning of the family as a biosocial unit in relation to mental health. The impact and full implications of these efforts have only begun to be appreciated. Many agree with Framo's (1973) assertion that "the view that craziness or odd behavior is an adaptive and socially intelligible response to a disordered or crazy context has a significance as momentous as the shift from demonological thinking several centuries ago."

In subsequent sections, the discussion turns to methods of evaluating families, to techniques for corrective intervention, and then to the assessment of results. The final section is devoted to the topic of ethical issues.

ASSESSMENT OF FAMILIES

In this section major trends in family assessment, illustrative examples of promising approaches, and difficulties inherent in the family approach to assessment are covered. For a more complete cataloging and evaluation of family assessment techniques, the reader is referred to excellent reviews by Bodin (1968) and L'Abate (1974).

In determining the utility of the various family assessment techniques, it is important to bear in mind the associated conceptual and procedural problems. As Bodin (1968) has pointed out,

The majority of our present techniques focus, either explicitly or implicitly, on *traits* as inherent characteristics of and in individuals. A new view is emerging, however, that gives increased emphasis to the social learning context in which maladaptive behaviors are instigated and maintained as inappropriate response patterns.

This "new view" requires not only different assessment instruments, but new conceptualizations as well. In traditional assessment the focus is on the individual, whereas in family assessment the focus is on the interaction patterns of family systems. Roman and Bauman (1960) have demonstrated that observed intellectual and personality characteristics change dramatically from individual to family settings when members are tested (Wechsler, Rorschach, TAT) both individually and jointly. The authors correctly point out that the group is a unique entity and that the group methods of assessment are needed to understand it.

One difficulty in devising appropriate assessment techniques can be traced to the number of competing theories of family pathology. Some theories give primary importance to disturbances in communication patterns (Jackson, 1959), others to distorted alliances or coalitions (Minuchin, 1974), and others to shared unconscious fantasies (Wynne, 1971) or failures in differentiation of individuals from the family identity (Bowen, 1966). Each theory demands different techniques to assess different variables presumed to be important. Bodin (1968) has accurately summarized the situation:

> . . . Enthusiasts for both intro- and inter-personal points of view sometimes abandon their scientific objectivity and engage in polemics about which of their special vocabularies is the "right" one to reflect "reality" accurately. Those who prefer to focus on the family are still handicapped in such disputes by the fact that there are not yet very many terms that are specifically suited to describing what goes on between individuals in a social system.

In this context, it is impossible to conceive of a single assessment technique, or even a manageable battery, that could hope to achieve widespread acceptance among adherents to diverse theoretical persuasions. Each theorist has attempted to develop his own methods of assessment, focused on variables he deems important. As a result, it is often difficult to compare the kinds of families and family problems being treated by different types of family therapists, much less develop a uniform system of classification.

Another major difficulty lies in the fact that the very act of assessment can change the object of assessment. A family interacting under the watchful eye of an expert or via contrived communication modalities or in an unfamiliar setting may not interact at all as they do with only each other to observe and with no restrictions on modes of communicating. Whether the differences are significant remains to be determined, but in the meantime they cannot be ignored. Naturalistic observation of the family introduces the least bias, but provides the least precision and allows for maximum distortion via observer reports; highly structured tasks, however, may offer precision at the cost of introducing bias (e.g., a family's customary use of withdrawal and other physical means to resolve conflict may not be sampled by an experimental situation requiring a verbal resolution). In this latter regard, O'Rourke (1963) studied the decision-making behavior of family groups in both laboratory and home settings. When seen at home, families showed less disagreement and less activity, but more efficiency in decision making and more emotionality than when seen in the laboratory. Bodin (1968) has correctly pointed out that lack of a counterbalanced order in O'Rourke's research design may seriously compromise the validity of his conclusions. Nevertheless, the study does raise the issue of contextual effects on family performance, and this issue has not been put to rest.

A third difficulty in assessing families is the problem of defining features that are characteristic of normal families as opposed to "artificial" families composed of unrelated individuals. Compared to the amount of knowledge we possess about the natural development of individuals, what we know about the developmental stages of families and about normative family interaction is extremely limited. Before the assessment of pathological families can go very far, our knowledge of what normal families are like must be vastly increased. In turn, normal families cannot be understood simply in terms of how they differ from abnormal or unusual or atypical ones. We must understand some of the essence of what it means to be "in a family." To be a member of a family is obviously different from being in an artificial family of strangers, even though certain instrumental behaviors may be found in each. What the crucial differences are, in terms of transactional behaviors, between real and artificial families have not been adequately delineated, and this in turn hampers the development of techniques designed to test for differences between families.

Additional problems are encountered when it is noted that a normal family asked to interact together for purposes of study is in a situation with demand characteristics different from those facing a family that has come for help because of problems. The test situation for the former implies approval, whereas for the latter there is a covert accusation, usually about the parents. This cannot help but influence the candor and openness of the respective groups.

A final problem in assessment lies in the richness and wealth of the data generated in even a small sample of family behavior. Consider a single, simple example. A father says to his wife, "Women who wear lipstick are all tramps." His wife replies, "I don't wear lipstick." The daughter, who is wearing lipstick, is silent. At one level, this can be taken as a simple statement of belief by the husband with which the wife agrees. However, if it is noted that these comments are made in the presence of their daughter who is wearing lipstick, the matter becomes complicated. Although the father appears to be addressing the mother, indirectly he may be addressing the daughter. Commenting to the mother on something he does not like about the daughter may be a reflection of his inability to deal with the daughter directly. Moreover, he may be blaming the mother for condoning or allowing something to be done by the daughter of which he disapproves. His comment, then, becomes a rebuke rather than a simple statement of fact—and the rebuke may be directed at either or both of the other two persons.

Or, as another possibility, this may be a father who is prone to provoking "friendly" arguments between others. By calling attention to a source of disagreement between them, he can start the argument he wants and thereby divert attention from himself, or set up a conflict that allows him to be the wise arbiter, or whatever. Conversely, the mother may be agreeing in order to avoid a fight. Or she may be waiting to see what the daughter's response will be. Or she may be trying to establish a coalition with her husband against the daughter. The possibilities are almost limitless, even without attending to variables such as the complex of nonverbal behaviors that can significantly alter the meaning of any verbal message. A simple measure of who is talking to whom in the family is not always simple, as can be seen from the above example. Given the complexity of the data and the multifaceted nature of human interaction, it is little wonder that the assessment of family interaction patterns is in a primitive state.

Bodin (1968) has listed three broad approaches to family assessment:

1.   Individual approaches in which each family member is assessed individually and scores are compared to produce an indirect picture of family interaction. Some commonly used instruments are the Interpersonal Check-List (ICL) (LaForge & Suczek, 1955) and the FIRO-B (Schutz, 1958).

2.   Conjoint approaches consisting of both objective and subjective methods for assessing family groups as interacting systems.

3.   Combined approaches which utilize both individual and conjoint data. A prominent example of this approach is Strodtbeck's (1951) "revealed differences" technique. In this technique, couples respond to a series of questions administered separately. They are then asked to respond together as a couple to those items on which their individual answers differed. The couple is thus forced to deal with their revealed differences.

Individual assessment techniques are covered elsewhere in this volume (see Chapters 1–5). Hence the present discussion is limited to conjoint and combined approaches. The techniques most widely used in these approaches are interviews (structured and unstructured), projective and objective tests, and controlled experimental studies utilizing specific interaction tasks.

Interview Techniques

Unstructured family interviews are widely used by clinicians to determine the suitability of a family for therapy, to assess a family's interaction style, and to identify family strengths and weaknesses. As in unstructured individual diagnostic interviews, each clinician has his own style, with favorite questions and preferred areas of functioning about which he wishes information. Diversity abounds, and comparability of findings is thereby rendered elusive. Nevertheless, such interviews have high utility for the practicing clinician in making practical decisions about whom to see and what to do. Fitzgerald (1973) uses a combined method of individual and conjoint interviews. Individual sessions are utilized to obtain a traditional history, formulate dynamics, and gather each person's view of the family problems. Joint interviews are then begun, with each person being given the feeling that there has been ample opportunity to present his own viewpoint. Joint diagnostic sessions are designed to relate individual dynamics to family transactions and to formulate treatment goals in conjunction with the family unit.

A similar use of both individual and conjoint interviews in assessment is used by a team of clinicians in the multiple-impact family therapy approach reported by MacGregor et al. (1964). Families spend up to 2½ days with the clinic team, during which the family members meet with all clinic team members conjointly and in various combinations with one or more clinicians. The power of this technique lies in the opportunity it presents for the family to be seen with different therapists in different combinations, while information gathered from any component group is constantly shared with the others for corrective information or reaction. In such a context stylized interaction patterns quickly become apparent, and the sheer pressure of events forces the family to test alternative methods of relating and challenges it to discover new resources. This approach is expensive in professional time, and the nature of the information gathered may vary considerably from one family to another since there are no formal guidelines for conducting the interviews. Emphasis is placed on flexibility, so as to gear the diagnostic study and the treatment as much as possible to the specific needs of each family.

The line between unstructured diagnostic interviews and therapy is a thin one. In many respects, it appears as if many family therapists have simply adopted the typical language of individual therapy to work with families; that is, arbitrarily referring to the initial interview or interviews as diagnosis and subsequent sessions as therapy, even though demonstrable differences between the two may be more apparent than real. As far as I am aware, there exists not a single study that compares the utility of the unstructured family diagnostic interview with other methods of assessment, in spite of the fact that it is without doubt the most widely used diagnostic approach. In most clinical settings advantages such as flexibility and relative low cost compared to other techniques are apparently sufficient to offset disadvantages such as the risk of subjective bias in the interpretation of the findings.

Structured or focused interviews have also received wide attention in family evaluation efforts, however. The structure is provided by either a standardized set of questions or by focus on a particular event or laboratory situation. The disadvantages of structured interviews are similar to those of questionnaires, especially in restriction of coverage to the questions asked, which may not be appropriate to a particular family situation. A further problem may occur in quantifying results when answers are not restricted to a simple "yes" or "no" response. However, the structure does provide common experiences across subjects and thus make comparisons easier. Also, respondents can be subjected to a particular experience and then interviewed concerning their feelings and reactions. The combination of (a) common tasks or questions and (b) open-ended (nonrestricted) responses has proved particularly popular. Two examples are considered here: the Wiltwyck Family Task and the MRI Structured Family Interview.

The Wiltwyck Family Task (Elbert et al., 1964) consists of eight tasks for the whole family. The first six tasks are presented via a tape recorder with the examiner watching through a one-way screen. As one feature of the evaluation process, this nonparticipant observer model is useful in that it is possible to observe the family interact without the distortion inevitably introduced by an outsider. The tasks prescribed via audiotapes are: (a) agreeing on a meal everyone would enjoy; (b) discussing "who's the most bossy," "the biggest troublemaker," "the one who gets away with most," and "the biggest cry baby" in the family; (c) discussing a remembered argument at home, including how it started, how it developed, and what the outcome was; (d) agreeing on a way to spend a hypothetical $10 gift that would be satisfying to all; (e) asking each member to tell what things every other member does that please him most and make him feel good, and what things each one does that displease him most and make him feel unhappy or mad; and (f) reassembling as asymmetric construction, each member starting with an equal number of pieces.

The remaining two Wiltwyck tasks are presented by the observer, who leaves the room after offering gifts about which the family must make decisions: (a) the family is offered its choice of a single gift, valued at $1.00 to $1.50, from a group of three, a group game, an individual game, and an age- or sex-specific game; and (b) the family is offered refreshments but provided one cupcake, one coke, and one cup less than the number of members present. The family is left to decide how to dispense the food and, as in the previous task, must live with the decision made. As Bodin (1968) points out, real rather than hypothetical outcomes may be important in such assessments. He cites a study by Gallo (Gallo & McClintock, 1965) showing that in two-person, mixed-motive games outcomes were quite different, depending on whether the payoff was real or imaginary. When playing for imaginary money, dyads lost an average of $38.80 over 20 trials. But when playing for real money, dyads averaged winnings of $9.92. Thus ". . . game behavior cannot be generalized to the players' actual life situation unless they are intensely motivated in the game by the announced availability of some reward having authentic value for them" (Bodin, 1968).

The Structured Family Interview was developed by Bateson, Haley, and Weakland at the Mental Research Institute (MRI) in Palo Alto and has been the subject of much attention (see Watzlawick, 1966, for the most complete discussion of this method). Designed to give observers valuable clinical impressions in the space of an hour, the interview is conducted by an interviewer and observed by the therapist. After completion of the interview, the therapist is introduced to a family already keyed to looking at themselves as an interacting unit. The procedure was created as a clinical tool to provide a catalyst in the initial stage of therapy and to provide the therapist with early information which might be more difficult to obtain through direct questioning. The five tasks in the interview utilize individual, dyadic, and whole-family observations. First, each member is asked individually, "What do *you* think are the main problems in your family?" Then the group is assembled, told that several discrepancies arose in the individual responses (whether they did or not), and asked to discuss the question together. The interviewer observes the discussion through a one-way screen. As their second task, the family group is asked to plan something together, such as an outing. Third, with the children excused the parents are asked to describe how they met each other. Fourth, the parents are asked to discuss the meaning of a proverb and then to bring the children into the room and teach them the meaning of the proverb. Fifth, the interviewer gives each person an index card and a pencil. Each member is asked to write down the main fault of the person on his left. The interviewer collects the cards and announces that he is adding two statements to the group. His statements are always "too good" and "too weak," but this fact is not revealed. After shuffling the cards, the interviewer reads each one to every member in turn, beginning with the father, and asks, "To whom do you think this applies?"

L'Abate (1974) has noted several values of the MRI Structured Family Interview for research purposes. These include its having a set form of administration for comparing results, obtaining input from all family members, allowing a view of family as process, having an empirical basis for portions of the interview and some objective scoring procedures, providing guidelines for administration (which helps standardization), and offering suggestions for how to evaluate the interaction patterns elicited. However, the objective measures rely on judges' ratings, which are a particular problem in family assessment. Any outside observer is severely limited in his capacity to judge a system that has a shared history, traditions, and way of communicating.

Satir (1966) is one of several clinicians who has introduced modifications of the Structured Family Interview. To look at effectiveness as a function of various relationships in the family, Satir asks the family to plan something together in a series of overlapping stages: (a) all together, (b) all but father, (c) all but mother, (d) children only, (e) mother and daughter(s), (f) mother and son(s), (g) father and son(s), (h) father and daughter(s), and, finally, (i) husband and wife. To help understand the identifications within the family, Satir uses a series of questions (with all members present) which begins with asking each parent which child is most like himself and his spouse. Each child is asked which parent he is most like, and then how he is alike and different from the parent he did not select. Finally, spouses are asked to describe how they are alike and different from each other.

A more recently reported structural interview technique developed by Wells and Rabiner (1973) may prove useful for gathering comparable data on problem families and for training family therapists. However, the quantification of the results with this technique is still based on rather complicated subjective ratings by judges.

Interviews are valuable tools for establishing rapport, conveying empathy, and gaining knowledge regarding family interaction. But further developments and research are necessary, including several listed by L'Abate (1974) as crucial:

. . . The major needs of this field include a systematic theory of family interviewing, construction of appropriate instruments and the development of well designed statistical studies to assess the facility and effectiveness of the instruments. . . . A sharper delineation of the purposes, goals and methods of family interviews is needed.

Projective Tests

Projective tests utilized in family assessment run the gamut from drawings (Kwiatkowska, 1967) and a marbles test (Usanidivaras et al., 1963) to traditional materials such as the TAT and Rorschach. The latter two are the most frequently used, perhaps because of their greater familiarity as popular individual assessment techniques. Family projective tests are more time-consuming to administer and more difficult to score than objective tests. In addition, they are subject to the same criticisms concerning subjectivity and validity that have been raised about their use as individually administered instruments (see Chapter 2).

Initially, projectives were given to individual family members and subjected to the same kind of content analysis used in the usual scoring of Rorschachs or TATs. Interpretations were focused on individual dynamics and on attempts to reconstruct relationships within the family [see Fisher & Mendell (1956) and Singer & Wynne (1965) for examples of this approach at its best]. Later observers adapted the tests for group administration, so that interaction could be observed more directly in the production of fantasy material. Some examples of the latter approach are given below.

Winter, Ferreira, and Olson (1965) asked family triads to produce three TAT stories based on nine cards. Using standardized scoring methods developed by others, these investigators differentiated between normal and abnormal families on the basis of their stories. In a subsequent study Winter and Ferreira (1969) subjected TAT stories to a factor analysis. Subjects were 33 abnormal family triads and 22 normal control triads. Seven factors were identified that differentiated the two groups: (a) middle-class good adjustment, (b) task orientation, (c) silence, (d) emotionality, (e) inefficiency, (f) pathological productivity, and (g) dependency.

There have been few attempts to develop stimulus cards specifically designed for conjoint family use. A notable exception is the Family Interaction Apperception Test (FIAT) developed by Elbert, Rosman, Minuchin, and Guerney (1964) for use with the Wiltwyck Family Task discussed earlier. The FIAT consists of 10 cards depicting familiar, recognizable family scenes which are sufficiently concrete to be usable with relatively uneducated, nonverbal subjects as well as typical middle-class families. Another excellent feature of the FIAT is that the people depicted are drawn with ambiguous racial characteristics so as to permit identification with the figures by a side range of ethnic groups.

The Rorschach has enjoyed even wider family assessment use than the TAT, in keeping with its greater popularity in clinical use. Levy and Epstein (1964), in a typical example of the conjoint use of the test, administered Rorschachs to each family member individually, following which the whole family was asked to discuss each plate and decide on consensus responses. In addition to the responses, the discussions were recorded so that family interactions and communication patterns could be studied. A less time-consuming approach has been reported by Behrens, Rosenthal, and Chodoff (1968). Using only Plates I, II, and III, these authors dispensed with the individual administration. Clinicians' blind analyses of the protocols were able to differentiate white families from black families and "schizophrenic families" from "normal families" at a statistically significant level. Statistically reliable ratings of communication and pathological interaction were also possible. (For a more thorough discussion of family Rorschach procedures and issues, see the report of a Consensus Rorschach Symposium, *Journal of Projective Techniques and Personality Assessment,* 1968.)

The advantages of the family Rorschach include its being a standard procedure, the noninvolvement of the experimenter, the opportunity it offers to observe interaction and communication patterns, and a data yield that taps both conscious and unconscious processes. Its disadvantages, as previously mentioned, include subjectivity of interpretation, overwhelming richness of data, and inordinate expense in terms of professional time. Loveland, Wynne, and Singer (1963) provide a thorough discussion of the advantages and disadvantages of the family Rorschach.

Objective Tests

Objective tests have not been used to a significant extent in conjoint family assessment. The clear trend has been to use objective tests in what Bodin (1968) called individual approaches to family assessment and to use projective or task interaction devices in the conjoint sessions. A notable exception to this trend is the ingenious work of Bauman and Roman (1966), who have developed interaction scores based on the Wechsler-Bellevue Intelligence Scale. The procedure is a simple one; the Wechsler is administered to each member of the family in the typical fashion and then readministered to the family together. Only the Comprehension and Similarities subtests are used, but Forms I and II of the W-B are combined to increase the number of items. Several interesting comparisons are possible. For example, prorated IQ scores can be computed for each individual and for the family as a whole. Also, by taking the best answer any individual gave to each item, it is possible to compute a "potential IQ" score for the family. Theoretically, a family that is efficient at recognizing and utilizing information known to be available in the system should achieve an actual conjoint score close to the potential IQ score. In fact, many families do not. Using the procedure in the Family Therapy Clinic at Ohio State University, I have found occasional disturbed families who scored more poorly together than any family member scored alone. It is also common to encounter couples whose conjoint score is lower than the individual scores of one of the spouses.

Bauman and Roman have operationally defined four interaction processes that can be scored with high reliability from Wechsler protocols obtained from families:

1. Dominance—scored when the conjoint response contains one member's individual response, but not the other's.
2. Combination—scored when elements of each individual's response are found in the conjoint response.
3. Emergence—refers to a new idea in the conjoint response that was not present in either individual response.
4. Reinforcement—which is scored when the same response is given in each individual protocol and in the joint response.

Examining the dominance scores for 50 couples in which one spouse had been hospitalized, they found:

Husbands dominated significantly more than wives, more competent members (more intelligent) dominated significantly more than less competent members, nonpatients dominated significantly more than patients, and recorders (i.e., the spouse chosen by the couple to record conjoint answers) dominated significantly more than those who were not recorders.

Bauman, Roman, Borello, and Meltzer (1967) presented further analysis of the results with the couples in the initial study and concluded that the technique "appears to be a feasible and reliable technique for the investigation of marital intelligence and decision making, and offers to be of use in family diagnosis and research." At Ohio State we have found it relatively easy to train assistants to administer and score the tests, and that the information yielded is highly useful in screening families for family therapy.

Experimental and Interactional Tasks

Rigged conflicts used to assess the family's method of resolving differences appear to be promising methods of tapping important aspects of family life. An excellent example of the use of this technique is provided by Goodrich and Boomer (1963), who used a color-matching technique. Couples were seated on opposite sides of an easel which blocked their view of each other and were told that their ability to discriminate five gradations of color was being evaluated. The couples were asked to compare one of their numbered panels to individual panels presented by the experimenter and arrive at an agreement on the best match. Ten of the 20 matches were rigged to make agreement impossible, since the couples' panels were designed to be contradictory. The authors identified several patterns that couples used to cope with disagreement: agreeing to disagree, taking turns on whose answer to use, attempting to reformulate standards against visible colors in the room, considering the possibility that discrepancies were built into their panels making agreement impossible, and engaging in mutal assault. This work has been twice replicated by Ryder (1966).

Another method of assessment was developed by Ferreira and Winter (1965) to study differences in family decision making. Comparisons were made of decision making in 125 families divided into normal, schizophrenic, delinquent, and maladjusted (neurotic, phobic, etc.) groups. Each member of a family triad was asked to fill out a questionnaire in which 7 situations were described, each with 10 alternatives or choices: famous people they might want to meet at a party, foods to eat if going out for dinner, films they would want to see, countries they might like to live in for a year, sports events they might desire to attend, magazines to which they might wish to subscribe, and two-tone colors they would prefer for their next family car. For each situation, the individual was asked to rank his first three choices of the 10 alternatives listed and to cross the 3 least favored choices. After completing the questionnaire individually, the family was assembled and asked to fill out the questionnaire as a family, choosing alternatives on which they could all agree.

In this "unrevealed differences" technique it was left to each individual to decide whether or not to disclose his personal choices made in the initial session. The protocols were scored for spontaneous agreement (degree of overlap between two or three family members' choices by comparing individual questionnaires); decision time (defined as the mumber of minutes spent by the family in completing the joint questionnaire); and choice fulfillment of the family as a group and of its individual members, which was defined as the degree to which family choices matched the individual choices of its members. As predicted, abnormal families scored significantly lower on spontaneous agreement and choice fulfillment and longer on decision time than normal families. Among the abnormal subgroups, the schizophrenic families appeared to have the least efficient decision-making ability. In a separate study using a different questionnaire, Bodin (1966) also found that spontaneous agreement in family triads exceeds chance expectations and that spontaneous agreement is higher in normal than in abnormal families. This independent confirmation of some of the earlier findings lends support to the potential use of the technique in family assessment.

Game applications have sometimes been used to good advantage in assessing family cooperation. Ravich, Deutsch, and Brown (1966) used a game involving toy trucks in which each person was to attempt to reach a specified destination in the shortest possible driving time. Since the shortest routes always involved a common stretch of one-way road usable by only one truck at a time, the couple was thus confronted with making decisions regarding cooperation. Five distinct categories of play were developed by the couples studied: (a) sharing in the use of one-lane sections; (b) dominating and submitting, in which one member consistently came out ahead; (c) inconsistent use of the first two strategies; (d) intense competition, in which individual members were willing to sustain both individual and joint losses in order to "win"; and (e) dysjunctive, in which individuals played games having no apparent relationship to each other.

Haley has contributed two investigations designed to assess family differences in the formation of coalitions (Haley, 1962) and in the patterning of speech sequences (Haley, 1964). To assess coalition differences, Haley used a device whereby any pair of family members could form an alliance by simultaneously pressing their coalition buttons. Fifteen of 30 schizophrenic families failed to carry out their own plan of having a certain member "win" by accumulating the most time spent in coalition. Only 2 of 30 normal families failed to carry out their plans.

In the second study Haley (1964) kept a running tally of all dyadic speech sequences (mother followed by father, mother followed by child, father followed by mother, etc.) in 40 normal and 40 abnormal family triads. He found that the normal families used more of the possible sequences more often, and the disturbed families used fewer of the possibilities and used some of them more often than others. Bodin (1968) reports a subsequent study by Haley, which attempted to extend these findings to families with two children present and found no evidence of greater flexibility in the normal families. This finding raises questions regarding possible group process differences between triads and tetrads, which need further exploration.

Schlamp (1964) has taken issue with Haley's (1962) interpretation of the results of the coalition study. He points out that a schizophrenic child, even in remission, is rather apathetic and that such a condition could easily account for the obtained result; a slower, more apathetic rate of button pressing could account for less time spent in coalition. In essence, Schlamp raises the question whether the result might not have been "caused" by the presence of a disturbed family member. Haley (1964), in responding to this criticism, correctly points to the essential dilemma: " . . . If the psychotic child is included in the test interacting with his parents, it can always be argued that he 'caused' whatever results are obtained, yet the child must be included if we are to test the way he deals with his parents and they with him." Labeling the argument that the disturbed child causes the differences between families an "irrefutable argument," Haley (1964) wryly comments, "Characteristically, irrefutable arguments persist over long, perhaps indefinite, periods of time. Two such arguments come to mind: the existence of God and the idea that insight causes therapeutic change." Although this assessment may be unduly pessimistic, it is true that to date no one has been able to design a satisfactory method for resolving the dilemma.

The problems with the assessment techniques thus far developed are numerous and glaring: differing classification schemes are used, the mode of communication studied varies from one approach to another, the unit of analysis varies, and differing definitions of "abnormal" are applied. All these problems seriously hamper the generalizability and practical utility of the several family assessment methods currently in use. In addition, reliability tends to be defined differently from one method to the next, validity is typically ignored, and replications are practically nonexistent. In view of these problems one can conclude that, as of the present, family assessment is more a goal than an accomplished fact, more an artistic tool than a scientific technique.

THEORIES OF FAMILY INTERVENTION

This section describes and summarizes the major concepts of the leading family theorists: the Palo Alto group, Lidz, Wynne, and Bowen.

The Palo Alto Group

As mentioned previously, the members of this group have been the leaders in conceptualizations of psychopathology that place primary emphasis on disturbances in communication. The two major concepts they have contributed to the literature are the *double bind hypothesis* and the notion of *family homeostasis*.

The basic ingredients of the double bind as originally formulated by Bateson, Jackson, Haley, and Weakland (1956) are: (a) two or more persons; (b) repeated experiences; (c) issuance of a primary injunction taking either of two forms: "Do not do this or I will punish you," or "If you don't do this, I will punish you"; (d) a secondary injunction conflicting with the first at a more abstract level and also enforced by punishment. This secondary injunction is generally nonverbal and disqualifies some important aspect of the first injunction, for example, "Do not see this as punishment. Do not think of what you must not do"; and (e) a tertiary negative injunction prohibiting "the victim" from escaping from the field. When the victim has learned to perceive his universe in such double-bind patterns, the complete set of ingredients is no longer necessary to elicit and maintain the behavior.

In order to understand this concept fully, it must be realized that it is grounded in

> . . . our most basic conception about communication as the chief means of human interaction and influence: that in actual human communication, a single and simple message never occurs, but that communication always and necessarily involves a multiplicity of messages, of different levels, at once [Jackson & Weakland, 1961]

The different messages may be conveyed verbally, with gestures, by facial expression or body posture, by tone and inflection of voice, by the context in which the message occurs, and so forth. Incongruity between messages sent at different levels seems part and parcel of the rich fabric of human communication and is sometimes used deliberately in order to achieve a desired reaction, as in irony and humor. But incongruities have also been seen as fundamental to the character a certain symptoms such as inappropriate affect. The essence of the double bind is not the fact that contradictory messages are issued, as this is a basic ingredient of much human communicative behavior; rather, it is the fact that other messages are also sent which conceal, deny, and otherwise prevent the recipient from noticing the incongruence and handling it effectively, such as by commenting on it. Within important relationships, such as the family, where messages cannot simply be ignored or avoided, the individual learns to respond in adaptive ways to the system, although his behavior might appear bizarre to the outside observer.

It was originally thought that the schizophrenic or "identified patient" was a victim of the family interaction style. Later this view was modified (Bateson, Jackson, Haley, & Weakland, 1963; Watzlawick, 1963), as it was seen that the double bind always binds both parties, so that there are at least two victims, rather than a single one; "The most useful way to phrase double bind description is not in terms of a binder and victim, but in terms of people caught up in an ongoing system which produces conflicting definitions of the relationship and consequent subjective distress" (Watzlawick, 1963). Additionally, the double bind is no longer seen as both a necessary and sufficient cause of schizophrenia. What can be said is that, where the double bind is the prevailing communication mode in a family and attention is limited to the ostensibly most disturbed individual, then the behavior of this individual satisfies the usual criteria of schizophrenia. Watzlawick (1963) describes three of the possible reactions of such an individual and points out their similarity to familiar symptomatic behaviors: (a) he can conclude that he is overlooking vital clues seen by others or that others are withholding and thus become obsessed with searching out the obscure or concealed information; (b) he can comply literally with all injunctions; or (c) he can withdraw from all human involvement.

An example of a double bind should help to clarify. Bateson et al., (1956) describe a brief interaction sequence which occurred between a hospitalized male schizophrenic patient and his mother. When visited by his mother, the young patient impulsively put his arm around her shoulders, only to feel her stiffen. When he quickly withdrew his arm, she asked, "Don't you love me any more?" When the patient then blushed, the mother admonished him, "Dear, you must not be so easily embarrassed and afraid of your feelings." Thus the son is in an impossible dilemma; if he shows his love, he is wrong; if he withholds his love, he is wrong; if he comments on the paradox (by blushing), he is wrong. In such a context so-called schizophrenic behavior such as withdrawal, irrelevant comments, nonsequiturs, and the like are adaptive in terms of maintaining the relationship while avoiding the trap of responding to either of the conflicting messages ("Love me," but "Do not show that you love me") and not commenting on the conflict in which he has been placed. It is believed that schizophrenic communication is learned as a result of continual experiences of the kind shown in the example.

Whereas incongruity of messages is basic to the theory and emphasis is thereby placed on the overt and the directly observable, fantasies and individual nonperceptions are implied. The basic dynamic in this theory is presumed to be a mother who is afraid of closeness, but unwilling to admit it or the consequent hostility generated, and masks it by assuming a too loving attitude toward the child. Further, there is an absence of a strong, insightful person (e.g., the father) who could support the child. In order to control her anxiety with the child, the mother manipulates the communication to produce a degree of tolerable emotional closeness, and the father collaborates in the deception. The child may become aware of the fact that mother's zealous concern masks a basic hostility, but he cannot communicate the awareness out of fear of losing the small amount of love that is provided. Thus he recognizes that it is incorrect to respond to her too-loving attitude, but that it is also incorrect to respond to her underlying hostility. He is damned either way, or caught in a double bind. The whole basis for the double bind, however, is embedded in hypothesized rather than directly observable behavior, and in this sense there is more overlap between this theory and psychoanalytic theory than the Palo Alto group is willing to admit. In terms of relative emphasis, it is true that this group has been instrumental in calling attention to the powerfulness of the current, ongoing, transactions in families in maintaining symptomatic behavior in one or more of its members.

The double-bind theory was initially formulated as a process believed to be important in the etiology of schizophrenia. Gradually, it was seen that the concept could be applied to much of our current thinking about psychopathology in general. Ferreira (1960) suggested that a double bind of a different variety was operative in the delinquent's family. Instead of the incongruent messages emanating from a single person or a single coalition, the incongruency is split and "the victim is caught in a sort of bipolar message in which A emanates from father, for instance, and B (a message about message A) from mother." The consideration of this different kind of double bind ". . . seemingly illuminates some important aspects in the communicational process that leads to delinquent behavior" (Ferreira, 1960). Thus schizophrenia appeared to result from a special type of double-bind situation rather than from the fact of double binding per se.

Haley (1963) and Watzlawick, Beavin, and Jackson (1967) have significantly extended the communicational approach to other types of families. In looking at double binds more broadly, Haley points out that conflicting messages can easily be viewed as attempts to define the relationship in terms of what type of communicative behavior is to take place on one level, while denying or qualifying the definition on another level. When the messages are incongruent, interpersonal difficulties are considered inevitable. He suggests that a primary issue in all human relationships has to do with who is going to set the rules for the relationship and, on a more abstract level, who is to decide who sets the rules. With this concept it is possible to see that the passive victim of an interpersonal exchange is in fact very powerful; by defining the relationship as one in which he is to be passive, the "victim," at a meta-communication level, is also saying, "I am in charge of saying who is in charge here and I decide that you must be in charge." In this way the "passive victim" may wield much control while appearing to be helpless. While controlling the relationship, the "victim" denies that this is so by attributing it to his illness rather than to a volitional choice. Haley (1963) listed several ways a person can define, or avoid defining, a relationship by pointing out that any message can be broken down into the following elements: (a) *I* (b) *am saying something* (c) *to you* (d) *in this situation.*

By negating or disqualifying any of these elements, a person can achieve control of a relationship while not appearing to do so. For example, the wife who refuses sexual advances with the excuse of a headache is indicating that she is not defining the relationship as one in which she refuses the husband; after all, it is the headache that prevents cooperation, not she. The extreme methods that can be used to disqualify the defining (i.e., controlling) of relationships is a list of schizophrenic symptoms (Haley, 1959): (a) a person may deny that *he* is communicating by claiming to be someone else; (b) he may deny that he is *saying something* by using meaningless language; (c) he may deny that he is *addressing another person* by claiming that he is talking to himself or that the other is "really" a secret agent; or (d) he may deny that he is saying something *in this situation* by claiming to be in some other place, such as Mt. Olympus. Haley also points out how other interesting interpersonal events such as hypnosis can be understood via this process; the hypnotist denies that he is controlling by claiming that the subject is doing it himself, and the subject complies by becoming "hypnotized" and claiming that the behavior is not under his control. That is, the subject "accepts" the hypnotist's definition of the relationship as one in which he will comply with the given instructions and not hold himself responsible. In effect, different ways of denying elements of a message appear to be varieties of double binds. In schizophrenia the pattern is simply more pervasive, the range of behaviors more restricted, and the denial more absolute than occurs in other types of pathological families.

Jackson's (1957) concept of *family homeostasis* emerged as a result of noting the rigidity and resistance to change that families evidence when attempts are made to point out, change, or interrupt double-bind sequences. He cited examples such as a husband who called his wife's therapist to express concern over her suicidal impulses. The therapist reassured him that his wife's depression was actually considerably improved. The next day the husband committed suicide by shooting himself. Jackson (1957) goes on to say that these observations

. . . suggested that a family forms a dynamic steady-state system; the characteristics of the members and the nature of their interaction—including any identified patient and his sick behavior—are such as to maintain a status quo of the family, and to react toward the restoration of the status quo in the event of any change, such as is proposed by the treatment of any member.

Similarly, Haley (1962) talks of an error-activated system for describing families. Noting that families often restrict themselves to repetitive patterns of behavior within a wider range of possibilities, as if confined to that pattern by a kind of governing process, he states, "No outside governor requires the family to behave in their habitual patterns, so this governing must exist within the family. . . ." When people interact, they establish rules for their joint behavior and thereby establish a system which appears to be error-activated. When one member "breaks the rules" of the family by exceeding the range of permitted behavior, the others are activated to pressure him into conforming to the rule. If he succeeds in establishing a new range of permitted behaviors, new rules are established and a new homeostasis achieved. Bateson (1960) used the homeostasis concept to explain how only one person may be symptomatic when the entire family is seen as schizophrenogenic. He hypothesizes that homeostasis in such families is achieved by only one member being overtly psychotic. Some evidence for this theory may be found in the frequently observed instance of the identified patient's improvement being followed by the emergence of psychological distress in another family member. Perhaps the homeostasis was upset by improvement in the identified patient, resulting in the creation of another "sick" person to restore the balance.

The development of family myths may also serve to maintain family homeostasis. Claiming that the family myth "is to the relationship what the defense is to the individual," Ferreira (1963) defines such myths as

. . . a series of fairly well-integrated beliefs shared by all family members, concerning each other and their mutual position in the family, beliefs that go unchallenged by everyone involved in spite of the reality distortions which they may conspicuously imply.

These shared beliefs and the struggle to maintain them is seen as part of the struggle to maintain the relationship. To expose the myth one must break certain implied rules concerning shared beliefs about the family, which threatens the homeostatic balance and is resented by other family members. An example of a three-generation, powerful, family myth has been reported by Ewing and Fox (1968). A teenage boy who was referred for treatment explained his behavior as the result of having a highly neurotic mother, which had in turn resulted from her having been raised in a family containing an alcoholic father. The boy's mother confirmed her son's story. When the grandparents were subsequently interviewed, their version of the family history was the same as their daughter's and grandson's. It emerged, however, that the grandfather was a successful member of his community (having been once elected mayor by write-in ballot) and did not have a drinking problem. What he did have was an immature, demanding wife and, in order to escape from her, he occasionally removed himself from her tirades to go for a drink. The wife would then complain to the children that, in addition to her other trials, she had a husband who drank. The entire family (including her husband) collaborated in supporting the mother by accepting her distorted version of reality, and the myth was still being used to explain the behavior of a boy two generations later. It was as if there were a family rule against criticizing the mother; a balance in relationships was achieved thereby, and a myth was created to lend credence to the entire construction. Family homeostasis has proven to be such a highly useful construct that Carson (1969) has labeled it "the central concept that, in my view, ties together all of this research. . . ."

The major problems some clinicians find with the "pure" communication approach of the Palo Alto group have been summarized by Mishler and Waxler (1966). First, there is a lack of precision and clarity with respect to the types of interaction sequences that do and do not fall within the definition of the double bind: "From the way the concept is used, it sometimes appears that all communication sequences may be interpretable, at some level of analysis, as double binds, and, if this is so, the concept loses all usefulness" (Mishler & Waxler, 1966). Second, by ignoring content and emphasizing the style of interaction that occurs irrespective of the topic being discussed, the theory has ignored the possibility that double binds centering around significant family norms may have more significance than ones involving trivial matters. However, Jackson for one is not impressed by this criticism, stating that, in his view, "the act itself alerts the participants that there is a conflict and in itself constitutes a kind of psychological trauma, whatever the substantive issue" (personal communication quoted in Mishler and Waxler, 1966). Third, the criteria for deciding whose perspective is to be used in determining the presence of incongruency are not specified. What appears contradictory to an observer may not appear so to an individual who shares a common communicative history with the rest of his family. Whose perspective is to be used and who decides which perspective is correct?

In reply to these criticisms Bateson (1966) admits, "Personally, I do not believe that the theory is at present subject to rigorous empirical testing." He also points out that this theory as well as many of the other currently popular ones are "really not theories in the ordinary sense, but are more like new languages or perhaps new epistemologies. A language can be confusing or enlightening. . . . convenient or clumsy. . . . But it cannot, in itself, be true or false."

Lidz

In many respects Lidz's formulations are psychoanalytic concepts applied to the family triad and as a result have the virtue of being easily understood by professionals used to thinking in these terms. Role differentiation in terms of both age and sex appropriateness play a central role in the Lidz group's analysis of family pathology. The basic problem in all family difficulties are seen in terms of distortions of normal parent-child role relationships:

> What appears to be essential can be stated simply. . . . The spouses need to form a coalition as members of the parental generation maintaining their respective gender-linked roles, and be capable of transmitting instrumentally useful ways of adaptation suited to the society in which they live [Lidz, 1963]

Two deviant types of marital relationships have been identified, each of which lead to impaired parenting and disrupted sex-role learning in the child: marital schism and marital skew.

Marital schism is used to describe relationships in which there is a state of severe, chronic discord and disequilibrium. Threats of separation are common and recurrent. Communication centers around power struggles, resistance, and fighting, and/or efforts to conceal or avoid facing the deep schism between the spouses. Having little to gain from each other, the parents tend to seek support from the child. In competition for his loyalty, each attempts to diminish the worth of the other to the child. Schizophrenia in females is believed to be particularly common in families marked by a schismatic marriage.

The other major pattern of disrupted relationships between the spouses is called *marital skew*. Here the relationship is not threatened by separation, but it is distorted or skewed toward meeting the needs of one member at the expense of the needs of others. Typically there is a domineering mother who forms an overly close relationship with one child at the expense of the other children and of the husband, who passively accedes to his wife's wishes. Schizophrenic males are believed relatively likely to come from such families.

In both types of marital relationship there is a failure to develop a reciprocally rewarding parental coalition. Age- and sex-appropriate role behaviors are impaired and poorly modeled for the children. Role reciprocity, which Lidz et al. (1957b) define as a "common understanding and acceptance of each others roles, goals, and motivation, and a reasonable sharing of cultural value orientations," is missing.

The theoretical constructs developed by Lidz and his colleagues have broad application in the understanding of many symptomatic behaviors, even though they were originally developed to help explain the phenomena of schizophrenia. For example, school phobic behavior can be seen as a situation in which the child has somehow taken for himself a decision that in most families is reserved for adults: whether or not the child is to attend school.

The major criticism of this theory is that its concepts are not integrated into a unified system. Concepts from several disciplines are used without being systematically related to each other. A second criticism is that it is individual- rather than family-oriented. Although frequent references are made to the family social system and social roles, the fact is that children develop problems because of poor marriages, which in turn result from psychological problems brought to the marriage by the individual spouses. In order to understand the family we have to understand the dynamics of the individuals. As Mishler and Waxler (1966) summarize the matter, ". . . it appears that we have to depend on an understanding of the psychodynamics of the parents; to the extent that this is necessary, the analysis of the family as a social system is superfluous." However, the appeal of Lidz's approach lies in calling attention to the concrete but powerful parameters of age- and sex-role behaviors, their development, and their vicissitudes.

Wynne

Wynne is interested in the impact of the family system as a unit on the quality and structure of the role relationships within that unit. He and his colleagues have identified four features of schizophrenic families, which seem to differentiate them from families in general (Wynne & Singer, 1964):

1. Patterns of handling attention and meaning that interfere with the capacity for purposive behavior and selective attention.
2. Erratic and inappropriate styles of relating leading to unpredictable closeness and distance.
3. Underlying feelings of meaninglessness, pointlessness, and emptiness, that pervade all interpersonal relationships.
4. A collusive family structure that serves to deny or reinterpret the reality of anxiety-producing feelings or events.

Although some of these features have been found in less seriously disturbed families as well, this discussion is limited to schizophrenic families for illustrative purposes. With respect first to describing patterns of handling attention and meaning (transactional thought disorders) in schizophrenic families, Wynne and Singer (1964) classify them along a continuum from amorphous to fragmented. Amorphous patterns are characterized by vague drifting and blurring of attention and meaning, so that attention and meaning are neither object-oriented nor specific. Fragmented patterns are poorly integrated messages resulting from the intrusion of unconscious thought processes, from using odd vantage points for communication, and from crypticness. The authors cite as an example of such fragmentation one parent's complete response to a Rorschach card: "If you read stories of Cossacks, that's self-explanatory." Amorphous or fragmented patterns are not seen as characteristics of a single parent, but are thought to be prominent features of the entire family system.

The second characteristic of disturbed families is an erratic and inappropriate style of relating which leads to unpredictable distance and closeness. Wynne and Singer are talking here not simply about interpersonal distance and affective functions; cognitive functions and distance from ideas are also included. The nature of the distance taken both from people and from ideas varies unpredictably, and often inappropriately, from too distant to too close.

Wynne and his colleagues believe that the schizophrenic family's patterns of handling meaning and attention and their erratic modes of relating function are defenses that help them deny or mitigate underlying feelings of helplessness and meaninglessness. Such feelings are thought to be pervasive in the family but not consciously experienced. Rather, it is when they threaten to come into awareness that the behaviors listed above are most likely to be brought into use.

Finally, the collusive family structure adopted serves to deny and reinterpret disturbing experiences and also to bolster the defensive patterns listed previously. Two structural patterns of this process that have been identified are *pseudomutuality* and *pseudohostility*. The difference between these two patterns is less important than their similarity, namely, that they are both pseudo states that are fixed and rigid. Pseudomutuality implies the opposite of mutuality and complementarity in interpersonal relationships. Energy is directed more toward maintaining a sense of reciprocity than toward the actual development of mutually acknowledged and supported individuation. Pseudohostility is defined as a fixed and rigid state of hostility which protects the family both from the threat of too much closeness and from any real anger and disillusionment that may emerge. Deviations from the family's rigid role structure are not permitted, but it is not obvious that they are not permitted. Rather, deviations from the family norm are either excluded from awareness or reinterpreted so that an illusion of harmony and closeness or an illusion of hostility is maintained. Family myths or legends may be used to communicate and teach the negative consequences attendant on divergence from the rigidly defined roles. Such efforts tend to cut off or sharply delimit separation from the family and involvement in the broader society. As a result, the possible corrective effects of extrafamilial influences are minimized, while the corrosive effects of the intrafamilial environment are maximized.

Summarizing Wynne's work, Mishler and Waxler (1966) point out that he tends to use concepts at several levels of analysis without specifying the interrelationships of the concepts. Consequently the theory is neither systematic nor complete. However, this group, perhaps more than any other, is empirically oriented—that is, they have attempted to accumulate data concerning which family patterns are found together rather than defining connections theoretically and then attempting to verify the hypothesized connections via observations.

Bowen

Bowen and his colleagues, who began studying hospitalized families at the National Institute of Mental Health in the mid-1950s, came to the view that families function as a single organism and that the identified patient is the part of the organism through which overt symptoms are expressed (Bowen, 1960). Bowen regards schizophrenia as the result of a family process which takes place over at least three generations. The process is as follows: grandparents may be relatively mature, but their combined immaturities are somehow acquired by one child (typically the one who is most attached to the mother); this child then marries a spouse of equal immaturity and their combined immaturities are also focused on a single child (again, the one most attached to mother); it is this child, carrying the collective immaturities of two prior generations, who is the most immature and the most likely candidate for the development of severe psychological symptoms.

Bowen's central theoretical concept is the *undifferentiated family ego mass*, which refers to the conglomerate emotional oneness that exists at various levels of intensity and shifts about within the family in definite patterns of emotional responsiveness. A mother-child symbiotic relationship is one example of part of a fragment of such a pattern. The point of the concept is that individual members do not act or react as autonomous, mature, differentiated individuals, but instead as subunits of a larger system. It is the system that reacts and thereby dictates and controls the reactions of individuals or subunits.

A prime example of how persons operate as part of an undifferentiated system is the relationship between spouses in which there may be an *emotional divorce*. Although both partners are immature, only one acts immaturely. The other denies the immaturity and functions with a facade of overadequacy. One appears more immature and the other more mature than is realistic. As part of the same ego mass, however, both components are expressed. The wife has adequacy as well as immaturity and, contrariwise, the husband is inadequate at times and adequate at others. In an undifferentiated ego mass each spouse takes on a role that expresses only half of the equation, and their roles are rigidly maintained. Between them they make a whole person. The emotional divorce allows them to maintain a relationship without meaningful interaction, which would threaten their respective roles, while appearing to be happily married.

In the families studied by Bowen, it was noted that the mother often had related well to the identified patient when he was an infant. It was as if the child's helplessness aided the mother in denying similar states in herself by projecting them onto the child. As an infant a child is realistically helpless but, as he matures and becomes more independent, the formerly fixed relationship is threatened, and the child is pressured by the system to remain helpless and immature in order to preserve the relationship and protect the mother.

Bowen feels that the mother in such a family makes two main demands on her child: (a) be helpless (usually communicated at the emotional level); and (b) be gifted, special, and mature (usually communicated at the overt, verbal level). Since the verbal message contradicts the emotional message, the child is placed in a situation in which he must talk one way while feeling another. The system bears close resemblance to those described by Bateson (double bind) and Wynne (pseudo).

A prominent feature of the mother-child relationship is projection whereby the mother focuses concerns about her own safety, competence, and helplessness on the child, and the child accepts this ascribed role. Further, the father complies with both the projection and the acceptance in order to preserve the family system. This paternal collusion is vital to the system, since the mother-child closeness could never develop without his functional approval. The mother ascribes her helplessness to the child and then "mothers" the helplessness in the child with her adequate self; thus what began as a feeling in the mother becomes a fact in the child. Sometimes anxiety in one person results in physical symptoms in the other. Bowen describes seesaw movements in several families in which improvement in one person led to physical illness in the other, and vice versa.

The theory leans heavily on psychoanalytic concepts such as projection, unconscious fears, and the like, but it lacks any precision. Although Bowen has developed a "scale" of ego differentiation to help define various levels of functioning (Bowen, 1966), the ratings are purely subjective. A major virtue of Bowen's theory lies in his delineation of the family ego mass concept. With this concept, it is easier for the therapist to see how changes in one individual's differentiation might force the family into a new equilibrium around a new level of separateness-connectedness. If the family, for some reason, cannot be treated as a unit, it still may be possible to effect needed changes in the system.

OBJECTIVES IN FAMILY INTERVENTION

In discussing the objectives of family intervention, some attention must be given first to the types of family problems that are most responsive to family intervention techniques. There is no universal agreement on this matter. At one extreme Williams (1967) essentially proposes using family therapy only as an adjunct or aid to individual therapy efforts, particularly when the identified patient is a child. Jackson and Weakland (1961), however, seem to imply that family intervention may be suitable for treating virtually any problem or type of family.

Among more denotative approaches to this question, Rabiner, Molinski, and Gralnick (1962) list several criteria for the appropriate selection of family cases in an inpatient unit. First, family intervention can be considered when current or anticipated family problems seem to significantly affect the inpatient's current adjustment and/or his potential adjustment. Second, the involved family members must be able to attend sessions at least once a week. Third, the staff must have sufficient knowledge about the family to judge that (a) serious decompensation will be unlikely to result in any member as a result of conjoint sessions; (b) unfulfilled but potentially mutually gratifying needs are present; (c) the stress generated by conjoint sessions will be therapeutically manageable; and (d) the primary patient's relationship with his therapist is sufficiently strong that it is unlikely to be jeopardized by family sessions.

Wynne (1971) has written cogently about indications for deciding to initiate exploratory family therapy. He recommends its consideration with the following types of family problems: (a) adolescent separation problems, which can also include older patients who have never effected a real separation; (b) families characterized by a trading of dissociations, such that each person locates the totality of a trait of feeling in another family member while being blind to similar traits in himself; (c) families characterized by collective cognitive chaos and erratic distancing; and (d) families marked by fixed interpersonal and cognitive distancing with eruptive threats and episodes.

Wynne (1971) also speaks of conditions that, if not met, limit the advisability or practicality of family therapy. First, there must be a family constellation available in which the members are emotionally invested and entangled and not simply intellectually interested in going along with the therapist. Wynne does not rigidly define which members are to be included, but only specifies that it should be "those who are functionally linked together, within discernible psychological boundaries." Second, the initiation of family therapy must fit constructively with the overall therapeutic process in which an identified patient is engaged. For example, in instances in which the family is very entangled, family sessions may precede any other therapeutic efforts. At other times individual therapy may best be interrupted to treat emerging family problems and resumed after the family therapy is completed. Such shifts must be carried out in a therapeutically strategic, rather than haphazard, manner if therapeutic trust is to be maintained. The author has provided elsewhere an example of a case that required several shifts from individual to family therapy and back again (Fox, 1974).

Third, the right kind of therapist must be available for conducting family therapy. Wynne (1971) lists as desirable qualities of the family therapist self-awareness, capacity for restraint, capacity for active limit-setting behavior, and capacity for sustained interest. To Wynne's list I add only a few considerations. A cotherapist is often highly useful with severely disturbed families and in families lacking an adequate, opposite-sex role model. Also, I like to structure therapy so that the form of treatment parallels the goals that are set. For example, in treating adolescent separation problems, I commonly obtain a different individual therapist for the adolescent. This treatment is in addition to the family therapy sessions. The adolescent is under no requirement to divulge the details of his individual therapy to either the rest of the family or to me. This treatment format emphasizes the adolescent's separateness, while at the same time recognizing his continuing ties to the family. Thus the treatment process, which aims at the achievement of separateness, proceeds by treating the adolescent separately.

It can be advanced as a general principle that the family therapist's techniques should be closely tied to his objectives, which in turn flow from some idea or theory about what families should be like and what is "wrong" with the unit at hand. In the face of considerable diversity, some broadly endorsed objectives of family therapy can be noted. Hess and Handel (1967), for example, have identified five objectives related to concerns common to all family units:

1.   Establishing patterns of separateness and connectedness.
2.   Establishing a satisfactory congruence of images through the exchange of suitable testimony, for example, of self, of others, of the family.
3.   Evolving modes of interaction in central family concerns or themes.

4. Establishing the boundaries of the family's world of experience.

5. Dealing with significant biosocial issues of family life, as in defining male and female and old and young.

All the theorists discussed in the preceding section point to the need to help troubled families meet one or more of the above goals. Three broad, related goals or objectives most theorists share are strengthening the family system, increasing separation-individuation, and strengthening the marital relationship.

Strengthening the Family System

The objective of strengthening the family system has several implications for the kinds of techniques employed in family therapy. First and foremost, the therapist attempts to help the system function better by helping the flow of communications. The techniques for doing this include modeling clear, direct, and open communication for the family, reinterpreting messages, checking out what message was sent and how it compares with the message received, forcing members to talk *to* each other rather than *about* each other through the therapist, directing members to rephrase questions as demands, and identifying and making overt emerging feeling tones (Satir, 1964). It is important to note here a common misconception of beginners that family therapy does not take place unless the family members constantly talk to each other. If excessive, this concern may lead the therapist to deprive the family of significant corrective experiences and allow them simply to repeat past interactive patterns. Even while not engaged in conversation directly, other family members may gain a great deal from hearing one member describe feelings to or interact intensely with the therapist in a manner different from anything they have seen before. In this sense it is proper to say that "individual therapy" conducted in the presence of the family has an impact far different from individual therapy conducted in isolation. The impact is different for the individual and for the others who witness his struggle. Some writers have speculated that the whole key to change in family therapy is communication in each other's presence, and not necessarily communication *with* each other (Beels & Ferber, 1969).

Naturally, the therapist cannot help the family system unless he first succeeds in making them view themselves as a system rather than as a family with a member who has a problem (identified patient). One of the basic methods for doing this is to see all the family together, at least in the initial treatment phase. Joint sessions help bring to light other family issues which may be important, and they dramatically illustrate the premise that the identified patient became disturbed in a social context and can best be understood and helped in that context. Another common misunderstanding of beginning therapists occurs at this point. In an effort to broaden the treatment context from an individual to a family one, the neophyte often ignores the identified patient. This is a mistake. Although the therapist wants to "get to the family," he cannot afford to ignore the pain in any of its members. The therapist's task is to keep both individual reactions and family processes in mind without allowing the family to exclude either one from attention. In this connection, Bell's (1963) admonition is appropriate: "Let it be recognized . . . that although family group treatment seeks the well-being of the family, secondarily it has important consequences for the states of individuals who make up the family."

As a rule, family therapists tend to place more emphasis on changing patterns of interaction than on increasing understanding. Thus for Zuk (1967) the goal is to "shift the balance of pathogenic relating among family members so that new forms of relating become possible." This is accomplished by the therapist's taking sides in order to intensify and then reduce conflicts (Zuk, 1971). Similarly, Jackson and Weakland (1961) believe that pointing out repetitive, self-defeating patterns does little good, and so they counsel therapists to pay less attention to noting and describing the content of patterns and more to influencing or changing the patterns. Not all therapists denigrate increased understanding to the extent that Jackson does, however. Laquer et al. (1964) list as a primary objective the development of better understanding of the reasons for the family members' disturbing behavior toward each other. Schaffer et al. (1962) also attach importance to increasing the family's understanding of maladaptive behavior patterns. The point is that all therapists emphasize the necessity of actively changing patterns rather than simply pointing them out. As Framo (1969) says, "Any therapist worth his salt knows that just pointing out, confronting, or interpreting things to people cannot work by itself." Some therapists feel that increased understanding helps bring about this change; others do not: "The goal of changing the family system of interaction is family therapy's most distinctive feature, its greatest advantage and, especially to those who come to it from other disciplines, its greatest stumbling block" (Beels & Ferber, 1969).

The deemphasis on increasing understanding is part of a general trend, both in individual and family therapy, to emphasize action and change rather than insight. Bell (1963) has best summarized the changing viewpoint: "Whereas formerly we assumed that insight ultimately led to action by some unknown process, we now concluded that action may be seen more fruitfully as coming before insight. Action has the primacy rather than insight." Accordingly, a family therapist may actively encourage the formation of a father-son coalition before anyone in the family "understands" that the mother and son have been "too close," that the father has assented by withdrawing, and that these actions protect each of them from acknowledging painful affects. Sometimes the understanding follows, but commonly it does not. This is different from a model that helps the family attain insight and then waits for them to put the understanding into practice, and it is a cardinal feature of the attitude of many family therapists.

Wynne (1969) suggests that the concept of insight is dead and should be left to die in peace, since it is no longer seen as the primary agent of change even by many classical psychoanalysts. Wynne feels that ". . . if the term is to be used at all, the gaining of 'insight' about the family may be useful to the therapist, rarely to the family." The changing ideas about the value of insight are not restricted to family therapists, who in this respect seem to be part of a new therapeutic *Zeitgeist*. Strupp (1973), a leading psychoanalytic scholar, recently labeled the idea that insight leads to therapeutic change a "convenient fiction" with no adequate empirical evidence to support it. While admitting that some patients during the course of therapy do gain understanding of motivations (particularly those that lead to neurotic entanglements), Strupp (1973) maintains that "such understanding may be intellectually satisfying and have an aesthetic appeal to certain patients. However, as far as behavior and personality change is concerned, I feel that, by and large, it is not a highly potent force in producing change."

Strengthening the family system as a system also has implications for the therapist. Once a systems approach is adopted, it then becomes as impossible to view therapy as something that involves only the family as it is to view pathology as something that involves only the identified patient. The therapist becomes involved in a system of interactions with the family as a participant rather than as a distant "healer." Such involvements makes it difficult to blame failures glibly on the family because they are "too defensive." Rather, the explanation has to be more along the following lines: Therapy failed because the therapist collaborated in establishing a relationship system in which several members were allowed to be less than candid and to continue to use rigid modes of interacting. Shapiro and Budman (1973), in a study of individual and family cases who continued treatment as opposed to those who terminated, found that the therapist's behavior was pivotal. A majority of "terminators," both individual and family, cited the therapist's behavior as an important factor in termination. Among "continuers" there was an important difference between individual and family cases. Family continuers lauded high levels of therapist activity, whereas terminators deplored therapist inactivity. Individual continuers, however, emphasized the therapist's empathy and concern.

Increasing Separation-Individuation

A second broad objective of family treatment is to help with the achievement of increased separation-individuation in each of the members. In a sense, this is a general objective of all psychotherapies. An increased sense of autonomy, of personal responsibility, and of being responsive to but not overly dependent on others is a primary goal of psychoanalysis, gestalt therapy, and a host of other approaches (see Chapter 6). In adopting this objective, therapists are reflecting an ideal of human behavior that has been seen as the key to happiness by widely varying cultures across several centuries. It has been knitted into the fabric of religions as diverse as Zen and Christianity (e.g., Buber, 1958), into sociological theories such as Riesman's (1950) ideal of the autonomous man, and into various other systems of thought such as that described in Castaneda's (1972) anthropological studies. The ancient Zen writers captured the essence of the idea as well as any (Kapleau, 1965). For them, man should strive to be as a stick in a river. The stick flows fast or slow as the water dictates, always responsive to its varying shifts. Yet the stick is always a stick, it never becomes water. This is very similar to Riesman's idea of the autonomous man who is keenly responsive and attuned to his interpersonal climate without ever sacrificing his own identity and separateness. It is this ideal that has been incorporated into many theories of psychotherapy, including most of the family approaches.

Bowen (1966) has probably placed more emphasis on this goal than any other writer in the family therapy literature. Ideally, he believes that the best results are obtained when family members can work together mutually to encourage and affirm higher levels of autonomy in each other. When this is impossible, the therapist can start the differentiation in one member, support his independence through the period of counterpressures from the family, and then help the family unit to develop a new homeostasis on a new level of differentiation. Bell (1963) states the objective here: "The therapist does not simply try to make the family more 'groupy,' more cohesive, but on the contrary, tries to promote its growth and differentiation." As differentiation is achieved, pressures to constrict behavior in order to protect or help some other member of the family are lessened and greater flexibility in the system is manifest. Szasz (1959) has reacted to the tendency of family members to hold each other responsible for their individual happiness:

. . . Given a certain (considerable) measure of autonomy, and therefore of separateness between people, it becomes quite impossible for anyone to "make someone [else] happy." The only person toward whose happiness we can contribute directly is our own. To the happiness of others, as I see it, we can contribute at most indirectly.

Strengthening the Marriage

The third broad objective of family therapy, strengthening the marital relationship, is not independent of the two previously mentioned objectives but is separated here for purposes of discussion. As Bowen (1966) has observed, intense marital conflict does not always cause emotional problems in the offspring and, conversely, children can develop serious impairment when the marital relationship of the parents is not disrupted. However, it is the general rule that in dysfunctional families impaired marital relationships are probable. Many family therapists see the marital relationship as the keystone on which all others in the family depend. Change in this relationship can thus lead to rapid and widespread changes throughout the family system:

. . . If the illness is in the family group, one should start with the group's leadership, and the parents are, in Satir's phrase, the architects of the family, the place where the main authority ought to be and where lasting sexual and contractual bonds should be cemented [Beels & Ferber, 1969]

In my experience, the families that make the most rapid and lasting changes are those in which there is an early identification of marital problems which the parents are willing to work at alleviating. At this point in the treatment children are typically excused, even when they are a part of the presenting problem. One reason for excusing the children is to emphasize thereby the separation of differing roles in the two generations. Parents handle adult problems without the unnecessary involvement of the children. If the therapist is successful in "getting to the marriage," he often has the battle more than half won. Dramatic changes in children almost regularly follow real changes in the parental relationship. Some families appear to contain a disruptive marital relationship which everyone in the family resists attending to. In such cases it is possible, on occasion, to help the family alter some interactions resulting in a particularly painful role for one of its members without changing the marital relationship. In this case the therapist helps the family "accommodate to the symptom" rather than change it.

FAMILY INTERVENTION TECHNIQUES

Jackson and Weakland (1961) list several aspects of the family therapist's attitude and behavior that are different from those of the individual therapist. The family therapist typically finds it necessary to be more active, assertive, and directive than individual therapists. If he is merely a passive listener, the therapist will typically find that the family either ignores his comments and reflections or incorporates them into their ongoing interaction pattern with no apparent change in behavior. Similarly, the therapist may find it necessary to intervene forcefully by directing one member to be silent or by encouraging another to rephrase a comment, or by asking for a change in the seating arrangement to facilitate or discourage certain interactions.

Typically the family's destructive interaction patterns are noticed very early, and the therapist becomes more interested in identifying and changing such patterns than in understanding individual dynamics. This means that his behavior is directed less toward individual motives or fantasies and more toward interpersonal perceptions and transactional sequences. This leads to a corresponding decrease in emphasis on asking the kinds of questions considered useful in establishing individual diagnoses. Thus, when confronted with profound sadness in one member, the therapist is less inclined to ask about such factors as changes in sleep patterns, loss of appetite, changes in memory, and the like, and more inclined to look for the function of the sadness in the family system. A family seen by the author was referred because of a 13-year-old son who was expressing suicidal thoughts. It was subsequently learned that the behavior emerged following the loss of his maternal grandmother, to whom he had not been particularly close. However, his mother had been very close to the grandmother and, as she began to experience and work through her own profound sadness and loss, the boy's depression lifted. In terms of the system, concern over the son's "depression" made it possible for the family to ignore a more serious depression in the mother.

Another technique sometimes used involves working with one member alone to help him make essential changes that force changes in crucial family interactions. Bowen (1966) describes this process as one in which one member is helped to become an expert on how the family system operates and thus is in a position to effect important changes in times of family disequilibrium. Ewing and Fox (1968) report in this regard working with wives of alcoholics to help them change their frequent pattern of rescue, protection, and belittling behavior vis-à-vis their husbands. As these wives' behavior changed, there were often changes in their husbands' drinking behavior, even though they had not been in therapy themselves.

This technique is sometimes especially useful in circumventing therapeutic impasses. Recently I saw a couple on the verge of divorce because of the husband's infidelity, his confusion over whether or not he still wanted to be married, and his inability to escape from a domineering father who owned the business in which he worked. The husband felt pressured from all sides to make important decisions concerning marriage, work, and the future of his relationship with his paramour. In this context, therapy was seen by him as further pressure to explain himself and take responsibility. His response to the various pressures was to withdraw into a very schizoidlike state, which served to stimulate the wife into more desperate requests for reassurance concerning the viability of the marriage. In conjoint sessions he became progressively more silent as his wife's attempts to make him discuss his feelings steadily escalated. When initial attempts to break through the husband's resistance to therapy failed, I excused him and worked with the wife. The aim was to help the wife change her desperate attempt to secure some sign of love from her husband. After three sessions she had been highly successful in altering her interactions with her husband, and he had changed dramatically for the better. Friends who knew the couple was in therapy but who were unaware of the approach being used commented on the obvious changes that had taken place in them. These comments helped to reinforce the new pattern and encouraged the husband to reenter the therapy. He requested joint sessions in order to enhance further the marital relationship, and a major resistance to treatment was thus avoided.

Still another method of altering pathological family alliances is through the encouragement of new coalitions that make maintenance of the original, pathological one more difficult. Hoffman (1971) cites as an example the changing of the role of a family scapegoat by creating a new scapegoat (i.e., by emphasizing problems and/or disruptive behaviors present in another member, which have been ignored by the family). Minuchin (1974) presents a comprehensive and lucid description of how to understand family coalitions and then use this understanding to effect more functional patterns of interaction.

Recently family therapists have begun to use teaching methods oriented toward improving communication skills as a method of effecting changes in the family. Ely, Guerney, and Stover (1973) describe a training program which involves 8 to 10 two-hour sessions focusing on communication skills (such as listening for and reflecting feeling tones). This is supplemented by scheduled practice sessions at home (½ hour per week) and by 1 hour per week for 6 weeks working through a programmed text. The therapist is clearly in the role of a teacher helping each spouse to be an effective, empathic listener. This approach prevents family members from seeing the therapist as the only one who can truly understand them and thereby becoming increasingly resentful toward each other. Such training has been found to be highly effective in bringing about communication pattern changes highly correlated with improved marital adjustment.

In a similar vein, I have had some success in teaching family members to listen for the statement about self that is implicit in practically every interpersonal statement and in all accusations. For example, when a wife angrily says to her husband, "You think more of your job than you do of me," she is making a statement both about the husband and about herself. Besides accusing the husband of neglect, she is also expressing hurt over not being more important to him. If the husband can be helped to listen for and respond to his wife's hurt and desire for affection rather than to the accusation, a meaningful discussion rather than a fight is likely to ensue. If he responds only to the statement about himself, a cycle of defense, charge, and countercharge is likely. By responding to the part of the message that reflects something about the sender's feelings, the receiver can avoid cyclical, self-defeating patterns of interaction. Fitzgerald (1973) has also pointed out the positive benefits of increased willingness to listen in highly conflicted couples. As mentioned previously, this may help account for the fact that having a spouse present and listening while the therapist works with the partner is highly beneficial to the relationship.

The ability to listen effectively is in turn highly dependent on the ability to disengage oneself sufficiently from the interaction process to be able to observe its pattern and effects. If one is only an observer or only a participant, he loses the ability to be a participant observer—a role therapists have long used to good effect in promoting important changes in others. Bowen, as described by Beels and Ferber (1969), seems to help patients achieve this role by instructing them to visit their parents and take an extensive family history from them. Beels and Ferber (1969) note that this process often has a "surprisingly powerful effect on the mutual understanding of both parties: it must be tried to be appreciated." It may be that the technique gains some of its effectiveness from emphasizing the patient's role as observer rather than merely as an unwitting participant.

Another method of helping a person be more observant and not simply a participant has been described by Minuchin and Montalvo (1967). These authors sometimes ask a family member to observe from behind a one-way screen while others in the family interact. Minuchin

(1974) also asks members of a family coalition to interact in the middle of the room while other members observe from an outer circle. Perlmutter et al. (1967) use videotape playbacks of portions of family sessions as material in subsequent family sessions. All these are methods for creating distance in order to increase the ability to observe, understand, and, hopefully, change.

The use of multiple therapists is another technique that has been reported by several clinicians. The technique seems especially useful in time-limited approaches in which intensive interaction over brief periods is indicated. The multiple-impact approach employed by MacGregor et al. (1964) necessitates intense interaction with various combinations of family members with different therapist. Similarly, the highly successful crises model developed at the University of Colorado Medical Center (Langsley et al., 1968) utilizes several therapists in flexible combinations with various family groupings to prevent hospitalization of the identified patient. Using this approach, the team prevented hospitalization in over 90% of the acute crises in which an independent expert had already deemed hospitalization necessary.

Many clinicians prefer to work with a cotherapist when treating families, although there is as yet no empirical evidence that two therapists obtain better results than one therapist (Gurman, 1973). There are numerous potential advantages to this technique, however:

1.   The family is provided with multiple models of interaction styles.

2.   If the cotherapists are male and female, the family has a model of a healthy adult heterosexual relationship, which enriches potential transference effects.

3.   General clinical expertise and therapeutic power is enhanced.

4.   Differing vantage points allow for cross-validation of hypotheses and observation.

5.   The therapists' willingness to expose and openly deal with their differing perceptions is an effective modeling technique.

Woody and Woody (1973) list three essential prerequisites for cotherapists to work together effectively. First, there must be full understanding of the other's style of functioning, so that each therapist can almost predict how his cotherapist will respond in a given interaction. Second, there must be professional respect sufficient to appreciate why the other functions as he does and how this is justified theoretically. Third, and most important, there must be a relationship characterized by "honest, personalized intimacy." Mutual knowledge, professional acceptance, and shared respect are not sufficient; there also must be an open, frank, and genuinely positive relationship.

Behavior modification techniques have been used extensively by some

family therapists. Haley (1971), somewhat incorrectly, feels that behavior therapists think only in terms of dyads and not in terms of larger
units. Thus, he comments, they speak of the manner in which one
parent or the other reinforces the child and not in terms of conflicts
between parents about the child. This is not completely true, even in
relatively simple instances of increasing the frequency of desired behavior through reinforcement. Liberman (1970), for example, observes
that family behavior therapy progresses best when each member of an
interlocking, rigid family system learns to change his behavior (response) to other members: "Instead of rewarding maladaptive behavior
with attention and concern, the family members learn to give each other
recognition and approval for desired behavior." Liberman is clearly
talking about the whole family system rather than about specific dyads.

Desensitization procedures have been employed in families to change
behaviors such as sexual inhibitions. Some techniques utilized by Masters and Johnson (1970) and Kaplan (1974) can easily be conceptualized
as desensitization, for example, when couples are instructed to work on
sexual inhibitions via a programmed sequence of exercises involving
increasing intimacy. Other types of hierarchies can be developed for
several members of the family and worked through (deconditioned) in
the actual family setting. This is superior to the usual practice of asking
an individual patient to fantasize increasingly fearful scenes while in a
relaxed state. Used in a family context, the technique can be particularly
powerful in that the interpersonal milieu in which one undergoes change
is the very one with which each individual must deal daily on a face-to-
face basis.

Role playing is a further behavioral technique that has enjoyed widespread use in work with families. Family members can be assigned roles
designed to help them deal directly with alternative interaction styles.
Another variation is to ask members to switch roles, so as to increase
their appreciation of how the other is behaving. Role playing has proved
particularly effective in reinforcing desired assertive behaviors for a
particular family member (Lazarus, 1971). Again, it is worth emphasizing that practicing such behavior with one's family in a context of
mutual understanding and support often has far greater impact than
similar practice with the therapist alone.

A misconception commonly found in criticisms of behavior modification approaches is that the therapist relies on prescribed formulas for
particular symptoms, which are then applied more or less blindly. In
fact, however, the behavior therapist relies as much on what others
would call "clinical skills" (e.g., intuitive judgement) as do other types
of therapists. After observing behavior therapy as practiced at one
leading center, Klein, Dittman, Parloff, and Gill (1969) reported:

. . . The selection of problems to be worked on seemed quite arbitrary and inferential. We were frankly surprised to find the presenting symptomatic complaint was often sidestepped for what the therapist intuitively considered to be more basic issues. Most surprising to us, the basis for this selection seemed often to be what others would call dynamic considerations [p. 261]

For a thorough discussion of behavioral approaches in family treatment, the interested reader should consult the appropriate chapter in Woody and Woody (1973). For our purposes, it is sufficient to say that behavior modification has contributed numerous techniques whose application to family difficulties seem limited only by the ingenuity of the therapist. Typically, family therapists as a group demonstrate a pragmatic willingness to draw techniques from any theory if that technique promises to be of help. Behavior modification has proved to be a rich source of techniques and of theoretical insights.

Before concluding the discussion of techniques, a word of caution concerning their use is in order. Many techniques from widely divergent theoretical systems seem to produce results. Any family therapist who is willing to make the effort to learn and use different methods of dealing with the same problem can easily demonstrate this to his own satisfaction. An example may be helpful:

A 26-year-old woman, married for 2 years, was referred to an outpatient clinic because of a paralysis of the lower right arm and hand. Neurological and physical examinations were negative. Psychological testing and diagnostic interviews revealed "sexual conflicts, guilt over masturbatory practices, and strong but poorly recognized dependency needs." The paralysis was believed to be a result of her conflicts, and intensive, depth-oriented psychotherapy was recommended. Since no individual therapist was available, the social worker in charge of the case decided to interview the patient's husband for further study and clarification. New material was discovered that made it possible to conceptualize the problem in a completely different manner. The patient's husband was a dependent person who was still very attached to his mother. Shortly after his marriage he was discharged from the service and returned with his wife to live with his mother. He was unable to decide whether to return to college or go to work and had delayed a decision for almost 2 years. The eventual living pattern of the triad involved the husband and his mother doing the household shopping, taking short trips together, and the like, while the wife worked to support them. The wife resented her husband's lack of direction and his closeness to his mother, but never refused to provide financial support. After 2 years, the sudden arm paralysis prevented her continued work as a typist. Family therapy was initiated with the aim of helping the couple to establish more independence from the mother. This was accomplished rather quickly and was followed a few weeks later by the husband deciding on a career goal and a disappearance of the wife's paralysis.

The point here is not that family therapy is superior to individual therapy. Hysterical conversion symptoms are frequently treated in dynamic psychotherapy with good results. The point is that the explanations for the cause of the symptom are quite different from different theoretical vantage points, and thus different approaches (techniques) are indicated. Psychoanalysis would explain the symptom as a sexual conflict (which was certainly present in this instance) and propose individual psychotherapy. A family systems theorist would explain the symptom in interpersonal-interactional terms and propose the treatment that was in fact used. I have little doubt that either approach would have worked. But, in view of the fact that different approaches based on divergent explanations often yield similar results, the neophyte would do well to avoid dogmatic adherence to any particular system or set of techniques. Strupp (1973) has summarized this point very well. Although he was speaking of individual psychotherapy, his comment is no less true of family therapy approaches:

> While every professional psychotherapist has deep commitments to some theoretical framework within which his therapeutic work is embedded, there is no evidence that one set of theoretical assumptions is more satisfactory than another—either in terms of what it permits the therapist to do or the outcomes to which it gives rise [p. 282]

RESULTS OF FAMILY THERAPY

The results of family therapy have been the subject of several critical reviews (Framo, 1965; Hill, 1964; Howells, 1971; Olson, 1970; Pool & Frazier, 1973; Walters, 1962; Wells, Dilkes, & Trivelli, 1972; Winter, 1971). The substance of these reviews is not reproduced here. Rather, this section attempts to summarize the major findings and remaining problems in this area of work. Finally, some examples of the better methodological studies are presented.

Family therapy researchers face all the problems attendant on research in individual psychotherapy (see Chapter 6), together with other problems particular to this field:

1. The unit of study is larger and more complex.
2. Events that transpire are often the result of many factors.
3. The identification and control of variables is complex and difficult.
4. The unit of study is in a state of continuous change.
5. The observer is often part of the system he observes and may change with it.
6. The area of study is wider, encompassing intrapsychic, relation-

ship, communication, and group variables, as well as contextual variables such as community, cultural, and social pressures.

The familiar problems of all outcome research are also to be found here. There are no adequate criteria measures with which to assess change. There is no adequate diagnostic or classification system for the clinical conditions being studied. And no empirical method exists for comparing treatment methods. In short, outcome studies are plagued by major problems at every stage of the scientific enterprise, from specification of the important antecedent conditions in the participants, through precise delineation of the intervening treatment variables, to measures of specific results. Noting these problems, the lack of sophistication in the overwhelming majority of studies, and the wariness of many clinicians toward research, Winter (1971) felt forced to conclude, "Perhaps family therapy simply does not work." Perhaps it does not, but this has not been demonstrated either. The best that can be said at present is that family therapy outcome studies enjoy the same inconclusive results as have characterized attempts to evaluate all other known forms of psychotherapeutic intervention. "Despite decades of persistent debate, the advent of new techniques, theoretical writings, and—alas— voluminous empirical studies, the basic issue concerning specific effects as a function of specific interventions remains as foggy as ever" (Strupp, 1973).

Realizing that the evidence for the efficacy of family therapy is short of overwhelming, let us look at the empirical studies that have been reported. The review can be short, because the number of such studies is small. Olson (1970) found that only 3% of approximately 250 published studies of marital and family therapy qualified as research studies. Beels and Ferber (1969) believed that there were only three reported studies of any substance dealing with outcome in family therapy. Probably the best review of the literature thus far is that of Wells, Dilkes, and Trivelli (1972) covering the period 1950–1970 and most of the major journals in the fields of social work, psychology, and psychiatry. Using the minimal search criteria of including only studies that (a) reported on at least three cases and (b) clearly specified the outcome measures used, they found only 18 studies. Of these 18 studies, 15 had an obvious methodological flaw—the omission of a control group. Another study was flawed by a sample size of only four, leaving only 2 studies with a satisfactory experimental methodology.

The 15 studies considered inadequate because of the lack of a control group also relied on subjective clinical judgments and client reports as their sole measure of outcome. Some neglected either pretherapy or follow-up measurement, and others included neither. Nevertheless, there is some merit in these studies. The realities of clinical work being what they are, unwanted compromises are almost inevitable and the researcher must simply do the best he can under the circumstances. Wells et al. (1972) have summarized the results of these studies, which are identified in Tables 1 and 2. It was not possible to include all studies in these tables, since some investigators have not reported evaluations in a form that is in any way comparable to the others.

Table 1 identifies outcome studies of family therapy with adults. Wells et al. point out that, although these studies were uncontrolled, the results are comparable to similar surveys of uncontrolled studies of individual psychotherapy. Thus the combined "improved" and "some improvement" rate is 69%, which is close to an overall success rate of 66% for individual therapy with adults reported by Frank (1961) and a 66% success rate for martial counseling reported by Gurman (1973). The success rate of family therapy with children (see Table 2) is 79%, which approximates a 73% improvement rate reported for individual therapy with children (Levitt, 1957). One of the above studies (Sigal, Rakoff, & Epstein, 1967) should be singled out for special attention, because of a particularly sophisticated use of clinical judgment as a criteria of outcome—the use of independent judges.

The two studies that Wells et al. (1972) found to have adequate methodology actually are an early and a final report of the same project

Table 1. Outcome Studies of Family Therapy with Adults

Nature of Problem	N	Improved	Some Improvement	No Change	Worse
Hospitalized schizophrenics (Bowen, 1961)	7	—	3	4	—
Outpatient schizophrenics (Bowen, 1961)	8	1	4	3	—
Outpatient neurotics (Carroll, 1963)	6	4	2	—	—
Adults with "work phobia" (Pittman, 1971)	5	5	—	—	—
Marital conflict (Belleville, 1969)[a]	44	26	—	18	—
Marital conflict (Fitzgerald, 1969)	49	37	—	12	—
Total	119	73	9	37	—
Percent	100	61	8	31	—

[a] Only one "improved" category was used; "no change" and "worse" were combined as "not successful."

Table 2. Outcome Studies of Family Therapy with Children

| Nature of Problem | N | Results at Termination | | | |
		Improved	Some Improvement	No Change	Worse
Adolescent behavior problems (MacGregor, 1962)[a,b,e]	50	43	—	7	—
Child & adolescent behavior problems (Kaffman, 1963)[c,d]	29	21	4	4	—
Adolescent behavior problems (Freeman, 1964)[a,i]	13	11	—	1	1
Child & adolescent behavior problems (Safer, 1966)[e,f,g]	29	12	9	8	—
Child behavior problems (Sigal, 1967)[h]	19	5	9	5	—
Delinquent adolescents (Minuchin, 1967)[a]	12	7	—	5	—
Adolescent behavior problems (Coughlin, 1968)[a,c]	10	8	—	2	—
Parent-child conflict (Wells, 1971)[i]	9	2	4	3	—
Total	171	109	26	35	1
Percent	100	64	15	21	—

[a] Only one "improved" category used.
[b] "No change" and "worse" combined as "not successful."
[c] "No change" includes cases that withdrew from treatment.
[d] "Considerable improvement" and "total improvement" combined.
[e] Evaluation conducted on follow-up, not at termination.
[f] "Some improvement" and "partial improvement" combined.
[g] Two instances of "symptomatic remission unrelated to therapy" included.
[h] "Slight improvement" and "no improvement" combined.
[i] Some marital conflict cases included.

(Langsley et al., 1968, 1969). In this project 150 families residing in the metropolitan Denver area for whom hospitalization had been recommended for one of its members were randomly assigned to a short-term, crisis intervention treatment group. The control group comprised 150 similar families with a patient who was admitted for conventional psychiatric inpatient treatment. The criterion measures were hospitalization rates, days lost from functioning, and performance on two rating scales. The scales were called the Social Adjustment Inventory and the Personal Functioning Scale and were apparently devised by the research group for this study. Six-month follow-up data are available for 90% of the subjects.

All the 150 family therapy cases were treated without admission to the hospital. Over the subsequent 6-month period following treatment, 13%

were hospitalized. This result compared favorably with a 29% readmission rate among the hospitalized controls. Days lost from functioning had a median of 5 for the family therapy cases and 23 for the control group. Both groups showed improvement on the two rating scales used, but there were no significant differences between the groups. Thus patients treated by family therapy rather than being admitted to a hospital returned to functioning an average of 2 weeks earlier, were functioning as well 6 months later, and were less likely to have spent part of the 6 months since treatment in the hospital in comparison to similar patients who had been hospitalized initially.

It should be emphasized that the basic tenets of sound research methodology were observed in this study. The families were randomly assigned to experimental and control groups, the groups were found to be statistically equal in all major respects, several outcome measures were utilized, and measures were obtained prior to and at the conclusion of treatment as well as at the end of a 6-month follow-up period. As Wells et al. (1972) correctly note, however, the independent variable employed in the study is extremely complex: "Whether the outcome measurements relate to the short-term nature of the treatment, the crises orientation, or the family therapy methods, cannot be distinguished in a non-factorial design." Another criticism is that the rating scales used were of questionable validity. Nevertheless, the study is on the whole impressive. Avoiding hospitalization for 150 seriously disturbed individuals is no mean accomplishment, and the differential readmission rates following treatment indicate that hospitalization was averted rather than simply delayed.

Further research in this area will have to become more specific and less broad-gauged than has been the case thus far. The question of whether family therapy "works" is not only too general to be meaningful, but is also simply unanswerable. The real question for future research is which kind of therapy administered by which therapist is likely to lead to what specific result in specified types of families. Obviously, we are a long way from achieving this kind of precision, but knowledge proceeds, and increasingly sophisticated research is being done. An example of the kind of precision needed in one aspect of study (patient characteristics) has been reported by Minuchin (1974). Although it is not an outcome study, it is reported here as an excellent example of the increasingly sophisticated research that is beginning to emerge.

Both children in the family Minuchin studied were diabetic, but they presented quite different medical problems. Dede, the older, was a "superlabile diabetic" who had been admitted to the hospital for treatment of ketoacidosis 23 times in 3 years. The younger sister, Violet, had some behavioral problems but they were not severe, and her diabetes was under good control. It was possible to demonstrate that each child responded differentially to family stress by measuring the level of plasma-free fatty acids (FFA) in the blood from samples drawn during structured interviews. Minuchin states that the blood samples were drawn from each family member in such a way that obtaining the samples did not interfere with ongoing interactions.

The sisters watched through a one-way screen while their parents were subjected to stress conditions. Even though not directly involved, each showed marked increases in FFA levels. When they were brought into the room with the parents, the levels rose still higher, but much more so for Dede than for her younger sister. When with the parents, the more responsive girl, Dede, was seen to play a different role from that of her sister. Dede's support was frequently sought by each parent in such a way that she could not respond to one without seeming to side against the other. This was not true of the younger sister, whose support was not sought by either parent. After the interview with the parents, Violet's FFA level returned promptly to baseline, whereas Dede's remained elevated for the next 1½ hours. Significantly, both parents showed elevated FFA levels in the latter part of their stress interview, but these levels lowered when the children entered the room. Apparently, interspouse conflict and stress were reduced when the conflict was detoured through the children and the usual parental roles were assumed.

ETHICAL ISSUES IN FAMILY THERAPY

In the opinion of many experts, family therapy raises unique ethical issues for the therapist in addition to those present in individual settings (see Fitzgerald, 1973; Fox, 1967; Grosser & Paul, 1964; Williams, 1967; Woody & Woody, 1973; Wynne, 1971). Generally speaking, these ethical issues have broadly to do with (a) potential conflicts with prevailing social values and (b) potential conflicts with traditional professional ethics.

The potential conflicts with prevailing social values mostly involve concerns that family therapy constitutes a threat to the family unit. The threat is seen in the encouragement of strong negative feelings and in the possibility of loss of parental authority and respect. Expression of strong hostility is specifically apt to be seen as a threat, since it may lead to unnecessary hurt through verbal acting-out and, possibly, to physical violence when away from the therapist. In fact, however, negative feelings are not new to families, even though expressing such feelings in the presence of an outsider may be. Such feelings are a threat to the family unit only if poorly handled by the therapist (Charny, 1972). The therapist's task is to place such feelings in the context of realistic ambivalence and to neutralize harmful effects through establishing an atmosphere of empathy for the feelings of others. As negative affects are made less fearful and anxiety-producing, positive affects become richer and the family unit is enhanced rather than weakened.

Similarly, concerns about the loss of parental respect and authority are groundless if the appropriate therapeutic atmosphere is established. Empathy and support for others' failings, fears, and weaknesses lead to greater tolerance and recognition of personal worth. Parental authority based purely on social roles may be lost by admission of inadequacies but, if empathy and compassion are established, the need to see or be seen as omnipotent gives way to a relationship built on mutual tolerance and respect for each individual as a person. With families who place a high value on the traditional hierarchial system of family life, it is important for the therapist to prepare the family by focusing on the potential gains that can follow the abdication of the omnipotent position of the parents. Grosser and Paul (1964) have presented a comprehensive discussion of this issue.

With respect to the potential for violence between sessions as a result of the material raised in the therapy, Grosser and Paul (1964) feel that the therapist must explain what might be involved before family therapy is initiated, pointing out possible disagreeable situations and the potential rewards. This is good advice.

Contrary to fears that family therapy threatens the integrity of the family unit, some clinicians have argued that individual therapy poses even more of such a threat. Fitzgerald (1973), for example, points out that in individual therapy it is often noted that improvement in the patient is followed by deterioration in some other family member. I have reviewed several studies showing deleterious effects that individual therapy often has on other family members, particularly spouses (Fox, 1967). If the family members are all present, it is easier for the therapist to monitor changes in each and to work toward helping each effect changes that are not perceived as harmful by the others. Similarly, Hurvitz (1967) has noted that individual therapy patients are able to criticize their spouses with impunity before a sympathetic therapist. In such contexts negative feelings often flourish, making the emergence of marital conflicts more likely and their resolution more difficult.

In all therapies personal values, social values, and the conflict between them arise of necessity. In family therapy, encompassing as it does man's oldest social institution, the conflicts are more pronounced.

"Women's lib" and the "sexual revolution" are but two simple examples of social phenomena that have serious implications for traditional family values and that affect patients and therapists alike. It is the responsibility of the therapist to be aware of such changing phenomena, to explore their impact on his personal life, to examine their validity in light of the best available knowledge, and to be aware of their place in his personal and professional roles: "The professional helper should recognize that values do get transmitted in therapy, and that this transmission must be an open and conscious process" (Woody & Woody, 1973).

The second broad category of ethical problems concerns issues that may place the family therapist in conflict with the professional ethics developed for individual patient-therapist relationships. One such issue is confidentiality of information. In traditional psychotherapy confidentiality is a relatively straightforward matter. Any information the patient reveals in the context of the help-seeking relationship is privileged information and may not be divulged without his consent. This is not only an ethical matter; in many states it is also a matter of law. The family therapist sometimes finds himself on the horns of a dilemma; one member of a family may reveal information he instructs the therapist not to reveal to other family members. The therapist must of course honor such requests. However, doing so may conflict with another ethical-moral principle according to which the therapist must not withhold information from clients he feels would be helpful to them. Thus the need to honor one person's right to privacy may conflict with another's right to know. Since both parties are patients of the same therapist, the therapist may be caught in the middle.

Generally, the therapist will do well to discuss this issue with the family beforehand. Some therapists frankly instruct people not to tell them anything they do not wish others to know, since they feel that their responsibility is to the family as a whole and that they will therefore share any information given to them. Others bypass the issue by refusing to talk to any family member alone. Yet it is almost impossible to avoid such issues at all times.

For example, the husband of a couple I was seeing confessed an extramarital affair through a letter and asked that his wife not be told. It was my judgment that the confession was an attempt to alleviate his guilt and that a revelation of this long past incident would do nothing more than upset his wife. I withheld the information. At other times the matter is not so simple. Generally, when people insist on telling me things they wish kept secret from the family, I follow the recommendation of Grosser and Paul (1964) and honor the request for silence while insisting that the person explore with me his reasons for wanting secrecy. Typically, it is a maneuver to secure special status with the therapist through a shared secret or an attempt to block the emergence of certain material in the conjoint sessions. As these motives are revealed and discussed, the patient generally decides to divulge the withheld information himself.

A final ethical problem or group of problems center around the question of who is to be regarded as the patient. Grosser and Paul (1964) think that the answer depends on the nature of the problem and the referral. When a disturbed individual comes to the attention of a therapist who then recommends that family members be included in the treatment in order to help the patient, the client is clearly the original patient. Grosser and Paul believe this is particularly true if a period of individual therapy has preceded the initiation of family sessions. There is some merit to this line of thought, but it is not a clear-cut matter. Patients are often referred for family treatment while one member is in the hospital or is about to be released. Although one person may appear to be more distrubed by virtue of having been hospitalized, a new therapist beginning with the family can easily begin with its being clearly understood that his client is the family. If the therapist who had been treating the individual in the hospital is to be the family therapist, some transition sessions will be necessary to resolve any feelings concerning a supposed patient-therapist alliance.

Finally, several authors have commented on the rich opportunities provided by family sessions for the therapist to act out his own unresolved interpersonal difficulties (Grosser & Paul, 1964; Williams, 1967; Wynne, 1971). Different family members inevitably seek the therapist's support and sympathy. Without thorough understanding of his own needs, awareness of the effects of his own family of origin on his current behavior, and an appreciation of the need-satisfaction system in his own present family, the therapist is hard-put to avoid the many potentials for being drawn into covert alliances which will subvert the therapeutic process. Although it is generally a good idea to announce a policy of neutrality, I also make it clear that at any point in time I may very well side with one person against another. In the long run, the family discovers that my allegiance shifts and is rather evenly distributed, but this even-handedness does not necessarily characterize each session.

Although there are potential problems, ethical conflicts, and more than enough opportunities for mistakes in this method of intervention, therapists should not be timid about working with families. Family units also have considerable cohesiveness and mutual support, which helps them to survive external stress, including many therapeutic errors. As

Wynne (1971) somewhat ruefully puts it, "I have been far more impressed with the difficulty of bringing about genuine and lasting change in family patterns than in the dangers of unintentionally disorganizing them. . . . Indeed, *families have a staggering capacity to remain the same.*"

TRAINING IN FAMILY THERAPY

The essential ingredients in learning family therapy are basically the same as those involved in learning individual therapy: conceptual knowledge, observation, practice under supervision, and self-understanding. At the Ohio State University Family Therapy Clinic, the training program is oriented toward the achievement of these objectives. Trainees (psychology interns, psychiatry residents, graduate social work students, and graduate nursing students) are given the opportunity to participate in a family therapy course which covers the major theoretical positions and uses role playing to illustrate specific techniques. Videotapes provide live material for discussion of clinical applications. (See Bodin, 1969, for a discussion of the use of videotapes in training family therapists.) The seminar shares several features in common with a format suggested by Ferber and Mendelsohn (1969). Trainees unable to take the course are furnished with a reading list similar to the bibliography at the end of this chapter. They are encouraged initially to read broadly across differing theoretical positions and then to proceed in depth into those authors who seem particularly cogent to them. Thus the trainee is encouraged to learn one system well as a framework to guide his own observations and interventions.

In the clinic trainees begin by observing sessions conducted by cotherapists and participating in the follow-up discussions. Often role playing is used in these "debriefing" sessions to explore other interventions that might have been used, or to concretize the effect that might eventuate from a change in one of the family members. After experience in observing, the trainee is assigned to a case as a cotherapist with a member of the staff. Miyoshi and Liebman (1969) describe further the problems and advantages of family therapy training in a medically oriented clinic setting of this kind. Finally, with regard to training, anyone seriously interested in becoming a therapist should sooner or later see the need for the personal therapy experience. We encourage, but do not require, personal therapy. In practice, most of our trainees seek out personal therapeutic experiences, but we prefer to respect each person's judgment as to when it is most appropriate for him.

For me, psychotherapy is not so much a set of techniques as it is a way of life—a method of living which is committed to open communication and the seeking out and fostering of mutually enhancing interpersonal relationships. Family therapy is a particularly fulfilling way for me to pursue such a way of life. The pace is fast, the feelings generated are intense, and the rewards are numerous. I have become so attuned to the pervasive effects of the family on each person's daily life that it is impossible for me to talk to an individual patient without "seeing" his family beside him. In this sense, individual therapy has become a special case of family therapy. There are persistent questions yet to be answered, and challenges to one's ingenuity constantly abound; but for sheer professional and personal gratification, the various mental health professions offer no other role that can compete with that of family therapist.

REFERENCES

Ackerman, N. W. *Psychodynamics of family life.* New York: Basic Books, 1958.

Bateson, G. Minimal requirements for a theory of schizophrenia. *Archives of General Psychiatry,* 1960, **2**, 477–491.

Bateson, G. Slippery theories. *International Journal of Psychiatry,* 1966, **2**, 415–417.

Bateson, G., Jackson, D. D., Haley, J., & Weakland, J. H. Toward a theory of schizophrenia. *Behavioral Science,* 1956, **1**, 251–264.

Bateson, G., Jackson, D. D., Haley, J., & Weakland, J. H. A note on the double bind—1962. *Family Process,* 1963, **2**, 154–159.

Bauman, G., & Roman, M. Interaction testing in the study of marital dominance. *Family Process,* 1966, **5**, 230–242.

Bauman, G., Roman, M., Borello, J., & Meltzer, B. Interaction testing in the measurement of marital intelligence. *Journal of Abnormal Psychology,* 1967, **72**, 489–495.

Beels, C., & Ferber, A. Family therapy: A review. *Family Process,* 1969, **8**, 280–318.

Behrens, M., Rosenthal, A., & Chodoff, P. Communication in lower-class families of schizophrenics: II. Observations and findings. *Archives of General Psychiatry,* 1968, **18**, 689–696.

Bell, J. E. *Family group therapy.* Public Health Monograph No. 64. Washington, D.C.: Department of Health, Education and Welfare, 1961.

Bell, J. E. Promoting action through new insights: Some theoretical revisions from family group therapy. Paper presented at the annual meeting of the American Psychological Association, 1963.

Bellville, T., Raths, O. N., & Bellville, C. J. Conjoint marriage therapy with a husband and wife team. *American Journal of Orthopsychiatry*, 1969, **39**, 473–483.

Bodin, A. M. Family interaction: A social-clinical study of synthetic, normal, and problem family triads. Paper presented at the meeting of the Western Psychological Association, 1966.

Bodin, A. M. Conjoint family assessment. In P. McReynolds (Ed.), *Advances in psychological assessment*. Palo Alto, Calif.: Science and Behavior Books, 1968.

Bodin, A. M. Videotape applications in training family therapists. *Journal of Nervous and Mental Disease*, 1969, **148**, 251–261.

Bowen, M. Family relationships in schizophrenia. In A. Auerback (Ed.), *Schizophrenia*. New York: Ronald Press, 1959. Pp. 147–178.

Bowen, M. A family concept of schizophrenia. In D. D. Jackson (Ed.), *Etiology of schizophrenia*. New York: Basic Books, 1960. Pp. 346–372.

Bowen, M. The family as the unit of study and treatment. *American Journal of Orthopsychiatry*, 1961, **31**, 4–60.

Bowen, M. The use of family therapy in clinical practice. *Comprehensive Psychiatry*, 1966, **7**, 345–374.

Brodey, W. On family therapy—A poem. *Family Process*, 1963, **2**, 280–287.

Buber, M. *I and thou*. New York: Scribner, 1958.

Carroll, E., Cambor, G. C., Leopold, J. V., Miller, M. D., & Reis, W. J. Psychotherapy of marital couples. *Family Process*, 1963, **2**, 25–33.

Carson, R. C. *Interaction concepts of personality*. Chicago: Aldine, 1969.

Castaneda, C. *Journey to Ixtlan*. New York: Simon & Schuster, 1972.

Charny, I. *Marital love and hate*. New York: Macmillan, 1972.

Coughlin, F., & Winberger, H. C. Group family therapy. *Family Process*, 1968, **7**, 37–50.

Elbert, S., Rosman, B., Minuchin, S., & Guerney, B. A method for the clinical study of family interaction. Paper presented at the meeting of the American Orthopsychiatric Association, Chicago, March 1964.

Ely, A. L., Guerney, B. G., Jr., & Stover, L. Efficacy of the training phase of conjugal therapy. *Psychotherapy: Theory, Research and Practice*, 1973, **10**, 201–207.

Ewing, J. A., & Fox, R. E. Family therapy of alcoholism. In J. Masserman (Ed.), *Current psychiatric therapies*. Vol. 8. New York: Grune & Stratton, 1968. Pp. 275–280.

Ferber, A., & Mendelsohn, M. Training for family therapy. *Family Process*, 1969, **8**, 25–32.

Ferreira, A. J. The "double-bind" and delinquent behavior. *Archives of General Psychiatry*, 1960, **3**, 359–367.

Ferreira, A. J. Family myth and homeostasis. *Archives of General Psychiatry*, 1963, **9**, 457–463.

Ferreira, A. J., & Winter, W. D. Family interaction and decision-making. *Archives of General Psychiatry*, 1965, **13**, 214–223.

Fisher, S., & Mendell, D. The communication of neurotic patterns over two and three generations. *Psychiatry*, 1956, **19**, 41–46.

Fitzgerald, R. V. Conjoint marital psychotherapy: An outcome and follow-up study. *Family Process*, 1969, **8**, 260–271.

Fitzgerald, R. V. *Conjoint marital therapy*. New York: Jason Aronson, 1973.

Fox, R. E. The effect of psychotherapy on the spouse. *Family Process*, 1967, **7**, 7–16.

Fox, R. E. . . . In love with an inch. *Voices: The Art and Science of Psychotherapy*, 1974, **10**, 32–34.

Framo, J. Review. *Contemporary Psychology*, 1973, **18**, 523–524.

Framo, J. L. Systematic research on family dynamics. In I. Boszormenyi-Nagy & J. Framo (Eds.), *Intensive family therapy: Theoretical and practical aspects*. New York: Hoeber/Harper, 1965. Pp. 407–462.

Framo, J. L. Comment. *Family Process*, 1969, **8**, 319–322.

Frank, J. *Persuasion and healing*. Baltimore: Johns Hopkins University Press, 1961.

Freeman, V. J., Klein, A. F., Riehman, L. M., Lukoff, I. F., & Heisey, V. E. Allegheny General Hospital study project, final report. Pittsburgh, Pa.: Mimeographed, 1964.

Gallo, P. S., & McClintock, C. G. Cooperative and competitive behavior in mixed motive games. *Journal of Conflict Resolution*, 1965, **9**, 68–78.

Goodrich, D. W., & Boomer, D. S. Experimental assessment of modes of conflict resolution. *Family Process*, 1963, **2**, 15–24.

Green, B. L. (Ed.) *The psychotherapies of marital disharmony*. New York: Free Press, 1965.

Grosser, G. H., & Paul, N. L. Ethical issues in family group therapy. *American Journal of Orthopsychiatry*, 1964, **34**, 875–885.

Grotjahn, M. Clinical illustrations from psychoanalytic family therapy. In B. Green (Ed.), *The psychotherapies of marital disharmony*. New York: Free Press, 1965. Pp. 169–186.

Gurman, A. S. The effects and effectiveness of marital therapy: A review of outcome research. *Family Process*, 1973, **12**, 145–170.

Haley, J. Family of the schizophrenic: A model system. *Journal of Nervous and Mental Disease*, 1959, **129**, 357–374. (a)

Haley, J. An interactional description of schizophrenia. *Psychiatry*, 1959, **22**, 325–331. (b)

Haley, J. Family experiment: A new type of experimentation. *Family Process*, 1962, **1**, 265–293.

Haley, J. *Strategies of psychotherapy*. New York: Grune & Stratton, 1963.

Haley, J. Research on family patterns: An instrument measurement. *Family Process*, 1964, **3**, 41–65.

Haley, J. A review of the family therapy field. In J. Haley (Ed.), *Changing families: A family therapy reader*. New York: Grune & Stratton, 1971. Pp. 1–12.

Handlon, J. H., & Parloff, M. B. Treatment of patient and family as a group: Is it group therapy? *International Journal of Group Psychotherapy*, 1962, **12**, 132–141.

Hess, R. D., & Handel, G. The family as a psychosocial organization. In G. Handel (Ed.), *The Psychosocial interior of the family*. Chicago: Aldine, 1967.

Hill, R. Methodological issues in family development research. *Family Process*, 1964, **3**, 186–194.

Hoffman, L. Deviation-amplifying processes in natural groups. In J. Haley (Ed.), *Changing families: A family therapy reader*. New York: Grune & Stratton, 1971.

Howells, J. G. *Theory and practice of family therapy*. New York: Brunner/Mazel, 1971.

Hurvitz, N. Marital problems following psychotherapy with one spouse. *Journal of Consulting Psychology*, 1967, **31**, 38–47.

Jackson, D. D. The question of family homeostasis. *Psychiatric Quarterly Supplement*, 1957, **31**, 79–90.

Jackson, D. D. Family interaction, homeostasis and some implications for conjoint family psychotherapy. In J. Masserman (Ed.), *Individual and familial dynamics*. New York: Grune & Stratton, 1959.

Jackson, D. D. The monad, the dyad, and the family therapy of schizophrenics. In A. Burton (Ed.), *Psychotherapy of the psychoses*, New York: Basic Books, 1961. Pp. 318–328.

Jackson, D. D., & Satir, V. A review of psychiatric development in family diagnosis and family therapy. In N. Ackerman, F. Beatmore, & S. Sherman (Eds.), *Exploring the base for family therapy*. New York: Family Service Association of America, 1961.

Jackson, D. D., & Weakland, J. H. Conjoint family therapy: Some considerations on theory, technique, and results. *Psychiatry*, 1961, **24**, 30–45.

Kaffman, M. Short term family therapy. *Family Process*, 1963, **2**, 216–234.

Kaplan, H. S. *The new sex therapy*. New York: Brunner/Mazel, 1974.

Kapleau, P. *The three pillars of Zen*. Boston: Beacon Press, 1965.

Kempler, W. Experiential family therapy. *International Journal of Group Psychotherapy*, 1965, **15**, 57–71.

Klein, M. H., Dittman, A. T., Parloff, M. B., & Gill, M. M. Behavior therapy: Observations and reflections. *Journal of Consulting and Clinical Psychology*, 1969, **33**, 259–266.

Kwiatkowska, H. Family art therapy. *Family Process*, 1967, **6**, 37–55.

L'Abate, L. Understanding and helping the family. Atlanta: Author (mimeographed), 1974.

LaForge, R., & Suczek, R. The interpersonal diagnosis of personality: III. An interpersonal checklist. *Journal of Personality*, 1955, **24**, 94–112.

Langsley, D. G., Flomenhaft, K., & Machotka, P. Follow-up evaluation of family crises therapy. *American Journal of Orthopsychiatry*, 1969, **39**, 753–760.

Langsley, D. G., Pittman, F. S., Machotka, P., & Flomenhaft, K. Family crisis—Results and implications. *Family Process*, 1968, **7**, 145–158.

Laquer, H. P., Laburt, H. A., & Morong, E. Multiple family therapy: Further developments. *International Journal of Social Psychiatry*, 1964, Congress Issue, 70–80.

Lazarus, A. A. *Behavior therapy and beyond.* New York: McGraw-Hill, 1971.

Levitt, E. E. The results of psychotherapy with children. *Journal of Consulting Psychology*, 1957, **21**, 189–196.

Levy, J., & Epstein, N. B. An application of the Rorschach test in family investigation. *Family Process*, 1964, **3**, 344–376.

Liberman, R. Behavioral approaches to family and couple therapy. *American Journal of Orthopsychiatry*, 1970, **40**, 106–118.

Lidz, T. *The family and human adaptation.* New York: International Universities Press, 1963.

Lidz, T., Cornelison, A., Fleck, S., & Terry, D. Intrafamilial environment of the schizophrenic patient. I: The father. *Psychiatry*, 1957, **20**, 329–342. (a)

Lidz, T., Cornelison, A., Fleck, S., & Terry, D. Intrafamilial environment of schizophrenic patients. II: Marital schism and marital skew. *American Journal of Psychiatry*, 1957, **114**, 241–248. (b)

Loveland, N. T., Wynne, L. C., & Singer, M. T. The family Rorschach: A new method for studying family interaction. *Family Process*, 1963, **2**, 187–215.

MacGregor, R. Multiple impact psychotherapy with families. *Family Process*, 1962, **1**, 15–29.

MacGregor, R., Ritchie, A., Serrano, A., & Shuster, F., Jr., *Multiple impact therapy with families.* New York: McGraw-Hill, 1964.

Masters, W. H., & Johnson, V. E. *Human sexual inadequacy.* Boston: Little, Brown, 1970.

Midelfort, C. F. *The family in psychotherapy.* New York: McGraw-Hill, 1957.

Minuchin, S. *Families and family therapy.* Cambridge: Harvard University Press, 1974.

Minuchin, S., & Montalvo, B. Techniques for working with disorganized low socioeconomic families. *American Journal of Orthopsychiatry*, 1967, **37**, 880–887.

Minuchin, S., Montalvo, B., Guerney, B. G., Jr., Rosman, B. L., & Shumer, F. *Families of the slums.* New York: Basic Books, 1967.

Mishler, E., & Waxler, N. Family interaction processes and schizophrenia: A review of current theories. *International Journal of Psychiatry*, 1966, **2**, 375–415.

Miyoshi, N., & Liebman, R. Training psychiatric residents in family therapy. *Family Process*, 1969, **8**, 97–105.

Olson, D. H. Marital and family therapy: Integrative review and critique. *Journal of Marriage and the Family*, 1970, **32**, 501–538.

O'Rourke, J. F. Field and laboratory: The decision-making behavior of family groups in two experimental conditions. *Sociometry*, 1963, **26**, 422–435.

Parloff, M. B. The family in psychotherapy. *Archives of General Psychiatry*, 1961, **4**, 445–451.

Perlmutter, M., Loeb, D., Gumpert, G., O'Hara, F., & Higbie, I. Family diagnosis and therapy using video playback. *American Journal of Orthopsychiatry*, 1967, **37**, 900–905.

Pittman, F. S., Langsley, D. G., & DeYoung, C. D. Work and social phobias. A family approach treatment. *American Journal of Psychiatry*, 1968, **124**, 1535–1541.

Pool, M., & Frazier, J. R. Family therapy: A review of the literature pertinent to children and adolescents. *Psychotherapy: Theory, Research and Practice*, 1973, **10**, 256–260.

Rabiner, E. L., Molinski, H., & Gralnick, A. Conjoint family therapy in the inpatient setting. *American Journal of Psychotherapy*, 1962, **16**, 618–631.

Ravich, R., Deutsch, M., & Brown, B. An experimental study of marital discord and decision-making. In I. Cohen (Ed.), *Family structure, dynamics and therapy*. Psychiatric Research Report 20. Washington, D.C.: American Psychiatric Association, 1966.

Riesman, D. *The lonely crowd*. New Haven: Yale University Press, 1950.

Roman, M., & Bauman, G. Interaction testing: A technique for the psychological evaluation of small groups. In M. Harrower et al. (Eds.), *Creative variations in the projective techniques*. Springfield, Ill.: Charles C Thomas, 1960.

Ross, W. D. Group psychotherapy with patients' relatives. *American Journal of Psychiatry*, 1948, **104**, 623–626.

Ryder, R. G. Two replications of color matching factors. *Family Process*, 1966, **5**, 43–48.

Safer, D. J. Family therapy for children with behavior disorders. *Family Process*, 1966, **5**, 243–255.

Satir, V. The family as a treatment unit. *Confinia Psychiatrica*, 1965, **8**, 37–42.

Satir, V. Notes on the structured interview. Palo Alto: Author (mineographed), 1966.

Satir, V. *Conjoint family therapy*. Palo Alto, Calif: Science and Behavior Books, 1964.

Schaffer, L., Wynne, L. C., Day, J., Ryckoff, I. M., & Halperin, A. On the nature and sources of the psychiatrist's experience with the family of the schizophrenic. *Psychiatry*, 1962, **25**, 32–45.

Schlamp, F. T. Family experiments: Some alternative hypotheses. *Family Process*, 1964, **3**, 229–243.

Schutz, W. C. *FIRO: A three-dimensional theory of interpersonal behavior.* New York: Rinehart, 1958.

Shapiro, R. J., & Budman, S. H. Defection, termination, and continuation in family and individual therapy. *Family Process*, 1973, **12**, 55–68.

Sigal, J., Rakoff, V., & Epstein, N. Indicators of therapeutic outcome in conjoint family therapy. *Family Process*, 1967, **6**, 215–226.

Singer, M. T., & Wynne, L. C. Thought disorder and the family relations of schizophrenics: III. Projective test methodology. *Archives of General Psychiatry*, 1965, **12**, 187–201.

Strodtbeck, F. L. Husband-wife interaction over revealed differences. *American Sociological Review*, 1951, **16**, 468–473.

Strupp, H. H. Toward a reformulation of the psychotherapeutic influence. *International Journal of Psychiatry*, 1973, **11**, 263–365.

Szasz, T. S. The communication of distance between child and parent. *British Journal of Medical Psychology*, 1959, **32**, 161–170.

Usandivaras, R., Issaharoff, E., Hammond, H., Ramanos, D., Mouján, O. F., & O'Farrel, J. Un neuvo test para estudiar los pequenos grupos. *Revista de Psicologia y Psichotherapia de Grupos*, 1963, **II** (3).

Vincent, C. E. *Sexual and marital health: The physician as a consultant.* New York: McGraw-Hill, 1973.

Walters, J. A review of family research in 1959, 1960 and 1961. *Marriage and Family Living*, 1962, **24**, 158–169.

Watzlawick, P. A review of the double-bind theory. *Family Process*, 1963, **2**, 132–153.

Watzlawick, P. A structured family interview. *Family Process*, 1966, **5**, 256–271.

Watzlawick, P., Beavin, J., & Jackson, D. D. *Pragmatics of human communication.* New York: Norton, 1967.

Wells, R. A. The use of joint field instructor-student participation as a teaching method in casework treatment. *Social Work Education Reporter*, 1971, **19**, 58–62.

Wells, R. A., Dilkes, T. C., & Trivelli, N. The results of family therapy: A critical review of the literature. *Family Process*, 1972, **11**, 189–207.

Wells, C. F., & Rabiner, E. L. The conjoint family diagnostic interview and the family index of tension. *Family Process*, 1973, **12**, 127–144.

Williams, F. S. Family therapy: A critical assessment. *American Journal of Orthopsychiatry*, 1967, **37**, 912–919.

Winter, W. D. Family therapy, research and theory. In C. D. Spielberger (Ed.),

Current topics in clinical and community psychology. New York: Academic Press, 1971.

Winter, W. D., & Ferriera, A. J. (Eds.) *Research in family interaction: Readings and commentary*. Palo Alto, Calif.: Science and Behavior Books, 1969.

Winter, W. D., Ferriera, A. J., & Olson, J. L. Story sequence analysis of family TATs. *Journal of Projective Techniques and Personality Assessment*, 1965, **29**, 392–397.

Woody, R. H., & Woody, J. D. *Sexual, marital and familial relations: Therapeutic interventions for professional helping*. Springfield, Ill.: Charles C Thomas, 1973.

Wynne, L. C. Comment. *Family Process*, 1969, **8**, 326–328.

Wynne, L. C. Some guidelines for exploratory conjoint family therapy. In J. Haley (Ed.), *Changing families: A family therapy reader*. New York: Grune & Stratton, 1971.

Wynne, L., Ryckoff, I., Day, J., & Hirsch, S. Pseudomutuality in the family relations of schizophrenics. *Psychiatry*, 1958, **21**, 205–220.

Wynne, L., & Singer, M. Thinking disorders and family transactions. Paper presented at the annual meeting of the American Psychiatric Association, 1964.

Zuk, G. H. Family therapy. *Archives of General Psychiatry*, 1967, **16**, 71–79.

Zuk, G. H. *Family therapy: A triadic-based approach*. New York: Behavioral Publications, 1971.

Zuk, G. H. & Rubinstein, D. A review of concepts in the study and treatment of families of schizophrenics. In I. Boszormenyi-Nagy & J. Framo (Eds.), *Intensive family therapy*. New York: Hoeber, 1965. Pp. 1–31.

CHAPTER 9

Behavior Modification[1]

PETER E. NATHAN AND AGNES D. JACKSON

As emphasized in each of the preceding chapters on methods of intervention, helping techniques in clinical psychology depend for their effectiveness and continued refinement on being tied to conceptual frames of reference which link the method to some broad understanding of the nature of the problems they are used to alleviate. Perhaps more than individual, group, or family therapy, behavior modification as a formal treatment approach emerged primarily as a direct outgrowth of conceptualizing normal and abnormal behavior in a certain way, namely, as *learned* behavior. This chapter begins with brief discussions of learning theory views of psychopathology and of the nature of behavior therapy. Following this introductory material, attention is given in separate sections of the chapter to behavioral approaches to neuroses, schizophrenias, depression, alcoholism and drug dependencies, sexual disorders, child psychopathology, and mental retardation.

PSYCHOPATHOLOGY AS LEARNED BEHAVIOR

The behavioral model of psychopathology posits that psychopathology is largely a set of learned maladaptive behaviors rather than the product of physical disease or deep-seated psychological trauma. Behavioral treatment, according to the behavioral model, involves applying procedures derived from known principles of learning to modify or eliminate maladaptive behavior and to foster acquisition of more adaptive behavior patterns. Although clinical application of learning theory began in the late 1930s with the Mowrers' "bell-and-pad" device for bed wetters (Mowrer & Mowrer,

[1]Preparation of this chapter was aided by a U.S. Public Health Service Grant AA00259-04, National Institute on Alcoholism and Drug Abuse, to Peter E. Nathan. The authors are grateful to Sandra L. Harris for her contributions to this chapter.

1938), the behavioral model attained recognition as a legitimate system for the modification of behavior in its own right only early in the 1960s. Interestingly enough, many early behavior modifiers were laboratory-trained experimental psychologists who chose to apply laboratory-based findings to the solution of human problems. They were often outspokenly vocal in their rejection of psychoanalysis, which they considered unproven theory rather than fact established by vigorous experimentation. The newer generation of behavior modifiers, more often trained within a behavioral clinical psychology program, probably have a greater appreciation for the clinical skills of the dynamically trained therapist even while retaining skepticism regarding the validity of the theory underlying his practice.

Behavioral models of mental disorder have generated a variety of innovative treatment methods to bring about behavioral change in persons carrying virtually the full range of diagnostic labels. These procedures, detailed later in the chapter, emphasize efforts to confront maladaptive behavior *in the here and now* rather than, as with many dynamic therapies, by attending to contemporary behavior only as it relates to long-past traumatic events. In this way the behavioral model highlights the impact of the environment and the family on the development of psychopathology, an emphasis very much in keeping with the *Zeitgeist* in contemporary America. Because the behavioral model originated in the experimental laboratory, it places great emphasis on the necessity for experimental confirmation of clinical observations. This emphasis appeals to many clinicians who are frustrated by the inaccessibility of other theoretical systems to validation by empirical methods.

Perhaps the greatest problem the behavioral movement has posed has been the unwarranted optimism it has instilled in laymen regarding the treatability of all mental disorders and in professionals vis-à-vis its potential capacity to modify virtually all pathological behavior. Despite the new treatment methods and insights into etiology the behavioral model has generated, many mental disorders—even nonorganic ones—remain inaccessible to substantive modification with present behavioral knowledge and procedures.

Behavioral models of personality and psychopathology encompass a variety of the mechanisms of learning by which human beings acquire complex behavioral patterns. The broadly based behavioral theories of personality formulated by Bandura, Kanfer, and Mischel, among others, and termed "social learning theories" because of their breadth, share important common elements. *In particular, all assume that most human behavior is learned, that the laws that govern its acquisition are knowable and measurable, and that both normal and abnormal behavior are acquired by the same fundamental learning mechanisms.* These models of learning include classical conditioning, operant conditioning, and observational learning, a brief review of which may be helpful.

Classical Conditioning

The Russian physiologists Sechenov, Bekhterev and, most importantly, Pavlov were largely responsible for setting forth the principles of what we now call classical or Pavlovian conditioning in the nineteenth and early twentieth centuries.

Ivan Pavlov, professor of physiology at the Military Medical Academy of St. Petersburg between 1895 and 1924, won a Nobel prize in 1904 for his pioneering research on digestive mechanisms. That work alerted him to the surprising degree to which environmental and psychological phenomena affect the volume of gastric and salivary secretions. In research stemming from this observation, Pavlov found that the volume of a dog's salivary response to food seemed to depend not only on its state of hunger and the kind of food presented it but also on environmental stimuli associated with the food presentation itself.

To formalize his observations, Pavlov performed a variety of experiments which laid the groundwork—and ultimately established the laws—of classical conditioning. His most famous experiment, taught to every beginning student of psychology, showed that repeatedly pairing a neutral stimulus with one that already had the capacity to elicit salivation ultimately enabled the neutral stimulus itself to elicit salivation. To this end, Pavlov sounded a tone immediately before presenting a small portion of meat powder to a dog; the tone ultimately acquired the capacity by itself to elicit salivation, a response that had previously been associated only with the meat powder.

The essential elements of the classical conditioning paradigm which this simple experiment illustrated so simply and yet so elegantly are:

1.   An originally neutral stimulus—the *conditioned stimulus* (e.g., a tone)—becomes temporally associated with

2.   Another stimulus—the *unconditioned stimulus* (e.g., meat powder)—which naturally evokes an unlearned, innate reflex response.

3.   The reflex response to the unconditioned stimulus (e.g., salivation) is called the *unconditioned response*.

4.   When sufficient repeated pairings of the conditioned and unconditioned stimuli have caused the conditioned stimulus by itself to elicit the reflex response, the response is renamed the *conditioned response*.

5.   The total stimulus-response reflex is the *conditioned reflex*.

Following Pavlov's pioneering work, which explored other conditioned reflexes besides the tone–meat powder–salivation reflex, many researchers worked to extend the parameters of the basic paradigm. Other investigators have more recently begun to explore the role of classical conditioning in normal emotional behavior (Gormezano & Coleman, 1973; Kimmel, 1973) and in psychopathology. As a result, the classical conditioning paradigm has become a popular etiological model for explaining neurotic behavior, drug dependencies and alcoholism, and psychophysiological disorders. The classical conditioning model has also influenced development of aversive conditioning procedures employed by some behavior therapists with alcoholics, sexual deviants, and autistic children. The model is also pointed to by Wolpe, the developer of systematic desensitization, as central to the effectiveness of that important behavior therapy procedure.

Operant Conditioning

When B. F. Skinner put forth the basic principles of operant conditioning in *The Behavior of Organisms* (1938), he set down the rules by which behavior not falling within the purview of classical conditioning could be explained. Noting early in the book that "there is a large body of behavior that does not seem to be elicited, in the sense in which a cinder in the eye elicits closure of the lid" (Skinner, 1938, p. 38), Skinner went on to identify the broad range of behaviors that seem to be largely a function of their *consequences* rather than their antecedents (as in the classical conditioning paradigm) and then to describe the basic laws by which these *operant behaviors* seem to be governed.

The basic operant conditioning paradigm establishes important functional relationships among three key components of the paradigm:

$$S^D \rightarrow R \rightarrow S^R$$

The first term in this formula, S^D, refers to the *discriminative stimulus*, an element of the environment in whose presence an operant response has been or will be reinforced. The discriminative stimulus sets the occasion for the operant response, because it indicates to the organism with what probability a response of a particular kind will be reinforced. R denotes the *operant response* itself. The final term in the operant equation, S^R, stands for the *reinforcing stimulus*, the all-important consequence of responding which, operant conditioners aver, determines the frequency with which the organism will emit similar responses in the future. Concluding that the temporal and quantitative relationships between responses and consequent reinforcers are more complex than originally thought, Skinner and Ferster, one of his students, investigated an exhaustive series of *schedules of reinforcement* (Ferster & Skinner, 1957), and concluded that each has its own particular effect on responding. The four basic schedules of reinforcement include *Fixed Ratio (FR) Schedules* (reinforcement follows emission of a specific number of consecutive responses of a particular kind by the organism), *Fixed Interval (FI) Schedules* (the organism must wait for a given interval of time to elapse before emitting the response that will be reinforced), *Variable Ratio (VR) Schedules* (the number of responses the organism must emit varies from reinforcement to reinforcement in a pattern clustering around an average number), and *Variable Interval (VI) Schedules* (reinforcement is available at irregular, unpredictable intervals which, however, cluster around an average reinforcement interval).

Although operant conditioning research at first centered on study of the acquisition, maintenance, and extinction of behavior by rats and pigeons in the face of a variety of different discriminative stimuli, reinforcers, and schedules, it has more recently expanded its applications enormously. The operant conditioning model is now employed to investigate the effects of new drugs on animals (Boren, 1966; McMillan, 1973), to study basic learning processes in animals that have relevance to human learning (Catania, 1973; Morse, 1966), to explore in animals such important human social behaviors as "mothering" and aggression (Azrin & Holz, 1966; Cherek, Thompson, & Heistad, 1973; Van Hemel, 1973), and to study such additional social variables as cooperation, competition, and nurturance in humans (Cohen, 1962; Hake, Vukelich, & Kaplan, 1973).

Of greater relevance to the readers of this book is that operant mechanisms are now seen as prime etiological factors in such diverse psychopathological conditions as schizophrenia, depression, drug dependencies, psychophysiological disorders, and certain so-called conduct disorders in children. Operant conditioners have also begun to play increasingly important roles in the remediation of important psychopathological disorders. Token economies, now "all the rage" for the treatment of chronic schizophrenia, the asocial behavior of retarded and autistic children, and the antisocial behavior of juvenile delinquents, is based on operant technology. A variety of operant approaches has also been employed to modify the behavior of neurotic patients and alcoholics.

Observational Learning

Until the early 1960s most learning theorists believed that the classical and operant models of learning were responsible for the acquisition and maintenance of virtually all behavior. Between 1961 and 1963, however,

Albert Bandura and his colleagues at Stanford (Bandura, Ross, & Ross, 1961, 1963; Bandura & Walters, 1963) reported several studies demonstrating that, simply by watching other persons modeling certain kinds of behavior, subjects could acquire response patterns that had not been theirs before. In one of these early studies (Bandura et al., 1961) a group of school children watched a live model being very aggressive toward a large inflated plastic doll, while another group watched the same model being very gentle and calm with the same doll. When members of both groups were later mildly frustrated, the children who had watched the aggressive model were themselves more aggressive than the children who had seen the more passive model.

Later research by Bandura's group (Bandura et al., 1963) revealed that this "modeling" effect holds for models seen in movies and cartoons as well as in real life. Bandura and Walters (1963) point out additional subject variables that influence the degree to which an observer models a model's behavior. These include the observer's sex and age in relation to the model, social reinforcement experiences he may have just had (e.g., having just been reinforced or punished for aggressive or submissive behavior), and his history of reinforcement or punishment for being either independent of or dependent on modeling as a mode of learning. Later experiments have since demonstrated that many of the most complex cognitive, verbal, emotional, and psychomotor behaviors of which human beings are capable can be learned, maintained, altered, and otherwise influenced by modeling (Bandura, Grusec, & Menlove, 1966; Mischel & Liebert, 1966; Staub, 1965).

Although many additional basic studies of observational learning and modeling have been published since the first reports of this work in the early and middle 1960s, empirical research in the area is now beginning to move more and more in applied directions, that is, toward using the insights gained from basic research to help disturbed people. Some of this work is discussed below in connection with neurotic disorders.

On Diagnosis and Diagnostic Labels

Although the unreliability and unproven validity and utility of psychopathological labels is well recognized, we use these labels in this chapter. We use them, however, in full recognition of the fact that they are probably best used when they serve as "shorthand" behavioral descriptions whose value beyond that purpose is essentially unestablished.

THE NATURE OF BEHAVIOR THERAPY

Behavior therapy, although still in its lusty youth, has come to mean very different things to many different people. To Joseph Wolpe, whose systematic desensitization technique was one of the earliest and is one of the most widely used behavior therapy procedures, the term is limited to "the use of experimentally-established principles of learning for the purpose of changing unadaptive behavior" (1969). Arnold Lazarus, originator of "broad-spectrum behavior therapy," defines the term more broadly; to him behavior therapy involves ". . . all the usual psychotherapeutic techniques, such as support, guidance, insight, catharsis, interpretation, environmental manipulation, etc., but in addition . . . the behavior therapist applies objective techniques which are designed to inhibit specific neurotic patterns" (1971a). To those who view behavior in its social learning context (psychologists such as Kanfer, Ullmann, Krasner, and Bandura), it is most important that behavior therapists consider the relevant social learning histories of their patients when they plan strategies for behavioral treatment. The social learning theorists can be said to occupy a position somewhere between Lazarus and Wolpe in this controversy over the scope and reach of behavior therapy.

Although these definitional differences partly reflect professional "power politics," they do have real consequence. Specifically, Wolpe's view of behavior therapy prohibits use of certain procedures which might in fact be effective, whereas Lazarus' much broader view of behavior therapy legitimizes techniques that might not actually contribute to the therapeutic gains achieved with "proven" behavioral procedures. Leonard Krasner, a thoughtful early figure in the field, sees the dilemma this way: "It is especially crucial to determine the scope and limitation of the field of behavior therapy since too comprehensive a view (e.g., equating it with all of psychology) tenders it meaningless, and too narrow a view (e.g., equating it with a specific technique) will render it useless" (1971, p. 484).

In a provocative recent article London (1972) restates the controversy:

> The early growth of behavior therapy as a professional speciality was largely polemical and political, not theoretical, and most of its scientific hoopla evolved to serve the polemical needs of the people who made it up. . . . The study of learning for behavior therapists, in fact, was always more for the purpose of metaphor, paradigm, and analogy than for strict guidance about how to operate or about what it all means [p. 914]

From this basic premise, London ultimately concludes that what is most important is to know which techniques work and which do not work, rather than to focus on the theoretical underpinnings of a therapy method or the hows and whys of its effectiveness.

It is, finally, important to note in this section that rather dramatic distinctions have been drawn between behavior therapy and psychoanalysis. In our view some of these distinctions are real, whereas others are not. Behavior therapy and psychoanalysis are alike in that they both aim ultimately for behavior change, enhanced personal effectiveness, and an increase in the satisfaction one derives from life. Neither is associated with physical manipulations or the use of drugs. Both require extensive training and experience.

Psychoanalysts and behavior therapists differ in their fundamental view of how mental disorders come about. Psychoanalysts view them as products of early traumatic experiences which result in deep-seated psychological malfunctioning; behavior therapists consider psychopathological behaviors to be either learned maladaptive responses or behaviors of unknown etiology. The immediate therapeutic aims of the two clinical approaches also differ. Psychoanalysis is structured to uncover repressed memories of early trauma in order to "cut out" the diseased core of unconscious conflicts causing the symptoms, whereas behavior therapy aims to modify or eliminate unwanted maladaptive behaviors. Finally, the two treatment methods employ very different procedures to bring about their aims. The psychoanalytic psychotherapist is relatively inactive. He relies primarily on the natural development of transference, resistance, and insight for therapeutic gain, although he helps them along with occasional interpretations. By contrast, the behavior therapist is more active, and the relationship between patient and therapist in behavior therapy is more collaborative. It is common for patient and behavior therapist together to identify and then employ a range of behavioral methods to confront specific unwanted behaviors—although it is of course the therapist's job to be the "expert consultant" in these efforts.

BEHAVIORAL APPROACHES TO NEUROSES

Publication in 1950 of Dollard and Miller's *Personality and Psychotherapy* marked psychology's first coherent attempt to apply the principles of learning theory to the etiology and treatment of abnormal behavior. Although the work benefited considerably from Clark Hull's prior learning theory and research (1943), Dollard and Miller's book set off on its own in an important new applied direction. This new direction, however, was only a partial departure from the mental health profession's prevailing preoccupation with dynamic approaches to psychopathology; Dollard and Miller proposed a model of psychopathology that was still based on psychoanalytic concepts, albeit translated into behavioral terms and concepts.

The immediate effect of *Personality and Psychotherapy* was to stimulate heated discussion of its premises, which were radical at the time. A delayed reaction to the book was the effort to develop a "purer" theory of psychopathology which would be independent of psychoanalytic influence. One of the earliest of those bent on the latter course was Hans Eysenck, Professor of Psychology at the Institute of Psychiatry, London, who took the position in 1957 that neurosis can be defined according to two objective behavioral dimensions: neuroticism/nonneuroticism and extroversion/introversion. Claiming that both dimensions of neurosis have strong underlying genetic components, Eysenck (1961) went on to characterize neuroticism as "an inherited autonomic over-reactivity" and to conclude from his own research and that of others (e.g., Franks, 1960) that introversion is characterized "by strong conditionability." Hence, he concluded, the focal neurotic symptom of anxiety appears most often in "dysthymics," his label for neurotic introverts.

Despite the elegance of much of his research and the volume, brilliance, and wit of his writings, Eysenck has had little direct influence on current behavioral conceptions of the etiology of neuroses, primarily because his commitment to his own theories has sometimes prevented him from being objective about others'. By contrast, the views of Joseph Wolpe, who began working in the area at about the same time, have had a major impact on behavioral approaches to the etiology and treatment of phobias, anxiety reactions, and obsessions. At the same time, however, Wolpe has been thoroughly criticized for performing what many researchers (e.g., Bandura, 1969; Eysenck, 1972; Wilson, 1973; Wilson & Davison, 1971) consider unwarranted extrapolation from the animal laboratory to the consulting room. In essence, Wolpe believes that human neuroses are parallel to experimental neuroses in animals in three crucial respects: (a) acquisition by learning; (b) primary stimulus generalization; and (c) elimination by unlearning. Following demonstration of these variables in the experimental neuroses of cats (Wolpe, 1952, 1958), Wolpe systematically observed a series of neurotic patients and concluded that human neuroses follow the same laws of learning and unlearning (Wolpe, 1969).

Wolpe's views on the etiology of neurotic behavior have also been attacked on grounds other than those having to do with the legitimacy of extrapolating from animals to humans. Dynamic theorists question Wolpe's unitary explanation for the complex, multifaceted phenomenon that is neurosis (Freeman, 1968), his apparent unwillingness to attend to cognitive, interpersonal, and unconscious determinants of behavior (Birk, 1970), and the essentially ahistorical view of human behavior he takes (Breger & McGaugh, 1965). Behaviorists, while they acknowledge Wolpe's central role in the development of rational alternatives to psychoanalytic treatment, fault what they say is his confused intermingling of classical and operant learning paradigms (Davison, 1968; Davison & Wilson, 1973), and the fact that, in speaking of "human neurotic reactions," Wolpe clings to an outmoded medical model of psychopathology which views maladaptive behavior as symptomatic of underlying pathology rather than as an inappropriate learned response to the environment (Ullman & Krasner, 1969).

Bandura takes a broader view than Wolpe of the behavioral determinants of neurosis. So far as he is concerned, the potential complexity of any given neurotic patient's relevant social learning history is much greater than that of the restricted classical conditioning model proposed by Wolpe. Modeling, classical conditioning, and operant conditioning all play roles in the development of neurotic behavior according to Bandura, as do other behavioral mechanisms including "response feedback processes" (self-reinforcement) and "internal symbolic central mediational processes" (hypotheses about the principles governing the occurrence of rewards and punishments).

Convinced that each of these learning mechanisms plays an important role in the etiology of the neuroses, but equally sure that their precise configuration and patterning vary from one neurotic patient to another, Bandura fails to hold to the prevailing view held by behavioral as well as nonbehavioral clinicians, namely, that neuroses are best explained by a single unifying concept (e.g., anxiety, conditioned avoidance, or underlying sexual disorder). Instead, Bandura views the neuroses as maladaptive behaviors which do not share common antecedents and will not respond magically to one or another specific treatment approach. Even the degree to which neurotic patients are labeled maladaptive, sick, or troublesome is subject, according to Bandura, to a variety of subjectively determined criteria including ". . . . the aversiveness of the behavior, the social attributes of the deviator, the normative standards of persons making the judgments, the social context in which the behavior is performed, and a host of other factors" (1969, p. 62). Although not without its vocal critics, Bandura's position on neuroses represents the etiological thinking of many currently active behavioral clinicians.

Systematic Desensitization

Although others before him attempted to treat neuroses by substituting preferred incompatible behaviors for unwanted neurotic ones (Jones, 1931; Holmes, 1936; Terhune, 1949), it was Wolpe's "reciprocal inhibition therapy" that generated the positive therapeutic outcomes to establish what is better known as *systematic desensitization* as a viable treatment for many neurotic behaviors. Wolpe's basic premise, that human neuroses are "persistent unadaptive learned habits of reaction" whose "unlearning can be procured only through processes which involve this primitive level," leads him to conclude that ". . . elimination of anxiety response habits is usually accomplished by the inhibition of anxiety by a competing response," and to believe that "if a response inhibitory of anxiety can be made to occur in the presence of anxiety-evoking stimuli it will weaken the bond between these stimuli and the anxiety" (Wolpe, 1969, p. 15).

The stimulus most often used to compete with or "countercondition" anxiety is deep muscle relaxation. For this reason, a behavior therapy relationship employing systematic desensitization generally allots regular periods of relaxation training to its earliest stages. The most common technique for teaching deep muscle relaxation is Jacobson's (1964) "progressive relaxation" method. The Jacobson method, as adapted by Wolpe, requires alternating contraction and relaxation of successively selected muscle groups in order to teach patients to discriminate gradations in tension level. The first of these exercises teaches relaxation of muscle groups in the hands and arms. Its initial instructions include:

I am now going to show you the essential activity that is involved in obtaining deep relaxation. I shall again ask you to resist my pull at your wrist so as to tighten your biceps. I want you to notice very carefully the sensations in that muscle. Then I shall ask you to let go gradually as I diminish the amount of force exerted against you. Notice, as your forearm descends, that there is decreasing sensation in the biceps muscle. Notice also that the letting go is an activity, but of a negative kind—it is an "uncontracting" of the muscle. In due course, your forearm will come to rest on the arm of the chair, and you may then think that you have gone as far as possible—that relaxation is complete. But although the biceps will indeed be partly and perhaps largely relaxed, a certain number of its fibers will still, in fact, be contracted. I shall therefore say to you, "Go on letting go. Try to extend the activity that went on in the biceps while your forearm was coming down." It is the act of relaxing these additional fibers that will bring about the emotional effects we want. Let's try and see what happens [Wolpe, 1969, p. 102]

Successive relaxation exercises focus on face and shoulders, trunk and abdomen, thighs, legs, and feet. Typically, portions of several early therapy sessions are given over to relaxation training exercises which are also practiced daily at home.

Training in assertive behavior is usually an important part of the systematic desensitization "package." Although a useful technique in its own right for patients who lack appropriate assertive behaviors but are not phobic or anxious, assertive training is also a useful adjunct to systematic desensitization. One reason for this is that assertive behavior—effective self-expression, self-control and/or self-assertion in interpersonal situations—appears to inhibit interpersonal anxiety as reliably as deep muscle relaxation does. Assertive training can take several forms. Most commonly it involves the teaching, usually by role-playing and behavior rehearsal, of properly assertive responses to the role-played verbal behavior of some person, often a parent, spouse, or employer, with whom the patient has difficulty being appropriately assertive.

The following case excerpt illustrates many of the techniques of assertive training. The patient is a teenage girl about to graduate from high school. She has no strong wish to go on to college but finds her life being made impossible by her mother, who insists that she attend college:

Therapist: Well, it is apparent to me that you really don't want to go to college. Now what happens when you discuss this with your mother?

Client: We don't exactly *discuss* it. She tells me what is best for me, and that I am immature and don't know my own mind, and that I'll regret not going to college for the rest of my life.

Therapist: Just to see how you do come across in this situation, let me play your mother and you be yourself. You direct the play and make sure I act like your mother. Ready? Here goes. (As mother): When are you going to apply to State? You haven't done it yet, have you?

Client: No. You know, I don't really want to go.

Therapist: I know you are not old enough to know your own mind! You are very immature and you'll regret not going to college the rest of your life. If I didn't love you I wouldn't say these things. Now, I insist that you apply!

Client: (Long sigh) Oh, all right. (Role play ended). That's actually what I'd say. To get her off my back.

Therapist: Well, you began by telling your mother how you really felt and that sounded good. But then, after she said her piece, you backed down, angry and frustrated. Let's try reversing roles for a minute. You be your mother and I'll be you. You start.

Client: O.K. . . . (As mother) Why haven't you applied to State College yet?

Therapist: (As client) To tell you the truth, Mom, I've thought about it a great deal, and I don't want to go to college.

Client: (As mother) I absolutely insist that you apply. You aren't really very grown up and you don't know your own mind. Do as I say. I love you and it's for your own good.

Therapist: (As client) Mom, I know you care a great deal about me and that is important. But, like I said, I thought it over very carefully. I wouldn't enjoy college and I know I wouldn't do well.

Therapist: Now, why don't you try something like that? You be yourself and I'll be your mother. (As mother) I insist you apply to State. I love you and it's for your own good.

Client: (As client) I know you love me and I appreciate it. But I've thought about it a lot and know I won't do well. I really don't think it would be a good idea. I'm sure it wouldn't be.

Therapist: That was certainly much better! How did you feel?

Client: A little anxious.

Therapist: Let's try it again.

The interaction continues until the client reports little or no anxiety while engaging in the interchange.

Therapist: Would the conversation end with that?

Client: No, I don't think so. She'd probably say I was a disappointment to her. That really gets to me, and she knows it, and I wouldn't know what to say.

Therapist: (As therapist) Let's try to reverse roles again. You begin with the statement about disappointment.

Client: (As mother) Why do you insist on disappointing me?

Therapist: (As client) Well, I don't want to disappoint you and, if I am, that makes me feel bad. But this is an important decision that I have to make for myself. You know I value your opinion and I don't want to seem disrespectful, but I've looked at this from all angles, and I know it would be best if I take that job instead of going to college.

Therapist: How did that sound?

Client: Really good. It was like you were disarming her. Putting it that way would have made her less angry.

Therapist: Now, you try it. Just the last part. (As mother) Why must you disappoint me?

Client: (As client) Well, that isn't what I want to do and I'm really sorry if I am. You know I respect your opinion very much, but this is an important decision and it has to be made by me. I've really thought it over and over and know it would be best if I took the job and didn't go to college.

Therapist: Very good. You came across forcefully, but you didn't sound harsh or unkind. Also, your eye contact is getting much better and that is important. Did you feel anxious at all?

Client: No, as a matter of fact, I felt pretty good while I was talking.

Therapist: How would your mother respond to what you just said?

Client: I really don't know. I've never asserted myself that much before [Rimm & Masters, 1974, p. 96–97]

Recent reports on the use of assertive training to deal with compulsive behavior (Tanner, 1971), homosexual pedophilia (Edwards, 1972), and interpersonal anxiety in group settings (Rathus, 1972) support extension of the utility of this behavior therapy procedure beyond simply traditional neurotic behaviors (Lazarus, 1971(a); Wolpe, 1969; Yates, 1970).

Although deep muscle relaxation and assertive training typically predominate during the early stages of systematic desensitization therapy, therapist and patient also generally begin to develop *anxiety and/or fear hierarchies* during early therapy sessions for use in the coming desensitization. These lists encompass those environmental situations that precipitate the anxiety or fear for which many neurotic patients first seek behavior therapy. The separate items on these lists are often arranged in the order of their capacity to elicit fear or anxiety.

Hierarchies have been described in recent reports on the successful application of systematic desensitization to a wide range of neurotic behaviors, including fear of childbirth—"Typical themes were the obstetrical examination, leaving home for the maternity hospital, receiving injections, feeling uterine contractions, being in the labor ward, and experiencing the phases of childbirth" (Kondas & Scetnicka, 1972, p. 52); fear of flying—"A desensitization hierarchy of 56 items, based on the temporal sequence involved in planning, anticipating and executing a commercial flight, was constructed. The items ranged from deciding to make a flight, getting tickets, making preparation, and going to the airport, to various aspects of taking off, flying, and landing" (Bernstein & Beaty, 1971, p. 260); handwashing compulsion—"Picking up objects from the floor without touching floor, picking up objects from the floor with touching floor, emptying dirty ash tray, picking up dirty clothes, touching husband's genitals, cleaning commode, vacuum cleaning, having dirty hands" (Rackensperger & Feinberg, 1972, p. 124); and "situational anxiety"—"(1) Sitting in a dorm room thinking of the banquet (to which her boyfriend was bringing another girl); (2) Dressing and putting on make-up in preparation for the banquet; (3) Riding to the banquet in a car with her sorority sisters; (4) Entering the banquet; and, (5) Sitting in the banquet room and seeing her boyfriend enter with date" (Ventis, 1973, p. 121).

The desensitization procedure itself is quite straightforward. After the patient, now able to induce relaxation on his own, informs the therapist that he has relaxed completely, he is asked to imagine a neutral "control" scene (e.g., lying on a deserted beach on a warm summer day). This scene serves as a nonanxiety-provoking relaxing image to which the patient can return from time to time as desensitization proceeds. The therapist then initiates desensitization by describing in detail the scene in one of the patient's hierarchies that causes him least anxiety or fear. If the patient—by now fully relaxed—can imagine that scene in detail without also experiencing anxiety, patient and therapist "go up" the hierarchy one scene. When anxiety to a scene is experienced, return to the control scene or to a scene lower on the hierarchy is made. Desensitization continues until the patient can imagine the entire hierarchy without experiencing the anxiety or fear it previously elicited. According to Wolpe (1969), desensitization to most anxiety- or fear-provoking stimuli takes as few as 15 therapy sessions.

Behavior therapists point with pride to the relative accessibility of their techniques to experimental investigation. Although much of this is comparative, outcome-oriented research, the desensitization process also lends itself to the empirical study of factors that relate directly to outcome—largely because it encompasses readily separable, hence manipulable elements. To this end, recent studies have explored therapist and client variables that influence therapeutic outcome (Borkovec, 1972; Lang, 1970; Lomont & Brock, 1971); relationships between hierarchy scene duration, timing and sequencing, and outcome (McNamara & MacDonough, 1972; Paul, 1969); and the extent to which relaxation training is necessary for successful desensitization (Garlington & Cotler, 1968; Hyman & Gale, 1973; Sue, 1972). Although results of these studies must still be regarded as tentative, they do suggest that the rather rigid format for desensitization advocated for many years by Wolpe and his colleagues may in fact be unnecessary to the overall success of the method.

Comparative studies contrasting the efficacies of systematic desensitization and psychotherapy conclude that systematic desensitization is clearly superior to no treatment as well as to dynamic treatment (Eysenck, 1971, 1973; Krasner, 1971; Marks & Gelder, 1968; Paul, 1969a, 1969b). The authors of these reviews, however, are all committed behavioral psychologists. Further, most of the studies they review evaluated the efficacies of systematic desensitization and dynamic therapy with specific behavior problems akin to speech anxiety, rather than with more clinical problems such as diffuse anxiety, depression, or obsessions. Consequently, as promising as these early studies have been, we must await the results of additional research to permit unequivocal positive answers about the limits of systematic desensitization's apparent utility.

Implosion Therapy and Flooding

Implosion therapy is a dramatic distant cousin of Wolpe's desensitization paradigm. As described by its originators, Stampfl and Levis (1967,

1968), implosion therapy involves exposing patients for prolonged periods of time to the most fear- or anxiety-arousing scenes in their hierarchies in order for them to experience the fear and/or anxiety at full intensity. Stampfl and Levis' research, as well as that of others (e.g., Boudewyns & Wilson, 1972; Fazio, 1970, 1972), suggests that implosion therapy can be useful—with those phobic or anxious patients who can withstand its rigors. Flooding, a variant of implosion therapy, differs from it in that it involves exposing patients to actual fear- or anxiety-arousing situations. A dramatic instance of the successful use of flooding is contained in the following brief excerpt from a longer report:

The patient was a 29-year-old English woman who had suffered from the age of four from a "fear of worms, snakes and anything that wriggles." Because of these fears, she could not walk in the rain without experiencing profound anxiety lest she see a worm flushed from his burrow. Even in dry weather she had to keep looking at the ground in front of her to prevent approaching too closely a worm. She had nightmares about worms and snakes crawling on her. She did not eat fish, lettuce, or celery for fear that she would find worms in these foods. If she happened to touch or even stand near a worm, she felt the need to wash repeatedly to decontaminate herself. Her fears, clearly, had assumed neurotic proportions. Their modification was achieved by the following *in vivo* flooding procedure:

After modeling by the therapist, the patient was asked to stand in front of the box of worms at a distance of 3 meters and continue to look at them. Jumping back was discouraged but the venting of anxiety by other methods such as screaming was permitted. Thus, the patient was kept in the phobic situation and could not receive the reinforcement of anxiety reduction that would ensue on running away from the worms. Actually, she gradually moved closer. After 1½ hr of continuous exposure she stood within a meter of the box and after an additional 1½ hr was able to touch the edge of the box, but neither the mud nor the worms. The second 3-hr session of the first phase began with the patient standing one meter from the box. Within ½ hr she returned to the point where she had left off at the previous session. After two more hours she touched the wriggling worms in the box, and in the final ½ hr rapidly progressed through holding the wriggling worms in her hand, letting them wriggle on her thigh and running them through her hair. Since the patient reported nearly negligible anxiety to live worms at this stage, the second phase of the therapy was commenced.

I.L. was instructed to search for worms in the ground with her shovel and remove them from the wet earth into a cardboard box. All aspects were modelled for her initially by the therapist. After digging in the hospital garden for ½ hr the patient encountered a worm at a depth of 18 inches. For 1 hr the patient transferred the worm from the ground to the box and back again. This procedure was repeated in a second session lasting ½ hr, and the second phase of therapy therefore lasted for a total of 2 hr. It was considered to be concluded when she could remove the worms from the ground without fear.

The third phase of therapy was the same as the first, but with the box of worms replaced by a grass snake and cloth sack, initially at a distance of 3 meters. After 20 minutes I.L. sat with the snake in the sack on her lap, and by 1½ hr she calmly held the snake in her hand. In the second session of the third phase, the sixth and final session of her therapy, she spent ½ hr handling the snake and concluded by placing it in the sack fastening the string. Since the patient could handle both worms and snakes, therapy was terminated [Antman, 1973, pp. 275–276]

Though implosion therapy and flooding have proven their utility with some patients, other reports (e.g., Borkovec, 1972; Morganstern, 1973) suggest that they are not universally applicable to all phobic patients. One of us had a patient, for example, who tried to cure a pronounced subway/bus travel phobia by spending long Saturdays riding buses and subways for great distances. Overwhelmed by anxiety and panic during many of these rides, he ultimately had to stop this effort at self-administered flooding because his fears and anxieties seemed to be getting worse rather than better.

Positive Reinforcement and Extinction

As is indicated in subsequent sections of the chapter, most clinical applications of the operant mechanisms of positive reinforcement and extinction have been either with schizophrenic and other psychotic patients or with children in classrooms, at home, or in institutions. Efforts have also been made, however, to use operant reinforcement and extinction to alter neurotic behaviors. Assertive training is such an effort in which neurotic patients initially learn and then practice assertive skills following direct therapist reinforcement. They are subsequently reinforced for appropriate assertive behavior by social approval from persons in their environment if their assertive behavior is appropriate and adaptive. Finally, if these two steps have been successfully traversed, assertive responding will be maintained by the patient's own internal "self-reinforcement" system (as with the college-age girl whose deficient assertive behavior was illustrated above).

One of the most innovative continuing research programs involving operant treatment for neurotic and other similar problems is that undertaken collaboratively by Leitenberg, Agras, Barlow, and their colleagues at the University of Vermont. One early study by this group (Leitenberg et al., 1968a) employed positive reinforcement to treat two female adolescents suffering from anorexia nervosa, an uncommon psychiatric syndrome characterized by severe and rapid weight loss. When verbal praise from a therapist was made contingent on a gradual increase in intake of food, food intake increased dramatically and remained at adequate levels during a prolonged follow-up.

Other studies by this group employed positive reinforcement and extinction procedures with a variety of "chronic neurotic patients." Agoraphobic patients (who feared open spaces), when reinforced with therapist's praise for making increasing progress along a 1-mile "course" from the medical center to a downtown area (Agras et al., 1968), made significant progress along this course. When contingent reinforcement was withdrawn, however, therapeutic progress stopped—to resume only when contingent praise was reintroduced. A related study by this group (Leitenberg et al., 1968b) reported that contingent praise for time spent in a small room by a severely claustrophobic woman had a profound positive effect on the phobia.

In a recent summary paper Leitenberg (1972) summarizes the strategy underlying this line of applied research: "When expectations of success are combined with repeated practice in the feared situation together with praise and feedback, all the ingredients for an effective treatment of phobia are present." This treatment approach, called *reinforced practice,* continues to be developed (Callahan & Leitenberg, 1970; Leitenberg et al., 1971, Leitenberg, 1973), although it currently centers on treatment of *nonclinical fears*—those that are not disabling (e.g., fear of heights, of animals, of thunder, of darkness, and of lightening.)

Modeling

As noted above, Bandura and his co-workers carried out an ambitious research program during the 1960s which focused on the functions of modeling, imitation, vicarious learning, and vicarious reinforcement in normal learning. As the decade drew to an end, Bandura and his colleagues turned their attention to a more applied project, the development of an experimental treatment procedure for use with adolescent and adult snake phobics whose phobias were so severe that some could not accept jobs that ran the risk of their coming into contact with snakes, and others could not garden or hike for the same reason (Bandura, Blanchard, & Ritter, 1969). This group of patients was divided into four matched groups. The first group, the "symbolic modeling" group, was shown a movie in which children, adolescents, and adults came into increasing physical contact with a large king snake. Members of the same group had also been taught deep muscle relaxation to use during the film. These subjects could also regulate the speed at which the film was projected, giving them a measure of control over their exposure to the feared stimuli. Armed with these desensitization and self-control skills, the subjects watched the film again and again until they could view it from beginning to end without experiencing anxiety.

A second group of subjects received "contact desensitization" treatment. They first watched a live model touch, hold, fondle, and stroke a king snake with gradually increasing intensity and fearlessness. Then the subjects themselves were led by the model to perform the same behaviors, albeit more gradually. This continued until subjects reported no anxiety even while engaged in a wide range of snake-touching behavior. Subjects assigned to the third group received standard systematic desensitization until they no longer experienced anxiety while imagining prolonged physical contact with a snake. Subjects in the fourth (control) condition completed the full battery of behavioral and attitudinal assessment instruments given all subjects before and after treatment, but did not receive therapy for their phobias.

As expected, the control subjects showed essentially no change in the intensity and severity of their phobic avoidance behavior, and members of the symbolic modeling and desensitization groups showed a moderate reduction in avoidance. By contrast, subjects who had received both live modeling and guided participation showed a marked decrease in avoidance behavior. At a 1-month follow-up, these therapeutic gains had been maintained.

Since publication of these findings, moderate growth in the use of modeling to treat neurotic behaviors has taken place (Kazdin, 1973; Rappaport, Gross, & Lepper, 1973; Ross, Ross, & Evans, 1971). The results of one of the most interesting of these studies are reviewed briefly here. Ross et al., colleagues of Bandura, employed modeling and guided participation to modify a 6-year-old boy's extreme social withdrawal. The boy's withdrawal was so extreme that his entry into public school had been delayed by his unwillingness to interact with peers. The boy was, however, of normal intelligence and of otherwise normal psychological development. A 7-week treatment program was conducted, with the patient being seen three times a week. During the first four individual therapy sessions, the patient received "tangible and social rewards" for imitating a variety of social behaviors first modeled by the experimenter. At the end of the fourth of these sessions, the boy showed a strong attachment to the experimenter and readily imitated him.

Following this phase of treatment, the experimenter began a graduated series of social interactions with other children at the patient's school, which the patient observed. Verbal techniques designed to teach the boy to employ "cognitive behavior rehearsal" and desensitization whenever reexperiencing his fears of social involvement were also taught at this time. At the same time the experimenter and patient role-played potential social situations into which the boy might be drawn at school. After these three separate behavior therapy procedures had been completed, the experimenter initiated actual social interaction with other children into which the patient was gradually brought, so that the two of them fully shared the social interaction by the end of the seventh week of therapy. Posttreatment assessment measures revealed that "treatment was effective in increasing subject's social interactions to approximate those of the socially competent baseline control children. . . . Treatment was also effective in reducing the frequency of subject's avoidance behavior" (Ross et al., 1971). A 2-month follow-up indicated that the patient had maintained his gains in social competence.

Self-Control

Self-control procedures, consisting of behavioral methods for self-management, self-reinforcement, and self-regulation, have been developed intensively during recent years as a means of helping some persons handle anxiety, depression, fears, and other neurotic behaviors. Kanfer (1970a, 1970b), Kanfer and Karoly (1972), and Bandura (1971) have done important basic work in this area. In a recent critical review of self-control research, Mahoney (1972) divides what he calls the self-management area into three subareas: (a) *self-reinforcement*—"any self-management (SM) enterprise designed to increase the probability of some target behavior either by the self-presentation of positive consequences or by the removal of negative consequences"; (b) *self-punishment*—"any SM enterprise designed to decrease the probability of a target behavior via the self-presentation of negative consequences or the removal of positive consequences"; and (c) *auxiliary techniques*—"SM procedures which emphasize stimulus variables and incompatible response."

Positive self-reinforcement has been employed successfully to treat "social anxiety," by a gradual increase in self-exposure to social situations for which self-reinforcement is given (Rehm & Marston, 1968), and obsessional thoughts of worthlessness, by increasing the frequency of interfering positive self-references (Mahoney, 1971). Positive self-reinforcement has also been used to treat problem behaviors in classrooms (Glynn, 1970), obesity (Mahoney, 1974), and study problems (Lovitt & Curtiss, 1969). No studies reporting on the use of negative self-reinforcement or negative self-punishment to treat neurotic behaviors have yet been reported, although positive self-punishment (berating or condemning oneself after behaving badly) is a common and very human behavior pattern.

Broad-Spectrum Behavior Therapy

Broad-spectrum behavior therapy is the term applied to the complex of different therapeutic techniques Lazarus and others who embrace his treatment philosophy use to deal with a wide range of behavior disorders including neurotic ones. As described in his recent book (Lazarus, 1971a), these techniques include conventional behavior therapy procedures, such as systematic desensitization, behavior rehearsal, modeling, assertive training, and aversive conditioning, along with pragmatically derived methods which hew less closely to the learning-theory base from which the behavioral methods derive. Although Lazarus has been severely criticized by some clinicians (Edwards, 1972; Franks & Wilson, 1974; Wolpe, 1969) for deviating from Wolpe's laboratory-derived reciprocal inhibition model, he and others have argued persuasively against such a restrictive view of behavior therapy, basing their arguments on promising therapeutic results rather than strict adherence to a doctrinal model.

Although the interested reader should consult Lazarus' *Behavior Therapy and Beyond* (1971) or a more recent paper in which he renames his approach *multimodal therapy* (Lazarus, 1973), one of his broad-spectrum techniques is detailed here to give the reader a flavor of the approach he espouses. Lazarus illustrates *rational imagery,* a broad-spectrum technique of appealing simplicity and apparent effectiveness, as follows:

Patient: Is it irrational to feel upset about losing my job?

Observer: No, there are a number of inherent frustrations about which you probably can't help telling yourself some realistically negative things. So to feel "rather frustrated" under the circumstances is a logical reaction. But you feel more than "rather frustrated." Look at yourself. To feel so dreadful about it surely means that you are compounding the facts with irrational assumptions.

Patient: Losing one's job is more than "rather frustrating."

Observer: Why? Is it a catastrophe? Would you say that losing one's job is worse than losing an eye?

Patient: Losing an eye is far worse.

Observer: But your grief and anguish seemed to fit the situation of someone who had just lost both eyes, 50% of his hearing, plus an arm and a leg, and who was in acute physical agony from his festering wounds.

Patient: Well, at least he'd have everyone's sympathy, whereas everyone will know that I am a failure.

Observer: It sounds as though you want to be pitied. However, are you a total failure or have you merely failed in a few specific situations?

Patient: Well, it is very upsetting.

Observer: It is not so upsetting. You are upsetting yourself.

Patient: So then what would be a rational course of action?

Observer: First, start looking for another job. Second, try to determine what acts of omission or commission caused you to lose your last job. Third, try to correct these errors in the future. Above all, stop telling yourself that because you are a fallible human being this means that you are worthless, useless, and a complete failure. [1971a, pp. 179–180]

Lazarus' multifaceted approach to neurotic disorders is similar in many ways to Ellis' rational-emotive therapy, a fact both men acknowledge. Ellis has stated repeatedly that rational-emotive therapy has three goals, all of which are clearly similar to the aims of broad-spectrum behavior therapy. These include (a) helping the patient identify the irrational beliefs and assumptions that determine his inappropriate emotional reactions to the world, (b) enabling him to challenge those beliefs and assumptions, and (c) encouraging him to modify his philosophy of life in order to regain rational control over his emotions. The procedures and techniques Ellis uses to bring about these therapeutic goals are like many of Lazarus'. In some cases his contributions predate Lazarus', in others they postdate his.

BEHAVIORAL APPROACHES TO SCHIZOPHRENIA

Bandura's Social Learning Theory of Schizophrenia

Bandura is convinced that most of the common behavioral signs and symptoms of schizophrenia can be explained by basic learning principles (Bandura, 1969). On reviewing Lidz' influential findings (1957a,b) relating disordered family structure to the development of schizophrenia, for example, Bandura concludes that Lidz' data "provide ample evidence that delusions, suspiciousness, grandiosity, extreme denial of reality, and other forms of schizophrenic behavior are frequently learned through direct reinforcement and transmitted by parental modeling of unusually deviant behavior patterns" (p. 295).

Bandura (1969) also maintains that schizophrenic behavior

. . . can become completely controlled by fictional contingencies and fantasied consequences powerful enough to override the influence of the reinforcement available from the social environment. . . . It is important to bear in mind that fantasied consequences are no less real, or less aversive, to the people who fear them than those associated with external aversive stimuli [p. 309]

Although he fails to detail the precise mechanisms by which the full range of behaviors associated with schizophrenic disturbance are acquired, Bandura's presumption that virtually all such behaviors can be explained according to the lawful operation of the three basic modes of learning is shared by many behavioral psychologists. Interestingly, widespread acceptance of this view has taken place in the absence of convincing empirical data in its support.

Ullmann and Krasner's "Sociopsychological Model" of Schizophrenia

One of the most comprehensive and provocative learning theory–based views of schizophrenic behavior was first advanced by Ullmann and Krasner in 1969. In essence, their view of schizophrenic behavior is that it is a product of "the failure of reinforcement for a sequence of behavior," such that after repeated failure of reinforcement the schizophrenic patient learns to stop paying attention to the environmental cues to reinforcement to which nonschizophrenics attend: "The crucial behavior, from which other indications of schizophrenia may be deduced, lies in the extinction of attention to social stimuli to which normal people respond" (p. 383). This view of etiology explains best the attention and thinking deficits characteristic of schizophrenia; that is, patients attending to internal cues or to uncommon external cues cannot respond appropriately to other people.

Other schizophrenic behaviors are explained less adequately by the sociopsychological model. Thus, although Ullmann and Krasner believe the schizophrenic's important affective disabilities to be the result of a long history of inadequate reinforcement for appropriate affective expression, they fail to delineate the nature and extent of that hypothesized history, and they omit to cite empirical data that support their view. Similarly, delusions are seen as dramatic—albeit maladaptive—ways to elicit attention and concern from the environment. Whereas this explanation clearly applies to some delusional behavior, it has only limited explanatory appeal because it can only explain overt delusions, those made obvious to persons with whom the delusional patient comes in contact.

Even less satisfactory is Ullmann and Krasner's explication of hallucinations, which they believe are learned from the mass media, from watching other patients, and from the questions of mental health professionals. But any clinician who has worked with hallucinating patients would find it hard to accept the view that hallucinations are maintained by such weak environmental contingencies. Despite the modest gains they may yield the patient, hallucinations also exact monstrous penalties from those who experience them, costs that far outweigh the modest reinforcers they may enable the patient to solicit from the environment.

The Nathan and Jackson View

We believe that persons who are labeled schizophrenic were born with an inherited predisposition to the development of the disorders included within the umbrella term "schizophrenia." This predisposition is characterized by one or another of several biochemical abnormalities capable of altering the proper functioning of the central nervous system. Persons predisposed to these disorders may emit "schizophrenic behavior" when they experience the normal stresses of life with which nonpredisposed persons deal adequately and easily. More commonly, these behaviors appear when the predisposed individual is under unusual or prolonged stress. In our view, many schizophrenic behaviors are in fact acquired during these times of stress, particularly those associated with disturbances in attention and affect. The same behaviors are probably maintained by many of the environmental contingencies to which Bandura, Ullmann, and Krasner refer. Other schizophrenic behaviors, however, notably delusions, hallucinations, and some cognitive dysfunctions, seem to us to be more likely the result of chronic brain disorder associated with inborn biochemical lesion (Nathan, Robertson, & Andberg, 1969; Nathan et al., 1968, 1969). In other words we think that the development of schizophrenic behavior is a dual function of environmental and physiological factors. Its maintenance probably depends on a similar interplay of these two sets of variables, although the environment may well bulk larger than physiology in determining the precise form of symptoms maintained over time.

Lindsley: The Roots of Behavior Modification

Many clinicians regard the work of Ogden Lindsley at the Metropolitan State Hospital outside Boston between 1953 and 1965 as marking the beginnings of behavior modification with schizophrenic patients. Believing that his operant research paradigm was "particularly appropriate in analyzing the behavior of non-verbal, lowly motivated, chronic psychotic patients" (1956, p. 118–119), Lindsley undertook studies which revealed that schizophrenic patients are apparently subject to the same basic laws of conditioning to which animals and nonpsychotic humans are also subject. This discovery, and Lindsley's refusal to back down under pressure from uninformed bureaucrats who thought he was being inhumane to psychotics by wanting to study their behavior, represent this pioneering researcher's most important legacies to the modern behavior modifier. Although he devoted his efforts to what we would now call behavioral assessment rather than behavior modification, Lindsley's work continues to shape current applied programs by virtue of his direct influence on those behaviorists who tried first to modify schizophrenic behavior.

Ayllon: Individualized Behavior Modification

Lindsley's work had considerable influence on Teodoro Ayllon, senior author of the first report on the successful application of operant methods within a mental hospital setting (Ayllon & Michael, 1959). That paper described the "commonsense" behavioral techniques that Ayllon taught to the psychiatric nurses and aides working with him at the Weyburn, Sasketchewan, Provincial Hospital. Prominent among these techniques were systematic withdrawal of attention from unwanted behavior and a systematic increase in attention to wanted behavior. "Psychotic" behaviors successfully treated in this way included bizarre, psychotic talk and unnecessary, time-consuming visits by patients to the nurses' stations. Although the point may seem a trifle obvious to us now, one of Ayllon's major contributions then was his powerful demonstration that attending to a maladaptive behavior, even attending to it critically, usually increases its frequency, whereas ignoring it instead of trying to punish it often makes it go away. Other target behaviors and treatment procedures reported by Ayllon and Michael in the same ground-breaking report included assaultive behavior, which was eliminated by reinforcing behavior incompatible with assaults, such as talking with nurses; refusal to feed oneself, which was modified by social reinforcement for self-feeding and punishment for refusal to do so; and "hoarding" of towels and clothing, which was extinguished by satiating the patient with those items.

Azrin and Ayllon: The First Token Economy

In 1965 Nathan Azrin, an experimental psychologist, and Ayllon reported on development of a "token reinforcement system" on a ward for chronic schizophrenic patients at the Anna (Illinois) State Hospital. Their token reinforcement system—and the multitude of similar token economy systems that have proliferated since their report—transferred responsibility for delivery of reinforcement for desired behavior from a caretaker (e.g., nurse, psychologist, ward attendant) to the patient, who must assume responsibility for earning and maintaining a supply of tokens. Tokens earned for emission of appropriate behaviors can then be used to purchase a variety of reinforcers including food, privacy, recreation, and sustained, scheduled attention from a therapist.

Azrin and Ayllon focused their developmental study of token reinforcement on a restricted group of target behaviors, including successful performance of selected ward duties and off-ward work and significant reduction in discrete units of "psychotic" behavior. Tokens given for these behaviors could be redeemed for six kinds of reinforcers: privacy (a single or double bedroom rather than a ward bed), the chance to leave the ward on pass, the opportunity for regular social interaction with staff, devotional opportunities, recreational opportunities (access to movies, television, a radio, etc.), and the opportunity to buy candy, cigarettes, toilet articles, clothing, reading materials, and room furnishings at the hospital commissary.

Most of the chronic schizophrenic patients who took part in Ayllon and Azrin's pilot studies met the token economy requirements despite the complexity of these requirements. As a result, the investigators were able to perform an elaborate behavioral analysis of the reinforcing properties of the token economy system. Many of their early findings remain relevant to the operation of the more sophisticated token economies now in widespread use. Among these findings were that tokens given for jobs patients initially rejected were able to generate high rates of adequate performance at these jobs, that reinforcement given regardless of the rate at which patients performed a preferred job (noncontingent reinforcement) resulted in a decrease in the adequacy of that job, and that the quantity of reinforcement provided for a job directly determined the adequacy of performance on that job. In other words Azrin and Ayllon affirmed that, true to predictions from basic operant laboratory research, the consequences of complex human work-related behavior determine the adequacy of these behaviors, even when psychotics are asked to perform these behaviors. This demonstration was necessary to permit incorporation of the token reinforcement system into the body of experimentally-derived behavior modification literature.

Atthowe and Krasner: Development of Sophisticated Token Economies

Ayllon and Azrin's report inspired rapid development of more sophisticated token economy systems. One such "second generation" token system, described by Atthowe and Krasner in 1968, was first established in 1963 on an 86-bed ward at the Palo Alto (California) Veterans Administration Hospital. The token ward, in operation for 2 years, housed 60 patients, most of whom were chronic schizophrenics who "had, for the most part, obvious and annoying behavioral deficits." Atthowe and Krasner's demonstration project is widely regarded as a definitive test of the long-term efficacy of the token economy approach with chronic schizophrenics, because of the length of time the ward operated, the large number of patients who lived on it, and the thorough, sophisticated research design incorporated in the operation of the ward.

Important similarities and differences between Ayllon and Azrin's earlier token economy and Atthowe and Krasner's can be noted in the following description:

Cigarettes, money, passes, watching television, etc., were some of the more obvious reinforcers, but some of the most effective reinforcers were idiosyncratic, such as sitting on the ward or feeding kittens. For some patients, hoarding tokens became highly valued. This latter practice necessitated changing the tokens every thirty days. In addition, the tokens a patient still had left at the end of each month were devaluated 25 percent, hence the greater incentive for the patient to spend quickly. In general, each patient was reinforced immediately after the completion of some "therapeutic" activity, but those patients who attended scheduled activities by themselves were paid their tokens only once a week on a regularly scheduled pay day. Consequently, the more independent and responsible patient had to learn "to punch a time card" and to receive his "pay" at a specified future date. He then had to "budget" his tokens so they covered his wants for the next seven days.

In addition, a small group of twelve patients was in a position of receiving what might be considered as the ultimate in reinforcement. They were allowed to become independent of the token system. These patients carried a "carte blanche"which entitled them to all the privileges within the token economy plus a few added privileges and a greater status. For this special status, the patient had to work 25 hr. per week in special vocational assignments. In order to become a member of the "elite group," patients had to accumulate 120 tokens which entailed a considerable delay in gratification [Atthowe & Krasner, 1968, p. 38]

This brief excerpt from Atthowe and Krasner's extended report sets the stage for an understanding of the behavioral analysis that ensued. That analysis permitted an evaluation of the mechanics of the token economy method, as well as an assessment of the power of the method as a therapeutic tool. To undertake this analysis Atthowe and Krasner established a 6-month baseline period at the start of their project, during which observers gathered reliable data on the rate at which patients naturally emitted a wide variety of "target" (symptomatic) behaviors. During the 3-month "shaping" period that followed, tokens contingent on specified behavior change were introduced. Shaping of the behavior of patients who required gradual introduction to the token system was instituted at this time.

At first, the availability of canteen booklets, which served as money in the hospital canteen, was made contingent upon the amount of scheduled activities a patient attended. It soon became clear that almost one-half of the patients were not interested in money or canteen books. They did not know how to use the booklets, and they never bought things for themselves. Consequently, for 6 wk. patients were taken to the canteen and urged or "cajoled" into buying items which seemed to interest them (e.g., coffee, ice cream, pencils, handkerchiefs, etc.) Then all contingencies were temporarily abandoned, and patients were further encouraged to utilize the canteen books. No one was allowed to purchase items in the ward canteen without first presenting tokens. Patients were instructed to pick up tokens from an office directly across the hall from the ward canteen and exchange them for the items they desired. After 2 wk. tokens were made contingent upon performance and the experimental phase of the study began [Atthowe & Krasner, 1968, p. 39]

The introduction of tokens into the ward routine of these 60 chronic schizophrenic patients increased their involvement in group activities enormously. Equally as important, a marked increase was observed in the number of patients receiving passes to leave the hospital on weekends, drawing weekly cash, and using the ward canteen. Unexpectedly, although patients were much more active during the study, infractions of hospital rules decreased sharply. Most important, as compared with 11 discharges and no transfers during the 11-month period before the study began, 24 patients were discharged and 8 were transferred to other more active wards during the period of the study.

Current Trends in Behavior Modification with Schizophrenics

The promise of meaningful therapeutic success provided by Atthowe and Krasner's study has been substantially but not entirely realized by more recent developments in behavior modification/token economy approaches to schizophrenia. Among important current trends we have observed are:

1. Token economies have been extended far beyond the back wards of state hospitals where they began to classrooms of normal children, whose learning has been accelerated by competition-inducing token systems (O'Leary & O'Leary, 1972); to retarded children in special classrooms, whose attentional and motivational deficits have been overcome in part by token reinforcement systems (Kaufman & O'Leary, 1972); and to institutionalized delinquents, whose aggressive, destructive behavior has been modified sufficiently by these methods to enable them to begin to do schoolwork (Burchard & Barrera, 1972; Cohen, 1968).

2. Token economies and other behavioral approaches to schizo-

phrenia have been extended directly to the community, where they have permitted patients to forsake the degradation and despair of the hospital for the hopefulness of halfway houses or foster homes in their home communities. Spruce House in Philadelphia, "established as an alternative to treatment in a state hospital," is one of the most successful of these facilities (Henderson & Scoles, 1970). As related by Henderson, its founder, Spruce House adopted the token economy system for three reasons: its complexity and rigidity help patients reacquire experience with the "rules" of real work; the system helps them relate more effectively to persons in a vastly expanded environment by involving many persons in its implementation; it helps prevent reappearance of the maladaptive behaviors that precipitated original hospitalization by differentially reinforcing maintenance of adaptive behaviors inimical to psychosis. Although data attesting to the long-term ability of places such as Spruce House to keep schizophrenic patients out of the hospital and in productive work have not been published, preliminary data from them continue to be promising.

3. The efforts of behavior modifiers have been shifting from exclusive concern with attempts to confront the totality of the schizophrenic patient's psychotic disorganization to new-found therapeutic attention to discrete types of psychotic behavior. Such specifically schizophrenic behaviors as delusional speech (Liberman et al., 1973), apathy (Weinman et al., 1972), interpersonal isolation (Ravensborg, 1972), and hallucinations (Haynes & Geddy, 1973) have recently been modified or eliminated by the efforts of behavior modifiers.

4. Along with its early successes, behavior modification has also come in for its share of criticism. Among the most thoughtful of these questions about the use of the token economy and other behavioral approaches to schizophrenia have been those asking whether token economies reinforce undesirable social values such as docility and obedience to authority (O'Leary, 1972; Winett & Winkler, 1972), and whether the individual behavior modification methods are worth the inordinate expenditure of time they require for the modest behavioral gains they produce in some schizophrenic patients (Kazdin & Bootzin, 1972). Only time will reflect the legitimacy of these concerns.

On balance, behavioral techniques have yielded extremely encouraging results with some schizophrenic patients. Nonetheless, it is clear that comparative research on the cost effectiveness of behavioral procedures as against drug treatment, traditional milieu therapy, psychoanalytic psychotherapy, and the other therapies for schizophrenia is required before comparative claims can justifiably be made. It is just as clear—

and necessary—that long-term outcome studies be undertaken to compare behavioral techniques to other *prosthetic* methods, so that we can be sure that the behavioral methods are as useful for keeping schizophrenic patients in the community as they seem to be for putting them there in the first place.

Behavioral clinicians, like their nonbehavioral colleagues, have begun to pay increasing attention to ways of providing better services in and to the community. A central component of this new thrust is development of ways to train significant community members (including parents, police, probation officers, and teachers) to assume direct responsibility for implementation of behavioral contingencies. The goals of this effort are to maintain the effective behavioral control over psychotic behavior first achieved in the hospital, while exerting control over the variables in the patient's home community that were associated with development of his maladaptive behavior in the first place. Giving responsibility for direct management of behavioral programs to nonprofessional persons in that environment has also been a component of the behavioral treatment of child psychopathology, alcoholism, and drug addiction, as discussed later in the chapter.

The following constitutes a convincing—albeit modest—demonstration of effective behavioral intervention on an outpatient basis into important socialization problems of outpatient chronic schizophrenic patients:

The decision to apply assertive training to an outpatient group of chronic schizophrenics arose from the observation that these patients are usually excessively compliant, submissive, and socially inhibited. Despite warnings from senior colleagues as to the fragility of the "schizophrenic ego," it was decided to employ assertive training in an endeavor to decrease social anxiety and increase interpersonal skills.

Composition of the Group

Assertive training is still in progress, but significant gains have already been achieved. The group is open-ended, consisting of eight to ten patients, males and females, with a mean age of about forty. All have been hospitalized at least twice for acute schizophrenic episodes prior to joining the group, and all carry the diagnosis of chronic schizophrenia. The group meets once weekly for an hour, a psychiatry resident and nurse serving as cotherapist. All of the patients are on major tranquilizers on a longterm basis. The patients are actively encouraged to take their medication as prescribed to help avoid the necessity for future hospitalizations. Group therapy provides these patients with a supportive and encouraging atmosphere in which to increase their interpersonal competence, self-acceptance, and self-esteem. Assertive training is a major technique for achieving these goals.

Example of Assertive Training with One of the Group Members

J.C. was an unmarried, 33-year-old female who had presented a very fragile and compliant picture of herself since coming into the group a few weeks earlier. At one group meeting she reported having difficulties with her downstairs neighbor, Ann, a demanding woman who was a light sleeper. Ann had repeatedly been knocking on her ceiling and complaining that J.C. was making "too much noise and commotion." Ann complained about the noise from J.C. walking in her apartment, playing with her cat, and even writing a letter as "late" as 8:30 PM! Ann continued her complaining and ceiling-knocking despite the fact that J.C. had already tried to be reasonably quiet. J.C. had not confronted Ann and continued to greet her with pleasant "hello's" in the hall. J.C. was becoming increasingly anxious, depressed and suspicious of "rumors" that Ann might be starting among the other tenants. J.C. felt unable to cope with this situation and was afraid that she would soon require rehospitalization. The sequence of the intervention made by the therapists was as follows:

(1) The therapists identified J.C.'s inappropriate compliance, timidity, submissiveness, and withdrawal that called for assertive training. Other group members helped J.C. recognize her maladaptive and inappropriate responses to Ann's complaints.

(2) The adverse consequences of J.C.'s compliance, including her recent symptomatology, were further documented. Differences between assertive and aggressive behavior were emphasized. Successful examples of other group members' assertiveness were discussed to encourage J.C.'s active participation. J.C. was encouraged by the group to recognize her rights in this situation and to practice assertion herself.

(3) The general instigation to more assertive behavior gave way to more specific behavior rehearsal, including role reversal. First, the psychiatry resident assumed the role of Ann. J.C. was instructed to try to assertively confront "Ann" as played by the therapist. Even with gentle prodding J.C. was unable to carry this out. The therapist then assumed the role of J.C. while J.C. played Ann. She played the role of Ann with enthusiasm while the therapist actively modelled assertive behaviors. Following some discussion, another female group member volunteered to role-play Ann and suggested that J.C. now play herself. This was practiced with several different members of the group.

(4) During rehearsal procedures, J.C.'s verbal content and mode of expression were carefully monitored. J.C. was given feedback from the therapists and group members as to her verbal content, tone of voice, inflection, resonance, posture, eye-contact and facial expressions. Group approval served as a positive reinforcer for this behavior-shaping process.

(5) The most useful assertive response is one in which the patient is taught not only to express displeasure, but also to provide information that would facilitate a more acceptable interaction. Thus, after a series of increasingly more exacting scenes, J.C. became proficient in the following assertive stance.

"Ann, I wish you would stop knocking on my floor at night; it annoys and irritates me. If you approached me more gently, you would find me trying to be cooperative rather than irritable. I can appreciate that you are a light sleeper but I cannot build my evening activities entirely around that fact, I would be willing to make some compromises with you but they will have to consider not only your needs and rights, which I can appreciate, but also my own. Rather than be angry with each other perhaps our anger is better channeled at the construction of our apartment building with its paper-thin walls. In many ways, Ann, you and I are both lonely people. Instead of bickering, why don't we try to be of mutual help to one another. . . ."

(6) It should be stressed that, especially when training potentially psychotic patients in assertive behavior, precautions must be taken to ensure that feedback from the environment will be supportive and positively reinforcing, whenever possible. Fortunately, one of the other group members had had Ann as a teacher in high school. He felt that Ann was "basically a nice person" and would respond well to J.C.'s assertiveness. Also, behavior rehearsal was refined and repeated until J.C., the therapists and the other group members felt fairly certain that punitive consequences were most unlikely to follow J.C.'s real-life stories. In addition, J.C. was prepared for the possibility that her assertiveness might not be received well. Thus, by the end of the session J.C. felt confident in her ability to assert herself and felt prepared to deal with any of Ann's possible reactions. J.C. spontaneously volunteered that she would confront Ann at the next opportunity. J.C. was asked to take careful notes of their interaction so that we could do a detailed assessment of her "performance." It was stressed that this was but a first step, and a rather difficult one at that. All of the group members participated actively in this session and many reported that they had benefited vicariously.

Over the next few weeks, J.C. reported a successful series of interchanges with Ann. They reached a mutual understanding and had begun to lay down the groundwork for a more amicable relationship. J.C. reported that she no longer was suspicious or as depressed or anxious. Instead, she felt better able to trust her emotions. In the long run, she felt hopeful about gaining pleasure and meaning from her human encounters through continued assertiveness.

Our group has dealt with the full spectrum of assertive behavior, from forthright statements of anger and resentment to genuine expression of love and appreciation. Other examples of specific situations that were dealt with by assertive training are as follows: difficulties with employers; problems in expressing emotion, especially towards spouses; and particular ways and means of achieving a more spontaneous and outgoing manner. Also, assertive training has been especially effective in the "here and now" of the group, where members have learned to express feelings of warmth and approval as well as annoyance and irritation for one another [Bloomfield, 1973, pp. 278–280]

Behavioral group therapy with schizophrenic patients who have returned to the community—and are making suitable adjustment to it—represents a most appropriate demonstration of the newly emerging emphasis behavioral clinicians are placing on explicit efforts to extend the efficacy of their methods and procedures beyond the hospital and consulting room.

BEHAVIORAL APPROACHES TO DEPRESSION

Only very recently have behavioral theories of depression been proposed. In one of the first of these, depression is viewed as "a function of inadequate or insufficient reinforcers" (Lazarus, 1968), resulting in a weakened or impoverished behavioral repertoire. In other words, the depressed person's behavior is no longer positively reinforced because some important reinforcer has been withdrawn or lost. Studies by Lewinsohn and Libet (1972) and Lewinsohn and Schaffer (1971) support the essentials of this theory.

Costello (1972) has more recently formulated a somewhat divergent behavioral view of the etiology of depression. While acknowledging Lazarus' "loss of reinforcers" as a prime etiological factor, Costello proposes another such factor, ". . . a general loss of reinforcer effectiveness." Costello maintains that "loss of reinforcers" alone cannot explain why the depressed person loses interest in positive reinforcers that were previously of great interest and value to him. How do reinforcers lose their effectiveness? Costello posits two mechanisms: (a) biochemical or neurophysiological events occurring in the brain, and (b) disruption of the usual chain of reinforcing events.

A behavioral treatment plan for depression was first proposed by Lazarus in his 1968 paper. In that paper he outlined a variety of treatment approaches to be employed directly to combat the depressed person's loss of reinforcement. In a more recent paper Lazarus (1974) proposes a complementary multimodal behavioral approach for use with severely and chronically depressed patients for whom drugs, electroconvulsive therapy, or both have been ineffective. The approach involves continuous monitoring and modification of seven behavioral modalities: overt behavior, affective processes, sensory reactions, emotive imagery, cognitive components, interpersonal relationships, and a medical modality. Multimodal treatment of depression begins with attempts to construct baseline graphs of the depressed person's activity level. The behavior therapist, in so doing, tries to identify at least 50 potentially high-frequency (reinforcing) behaviors from which to work: riding a bicycle, grocery shopping, reading, and so on. The therapist "prescribes" from this graded series of potentially reinforcing responses in an effort to replace the lost reinforcers that are at the root of the depression. If the client remains unmotivated to try any of them, it may be necessary for the therapist to make home visits and observations, which are described by Lewinsohn as a "most powerful procedure."

Lazarus has also treated reactive (neurotic) depression with a combination of three other behavioral techniques. The common notion that time heals many depressions by giving patients the chance to replace their lost reinforcers with newly acquired ones is the concept underlying Lazarus' "time projection with positive reinforcement." The patient is projected into a future time and setting that is full of increased activity and enjoyment of old and new activities. Lazarus also prescribes "affective expression"—deliberate elicitation of anger, amusement, affection, sexual excitement, and/or anxiety—in attempting to break the depressive cycle. He assumes that, although depressed patients infrequently respond to affective stimuli, those stimuli that do somehow "break through" the depression should have at least a temporarily positive uplifting effect. Lazarus also recommends "behavioral deprivation and retraining," a procedure that involves enforcing a prolonged period of inactivity to the point of sensory deprivation. Following such a stressful period, almost any stimulation is positively reinforcing. When patients are then exposed to a graduated sequence of tasks reintroducing them to daily stresses, their depression may attenuate. Although Lazarus has used all these techniques with his own depressed patients (Lazarus, 1971a, 1973), they remain largely unproven on an independent basis.

Although Lazarus' techniques are theoretically applicable to psychotically depressed patients, the case examples he gives in his 1968 and 1974 papers describe only less seriously depressed patients. Only one recent paper, by Todd (1972), describes the behavioral treatment of psychotic depression. By contrast, numerous behavior therapists have written about their use of more-or-less standard behavior therapy methods to deal with mild to moderate depressions. Among the methods employed in this context have been reinforcement reinstatement, contingency management, and task completion (Burgess, 1969); interpersonal feedback (Lewinsohn & Shaw, 1969); assertive training and self-reinforcement (Todd, 1972); self-reinforcement (Jackson, 1972, Robinson & Lewinsohn, 1973); and desensitization (Wanderer, 1972).

One of the more interesting recent developments in the behavioral approach to depression is development of a behavioral rating scale for depression by Williams, Barlow, and Agras (1972). This scale, which depends on reliable, observable behavioral correlates of depression as primary data, successfully measured the therapeutic efficacy of behavioral treatment given to three male veterans with presenting histories of reactive depression on the token economy ward of a Veterans Administration

Hospital (Hersen, Eisler, Alford, & Agras, 1973). The scale reflected an increase in behavioral indices of depression during a baseline (no treatment) condition and a decrease in the same indices during token reinforcement. The authors of the 1973 report conclude that the token economy's contingent reinforcement procedures increased depressed patients' activity levels and social stimulation—which in turn decreased the frequency of target behaviors included on the behavior rating scale.

Despite recent increased interest in and application of behavioral techniques for the treatment of depression, the need for development of more creative approaches to the more serious depressions clearly remains. What is also clearly needed is replication of standard techniques and follow-up of patients for standard periods of time to establish the comparative efficacy of these procedures on a broader scale.

BEHAVIORAL APPROACHES TO ALCOHOLISM AND DRUG DEPENDENCIES

Most behavioral theories of alcoholism are variations on the basic theme that excessive drinking is an acquired means for reducing conditioned anxiety. Variations on this theme stem from differences as to precisely which learning mechanisms are responsible for the development and maintenance of the anxiety alcohol is supposed to reduce. A major problem with the anxiety-reduction model of alcoholism is its assumption that alcohol invariably reduces prevailing high levels of anxiety in the alcoholic. Unfortunately, recent data suggest that this popular theory is quite invalid.

A recent study comparing alcoholics and matched nonalcoholics on a variety of behavioral dimensions, for example, revealed that alcohol actually *increases* levels of anxiety and depression in alcoholics following an initial 12- to 24-hour period of drinking during which levels of anxiety do decrease (Nathan & O'Brien, 1971). Another recent study (Okulitch & Marlatt, 1972) makes the same observation, concluding in addition that alcohol probably acts as a discriminative stimulus with both positive and negative properties for the alcoholic.

Although these and other similar findings do not completely invalidate the common behavioral view of the etiology of alcoholism, they do paint a picture of alcoholism etiology more complex than the simple "anxiety-reduction" model. This more elaborate model of alcoholism explains the alcoholic's decision to drink again by assuming that he remembers that drinking immediately lifts his anxiety and depression but forgets that it increases his anxiety later on. This hypothesized "dual action" of alcohol reflects the influence of "blackout," a deficit in short-term memory function associated with chronic alcoholism, which is brought on by sustained high blood alcohol levels (Lisman, 1974; Nathan et al., 1972).

Abraham Wikler, who has used a behavioral model to explore both alcoholism and drug addiction, was the first clinician to put forth a distinctly behavioral theory of drug dependence. In 1965 Wikler wrote that hard-drug addiction is a product of instrumental learning, and that each injection or ingestion of a drug reinforces drug-seeking behavior by providing immediate and powerful positive reinforcement for it. "Hustling" for drugs becomes a secondary reinforcer via its association with the primary reinforcement of drive reduction afforded by injection or ingestion of the drug. Wikler explains the extremely high rate of return to drug dependence by detoxified addicts in like terms, as "due simply to incomplete extinction of reinforced drug-seeking behavior" (Wikler, 1965).

This theory of drug dependence, although cast within the operant framework, is directly analogous to the anxiety-reduction model of alcoholism. And as with the anxiety-reduction model of alcoholism, Wikler's theory of drug dependence cannot explain maintenance of addiction in the face of a tolerance-induced decrease in the reinforcement value of the drug. Another mechanism is clearly needed to explain the fact that alcohol and drug abuse continue long after these drugs have lost their initial reinforcement value. It is possible that this necessary addition to theory will derive from the fact that continued drug taking and ingestion of alcohol effectively postpone the pains of withdrawal; such an addition to theory could certainly be framed from the learning-theory point of view.

The possible role of modeling in the development of patterns of drug use has also recently begun to be explored. Smart and Fejer (1972), for example, studied relationships between adolescent and parental drug use among 8865 Canadian high school students. They identified a positive relationship between students' use of psychoactive and hallucinogenic drugs and parents' use of prescription and patent medication. This relationship was strongest when both students and parents used psychoactive drugs. The authors of this study conclude that many adolescents do model their own drug use after that of their parents. For this reason, they believe that the use of drugs by these adolescents can be reduced only when and if their parents' use of drugs is reduced. Similar conclusions about the role drinking by parents plays in the development of problem drinking by adolescents have been drawn by Jessor and Jessor (1973).

Behavior Therapy for Alcoholism

Alcoholism has been a favorite target disorder in the upsurge of activity and interest in behavior modification that has characterized the last decade. Franks observed in 1970 that behavioral approaches to alcoholism had passed through three distinct phases to that time. The first and earliest of these phases, the direct application of techniques derived from classical conditioning, involved efforts to pair the sight, taste, or smell of alcohol with an aversive agent to establish a condition avoidance to alcohol. In an early classical study within this category, Sanderson and his colleagues (1963) subjected 15 alcoholic patients to what seems now to have been a drastic conditioning procedure. Each patient was first given a bottle containing his favorite beverage and told to hold it, look at it, smell it, and then put it to his lips and taste it. After five such "familiarization" trials, the paralytic drug succinylcholine was injected intravenously. The patient was then rehanded the bottle—at which point the overwhelming effects of this curarelike drug made their dramatic entry. The patient became totally paralyzed, unable to move and unable to breathe, a fearsome condition which lasted a full minute. After a few such conditioning trials, the authors of the study report, the majority of the patients "developed a conditioned aversion to alcohol in any form," such that the sight, taste, or smell of the substance brought back the feelings of fear of imminent death they had experienced during the pairing of alcohol and succinylcholine. Despite these findings and the resultant conclusion that "favorable recovery rates" are associated with use of this drug, other studies of the drug with more extensive follow-up (Farrar, Powell, & Martin, 1968; Holzinger, Mortimer, & Van Dusen, 1967) have not been so enthusiastic in their assessment of its effects.

Because the continued use of succinylcholine presents moral and medical problems along with those of efficacy, behavior therapists attempting aversive conditioning with alcoholics have largely chosen to use other aversive agents, such as electric shock, emetic drugs, or unpleasant covert stimuli, instead. The classical application of electrical aversion conditioning to alcoholism was undertaken by MacCulloch et al. (1966). Modeled after the same investigator's use of a similar paradigm to treat homosexuality (Feldman & MacCulloch, 1965), treatment began with the alcoholic being shown photographs of beer and liquor bottles, the sight of an actual (sealed) bottle, the sight of an open bottle of alcohol, and the sight of an alcoholic beverage in a glass while a tape repeating an invitation to have a drink of the patient's favorite beverage was played. When actual conditioning began, the patient was shown one of the alcohol-related stimuli. If he pushed a switch to remove the stimulus within 8 seconds of its onset, he avoided an electric shock. In so doing, he also illuminated a non-alcohol-related stimulus (a picture of a soft drink) which presumably signaled aversion relief to him. This sequence continued through lengthy daily conditioning sessions. In essence, MacCulloch, Feldman, and their co-workers were attempting to use painful shock here the same way Sanderson and his colleagues had used succinylcholine: to create a conditioned reflex linking sight and smell of alcohol to the aversive stimulus of electric shock.

Although theirs was a more sophisticated use of the aversive paradigm than the succinylcholine project, because it aimed to instill both conditioned aversion to alcohol and conditioned attraction to non-alcohol-related stimuli, MacCulloch and his colleagues claimed only limited results with this procedure, in part because its positive effects remained in force for only limited periods of time. Although more sophisticated applications of electrical aversion to excessive alcohol consumption have been undertaken since this report (e.g., Blake, 1967; Miller & Hersen, 1972; Vogler, Lunde, Johnson, & Martin, 1970), the method is no longer widely used, largely because long-term follow-up reports have failed to show that positive changes in drinking behavior were maintained over time. Data from a recent study in our laboratory suggest, in fact, that there is serious reason to question even the immediate suppressive effects of electric shock on drinking when shock is not directly contingent on drinking (Wilson, Leaf, & Nathan, 1975).

Other researchers have attempted to induce conditioned aversion to alcohol in alcoholics by pairing the taste of alcohol with actual feelings of nausea and the actual experience of vomiting. Injection of an emetic drug such as apomorphine or emetine just before the patient takes a sip of an alcoholic beverage permits simultaneous pairing of the taste of the beverage with the onset of severe vomiting. Although Voegtlin and his colleagues claimed considerable long-term success with this method in the 1940s, other behavior therapists have been unable to replicate their findings. One reason for this failure to replicate may be that Voegtlin's patients probably had better prognoses for successful outcome than more typical subjects of usual alcoholism treatment research, chronic skid-row alcoholics, because Voegtlin's patients were still working, still within the family, and of sufficient means to afford treatment that had to be given in a private hospital.

Covert sensitization (Cautela, 1970) is another behavioral approach to the treatment of alcoholism. Cautela suggests asking alcoholics to imagine the following covert sensitization scene: "You are walking into a bar. You decide to have a glass of beer. You are now walking toward the bar. As you are approaching the bar you have a funny feeling in the pit of your stomach. Your stomach feels all queasy and nauseous. Some liquid comes up your throat and it is very sour. You try to swallow it back down, but as you do this, food particles start coming up your throat to your mouth. You are now reaching the bar and you order a beer. As the bartender is pouring the beer, vomit comes to your mouth." A graphic, detailed description of the mechanics and sensations of vomiting then ensues, followed by, ''As you run out of the barroom, you start to feel better and better. When you get out into the clean, fresh air you feel wonderful. You go home and clean yourself up'' (Cautela, 1970, p. 85). Although preliminary data on the efficacy of this procedure with alcoholics has been promising, independent confirmation of these positive results by investigators other than Cautela and his students has not yet been reported.

A multifaceted approach to the behavioral treatment of alcoholism, one that attempts to modify other of the alcoholic patient's maladaptive behaviors besides his drinking, has been developed during the past few years. One exciting trend in this regard involves the possibility of training alcoholics who have tried and failed repeatedly to achieve abstinence to become controlled drinkers. In one of the first studies with this goal, Lovibond and Caddy (1970) first taught alcoholics to estimate their own blood alcohol level (BALs) by alerting them to their subjective feelings of disorientation and euphoria at various levels of intoxication, as well as by relating the number of drinks consumed to the same subjective sensations. During the second phase of the study, subjects were given beverage alcohol to drink according to a predetermined schedule in order to generate moderate BALs. When subjects then drank more than moderate amounts of alcohol and reached BALs above moderate levels, they received painful electric shock on a variable ratio punishment schedule. A control group of alcoholics received random shocks instead of shocks contingent on high BALs. During a follow-up period lasting almost a year, subsequent data revealed that the alcohol intake of the experimental group was lower than that of the control group.

In a study designed to replicate and extend Lovibond and Caddy's findings, Silverstein, Nathan, and Taylor (1974) compared alcoholic subjects' ability first to discriminate BALs and then to maintain predetermined moderate levels of blood alcohol with and without explicit feedback on BALs and with and without reinforcement for accurate estimates. These authors concluded from their study that alcoholics can estimate BALs accurately and can maintain moderate BALs satisfactorily only as long as they receive occasional accurate feedback on the exact status of their BALs. In other words, Silverstein and his co-workers maintained that their subjects (and, by extension, Lovibond and Caddy's subjects) did not rely largely on visceral cues—on subjective feelings—for estimation accuracy. Rather, they relied on occasional feedback of their BALs for this purpose. A study designed to resolve this important controversy about the locus of blood alcohol estimation capability (internal or external) is currently underway in our laboratory (Huber, Karlin, & Nathan, 1975).

Sobell and Sobell (1973) have reported recently on the development of "individualized behavior therapy" for alcoholism which employed assertive training, aversive conditioning, and behavioral training in social skills within a 17-session format. The strength of this behavioral approach to alcoholism lies in its capacity for individualized training, especially individualized training in social skills. Individualization built into other parts of the program ensured that patients received assertive training directed specifically to the persons and situations with which they lacked these behaviors. It also meant that aversive conditioning took place in settings designed to be like those in which the patients typically drank. Training in social skills—required in one-to-one social situations, in groups, on the job, in the family—meant that subjects were taught effective coping skills designed to make drinking less attractive as an ineffective coping device. Modeling, role playing, and behavioral rehearsal were all components of the social skills training. At the 2-year follow-up of the 70 treatment and control patients included in this project, those patients given training explicitly designed to permit a return to controlled drinking were drinking significantly less and working significantly more than patients not given such training. In view of the apparent care with which this project's treatment and follow-up were designed, these results encourage the view that controlled drinking may well be a viable goal for chronic alcoholics for whom abstinence has repeatedly failed.

Behavior Therapy for Drug Dependencies

Behavior therapy for drug addiction has a very recent history. One of the first reports on the use of behavioral procedures with a drug addict (Lesser, 1967) described the treatment of a 21-year-old college senior who was taking morphine two or three times a week but had not become fully addicted. Treatment included training in relaxation to overcome tension and as a substitute for drug-induced relaxation, training in self-assertion to overcome the need for drugs and to help say "no" to the pusher, and electrical aversion to establish a conditioned aversion to behaviors associated with drug ingestion. Follow-up 7 and 10 months after the 4½-month treatment revealed that the patient had not returned to drugs and was leading an apparently productive life.

Behavior therapists have continued to employ aversive conditioning by itself (Gotestam & Melin, 1974; Liberman, 1968; Thomson & Rathod, 1968) and in conjunction with other behavioral techniques including desensitization and assertive training (O'Brien, Raynes, & Patch, 1972; Wisocki, 1973) to treat drug dependence. Preliminary results from the use of these procedures have been positive, in that significant proportions of addicts treated by these techniques achieve abstinence quickly and maintain it through follow-up periods. However, comparative studies of behavioral and other treatments employing much longer follow-up periods are necessary before one can conclude that behavior therapy has unequivocal promise in this application.

One of the most exciting new applications of the behavioral approach to drug addiction involves the use of contingency contracting, a behavioral technique used most often heretofore with families in discord. The first published report on the use of contingency contracts with a drug addict (Boudin, 1972) describes the treatment of a female graduate student at a midwestern university who had become addicted to amphetamines originally prescribed for a physical disability. A contingency contract, lasting for 3 months and signed by both patient and therapist, required the patient to keep the therapist continuously informed of her whereabouts, to call him three times a day to report on her activities, to call him "in addition" whenever she became involved in situations exposing her to possible drug use, and to give up all drug use. The therapist, in turn, rearranged his schedule so that the patient knew where he was at all times. A joint bank account was established in the names of both patient and therapist in the amount of $500 (all of the patient's money). Therapist and patient agreed that any actual or suspected drug use by the patient would result in a $50 check being made out to the Ku Klux Klan. This was presumed to be an effective contingency, since the patient was black.

Although the ensuing therapy had its inevitable trials, the patient did remain almost drug-free—with but one "slip"—over the 3-month contract period. Follow-up of the patient well beyond the initial 3-month period revealed that she had remained abstinent and was making satisfactory progress toward a Ph. D. degree. Given the positive outcome of this trial of contingency contracting, it is disappointing that neither Boudin nor other clinicians have applied the technique to other addicted patients.

BEHAVIORAL APPROACHES TO SEXUAL DISORDERS

McGuire, Carlisle, and Young (1965) were the first to advance a coherent behavioral theory of sexual deviation. After examining the case histories of 45 sexually deviant patients, they concluded that the early thoughts, fantasies, and experiences that first become associated with intercourse or masturbation during adolescence later become specific sexual cues to adult sexual behavior. As a result, if early sexual stimuli are predominantly heterosexual, adult sexual behavior is likely to be normal; by the same token, if early sexual stimuli are homosexually oriented, adult sexual behavior may be deviant:

> Any stimulus which regularly precedes ejaculation by the correct time interval should become more and more sexually exciting. The stimulus may be circumstantial (for example, the particular time or place in which masturbation or intercourse is commonly practiced) or it may be deliberate (for example, any sexual situation or a fantasy of it, be it normal intercourse, or wearing female apparel) [McGuire et al., 1965, p. 186]

Evans (1968) later reported modest laboratory analog support of McGuire's theory, and Davison (1968a) and Marquis (1970) have also confirmed it in the clinic.

Bandura delineated three different social learning mechanisms relevant to the development of deviant sexual behavior in his 1969 redefinition of psychopathology in social learning terms. The first of these mechanisms involves parents who may model sexually deviant behavior in overt or subtle ways in front of their children. As an example, Bandura cites a case study by Giffin, Johnson, and Litin (1954) linking development of exhibitionistic behavior in a 17-year-old boy to his mother's seductive behavior toward him as a child; this early behavior included showering with him, engaging in involved discussions of sex with him, and telling him how much she enjoyed looking at his naked body, especially his "beautiful masculine endowment."

Bandura also emphasizes the importance of events that cause new and deviant sexual responses to become associated with positive reinforcement. He concludes that if early deviant behaviors are associated with affection, physical intimacy, or other specifically positive reinforcement by parents or friends, they are likely to remain a part of the adult's sexual repertoire. A study by Stoller (1967) of the mothers and wives of 32 transvestites provides support for this presumed etiological mechanism. Stoller found that the wives and mothers of these men had both rewarded their growing sexual deviance and "taught" them how to dress as women, to apply cosmetics, and to emit "feminine" behavior.

The third mechanism in Bandura's portrayal of the social learning roots of sexual deviance operates as follows: once sexually deviant behavior acquires stress-reducing properties, that is, once it becomes strongly self-reinforcing, it is likely to be maintained despite aversive external feedback from others about it. Elaborating on this mechanism, Bandura draws the following conclusions:

> First, sexual activities can produce sufficient internal pleasurable experiences to contravene feelings of apprehension or frustration. Secondly, performance of sexual behavior also changes the stimulus situation by temporarily directing the person's attention away from stress-producing events [1969, p. 514]

Behavior Therapy for Sexual Deviations

Aversion Therapy. In an odd alliance, homosexuals and dynamic therapists alike strongly object to the increasing use of behavior therapy for treatment of sexual deviations. Their objections center on aversion therapy, the behavioral technique first used by behavior therapists to modify homosexual behavior. The first clinical application of aversion therapy in this context was reported by Max (1935), who successfully treated a male homosexual by pairing electric shock with pictures of nude males. Despite this initial success, however, it was not until 1956 that aversive conditioning was again employed to modify homosexual behavior. In that year Raymond used apomorphine, an emetic drug which induces nausea and vomiting, in a classical conditioning paradigm to treat a fetishist. Subsequent efforts to use the aversive paradigm alone to create lasting conditioned aversion to homosexual stimuli have largely failed, however. In the most ambitious study examining the efficacy of aversion therapy for homosexuality (Freund, 1960), fewer than 25% of 47 homosexual patients changed their deviant sexual patterns for even a short period of time after a course of apomorphine aversive conditioning.

Aversion-relief therapy, a modification and extension of aversion therapy, was developed by Thorpe and his colleagues (1964) in response to Freund's discouraging report. Aversion-relief therapy supplements aversive procedures designed only to extinguish unwanted homosexual responses by adding a reinforcement component designed to "build in" desired heterosexual responses.

Aversion-relief therapy received its name from the fact that a patient undergoing this behavioral treatment achieves relief from an aversive event (e.g., a painful electric shock) only when he chooses to switch off the homosexual stimulus with which the shock is paired. Repetitive pairings of aversive events with homosexual stimuli and aversion relief with heterosexual stimuli were presumed by Thorpe to represent a promising advance over straight aversive conditioning for homosexual behavior. Although all five of the patients treated by Thorpe with aversion relief immediately altered their sexual orientation, a long-term follow-up of these patients was unfortunately not completed.

Anticipatory Avoidance Learning. Feldman and MacCulloch (1965, 1967, 1971) subsequently developed a new behavioral procedure— anticipatory avoidance learning—based both on the aversion-relief paradigm and on data from laboratory studies of avoidance conditioning. Anticipatory avoidance learning works as follows. Slides of nude males and females, ranked in terms of their capacity to elicit sexual arousal, are presented randomly to a patient seated before a screen. The patient is told before treatment begins that, when a "homosexual" slide appears, an electric shock will begin within 8 seconds unless he switches off the slide. Switching the slide off before the shock begins brings on a "heterosexual" slide—which presumably becomes associated with reinforcing feelings of relief at shock avoidance. In their treatment setting Feldman and MacCulloch arranged it so that avoidance of the homosexual slide brought on one of three behavioral consequences in random order: (a) reinforced, in which as before the learned avoidance response immediately succeeds; (b) delayed, in which the avoidance response does not work immediately but does work before the 8-second interval has elapsed; and (c) nonreinforced, in which the avoidance response does not work and the patient receives a brief painful shock which terminates when the homosexual slide disappears. These three consequences of the decision to terminate the homosexual stimulus were made part of treatment to heighten generalization of the effects of the procedure from the laboratory to the real world.

Forty-three homosexual patients, all volunteers who wanted to eliminate deviant sexual behavior from their sexual repertoires, were treated by MacCulloch and Feldman's anticipatory avoidance learning procedure. Following completion of treatment the sexual behavior of all patients was monitored systematically during the ensuing year, and appropriate "booster" treatment sessions were provided for those patients who needed them. At the end of the year it was found that the technique had apparently been successful with nearly 60% of the 43 patients. Success was defined as cessation of all overt homosexual behavior, only occasional or mild homosexual fantasies, and strong heterosexual fantasies and overt heterosexual behavior.

Although researchers have criticized the Feldman and MacCulloch procedure for design shortcomings (MacDonough, 1972; Rachman & Teasdale, 1969), lack of terminological accuracy (Lovibond, 1970; Wilson, 1972), and insensitivity to ethical issues, anticipatory avoidance conditioning does seem to hold promise for successful treatment of homosexuality. In particular, reports of successful use of variants of this treatment approach by Bancroft (1971), Birk et al. (1971), and Callahan and Leitenberg (1973) encourage us to recommend continued exploration of methods derived from the anticipatory avoidance learning paradigm.

Other Behavioral Techniques for Treating Sexual Deviations. More recently, direct efforts have been made to train heterosexual behavior without first attempting to extinguish homosexual arousal and behavior. In one such effort a young male preoccupied with a sadistic fantasy was gradually taught to become aroused by previously neutral (for him) stimuli, magazine nudes, in the context of a carefully directed progressive sequence of masturbation (Davison, 1968a). Davison's "*Playboy* therapy" first permitted the patient to reach a preorgasmic state of sexual arousal via his usual sadistic fantasies before he started viewing the magazine's heterosexual stimuli, which were presumed as a consequence to become associated with the final, highly reinforcing event of orgasm. Introduction of the heterosexual stimuli then occurred earlier and earlier in the masturbation sequence until finally the nude pictures themselves attained the capacity to induce erection and, ultimately, orgasm. A follow-up at the 16-month mark revealed the following:

> The client reported that, since the therapy had so readily eliminated the arousal from sadistic fantasies, and, most importantly, had altered his outlook for "normal" sexual behavior, he allowed himself, "premeditatedly," to return to the use of the sadistic fantasies 6 mo. after termination, ". . . resolving to enjoy my fantasies until June 1, and then to reform once more. This I did. On June 1, right on schedule, I bought an issue of *Playboy* and proceeded to give myself the treatment again. Once again, it worked like a charm. In two weeks, I was back in my reformed state . . . . I have also been pursuing a vigorous (well, vigorous for *me*) program of dating [Davison, 1968, p. 89]

Lazarus (1971b) has applied his broad-spectrum behavior therapy approach to sexual deviations. As noted earlier, this multifaceted treatment approach comprises a variety of complementary behavioral techniques, including modeling, behavioral rehearsal, assertive training, and practice (homework) assignments. It is, however, with the sexual dysfunctions rather than the sexual deviations that broad-spectrum behavior therapy has had its widest application. A report on one of those applications concludes this section of the chapter.

It is important to emphasize at this point that behavior therapists, like nonbehavior therapists, do not and cannot modify the homosexual behavior of persons who do not desire modification of that behavior. The notion that a behavior therapist can alter behavior in a person who does not wish to have that behavior altered is to accord behavior modification procedures far more efficacy and power than they do (and, perhaps, should) possess. Even studies reporting the successful use of behavior therapy with institutionalized homosexuals, on close perusal, generally reveal these homosexuals subjects to have desired a change in sexual orientation; although the demand characteristics of such restricted settings suggest the absence of freely given consent, one can presume that patients whose behavior did change were those who initially wished it to do so.

Where behavior therapists may have extended their purview beyond usual limits of therapeutic applicability is in the willingness of some to try to improve the homosexual functioning of homosexuals whose sexual functioning is maladaptive or inadequate. Wilson and Davison (1974) argue convincingly for the legitimacy and ethicalness of such efforts, and Lazarus (1971b) and Kohlenberg (1974) have demonstrated their apparent success. Kohlenberg's successfully attained treatment goal, for instance, was to decrease a homosexual pedophiliac's attraction to male children and to increase it to adult males; the therapist successfully achieved his goal following 4 weeks of aversive conditioning and 12 weeks of "*in vivo* desensitization" involving increasing sexual contact with another adult male. Interestingly, while lauding Kohlenberg's treatment goals, Davison and Wilson (1974) find fault with his treatment regimen, concluding that he had no right to assume that a decrease in the patient's attraction to children had to precede explicit efforts to increase his attraction to adults. Davison and Wilson also point out, as does Silverstein (1972), that the behavior therapist should also consider the nonsexual behavioral problems of homosexuals in delineating a treatment plan for them. Often included among these are deficits in assertive behavior and self-esteem and inadequate or unrealistic criteria for self-approval and self-reinforcement.

Behavior Therapy for Sexual Dysfunctions

Sexual dysfunctions have also been treated effectively by behavioral methods. The most common male dysfunctions, impotence and premature ejaculation, have both been treated successfully with a combination of (a) systematic desensitization to reduce anxiety accompanying sexual arousal and intercourse, and (b) assertive training to help the male feel an increasing sense of control in relationships with women. Among others, Wolpe (1958), Kraft and Al-Issa (1968), Friedman and Lipsedge (1971), and Lazarus (1974) have used these techniques to treat male sexual dysfunctions. Brady (1966) and Lazarus (1963), among others, have also used systematic desensitization to treat frigidity in women.

An important adjunct to treatment of sexual dysfunctions via systematic desensitization and relaxation training is graded exposure to actual sexual experiences. A man who is unable to maintain an adequate erection through to complete sexual intercourse may be able to keep that erection when he and his partner are instructed to proceed to a certain point in the sexual sequence and no further. Then, as confidence and proficiency are gained from such successful partial experiences, the sexual sequence can be moved farther along until sexual intercourse itself is successfully achieved. A woman who finds intercourse too painful to bear might be able to sustain a brief intromission, especially if she can do so while she is fully relaxed. This being possible, intromission can then be successively prolonged until intercourse—and orgasm—result. Because these behavioral

methods are incorporated in important components of the widely pub-
licized Masters and Johnson (1970) approach to the sexual dysfunctions,
we review their techniques in some detail.

Although Masters and Johnson's techniques deal with the full array of
sexual dysfunctions, the preliminaries to treatment for all these disorders
are the same. They are based on the basic premise that both marital
partners bear responsibility for either partner's sexual inadequacy. Accordingly, Masters and Johnson's 2-week treatment program always begins with a brief initial interview during which the couple is welcomed and
given an outline of the treatment program to come. The first 3 days of the
program are given over to history taking and a medical/laboratory workup.
The couple is asked to refrain from any sexual activity during this time,
largely because such activity would almost certainly be as self-defeating
and unsuccessful as it had been before. On the fourth day a round-table
session attended by both marital partners and both therapists (Masters and
Johnson) permits the therapists to tie together their knowledge of human
sexual function and dysfunction with the couple's individual and joint
personal, social, and sexual histories.

Treatment then shifts to instruction and practice in *sensate focus* training, during which both marital partners learn to touch and explore each
other's bodies with the sole goal of pleasing each other by touch and
presence, rather than simply proceeding in haste, as before, to the final
orgasmic goal. Sensate focus training also includes regular meetings with
the therapists to discuss apprehensions, guilt feelings, and/or inadequate
understanding of the goals of sensate focus training or of the overall
program. At the successful conclusion of sensate focus training, the focus
of therapy shifts to the couple's specific sexual dysfunction.

Premature ejaculation is treated by teaching both partners ways to
reduce sensory stimulation to the penis during intercourse as well as how to
use the "squeeze technique," a manual procedure, to inhibit imminent
ejaculation. The squeeze technique, involving strong pressure to the top
and bottom surfaces of the penis immediately below the glans penis, causes
the male immediately to lose his urge to ejaculate.

Masters and Johnson's treatment plan for *male impotence* has four
major goals: (a) removal of fears surrounding sexual performance generated by past failures; (b) return to a more active sexual role for the male;
(c) removal of the woman's fears regarding her partner's sexual performance; and (d) strengthening of communication between partners, especially as it relates to communication about sexual desires and preferences.

The couple is specifically requested not to attempt sexual intercourse
during the early stages of treatment for impotence. Instead, sensate focus

training—designed to provide the "opportunity to think and to feel sexually without orientation to performance"—may allow the male to achieve and maintain an erection without having to worry about how long and under what circumstances he will keep it. Once "erection control" has been attained, a variety of graduated sexual exercises involving greater and greater penetration, all free from time or performance demands, are prescribed. Successful, prolonged intromission is programmed only after the performance fears that previously prevented intromission have disappeared.

Of 32 cases of primary impotence (defined as failure ever to achieve or maintain an erection sufficient for intercourse) treated by Masters and Johnson and reported on in 1970, 13 (41%) failed to respond to treatment. By contrast, 157 (74%) of 213 cases of secondary impotence (failure in sexual performance after a period of successful performance) responded successfully to treatment.

Masters and Johnson's treatment for female *orgasmic dysfunctions* (including frigidity, vaginismus, and dyspareunia) is predicated on the assumption that these conditions are strongly influenced by a woman's feelings about her body, about the legitimacy of sexual pleasure for women, and about the function of sex in her marriage. In other words, if a woman has been conditioned to view sex as distasteful, loathsome, or a duty, it is likely that this view has strongly affected her sexual performance.

Sensate focus training, which is of crucial importance to the frigid woman, teaches her that she can feel and enjoy a whole variety of new physical sensations with her mate, which do not necessarily have to be linked to intercourse. As a result, the woman can enjoy physical closeness and touching, often for the first time in her life, without having to deal simultaneously with all her conflicting feelings about intercourse. Graduated instruction and practice in a variety of new, hopefully stimulating coital positions follows, in the effort to provide the woman with maximum sensate pleasure. Attesting to the efficacy of these methods, only 66 (19%) of 342 orgasmically dysfunctional women treated by Masters and Johnson (1970) failed to benefit immediately from these therapeutic procedures.

Lazarus (1974) has developed a multimodal approach to treating sexual dysfunctions which combines many distinctly behavioral techniques with some used by Masters and Johnson. The following abbreviated case study illustrates Lazarus' approach to sexual dysfunction:

Leon and Carol were in love. They had been dating for the past year, and they planned to marry soon. Both were virgins eager to have premarital sex. Although Leon had seen various girls for five years, Carol was his first serious involvement. He enjoyed kissing and caressing her, but as soon as the amorous activities became more serious, he became tense and agitated. Leon was impotent.

The most logical imagery technique in this case was systematic desensitization. I lent Leon a series of cassette recordings on deep muscle relaxation so that he could learn to relax his entire body. Meanwhile, I asked him to picture a range of non-threatening images; they included seeing Carol, dancing with her, holding her hand, rubbing her back, and stroking her hair. We began the desensitization process by asking Leon to imagine himself fondling Carol's breasts while she was fully clothed. He pictured this image clearly and reported no anxiety. I then asked him to imagine kissing, hugging, fondling of naked breasts while otherwise fully clothed; mouth contact with breasts; undressing completely; lying together in the nude; touching Carol's genitals. We could not proceed beyond the last item without evoking high levels of anxiety in Leon. This block prevented me from adding progressively more intimate images. I switched to those that involved Carol as the more active partner; Leon was soon able to visualize her caressing *his* genitals without anxiety. But the moment *her* genitals came into the picture, Leon became highly anxious. Leon and I searched vainly for reasons for his overwhelming aversion. I asked him to picture his mother's genitals. . . . He found the idea abhorrent. He then recalled the following incident.

Leon: My mom and dad had a double bed and I used to cuddle with them on Sunday mornings. One day I noticed an unpleasant odor and saw blood on the sheets. . . . I guess that she was menstruating.

Therapist: Well, can you get into that image? Pretend you are eight or nine years old. It is a Sunday morning and you are cuddling in bed with your parents. Can you picture that vividly?

Leon: (pause) Yes.

Therapist: Now you mentioned an odor.

Leon: Yeah. Carol sometimes smells like that.

Therapist: When she menstruates?

Leon: I don't know.

Therapist: Okay. Let's get back into the image.

Leon had difficulties suspending his adult faculties at this point. I then asked him to imagine himself in bed with Carol when she was menstruating. (Leon) "That makes me uptight."

I instructed Leon to relax and go through the last scene several times. At the next session, Leon was able to visualize himself touching and caressing Carol's genitals without experiencing anxiety; even with the imagery of menstruation added, the desensitization proceeded swiftly.

Leon and I had met 10 times over a period of 6 weeks; it was now time to bring Carol to therapy. She appeared tense but eager to help by going through a modified Masters and Johnson program with him. I decided to work on their problems in the *sensory* modality by applying Masters and Johnson's method of sensate focus.

One week later they reported they both had become aroused during noncoital sensual exchanges, and that they had sexual intercourse on three separate occasions. They were jubilant . . . . Leon stated that his sexual prowess exceeded his wildest dreams. They had set a date for their wedding, and had replaced the initial atmosphere of gloom and desperation with one of joy and optimism in less than four months of therapy [Lazarus, 1974, p. 60–61]

BEHAVIORAL APPROACHES TO CHILD PSYCHOPATHOLOGY

A fundamental tenet of the behavioral approach to psychopathology in children is that parents often unintentionally reward their children's most undesirable behavior. A child who finds that he can get his parents' attention only by having a temper tantrum, for example, is being reinforced for this maladaptive behavior even while he is being "punished" for it. The same child may find that more appropriate behavior, such as obedience and cooperation, receives much less attention, hence is much less reinforcing. Such a common behavioral paradox is virtually guaranteed to establish a behavioral pattern characterized by frequent, disruptive temper tantrums.

Another behavioral mechanism by which childhood behavioral disorders are probably acquired is modeling. Promiscuous sexual behavior by children or teenagers, for example, is often associated with promiscuous sexual behavior modeled by parents (Scharfman & Clark, 1967), although this behavior may also represent a response to peer group pressure or an attempt to "prove" sexual attractiveness or sexual potency. In both instances, reinforcement for maladaptive behavior is available, in the first instance from peers and in the second from sexual partners as well as from the self. Conduct disorders reflected in acts against other people or things can similarly provide children with tangible immediate reinforcers. Stealing, swearing, cheating, behaving poorly in class, and lying all possess immediate reinforcement value. Reinforcers include teacher's attention, peer approval, stolen goods, and drugs, alcohol, and sex.

Ferster (1961) has advanced a theory of autism and childhood schizophrenia, based on learning principles, which is concerned more with behavioral techniques for modifying autistic behavior than with etiological issues, but also touches on etiology. Central to its etiological component is the assumption that the autistic child's behavior differs from the normal child's in frequency but not in range, kind, or quality; as a corollary, Ferster's theory concludes that the autistic child's behavioral repertoire is deficient in complex social behaviors and excessive in simple asocial behaviors. These behavioral deficits and excesses, according to Ferster, result from absence of the consistent parental reinforcement necessary for the development of appropriate social behavior. Ferster's theory of autism is similar in its essentials to Ullmann and Krasner's previously mentioned "sociopsychological model" of schizophrenia. Like that theory, however, it has not been the subject of independent experimental validation. This is unfortunate, because the theory has a coherence and parsimony appealing to those who want to understand the puzzling, paradoxical disorder that is childhood autism.

Behavior Therapy for Children's Behavioral Problems

Behavior therapy is increasingly being used to treat a wider and wider array of children's behavioral problems. Such diverse childhood problems as sibling rivalry (O'Leary, O'Leary, & Becker, 1967), inappropriate aggressive behavior (Wiltz & Patterson, 1974), enuresis (Lovibond & Coote, 1970; Yates, 1970), tantrums (Martin & Iaqulli, 1974), thumbsucking (Davidson, 1970), hyperactivity (Werry & Sprague, 1970), school phobia (Gordon, 1974; Lazarus, Davison, & Poletky, 1965) and childhood psychosis (Merbaum, 1973; Saposnek & Watson, 1974; Yates, 1970) have all been treated by behavioral techniques.

Many behavioral treatment programs for children are now carried out by parents under supervision from professionals (Ferber, Keeley & Scheinberg, 1974). Basically, parents are taught the basic tenets of reward and punishment to allow them to analyze their interactions with their children in keeping with these principles (Kozloff, 1973). In essence, the parent learns *not* to give positive reinforcement for inappropriate behavior, as well as how to reinforce appropriate behavior. When love and expressions of affection are given consistently for appropriate behavior rather than inappropriate behavior, they more effectively maintain the child's appropriate behavior; as important, they increase the parent's sense of his own competence as a parent.

Behavioral Treatment of Childhood Psychoses

During the past few years the use of behavioral techniques with psychotic children has grown in quantum jumps. Ivar Lovaas, an important figure in this endeavor, pioneered the early use of operant techniques to develop speech (Lovaas et al., 1966), to encourage social interaction (Lovaas et al., 1965), and to eliminate self-destructive behavior (Lovaas & Simmons, 1969), all with psychotic children.

In one of these early studies (Lovaas et al., 1966), Lovaas and his colleagues successfully established functional speech in two virtually mute 6-year-old schizophrenic boys, Chuck and Billy. Before behavioral training began Chuck and Billy uttered only infrequent, noncommunicative vowel sounds. Most of the time they were withdrawn and isolated, tantrumed frequently, and spent inordinate periods of time rocking and twirling. Chuck and Billy received 7 hours a day of training 6 days a week for 4 weeks. During these sessions small bites of meals served as rewards for appropriate behavior, while spanking and shouting were used to punish tantrums, self-destructive behavior, and failure to pay attention.

A four-step discrimination-shaping training procedure characterized the behavior modification. At first the children were rewarded with food for all vocalizations. They were also rewarded at this time for visually focusing on the therapist's mouth. Next, the children were rewarded for all vocalizations made within a certain period of time after the therapist had emitted a sound. Next, the children were rewarded only if their sound matched (modeled) the adult's vocalization; this sometimes required the therapist to prompt the child by forming his lips correctly. Finally, different sounds from those used before were introduced. At this point the child had first to discriminate between the two sounds and then to imitate the correct one. New words could now be successively introduced at this point in the training sequence.

After 26 days of imitation training, both boys were learning new words so rapidly that a new training program was designed; it was to teach them to use the words they had learned communicatively rather than simply imitatively. Shortly thereafter both boys were reinstitutionalized. Although both lost some of the words they had learned while back in the hospital, Billy had made enough progress overall to make a subsequent marginal adjustment to a foster home. Further, it seemed likely at a final follow-up that Chuck's mother would take him home. Although neither boy stopped being psychotic as a result of Lovaas' behavioral interventions, both made sufficient behavioral gains—gains clearly impossible without that intervention—to enable them to lead lives more satisfying to their loved ones and, probably, to themselves.

The following case report by Merbaum (1973) shows how a psychotic child's self-destructive behavior was successfully eliminated by use of aversive stimulation. It suggests that this use of contingent electric shock, a most controversial behavioral procedure, may ultimately be its most promising application.

Andy was a 12-year-old boy . . . who had been variously diagnosed as autistic, schizophrenic, retarded, brain damaged or combinations of these. His behavior was extremely primitive. . . . Andy's self-abusive behavior had been a constant problem at home and in school for at least five years. With both hands he would beat his face furiously and, as a result, his face was terribly bruised and his cheeks grotesquely swollen. During the past five years, intensive therapeutic programs had all failed completely (including chemotherapy, mega-vitamins, patterning, physical restraints and conventional psychotherapy) . . . . Parents and teachers reported that the problem was becoming more severe and they were fearful that more serious damage might occur to his head.

A time sampling procedure consisting of a series of 10-minute intervals was arranged to determine the frequency of blows to the face. The average number of blows was 221 per 10-min. period.

The punishment contingency was administered by a Hot Shock stock prod. The prod, 18 inches in length with two end terminals about five inches apart, is battery operated and gives off 150–300 ma. peak amperage with output from 200–500 V.

The therapist waited until Andy hit himself and then presented the shock. Andy's initial reaction to this experience was surprise, a cry of pain and immediate fear of the device. Paradoxically, his reaction to the therapist was one of approach and desire for closeness. Tenderness and affection were freely expressed by the therapist and Andy responded warmly to this attention. For the next 2 hr., with the shock prod visible to him, there was not one instance of self-abusive behavior.

Andy's teachers, carefully instructed in the use of the shock device, played an essential role in the treatment program. The shocker, carried around constantly, was immediately available when Andy began to beat his face. On those rare occasions on which he would hit himself, a shock was immediately forthcoming along with a resounding *no* from the teacher. It was estimated that Andy received no more than seven shocks at school before the behavior appeared to be under tight stimulus control. Throughout subsequent weeks the teachers continued to carry the shock prod wherever they went and Andy was constantly exposed to the threat of shock.

During the school program continual communication with his parents indicated that not only was the amount of self-destructive behavior at home the same, there even seemed to be a slight increase in its frequency. At this juncture a second program was established. Andy's mother was trained to use the shock apparatus. In addition, the practical value of positive reinforcement was explained and the behavior contingencies for the presentation of punishment and positive reinforcement worked out. The mother was instructed to use shock on a response contingent basis, and to take a frequency count of the target behavior twice a day prior to the introduction of the shock.

The first day the mother took two 15-minute time samples, during which periods Andy hit himself 253 and 358 times. Following these time samples she produced the shock with a simultaneous *no* as the shock was presented.

The following is the mother's summary of July and August: "Andy responds very quickly to the shock stick. I have used it about eight times."

Finally, a year later, I (therapist) contacted her (Mother) and the following report was given: "I haven't used the shock stick since some time back in the winter. . . . They used it at the school only once this summer. The frequency of hitting is almost nil. He is quieter, happier, and wonderful around the house."

The mother estimates that she has used the shock stick about 25 times through the entire treatment program. When he does start to hit, and this is very infrequent now, a strong *no* is sufficient to stop the behavior [Merbaum, 1973, pp. 443–445]

The application of aversive stimulation in this instance eliminated a problem that was potentially very harmful to the *S* as well as being very disruptive to his entire family. Three points justify choice of what was certainly a high-risk treatment method: (a) other behavioral and non-behavioral techniques had repeatedly failed to suppress Andy's self-injurious behavior; (b) Andy's own self-injurious behavior was potentially more harmful to him than the electric shock; and (c) although nonprofessionals administered the shock, they were under close supervision. The cooperation of the mother and school personnel with the primary therapy was essential. Although aversive conditioning should always be used judiciously, its use in this situation seems to have been an especially wise choice. It eliminated a serious problem of long-standing in just a few months.

Behavioral Treatment of Phobias in Children

Several behavioral techniques have been developed specifically to treat children's phobias. Lazarus has developed what he calls *emotive imagery* for the specific purpose of helping children who are anxious, phobic, or both to relax. The underlying axiom of emotive imagery is the same as that of systematic desensitization; no one can feel anxious and relaxed at the same time. In one of the best known reports on the use of this behavioral technique, Lazarus and Abramovitz (1962) used emotive imagery to treat a 14-year-old boy who was intensely afraid of dogs. The boy was asked first to construct an elaborate fantasy involving a favorite hero, activity, or ambition. He chose to create a fantasy in which he drove an Alfa Romeo to victory in the Indianapolis 500 road race. Thoughts about the feared stimulus object were then interwoven with the fantasy (dogs were in the stands, "in the pit," and by his side at the racetrack). Each scene involving both the favorite fantasy and the feared object was painted in vivid verbal detail by the therapist. As a consequence, the more powerful competing stimulus of the fantasy inhibited anxiety produced by the feared object, ultimately allowing the boy to approach and touch live dogs without feeling anxious. Lazarus and Abramovitz report complete recovery by seven of nine phobic children treated with emotive imagery. The absence of a prolonged follow-up of these subjects, however, and few replicating reports on use of the method detract from the enthusiasm with which one might otherwise view emotive imagery.

Modeling has also emerged as an important behavioral approach to children's phobias. The impetus for that development came both from Bandura's early research on modeling mechanisms and from his later more applied research on the remediation potential of some of these mechanisms. In one of the latter studies Bandura, Grusec, and Menlove (1967) reported on the successful treatment of children's dog phobias by modeling, along with other behavioral procedures. In that study, dog phobic preschool children were randomly assigned to one of four treatment conditions: a *modeling–positive context* group, which observed a fearless child play with a dog in a party-type atmosphere; a *modeling–neutral context* group, which saw the same model play with the same dog but not in the party atmosphere; an *exposure-positive context* group, which went to parties with the dog present but saw no fearless peer interact with the animal; and a *positive context* group, which went to parties where no dog was present. The two groups who had seen a fearless child interact with the dog showed a stable decrement in their own fear of dogs. The positive context groups, by contrast, did not have a more positive outcome than the neutral groups, indicating that the model, not the context, was responsible for the therapeutic effect.

Outpatient Behavioral Treatment

Little controlled research on behavioral techniques with children in outpatient clinics has been reported thus far. Although a variety of case studies involving a child as his own control have reported success with standard behavioral techniques, this kind of treatment design represents a restricted test of efficacy. A recent controlled study comparing play therapy with reciprocal inhibition in the reduction of children's phobias was an exception to this rule; both behavioral techniques were equally effective (Miller et al., 1972). Operant techniques were found to be more effective than play therapy in modifying the schizophrenic behavior of a group of schizophrenic boys in another controlled study (Ney, Palvesky, & Markley, 1971). Nonetheless, more controlled research to evaluate all therapeutic approaches including behavior therapy with children's behavioral problems is needed.

Token Economies

Phillips et al. (1971) have recently described a successful token economy at Achievement Place, a halfway house for young predelinquent boys in Kansas. The byword at Achievement Place is consistent reinforcement for appropriate behavior and equally consistent punishment for inappropriate behavior or behavioral omissions. Residents of Achievement Place are given small cards which indicate how many points they have accumulated for desirable behavior. Rewards are given for such behaviors as getting up on time, behaving properly during school hours, keeping their rooms clean, and saving allowance money. Points are lost for a variety of antisocial behaviors including fighting, swearing, and truancy from school. Achievement Place functions via a semi-self-government system by which its residents establish many of their own rules; "semi-" means, however, that certain limits are set on the boys' autonomy based on experience with the system (Brown et al., 1974; Fixen et al., 1973). More than 5 years of treatment research at Achievement Place suggests strongly that this halfway house for predelinquent boys organized around behavioral principles has succeeded well in its purposes—to prevent predelinquent boys from becoming mature criminals. Much of the success of the institution is thought to rest on the fact that its behavioral underpinnings make the consequences of wanted and unwanted behavior crystal clear, perhaps more clear than they have ever before been to its troubled residents.

BEHAVIORAL APPROACHES TO
MENTAL RETARDATION

Behavioral approaches to mental retardation are directed above all toward structuring the environment to provide small reinforced steps which will build self-confidence and motivate further self-help efforts by mentally retarded persons. Zigler's 1967 study of motivational and environmental influences on the performance of institutionalized cultural-familial retardates provides empirical support for this approach to therapy. Focusing on the frequent failure experiences of retarded individuals, Zigler and his colleagues pointed out that retarded persons probably experience more failure in a day than normal persons do in a week or more. As a consequence, the retarded learn to expect failure and become reluctant to tackle new problems. By structuring the environment around successive approximations that will shape the retarded individual's behavior to its desired form, behaviorists can combat the negative effects of prior frequent failure experiences by promoting deserved and consistent, if modest, success experiences.

Teaching Self-Care Skills

Over the relatively few years that operant techniques have been employed extensively with mentally retarded individuals, they have been used most often to teach institutionalized individuals practical self-care skills such as washing, dressing, and eating (Mahoney & Craighead, 1973). They have also been used with success to teach academic subjects to the retarded (O'Leary & O'Leary, 1972). Token economies have also been prominent components of behavioral self-care programs for institutionalized retarded persons (Bricker et al., 1972; Musick & Luckey, 1970; Roberts & Perry, 1970).

Whitney and Barnard (1966) employed operant techniques to modify the behavior of a severely retarded 15-year-old girl who was unable to sit alone or grasp objects. Using successive approximation methods, the girl was first trained to spoon-feed herself. Food, the reinforcement for each successively more correct spoon-handling behavior, was withdrawn whenever the spoon was used inappropriately. Employing the same technique, the girl was also taught to hold and then to drink from a cup and, eventually, to sit and eat with other patients. In a few short weeks of behavioral treatment this severely retarded girl was able to learn more self-care skills than she had acquired in 15 years of traditional care.

Nine incontinent adult retardates with a median IQ of 14 and an average age of 43 years were successfully toilet-trained by Azrin and Foxx (1971) after a combined total of more than 250 years of incontinence before behavioral treatment began. Treatment centered on use of moisture-sensitive pairs of shorts, which activated a buzzer whenever the patient urinated or defecated in them, and a specially designed toilet bowl which provided an auditory signal whenever it was used. These pieces of equipment enabled immediate recognition by both patient and experimenter of inappropriate toileting (initial incontinence) and appropriate toileting (finally urinating or defecating in the toilet). Following inappropriate toilet behavior with a lengthy corrective sequence which involved what amounted to a punishment contingency and following appropriate toileting behavior with reinforcement permitted the experimenters to report near-complete continence for all patients within a mean of 6 days. This report by Azrin and Foxx is of special interest, because it employed a variety of sophisticated shaping procedures to heighten the effectiveness of new prosthetic equipment. The success of what seem to have been necessary components of this behavior-modification program suggests that behavioral programs that attempt to modify complex human behaviors in one or two steps, without explicit efforts at shaping or successive approximation, may well be doomed to failure.

Teaching Vocational Skills

Behavioral techniques have also been used to teach useful vocational skills to mentally retarded persons. In one of the first such efforts, Clarke and Hermelin (1955) successfully taught six retardates with IQs between 22 and 42 to fold and glue cardboard boxes, a fairly complicated sequence of behaviors. Although their retarded subjects were initially unable to perform this task as well as individuals of normal intelligence, by the end of the training period they were producing a product that passed industrial inspection standards. The prime behavioral mechanism employed was simply reinforcement for successively more appropriate folding and gluing behavior.

Retarded individuals have also been taught to wire electrical components, assemble mechanical devices, count and sort money, do office filing, and use simple office machines (Neuhaus, 1967; Tate & Baroff, 1967), although sometimes only after the introduction of technological aids for initial assessment of behavioral deficits and final assessment of behavioral improvement (Tate, 1968; Schroeder, 1972). Interestingly, performance by retarded individuals of many simple tasks has been shown to be influenced as much by personality variables such as perseverence as simply by IQ (Sali & Amir, 1971). In any event, the overwhelming bulk of studies reporting on the use of behavioral techniques to teach vocational skills to the retarded strongly suggest that these techniques can be employed on a wider scale to enable more of the retarded to become self-supporting and independent.

Treatment of Speech Problems

The speech problems of the retarded—common accompaniments of retardation—have also been attacked by behavior modifiers. Recent examples include studies by Garcia (1974), Guess and Baer (1973), and Rubin and Stolz (1974). The following case study, reported by Butz and Hasazi (1973), demonstrates the range of differential reinforcement procedures behaviorally trained clinicians can now bring to bear on the maladaptive speech of retarded children:

Seven-year-old John enrolled in a special education classroom for educable mentally retarded children was the subject of this study. He functioned adequately and appropriately in most situations, and possessed an extensive verbal repertoire. He used complete sentences, could imitate speech and was able to ask coherent, appropriate questions. However, John's appropriate verbal responses were typically followed by periods of perseverative speech. . . .

[Treatment] sessions were held on each school day throughout the study and were 20 min. in length. All sessions involved a structured questioning procedure to maximize the opportunities for perseverative speech. John was shown a number of magazine pictures, each presented only once per session, and was asked who or what was depicted. Three questions were asked per 30 sec. period. Any amount of perseverative speech within a 30-sec. period was considered a single instance (Perseverative speech was defined as any verbalization which was unrelated to the previous question, was repetitive, or was unintelligible to the E.)

The experiment consisted of four phases; the first, or Baseline, phase was 3 days long and designed to assess the frequency of perseverative speech without intervention from the E. Phase 2, a Contingent Reinforcement phase, followed and included sessions 4–14. In this phase, each 30-sec. period in which perseverative speech did not occur was reinforced by presenting the child with a penny and providing verbal praise at the end of the period. Periods containing any perseverative speech were not reinforced and were otherwise ignored by the E regardless of the extent of appropriate speech.

A third experimental phase, the Noncontingent Reinforcement phase, followed and was eight days in length. Here the purpose was to determine whether changes in the child's verbal behavior during the previous phases were under the control of experimenter-mediated consequences. In this phase, both appropriate and perseverative speech were ignored by the E, as in Phase 1. Additionally, reinforcement was provided at the end of each 30-sec. period on a noncontingent basis, i.e., regardless of the child's verbal performance in the previous period.

The fourth phase of the experiment followed and was eight sessions in length. This phase, a second Contingent Reinforcement phase, was a replication of Phase 2 of the experiment.

Reliability judgments were obtained by having an independent judge rate tape recordings of the sessions for perseverative speech. Percent agreement varied from 85 per cent to 98 per cent, with a mean of 93 per cent.

In the baseline phase. . . perseverative speech occurred at a high rate . . . averaging 72 percent for the 3 days of this phase. When reinforcement contingent upon the absence of perseverative speech was introduced, John continued to speak perseveratively at a high rate for 3 days. The rate then dropped off drastically, with the percent of perseverative speech less than 10 percent on each of the last 3 days of this period.

After the fifteenth session (Noncontingent Reinforcement Phase) . . . the percent of perseverative speech steadily increased over sessions. In the last three sessions of this phase . . . it averaged 58 percent. . .

The second contingent Reinforcement Phase was also characterized by a sharp drop in the rate of perseverative speech. By the second day of this phase, the percentage had dropped to 5 percent, and remained under 10 percent for the last four days. The significant changes in the rate of perseverative speech occurring in this and in the preceding experimental phase provide further evidence of the strong control operated over this behavior by contingent reinforcement [Butz & Hasazi, 1973, pp. 167–169]

Thus, a mentally retarded child's perseverative speech, a frequent speech problem with the retarded, was effectively and quickly modified without the use of punishment.

Behavioral Techniques for Use with Deprived Children

Only recently have behavioral techniques been used with deprived children for whom an enriched environment—perhaps achieved via behavioral means—may mean the difference between normal intelligence and cultural-familial retardation. A variety of learning problems typical of preschool children in day care and Head Start programs have been studied by Risley and his colleagues at the University of Kansas. They report that behavioral procedures can improve the correspondence between what a Head Start child says he does and what he actually does (Risley & Hart, 1968), increase the amount of time a child spends at various work-related tasks (Jacobson, Buschell, & Risley, 1969), and increase verbal imitation skills (Risley & Reynolds, 1970). These successes led the same investigators to organize local day care centers along completely behavioral lines (Doke & Risley, 1972; LeLaurin & Risley, 1972). Although such psychologists as Arthur Jensen and Richard Herrnstein have concluded that compensatory education has failed (see Cronbach, 1975), the judgement seems premature considering that behavioral techniques, only recently employed in this area, have been shown to be surprisingly effective. Nonetheless, much additional research and development of behavioral techniques tailored to preschool deprived children is required before what is now a promise becomes a reality.

REFERENCES

Agras, W. S., Leitenberg, H., & Barlow, D. H. Social reinforcement in the modification of agoraphobia. *Archives of General Psychiatry*, 1968, **19**, 423–427.

Antman, E. M. Flooding *in vivo* for a case of vermiphobia. *Journal of Behavior Therapy and Experimental Psychiatry*, 1973, **4**, 275–278.

Atthowe, J. M., & Krasner, L. Preliminary report on the application of contingent reinforcement procedures (token economy) on a "chronic" psychiatric ward. *Journal of Abnormal Psychology*, 1968, **73**, 37–43.

Ayllon, T., & Azrin, N. H. The measurement and reinforcement of behavior of psychotics. *Journal of the Experimental Analysis of Behavior*, 1965, **8**, 357–383.

Ayllon, T., & Michael, J. The psychiatric nurse as a behavioral engineer. *Journal of the Experimental Analysis of Behavior*, 1959, **2**, 323–334.

Azrin, N. H., & Foxx, R. A rapid method of toilet training the institutionalized retarded. *Journal of Applied Behavior Analysis*, 1971, **4**, 89–100.

Azrin, N. H., & Holz, W. C. Punishment. In W. K. Honig (Ed.), *Operant behavior: Areas of research and application.* New York: Appleton-Century-Crofts, 1966, pp. 380–447.

Bancroft, J. H. J. The application of psychophysiological measures to the assessment and treatment of sexual behavior. *Behaviour Research and Therapy*, 1971, **9**, 119–130.

Bandura, A. *Principles of behavior modification.* New York: Holt, 1969.

Bandura, A. Vicarious and self-reinforcement processes. In R. Glaser (Ed.), *The nature of reinforcement.* New York: Academic Press, 1971.

Bandura, A., Blanchard, E. G., & Ritter, B. Relative efficacy of desensitization and modeling approaches for inducing behavioral, affective, and attitudinal changes. *Journal of Personality and Social Psychology*, 1969, **13**, 173–199.

Bandura, A., Grusec, J. E., & Menlove, F. L. Observational learning as a function of symbolization and incentive set. *Child Development*, 1966, **37**, 499–506.

Bandura, A., Grusec, J. E., & Menlove, F. L. Vicarious extinction of avoidance behavior. *Journal of Personality and Social Psychology*, 1967, **5**, 16–23.

Bandura, A., Ross, D., & Ross, S. A. Transmission of aggression through imitation of aggressive models. *Journal of Abnormal and Social Psychology*, 1961, **63**, 575–582.

Bandura, A., Ross, D. M., & Ross, S. A. Imitation of film-mediated aggressive models. *Journal of Abnormal and Social Psychology*, 1963, **66**, 3–11.

Bandura, A., & Walters, R. *Social learning and personality development.* New York: Holt, 1963.

Bernstein, D. A., & Beaty, W. E. The use of *in vivo* desensitization as part of a total therapeutic intervention. *Journal of Behavior Therapy and Experimental Psychiatry*, 1971, **2**, 259–266.

Birk, L. Behavior therapy—Integration with dynamic psychiatry. *Behavior Therapy*, 1970, **1**, 522–526.

Birk, L., Huddleston, W., Miller, E., & Cohler, B. Avoidance conditioning for homosexuality. *Archives of General Psychiatry*, 1971, **25**, 314–323.

Blake, B. G. A follow-up of alcoholics treated by behaviour therapy. *Behaviour Research and Therapy*, 1967, **5**, 89–94.

Bloomfield, H. H. Assertive training in an outpatient group of chronic schizo-phrenics: A preliminary report. *Behavior Therapy,* 1973, **4,** 277–281.

Boren, J. J. The study of drugs with operant techniques. In W. K. Honig (Ed.), *Operant behavior: Areas of research and application.* New York: Appleton-Century-Crofts, 1966, 531–564.

Borkovec, T. D. Effects of expectancy on the outcome of systematic desensitization and implosive treatments for analogue anxiety. *Behavior Therapy,* 1972, **3,** 29–40.

Boudewyns, P. A., & Wilson, A. E. Implosive therapy and desensitization therapy using free association in the treatment of inpatients. *Journal of Abnormal Psychology,* 1972, **79,** 259–268.

Boudin, H. M. Contingency contracting as a therapeutic tool in the deceleration of amphetamine use. *Behavior Therapy,* 1972, **3,** 604–608.

Brady, J. P. Brevital-relaxation treatment of frigidity. *Behaviour Research and Therapy,* 1966, **4,** 71–77.

Breger, L., & McGaugh, J. L. A critique and reformulation of "learning theory" approaches to psychotherapy and neurosis. *Psychological Bulletin,* 1965, **63,** 335–358.

Bricker, W., Morgan, D., & Grabowski, J. Development and maintenance of a behavior modification repertoire of cottage attendants through T.V. feed-back. *American Journal of Mental Deficiency,* 1972, **77,** 128–136.

Brown, W. G., Turnbough, D. P., Fixsen, D. L., Phillips, E. L., & Wolf, M. M. Achievement Place: Reduction of parental disapproved behaviors in the natural home by contingencies applied in a community-based residential group home. Paper presented at the meeting of the American Psychological Association, New Orleans, 1974 August.

Burchard, J. D., & Barrera, F. An analysis of timeout and response cost in a programmed environment. *Journal of Applied Behavior Analysis,* 1972, **5,** 271–282.

Burgess, E. P. The modification of depressive disorders. In E. D. Rubin & C. M. Franks (Eds.), *Advances in behavior therapy.* New York: Academic Press, 1969.

Butz, R. A., & Hasazi, J. E. The effects of reinforcement on perseverative speech in a mildly retarded boy. *Journal of Behavior Therapy and Experimental Psychiatry,* 1973, **4,** 167–170.

Callahan, E. J., & Leitenberg, H. Reinforced practice as a treatment for acrophobia: A controlled outcome study. *Proceedings of the American Psychological Association,* 1970, **5,** 533–534.

Callahan, E. J., & Leitenberg, H. Aversion therapy for sexual deviation: Contingent shock and covert sensitization. *Journal of Abnormal Psychology,* 1973, **81,** 60–73.

Catania, A. C. Self-inhibiting effects of reinforcement. *Journal of the Experimental Analysis of Behavior,* 1973, **19,** 517–526.

Cautela, J. R. The treatment of alcoholism by covert sensitization. *Psychotherapy: Theory, Research and Practice,* 1970, **7,** 83–90.

Cherek, D. R., Thompson, T., & Heistad, G. T. Responding maintained by the opportunity to attack during an interval food reinforcement schedule. *Journal of Experimental Analysis of Behavior,* 1973, **19,** 113–123.

Clarke, A., & Hermelin, B. Adult imbeciles: Their abilities and trainability. *Lancet,* 1955, **2,** 337–339.

Cohen, D. J. Justin and his peers: An experimental analysis of a child's social world. *Child Development,* 1962, **33,** 697–716.

Cohen, H. L. Educational therapy: The design of learning improvements. In J. M. Shlien (Ed.), *Research in psychotherapy.* Vol. III, Washington, D.C.: American Psychological Association, 1968, pp. 21–53.

Costello, C. G. Depression: Loss of reinforcers or loss of reinforcer effectiveness? *Behavior Therapy,* 1972, **3,** 240–247.

Cronbach, L. J. Five decades of public controversy over mental testing. *American Psychologist,* 1975, **30,** 1–14.

Davidson, P. Thumbsucking. In C. Costello (Ed.), *Symptoms of psychopathology.* New York: Wiley, 1970.

Davison, G. C. Elimination of a sadistic fantasy by a client-controlled counterconditioning technique: A case study. *Journal of Abnormal Psychology,* 1968, **73,** 84–90.

Davison, G. C. Systematic desensitization as a counterconditioning process. *Journal of Abnormal Psychology,* 1968, **73,** 91–99.

Davison, G. C., & Wilson, G. T. Processes of fear-reduction in systematic desensitization: Cognitive and social reinforcement factors in humans. *Behavior Therapy,* 1973, **4,** 1–21.

Davison, G. C., & Wilson, G. T. Goals and strategies in behavioral treatment of homosexual pedophilia: Comments on a case study. *Journal of Abnormal Psychology,* 1974, **83,** 196–198.

Doke, L., & Risley, T. The organization of day-care environments: Required vs. optional activities. *Journal of Applied Behavior Analysis,* 1972, **5,** 405–420.

Dollard, J., & Miller, N. *Personality and psychotherapy.* New York: McGraw-Hill, 1950.

Edwards, N. B. Case conference: Assertive training in a case of homosexual pedophilia. *Journal of Behavior Therapy and Experimental Psychiatry,* 1972, **3,** 55–64.

Evans, D. R. Masturbatory fantasy and sexual deviation. *Behaviour Research and Therapy,* 1968, **6,** 17–19.

Evans, R. B. Physical and biochemical characteristics of homosexual men. *Journal of Abnormal Psychology,* 1972, **39,** 140–147.

Eysenck, H. J. *The dynamics of anxiety and hysteria.* London: Routledge & Kegan Paul, 1957.

Eysenck, H. J. Classification and the problems of diagnosis. In H. J. Eysenck (Ed.), *Handbook of abnormal psychology*. New York: Basic Books, 1961.

Eysenck, H. J. Counterconditioning and related methods in behavior therapy. In A. E. Bergin & S. L. Garfield (Eds.), *Handbook of psychotherapy and behavior change*. New York: Wiley, 1971.

Eysenck, H. J. Behavior therapy is behavioristic. *Behavior Therapy*, 1972, **3**, 609–613.

Eysenck, H. J. (Ed.) *Handbook of abnormal psychology*. (2nd ed.) London: Pitman, 1973.

Farrar, C. H., Powell, B. J., & Martin, K. L. Punishment of alcohol consumption by apneic paralysis. *Behaviour Research and Therapy*, 1968, **6**, 13–16.

Fazio, A. F. Treatment components in implosive therapy. *Journal of Abnormal Psychology*, 1970, **76**, 211–219.

Fazio, A. F. Implosive therapy with semiclinical phobias. *Journal of Abnormal Psychology*, 1972, **80**, 183–188.

Feldman, M. P., & MacCulloch, M. J. The application of anticipatory avoidance learning to the treatment of homosexuality. 1. Theory, technique, and preliminary results. *Behaviour Research and Therapy*, 1965, **3**, 165–183.

Feldman, M. P., & MacCulloch, M. J. *Homosexual behaviour: Therapy and assessment*. Oxford: Pergamon Press, 1971.

Fensterheim, H. The initial interview. In A. A. Lazarus (Ed.), *Clinical behavior therapy*. New York: Brunner/Mazel, 1972.

Ferber, H., Keeley, S. M., & Scheinberg, K. M. Training parents in behavior modification: Outcome of and problems encountered in a program after Patterson's work. *Behavior Therapy*, 1974, **5**, 415–419.

Ferster, C. B. Positive reinforcement and behavioral deficits of autistic children. *Child Development*, 1961, **32**, 437–456.

Ferster, C. B., & Skinner, B. F. *Schedules of reinforcement*. New York: Appleton-Century-Crofts, 1957.

Fixsen, D. L., Phillips, E. L., & Wolf, M. M. Achievement Place: Experiments in self-government with pre-delinquents. *Journal of Applied Behavior Analysis*, 1973, **6**, 31–48.

Franks, C. M. Conditioning and abnormal behaviour. In H. J. Eysenck (Ed.), *Handbook of abnormal psychology*. New York: Basic Books, 1960.

Franks, C. M. Alcoholism. In C. G. Costello (Ed.), *Symptoms of psychopathology*. New York: Wiley, 1970.

Franks, C. M., & Wilson, G. T. (Eds.), *Annual review of behavior therapy*. New York: Brunner/Mazel, 1974.

Freeman, T. A psychoanalytic critique of behavior therapy. *British Journal of Medicine and Psychology*, 1968, **41**, 53–59.

Freund, K. Some problems in the treatment of homosexuality. In H. J. Eysenck (Ed.), *Behaviour therapy and the neuroses*. London: Pergamon Press, 1960.

Friedman, D. E., & Lipsedge, M. S. Treatment of phobic anxiety and psychogenic impotence by systematic desensitization employing methohexitone-induced relaxation. *British Journal of Psychiatry*, 1971, **118**, 87–90.

Garcia, E. The training and generalization of a conversational speech form in nonverbal retardates. *Journal of Applied Behavior Analysis*, 1974, **7**, 137—149.

Garlington, W. K., & Cotler, S. B. Systematic desensitization of test anxiety. *Behaviour Research and Therapy*, 1968, **6**, 247–256.

Giffin, M. W., Johnson, A. M., & Litin, E. M. Antisocial acting out: 2. Specific factors determining antisocial acting out. *American Journal of Orthopsychiatry*, 1954, **24**, 668–684.

Gordon, S. Unpublished manuscript, Rutgers University, 1975.

Gormezano, I., & Coleman, S. R. The law of effect and CR contingent modifications of the USC. *Conditional Reflex*, 1973, **8**, 41–56.

Gotestam, K. D., & Melin, L. Covert extinction of amphetamine addiction. *Behavior Therapy*, 1974, **5**, 90–92.

Guess, D., & Baer, D. M. An analysis of individual differences in generalization between receptive and productive language in retarded children. *Journal of Applied Behavior Analysis*, 1973, **6**, 311–329.

Hake, D. F., Vukelich, R., & Kaplan, S. J. Audit responses: Responses maintained by access to existing self or coactor scores during non-social, parallel work, and cooperation procedures. *Journal of Experimental Analysis of Behavior*, 1973, **19**, 409–423.

Haynes, S. N., & Geddy, P. Suppression of psychotic hallucinations through timeout. *Behavior Therapy*, 1973, **4**, 123–127.

Henderson, J. D., & Scoles, P. E. Conditioning techniques in a community-based operant environment for psychotic men. *Behavior Therapy*, 1970, **1**, 245–251.

Hersen, M., Eisler, R. M., Alford, G. S., & Agras, W. S. Effects of token economy on neurotic depression: An experimental analysis. *Behavior Therapy*, 1973, **4**, 392–397.

Holmes, F. B. An experimental investigation of a method of overcoming children's fears. *Child Development*, 1936, **7**, 6–30.

Holzinger, R., Mortimer, R., & Van Dusen, W. Aversion conditioning treatment of alcoholism. *American Journal of Psychiatry*, 1967, **124**, 246–247.

Huber, H., Karlin, R. A., & Nathan, P. E. Blood alcohol level discrimination in normals: Role of internal and external cues. Unpublished manuscript, Rutgers University, 1975.

Hull, C. L. *Principles of behavior*. New York: Appleton, 1943.

Hyman, E. T., & Gale, E. N. Galvanic skin response and reported anxiety during systematic desensitization. *Journal of Consulting and Clinical Psychology*, 1973, **40**, 108–114.

Jackson, B. Treatment of depression by self-reinforcement. *Behavior Therapy*, 1972, **3**, 298–307.

Jacobson, E. *Self-operations control*. New York: Lippincott, 1964.

Jacobson, J., Buschell, D., & Risley, T. Switching requirements in a Head Start classroom. *Journal of Applied Behavior Analysis*, 1969, **2**, 43–47.

Jessor, R., & Jessor, S. L. Problem drinking in youth: Personality, social, and behavioral antecedents and correlates. Boulder, Colo.: Institute of Behavioral Science, 1973.

Jones, H. E. The conditioning of overt emotional responses. *Journal of Educational Psychology*, 1931, **22**, 127–130.

Kanfer, F. H. Self-regulation: Research, issues and speculations. In C. Neuringer & J. L. Michael (Eds.), *Behavior modification in clinical psychology*. New York: Appleton-Century-Crofts, 1970.

Kanfer, F. H. Self-monitoring: Methodological limitations and clinical applications. *Journal of Consulting and Clinical Psychology*, 1970, **35**, 148–152.

Kanfer, F. H., & Karoly, P. Self-control: A behavioristic excursion into the lion's den. *Behavior Therapy*, 1972, **3**, 398–416.

Kaufman, K. F., & O'Leary, K. D. Reward, cost, and self-evaluation procedures for disruptive adolescents in a psychiatric hospital school. *Journal of Applied Behavioral Analysis*, 1972, **5**, 293–310.

Kazdin, A. E. Covert modeling and the reduction of avoidance behavior. *Journal of Abnormal Psychology*, 1973, **81**, 87–95.

Kazdin, A. E., & Bootzin, R. R. The token economy: An evaluative review. *Journal of Applied Behavior Analysis*, 1972, **5**, 343–372.

Kimmel, H. D. Reflex habituality as a basis for differentiating between classical and instrumental conditioning. *Conditional Reflex*, 1973, **8**, 10–27.

Kohlenberg, R. J. Treatment of a homosexual pedophiliac using *in vivo* desensitization: A case study. *Journal of Abnormal Psychology*, 1974, **83**, 192–195.

Kondas, O., & Scetnicka, B. Systematic desensitization as a method of preparation for childbirth. *Journal of Behavior Therapy and Experimental Psychiatry*, 1972, **3**, 51–54.

Kozloff, M. *Reaching the autistic child: A parent training program*. Champaign, Ill.: Research Press, 1973.

Kraft, T., & Al-Issa, I. The use of methohexitone sodium in the systematic desensitization of premature ejaculation. *British Journal of Psychiatry*, 1968, **114**, 351–352.

Krasner, L. Behavior therapy. *Annual Review of Psychology*, 1971, **22**, 483–532.

Lang, P. J. Stimulus control, response control, and the desensitization of fear. In D. J. Levis (Ed.), *Learning approaches to therapeutic behavior change*. Chicago: Aldine, 1970.

Lazarus, A. A. The treatment of chronic frigidity by systematic desensitization. *Journal of Nervous and Mental Disease*, 1963, **136**, 272–278.

Lazarus, A. A. Learning theory and the treatment of depression. *Behaviour Research and Therapy*, 1968, **6**, 83–90.

Lazarus, A. A. *Behavior therapy and beyond.* New York: McGraw-Hill, 1971. (a)

Lazarus, A. A. Behavioral therapy for sexual problems. *Professional Psychology*, 1971, 349–353. (b)

Lazarus, A. A. Multimodal behavior therapy: Treating the "basic id." *Journal of Nervous and Mental Disease*, 1973, **156**, 404–411.

Lazarus, A. A. Multimodal therapy: "Basic id." *Psychology Today*, 1974, **7**, 59–64. (a)

Lazarus, A. Multimodal behavioral treatment of depression. *Behavior Therapy*, 1974, **5**, 549–554. (b)

Lazarus, A. A., & Abramovitz, A. The use of "emotive imagery" in the treatment of children's phobias. *Journal of Mental Science*, 1962, **108**, 191–195.

Lazarus, A. A., Davison, G., & Poletky, K. Classical and operant factors in the treatment of school phobia. *Journal of Abnormal Psychology*, 1965, **70**, 285–289.

Leitenberg, H. Positive reinforcement and extinction. In W. S. Agras (Ed.), *Behavior modification: Principles and clinical applications.* Boston: Little, Brown, 1972.

Leitenberg, H. The use of single-case methodology in psychotherapy research. *Journal of Abnormal Psychology*, 1973, **82**, 87–101.

Leitenberg, H., Agras, S., Butz, R., & Wincze, J. Relationship between heart rate and behavioral change during the treatment of phobias. *Journal of Abnormal Psychology*, 1971, **78**, 59–68.

Leitenberg, H., Agras, W. S., & Thomson, L. E. A sequential analysis of the effect of selective positive reinforcement in modifying anorexia nervosa. *Behaviour Research and Therapy*, 1968, **6**, 211–218.

Leitenberg, H., Agras, W. S., Thomson, L. E., & Wright, D. E. Feedback in behavior modification: An experimental analysis in two phobic cases. *Journal of Applied Behavior Analysis*, 1968, **1**, 131–137.

LeLaurin, K., & Risley, T. The organization of day-care environments: "Zone" versus "man to man" staff assignments. *Journal of Applied Behavior Analysis*, 1972, **5**, 225–232.

Lesser, E. Behavior therapy with a narcotics user: A case report. *Behaviour Research and Therapy*, 1967, **5**, 251–252.

Lewinsohn, P. M. Clinical and theoretical aspects of depression. In K. S. Calhoun, H. E. Adams, & K. M. Mitchell (Eds.), *Innovative treatment methods in psychopathology.* New York: Wiley, 1974.

Lewinsohn, P. M., & Libet, J. Pleasant events, activity schedules, and depressions. *Journal of Abnormal Psychology*, 1972, **79**, 291–295.

Lewinsohn, P. M., & Shaffer, M. Use of home observations as an integral part of the treatment of depression. *Journal of Consulting and Clinical Psychology,* 1971, **37,** 87–94.

Lewinsohn, P. M., & Shaw, D. A. Feedback about interpersonal behavior as an agent of behavior change: A case study in the treatment of depression. *Psychotherapy and Psychosomatics,* 1969, **17,** 82–88.

Liberman, R. P. Aversive conditioning of drug addicts: A pilot study. *Behaviour Research and Therapy,* 1968, **6,** 229–231.

Liberman, R. P., Teigen, J. R., Patterson, R., & Baker, V. Reducing delusional speech in chronic, paranoid schizophrenics. *Journal of Applied Behavior Analysis,* 1973, **6,** 57–64.

Lidz, T., Cornelison, A. R., Fleck, S., & Terry, D. The intrafamilial environment of the schizophrenic patient: I. The father. *Psychiatry,* 1957, **20,** 329–342. (a)

Lidz, T., Cornelison, A. R., Fleck, S., & Terry, D. The intrafamilial environment of schizophrenic patients: II. Marital schism and marital skew. *American Journal of Psychiatry,* 1957, **114,** 241–248. (b)

Lindsley, O. R. Operant conditioning methods applied to research in chronic schizophrenia. *Psychiatric Research Report,* 1956, **5,** 118–139.

Lisman, S. A. Alcoholic "blackout": State-dependent learning? *Archives of General Psychiatry,* 1974, **30,** 46–53.

Lomont, J. F., & Brock, L. Stimulus hierarchy generalization in systematic desensitization. *Behaviour Research and Therapy,* 1971, **9,** 197–208.

London, P. The end of ideology in behavior modification. *American Psychologist,* 1972, **27,** 913–920.

Lovaas, O. I., Berberich, J., Perloff, B., & Schaeffer, B. Acquisition of imitative speech by schizophrenic children. *Science,* 1966, **151,** 705–707.

Lovaas, O. I., Schaeffer, B., & Simmons, J. Building social behavior in autistic children by the use of electric shocks. *Journal of Experimental Research in Personality,* 1965, **1,** 99–109.

Lovaas, O. I., & Simmons, J. Q. Manipulation of self-destruction in three retarded children. *Journal of Applied Behavior Analysis,* 1969, **2,** 143–157.

Lovibond, S. H. Aversive control of behavior. *Behavior Therapy,* 1970, **1,** 80–91.

Lovibond, S. H., & Caddy, G. Discriminated aversive control in the moderation of alcoholic drinking behavior. *Behavior Therapy,* 1970, **1,** 437–444.

Lovibond, S., & Coote, M. Enuresis. In C. Costello (Ed.), *Symptoms of psychopathology.* New York: Wiley, 1970.

Lovitt, T. C., & Curtiss, K. Academic response rate as a function of teacher- and self-imposed contingencies. *Journal of Applied Behavior Analysis,* 1969, **2,** 49–53.

MacCulloch, M. J., Feldman, M. P., Orford, J. F., & MacCulloch, M. L. Anticipatory avoidance learning in the treatment of alcoholism: A record of therapeutic failure. *Behaviour Research and Therapy,* 1966, **4,** 187–196.

MacDonough, T. S. A critique of the first Feldman and MacCulloch avoidance conditioning treatment for homosexuals. *Behavior Therapy,* 1972, **3,** 104–111.

Mahoney, M. J. The self-management of covert behavior: A case study. *Behavior Therapy,* 1971, **2,** 575–578.

Mahoney, M. J. Research issues in self-management. *Behavior Therapy,* 1972, **3,** 45–63.

Mahoney, M. J. Self-reward and self-monitoring techniques for weight control. *Behavior Therapy,* 1974, **5,** 48–57.

Mahoney, M. J. & Craighead, B. K. Self-control techniques in behavior modification with the mentally retarded. Paper presented at the meeting of the American Association on Mental Deficiency, Atlanta, June, 1973.

Marks, I. M., & Gelder, M. G. Controlled trials in behaviour therapy. In R. Porter (Ed.), *The role of learning in psychotherapy.* London: Churchill, 1968.

Marquis, J. N. Orgasmic reconditioning: Changing sexual object choice through controlling masturbation fantasies. *Behavior Therapy and Experimental Psychiatry,* 1970, **1,** 263–271.

Martin, J. A., & Iagulli, D. M. Elimination of middle-of-the-night tantrums in a blind, retarded child. *Behavior Therapy,* 1974, **5,** 420–422.

Masters, W. H., & Johnson, V. E. *Human sexual inadequacy.* Boston: Little, Brown, 1970.

Max, L. W. Breaking up a homosexual fixation by the conditional reaction technique. A case study. *Psychological Bulletin,* 1935, **32,** 734.

McGuire, R. J., Carlisle, J. M., & Young, B. G. Sexual deviations as conditioned behavior: A hypothesis. *Behaviour Research and Therapy,* 1965, **2,** 185–190.

McMillan, D. E. Drugs and punished responding. I: Rate dependent effects under multiple schedules. *Journal of Experimental Analysis of Behavior,* 1973, **19,** 133–145.

McNamara, J. R., & MacDonough, T. S. Some methodological considerations in the design and implementation of behavior therapy research. *Behavior Therapy,* 1972, **3,** 361–378.

Merbaum, M. The modification of self-destructive behavior by a mother-therapist using aversive stimulation. *Behavior Therapy,* 1973, **4,** 442–447.

Miller, L., Barrett, C., Hampe, E., & Noble, H. Comparison of reciprocal inhibition, psychotherapy, and waiting list control for phobic children. *Journal of Abnormal Psychology,* 1972, **79,** 269–279.

Miller, P. M., & Hersen, M. Quantitative changes in alcohol consumption as a function of electrical aversive conditioning. *Journal of Clinical Psychology,* 1972, **28,** 590–593.

Mischel, W., & Liebert, R. M. Effects of discrepancies between observed and imposed reward criteria on their acquisition and transmission. *Journal of Personality and Social Psychology,* 1966, **3,** 45–53.

Morganstern, K. P. Implosive therapy and flooding procedures: A critical review. *Psychological Bulletin*, 1973, **79**, 318–334.

Morse, W. H. Intermittent reinforcement. In W. K. Honig (Ed.), *Operant behavior: Areas of research and application*. New York: Appleton-Century-Crofts, 1966.

Mowrer, O., & Mowrer, W. Enuresis: A method for its study and treatment. *American Journal of Orthopsychiatry*, 1938, **8**, 436–449.

Musick, J., & Luckey, R. A token economy for moderately and severely retarded. *Mental Retardation*, 1970, **8**, 35–36.

Nathan, P. E., Goldman, M. S., Lisman, S. A., & Taylor, H. A. Alcohol and alcoholics: A behavioral approach. *Transactions of the New York Academy of Science*, 1972, **34**, 602–627.

Nathan, P. E., & O'Brien, J. S. An experimental analysis of the behavior of alcoholics and nonalcoholics during prolonged experimental drinking: A necessary precursor of behavior therapy? *Behavior Therapy*, 1971, **2**, 455–476.

Nathan, P. E., Robertson, P., & Andberg, M. M. A systems analytic model of diagnosis: IV. The diagnostic validity of abnormal affective behavior. *Journal of Clinical Psychology*, 1969, **25**, 235–242.

Nathan, P. E., Samaraweera, A., Andberg, M. M., & Patch, V. D. Syndromes of psychosis and psychoneurosis. *Archives of General Psychiatry*, 1968, **19**, 704–716.

Nathan, P. E., Simpson, H. F., Andberg, M. M., & Patch, V. D. A systems analytic model of diagnosis: III. The diagnostic validity of abnormal cognitive behavior. *Journal of Clinical Psychology*, 1969, **25**, 120–130.

Neuhaus, E. Training the mentally retarded for competitive employment. *Exceptional Children*, 1967, **33**, 625–628.

Ney, P., Palvesky, A., & Markley, J. Relative effectiveness of operant conditioning and play therapy in childhood schizophrenia. *Journal of Autism and Childhood Schizophrenia*, 1971, **1**, 337–349.

O'Brien, J. S., Raynes, A. E., & Patch, V. D. Treatment of heroin addiction with aversion therapy, relaxation training and systematic desensitization. *Behaviour Research and Therapy*, 1972, **10**, 77–80.

Okulitch, P. V., & Marlatt, G. A. Effects of varied extinction conditions with alcoholics and social drinkers. *Journal of Abnormal Psychology*, 1972, **9**, 205–211.

O'Leary, K. D. Behavior modification in the classroom: A rejoinder to Winett and Winkler. *Journal of Applied Behavior Analysis*, 1972, **5**, 505–510.

O'Leary, K. D., & O'Leary, S. G. (Eds.), *Classroom management: The successful use of behavior modification*. New York: Pergamon Press, 1972.

O'Leary, K. D., O'Leary, S., & Becker, W. C. Modification of a deviant sibling interaction pattern in the home. *Behaviour Research and Therapy*, 1967, **5**, 113–120.

Paul, G. L. Outcome of systematic desensitization. I. Background, procedures, and uncontrolled reports of individual treatment. In C. M. Franks (Ed.), *Behavior therapy: Appraisal and status.* New York: McGraw-Hill, 1969, pp. 63–104. (a)

Paul, G. L. Outcome of systematic desensitization. II: Controlled investigations of individual treatment, technique variations and current status. In C. M. Franks (Ed.), *Behavior therapy: Appraisal and status.* New York: McGraw-Hill, 1969, pp. 105–159. (b)

Phillips, E., Fixen, D., & Wolf, M. Achievement Place: Modification of the behaviors of pre-delinquent boys within a token economy. *Journal of Applied Behavior Analysis,* 1971, **4**, 45–59.

Rachman, S., & Teasdale, J. *Aversion therapy and behaviour disorders: An analysis.* Coral Gables, Fla.: University of Miami Press, 1969.

Rackensperger, W., & Feinberg, A. M. Treatment of a severe handwashing compulsion by systematic desensitization: A case report. *Journal of Behavior Therapy and Experimental Psychiatry,* 1972, **3**, 123–128.

Rappaport, J., Gross, T., & Lepper, C. Modeling sensitivity training, and instruction. *Journal of Consulting and Clinical Psychology,* 1973, **40**, 99–107.

Rathus, S. A. An experimental investigation of assertive training in a group setting. *Journal of Behavior Therapy and Experimental Psychiatry,* 1972, **3**, 81–86.

Ravensborg, M. R. An operant conditioning approach to increasing interpersonal awareness among chronic schizophrenics. *Journal of Clinical Psychology,* 1972, **28**, 411–413.

Raymond, M. J. Case of fetishism treated by aversion therapy. *British Medical Journal,* 1956, **2**, 854–857.

Rehm, L. P., & Marston, A. R. Reduction of social anxiety through modification of self-reinforcement. *Journal of Consulting and Clinical Psychology,* 1968, **32**, 565–574.

Rimm, D. C., & Masters, J. C. *Behavior therapy.* New York: Academic Press, 1974.

Risley, T., & Hart, B. Developing correspondence between the non-verbal and verbal behavior of preschool children. *Journal of Applied Behavior Analysis,* 1968, **1**, 267–281.

Risley, T., & Reynolds, N. Emphasis as a prompt for verbal imitation. *Journal of Applied Behavior Analysis,* 1970, **3**, 221–222.

Roberts, C., & Perry, R. A total token economy. *Mental Retardation,* 1970, **8**, 15–18.

Robinson, J. C., & Lewinsohn, P. M. Behavior modification of speech characteristics in a chronically depressed man. *Behavior Therapy,* 1973, **4**, 150–152.

Ross, D. M., Ross, S. A., & Evans, T. A. The modification of extreme social withdrawal by modeling with guided participation. *Journal of Behavior Therapy and Experimental Psychiatry*, 1971, **2**, 273–280.

Rubin, B. K., & Stolz, S. B. Generalization of self-referent speech established in a retarded adolescent by operant procedures. *Behavior Therapy*, 1974, **5**, 93–106.

Sali, J., & Amir, M. Personal factors influencing the retarded person's success at work: A report from Israel. *American Journal of Mental Deficiency*, 1971, **76**, 42–47.

Sanderson, R. E., Campbell, D., & Laverty, S. G. An investigation of a new aversive conditioning treatment for alcoholism. *Quarterly Journal of Studies on Alcohol*, 1963, **24**, 261–275.

Saposnek, D. T., & Watson L. The elimination of the self-destructive behavior of a psychotic child: A case study. *Behavior Therapy*, 1974, **5**, 79–89.

Scharfman, M., & Clark, R. Delinquent adolescent girls. *Archives of General Psychiatry*, 1967, **17**, 441–447.

Schroeder, S. R. Automated transduction of sheltered workshop behaviors. *Journal of Applied Behavior Analysis*, 1972, **5**, 523–525.

Silverstein, C. Behavior modification and the gay community. Paper presented at the Annual Convention of the Association for the Advancement of Behavior Therapy, New York, October, 1972.

Skinner, B. F. *The behavior of organisms*. New York: Appleton-Century-Crofts, 1938.

Smart, R. G., & Fejer, D. Drug use among adolescents and their parents: Closing the generation gap in mood modification. *Journal of Abnormal Psychology*, 1972, **79**, 153–160.

Sobell, M. B., & Sobell, L. C. Individualized behavior therapy for alcoholics. *Behavior Therapy*, 1973, **4**, 49–72.

Stampfl, T. G., & Levis, D. J. Essentials of implosive therapy: A learning-theory-based psychodynamic behavioral therapy. *Journal of Abnormal Psychology*, 1967, **72**, 496–503.

Stampfl, T. G., & Levis, D. J. Implosive therapy: A behavioral therapy? *Behaviour Research and Therapy*, 1968, **6**, 31–36.

Staub, E. The effects of persuasion, modeling, and related influence procedures on delay of reward choices and attitudes. Unpublished doctoral dissertation, Stanford University, 1965.

Stoller, R. J. Transvestites' women. *American Journal of Psychiatry*, 1967, **24**, 333–339.

Sue, D. The role of relaxation in systematic desensitization. *Behaviour Research and Therapy*, 1972, **10**, 153–158.

Tanner, B. A. A case report on the use of relaxation and systematic desensitization to control multiple compulsive behaviors. *Journal of Behavior Therapy and Experimental Psychiatry*, 1971, **2**, 267–272.

Tate, B. G. An automated system for reinforcing and recording retardate work behavior. *Journal of Applied Behavior Analysis,* 1968, **1,** 347–348.

Tate, B. G., & Baroff, G. Training the mentally retarded in the production of a complex product: A demonstration of work potential. *Exceptional Children,* 1967, **33,** 405–408.

Terhune, W. B. Phobic syndrome. Study of 86 patients with phobic reactions. *Archives of Neurology and Psychiatry,* 1949, **62,** 162–172.

Thomson, I. G., & Rathod, N. H. Aversion therapy for heroin dependence. *Lancet,* 1968, **2,** 382–384.

Thorpe, J. G., Schmidt, E., Brown, P. T., & Castell, D. Aversion-relief therapy: A new method for general application. *Behaviour Research and Therapy,* 1964, **2,** 71–82.

Todd, F. J. Coversant control of self-evaluative responses in the treatment of depression: A new use for an old principle. *Behavior Therapy,* 1972, **3,** 91–94.

Ullmann, L., & Krasner, L. *A psychological approach to abnormal behavior.* Englewood Cliffs, N.J.: Prentice-Hall, 1969.

Van Hemel, S. B. Pup retrieving as a reinforcer in nulliparous mice. *Journal of Experimental Analysis of Behavior,* 1973, **19,** 233–238.

Ventis, W. L. Case history: The use of laughter as an alternative response in systematic desensitization. *Behavior Therapy,* 1973, **4,** 120–122.

Voegtlin, W. L., & Lemere, F. The treatment of alcohol addiction: A review of the literature. *Quarterly Journal of Studies on Alcohol,* 1942, **2,** 717–803.

Vogler, R. E., Lunde, S. E., Johnson, G. R., & Martin, P. L. Electrical aversion conditioning with chronic alcoholics. *Journal of Consulting and Clinical Psychology,* 1970, **34,** 302–307.

Wanderer, Z. W. Existential depression treated by desensitization of phobias: Strategy and transcript. *Journal of Behavior Therapy and Experimental Psychiatry,* 1972, **3,** 111–116.

Weinman, B., Gelbart, P., Wallace, M., & Post, M. Inducing assertive behavior in chronic schizophrenics: A comparison of socioenviromental, desensitization, and relaxation therapies. *Journal of Consulting and Clinical Psychology,* 1972, **39,** 246–252.

Werry, J., & Sprague, R. Hyperactivity. In C. Costello (Ed.), *Symptoms of psychopathology.* New York: Wiley, 1970, pp. 397–417.

Whitney, L., & Barnard, K. Implications of operant learning theory for nursing care of the retarded child. *Mental Retardation,* 1966, **4,** 26–29.

Wikler, A. Conditioning factors in opiate addiction and relapse. In D. M. Wilner & G. G. Kassebaum (Eds.), *Narcotics.* New York: McGraw-Hill, 1965, pp. 82–117.

Williams, J. G., Barlow, D. H., & Agras, W. S. Behavioral measurement of severe depression. *Archives of General Psychiatry,* 1972, **27,** 330–333.

Wilson, G. T. Behavior therapy and homosexuality: A critical perspective. Unpublished manuscript, Rutgers University, 1972.

Wilson, G. T. Counterconditioning versus forced exposure in the extinction of avoidance responding and conditioned fear in rats. *Journal of Comparative and Physiological Psychology*, 1973, **82**, 105–114.

Wilson, G. T., & Davison, G. C. Processes of fear reduction in systematic desensitization: Animal studies. *Psychological Bulletin*, 1971, **76**, 1–14.

Wilson, G. T., & Davison, G. C. Behavior therapy and homosexuality: A critical perspective. *Behavior Therapy*, 1974, **5**, 16–29.

Wilson, G. T., Leaf, R. C., & Nathan, P. E. The aversive control of excessive alcohol consumption by chronic alcholics in the laboratory setting. *Journal of Applied Behavior Analysis*, 1975, **8**, 13–26.

Wiltz, N. A., & Paterson, G. R. An evaluation of parent training procedures designed to alter inappropriate aggressive behavior of boys. *Behavior Therapy*, 1974, **5**, 215–221.

Winett, R. A., & Winkler, R. C. Current behavior modification in the classroom: Be still, be quiet, be docile. *Journal of Applied Behavioral Analysis*, 1972, **5**, 499–504.

Wisocki, P. A. The successful treatment of a heroin addict by covert conditioning techniques. *Journal of Behavior Therapy and Experimental Psychiatry*, 1973, **4**, 55–62.

Wolpe, J. Experimental neuroses as learned behavior. *British Journal of Psychology*, 1952, **43**, 243–268.

Wolpe, J. *Psychotherapy by reciprocal inhibition*. Stanford, Calif.: Stanford University Press, 1958.

Wolpe, J. *The practice of behavior therapy*. New York: Pergamon Press, 1969.

Yates, A. J. *Behavior therapy*. New York: Wiley, 1970.

Zigler, E. Familial mental retardation: A continuing dilemma. *Science*, 1967, **155**, 292–298.

CHAPTER 10

Crisis Intervention[1]

JAMES N. BUTCHER AND GAIL R. MAUDAL

Traditional sources of psychological help are frequently unavailable to persons undergoing emotional or situational stress. The following cases illustrate the situation:

One evening Bob, a 24-year-old unemployed male, appeared looking disheveled and quite depressed. He did not maintain eye contact with the interviewer, but mumbled several times that his wife had left him for good and that he was going to kill himself.

Andrea, an attractive 27-year-old woman with "no other place to turn," reported that a week earlier she had been assaulted and almost raped. She was experiencing a great deal of difficulty sleeping, fear at being alone, and morbid ruminations about the incident. She had contacted a mental health center the day after the attempted assault and was given a therapist appointment date about 2 weeks away. She felt like she was "losing control" and could not wait for her appointment.

Esther, a 63-year-old outpatient from a mental health clinic, presented herself one evening complaining that she had had a "breakdown" and could not continue working. She was very agitated, depressed, and mildly confused. She wanted to be hospitalized. She thought she had taken a large number of pills earlier in the evening.

The critical nature of these situations is reflected in the immediacy and urgency of the real-life problems facing each individual, and by the apparent "immobility" or inability of the person to move toward a satisfactory resolution by himself. A crisis situation is one in which an outcome of some sort is inevitable, and prompt, correct action is consequently important. An effective intervention, which is aimed at al-

[1]We gratefully acknowledge the following colleagues for their helpful comments on an earlier version of this chapter: Irving Benoist, A. Jack Hafner, Maria Milillo, Gary Schoener, and Zigfrids Stelmachers.

leviating the crisis or better yet enabling the person to act decisively, may prevent further and perhaps more severe consequences from developing. A timely positive intervention at the point of crisis may prove more effective than many hours of therapy later on.

Justification for the concept of crisis intervention is not difficult to find. Many individuals who are faced with a psychological crisis find traditional hospitals and clinics inaccessible when they are most needed—at the peak of the crisis. Situational crises frequently do not fit into the 9-to-5 working day that has characterized traditional mental health agencies. Similarly, some individuals have experienced rebuff or rejection from the more traditional and usually bureaucratically dominated treatment agencies, which may seem (to a person needing help) more concerned that forms are completed in triplicate than that a problem be heard. Institutions that are establishment-owned and operated may also not be sensitive to or willing to focus on certain human problems, for example, abortion counseling or runaway youths.

Crisis intervention and therapy using volunteer and paraprofessional personnel have been hailed as part of the third revolution in the mental health movement (Tapp & Spanier, 1973), the first two being the theory of the unconscious in the latter part of the nineteenth century and the discovery of the phenothiazines in the 1950s. In the beginning, crisis intervention originated as an attempt to serve unmet treatment needs of individuals, but now it has come into its own—not just as an emergency alternative but as a treatment of choice. The first section of this chapter reviews briefly the origins of crisis intervention, and subsequent sections are addressed to theoretical formulations of crisis intervention, goals of crisis therapy, assessment in crisis therapy, the tactics of crisis therapy, and follow-up and evaluation in crisis therapy.

ORIGINS OF CRISIS INTERVENTION

Treatment of the individual in crisis has several historical sources. In most instances in which emergency therapeutic interventions were initiated, the situation was such as to require immediate action or attention, usually for larger numbers of individuals than could be managed with typical therapeutic means, and generally with little opportunity for obtaining a great deal of personal historical information. Four major historical developments that have contributed to the present-day crisis intervention movement are the treatment of traumatic neuroses in World War II, attention to "grief work," interest in suicide prevention, and the free clinic movement.

Treatment of Traumatic Neuroses in World War II

The upheaval in family relationships and the personally stressful situations brought about by World War II created a great need for expanded psychological services. In order to meet the treatment needs of large numbers of soldiers who experienced stress-related neuroses, new treatment approaches were developed. Short-term treatment of the individual was undertaken as soon as possible after breakdown had occurred, before newly acquired maladaptive patterns of behavior could be consolidated and incorporated into the soldier's total adjustment (Grinker & Spiegel, 1944, 1945; Kardiner, 1941).

In order to prevent a collapse of self-esteem, the individual was kept in his unit and given less stressful duties. These early forms of crisis intervention were highly effective in relieving the symptoms of neurosis and in preventing the individual from retreating into more maladaptive behavioral patterns. They served to underscore one of the tenets of crisis theory, namely, that intervention at the time of disruption is not only effective, but in a sense preventive as well.

Grief Work and the Development of Early Crisis Clinics

The work of Erich Lindemann (1944), in which he described treatment of grief reactions of families of people who died in the Coconut Grove nightclub fire in 1943, is a classic study in crisis intervention. Lindemann compared brief and prolonged grief reactions in individuals and concluded that the duration of the grief reaction was a function of the bereavement process, or how the individual handled the grief. He delineated phases of grief work through which a person must go to free himself from the deceased and readjust to the environment without the presence of the deceased person.

Lindemann's contribution to understanding the normal process of grief and the demonstration that an individual may be helped during the process of grief work established the efficacy of crisis intervention treatment. One of Lindemann's most important formulations for crisis theory was that behavior in a crisis situation is unique—it is related to the crisis situation itself and not to the premorbid personality as postulated by traditional psychiatric practice (Kaplan, 1968). Lindemann described several characteristics associated with stress disorders: (a) they are usually acute in nature, with a specifiable onset and of relatively brief duration; (b) the number of alternative courses of action, whether adaptive or maladaptive, is limited; (c) the possible courses of action are usually identifiable and predictive of outcome; (d) the observable symptoms of stress are usually transitory features of the individual's struggles to overcome his problem situation rather than signs of "mental disorder"; and (e) characteristic psychological tasks posed by each situation are specifiable.

Since Lindemann's work other investigators have studied crises related to bereavement (Kraus & Lilienfeld, 1959; Madison, 1968; Parkes, 1964; Parkes, Benjamin, & Fitzgerald, 1969); transitional states (Tyhurst, 1958); and premature birth (Bibring, Dwyer, Huntington, & Valenstein, 1961; Caplan, 1964; Kaplan & Mason, 1965). These studies have supported Lindemann's theory of transitional pathology associated with crisis states.

The work of Lindemann and his collaborator, Caplan, not only contributed to the theoretical formulation of crisis work, but also influenced the development of the first crisis clinics. These were generally supported by and often attached to existing hospitals or clinics. Caplan began a project on the study of crisis at the Family Guidance Center at Harvard prior to 1954, and other crisis treatment facilities followed shortly in the early 1950s in Galveston (Ritchie, 1960); at Bellak's Trouble-Shooting Clinic in Elmhurst, New York (1958); at the Langley Porter Clinic in San Francisco (Kalis, 1961); at the Benjamin Rush Center in Los Angeles (Jacobson, Wilner, Morley, Schneider, Strickler, & Sommer, 1965); at Cincinnati General Hospital (MacLeod & Tinnin, 1966); and at Massachusetts General Hospital in Boston (Sifneos, 1964).

Suicide Prevention

The crisis of imminent suicide has for a long time occupied the position of being the most visible form of crisis state. Consequently much of the impetus for crisis intervention derived from the suicide prevention movement. In Britain, the "befrienders" or Samaritan Movement was organized in 1953. This group of concerned lay persons set forth the goal of preventing suicide by providing companionship to people who identified themselves as being in crisis (Bagley, 1971). In 1958 the first suicide prevention center was established in Los Angeles (Farberow & Shneidman, 1961). The successful management of suicide-related crises was made possible by some innovative "turning points" which were subsequently incorporated into the crisis intervention movement (Farberow, 1968). These included development of the telephone as the primary means of communicating with people who needed help, the initiation of an around-the-clock and weekend service, and the introduction of nonprofessional personnel into the role of providing direct patient contact (Helig, Farberow, Litman, & Shneidman, 1968).

The Free Clinic Movement

The development of free clinics represents the most recent contribution to the crisis intervention movement, and it provides the primary experiential base from which we have drawn in writing this chapter.

In just the past few years, the mental health scene has witnessed the growth of a large number of nontraditional treatment facilities. The focus of such helping agencies has been to provide crisis management assistance to individuals who would otherwise have no place to go. In several large metropolitan areas, a wide variety of agencies has opened to serve a specific group or problem situation, for example, gay rights, draft counseling, suicide hotlines, drug-related emergencies, venereal disease, and emergency counseling problems. Whereas some of these treatment or referral facilities have been initiated by professionals such as physicians, psychologists, and social workers, a large number of them were begun with the energies of concerned lay persons and students.

It was primarily the antiestablishment reaction accompanying the counterculture movement of the late 1960s that produced great diversity in free clinic innovations. This period of youth revolt against governmental policies in Viet Nam and of wide utilization and experimentation with drugs, particularly hallucinogens, produced not only a high level of tension and maladaptive life-style options, but also an acute mistrust for anything resembling authority or establishment. A large segment of the United States population was in the vulnerable position of being at high risk for developing psychological problems, but at the same time had no access to sources of help since establishment agencies were considered unsympathetic to their problems.

The philosophy of the free clinic movement is:

. . . that "free" is a state of mind, rather than an economic term. Characteristics of the free clinic philosophy are: health care is a right rather than a privilege; no proof of financial need is required, thus differentiating free clinics from charity facilities; a minimum of red tape is implied; and conventional labels and value systems applied to individuals who may be regarded as "deviant" by the general society are disregarded. No fee, no patronizing, and no moralizing on the staff's part are essential components of the free clinic philosophy [National Clearing House for Drug Abuse Information, 1974]

A primary value of the free clinics was to provide a nonestablishment staff who spoke the language and shared the values of the counselee

(Freudenberger, 1972; Smith, Luce, & Dernburg, 1970). This situation fostered the development of several free clinics across the country, which revolutionized thinking about the treatment and delivery of mental health services.[2] Free clinics introduced "rap sessions" in which "street people" came together at the facility without registering or otherwise identifying themselves. They became involved in group discussions which kept them together but did not make them "straight." Such self-treatment, at what was almost a mutual aid society for youth, was often all the help that was needed, but it sometimes served as a stepping stone into more systematic group or individual therapy.

Some free clinic facilities obtained sufficient community support to continue. For example, the Waikiki Drug Clinic and Huckleberrys for Runaways have grown into operations with large budgets running into many hundreds of thousands of dollars. Others, however, operated for a brief period of time and then closed down. In fact, in the Minneapolis–St. Paul area, 30 youth resource agencies closed down between 1973 and 1974. There were many reasons for the short life of some nontraditional agencies, including financial problems, personnel who did not maintain a sustained interest after the novelty wore off (Eisenberg, 1972), or target groups that no longer needed services, for example, draft evaders.

In spite of their difficulties, free clinics have been an important treatment development. In many communities, they have survived their troubled childhood and seem to be finding more stability and even respect from the same establishment whose insensitivity to changing times fostered their origin. The extent of this innovative clinic movement has been great, and the diversity in services rendered has been impressive.

One problem that still confronts the free clinic movement is that it has not completely achieved its goal of reaching unserved populations. Many free clinics were started with the hope of providing treatment for minority and poor people, and thus they were located in neighborhoods that were predominantly black, Puerto Rican, Indian, and Mexican. Although free clinics do provide services that many minority people need (especially medical clinics) (Health/PAC Bulletin, No. 34, October

[2]The recency of the free clinic movement is shown by two surveys of free clinics. Schwartz (1971) surveyed 30 medically oriented clinics opened between 1967 and 1969 to provide medical and counseling services and to deal with the increased drug problems among young people. A more recent survey by Freudenberger and Freudenberger (1973) indicated that 31 of 58 responding clinics had opened since January 1969, and that new clinics are being started at the rate of about 20 to 30 a year. Since the first free clinic was started in 1967 to serve alienated youth in San Francisco, over 250 free clinics have been opened, offering services to over 2 million patients each year (National Clearing House for Drug Abuse Information, 1974).

1971), available studies show that the free clinic movement, both in terms of its originators and the population it serves, is still essentially a white middle-class movement. One recent survey of an Indian community in Minnesota found that psychological resources were not considered to be among the most pressing "needs." Rather, housing, clothing, food, medical care, and education were considered the more critical problems requiring attention (Bloomfield, Levy, Kotelchuck, & Handelman, 1971). Stoeckle, Anderson, Page, and Brenner (1971) report that

Those clinics intending to serve diverse clients often do not. For example, the Black Man's Free Clinic (San Francisco) and the Cambridgeport Medical Clinic were both meant to serve local black residents as well as youth. However, they had more use by the white youth in their districts [p. 131]

Two recent reports (Freudenberger & Freudenberger, 1973; Schoener, 1972) suggest that, although free clinics are not reaching their original target population, they nevertheless still provide a needed source of psychological assistance for many individuals who feel that no other agencies could help them. It should also be noted that adequate funding for free clinics has been a problem from the beginning. Only one of the 58 clinics surveyed by Freudenberger and Freudenberger was started through a federal grant. Most clinics began with extremely limited funds, often just a few small donations, and subsequently limped along with fund-raising activities as varied as panhandling, opening hot dog stands, and sponsoring rock concerts. In more recent times, fortunately, many of the stable and well-run free clinics have been able to obtain broader community support, including funds from various federal and state government agencies (NIMH, LEAA, etc.). Many of these clinics have consequently flourished and have been able to compete with the more traditional health delivery programs for continuing operating funds. This development may to some extent support a conviction that many psychologists associated with free clinics have had for some time—that the "walk-in type" free clinic provides a valuable alternative to the present medical delivery system model. Stoeckle, Anderson, Page, and Brenner (1971) make the following apt observation:

While community health systems were planned, 100 million dollars spent on health centers and "free care" through national insurance debated, the free clinic movement began. Unplanned and left out of planning, supported only by volunteer work and sporadically by private funds and patient donations, community-based medical clinics scattered throughout the country have actually opened and provided "free care" [p. 127]

In summary, the articulation of crisis intervention methods and theory has stemmed from various originating sources. It would be incorrect to assume that the evolution has been a smooth or natural one. Yet despite its diverse origins and the inherent difficulties with any novel approach to human problem solving, crisis intervention therapy has established itself as a viable, useful vehicle of intervention. What began as an expedient, pressed on us because of varying external circumstances, has generated unanticipated and gratifying benefits. Today crisis work is no longer seen as a last alternative, far inferior to reconstructive, uncovering long-term treatment; it is looked at instead as a legitimate treatment alternative and even as the treatment of choice for certain kinds of problems and certain types of patients: "Crisis intervention is not a second-class psychotherapy, but a unique form of intervention, based on its own unique assumptions" (Goldenberg, 1973, p.350).

THEORETICAL FORMULATIONS OF CRISIS INTERVENTION

The theoretical formulation of crisis intervention was primarily the contribution of Gerald Caplan and derived from his work with Erich Lindemann at the Community Mental Health Project in Cambridge, Massachusetts (see Caplan, 1964). Crisis theory centers around the concept of a homeostatic equilibrium in which the individual is in a relative state of psychosocial balance. That is, his usual coping or adaptive techniques are operating sufficiently to handle his daily problems. When difficult problem situations present themselves, the individual calls into play the mechanisms that have worked successfully in previous situations. A crisis situation occurs, according to Caplan (1961), "when a person faces an obstacle to important life goals that is, for a time, insurmountable through the utilization of customary methods of problem solving." The obstacle may result in an emotionally hazardous situation when the individual perceives a potentially unmanageable threat surrounding it. The crisis is an internally experienced, acute disturbance resulting from the individual's inability to cope with ominous events encompassing him.

The crisis is usually followed by a period of disorganization and confusion, resulting in generally ineffective attempts at problem solution. In time, usually about 4–6 weeks according to Caplan, some outcome to the crisis situation (for better or worse) has been reached. This outcome can be positively directed with timely and effective crisis intervention techniques, and the individual at this point in a crisis situation is highly amenable to therapeutic intervention.

Caplan (1964) delineated four phases of a typical crisis situation.

When the crisis begins to develop and the individual feels the emotional tension and disorganization, he attempts to manage the situation by his previously learned coping mechanisms. In the second phase these coping efforts fail to resolve the problem, and further disorganization ensues. The third phase is characterized by a greatly increased tension level and further mobilization of internal and outside resources. The person may seek help or change his direction or goals. If these intensified efforts fail to resolve the crisis and lower the tension, then the fourth phase of crisis develops—extensive personality disorganization and perhaps emotional breakdown.

Crisis Intervention versus Crisis Therapy

One of the primary functions of many crisis centers has been to handle cases that do not readily fit into the more traditional mental health offerings. Although formal "treatment" of people in crisis is a relatively new professional endeavor, it has become apparent that not all emotional crises are of the same type and magnitude, and thus cannot be managed in the same way. Each situation requires careful evaluation to determine what form of intervention is needed and what kinds of outcomes can be expected.

Jacobson, Strickler, and Morley (1968) and Morley (1970) describe four levels of crisis intervention, all of which are considered effective. The first level is called *environmental manipulation*. At this level the helper serves as a referral source or puts the troubled person in touch with an appropriate resource. The second level, termed *general support*, involves working in a limited way with the troubled person—interested listening without threatening or challenging his statements. The third level, characteristic of Caplan's approach, Morley calls the *generic approach*. "This level requires that the helping agent have a thorough knowledge of crisis in general, specific crises in particular, and kinds of approaches which are particularly effective in resolving specific crises." The fourth level is called *individually tailored,* and it requires in addition to the specification of the first three levels that the crisis worker be trained in abnormal psychology and personality theory and have a thorough knowledge of psychodynamics. The intervention on this level assumes that the crisis is related to the individual's long-term personality dynamics.

For the purposes of this chapter, we distinguish between two types of crisis problem that appear at crisis centers or walk-in clinics: "dispositional crisis" cases and "crisis therapy" cases. This distinction will prove useful to the intake worker who is faced with the decision of evaluating for referral or further treatment. The following two cases illustrate some elements of the first general type of crisis problem.

Mary, a 31-year-old separated mother, called regarding a custody fight following an argument with her estranged husband. He refused to bring their 2-year-old child back after a visit. Following an interview, it became apparent that Mary was angry and frightened but generally well-functioning. She did not desire or require counseling regarding her life situation. Instead, the conflict she was faced with was a legal one. She was referred to legal aid and a follow-up was conducted to assure that the referral was successful.

An elderly woman was brought to the center by the police after they found her sitting on a curb in −20° weather. She was pleasant and smiling, but couldn't supply any information about herself. Nearby nursing homes were contacted to determine if they had "lost" anyone. The home was located and the police returned her. Follow-up indicated that she was receiving medical attention.

These cases represent dispositional crises. They illustrate the point that not all crises are psychological in nature. Neither Mary nor the elderly woman required nor stood to gain from crisis therapy. However, well-timed intervention may have prevented these crises from developing into ones that would have had more serious consequences.

It is useful, then, to draw a distinction between what might be called "crisis intervention" and what is termed "crisis therapy." This distinction somewhat parallels Bloom's (1963) distinction between a stressful situation and a crisis. Bloom notes that "crisis differs from stress in that there are time limits to a crisis, but, in general, acute stress is a crisis." The distinction is more clearly expressed through Klein and Lindemann's (1961) definitions of an "emotionally hazardous situation" and a "crisis." They define an emotionally hazardous situation as "a situation in which a sudden change in the field of social forces causes a person's relations with others, or his expectations of himself, to change." Crisis is "a term reserved for the acute, and often prolonged disturbance to an individual or to a social orbit as the result of an emotionally hazardous situation."

One theoretical consideration that helps clarify this distinction is the amount of ego investment a person has in a potential crisis situation. An individual's perceptions of events are "autistic," in the sense that they are highly influenced by his personal needs and values. If a person is "needy," requiring much outside support to sustain his quota of self-esteem, even a mildly stressful situation may plunge him into a crisis. Conversely, if a person is relatively need-free and has a healthy self-concept, even highly stressful situations may not represent a blow to his self-esteem. Strickler and Allgeyer (1967) view crises as occurring "only if the individual senses that he does not possess available means of coping with the hazard, which is seen consciously or unconsciously as a vital threat to his narcissistic, libidinal or dependency needs and supplies." In such cases crisis therapy is indicated. The person is encouraged to focus on the factors that precipitated the crisis and to explore new, potentially adaptive means of handling it. If a person's ability to cope is not threatened by a stressful situation, he is a candidate for crisis intervention, but not crisis therapy. The goal is not restoration of a psychic homeostasis, since the balance has not been upset. Instead the goal is that of adroit dispositional management, that is, meeting the nonpsychological needs of the situation. This can involve something as simple as locating a person a bed for the night, or something as complex as providing information about state commitment procedures.

The role of crisis interveners, although perhaps less glamorous than that of crisis therapists, should not be relegated to the status of second-class citizenship. Although the eventual disposition may be simple and clear-cut, the disposition results only after the crisis intervener has made a sufficiently thorough assessment of the stress situation to determine that the crisis is not psychological in nature, or that the stress is perceived as ego-alien in origin and not part of the person's own doing.

An assessment error illustrates this point. One crisis worker saw a 19-year-old male who complained that he suffered from flashbacks. He had taken LSD 9 months previously. Proceeding on the assumption that he was dealing with a typical flashback case, the crisis worker assured the youth that his symptoms were anxiety-related and would soon dissipate. He sent him home after encouraging him to call if difficulties persisted. Only in later case supervision did the crisis worker indicate that the flashbacks were periods during which the patient heard voices telling him he was the devil. Additionally, the patient was umemployed and was a "culture dropout" who strongly identified with the "Jesus freak" movement. Although none of these facts is pathognomonic in itself, together they are at least cause for concern and adequate basis for further assessment, probably entailing something more than dispositional management. It is important to note that the role of astute assessment is not only the first phase of crisis therapy, but constitutes an important part of every case, whether the clinician's response is eventually designated crisis intervention or crisis therapy.

Is a crisis situation always easy to identify? Golan (1969) noted that, although a worker sometimes encounters patients with clear-cut presenting problems, more often he faces an "undifferentiated, multifaceted problem situation" which is difficult to conceptualize. The components of a crisis situation defined by Sifneos (1960) provide a useful framework for conceptualizing crisis situations. He identified four elements in an emotional crisis: the hazardous event, the vulnerable state, the precipitating factor, and the state of crisis itself.

By what practical criteria might we distinguish between crisis intervention cases and crisis therapy cases? It is of course not possible to specify guidelines that would be applicable for every crisis intervention center, since particular staffing situations and typical presenting problems dictate treatment and referral policies. Nevertheless, it is important to recognize that there are factors that are relevant for deciding which cases should be seen in additional therapy sessions by a trained therapist and which cases may be terminated after an initial contact, with or without some provision for follow-up.

In most crisis intervention settings, time and staff resources limit the number of sessions an individual may be seen. However, the point we would like to make is that it is neither necessary nor desirable to see most cases for an extended period of time. Thus the prime consideration involves determining whether a limited, directive intervention, for example, finding the person a place to stay, getting a previously made decision crystallized, and the like, will restore the individual's adjustment to a previous satisfactory level. The essential consideration for continuing an individual in therapy is some determination that he or she may benefit from an extended number of sessions and the accompanying relationship with a therapist. This is a complex decision which must be made jointly by therapist and client on the basis of such factors as the following:

1. *Workability*. Are the problems such as to be manageable with the temporary aid of an outside opinion? That is, are the problems in large part internal and within the power of the individual to resolve?

2. *Capability of self-examination*. Does the individual have the ability to examine with the therapist the problem situation in the light of his own contribution to the crisis?

3. *Motivation*. Does the person have the motivation or personal resources to act on his or her own decision? Can he accept direction from a therapist? What action has he taken thus far to resolve the problems?

4. *Accessibility*. Is he presently in therapy elsewhere? In many instances a crisis patient may be in therapy elsewhere, which generally contraindicates setting up a new therapeutic contract.

5. *Advisability in terms of personality structure*. Would a therapeutic relationship (which is inherently directive in nature) be detrimental to the person's future adjustment? It may be that seeing the individual for a longer period of time would serve to define him as a "patient" who *needs* a lot of help from others—this may foster negative self-attitudes, which are an undesirable outcome of the intervention. Fostering depen-

dency in a person who prides himself on being "strong" may result in problems worse than those for which he originally sought help.

6. *Treatment history*. It is important to explore the patient's past therapeutic experience, both qualitatively and quantitatively. This can be an especially useful variable in helping the therapist determine if crisis therapy is indicated. If a patient reveals an extensive history of unsuccessful treatment attempts, one must entertain the hypothesis that he is dealing with a "doctor shopper" who terminates when therapy begins to look like work, or an obsessional intellectualizer who views therapy as an end in itself rather than a means which can be utilized to bring about a desired change. In such cases the therapist does well to scrutinize carefully what the patient's expectations of treatment were, what he tried to accomplish, what worked and did not work, and why.

However, some patients may have legitimately, and in good faith, sought out therapy in the past, and it may be quite reasonable for them to do so again. In these cases it is useful for the therapist to discern whether the current problem is similar in nature to the previous one, what factors helped the patient in the past, and what other resources were utilized to bring about problem resolution.

7. *Cost-benefit*. Would the benefit that might result from utilizing the available staff resources for this particular patient be worth the cost? This is a difficult question to answer (or even to ask ourselves). There are few clear-cut criteria to guide our judgment of potential "gain." More often the limited resources available restrict what we might like to recommend. The crisis therapist or intake interviewer may have to weigh the question before committing future staff time to a specific case.

Requirements of Capable Crisis Intervention

It is apparent that many crisis problems do not require the attention of highly specialized psychotherapists with advanced professional degrees. Many types of problems may be adroitly handled by an informed and attentive lay person. In the last few years paraprofessionals have become increasingly involved in both traditional and nontraditional treatment settings. Part of the impetus for paraprofessional involvement arose from mental health manpower needs, but an equally important stimulus was the dissatisfaction lay people felt toward the traditional therapeutic options. Paraprofessional mental health workers have been recruited from many ranks and strata of the population to perform a variety of therapeutic activities ranging from drug counseling to manning suicide telephones. This lay "therapist" movement has not been unique to the United States. Torrey (1971) reports on the development of emergency psychiatric ambulance services in the U.S.S.R. and, in Britain, a far-reaching suicide prevention system, the Samaritan Movement, was founded in 1953 (Bagley, 1971). There has been a rapid development of Samaritan units in many cities since then. The Samaritans offer day or night service-advice, friendship, and other forms of help. The people operating these units usually have no professional training in therapy but are frequently members of the clergy or intelligent lay persons who have been given some training relevant to the Samaritan work. The goal of the Samaritan work is to help prevent suicide and, according to recent studies in 15 towns where there are Samaritan units, the suicide rate declined by 5.85%, whereas in 15 control towns the rate increased by 15.84% (Bagley, 1971).

In some settings in which paraprofessionals have been utilized as therapists, an almost paradoxical situation is found; paraprofessionals are now assuming the traditional therapy roles they once rejected as narrow or inappropriate. In many instances the paraprofessional steps into this therapist role with very little in the way of traditional training or supervision. It is unfortunate that many paraprofessional groups in the United States have not developed roles or expended their energies in exploring some very unique contributions they might make to mental health work. This is not to imply that paraprofessionals have no useful role in the area of crisis intervention, but rather to suggest that perhaps their full potential and most useful roles have not been fully realized.

In many crisis centers paraprofessionals can provide useful services as crisis interveners, providing they possess or can acquire some skills necessary to the demands of the situation. The following are seen as essential minimum requirements:

1. The worker must possess an empathic ability which enables him to understand the problems being faced by the patient *as* they are being experienced.

2. He must be able to listen attentively and selectively for material relevant to the problem at hand, and to elicit appropriate material from reluctant or verbally-emotionally incapacitated persons.

3. He must be able to listen objectively without imposing his own needs, wishes, and values on the material.

4. He must be able to assess the individual's problems, conflicts, assets, and resources in the context of the crisis situation surrounding him. This requirement is the most important and the least often met. Before the interview is even half over, the crisis worker must have a tentative formulation of the problem, which allows him to determine whether the client is in need of some immediate crisis intervention or perhaps in need of crisis therapy. He must be able to evaluate such

things as premorbid level of functioning, mental status, suicidal potential, and change motivation. Although he need not be a trained psychiatric diagnostician, he must be well versed in the clinical significance of important behaviors or symptoms. Assessment in the initial interview is considered in greater detail in a later section.

5. He must have up-to-date knowledge of the community resources that might be potential referral options, and be aware of various administrative/legal procedures that may be encountered (e.g., categorical assistance qualifications, child abuse legislation, commitment procedures for mental illness, and emancipation rights).

6. One potentially valuable characteristic for the crisis worker is that he or she be a member of the particular subculture or counterculture group that might utilize the agency.

Distinctions between Crisis Therapy and Other Therapeutic Approaches

Crisis therapy can be distinguished from other forms of therapy including psychoanalytic psychotherapy, client-centered therapy, and even many "short-term" therapeutic approaches, on the basis of several variables such as time requirements, therapeutic goals, methods utilized, types of presenting problems, and characteristics of patients seen.[3]

Crisis therapy is generically a form of short-term therapy. Although it is still in the process of being defined and characterized, the broader issue of the legitimacy of short-term versus long-term, or traditional psychoanalytic, treatment is generally settled at this point. Several studies have found no support for the hypothesis that the number of treatment sessions is positively related to amount of therapeutic gain (Lorr, McNair, Michaux, & Raskin, 1962; Muench, 1965; Shlien, Mosak, & Dreikurs, 1962). In a well-controlled study, Shlien, Mosak, and Dreikurs (1962), employing the Q-sort technique, found that imposing time limits on two types of psychotherapy, client-centered and Adlerian, provided more immediate improvement than time-unlimited therapy, all three groups improved eventually, however, whereas no change was observed in a group of normals and a group of patients awaiting treatment. Shlien et al. found that time-limited therapy is not only as effective, but twice as efficient (20 sessions versus 37 sessions) as time-unlimited treatment. Their conclusion was that "time limits place emphasis where it belongs; on quality and process, rather than upon quantity."

[3]For an extended discussion of the distinctions between short-term emergency therapy and other therapeutic approaches, see Aguilera, Messick, and Farrell (1970).

Psychoanalytic Methods and Short-Term Treatment

Crisis and short-term therapy can be readily distinguished from traditional psychoanalysis on the basis of time requirements, since the process of psychoanalysis is generally a lengthy, intrapsychically complicated, and generally nondirective treatment method.[4] Yet many of the principles of psychoanalysis have been applied to short-term therapy. In the late 1930s Alexander (Alexander & French, 1946) conducted several studies in an effort to abbreviate psychoanalytic treatment, that is, to develop techniques of treatment from psychoanalysis that could bring about desired therapeutic results in a shortened time span. He believed that the way for a patient to be relieved of his neurotic conflicts was for him to undergo new emotional experiences that could undo the punishing effects of early (usually childhood) emotional experiences. He noted that emotional adjustment had become a problem for a large proportion of the population, and that "here lies the most vital function of psychotherapy: to give rational aid to all those who show early signs of maladjustment, a flexible approach based on sound principles of psychodynamics and adjustment to the great variety of those in need is therefore a pressing necessity of our day" (Alexander & French, 1946). He pointed out that psychodynamic principles can be used for therapeutic effect regardless of the duration of treatment, whether for just one or two interviews or for several years. More recently other psychoanalytically oriented but short-term approaches to psychotherapy have been published (e.g., Bellak & Small, 1965; Mann, 1973).

There are other factors that differentiate crisis therapy from short-term and traditional psychoanalysis besides length of treatment. Crisis therapy can be distinguished from both according to the characteristics of the presenting problem and the manner in which the problem is treated. The person in crisis, regardless of what his adaptive potential may be, presents himself at a time in life when his adaptive and creative capacities are inadequate to handle the change of input to his system. Phrased simply, something has changed with him so that he has lost a sense of mastery and in desperation is reaching out. He is different from the short-term or traditional long-term patient in that he is currently faced with a perceived (often reality-based) crisis that must be resolved. To understand the crisis and help the person resolve it, the therapist

---

[4]Interestingly, however, even Freud was not opposed to the idea of brief therapy and, in fact, successfully treated the noted conductor Bruno Walter for a neurotic reaction in six sessions (Sterba, 1951). Freud (1919) noted, "It is very probable, too, that the application of our therapy to numbers will compel us to alloy the pure gold of analysis plentifully with the copper of direct suggestion" (pp. 167–168).

begins by actively developing a rapid and clear-cut understanding of the precipitating factor and the personal relevance of that factor for the patient. Strickler and LaSor (1970) note that "without a clear picture of all the elements leading to a crisis, utilization of the crisis intervention model is impossible and the sessions begin to resemble conventional short-term therapy with the focus on pathology, rather than on the crisis itself." Whereas the psychoanalytic and other traditional approaches often deemphasize the focal symptoms and precipitating factors and place major importance on exposing the unconscious conflicts underlying them (Frank, 1966), placing the treatment focus on the precipitating factor is the most salient characteristic of crisis therapy.

Another dimension that distinguishes crisis therapy from traditional short-term psychotherapy is the characteristics of at least part of the patient population. Undoubtedly there is some overlap between the crisis population and the short-term therapy population, in part because anyone can at some time experience a crisis, and also because some people enter other forms of therapy as a result of successful crisis treatment. However, there are subsegments of the crisis population whose only contact with mental health treatment is during periods of crisis. Parad (1966), perhaps provocatively, once suggested that crisis intervention may be most validly applicable for the very strong or the very weak, for those requiring only short periods of help and for those not motivated for continuing services. The "weak" refers to those who have severely limited adaptive capacities resulting from constitutional endowment or pervasive early life experiences, such as the marginally compensated person who resists medication except for brief periods when he is overpowered by symptoms. The motivation for change in this group is limited, and the benefits received from longer contacts probably do not exceed the costs. The "strong" refers in contrast to those who have healthy adaptive potential, but who for a time are faced with nearly insurmountable real-life stress, such as death or financial setback.

Some authors have suggested that certain diagnostic types are particularly amenable or not amenable to crisis intervention therapy. Goldenberg (1973), for example, concludes that the following types are properly classified as psychiatric emergencies and are likely to require and benefit from crisis therapy: (a) severe depressive reactions; (b) acute psychotic states; (c) hyperactive excited states; (d) acute anxiety and panic reactions; (e) acute hysterical reactions; (f) miscellaneous groups of intoxications; (g) severe fear and hysterical manifestations as a result of sexual attack; (h) separation anxiety; (i) fire setting; and (j) grief and bereavement. Hoch (1965) recommends against brief intervention for patients who exhibit chronic psychiatric disorders for which they have never received treatment (e.g., long-standing obsessive compulsive neuroses or chronic psychosomatic reactions), for patients with marked sexual aberrations, and for patients with primary depression; he recommends it as the treatment of choice for anxiety states, hysterical reactions, homosexual panic, and acute psychosomatic disorders. Castelnuovo-Tedesco (1966) indicates that brief treatment does not work if the patient is outspokenly self-centered, passive-dependent, masochistic, or self-destructive.

Wolberg (1965) advocates long-term treatment for patients in the following circumstances: (a) where extensive personality reconstruction is the prime objective; (b) where dependency is so entrenched that prolonged support is essential; (c) where there are persistent and uncontrollable acting-out tendencies, as in some homosexuals, psychopaths, drug addicts, alcoholics, and individuals driven by repressed infantile needs to involve themselves in self-destructive and dangerous activities; and (d) where there is constant and irrestrainable anxiety. However, he recommends short-term treatment for patients in whom the breakdown is of recent origin and whose personality structure and defenses have enabled them to function satisfactorily prior to the present illness; where the goal is a resolution of an acute upset in a chronic personality; and where the goal is reconstruction of personality in cases unsuited for, or who are unable to avail themselves of, long-term therapy, for example, persons who possess strong dependency drives but are able to operate with some degree of independence and may become infantilized by prolonged therapy, or persons with a fragile "ego structure" which may shatter through the use of probing techniques or because of violent transference reactions.

The first two groups of patients that Wolberg considers appropriate for short-term therapy resemble the types of patients we consider appropriate for crisis therapy. Space limitations prevent a more extensive and comprehensive listing of patient characteristics for crisis therapy. Those presented here should serve only as general support for the idea that crisis therapy is not for every patient. Specifically, however, the crisis worker is best advised not to restrict his services along too many predetermined lines. Progress in crisis therapy depends more on the individual's ability and motivation to return to his former level of functioning than on his diagnostic label. Treatment focuses on the crisis itself, rather than on long-standing pathology or well-ingrained character problems. It is also important to remember that channeling a patient into a suitable form of therapy is a proper and often profitable therapeutic endeavor in itself.

One last group for whom crisis therapy has proved useful and for whom it is often the only kind of treatment available includes patients from lower sociocultural groups. Several studies have documented that lower-class persons are less likely than others to be accepted as patients to receive treatment beyond diagnostic workup, and less likely to stay in treatment through the prescribed duration of the therapy, (Brill & Storrow, 1960; Hollingshead & Redlich, 1958; Hunt, 1960; Lief, Lief, Warren, & Heath, 1961; Lorion, 1973, 1974; Rosenthal & Frank, 1958). These studies suggest that even when cost of treatment is not a factor, problems such as bus fares, babysitters, clinic hours, and residential mobility militate against involvement. It has also been suggested that the lower-class person's time perspective is limited, that he has difficulty conceptualizing delay of treatment rewards for lengthy periods, that he encounters an intense transference distortion, and that he does not value (or is less able to engage in) psychotherapeutic contracts in which the principal element is "talk."

Jacobson (1965) makes the following observation in this latter regard:

> The situation is very different when patient and therapist agree to meet around a specific crisis which the patient experiences. Any successful approach to psychotherapy when the therapist and patient are psychosocial strangers must, at least at first, minimize the difference between the persons involved and maximize what unites them. Everyone beyond a certain age has personally experienced the major and minor crisis connected with childhood and adolescence . . . . Since crisis experiences cut across cultural lines, the therapist, on the basis of his own experiences, can achieve empathy with the patient. The patient in turn senses that the therapist is able to respond empathically . . . . In other words, the motivating forces in crisis ontogenetically precede cultural differentiation and thus have universal elements.

Jacobson points out that special advantages are to be gained from crisis therapy for this population because the patient's crisis becomes the deliberate focus of treatment, whereas in many traditional psychiatric clinics this is not the case. The circumscribed nature of the therapy, the major emphasis on action versus "talk cure," and the brevity of the treatment are also likely to decrease the possibility of difficult transference distortions. Empirical studies at the Benjamin Rush Center bear out these ideas (Jacobson, 1965). About 54% of the center's patient population falls into social Classes IV and V, the two lowest classes in the Social Stratification System of Hollingshead and Redlich (1958). No relationship is found at the center between social class and either variables related to the therapeutic process or number of visits, percentages treated, and rating of improvement at termination. Furthermore, by meeting at first on the common ground of crisis, the therapist and client gradually work through the problems of their different backgrounds. One study (Chafitz, 1964) found that patients who are first seen on a walk-in basis are more motivated for longer-term treatment than those who are not.

GOALS OF CRISIS THERAPY

In crisis therapy it is of course necessary to work within the contstraints of some essential compromises. Goals must be somewhat abbreviated, however, we concur with Wolberg (1965) that "once a basic modification has been accomplished, irrespective of how tiny the adaptive equation becomes unbalanced and more substantial alterations can continue." The following four goals, though not exhaustive, provide a useful framework in which the crisis therapist can direct his efforts.

1. *Symptom relief.* "Symptom" refers to any complaint for which the patient seeks treatment (Battle, Imber, Hoehn-Saric, Stone, Nash, & Frank, 1966; Weiss & Schaie, 1964). These may include disturbances of performance or communicative behavior, or states of subjective distress.

Crisis therapy and other short-term therapies have often been characterized as directed at symptom relief, whereas long-term psychotherapy is seen as reconstructive, dealing with the uncovering of unconscious impulses and long-standing maladaptive trends. The implication that generally follows is that symptom relief is in itself a compromised goal. This distinction, however, is more apparent than real, and at best it represents an unfortunate dichotomy.

Wolberg (1965) maintains that it is time therapists overcame the "prejudice of depth," because "psychotherapy is no mining operation that depends for its yield exclusively on excavated psychic ore." He points out, "We have to accept the fact that no single form of therapy known today in psychiatry is anything but non-specific and hence is directed at symptoms." Furthermore, the empirical success using techniques of behavior modification (see Chapter 9) suggests that symptom removal can be a major stepping stone toward personality growth and reorganization. One might visualize, for example, a man who seeks help because he is virtually immobilized by anxiety attacks. The therapist is able to formulate a reasonable psychodynamic interpretation for his own understanding, but the patient is too immobilized to integrate it. Consequently the therapist provides the patient with medication, which perhaps is the purest form of symptom-relief treatment. Suppose, then, that the patient is now able to resume his job, take his rightful place as a contributing family member, regain some confidence and, recognizing that he is back in control, perhaps even confront the conflict that initially produced his anxiety. The goal of symptom relief has been attained, but it has resulted in such intangibles as increments in self-esteem and perhaps even changes in self-concept. It is apparent, then, that symptom relief is not a shabby goal. One may address symptoms as a means to an end, or as an end in themselves, but the results may be the same.

2. *Aid in restoration of the individual's adjustment balance.* There
are three restoration target goals the therapist might consider, depending
on the complexity of patient's problems and the resources at hand.
The scope of the therapy sessions and the projected modifications depend on the sights that are taken. These three goals are (a) prevention of
further decompensation, (b) restoration to the level of adjustment that
existed prior to the crisis, and (c) restoration to an optimal level of
functioning.

The appropriateness of goal (a) versus goal (b) or (c) depends in large part
on the goals the patient himself brings to crisis therapy and on his
availability and openness to intervention. We agree with Strickler and
Allgeyer (1967) that the minimum "goal of crisis intervention is preventive,
since the outcome can be affected significantly by the presence of timely
help."

It is apparent that the third level, restoration to or achievement of
the person's optimal level of functioning, represents the largest gain for
the patient. The achievement of goal (b) versus goal (c) depends largely on
the degree of skill of the therapist, specifically his ability to view the crisis
as the culmination of maladaptive coping and to help the patient acquire a
broader range of adaptive coping mechanisms.

3. *An understanding of the precipitating factors.* The doctrine of
psychic determinism is one of the oldest principles of psychological
thought. The applied psychologist proceeds from the assumption that
behavior is caused. Similarly, crises are not random occurrences, but
result from a particular interplay of forces in which the individual himself is a main character.

When people enter any form of therapy, there are usually precipitating
factors that precede and influence their decision to seek help. However,
the precipitating factor takes on added importance when a person is in
crisis. It is imperative that the therapist discern very rapidly what the
precipitants are, because this is where crisis therapy begins. The precipitating factor is often the proverbial "last straw." In a crisis, it
always exists, although its exact form and meaning may be submerged
and camouflaged. The veracity of this strong statement is upheld even
with patients who have a "chronically" poor adjustment and generally
poor prognosis.

Birley and Brown (1970), for example, studied 50 schizophrenic patients and discovered that 60% of them had experienced an event that
would be considered potentially disturbing within 3 weeks of their most
recent relapse. Oberleder (1970), examining 12 patients who were diagnosed as having senile psychosis or arteriosclerosis with psychosis and
had an average age of 76.4, found that *all* of them had precipitating

crises that preceded their hospitalization. In a well-controlled study comparing 185 depressed patients with normal controls, Paykel, Myers, Dienelt, Klerman, Lindenthal, and Pepper (1969) determined that depressed patients interviewed after substantial improvement reported almost three times as many life events in the 6 months immediately prior to the symptomatic onset of depression as did controls during a comparable 6-month period. Events generally regarded as undesirable and those involving losses or exits from the social field particularly distinguished the depressed patients from the controls. These included marital difficulties, deaths and illnesses, and work changes.

A unique study by Bloom (1963) suggests that a crisis is usually defined clinically primarily in terms of knowledge of a precipitating event and secondarily in terms of a slow resolution. In an effort to determine how clinicians identify a crisis, he presented eight expert judges with 14 case histories constructed so that it was possible to study the differential effects of five variables: (a) knowledge or lack of knowledge of a precipitating event; (b) rapidity of onset of reactions; (c) awareness or lack of awareness on the part of the patient of inner discomfort; (d) evidence of behavioral disorganization; and (e) rapidity of resolution. He found that the judgment of crisis is made significantly more often when there is a known precipitating event than when the precipitating event is unknown.

4. *Knowledge of the origin of the crisis in past experiences and prevailing personality problems.* We have noted previously that the most desirable goal of crisis intervention is not only to prevent further decompensation or restore a person to a prior level of adjustment, but to assist him in achieving or regaining his optimal level of functioning. To achieve this goal, it is necessary for the therapist and patient to formulate not only what the crisis is, but "why" it is. One often finds in examining the precipitating factors that there is nothing inherently "crisis-producing" about a certain set of precipitating events. There is no one event that pathognomonically suggests crisis. Of course, there are some life events such as unexpected deaths, military combat, or national disasters which would predictably result in crises for all but the most adaptable. But this type of crisis, with clear-cut, readily understood precipitants, represents only a fraction of the crises encountered. It is more often the case that the precipitating factors can only be understood in terms of their dynamic, symbolic, and personal meaning to the patient. One must ask why it is that one executive reacts to a business failure with overwhelming feelings of guilt, failure, and loss of esteem, while another integrates such an event, chalks it up to experi-

ence, and goes on about the business of living. It becomes apparent, then, that simply identifying and isolating the factors that precipitate the request for help is only the beginning step.

We believe that in many cases a successful resolution of an ego-invested problem cannot occur without an examination of the forces that produced the problem. Menninger (1954) comments in this regard that "the ego always does more than attempt to manage the immediate emergency. In spite of resistance implicit in the semistabilized emergency adjustment, the ego perennially endeavors to return to its original normal adjustment level." This is similar to the "adaptational" approach presented by Frank (1966). Frank explains that his adaptational approach can be best understood theoretically in terms of its relationship with the psychoanalytic and behavioral therapy models, which may be seen as occupying opposite ends of a continuum. In the psychoanalytic approach the focal symptom is seen as secondary to the unconscious conflicts underlying it. The goal of analysis is to produce insight and self-awareness, with the assumption that behavioral change will follow. At the other end of the continuum lie particular forms of behavior therapy that concentrate explicitly on the removal of focal symptoms by utilizing laws of learning.

The adaptational approach both resembles and differs from these two theoretical constructions. It assumes that symptoms—and we would add crises—are meaningful communications. Hence the therapeutic aim is not solely to remove the stress, but to understand the communication. The focus is on precipitating factors rather than historical intrapsychic causes of the crisis per se, but the emphasis is not completely ahistorical, because the therapist understands that behavior is multiply determined and actively seeks out any intrapsychic causes that give meaning to the currently encountered symptoms and precipitating factors. As Harris, Kalis, and Freeman (1963) note, "The most apparent difference between this type of brief treatment and more traditional forms of psychotherapy is in the systematic focussing on the current situation, with historical material utilized only as it arises spontaneously and relates directly to the current problems."

This approach does not assume that there is any "basic" conflict that must be discovered before a crisis can be resolved. It suggests instead that, in order to understand and consequently deal with the personal nature of the precipitating factors, one must also look beyond them to potential antecedents such as child-rearing patterns, past traumas, or simply personality trait patterns and the other people with whom the patient interacts.

The Legitimacy of Single-Contact Therapy

Psychotherapeutic intervention need not entail a long series of contacts. Actually, most patients beginning psychotherapy expect the therapy to require only 5 to 10 sessions (Garfield, 1971), and several recent studies show that many patients do not remain in therapy beyond that. Rubenstein and Lorr (1956) reported that between 30 and 60% of patients accepted for therapy terminate within the first six sessions. Rogers (1960) reported that over half of the clinic populations he surveyed dropped out before the eighth session. A large-scale survey of 979,000 patients who had received some type of psychiatric treatment found an average of 4.7 contacts with the therapist (National Center for Health Statistics, reported in Lorion, 1974).

Two studies by Goin, Yamamoto, and Silverman (1965) and Yamamoto and Goin (1965) suggest that patients usually leave treatment at clearly defined points and not just in the middle of treatment. It not only seems to be the case that individuals expect a brief therapeutic experience and usually receive it, but that they frequently leave when they have arrived at some subjectively defined end point. Many individuals seek short-term help because they feel less threatened in the relative anonymity of a brief therapeutic encounter; because they have worked through the problem situation, weighed all alternatives, and simply need an outside opinion and a boost to get started; or because they do not wish to reevaluate the long-gone past, but simply need an evaluation or opinion from an objective outsider. Many people seek reassurance that a decision they have made was the correct one.

All crisis psychotherapy sessions should be conducted as though they may be the last contact with the patient. A large number of individuals do not return for additional sessions, even when the therapist asks them to return. Ideally, the crisis therapist should consider all cases as single contacts and assume that the individual will, after some redefinition of his situation and remotivation, be able to modify his life events without continued support of the therapist. It may be necessary for the therapist to schedule additional sessions (and the patient *may* return) to work on other problems or to do a follow-up; however, the therapist should not bank on having the person in for another session next week. In crisis therapy, next week is now.

What can be accomplished in a single session? The answer is plenty—if the therapist keeps his eye on the goal. The fact that single contacts with a therapeutic agent can be beneficial has been well documented in social work literature (Parad, 1971). Early social workers such as McCord (1931) and Reynolds (1932) noted that the "short contact" or the single-interview case can produce positive results by clearing up problems that are of immediate concern. Wayne (1966) stated, "We consider it significant, conceptually, if not statistically, that some patients undergoing crisis therapy show prompt and relatively lasting improvement as the result of a single interview" (p. 114). The philosophy of short-term clinical intervention in social casework was summed up nicely by Taft (1933): "If there is not therapeutic understanding and use of one interview, many interviews, equally barren, will not help. In the single interview. . . there is no time to hide behind material, no time to explore the past or future. I myself am the remedy at this moment, if there is any. . . ."

The Modus Operandi of the Crisis Therapist

When a person in crisis appears for an initial interview at a crisis center, he may be emotionally distraught or blunted after having tried "everything else possible" and failed. He is usually desperate for help and hopeful that a solution can be provided. He may arrive with preconceived ideas of what to expect from a crisis therapist, or he may be so preoccupied with the situation that he is almost surprised when he finds himself discussing his private life with a stranger. What kind of a person does the patient find? How can he immediately and quite openly discuss often sensitive and usually painful matters? Are there definable attributes of a good crisis therapist that encourage "instant" rapport and trust? Or is the crisis situation itself usually so urgent and overwhelming that just *any* person will suffice in that role? We think not. Bellak and Small (1965) observe that, by definition, brief psychotherapy involves intervention within the shortest possible period of time, and thus it cannot be haphazard. Crisis therapy, by virtue of its fast-moving pace and very time-limited structure, requires a highly confident, skillful, and directive therapist.

The crisis therapist should present the image of one who has the capacity to understand the patients's problems. He should appear human and concerned about the patient's felt conflict, but at the same time businesslike about the information he needs to acquire rather quickly. Traditional attitudes of therapists as "objective" (aloof), "disinterested" (noninvolved), and "nondirective" (inefficient) are not appropriate in the crisis context. Abroms (1968) comments correctly that a therapist is more than just a catalyst—"A catalyst influences only the rate of a process, not its end products." This underlines the importance of activity and direction-pointing in crisis therapy. In Abroms' words, "we assume that all effective therapists are directive." The therapist must be in command all the time—thus there is no substitute for experience and the acquired ability to size up problems rapidly, to articulate the relevant dynamics, and to initiate affirmative action. It is necessary to obtain relevant background information quickly without being caustically intrusive. The crisis therapist, during the early phases of the first interview, is a diagnostician who, in Brantner's (1973) words, becomes a "sponge" and absorbs everything about the person. He may delay giving feedback until later in the interview, when a full picture of the individual in crisis is acquired, or it may be necessary to begin tentative therapeutic interventions, for example, support, before all the assessment information is in.

The crisis therapist must be flexible and sensitive to the roles he may be required to play to effect the desired cognitive and hopefully behavioral reorientation of the patient. Depending on the demands of the situation, he may need to be supportive or confronting, friendly or antagonistic, accepting or rejecting of the patient's ideas, and so forth. The therapist must be able to call forth the appropriate "stimulus conditions" (through his response to the patient's problems) from a variety of available roles or attitudes and bring them to bear on the patient's problem situation. One way in which the crisis therapist differs from other therapists is that he *is* involved in the session. As Seabolt (1973) states, "The crisis therapist is there to reflect reality, and reality does not sit passively and mirror feelings back to the client. The crisis therapist responds as a person giving pertinent feedback to the client as to how he comes across, is perceived and is responded to by others" (p. 69).

When the time comes to move toward an intervention (after a satisfactory assessment is obtained), the therapist must aggressively take hold of the session. Again in Seabolt's well-chosen words, the therapist "conveys an important message of being in command of the situation." The therapist must act positively and decisively toward the definite goal or goals he determines will alleviate the crisis situation. Whether the situation demands supporting the patient's present efforts, confronting his unrealistic expectations, exploring more workable options, or whatever, the therapist must call the plays. He may need to take a strong stand on an issue or an action. If he is right, it may reinforce a patient's basic leaning; if he is wrong, it may help the patient clarify and crystallize an opposite though workable, acceptable alternative.

Throughout the session the crisis therapist operates as a goal setter, helping the patient chart new strategies, clarify previously unworkable adaptive mechanisms, and shelve or give up on unattainable goals. He may not only suggest new goals or strategies, but persuade the patient concerning what the only viable options are. It is usually valuable for the therapist to work through possible factors that could interfere with these plans and to develop rebuttals to such obstacles.

Many roles and requirements are placed on the crisis therapist. To work out an effective intervention in the brief time available, he must carry out several activities almost simultaneously: assessing the nature and extent of the problem and the individual's potential response; inquiring about relevant facts; offering encouragement and support if needed; and evaluating how the patient integrates feedback. The next two sections of the chapter deal in some detail with the two major activities of the crisis therapist—assessment of the individual in crisis and implementation of the tactics of crisis therapy. Isolating these activities out of the therapeutic process for separate discussion is artificial, since both processes are intertwined in the typical crisis therapy situation. Yet a separate exploration of assessment and intervention will hopefully provide the reader with an awareness of the range of skills required of a crisis therapist. The structure of the presentation that follows should not be taken as the suggested order for conducting crisis therapy.

ASSESSMENT IN CRISIS THERAPY

The critical nature of the situation, the time constraints, and the necessity for therapeutic intervention to begin almost immediately make it impossible for the therapist to conduct a detailed assessment apart from actual treatment. Within the space of just the first interview, several objectives must be accomplished:

1. Establishing a relationship with the patient.
2. Gathering assessment information necessary for treatment planning.
3. Arriving at a tentative formulation of the problem incorporating the precipitating problem together with the personality structure. This involves arriving at a working hypothesis of the precipitant and its subsequent hazardous meaning to the individual.
4. Giving the patient some perspective on the problem, including an understanding of his adaptive and maladaptive coping mechanisms in relation to it.
5. Exploring new adaptive ways the patient can deal with the problem.
6. Arriving at a strategy for achieving the agreed-upon goals and making a therapeutic "contract" if additional sessions are planned.
7. Arranging for future visits.

The second of these objectives, the gathering of assessment information, is the one addressed in this section. The remaining objectives, which are less defined and more likely to vary with each individual situation, are addressed in the next section on tactics the therapist may choose to use.

In considering assessment in crisis therapy, it is first helpful to distinguish assessment from diagnosis. Formal psychiatric diagnosis is not particularly useful in crisis therapy and may in fact be detrimental, in that it may orient the therapist toward seeing and planning for "chronic pathology" and blind him to important and manageable critical events. Although a reaction to crisis is often seen as indicative of the person's prestress personality, evidence from studies that have attempted to predict the outcome of a stress situation solely on the basis of personality has tended to disconfirm this belief (Aita, 1949; Bibring, 1961; Glass, 1956; see also Kaplan, 1968).

It is important to keep in mind that the primary goal of crisis work is to restore the patient's functioning to the level of adjustment that existed prior to his recent decompensation. Consequently, the focus of treatment is not on whatever long-standing pathology may be present, but rather on "the patient's failure to cope in the here-and-now problem" (Jacobson et al., 1965). There is little relationship between diagnosis and the ability of a person to return to his optimal level of functioning, although there is some relationship between diagnosis and the capacity for reconstructive change. As Kaplan (1968) notes, "The person's prestress personality is likely to influence his response to a crisis, but his personality alone does not determine the outcome, which is markedly affected by his current relationships." Crisis treatment assumes, then, that a crisis is distinct from a chronic condition, although it may be affected by it. This assumption indicates a need for thorough and accurate assessment rather than diagnosis in the traditional sense.

The importance of assessment in crisis work cannot be overemphasized. Klopfer (1964) has critically questioned the value of initiating any psychotherapy without first obtaining as much assessment information as possible, and DeCourcy (1971) has underscored the importance of adequate assessment by reporting a case in which a woman patient was being seen in a short-term directive counseling situation for problems centering around her husband's alleged homosexual practices. An incidental assessment study uncovered a severe paranoid schizophrenic reaction in the woman and a relatively problem-free husband. Other case excerpts vividly demonstrating the importance of adequate assessment in crisis intervention are reported by Lambley (1974) and Small (1972).

Compared to traditional psychotherapies, crisis therapy occurs in settings that are relatively more casual and that call for relatively more active and directive therapist roles. However, none of these factors gives the therapist license to disregard important therapeutic content. In spite of time pressures and apparent urgencies of the situation, one cannot afford to abandon guidelines that constitute part of any good clinical interview (see Chapter 1). The therapist should be as nonobtrusive as possible and allow the psychological content to be contributed by the patient and not by the therapist. Every attempt should be made to facilitate the "flow" of therapeutically relevant personal history information without the therapist prematurely imposing a framework (perhaps an incorrect one) or structuring the interview in such a way that some types of important information are not divulged. For example, if the therapist initially comes across as a happy and cheerful extrovert, the patient may feel reluctant to discuss his problems because "surely he wouldn't be interested." Sometimes the therapist needs to do nothing more than say, "Tell me about the problem that brings you in." If the patient is withdrawn, frightened, or anxious, some additional responses may be necessary to bring the patient to a point where he is able to tell his own story.

At the beginning the clinician should do no more than this, since superfluous activity at this stage serves only to contaminate needed clinical data. The initial interview is not the place for giving casual reassurance, making glib remarks on the patient's physical appearance, or even initiating a friendly handshake. All these perhaps "socially appropriate" behaviors have no place in the therapist's initial stimulus projection. The therapist should begin his observation of the patient immediately—noting, for example, whether the patient is seeking reassurance and whether he, in a friendly manner, shakes hands. Before the therapist can assist the patient in formulating his problem, he must be able to assess its important dimensions. One can generally gain most of the initially necessary assessment information by listening and briefly encouraging the patient to present the problem as he sees it. Especially in crisis therapy one should guard against the inclination to do or to say too much too soon. Astute listening and observation are absolutely necessary to formulating the problems adequately.

More specifically, adequate assessment for crisis therapy should include the following eight kinds of observation and data collection:

Determining Whether or Not the Patient Can Be Adequately Assessed at the Time

Some patients may have contributing features that augment or stimulate their crisis, but which also interfere with making an accurate assessment of it. Patients who are currently in toxic states due to drug or alcohol use often fall into this category, as do patients who have overdosed on barbiturates or tranquilizers. In this situation the foremost crisis that must be dealt with is the physical risk. To handle this type of crisis efficiently, some crisis centers cooperate with hospital emergency rooms or make arrangements for medical consultation on an on-call basis.

If the physical risk factor in an intoxicated patient does not require acute medical attention or hospitalization, it may still be necessary to provide the patient with a place where he can detoxify, pending assessment. This may be provided by working out arrangements with detoxification centers or drug treatment units. Some centers provide certain patients with beds right at the center, to insure that the patient is not lost or injured during the referral process.

A second set of patients for whom assessment may have to be deferred includes those who are currently and perhaps temporarily overcome by the crisis, and are consequently too agitated or physically exhausted to provide necessary assessment information, but for whom there are known factors that militate against immediate hospitalization. These might be people in severe anxiety states, people who have had previous psychiatric hospitalization without benefit, or people who are known to have fast recovery potential. Providing such people with medication and an opportunity to recuperate may be an important first step which can precede the actual full assessment of the crisis situation.

Gathering Essential Demographic Information

Essential demographic information includes such items as the patient's name, age, place of residence, marital status, occupation, and education, the names of key relatives or friends, and whether the patient is currently in treatment elsewhere. Many crisis centers use brief forms so that this information is readily available to the therapist before he begins the initial interview. As a result, some data-gathering questions may be separate from and not interfere with collecting the more "clinical information.

The clinical utility of these demographic variables defies specific description; however, the astute clinician can formulate various hypotheses about factors such as intelligence, motivation, interpersonal relationships, and subcultural mores on the basis of information about a patient's name, place of residence, occupation, and education. A well-dressed and articulate surburban housewife who comes in to talk about her fear of dying probably requires a different strategy from an inner-city welfare recipient who presents with the same problem. Needless to say, all hypotheses formed on the basis of such demographic information must be rigorously explored before they are presumed to represent fact.

Assessing the Current Level of Function

The patient's current level of functioning is most efficiently assessed by direct observations that follow a standard mental status examination format (see Wells & Ruesch, 1972) covering the following:

Appearance and Behavior. Take note of apparent state of health, body type, manner of dress, care of appearance, facial expressions, and motor activity such as posture, gait, tremulousness, and clenching of fists. There is a wealth of information in the appearance and behavior of patients, which is useful in confirming or generating hypotheses about the individual. Do the inferences about the patient from the way he appears seem consistent with what the patient says about himself?

Speech and Verbal Behavior. Verbal behavior and the structure of speech are important areas of assessment, because they may reveal disordered thinking or powerful feelings of which the patient is not aware. The structure and styles of verbal behavior are often rather subtle, and consequently difficult for an inexperienced crisis therapist to assess—especially when the "content" the patient presents is, itself, complex and difficult to organize. However, this is an important fund of information which should not be ignored.

The clinician should also note such things as the freedom with which the patient speaks. Some patients may be evasive, halting, noncommittal, monosyllabic, or even mute, whereas others may be spontaneous, garrulous, effusive, or display great pressure of speech. Qualitatively, speech may be coherent and precise, or it may be circumstantial, dissociated, and illogical. In this regard, one must be careful to note flight of ideas, perseveration, neologisms, "word salads," or bizarre statements.

Thought Content. It is essential to determine the predominant ideas occupying the patient's mind. One should note in particular those ideas that the patient spontaneously relates to the therapist. More specific inquiry may be used to reveal his thoughts about what he thinks the problem is and what is the cause of his distress. The therapist should be aware that the thoughts, attitudes, and concerns carrying the most emotional significance are often not stated directly, but can be detected in the patient's illogical, irrational, unguarded, and loosely considered productions.

Observing the Patient's Emotional State

In observing a patient's emotional state, one should consider both mood and affect. Mood refers to the individual's general, overall, more-or-less prolonged emotional tone, whereas affect refers to his momentary emotional responsiveness, which may vary during the interview in relation to changing thought content. It may be important to determine if the particular emotion the patient is expressing, for example, anger, is primarily a situationally induced and transitory state, or is rather a "sign" or representative instance of more persistent behavior trends, for example, chronic hostility. Further questioning may be required to make such determinations. One should note not only the patient's direct statements regarding his feelings, but also any revealing indirect statements, facial expressions, and motor activity. Frequently, patients may express verbally a set of attitudes or feelings that do not correspond with the emotions they are actually experiencing. A therapist who detects such disparity in the patient's manner of presentation may find fruitful therapeutic terrain. Finally, the therapist should to some extent monitor his own empathic feelings for clues to the patient's emotions.

Observing the Patient's Manner of Relating

One should observe the manner in which the patient relates to the therapist and to others around him, as this provides important information about how he gets along with other people. Does he seem sullen, resentful, sarcastic, or uncooperative? Does he appear cool and distant, warm and friendly, flat, indifferent, ingratiating, or seductive? One can assume during the initial interview that any such attitudes and modes of behavior derive mainly from the patient's own personality style and way of relating to people, providing that the therapist's own inputs are minimal.

Assessing Premorbid Adjustment as Distinct from Current Stress

This assessment area is illustrated by the following model.

As the model suggests, crises result from an interplay of stressful life experiences with congenital or acquired vulnerabilities. Some populations distinguish themselves as being particularly high on one or the other axis, and the probability of their confronting a crisis is consequently very high. For example, the genetic component in schizophrenia has now been well documented (Gottesman & Shields, 1972). Because many schizophrenics have genetic predispositions toward decompensation, it is probable that relatively innocuous life experiences may be perceived as crises—point A in the diagram. Such is the case with a schizophrenic lady who presents herself because she has left her keys to her apartment at work and does not know what to do.

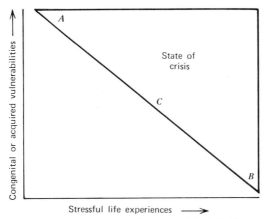

Fig. 1.   A Vulnerability/Stress Model of Crisis

On the other axis one finds relatively well-functioning people, depicted at point *B* who are faced with threatening life experiences such as aging, poverty, discrimination, and unexpected deaths.

The middle ground, point *C*, is occupied largely by people who have specific congenital or acquired vulnerabilities or "weak spots." These vulnerabilities are subject to being reactivated when the person confronts particular life experiences, as in the case of a woman reared by alcoholic parents who finds that her husband has an uncontrolled drinking problem. When a therapist begins to work with a patient in crisis, it is necessary for him to be able to assess accurately the particular combination of forces resulting in the crisis. The appropriate plan of action depends in large part on this assessment.

To assess the premorbid level of adjustment or adaptive potential, it is useful to explore the manner in which the patient has handled past crises and the current crisis before coming for treatment. Erikson (1953) focused in this regard on the difference between "accidental crises" and "developmental crises." Patients are often able to describe past accidental crises in response to the question, "Has anything like this happened to you in the past?" or "What have you done when you felt like this in the past?" If there are no apparent accidental crises, one can explore standard developmental crises such as school entry and exit, marriage, first job, and the like. The methods in which crises were handled previously can then be analyzed according to their affective, perceptive-cognitive, behavioral, and biophysiological content, as suggested by Golan (1969).

As a result of her research Golan (1968) concluded that most responses to crises can be classified according to the following eight categories:

1. Carried on as usual; made no new effort.
2. Expressed grief in words or actions or both (adopted depressive behavior).
3. Expressed anger by words or actions or both (adopted aggressive behavior).
4. Escaped reality by words or actions or both (slept excessively; fantasized; became psychotic; used alcohol or drugs).
5. Developed neurotic symptoms (adopted phobic behavior, compulsive rituals, hysteric manifestations).
6. Developed somatic symptoms (suffered from migraine, ulcers, dermatitis).
7. Engaged in reality-oriented efforts to deal with the situation (cut down expenses; looked for a job; returned to the parental home).
8. Mobilized energies for new, growth-producing activities (started training for a new career; innovated basic changes in the home).

Rapaport (1962) has suggested that it is also useful to classify the way in which a crisis is perceived, since this allows one to understand better the response, adaptive or maladaptive, that ensues. She notes that the "initial blow" may be seen as (a) a threat, either to instinctual needs or to the sense of physical or emotional integrity; (b) a loss, either of a person or of an ability or capacity; or (c) a challenge. Strickler and LaSor (1970) have further delineated her second category of loss into (a) loss of self-esteem, particularly in regard to the person's ability to function well in certain social roles or relationships; (b) loss of sexual role mastery in terms of performance in vocational and heterosexual areas for males, and maternal and vocational areas for women; and (c) loss of nurturing by virtue of loss of nurturing objects or roles.

Rapaport's categories bear some resemblance to those of Pollack (1971), who classified crises in students as external stress, frustration, and conflict. Rapaport noted that threat calls forth a high level of anxiety, loss or deprivation is accompanied by depression or mourning, and challenge stimulates moderate anxiety, some hope, and a release of energy for problem solving.

It is also possible to assess the premorbid level of adjustment by relying in part on the personal history data already available. Work history, educational success, and marital and interpersonal relationships provide important clues to the premorbid level of adjustment. It is usually necessary to do more specific questioning in areas such as previous psychiatric history, medical history, medication, and use of drugs and alcohol. It is also useful, if possible, to talk with family members, friends, or professional colleagues who are directly familiar with the patient's previous level of adjustment. Information from these various sources can facilitate identifying the strengths and coping

mechanisms the patient brings to the crisis situation, as well as wh
has not been able to cope adaptively with the current crisis.

Assessing Current Life Stresses

While the therapist is assessing the aforementioned areas, the focus of
the interview for the most part is in the area of the current life stresses
precipitating the crisis. After being asked to state what the problem is
that brings him in, the patient is encouraged to relate the current crisis to
past problems or to particular personality styles he has observed in
himself. The interviewer should draw on this information to delineate as
best he can the psychological hazards confronting the patient and the
precipitating event that has brought him for help. At this point it is also
necessary to determine whether the problem is a *chronic* one which has
persisted for some time, a continuing situation which has existed for a
long time but has only recently become a problem, or a psychological
difficulty of entirely recent origin. The assessment made in this regard
bears directly on decisions about referral, as is more fully elaborated in
the previous section on goals of crisis therapy.

Assessing the Patient's Level of Motivation

This area of assessment is concerned with elucidating the patient's
expectations regarding his and the therapist's role in crisis therapy.
Rado (1965) has described four motivational levels which are useful to
keep in mind in making this assessment. The first and lowest level of
motivation, which he calls "magic craving," is represented by the completely discouraged and helpless adult who retreats to the hope that the
physician-parent will do miracles for him. Such motivation is exemplified by the thought, "The doctor must not only cure me, he must do
everything for me, by magic." This regression is triggered by the distress and helplessness of the patient, and it is not adaptive.
    The second level of motivation is called "parental invocations" and is
exemplified by the thought, "What can the doctor do for me? He should
do everything for me. I want to be his favorite child." Although this
kind of response suggests regression to the period of infantile reliance on
parents, it is at least potentially an adaptive response compared to that
of "magic craving."
    The third level, "cooperative striving," is even more adaptive than
reaching out for a parent or magician. It is exemplified in the thought, "I
am ready to cooperate with the doctor. I must learn how to help myself
and do this for myself."
    The fourth and most adaptive level of motivation is "realistic self-

nplified by the thought, "I will cooperate with the
opportunity to make full use of all my potential
ve growth."

t the utility of any particular level of motivation
ılar circumstances; however, only at the third and
therapist help the patient acquire new emotional
to be self-perpetuating and independent of varia-
patient's feelings toward the therapist.

THE TACTICS OF CRISIS THERAPY[5]

What does a crisis therapist do to bring about relief of emotional distress
or behavioral change with an individual in crisis? The therapist has
several effective tools ranging from attentive listening to complimenting
or criticizing the patient's behavior, giving advice, enlisting environmental support, or interceding with concerned relatives. What power does a
therapist have that enables him to aid in the resolution of problems that
are out of the individual's control, that is, problems in which the patient
is intimately involved and aware of the complexities but is unable to
resolve himself? Perhaps the treatment situation, in which the therapist
is engaged as an interested but objective participant, is itself the most
valuable asset to the change-oriented relationship, since it allows the
therapist to perceive what new directions are required without being
bogged down with the futility and inactivity surrounding the patient.

An important factor in the therapist's ability to offer assistance lies in
the authoritative nature of the role he fills. The therapist is viewed as an
expert who has the knowledge or power to help, and the patient generally expects or at least hopes that the therapist will offer some relief.
This expectation is in itself a powerful change agent, and "placebo"
effects in bringing about patient changes have been well documented
(see pp. 356–357). Wolberg (1965) among others has pointed out that the
placebo effect is rooted in the individual's expectation that the person
whom he consults has the knowledge, the means, and the magic to bring

[5]The reader will find the following sources relevant and useful for gaining additional
familiarity with the tactics of crisis therapy: Aguilera, Messick, and Farrell (1970); Barten
and Barten (1972); Barten (1971); Beck and Robbins (1946); Bellak and Small (1965);
Bergin and Garfield (1971); Caplan (1961); Caplan (1964); Coleman (1960); Darbonne
(1968); Frank (1961); Golann and Eisdorfer (1972); Haley (1963); Koegler and Brill (1967);
Lerner (1972); Lewin (1970); Mann (1973); Massermann (1969); McGee (1974); Parad
(1965); Phillips and Wiener (1966); Reid and Shyne (1969); Rothman (1970); Sifneos (1972);
Small (1971); and Wolberg (1965).

his difficulties to a halt; in response to this expectation, Wolberg advises, "The therapist should neither exaggerate nor crush it, but accept it."

In this section we discuss some of the tactics that prove useful in the conduct of crisis therapy. It needs to be recognized, however, that these tactics vary in their effectiveness for treating different kinds of individuals who present in crisis situations. Hence the particular tactic to employ in a given situation cannot always be readily specified, and it is sometimes difficult for the crisis therapist to know precisely what to do. Because he intervenes initially on the basis of limited data, he must often rely on an educated guess and hope that his tactics produce the desired effect. Sometimes the result is immediately apparent, at other times feedback from the patient provides some information about the adequacy of the intervention, and in still other instances a therapist may not know whether his tactics have been effective until a follow-up is conducted. The brief exposition of tactics below is by no means exhaustive, and it is difficult to extract therapeutic tactics out of the process itself without greatly oversimplifying the therapist's task. We can, however, give the reader an idea of the more frequently used and useful procedures in crisis therapy.

Offering Emotional Support

An individual appearing for an initial crisis interview is often experiencing a heightened state of anxiety or depression and has almost always recently experienced failure at managing his own situation. He is probably preoccupied with the precipitating event and has difficulty focusing his attention on anything else. Before the patient can begin to consider alternative stategies of problem resolution, he may need to receive some clear *emotional support* from the therapist. This support may range in degree from simply acknowledging the existence of the problem (with the implicit communication that the problem "can't be too bad, since we are at least able to talk about it") to offering strong verbal reassurance ("I am quite certain that you did the right thing in leaving").

Several theorists (e.g., Truax & Wargo, 1966; Wolpe, 1958) have pointed out that the essential ingredients for therapeutic effectiveness comprise (a) sensitivity and understanding of the patient's situation and a manner of communicating this awareness, (b) the communication of nonpossessive warmth and acceptance of the patient, and (c) the communication of therapist genuineness and authenticity to the patient (see also Chapter 6). These are necessary conditions for communicating emotional support to a patient, and in crisis therapy these "ingredients" are just as essential as in other forms of psychotherapy for bringing about desired change—although they may be more difficult to attain since the duration of treatment, expecially if there is only a single contact with the patient, is all too brief.

The grief work involved in much of crisis therapy (Lindemann, 1944; Paul, 1966) is facilitated or, to be more exact, made possible by the therapist's providing strong emotional support to the patient. Having someone to rely on in times of severe stress encourages the patient to express overwhelming feelings he has been holding back. It is not a sign of weakness for individuals to utilize others in this way at such times, nor does it suggest that the therapist is encouraging dependency in the patient, since the time-bound structure, if correctly managed, helps to prevent this unwanted side effect.

Providing Opportunities for Catharsis

Several therapists have noted the *importance of catharsis* in successful psychotherapy (Breuer & Freud, 1895; Frank, 1961; Rosenzweig, 1936; Shoben, 1948). In some more recent behaviorally oriented therapeutic approaches as well, cathartic techniques are viewed as important procedures for bringing about successful behavioral change (Hogan, 1968;Lazarus, 1968; Stampl & Levis, 1967; Ullman & Krasner, 1965). It is especially important for individuals in crisis who may be experiencing a great deal of affect (or perhaps are unable to express their emotions directly) to be offered an opportunity to discharge such feelings in the relative safety of a therapeutic situation. Thus the therapist must be aware of the high arousal state of most individuals in initial crisis therapy sessions, and be sensitive to their cathartic needs.

The therapist must accordingly set the stage for the free expression of emotion by the patient. He must strive to elicit strong feelings, and he must give the patient permission to express intense emotions. With depressed patients who have difficulty letting their feelings out, even vicarious catharsis may help, since the patient may thereby be able to reverse the aggression and anger he has turned on himself (Bellak & Small, 1965). A response from the therapist such as "Some part of you must have wished your father dead," for example, has the advantage of not requiring the patient to take full responsibility for the hostility expressed. As Paul (1966) notes, "The client must be encouraged to 'experience' his emotions, to examine them, to 'own up' to them, to feel them fully as emotions." The therapist must also be prepared for possibly uncontrollable waves of emotion which may appear in effective crisis therapy. After such storms of expressed emotion, patients are frequently at their most receptive point for therapeutic input. Work by Nichols (1974) has confirmed that emotive psychotherapy is effective in producing catharsis, and that catharsis in turn leads to therapeutic improvement.

Communicating Hope and Optimism

The communication of hope and optimism to the patient is an important ingredient of effective psychotherapy (Frank, 1968). An optimistic attitude on the part of the therapist is especially effective in dealing with individuals in crisis, since the loss of hope in solving one's problems usually accompanies deterioration of adjustment during a crisis. As Aldrich (1968) has pointed out,

> If the therapist expects that the patient's capacity to respond favorably to short-term symptomatic treatment is evidence of his capacity to cope autonomously with residual unresolved conflicts, the therapist's optimistic expectations may cancel out the earlier expectations of failure the patient has perceived from others.

When the therapist *sincerely* communicates hope and the possibility of problem resolution to the patient, the individual may react positively and begin to view his options in a more flexible fashion. A "deadpan" therapist, or worse yet a pessimistic one, can do little to mobilize the action resources within the patient.

However, the crisis therapist must be cautious in committing himself to any such attitudes routinely. An important assessment must be made first. Is there a ray of hope in the patient's life that may be harnessed? If the therapist feels realistically hopeful, then some change leverage may be effected; if he is not sincere and provides superficial reassurance and false hope that the patient detects (and they usually do), then the outcome may be therapeutic failure. Few tactics provide greater credibility gaps between therapist and patient than reassurance when a therapist holds unrealistic expectations about outcome.

Being Interested and Actively Involved

To most patients in crisis, their problems are of the utmost importance at the moment. Consequently, *the therapist must be interested and actively involved* in the unfolding events, tedious though they might be to discuss. His "interest" in the patient's problem situation communicates positive feelings which may have the effect of mobilizing the individual to focus on particularly effective aspects of his life. One thing is fairly certain, namely, that the obverse—evident disinterest in the patient—generally has undesirable and unwanted effects. This is not meant to imply that the therapist must be exuberant over every minute detail of every case. On the contrary, the therapist, listening selectively, may even need to inform the patient of the irrelevance of some types of information. What we are saying is that the therapist must be interested and involved in the patient's situation, regardless of the particular tactics he uses at the moment.

Listening Selectively

The crisis therapist must cultivate an ear for workable material and ignore aspects of the case that are irrelevant, unmanageable, or beyond any practical grasp. Not everything the patient brings to the session can be dealt with. For the therapy to be short-term, only material that is immediately relevant can receive attention. Rusk (1971) notes in this regard that people in crisis are frequently unable to address the stress or conflict situation directly and may defensively launch into pseudocrises. These may take such forms as preoccupation with physical symptoms, reversion into explanation of long-standing difficulties, or focus on irrelevant concerns. *Selective listening is one of the most important tactics for a therapist to learn.* It is crucial for the therapist to sift out of the morass of multiplex trends and irrelevant material *only* that information that bears usefully on bringing about desired change.

The concept of "skillful or benign neglect," suggested by Pumpian-Mindlin (1953), describes this therapeutic tactic nicely. It is important for the therapist to keep the session moving and not become preoccupied with defensive entanglements of the patient. Castelnuovo-Tedesco (1966) observes,

In the brief treatment of these depressive disorders, it is important to recognize early the major characterological defenses and, in the main to respect them, to leave them alone, and not to become involved in premature attempts at character analysis which are not in keeping with the circumscribed goals of brief treatment [p. 206].

Rusk (1971) adds that anxiety too must be handled gently, leaving existing defenses intact unless others can be substituted.

Providing Factual Information

It is frequently necessary for the crisis therapist to provide *factual information* relevant to the patient's problem. It may be necessary to clear up misconceptions that cloud a session, as in the case of a patient who was fond of tossing out such "statistics" as, "I heard that 30% of all homosexuals have troubles with their sex glands." The myths that many people hold and sometimes use to sanction or excuse certain behaviors may need to be dispelled in order for the proper therapeutic focus to be obtained. A straightforward, nontechnical explanation which is both brief and authoritative works best for this purpose. The beginning therapist often falls into a habit of lecturing (frequently over the patient's head), rather than simply noting a fact. When the therapist provides any information, he is often in effect interrupting the flow of the session to do so. Thus he should be judicious in his interruptions, making sure that they are warranted and not just self-serving displays of his own knowledge and sophistication.

Formulating the Problem Situation

Therapy sessions, particularly those in which much factual information is first needed to make therapeutic decisions, are frequently cluttered with names, dates, facts, untruths, emotional discharges, and other unsorted things. The therapist must attempt to get a handle on all the material being presented and arrive at an agreement with the patient as to what are the problems to be dealt with, what goals are to be attained, and what potential mechanisms for attaining these ends are available. A preliminary *formulation of the problem situation,* in the form of a synthesis of forces acting on the patient, his experienced resulting conflicts, and his ineffective mechanisms, can help bring order into the material and sharpen a workable focus for the therapy. A synthesis that includes a statement of essential facts and some observations and tentative hypotheses enables the patient to integrate the elements considered important by the therapist and to correct or provide addenda to the therapist's perceptions of the situation.

This formulation represents an important stage in the session, since it in effect defines the "work area" for the session and provides the material for forming therapeutic contracts later on. Additionally, the realization that, if events can be explained, they can be handled, serves to diminish the patient's anxiety and fosters hope. As Rusk (1971) notes, verbalizing the circumstances, relationships, and feelings involved in a crisis situation externalizes them. Not only is a preliminary formulation essential, then, but subsequent formulations are useful in fostering the synthetic ability of the patient at various stages of therapy. Reviewing feelings and expressions manifested in earlier sessions is a helpful device for allowing the patient to develop an understanding of how today's needs for action relate to events just past.

Being Emphatic and to the Point

The crisis therapist should strive to *be emphatic and to the point* in providing feedback or interpretations to the patient. Irrelevant comments and off-target interpretations should be avoided—it is better to say nothing at all than to fill the room with unimportant observations and pointless questions. The beginning therapist should consciously determine the proportion of content the patient contributes compared with his own comments. This of course varies with the patient, but a good rule of thumb to follow is that during the early part of the session the therapist should limit his verbal input to about 10% of the time, and to eliciting information from the patient only. During the latter part of the therapy session the inputs from both therapist and patient may appropriately become more equal in amount. It is also important for the therapist to be "straight" with the patient when he does comment, since only by being a model of openness can he create an atmosphere conducive to honest communication between patient and therapist.

Predicting Future Consequences

It is frequently useful, especially when the patient has a characterologically disordered life-style, to *predict what will happen if the patient follows his present course of action*—spelling out in detail the possible consequences of his behavior. This is a useful technique for focusing on workable courses of action in that it helps to clarify what the patient may expect to occur if his life-style is not altered. The patient may be informed at the time that the purpose of the prediction is the hope of proving it false, as Bellak and Small (1965) recommend. Many individuals cannot or do not make such predictions about the outcomes of their own behavior; consequently they cannot weigh behavioral strategies to obtain desired outcomes. This ability to predict one's fate given a particular behavioral sequence is frequently impaired in individuals undergoing stress.

Giving Advice and Making Direct Suggestions

Advice giving and direct suggestions are effective therapeutic tools if properly and sparingly used. These techniques are useful because people seek out and accept the formulations of authorities they respect. Many individuals in crisis go to a therapist to obtain an opinion about their situation and to seek advice or suggestions for remedying it. This is especially true when the patient is of low-income status (see Lorion, 1973). Auld and Myers (1954) report in this regard that low-income patients tend to see the therapist as a magician or mind reader and to view their problems as organic (nerves) and as requiring physical treatment. Redlich, Hollingshead, and Bellis (1955) similarly comment that lower-class patients are relatively likely to seek advice and guidance in psychotherapy and to be disappointed when it is not offered.

As we have seen, the therapist has a "given" authority which provides him leverage to bring about change. The power of direct suggestion accordingly works to mobilize many patients to attempt new behaviors. If successful, these attempts will not only begin to relieve the patient's problem situation and give him confidence in his ability to change, but will provide an impetus for the therapist to initiate additional and perhaps more substantial changes. Thus it is important to make suggestions within the patient's power to succeed at and that, at the same time, contribute toward problem resolution. The therapist who gives either bad advice or too many suggestions finds that the patient may quickly lose confidence in his therapeutic powers. Furthermore, some patients are fond of playing the "Yes, but I've tried that already" role, which tends to generate a nonproductive power struggle. If the therapist finds that his "sage" advice is being ignored or attacked, then he must reevaluate the effectiveness of this therapeutic tactic or of the quality of his advice, or both.

Setting Limits

Sometimes it is not enough for the therapist just to be understanding and thoughtful in providing structure and advice to the patient. He may in addition have to be very *directive in setting limits* for the patient. Abrams (1968) describes several types of behavior that may require the therapist to set firm limits. These include destructive behavior, such as suicidal or homicidal threats; disorganized behavior, especially as found in regressed, psychotic individuals; acting-out or rule-breaking behavior; withdrawal; and excessive dependency. In such cases the therapist may need to establish explicit rules aimed at stopping the behavior and aiding the patient in placing these maladaptive behaviors under his own control.

Clarifying and Reinforcing Adaptive Mechanisms

It may be that all the elements for change are present within the experience and adaptive capacities of the patient, in which case the therapist needs merely to *clarify and reinforce these adaptive mechanisms*. This may involve determining what behaviors have worked in the past and strengthening them to meet the new adaptive requirements. Some patients come to a therapist with a good solution at hand, that is, they "really know what to do" but for some reason are reluctant or unable to do it. The therapist who recognizes this situation and believes that it is within the patient's power to carry out a reasonable plan of action may simply serve the patient by allowing him to adjust himself to the task at hand and encouraging him to be less timid about the decision. In other cases the patient may have no clear options and must adapt in some specific and perhaps limited way. Then the preferred treatment strategy is not to develop new alternatives, but to focus on making the only available alternatives more acceptable to the patient. Recognizing when there is limited power for behavior change is important, since it facilitates spending the available time on the most potentially fruitful therapeutic task.

Confronting the Patient

With respect to limited power for change, the crisis therapist frequently finds himself working with immobilized patients who have unrealistic goals or maladaptive life-styles which require frank and direct examination. Often such patients rigidly attempt to maintain their life stance despite persistent failures and accompanying psychological pain. The appropriate therapeutic tactic may then be the *direct and aggressive confrontation of the patient's ideas or behavior*. For the immobilized individual who does not know where to begin, the confrontation therapeutic technique frequently initiates a critical reappraisal of the problem (Garner, 1970). The use of confrontation, from relatively mild but pointed questions aimed at drawing the patient's attention to neglected or denied problem areas to more blatant and accusatory "attacking" statements, is aimed at forcing the patient to appraise his situation realistically. The rational-emotive techniques detailed by Ellis (1962) are perhaps the most useful guidelines to confrontation for a therapist to follow. Another useful technique for challenging a patient's beliefs is "paradoxical intention" (Frankl, 1960), which attempts to make the individual assume attitudes or practices diametrically opposed to his accepted ones.

An inexperienced or timid therapist may be reluctant to confront or challenge in an aggressive fashion the belief systems of the patient. Many beginning therapists find confrontation awkward and unsettling, because their "natural" response to the patient is acceptance and "unconditional positive regard." Hence they are seen by the patient as "nice and understanding,"but little else. In crisis therapy a "nice" person is not necessarily a "therapeutic" person. Very often the situation calls for the therapist's being critical of the behavior of the patient, and a therapist who cannot objectively and effectively confront patients when it is appropriate to do so is ineffective with many of the people in crisis he tries to help.

Terminating the Session Abruptly

A somewhat extreme form of confrontation is sometimes necessary to make an impact on certain patients. It occasionally happens that the patient's situation is such that *abrupt termination of the session* is not only necessary but in the long range therapeutic. Individuals who for various reasons (unwillingness, defensiveness, etc.) are not at the point of working on their problems may be best handled by an abrupt termination with an explanation from the therapist such as, "It is evident that you are not able to work on these problems at this time, even though I believe that you know what is necessary to make your situation better; if you decide to work on your problems, you may schedule another appointment." This tactic communicates to the patient that, although the therapist is interested in his welfare and wishes to be of help, it is necessary for him to come to terms with his immobility in the situation. For some types of patient this indicates that their present frame of mind does not facilitate problem resolution, and it may produce a prompt increase in their level of cooperation and participation in the session.

Making Concrete Demands

In the event that additional therapy sessions are planned or a follow-up is scheduled, it is usually a good idea to *place some concrete demands or requirements on the patient* before the next meeting or contact. This "expectation" should be something that emerges naturally out of the material as a task to be done and is, in both the therapist's and patient's judgment, a manageable request. The task, even if small, will communicate to the patient that, if treatment continues, the therapist will expect him to work on his problems. The patient may experience some feelings of immediate improvement if he is able to perform the task successfully, and the therapist will obtain an assessment of the patient's change-motivation from the way he manages his homework.

Working Out a Contract

Implicit in the previous point is the idea of working out a *therapeutic contract* or set of concrete goals for the treatment program. A "change plan" (Phillips & Wiener, 1966) should be formulated in which there is a clear "statement of what behavior has to change, how the change may be brought about, by whom the change can be wrought" (p. 68). In time-bound psychotherapy a contract between the patient and therapist is essential for a number of reasons. The patient should have a clear idea of the number of sessions that will be involved and what, explicitly, is to be accomplished in this time. The behaviors to be changed or the environmental conditions to be manipulated need to be charted, and the means for achieving these ends need to be clearly delineated.

Enlisting the Aid of Others

The crisis therapist often finds that the patient is so embroiled in and bound to his situation that little progress can be attained until significant environmental factors are alleviated or unless other persons, close to the patient, are involved. Lorion (1973) warns that "to ignore the social reality of a patient's existence while attempting to implement change in therapy may be self-defeating." The patient's economic, social, and family situation must be tied in with individual treatment plans. Parad (1961) considers crisis therapy distinct from traditional short-term therapy precisely in that it views work with significant others as very important. Hence the crisis therapist may do well to *enlist the aid of others in an effort to change* the pressures impinging on the patient. He may encourage the significant others in the patient's life to come in for a meeting or allow a home visit by the therapist. Employers may be contacted to work out more satisfactory work arrangements for some patients. Outside contacts should of course be worked out in detail with the patient.

FOLLOW-UP AND EVALUATION IN CRISIS THERAPY

Follow-up of the patient's progress after termination of treatment constitutes an important function of any therapeutic offering. It is especially important for crisis therapy to be guided by knowledge of results from follow-up studies, because the therapist's input in a case is usually great and the consequences of perseverating "errors" over future cases are profound. Brief crisis therapy lends itself particularly well to follow-up, since the therapeutic contracts that are arranged are usually concrete enough to allow the therapist to ascertain if the behavioral change strategies have been followed through.

The role of the therapist here is viewed in an entirely different light than in the therapeutic teachings of a few years ago. Psychologists have relinquished some of their cherished ideals such as, "The therapist is a mirror," or "A therapist never initiates contact with a patient." It is likely that the benefits of these ideals always existed more in the mind of the therapist than of the patient anyway. One effect of this shift is that crisis workers can feel quite comfortable doing fairly aggressive follow-ups. One can readily see that the same factors that call for therapist directiveness also call for directiveness and aggressiveness in follow-up. In crisis work follow-up can be broadly defined as any activity, other than the therapy sessions themselves, that enables the crisis worker to determine if he has mobilized all resources that might be instrumental in insuring a successful resolution of the crisis. Follow-up should not be limited to contacts made after therapy is successfully terminated. If this were the case, it is likely that at least half of the crisis population would never be followed up, since many fail to return for scheduled visits after their initial contact.

It is worth reiterating that some of the personality characteristics that cause people to find themselves in the midst of a crisis are equally operative in preventing them from successfully resolving the crisis. For example, a passive-dependent woman drops in with the complaint that her alcoholic husband beats her. The base rate expectations lead one to speculate that that same dependency and passivity may prevent her from confronting and handling this situation, in spite of the fact that she sincerely asserts at the moment that this is what she wants to do and knows she should do. If she fails to return for her next appointment, a well-timed follow-up may communicate to her that it is understandable why this is such a difficult step for her, and may present her with an opportunity to discuss and work through some of her feelings which have prevented her from dealing with her "presenting crisis" adaptively.

Follow-up can also be utilized to insure that referrals are successfully completed. As we have previously mentioned, crisis intervention often involves directing clients to already existing agencies and services. For example, one comprehensive crisis center found that nearly 50% of its contacts required referral as part of the final disposition (Stelmachers, 1972). Follow-up at this point insures that the referral contact is successfully made and communicates to the patient that the therapist, in making the referral, was not just "passing the buck." The concern expressed through this follow-up contact opens the door for further intervention if the referral is unsatisfactory or unsuccessful.

An important group of patients who need close follow-up are people who have attempted suicide. It has been well-documented that those patients who successfully commit suicide do so within 3 months after treatment termination, and most of them have made unsuccessful attempts previously. Although follow-up may not prevent suicide, it may communicate to the patient that his welfare is important and that immediate treatment options do exist. Despite the obvious importance of follow-up in crisis work, surveys indicate that most crisis centers are lax, if not negligent, in this respect (Bloomfield et al., 1971).

The follow-up of individual patients is closely related to the broader goal of evaluating the work accomplished by the crisis center itself. The necessity for evaluation of the therapeutic offerings is probably given as much lip service as is the necessity for follow-up; however, in most settings the actual yield is paltry, since few centers utilize a formal evaluation procedure that allows for quantitative analysis. The importance of accountability within the mental health field was recently highlighted by Senator Walter Mondale (1972):

We must design methods for filling the gaps in our information systematically. We must develop a coherent set of problem definitions, goals, and solutions. And this is a task to be addressed at all levels of national life. In short, planning and evaluation must proceed at the national and the local levels more or less simultaneously.

We would like to underscore the importance of follow-up in individual treatment and the necessity for evaluation of treatment programs by describing one extensive approach to implementing these ideals.

A brief description of one center that has engaged in extensive follow-up research and the evaluation of treatment programs (Kiresuk & Sherman, 1968) is presented as a model. The Crisis Intervention Center has been in existence since July of 1971. It is located within Hennepin County General Hospital, near the inner-city neighborhoods of Minneapolis, Minnesota. It is open 24 hours a day, 7 days a week, and offers assistance without regard to eligibility to any individual in need. Telephone, walk-in, and home visit services are available, and the center has direct access to medical and inpatient psychiatric facilities. The clinic is directed by a clinical psychologist. The staff of 25 consists of psychiatric nurses, psychiatric social workers, psychologists, community mental health workers, and on-call psychiatrists. Students of varying disciplines and volunteers are also utilized. The center emphasizes immediate crisis resolution through direct intervention and appropriate follow-up. Services include brief, reality-oriented therapy, medication, and appropriate referrals. During the first year of operation it sustained 14,000 telephone and 7,000 walk-in contacts (Lund, 1974).

The clinical effectiveness of the center has been measured by utilizing a set of procedures, consisting of goal attainment scaling and consumer satisfaction interviews, developed by Kiresuk and Sherman (1968). In goal attainment scaling, appropriate treatment goals are selected and scaled as a negotiated contract between client and clinician. If a client is unwilling or unable to participate in the negotiation, the clinician completes the follow-up guide alone. Clinicians specify behaviorally the expected level of treatment success, as well as degrees of "less than expected success" and "more than expected success." An example of some of the treatment goals is shown in Table 1 (Stelmachers, Lund, & Meade, 1972). The actual follow-up interviews to determine if the goals have been achieved are made by independent workers, often over the phone. Consumer satisfaction is assessed by the follow-up workers, who ask brief additional questions such as, "How satisfied were you with the services you received at the Crisis Intervention Center?," and "Would you return again?" Feedback is immediately made available to individual clinicians.

An evaluation of results of the first 109 clients followed up revealed a mean goal attainment score of 51.69 (a goal attainment score of 50 represents the "expected" level of goal attainment for a single client; the mean score represents a summary of goal attainment success across the various scales constructed). The mean scores for various staff disciplines were quite similar, the range being from 49.25 to 52.20. Of the follow-up guides constructed in the Hennepin County Crisis Intervention Center, 67.0% contained only one or two scales. This illustrates the fact that many crisis contacts are of a rather limited nature, which results in limited goal setting. Some preliminary data indicate that clients who actually receive crisis treatment have a larger number of scale goals (2.33) than clients who are referred for treatment elsewhere (1.54).

The client satisfaction survey, included as part of the follow-up, revealed that 79% of the crisis patients were either "very satisfied" or "satisfied" with the services they received. Only 10.3% of clients showed evidence of new mental or physical problems since the time of their contact.

The goal attainment scaling procedure can be further utilized in research by allowing a quantitative assessment of whether or not particular groups of patients attain the goals that have been worked out or whether specific therapists or therapeutic approaches are more or less successful at bringing about desired goals.

Table 1. Sample of Goal Attainment Scales[a]

Level of outcome	Attitude toward Treatment	Success of Referral	Depression	Manipulation
Most unfavorable treatment outcome thought likely	Patient does not keep intake appointment and refuses new appointment at follow-up	Detoxification center refuses to accept patient	Patient is immobilized by depression and apathy over death of wife, and is unable to care for self. Perhaps in an institution	Patient makes rounds of community service agencies demanding medication and refuses other forms of treatment
Less than expected success with treatment	Patient keeps intake appointment, but refuses further treatment	Detoxification center accepts patient but complains at follow-up that the referral was not appropriate	Patient is chronically depressed, but is able to function at a level necessary to continue living	Patient no longer visits CIC with demands for medication but continues with other community agencies and still refuses other forms of treatment
Expected level of treatment success	Patient keeps intake appointment and accepts treatment, but reports that he does not expect it to help him	Detoxification center accepts patient and comments at follow-up that, although the patient was difficult to handle, the referral was probably appropriate	Patient is still depressed and apathetic but reports periods of up to a day when he does not think of wife	Patient no longer attempts to manipulate for drugs at community service agencies but will not accept another form of treatment
More than expected success with treatment	Patient keeps intake appointment and accepts treatment, and makes some positive comments about his expectations (i.e., "I don't know; I suppose it might help")	Detoxification center accepts patient and comments at follow-up that the referral was definitely appropriate	Patient reports severe depression only on occasions which evoke special memories	Patient accepts nonmedication treatment at some community agency
Best anticipated success with treatment	Patient accepts treatment and expresses enthusiasm concerning his treatment expectations (i.e., "I think this really might help me")	Detoxification center accepts patient and comments at follow-up that the referral was definitely appropriate and compliments CIC unit's handling of case	Patient reports he is no longer depressed over death of wife, and realizes he must go on living without her	Patient accepts nonmedication treatment, and by own report shows signs of improvement

[a] Adapted from Stelmachers, Lund, and Meade (1972, p. 63).

REFERENCES

Abroms, G. M. Setting limits. *Archives of General Psychiatry,* 1968, **19,** 113–119.

Aguilera, D. C., Messick, J. M., & Farrell, M. S. *Crisis intervention: Theory and methodology.* St. Louis: Mosby, 1970.

Aita, J. A. Efficacy of the brief clinical method in predicting adjustments. *Archives of Neurology and Psychiatry,* 1949, **61,** 170–176.

Aldrich, C. K. Brief psychotherapy: A reappraisal of some theoretical assumptions. *American Journal of Psychiatry,* 1968, **125,** 585–592.

Alexander, F., & French, T. *Psychoanalytic therapy.* New York: Ronald Press, 1946.

Auld, F., & Myers, J. Contributions to a theory for selecting psychotherapy patients. *Journal of Clinical Psychology,* 1954, **10,** 56–60.

Bagley, C. An evaluation of suicide prevention agencies. *Life-threatening Behavior,* 1971, **1,** 245–259.

Barten, H. H., & Barten, S. S. (Eds.) *Children and their parents in brief therapy.* New York: Behavioral Publications, 1972.

Barten, H. H. (Ed.) *Brief therapies.* New York: Behavioral Publications, 1971.

Battle, C. C., Imber, S. D., Hoehn-Saric, R., Stone, A. R., Nash, E. H., & Frank, J. D. Target complaints as criteria of improvement. *American Journal of Psychotherapy,* 1966, **20,** 184–192.

Beck, B. M., & Robbins, L. L. *Short-term therapy in an authoritative setting.* New York: Family Service Association, 1946.

Bellak, L., & Small, L. *Emergency psychotherapy and brief psychotherapy.* New York: Grune & Stratton, 1965.

Bergin, A. E., & Garfield, S. L. (Eds.) *Handbook of psychotherapy and behavior change: An empirical analysis.* New York: Wiley, 1971.

Bibring, G. L., Dwyer, T. F., Huntington, D. S., & Valenstein, A. F. A study of the psychological processes in pregnancy and of the earliest mother-child relationship. *Psychoanalytic Study of the Child,* 1961, **16,** 25–72.

Birley, J. L., & Brown, G. W. Crises and life changes preceding the onset or relapse of acute schizophrenia: Clinical aspects. *British Journal of Psychiatry,* 1970, **116,** 327–333.

Bloom, B. L. Definitional aspects of the crisis concept. *Journal of Consulting Psychology,* 1963, **27,** 498–502.

Bloomfield, C., Levy, H., Kotelchuck, R., & Handelman, M. Free clinics. *Health PAC Bulletin,* 1971, No. 34, 1–16.

Brantner, J. The first interview. In J. Butcher, J. Ayers, & I. Benoist, *Role of assessment in crisis intervention: A video taped discussion.* Clinical Psychology Program, University of Minnesota, 1973.

Breuer, J., & Freud, S. (1893–1895) Studies on hysteria. *Standard Edition,* Vol. II. London: Hogarth Press, 1955. Pp. 1–305.

Brill, N. Q., & Storrow, H. A. Social class and psychiatric treatment. *Archives of General Psychiatry,* 1960, **3,** 340–344.

Caplan, G. *An approach to community mental health.* New York: Grune & Stratton, 1961.

Caplan, G. *Principles of preventive psychiatry.* New York: Basic Books, 1964.

Castelnuovo-Tedesco, P. Brief psychotherapeutic treatment of the depressive reactions. In G. J. Wayne & R. R. Koegler (Eds.), *Emergency psychiatry and brief therapy.* Boston: Little, Brown, 1966. Pp. 197–210.

Chafetz, M. E. The effect of an emergency psychiatric service on motivation for treatment. Paper presented at the annual meeting of the American Psychiatric Association, Los Angeles, May 1964.

Coleman, M. D. Emergency psychotherapy. In J. H. Masserman & J. L. Moreno (Eds.), *Progress in Psychotherapy,* Vol. V. New York: Grune & Stratton, 1960.

Darbonne, A. Crisis: A review of theory, practice and research. *International Journal of Psychiatry,* 1968, **6,** 371–379.

DeCourcy, P. The hazard of short-term psychotherapy without assessment: A case history. *Journal of Personality Assessment,* 1971, **35,** 285–288.

Eisenberg, H. Challenging fee for service: The free clinic movement. *Medical Economics,* October 1972, 95–130.

Ellis, A. *Reason and emotion in psychotherapy.* New York: Lyle Stuart, 1962.

Erikson, E. Growth and crisis of the healthy personality. In C. Kluckholn & H. Murray (Eds.), *Personality in nature, society and culture.* New York: Knopf, 1953.

Farberow, N. L. Suicide prevention: A view from the bridge. *Community Mental Health Journal,* 1968, **4,** 469–474.

Farberow, N. L., & Schneidman, E. S. (Eds.) *The cry for help.* New York: McGraw-Hill, 1961.

Frank, J. D. *Persuasion and healing: A comparative study of psychotherapy.* New York: Schocken, 1961.

Frank, J. D. Treatment of the focal symptom: An adaptational approach. *American Journal of Psychotherapy,* 1966, **20,** 564–575.

Frank, J. D. The role of hope in psychotherapy. *International Journal of Psychiatry,* 1968, **5,** 383–395.

Frankl, V. E. Paradoxical intention: A logotherapeutic technique. *American Journal of Psychotherapy,* 1960, **14,** 520–535.

Freud, S. (1919) Lines of advance in psycho-analytic therapy. *Standard Edition,* Vol. XVII. London: Hogarth Press, 1955. Pp. 159–168.

Freudenberger, H. J. The free clinic concept. *International Journal of Offender Therapy,* 1972, **15,** 121–125.

Freudenberger, H. J., & Freudenberger, A. F. 1973—The free clinic picture today: A survey. *Journal Supplement Abstract Service,* 1974, **4,** 21.

Garner, H. H. Brief psychotherapy and the confrontation approach. *Psychosomatics,* 1970, **11,** 319–325.

Garfield, S. L. Research on client variables in psychotherapy. In A. E. Bergin & S. L. Garfield (Eds.), *Handbook of psychotherapy and behavior change.* New York: Wiley, 1971. Pp. 271–298.

Glass, A. J. Psychiatric prediction and military effectiveness. Research Report WRAIR-64-65. Washington, D.C.: Walter Reed Army Institute of Research, 1956.

Goin, M., Yamamoto, J., & Silverman, J. Therapy congruent with class-linked expectations. *Archives of General Psychiatry,* 1965, **13,** 133–137.

Golan, N. When is a client in crisis? *Social Casework,* July 1969, 389–394.

Golann, S., & Eisdorfer, C. (Eds.) *Handbook of community mental health.* New York: Appleton-Century-Crofts, 1972.

Goldenberg, H. *Contemporary clinical psychology.* Monterey, Calif.: Brooks/Cole, 1973.

Gottesman, I., & Shields, J. *Schizophrenia and genetics: A twin study vantage point.* New York: Academic Press, 1972.

Grinker, R. R., & Spiegel, J. P. Brief psychotherapy in war neuroses. *Psychosomatic Medicine,* 1944, **6,** 123–131.

Grinker, R. R., & Spiegel, J. P. *Men under stress.* Philadelphia: Blakiston, 1945.

Haley, J. *Strategies of psychotherapy.* New York: Grune & Stratton, 1963.

Harris, M. R., Kalis, B. L., & Freeman, E. H. Precipitating stress: An approach to brief therapy. *American Journal of Psychotherapy,* 1963, **17,** 465–471.

Helig, S. M., Farberow, N. L., Litman, R. E., & Schneidman, E. S. The role of nonprofessional volunteers in a suicide prevention center. *Community Mental Health Journal,* 1968, **4,** 287–295.

Hoch, P. H. Short-term versus long-term therapy. In L. R. Wolberg (Ed.), *Short-term psychotherapy.* New York: Grune & Stratton, 1965. Pp. 51–66.

Hogan, R. The implosive technique. *Behavior Research and Therapy,* 1968, **6,** 423–431.

Hollingshead, A. B., & Redlich, F. C. *Social class and mental illness: A community study.* New York: Wiley, 1958.

Hunt, R. G. Social class and mental illness: Some implications for clinical theory and practice. *American Journal of Psychiatry,* 1960, **116,** 1065–1069.

Jacobson, G., Strickler, M., & Morley, W. Generic and individual approaches to crisis intervention. *American Journal of Public Health,* 1968, **58,** 339–343.

Jacobson, G., Wilner, D., Morley, W., Schneider, S., Strickler, M., & Sommer, G. The scope and practice of an early-access brief treatment psychiatric center. *American Journal of Psychiatry,* 1965, **121,** 1176–1182.

Jacobson, G. F. Crisis theory and treatment strategy: Some socio-cultural and psychodynamic considerations. *Journal of Nervous and Mental Disease,* 1965, **141,** 209–218.

Kalis, B. L., Harris, M. R., Prestwood, A. R., & Freeman, E. H. Precipitating stress as a focus in psychotherapy. *Archives of General Psychiatry*, 1961, **5**, 219–226.

Kaplan, D. M. Observations on crisis theory and practice. *Social Casework*, 1968, **49**, 151–155.

Kaplan, D. M., & Mason, F. A. Maternal reactions to premature birth viewed as an acute emotional disorder. In H. J. Parad (Ed.), *Crisis intervention: Selected readings*. New York: Family Service Association of America, 1965. Pp. 118–128.

Kardiner, A. *The traumatic neuroses of war.* New York: Hoeber, 1941.

Kiresuk, T. J., & Sherman, R. E. Goal attainment scaling: A general method for evaluating comprehensive community mental health programs. *Community Mental Health Journal*, 1968, **1**(1), 443–454.

Klein, D., & Lindemann, E. Preventive intervention in individual and family crisis situations. In G. Caplan (Ed.), *Prevention of mental disorders in children*. New York: Basic Books, 1961. Pp. 283–306.

Klopfer, W. G. The blind leading the blind: Psychotherapy without assessment. *Journal of Projective Techniques and Personality Assessment*, 1964, **28**, 387–392.

Koegler, R. R., & Brill, N. Q. *Treatment of psychiatric out patients.* New York: Appleton-Century-Crofts, 1967.

Kraus, A. S., & Lilienfeld, A. M. Some epidemiological aspects of the high mortality rate in the young widowed group. *Journal of Chronic Diseases*, 1959, **10**, 207–217.

Lambley, P. The dangers of therapy without assessment: A case study. *Journal of Personality Assessment*, 1974, **38**, 263–265.

Lazarus, A. A. Learning theory and treatment of depression. *Behavior Research and Therapy*, 1968, **6**, 83–89.

Lerner, B. *Therapy in the ghetto.* Baltimore: Johns Hopkins University Press, 1972.

Lewin, K. K. *Brief encounters: Brief psychotherapy.* St. Louis: Warren H. Green, 1970.

Lief, H. I., Lief, U. F., Warren, C. O., & Heath, R. C. Low dropout rate in a psychiatric clinic. *Archives of General Psychiatry*, 1961, **5**, 200–211.

Lindemann, E. Symptomatology and management of acute grief. *American Journal of Psychiatry*, 1944, **101**, 141–148.

Lorion, R. P. Socioeconomic status and traditional treatment approaches reconsidered. *Psychological Bulletin*, 1973, **79**, 263–270.

Lorion, R. P. Patient and therapist variables in the treatment of low income patients. *Psychological Bulletin*, 1974, **81**, 344–354.

Lorr, M., McNair, D., Michaux, W., & Raskin, A. Frequency of treatment and change in psychotherapy. *Journal of Abnormal and Social Psychology*, 1962, **64**, 281–292.

Lund, S. H. Program evaluation project report, 1969–1973. Program Evaluation Project Report—NIMH Grant #5 RO1 1678904, 1974.

Macleod, J. A., & Tinnin, L. W. Special service project: A solution to problems of early access and brief psychotherapy. *Archives of General Psychiatry,* 1966, **15,** 190–197.

Madison, D. The relevance of conjugal bereavement for preventive psychiatry. *British Journal of Medical Psychology,* 1968, **41,** 223–233.

Mann, J. *Time limited psychotherapy.* Cambridge, Mass.: Harvard University Press, 1973.

Massermann, J. H. (Ed.) *Current psychiatric therapies,* Vol. 9. New York: Grune & Stratton, 1969.

McCord, E. Treatment in short-time contacts. *The Family,* 1931, **12,** 191–193.

McGee, R. K. *Crisis intervention in the community.* Baltimore: University Park Press, 1974.

Menninger, K. Psychological aspects of the organism under stress. *Journal of the American Psychoanalytic Association,* 1954, **2,** 280–310.

Minneapolis Medical Research Foundation. *Health behavior and health needs of American Indians in Hennepin County,* 1971.

Mondale, W. F. Social accounting, evaluation, and the future of the human services. *Evaluation,* 1972, **1,** 29–34.

Morley, W. E. Theory of crisis intervention. *Pastoral Psychology,* 1970, **21,** 14–20.

Muench, G. A. An investigation of time limited psychotherapy. *Journal of Counseling Psychology,* 1965, **12,** 294–299.

National Clearing House for Drug Abuse Information. *Free Clinics,* 1974, March, Series 27, No. 1.

Nichols, M. P. Outcome of brief cathartic psychotherapy. *Journal of Consulting and Clinical Psychology,* 1974, **42,** 403–411.

Oberleder, M. Crisis therapy in mental breakdown of the aging. *The Gerontologist,* 1970, **10,** 111–114.

Parad, H. J. Preventive casework: Problems and implications. *The social welfare forum, 1961.* Papers from the National Conference on Social Welfare. New York: Columbia University Press, 1961.

Parad, H. J. (Ed.) *Crisis intervention: Selected readings.* New York: Family Service Association of America, 1965.

Parad, H. J. The use of time limited crisis intervention on community mental health programming. *Social Service Review,* 1966, **40,** 275–282.

Parad, L. Short term treatment: An overview of historical trends, issues and potentials. *Smith College Studies in Social Work,* 1971, **61,** 119–147.

Parkes, C., Benjamin, B., & Fitzgerald, R. Broken heart: A statistical study of increased mortality among widowers. *British Medical Journal,* 1969, **1,** 740–743.

Parkes, C. M. Effects of bereavement on physical and mental health—A study of the medical records of widows. *British Medical Journal,* 1964, **2,** 274–279.

Paul, L. Crisis intervention. *Mental Hygiene,* 1966, **50,** 141–145.

Paykel, E. S., Myers, J. K., Dienelt, M. N., Klerman, G. L., Lindenthal, J. J., & Pepper, M. P. Life events and depression: A controlled study. *Archives of General Psychiatry,* 1969, **21,** 753–760.

Phillips, E. L., & Wiener, D. N. *Short-term psychotherapy and structured behavior change.* New York: McGraw-Hill, 1966.

Pollack, D. Crisis and response in college students. *Journal of Abnormal Psychology,* 1971, **78,** 49–51.

Pumpian-Mindlin, E. Consideration in selection of patients for short-term therapy. *American Journal of Psychotherapy,* 1953, **7,** 641–652.

Rado, S. Relationship of short-term psychotherapy to developmental stages of maturation and stages of treatment behavior. In L. R. Wolberg (Ed.), *Short-term psychotherapy.* New York: Grune & Stratton, 1965. Pp. 67–83.

Rapaport, L. The state of crisis: Some theoretical considerations. *Social Service Review,* 1962, **36,** 211–217.

Redlich, F., Hollingshead, A., & Bellis, E. Social class differences in attitudes toward psychiatry. *American Journal of Orthopsychiatry,* 1955, **25,** 60–70.

Reid, W., & Shyne, A. *Brief and extended casework.* New York: Columbia University Press, 1969.

Reynolds, B. An experiment in short-contact interviewing. *Smith College Studies in Social Work,* 1932, **3,** 3–107.

Ritchie, A. Multiple impact therapy: An experiment. *Social Work,* 1960, **5,** 16–21.

Rogers, L. S. Drop-out rates of psychotherapy in government aided mental hygiene clinics. *Journal of Clinical Psychology,* 1960, **16,** 89-92.

Rosenthal, D., & Frank, J. The fate of psychiatric clinic outpatients assigned to psychotherapy. *Journal of Nervous Mental Disease,* 1958, **127,** 330–343.

Rosenzweig, S. Some implicit common factors in diverse methods of psychotherapy. *American Journal of Orthopsychiatry,* 1936, **6,** 412–415.

Rothman, T. (Ed.) *Changing patterns in psychiatric care.* New York: Crown, 1970.

Rubenstein, E., & Lorr, M. A comparison of terminators and remainers in outpatient psychotherapy. *Journal of Clinical Psychology,* 1956, **12,** 345–349.

Rusk, T. N. Opportunity and technique in crisis psychiatry. *Comprehensive Psychiatry,* 1971, **12,** 249–263.

Schoener, G. Walk-in counseling services. Memorandum to the Secretary, HEW (Elliott Richardson), May 4, 1972, pp. 4–7.

Schwartz, J. L. First national survey of free medical clinics: 1967–1969. *HSMHA Health Reports,* September 1971, **86.**

Shlien, J., Mosak, H., & Dreikurs, R. Effects of time limits: A comparison of two psychotherapies. *Journal of Counseling Psychology,* 1962, **9,** 31–34.

Shoben, E. J., Jr. A learning theory interpretation of psychotherapy. *Harvard Educational Review,* 1948, **18,** 129–145.

Sifneos, P. E. A concept of "emotional crisis." *Mental Hygiene,* 1960, **44,** 169–179.

Sifneos, P. E. Seven years experience with short term dynamic psychotherapy. *Proceedings of the Sixth International Congress of Psychotherapy*, London, 1964.

Sifneos, P. E. *Short-term psychotherapy and emotional crisis*. Cambridge, Mass.: Harvard University Press, 1972.

Small, L. *The briefer psychotherapies*. New York: Brunner/Mazel, 1971.

Small, L. The uncommon importance of psychodiagnosis. *Professional Psychology*, 1972, **3**, 111–119.

Smith, D., Luce, J., & Dernberg, E. The health of Haight-Ashbury. *Transaction*, April 1970, 35–45.

Stampfl, T. G., & Levis, D. J. Essentials of implosive therapy: A learning theory based psychodynamic behavioral therapy. *Journal of Abnormal Psychology*, 1967, **72**, 496–503.

Stelmachers, Z. T. Crisis Intervention Center: An interim report. *Program Evaluation Project Newsletter*, January 1972.

Stelmachers, Z. T., Lund, S. H., & Meade, C. J. Hennepin County Crisis Intervention Center: Evaluation of its effectiveness. *Evaluation*, Fall 1972, 61–65.

Sterba, R. F. A case of brief psychotherapy by Sigmund Freud. *Psychoanalytic Review*, 1951, **38**, 75–80.

Stoeckle, J., Anderson, W., Page, J., & Brenner, J. The free clinic movement: Present and future. In *The free clinic: A community approach to health care and drug abuse*. Beloit, Wis.: Stash Press, 1971.

Strickler, M., & Allgeyer, J. The crisis group: A new application of crisis theory. *Social Work*, 1967, **12**, 28–32.

Strickler, M., & LaSor, B. The concept of loss in crisis intervention. *Mental Hygiene*, 1970, **51**, 301–305.

Taft, J. *The dynamics of therapy in a controlled relationship*. New York: Macmillan, 1933.

Tapp, J., & Spanier, D. Personal characteristics of volunteer counselors. *Journal of Consulting Psychology*, 1973, **41**, 245–250.

Torrey, E. F. Emergency psychiatric ambulance services in the USSR. *American Journal of Psychiatry*, 1971, **128**, 45–49.

Truax, C. B., & Wargo, D. G. Psychotherapeutic encounters that change behavior: For better or for worse. *American Journal of Psychotherapy*, 1966, **20**, 499–520.

Tyhurst, J. S. The role of transitional states—including disaster—in mental illness. Symposium on Preventive and Social Psychiatry, Walter Reed Army Institute of Research. Washington, D.C.: U.S. Govt. Printing Office, 1958.

Ullman, L., & Krasner, L. (Eds.) *Case studies in behavior modification*. New York: Holt, Rinehart & Winston, 1965.

Wayne, G. J. The psychiatric emergency: An overview. In G. J. Wayne & R. R. Koegler (Eds.), *Emergency psychiatry and brief therapy*. Boston: Little, Brown, 1966. Pp. 3–8.

Weiss, J. M., & Schaie, K. W. The Psychiatric Evaluation Index. *American Journal of Psychotherapy,* 1964, **18,** 3–14.

Wells, F., & Ruesch, J. *The mental examiners handbook* (Rev. ed.). New York: Psychological Corporation, 1972.

Wolberg, L. R. The technique of short-term psychotherapy. In L. R. Wolberg (Ed.), *Short-term psychotherapy.* New York: Grune & Stratton, 1965. Pp. 127–200.

Wolpe, J. *Psychotherapy by reciprocal inhibition.* Stanford, Calif.: Stanford University Press, 1958.

Yamamoto, J., & Goin, M. On the treatment of the poor. *American Journal of Psychiatry,* 1965, **122,** 267–271.

Author Index

Wallach, M. A., 161
Wallhermfechtel, J., 256
Wallin, J. E. W., 133
Wallis, R. R., 64, 72, 103, 106, 201
Walsh, J. A., 224
Walsh, J. N., 250
Walters, J., 498
Walters, R., 522
Wanderer, Z. W., 550
Warbin, R. W., 210, 256-257
Warburton, F. W., 196
Wargo, D. G., 336, 627
Warner, A., 430
Warren, C. O., 609
Warren, N. C., 436
Watson, D., 312
Watson, L., 567
Watson, R. A., 248
Watzlawick, P., 466, 474-476
Waxler, N., 456, 479, 481, 483
Way, J. G., 141
Wayne, G. J., 615
Weakland, J. H., 466, 473-474, 485, 488, 492
Webb, E , 144
Webb, E. J., 19
Webb, J. T., 255-256, 258
Webb, W. B., 141
Wechsler, D., 125, 131, 135-137, 144-145, 158-159
Wechsler, I., 411-412
Weinberg, L., 315
Weiner, H. B., 430
Weiner, I. B., 72-73, 82, 84, 312, 349, 366, 368, 382
Weinman, B., 545
Weintraub, W., 24
Weisman, A. G., 127
Weiss, J. M., 610
Weisskopf-Joelson, E., 98, 101
Weitz, S., 30, 32
Welch, L., 149
Wells, F. L., 145
Wells, C. F., 467
Wells, F., 621
Wells, R. A., 498-500, 502
Welsh, G. S., 205-207, 252, 255-258
Wender, L., 395
Werry, J., 567
Wertham, F., 149

Wessler, R., 242
Westfield, D. R., 430
Westman, J. C., 424
Wexler, D. A., 351
Wexner, L. B., 98
Whally, M., 429
Wheeler, D. R., 91
Wheeler, W. M., 87
Wheelright, J., 344
Whipple, G. M., 62
Whitaker, D. S., 403, 405, 419, 433
White, K. M., 149
White, P. O., 144
White, R. K., 408-409
White, W. A., 153
Whitney, L., 573
Wickens, D. D., 301, 305
Wideman, H., 149, 151
Wiener, D. N., 346, 627, 636
Wiener, M., 30
Wiens, A. N., 7, 16-24, 45, 360
Wiggins, J. S., 65-66, 190, 196, 203, 210, 213, 227, 235, 242, 250, 253-254, 295
Wikler, A., 552
Wilkins, W., 357
Willett, A. B., 429-430
Williams, F. S., 485, 503, 506
Williams, H. L., 257
Williams, J. G., 550
Williams, J. H., 360
Williams, R. I., 360
Wilner, D., 594
Wilson, A. E., 532
Wilson, A. J., 432
Wilson, G. T., 525-526, 537, 554, 560, 562
Wilson, J. A. R., 143
Wilson, J. H., 128
Wilson, R. C., 127-128
Wiltz, N. A., 567
Winder, C. L., 295
Winer, M. F., 433
Winett, R. A., 545
Winick, C., 429
Winkel, G. H., 297
Winkler, R. C., 545
Winter, W. D., 468, 471, 498-499
Winthrop, H., 413
Wisocki, P. A., 556
Witenberg, M. J., 424
Witkin, H. A., 97, 161

Subject Index

racial influences on, 256-257
reliability of, 206-207
research activity on, 201
residential influence on, 258
scales of, 204, 213
sex influences on, 256
short forms of, 213-214
socioeconomic influence on, 257-258
usage of, 64, 201-202
Modeling, in behavior therapy, 534-536, 571
Mooney Problem Check List, 201
Motivation Analysis Test, 234
Multiple Affect Adjective Checklist, 309
Multiple-impact family therapy, 458
Multiple therapists, in family therapy, 495

National Training Laboratories, 410-412
Neo-Freudian analysis, 347-348
Nonstandardized interviews, 8-10
Nonverbal communication, in interviews, 25-39
Note-taking, in interviews, 10-11

Objective-Analytic Personality Test Battery, 197
Objective personality measures, as distinguished from projective measures, 195-196
  family assessment with, 469-470
  L data in, 196-197
  nature of, 195-197
  Q data in, 196-197
  T data in, 196-197
  see also specific personality measures
Observational assessment, 288-295
Observational learning, 521-522
Observer bias, 292-293
Omnibus Personality Inventory, 201
Operant conditioning, 520-521, 533-534, 573-574
Organizational activity, on Rorschach, 83
OSS Assessment Staff, 295
Outcome research, in family therapy, 498-503
  in psychotherapy, 377-382

Paradoxical intention, 634
Paraprofessionals, in crisis intervention, 603-605
Percentage of interruptions, in

interviews, 17-22
Personal Data Sheet, 198
Personality assessment, and age influence, 255
  automation of, 250-251, 253-254
  Barnum effect in, 258-261
  base rates in, 193-194
  basic steps in, 190-192
  blind analysis in, 98-99, 254-255
  configural models for, 252
  discriminative efficiency in, 192-193
  and education, 257-258
  false positives and negatives in, 192-193
  illusory correlation in, 251-252
  and intelligence, 257-258
  and invasion of privacy, 250
  linear models for, 252-253
  and place of residence, 258
  and racial influence, 256-257
  selection ratios in, 194-195
  and sex influence, 256
  and socioeconomic status, 257-258
  state vs. trait issue in, 250
  valid positives and negatives in, 192-193
Personality inventories, history of, 197-200
  research activity on, 201
  and response tendencies, 250
  usage of, 201-202
  see also specific inventories
Personality prediction, clinical vs. statistical, 250
Personality Research Form, aims of, 235
  construction of, 235-237
  factor analyses of, 239
  forms of, 237
  history of, 200
  intercorrelations in, 238-239
  interpretation of, 240-242
  psychometric properties of, 237-240
  reliability of, 239-240
  scales of, 237
Personal Orientation Inventory, 201
Pintner-Paterson Scale, 135-136
Placebo treatment, 356
Pleasant Events Schedule, 310
Porteus mazes, 134
Pre-School Questionnaire, 233
Primary mental abilities, 127-128
Process research, in psychotherapy, 377-379
Progressive relaxation, 527-528